Russia's l

Russia's Uncommon Prophet

Father Aleksandr Men
and His Times

WALLACE L. DANIEL

NIU PRESS
DeKalb

TO KAROL

Christ built His Church on the foundation of freedom—we never see Him on the side of power. . . . In Him there is nothing totalitarian, dictatorial, obtrusive—[but] always freedom.

—Fr. Aleksandr Men

At Novaia Derevnia a small flame flickered in an icy world; unfortunately, it left hidden in the shadows the forces intent on extinguishing it.

—Michel Evdokimov

Note on Transliteration

I have used the standard Library of Congress system of transliteration throughout this book, but have altered some Russian spellings of proper names. Russian surnames that are well known to an English-speaking public are given in their common spelling (for example, Tolstoi becomes Tolstoy, Iakunin is transliterated as Yakunin). In the text, Fr. Aleksandr Men's family name is written in its English form as Men. In the case of published works in English, I have used the writers' spelling of his name when they have written in English Alexander Men. The name Aleksandr Men has been used throughout the book, in the text, notes, and bibliography. The only exceptions are Russian language titles of books and articles.

Northern Illinois University Press, DeKalb 60115
© 2016 by Northern Illinois University Press
Printed in the United States of America
25 24 23 22 21 20 19 18 17 16   1 2 3 4 5

978-0-87580-733-1 (paper)
978-1-60909-194-1 (ebook)

Book and cover design by Shaun Allshouse

Library of Congress Cataloging-in-Publication Data
Names: Daniel, Wallace L., author.
Title: Russia's uncommon prophet : Father Aleksandr Men and his times /
    Wallace L. Daniel.
Description: First [edition]. | DeKalb : Northern Illinois University Press,
    2016. | Includes bibliographical references and index.
Identifiers: LCCN 2016004798 (print) | LCCN 2016005154 (ebook) | ISBN
    9780875807331 (pbk. : alk. paper) | ISBN 9781609091941 (ebook) | ISBN
    9780875807331 (paper)
Subjects: LCSH: Men, Aleksandr, 1935-1990. | Russkaia pravoslavnaia t͡serkov'—Clergy—
Biography. | Orthodox Eastern Church—Russia
    (Federation)—Clergy—Biography.
Classification: LCC BX597.M46 D36 2016 (print) | LCC BX597.M46 (ebook) | DDC
    281.9092—dc23
LC record available at http://lccn.loc.gov/2016004798

Contents

Preface

During the first half of my academic career, my research and writing focused on Russia in the eighteenth century. This research mainly centered on the social and economic history of the turbulent and colorful period of Empress Catherine the Great, a subject I had always found deeply engaging. But beginning in the mid-1990s, a much different topic became increasingly compelling. Concurrent with the end of the Soviet Union and Russia's attempts to redefine itself, I became interested in its efforts at reconstruction, and particularly in the role of the Orthodox Church in this process. Long suppressed, the victim of nearly seventy years of state opposition, and often viewed as an anachronism and an unnecessary holdover from the past, the Church had suffered one of its greatest assaults in modern European history. After the end of the Communist state, how the Russian Orthodox Church recovered from years of oppression, particularly its efforts to recover its cultural memory and reclaim its heritage, seemed to me to be significant, largely unexplored aspects of its national story. What parts of its historical memory the Church aspired to regain—whether the autocratic, xenophobic elements or those that were nonauthoritarian and outward-looking—would have a large bearing on how the country developed.[1]

Convinced that the subject warranted more attention than it had received in my field, I sought topics that were concrete, revealing practical, day-to-day realities. These endeavors led to a close look at individual parishes, the struggles of certain priests and their parishioners to rebuild, and their efforts to reconceive themselves during the years following the end of the Soviet Union. Whether these attempts either contributed to or undermined the creation of civil society became a primary subject of my research.

From October to November 2005, while in Moscow to participate in two international conferences on religion and society at the Russian Humanities University and the Institute of Sociology of the Academy of Sciences, I began thinking about the possibility of the present topic. I became interested in Fr. Aleksandr Men while researching my book on the Russian Orthodox Church and civil society.[2] Fr. Aleksandr's name and activities came up multiple times among leading proponents of civil society. I was intrigued by his story, and the more I read about him, the greater my interest became.

Returning to Moscow in the summer of 2006 for several weeks to do research in the National Library of Foreign Literature, I met Ekaterina Genieva, the distinguished director of the library and a close friend to Aleksandr Men, and Fr. Georgii Chistiakov, head of the library's research center on religious literature. Before his untimely death in June 2007, Chistiakov provided me with a great deal of assistance. A kindly, learned, and greatly respected Orthodox priest, Fr. Georgii was a disciple of Aleksandr Men. He allowed me several interviews, which have turned out to be extremely important to my study, particularly his discussion of the theme he considered most significant in Fr. Aleksandr's work: his ecumenical vision. This theme, Chistiakov claimed, was largely unexplored in writings about Fr. Aleksandr.

Chistiakov introduced me to Pavel Vol'fovich Men, Fr. Aleksandr's younger brother, the director of the Aleksandr Men Foundation in Moscow, and a rich source of information about the late priest. In the last decade, the foundation has published a large number of Men's lectures, papers, and letters, as well as his memoirs, which Pavel Men provided to me before their publication. These materials, inaccessible to previous biographers, contributed a great deal of information about Fr. Aleksandr's personal relationships and primary influences.

Since his death in September 1990, public interest in Aleksandr Men has not diminished, but rather has greatly increased. I have witnessed three events that surprised me with the breadth and depth of the desire to keep his memory alive and to explore the significance of his life and thought. The first took place in New York, in June 2007, at a conference organized by Seraphim Sigrist, then bishop of the Orthodox Church in North America. Devoted to Fr. Aleksandr Men's legacy, the gathering attracted about forty people—scientists, artists, priests, professors, writers, and others—most of them from New York, but also included some who had traveled from Russia and Great Britain to attend. This, it turned out, was an annual event attended by people who met to explore Fr. Aleksandr's teachings and writings.

The second and third events took place in Moscow and Moffat, Scotland, respectively. The former was a celebration convened on a frigid evening in January 2010, the eve of what would have been Fr. Aleksandr's seventy-fifth birthday. Held in the Great Hall of the Library of Foreign Literature, about four hundred people of all ages gathered that evening, large numbers of them arriving an hour-and-a-half early. When the program began, the crowd filled the auditorium to overflowing, with people standing two deep along the walls. Music, speeches, poetry reading, and reminiscences about Fr. Aleksandr completed a program that lasted nearly four hours, with most everyone remaining until the end.

The third event took place in September 2012. Held in the southern Scottish town of Moffat, the conference on "The Life and Significance of Alexander Men" was truly an international gathering, featuring participants from multiple countries, including Russia. Organized by Elizabeth Roberts, Ann Shukman, and Donald Smith, with the support of Ekaterina Genieva, the conference explored the contemporary religious and cultural relevance of Fr. Aleksandr's ideas. No one left Moffat without a greater awareness of this remarkable Russian parish priest, whose significance extended far beyond the country in which he had lived and served.

A common perception of the Russian Orthodox Church is that it has played only a marginal role in Russian life for most of the last century. Inward-looking and cut off from political and public affairs, the Church, according to this view, operated with little or no influence beyond its narrow, decaying walls. Its priests were an unimpressive lot—docile, poorly educated, and interested in preserving a defunct tradition—and they are often depicted as backward-looking, tied to the government, and with little to say to the modern world. But these general depictions of the Russian Orthodox Church neither tell the full story nor capture the lives of the men and women who moved in a much different direction. Such people present a more complex and paradoxical picture than the stereotypes commonly found in popular Western accounts.

One good reason for writing a book on Fr. Aleksandr Men (1935–1990) is that he challenges the common view of the Russian Orthodox Church as passive and submissive. There are also other reasons. He offers a way of looking at Russia's national story for most of the twentieth century other than strictly through the prism of politics and economics. Growing up during the Stalin era, where fear and ideological conformity dominated nearly all of Soviet life, he had every reason to accommodate himself to the regime. That he refused to take this route, choosing instead to follow an alternative course and to construct his own separate path, is a tale of uncommon strength of mind and spirit. Russian scholars speak of the process of looking inward, pursuing one's own version of truth, as "internal immigration" from the regime. Aleksandr Men represents an example par excellence of that phenomenon. Yet his story is compelling for still another reason: he cast his vision not only inward, but also outward—at his society, the struggles of other people, and the Church as an institution. In the United States, with few exceptions, Aleksandr Men remains nearly unknown. I am hopeful that the present work, in some small way, will help fill that gap.

This book is a study of Aleksandr Men's life and thought, particularly as it relates religion to science, culture, the state, Russian society, and freedom.

But the present work also has a broader focus than simply the study of ideas. It adheres to a chronological framework, tracing Aleksandr Men's origins and early life, his evolution as a person and as a seminal Russian Orthodox writer and thinker. It examines how a person, born as an ethnic Jew in the darkest years of the twentieth century, became a Russian Orthodox priest who commanded a large following.

I have not attempted to write a theological study, nor do I claim that this work is a definitive account of Fr. Aleksandr. A complete review of his voluminous writings and talks would require a lifetime of study, and some of the documents relating to his parish are still in the process of discovery and publication. This study is concerned, however, with the communal context in which his ideas evolved, his relationships with certain individuals who influenced him, his love affair with books and people, and his legacy.

Alexandre Men, un témoin pour la Russie de ce Temps, written by the French diplomat and scholar Yves Hamant more than two decades ago, is the standard biography of Fr. Aleksandr and the most accessible to an English-speaking public.[3] Translated into Russian, German, and English, Hamant's book is a warmly written appreciation of Fr. Aleksandr that primarily focuses on his relationship to the Soviet state. Since its publication, two additional biographies of Men have appeared, both written by members of his parish at Novaia Derevnia: Zoia Afanas'evna Maslenikova's *Zhizn' ottsa Aleksandr Menia* (Life of Father Aleksandr Men) and Andrei Alekseevich Eremin's *Otets Aleksandr Men': Pastyr' na rubezhe vekov* (Father Aleksandr Men: Pastor on the boundary of centuries).[4] Both volumes contain many valuable first-hand observations of parish life. Both, especially Eremin's account, heavily incorporate Fr. Aleksandr's own words. My work has a different focus, although all three of these biographies offer a wealth of primary and secondary source materials from which I have drawn.

In recent years, particularly in the last decade, the Aleksandr Men Foundation in Moscow has published a large number of primary materials on the subject of my study. I have made extensive use of these primary sources, which include Fr. Aleksandr's lectures on Russia's philosophical/theological writers, as well as his household conversations, letters, and public interviews. In addition, as I learned while writing my earlier book on civil society, face-to-face interviews with primary participants, when used with much care, offer important insights into thoughts and motivations. Such interviews with people who knew Fr. Aleksandr well have benefitted my own understanding of his life and the circumstances in which he served.

Aleksandr Men saw himself foremost as a parish priest, but his contributions went far beyond that designation: he was a social critic, a thinker of national and international importance, a primary interpreter of Orthodoxy and world religions to the Russian people, and a religious leader who commanded a large following and whose influence transcended his death. He was an apostle of freedom in Russia and a believer that Christianity is a "religion of freedom," which "rejects authoritarianism and paternalism" as antithetical to the spirit of faith.[5] In professing this belief and refusing to be ruled by fear, Fr. Aleksandr and his teachings have significant implications for Russia's future, and such implications go far beyond Russia's national boundaries.

On a personal level, the life of Aleksandr Men offers a window into themes the Russian Orthodox Church lived through in the twentieth century: its struggle to survive despite overwhelming political circumstances seeking its destruction; its efforts to speak convincingly to a people searching for historical, cultural, and religious roots in a world turned upside down; its attempts to regain its memory in a sea of competing voices; and more broadly, its relationship to a changing social and political landscape at the end of the Soviet period and beyond. His is an inspiring story of perseverance and triumph against formidable odds.

1

. . . .

Murder in the Semkhoz Woods

On most days, the winding path through the woods near the village of Semkhoz, close to the city of Sergiev Posad (Zagorsk in the Soviet era), presents a peaceful scene. The footpath, cut long ago from the railroad to the village, enables Semkhoz inhabitants to walk to the station and await the train connecting them to the outside world. Tall grasses and wildflowers grow on each side of the narrow path for several feet before merging into thick woods and their leaf-covered floor. Elegant birch trees, with their white bark and rich, green leaves, appear sporadically along the edge of the woods. In the early morning, with the sunlight coming through the tree branches, their autumn leaves golden, this is a lovely site, the stillness interrupted only by an occasional foot traveler going to the station or taking an early morning walk. In early September, with the fall season fast approaching, the warm days of summer have already begun to fade.

Between 6:30 and 6:45 a.m. on September 9, 1990, Fr. Aleksandr Men left his home at Semkhoz to walk to the station and travel the short distance to his nearby church at Novaia Derevnia where, for the last twenty years, he had served as priest. He fastened the gate at the edge of his yard and turned down the path through the woods to take the quarter-mile walk to the station. He had a long day ahead—the liturgy, confessions, baptisms at his church, and then another lecture scheduled in Moscow in the afternoon. He carried a leather briefcase, which held a manuscript on which he had worked for several months. It was a Sunday morning, and Fr. Aleksandr had arisen early to prepare for the services that morning and, as he had done since he was an adolescent, to spend some time in silence and prayer before the activities of the day began. The previous week had been an extremely busy time, each day filled with meetings, public talks, and scheduled discussions, mostly in Moscow. He relished the time to gather his thoughts, the quietness of his surroundings, and the peacefulness that this early morning walk normally provided. He did not hurry. He left in plenty of time to think and to walk at a normal pace along the pathway. He was unaware that this would be the final time he would traverse the wooded path to the station.

Aleksandr Men was fifty-five years old, an energetic, robust, and life-loving man, who was constantly in demand and who never had enough time to accomplish everything he wished to do. His reputation, especially among young people and intellectuals, had skyrocketed in the last five years. During Gorbachev's period of perestroika, and particularly following the end of state repression of the church in 1987–1988, his activities seemed to multiply. His appearances attracted large crowds of people who, heretofore, had showed little public interest in religion.

Extremely learned, articulate, and courageous, Fr. Aleksandr represented the spiritual voice of a democratic, nonauthoritarian Christianity. His actions and his words, including his vision of Orthodoxy, spoke sharply and eloquently against the ultranationalistic, anti-Semitic, and reactionary tendencies within the official church and certain political circles. He had not compromised either with the government or the police, even during the years when many church officials had done so. He was a strong, principled, and thoughtful advocate of the renewal of Orthodoxy at a moment in time unique in his life and, perhaps even more so, in Russia in the twentieth century.

On the previous evening, September 8, Fr. Aleksandr had delivered a major address at the House of Culture and Technology in Moscow. The lecture served as the culmination of a series of talks he had given on world religions that spring and summer, and it led to his final argument that Christ represented the conclusion, the ultimate product, of God's revelation. Fr. Aleksandr, according to Russian historian and librarian of Congress James H. Billington, was "the greatest preacher of his generation, who appeared in many ways to be a prophet of the Russia we had seen emerging" in the late 1980s.[1]

As Fr. Aleksandr set out early the next morning along the same path he had walked the night before, he could see no one coming toward him. But the evidence suggests that two men, who had likely waited for him in the woods sometime during the previous night, soon stepped out of the shadows. It appears that they approached him from the rear, called out to him, and showed him some printed materials.

As best as the scene can be reconstructed, Fr. Aleksandr took his glasses from his coat pocket and bent forward to read the materials. As he did so, one of the men struck him hard on the back of his head with a sharp instrument resembling a small axe, like the one sometimes carried by members of Russia's special forces. His glasses fell to the ground by the side of the path, where they would be found later. Fr. Aleksandr stumbled forward, bleeding profusely from his wound, and began walking toward the railway station, but then, as if understanding the severity of his wound, turning to painfully stumble back along the path to his home. Nearing the gate he had unlatched only minutes earlier, he fell against it, his robust body crumbling to the ground, his head and shoulders lying against the wooden fence, and his left hand trying to grasp the fence's siding.

Still asleep inside the house, Nataliia Fedorovna, Fr. Aleksandr's wife, was awakened by the groans and cries of a person lying outside, at the front. The window in the room where she slept opened onto the street, and she could hear the sounds clearly. Half asleep, unsure of what had happened, and unable to see distinctly through the gaps in the fencing, she saw a blood-soaked man lying in the road. She did not know that this man was her injured husband. Frightened by the evidence of violence, instead of opening the gate, Nataliia Fedorovna went back into the house and immediately called for an ambulance. It took nearly a half-hour before the ambulance arrived to find the body of the man lying against the fence. He was no longer alive.[2]

In the following months, many testimonies appeared both in the Russian and international press eulogizing Fr. Aleksandr Men. One of the most incisive of these post-mortem assessments came from Abkhaz native Fazil Abdulevich Iskander, author of *The Goatibex Constellation* (1966) and other well-known novels and short stories. Iskander was known in the former Soviet Union for his fictional depictions of Caucasian life and sharp satirical portraits of various social problems. He had met Fr. Aleksandr on several occasions, knew of his growing importance, and had witnessed firsthand his actions as a public figure. In his short account, Iskander focused on a recent conversation he had with Fr. Aleksandr at a social event, held in a private house, at which many other guests were present. Portraying Aleksandr Men as a charming person, easily met, and completely unpretentious, Iskander also described a man of penetrating intelligence and impressive aesthetic sensibilities.

How is it, Iskander had wanted to know, that the priest of a small church near Moscow had developed the capacity to write so compellingly for the Russian people? Use of language and ability to speak across the divisions of class and educational levels were unusual. Iskander felt himself in the rare presence of an independent mind, a person of great learning but also entirely natural, without the "pride of self esteem" and in possession of a unique spirit. The two men talked about humor and its importance for human beings; Fr. Aleksandr claimed humor to be among humanity's greatest and most distinctive gifts, an essential part of what it means to be human. They conversed about literature, particularly about Alexander Solzhenitsyn's works and Mikhail Bulgakov's *Master and Margarita*, which

Fr. Aleksandr knew well. As Iskander recalled their discussion, Aleksandr Men viewed Russia's renewal as greatly dependent on restoring the connections to its rich cultural and philosophical traditions, which looked outward, across religious and national boundaries, to the deepest expressions of the spirit. It was this aspiration, Iskander maintained, that also "provoked in some people a frenzied hatred."[3] Iskander said Fr. Aleksandr left the meeting early that evening. The priest had remembered his promise to visit one of his parishioners, "who had recently fallen into depression," and Fr. Aleksandr hoped to raise his spirits.[4] He departed about 9 p.m., going out into the rainy, windy night, even though he could easily have waited for another, more comfortable time. Fr. Aleksandr's departure that evening incited anxiety among some guests about his safety and the possibility of an attack on this solitary figure, walking along a dark, isolated road to call on a friend. But what struck Iskander most deeply was Aleksandr Men's care for people and his uncommon ability to reach out to them. On later occasions, while walking with Fr. Aleksandr near his parish, Iskander observed how his parishioners stopped him, "hailed him from a distance, almost ran to him" to discuss some problem in their lives.[5] Such a learned academic mind paired with a unique capacity to relate to people of every social rank presented a rare combination. "He was the light of our Homeland," Iskander concluded, the light whose "power will show itself only in the future. And if again darkness envelops our country, we will understand that from whence came the darkness, came also the murderer."[6]

The questions Iskander raised in his eulogy have resonated long after Fr. Aleksandr Men's death in the late summer of 1990. How did the Stalin era, known for its extreme violence and terror and its attempts to reeducate the entire Soviet population, somehow produce this prophetic figure who offered such a different view? How did this priest, who spent much of his career serving in a small village parish, develop a voice that spoke compellingly to such large numbers of people across social and religious boundaries? Upon what sources within Russian Orthodoxy and within Russian culture did Fr. Aleksandr draw, and which did he rediscover, and relate to the present? How did Fr. Aleksandr's vision of the church and its role in society compare and contrast with the view of the official Orthodox Church? With whom was he in conflict, both inside and outside the church, and was this conflict political, religious, or both? In reference to Iskander's concluding statement about the light and the dark, from whence came this darkness that produced Fr. Aleksandr's murderer? What is his legacy in present-day Russia: religious heretic or sacred martyr?

The pages that follow examine these interrelated questions about Fr. Aleksandr Men and the Russian Orthodox Church.

2

. . . .

Swimming against the Stream

The second half of 1977 was a perilous time in Fr. Aleksandr Men's life. In the fall, he began a series of experimental meetings in the Moscow homes of several of his parishioners. These sessions, clandestinely held, brought him a great deal of joy, but they also created much personal anxiety, given the circumstances in which he operated. Such meetings allowed him to expand his ministry beyond the boundaries of his church at Novaia Derevnia on the outskirts of the town of Pushkino, northwest of Moscow and near the traditional religious center of Sergiev Posad. At Novaia Derevnia, he had served for seven years as the second priest. While he worked in this small village parish, his ministry had already become well known among a significant number of the intelligentsia and other city people, many of whom traveled to Novaia Derevnia on Sundays to participate in the church's activities. News traveled quickly by word of mouth about this unusual Orthodox priest during one of the darkest periods of Soviet history. His ministry also attracted the attention of the KGB (the Committee for State Security, or *Komitet gosudarstvennoi bezopasnosti*).

Aleksandr Men called the sessions "gatherings," since to hold meetings without government approval constituted a crime and its participants would be arrested. "Gatherings" connoted something different, an informal, unplanned get together of friends, usually to celebrate birthdays or holidays, to share food, drink, and conversation. Held in someone's flat in one of Moscow's ubiquitous apartment buildings, these "gatherings," to some, might have emulated the illicit meetings of Russia's prerevolutionary circles of the intelligentsia, although Fr. Aleksandr's "gatherings" had much different goals; they had their roots in Russia's "catacomb church," the underground church that began in the late 1920s in an effort to preserve Orthodox traditions of worship during a time when the Bolshevik government unleashed a violent assault against all forms of religious expression.[1]

The "gatherings" Aleksandr Men organized existed in no less threatening circumstances, and the people who participated took precautions. They came separately, with no more than two of them arriving at the same time. They also departed at different times. Meeting weekly, gatherings rarely took place in the same apartment on consecutive weeks. Participants took special care not to attract attention, either by their dress or demeanor. The collection of men and women in an apartment resembled an informal, impromptu coming together of family members or friends who could easily be dispersed, should circumstances demand such action. But they seldom did, and the suspicious official or member of the police who followed a young, suspected member of the group had little reason to think that he or she had come to gather for an illicit discussion. The assembly of people did have a familial atmosphere, as the individuals, packed together into a small room, sat on the bed, on chairs, or, most often, on the floor. "My two sons were little at the time, and friends would bring their own children, too," recalled a participant in one of the earlier gatherings, held in his single room on Garibaldi Street. "Father [Aleksandr] would speak amid the sound of clanging cups and forks, and the cries of infants," a background symphony that seemed not to disturb him.[2]

While the young men and women who participated in these group sessions may have feared coming to Novaia Derevnia in the late 1970s and early 1980s, Fr. Aleksandr Men took the church into the city. This was a time, particularly in the early 1980s, when the Communist Party intensified its efforts to eradicate religion in the Soviet Union. KGB pressure on active church parishes, such as the Novaia Derevnia parish, grew more oppressive than it had been earlier in the 1970s, and Fr. Aleksandr faced multiple interrogations by the police. The leading antireligious journal *Nauka i religiia* (Science and religion) constantly hammered on the theme of science's superiority over religion, proclaiming religious belief as superstitious, a pillar of Russian backwardness that the Soviet state aimed to overcome.[3]

At the Moscow gatherings in 1977 and thereafter, Aleksandr Men aimed to expand the conversation about religion. He wanted to develop a new way of understanding the world, one much different from the teachings the Soviet state had sought to impart since the early 1920s. Education constituted one of his primary tasks. He knew that the participants in these sessions hungered for different approaches to life than those that the present educational system and the media sought to inculcate in Soviet citizens. A great deal of his voluminous teaching and writing aimed to reconnect his followers with a religious and cultural heritage whose organic process had been broken. "The fact that whole generations in our country were cut off from traditions, including ethical, religious and philosophical ones, dealt society a grievous blow," he said. "But since 'the oxygen was cut off' our culture became unbelievably impoverished."[4] In such an intellectual environment, he faced a daunting task.

The gatherings Fr. Aleksandr organized had another purpose that related to one of the main themes in his understanding of Orthodox tradition. He deeply believed that the church ought to foster a strong sense of community among believers, both within and outside the boundaries of the church. Since the state prohibited such groups from organizing without special permission and closely oversaw the church's own activities, Fr. Aleksandr had to find another way to provide this community. He wanted to connect individuals to each other, providing them support and a channel for dialogue, which he believed lay at the core of the church's mission.[5] He needed to find the means to overcome the atomistic, self-reliant existence in which individuals operated. He wanted to build trusting relationships.

As they grew in number, the gatherings focused on specific subjects, each of them designed not only to offer the opportunity for worship, but also to fill in the large educational gap. These subjects included the teachings of the church fathers, church history, theology, Biblical criticism, and Orthodox traditions. Fr. Aleksandr actively took part in the first sessions of each of the gatherings, during which he set the framework for their discussions. As the internal dynamics of the group developed, he moved to the site of another gathering, helping it become established. While they had no direct relationship, the gatherings Fr. Aleksandr created resembled the small groups founded in Western countries in the late 1970s, following the apostolic exhortation of Pope Paul VI, which set forth the guiding principles for local Roman Catholic communities, and kept such communities firmly attached to their local church.[6]

In Russia, however, the gatherings developed under different circumstances than in Western countries. They had to be kept hidden from the watchful eyes of the police. Most importantly, Fr. Aleksandr well understood that unless newcomers to the church had additional networks of support, they would find it nearly impossible to develop their knowledge in a vast ideological sea that assaulted them every day with very different ideas.

If Aleksandr Men had relied exclusively on his intellectual abilities to connect Orthodoxy with the lives of individuals who came to him, his success as a parish priest might well have existed only as a temporary phenomenon. He knew that the exploration of religious ideas was an overt challenge to Soviet ideology and could take place only in the most tenuous and dangerous circumstances. At the gatherings, Fr. Aleksandr introduced the idea of the church as a fellowship, a community not governed by an external power, but which bore witness to an internal authority. Here, he spoke about the "presence of the Mysteries. . . . so that our witness may not be a witness about ideology, but of the living presence of God in us."[7] His teachings addressed a different way of seeing the world than the members of the community had been taught elsewhere.

Fr. Aleksandr attempted to provide the framework and to offer the encouragement for participants to engage in a simple but difficult task: to discover the divine source that existed within each of them. Such an approach lay deep within Orthodox tradition, and Aleksandr Men had discovered it early in his life. He elaborated on that process in the gatherings and, extensively, in his parish activities. But, in addition, as Fr. Aleksandr modeled them, the gatherings were channels of exploration and discovery, places where the mind could be unfettered. This belief had little in common with the Western notion of independent thought, individualistic beliefs, or a consumerist religion that, later, he would sharply criticize. Rather, the quest for the divine spirit in each person took place within the fellowship of others, and the gatherings and the community he developed aspired to offer that fellowship.

To participants in these meetings, living in such difficult times, Fr. Aleksandr did not give comfort. What he offered was hope. He stressed the importance of imagination and the need to look at the world differently than through the materialist underpinnings that Soviet education emphasized as the proper means of interpreting society. In the social context of his times, Fr. Aleksandr was an outsider, a rebel who rejected the established social and political order. While he may have physically lived in that order, he existed apart from it mentally and spiritually, and the hope he projected called for a new way of being and relating. As the Russian Orthodox priest Alexi Vinogradov has pointed out, Fr. Aleksandr also lived in a world much different than that of Russian émigré theologians who taught and wrote in an "atmosphere of relative intellectual freedom" in Western Europe; "In Russia, however, unique figures like Fr. Aleksandr Men were lonely fish swimming against the stream."[8] He would not be the first in his family line to move in that direction and to challenge the social and religious surroundings in which he existed.

Family Heritage

Aleksandr Men traced his family roots to Poland, but he and other living family members knew few details about their predecessors or social circumstances. He belonged to a long line of Jewish families whose heritage extended into this region. It is likely that the partitions of Poland, which divided up the former sovereign state during the second half of the eighteenth century, incorporated the family into the Russian Empire during the reign of Catherine II (1762–1796), when the Russian government gained large swaths of Polish territory. In the second partition (1793), which aimed at preventing Poland from becoming a future military threat to Russia and Prussia, Russia acquired more than 100,000 square miles of new territory and more than three million citizens.[9] Russia absorbed this population in the second and third partitions (1795) and included large numbers of Jews, estimated at 289,022.[10] They came with religious traditions different from those of the Russian population, and over time proved difficult to assimilate. Having a long history of political and economic autonomy, they did not readily fit into the legal social estate categories that Catherine II and her immediate successors—Paul I and Alexander I—sought to enforce. These Russian rulers did not harbor religious prejudices against the new inhabitants, either in their rhetoric or in their state policies, at least until 1815, but such prejudices would not be long in emerging in the nineteenth century.[11] Separated from the rest of the population by their dress, their speech, and their religious practices, Jews came to be treated with both distrust and condescension. Protesting competition from Jewish traders who developed commercial networks between cities and villages, in 1790, the merchants of Moscow petitioned the government to restrict registration of Jews in the merchant guilds of the city.[12] In the mid-nineteenth century, the Pale of Jewish Settlement evolved, which fixed residential places and occupational choices for Jews, and, in the 1880s, further discriminatory legislation permitted Jews to secure permanent residence only in certain urban centers.[13] Although the application of the laws remained fluid, subject to individual appeal of these restrictions, thousands of Jews were expelled from their residences in the countryside. The imperial Russian government sought to segregate and isolate Jews from the larger part of the Russian population. Over time, a social and economic context evolved that led to anti-Jewish violence on a large scale in 1881–1882 and 1905–1906.[14]

In the Vasilevskaia family, his mother's line, one of Aleksandr's forefathers had already established himself in Russia in the early nineteenth century. He, therefore, left more information about himself than did the family members on his father's side. This individual served as an artilleryman in the reign of Alexander I (1801–1825), and his son spent twenty-four years in the army of Tsar Nicholas I (1825–1855). The Russian military thus played a significant role in Aleksandr's mother's side of the family, service that gave it an orientation different from the lineage of his father. He tells us little about that orientation, but it is likely that the family's life in the city exposed it to a larger cultural and educational world, as well as a chance to mingle with people of different nationalities and ways of thinking. The military service of this predecessor permitted his children to live in the capital city, unlike those who, because of their Jewish heritage, were excluded from the privilege of owning a place of residence in Moscow.

In the Vasilevskaia family, several personalities and events stand out as playing a significant role in shaping the family's memory and heritage. Aleksandr Men's great-grandmother Anna Osipovna (Iosifovna) Vasilevskaia was one of the personages whose life became an important part of family lore.[15] A strong-willed, spirited, and highly principled woman, Anna Osipovna lived in the Ukrainian city of Khar'kov. She had seven children, four boys and three girls, ranging in age from three to eighteen years of age, when her husband died and left her nearly penniless. She managed to raise them by virtue of hard work, steadfastness, and an indomitable will to persevere, despite the multiple hardships she faced. While still a young, widowed mother, Anna Osipovna had to deal with a life-threatening illness that caused her severe pain and anxiety. She developed a large lump on her breast, which continued to grow and to spread. Despite numerous consultations with local medical specialists, she found no one who could relieve her suffering or offer her proper treatment.

In 1890, the renowned Russian Orthodox priest Fr. John of Kronstadt (Fr. Ioann Kronstadtskii, 1829–1908) visited Khar'kov. Well known for his ministry among the poor of Kronstadt, the island naval base off the coast of Saint Petersburg, Fr. John's arrival created a stir among the townspeople, and large contingents of people greeted him wherever he appeared. A neighbor of Anna Osipovna's convinced her that she should attempt to approach Fr. John, despite Anna's Jewish religion. On the day of the priest's appearance in the city's center, an enormous crowd gathered around him. As Anna related the event, her friend pushed through the crowd, taking Anna by the hand and leading her to Fr. John. He looked at her, listened to her friend's pleas for help, and then said to Anna, "I know that you are Jewish, but I see in you a deep faith in God." Fr. John offered to pray with her for her health and assured her of God's help, saying to Anna that "within a month your illness will pass from you."[16] In the story passed down to Anna's descendants, "her swelling tumor began to recede, and after a month nothing remained of it."[17] In this family story, Fr. John had looked beyond the narrow religious distinctions that people commonly made and had reached out to the sick woman. He had recognized only her humanity, her belief, and her need.

The healing ministry that he projected would take a similar and yet different form in later generations of Anna's descendants. Fr. John's reception of the distressed Anna, his prayers for her, and the healing that resulted became part of a larger family story that would be retold many times.

Despite her meager economic resources, Anna Osipovna Vasilevskaia managed to educate all her children, three of whom became engineers. "They were men of great physical strength, with a good enlightened character," as Aleksandr Men later described them.[18] The last of her children, Tsetsiliia, would become his grandmother. All of Anna Osipovna's children became freethinking members of the Russian intelligentsia who grew up at a time when positivism and rationalism dominated university life, and most of Anna Osipovna's children fell in with these general trends. Few of them actively practiced their Jewish faith; not one learned Hebrew.[19] They were strongly attracted to the sciences and aspired to contribute to a world being rapidly remade through technology and the physical sciences.

Like her older siblings, Tsetsiliia, too, grew up in an environment where study of the sciences became a preeminent goal. In her schooling, she developed a passionate interest in chemistry, soon committing herself to this field for her life's work. Serious-minded, determined, and talented, she proved to be an excellent student, who, after completing her secondary education, earned a scholarship to study at the University of Berne, one of Europe's leading centers for research in the physical sciences. At the university, Tsetsiliia met Solomon Tsuperfein, a young man from Odessa who shared her love of the sciences. The two of them became fast friends, often studying together and talking about their future plans. Soon, their relationship developed into much more than friendship. Shortly thereafter, the two aspiring chemistry students married, promising to live in total commitment to each other and to their life's work. As Aleksandr Men recalled, his grandfather adored Tsetsiliia "and would do so to the end of his life."[20] The young couple finished the university at the same time in the chemistry faculty, both with doctoral degrees. In 1908, while students in Berne, they had a daughter (Elena), the future mother of Aleksandr Men, and, in 1912, a son (Leonid).

During the years preceding World War I, Switzerland became a home for many of the revolutionaries who had fled Russia after the 1905 Revolution and the government's ensuing harsh reprisals against all revolutionary political parties. In Russia, both liberalism and the revolutionary movement were in retreat as ultraconservative organizations, such as the Union of the Russian People, spearheaded a forceful, often violent assault on the advocates of constitutional government. Jews became the targets of these ultraconservatives, who used them as scapegoats for Russia's internal unrest. In 1911, the sensational case of Mendel Beilis, a Jewish citizen living in Kiev, drew international attention. Beilis was accused of the ritual murder of a young Christian boy, following the discovery of the boy's dismembered body. The case incited anti-Semitic, monarchical political parties, and extremist groups such as the Black Hundreds attempted to "provoke mass anti-Semitic pogroms in the country" then and after Beilis's acquittal by jury trial in October 1913.[21]

In these prewar years, while living abroad, Vladimir Il'ich Lenin often came to Berne, where he occasionally spoke and met with members of the Bolshevik Party. In 1909 he published *Materialism and Empirio-Criticism*, which he wrote during the political struggle with his rival, Aleksandr Bogdanov, a biological scientist, for the intellectual leadership of the Bolshevik Party. *Materialism and Empirio-Criticism* would later become a classic of Marxism-Leninism, a text that defined Lenin's approach to knowledge and laid out certain key principles of his materialist philosophy. In this work, Lenin sought to refute his opponents, whose orthodox views he challenged. Bogdanov argued that the physical world, as well as society itself, evolved from the human mind; without the human desire to form community, society would not have developed. Lenin branded such thinking as idealist; he dismissed the view that society had come into being as an expression of consciousness, and he claimed the primacy of matter over mind.[22] The exterior world, he maintained, existed independently of the mind's capacity to conceive it. Citing Friedrich Engels, whom he accused his opponents of misunderstanding, Lenin distinguished the materialist from the idealist, the "pure" thinkers from the "impure" thinkers.[23] He laid the foundation for his materialist worldview, a philosophy that rejected the scientific basis of religion.[24] In Berne, Lenin applied his materialist philosophy to the living and working conditions of laboring men and women, whose sufferings at the hands of the ruling class of exploiters the Bolshevik leader proposed to alleviate.

In Switzerland, Tsetsiliia Tsuperfein heard Lenin speak and found herself "strongly attracted" to his materialist philosophy.[25] She "soon became totally and sincerely pro-Soviet," and while Aleksandr Men's reminiscences did not reveal the revolutionary party that his grandmother supported, he underscored her sympathy with Lenin's empirical approach and with issues of social justice.[26] Politically, she strongly disagreed with the social and economic policies of the Tsarist government and its repressive agencies.

After graduation, Tsetsiliia and her husband planned to settle in Paris. But before they moved, they decided to make a trip home to visit their relatives, intending to give them a first view of their five-year-old daughter, Elena, and her younger brother, Leonid. The family left Berne in the early summer of 1914, traveling by train across the Austro-Hungarian Empire. Like most other people, they could not have known the future course of events that lay immediately before them and the unfortunate circumstances that would change the world forever. When World War I began on July 28, they were in Ukraine, caught behind the lines of battle that quickly developed and interrupted their plans to return to Western Europe to pursue their careers in the sciences. Solomon was recruited into the Russian army, and Tsetsiliia and the children remained in Khar'kov in order to be near her family. There she spent the war years, working to sustain herself and her two children during these years not only of war, but soon of revolution.

In 1914, on the eve of World War I, Khar'kov was Ukraine's second largest city, with a population of 244,700.[27] As a major industrial and railroad center, the city had seen rapid economic growth early in the twentieth century, especially in mechanical engineering, mining, and steel processing. During these years of war, revolution, and civil war the city and its surrounding areas witnessed intense fighting from all sides—from pro- and anti-Bolshevik armies, German units, Ukrainian national forces, and anarchists. In 1920, after the Red Army defeated its opponents, Khar'kov became the capital of Soviet Ukraine, a position it continued to hold until 1934, when the Soviet government returned the Ukrainian capital to Kiev.

In coming to power, the Bolsheviks championed a collective way of life in which private interests were to be sacrificed to the interests of the whole community. In part, the primary importance of the collective came out of the Bolsheviks' struggles with their enemies, first the Tsarist regime and later the oppositional forces of the revolution. But the focus on collective consciousness reflected the Party's ideological goals. The Bolsheviks fought for the liberation of humankind from social and economic oppression, aspirations requiring the submergence of the personal into the larger social good, as the Party conceived it. The New Soviet Man and Woman would be selfless, obliterating the distinction between private and public life. In his visit to Moscow from December 1926 until the end of January 1927, the German writer Walter Benjamin was struck with this new approach to social activity, this "withering away of private life."[28] "Everything is being rebuilt and every movement poses very critical questions," he wrote. "The tensions of public life—which for the most part are actually of a theological sort—are so great that they block off private life to an unimaginable degree."[29] He described the small amounts of living space, the communal apartments, and lives lived essentially in the office, the club, and on the street.[30] The Bolshevik Party's assault on the traditional family and on the Russian Orthodox Church aimed to destroy the roots of private interests and dissolve the self into a communal existence.

Thus, as recent scholars have pointed out, a large majority of diaries and memoirs written by Soviet citizens in the 1920s and '30s demonstrate, even glorify, this emphasis on the collective.[31] Private concerns and personal sensibilities play little role in these writings. Soviet diaries and memoirs attempt to set the individual in the context of political events, connect the person to those events, and highlight his or her contributions to Party successes. They show the drive to internalize the physical, external world, rather than to allow one's internal thoughts to determine one's actions.

In the life of Aleksandr's mother Elena Semenovna, who would become a major influence on him, the reverse was the case.[32] She, too, wrote a memoir about these years, although she composed some of it later in the Soviet period. Her memoir offered a rare, private view of her struggles. Unlike other such writers, she seldom spoke of external political events. She offered a personal recollection of her internal life, her thoughts and feelings in the process of self-discovery, her family, and her attempts to survive in a world outwardly hostile to her way of being.

In their studies of Soviet autobiographies from the 1920s through the 1940s, historians Igal Halfin and Jochen Hellbeck speak of an inner transformation that took place in the lives of the writers of these works. Both historians focused on language, "the medium that molds the new consciousness" of individuals, to show that such individuals shed their old individual selves and became members of an elect, the makers of a selfless, forward-looking, classless society.[33] In describing their conversion experiences, autobiographical writers proudly proclaimed how they extricated themselves from religious superstitions, how the state became the source of their new identity, and how they learned "to think correctly."[34]

In contrast to Halfin's and Hellbeck's analysis, Elena Men's autobiography offers a portrait of a young woman's personal experiences (entrance into adulthood). Like Halfin's and Hellbeck's protagonists, she writes about a personal transformation, but one that bears little resemblance to the worlds they describe. Elena Semenovna does not speak of a new social identity. She came to a new way of understanding the self and a different means of perceiving the world and her purpose in it. She sought to obey, she writes, not an external authority, but to listen to "an inner voice," and she speaks of an "independence of soul" that characterized her life.[35] She does not recognize "class enemies," the social and economic divisions that featured in the autobiographies of Party members. It is, therefore, not surprising that Elena's favorite Russian writer is Fedor Dostoevsky, whose protagonist Alyosha

Karamazov she calls her "favorite literary character," and whose love for all people and selfless service she greatly admired.[36] She would not have said that "she learned to think correctly." She had an "innate sense of mystery" about everything, including her own world.[37] She presents a more nuanced, more complex portrait than those found in the autobiographies that Helfin and Hellbeck describe.

A Different Road

In November 1917, when the Bolsheviks came to power, Elena Semenovna Tsuperfein was eight years old. That fall, she entered the private gymnasium in Khar'kov, matriculating into the oldest preparatory class in her school. The regimen of the school continued to follow the same plan as it had in the past, starting with religious instruction in the fundamentals of the Orthodox tradition. "In the beginning of the lessons," she later recounted, "the priest explained the foundations of the Orthodox faith, and offered to teach us the prayers."[38] The first class consisted of study of the Old Testament, and the second dealt with the New Testament. Not all students in the school were Orthodox, a distinction the teachers respected, allowing non-Orthodox students like Elena to leave the classroom during religion sessions and stand in the hallway outside or go down to the floor below, where an instructor gave them dance lessons. Although she was Jewish, Elena elected to remain in the classroom, where she "listened attentively" to the explanations of the priest, fascinated by his discussion of the Trinity, which she "absorbed," she said, and "took into my heart."[39]

At home, Elena's mother offered private French and German lessons to children and occupied herself all day and into the evening with her students. Needing the money to feed herself and her children, as well as her own mother, who lived with them during these difficult times, Tsetsiliia worked extremely hard to make ends meet; she left the household duties and care of the children largely in the hands of the grandmother. One day, near the end of the spring term, a student of Tsetsiliia's forgot a copy of the New Testament after it inadvertently slipped down behind her chair as she departed. Several days later, Elena discovered the book, but her mother's pupil had already gone to the countryside for the summer holidays, thus leaving it in Elena's safekeeping for the following several months.

In her memoir, Elena Semenovna describes her reading of the New Testament that summer and how it opened before her a whole new world, which she had only glimpsed before in the school instructor's talks. During

the summer, she read the book herself, as she wrote, fascinated by the stories it contained. But even more than the biblical stories, Elena felt herself
moved by the words and what they proclaimed, a feeling she had not experienced before: "The more I read, the more I became attracted, drawn to
its [the New Testament's] spirit, and the more the love for Christ grew in
me."[40] Elena claimed to have found that summer a different approach to
other people and to herself than she had known previously. In part, her
grandmother's tender disposition—the same grandmother whom Fr. John
of Kronstadt had allegedly healed—had prepared her for this moment. Living in the same household as her grandmother for several years had given
Elena many opportunities to observe her kind demeanor and rich spiritual
life. It was nothing explicit that her grandmother taught her, Elena noted,
but the example she set through her relationships with others, which "acted
in me to produce the strongest kind of moral sense."[41] In Elena Semenovna's
reading of the New Testament, she came to the Crucifixion, at which point
she confessed to being overcome with emotion, a kind of "shock, which I
had never before experienced, nor would I after that moment."[42] This image
and Christ's words about forgiveness during his Crucifixion would remain
with her, as well as the love for humankind that the event expressed, words
that she took literally and incorporated into her daily life.

What did she see in this Gospel story that she found so compelling? Was
it the suffering Christ, the Man of Sorrows, who died for suffering humanity? Or was it the hope that the story inspired? Elena Semenovna did not
say. One may suppose that both elements appealed to her, even in these
early years, but that she also found something more, which would come
out only in light of her later experiences: the courage to develop her own
distinctive voice, despite the strong social forces that powerfully moved in
a different direction.

Confused and with the need to talk with someone about her thoughts,
Elena found no one in whom she could confide. At first, she said, she sought
out an older cousin, who she thought would be sympathetic, but that effort
proved disappointing. Next, she approached her mother and revealed to her
the thoughts and emotions she had experienced in her reading. The discussion led to confrontation between them and then to an explosion of anger.
Her mother's reaction was devastating. Tsetsiliia regarded Elena's position
as a betrayal of her heritage, a foolish and irrational decision that she simply
found unacceptable. Elena's account of the confrontation reveals, even in its
retelling, the emotional eruption Elena's confession produced: "My words
struck momma like a bomb. She recoiled in horror, began to scream at me,
and then struck me."[43] The conflict became so intense that Elena's brother

tried to divert his mother's attention from beating his sister: he picked up a chair and broke a window in the next room. Still angry at her daughter's impudence, Tsetsiliia violently shoved her into a corner, where she remained for some time, softly crying and feeling herself alone. In retrospect, as the pages of Elena's memoir suggest, her mother's reaction hardened her resolve regarding the road she decided to follow, although she well understood the personal difficulties her choice entailed.

Elena Semenovna recalled this scene many years after its occurrence, perhaps incorporating convictions she developed later in life into the memory of an event deeply buried in her consciousness. It is noteworthy, however, that this event was not isolated from other circumstances in her environment. As mentioned above, the religion instructor at the school she attended presented a framework different from the one she encountered at home. Elena had examples in her life, whether spoken or unspoken, that encouraged her to reach out beyond the boundaries of her own heritage. Moreover, as she later displayed more fully, she had an inner life and personal disposition much different from the harsh physical and political realities of the world around her.

Elena Semenovna's developing spirituality challenged the political and social environment in which she lived, both internally within her family and externally within the larger world. Political currents in Russian society were moving away from the inner convictions she harbored. By late 1917 and early 1918, the Bolsheviks were coming to power in the capital cities of Russia, which led to a frontal assault on Russia's traditional prerevolutionary culture and heralded a new world in which religion played a minimal role, if any at all. Soon thereafter, Elena's father returned from the war, quickly learning of the conflict between his wife and daughter. According to Elena, he first responded by smothering her with kindness, believing that she was passing through a temporary phase in her development. He learned, however, that he was mistaken, and as Elena began to explore more deeply her convictions, her father, too, joined his wife in disappointment and dismay.

Lonely, curious about what she had read, and desirous of learning more about the development of Christianity, Elena Semenovna turned to the Khar'kov municipal library. That fall, she went often, locating on the shelves accounts of the early Christians and their struggles to survive persecutions in the Roman era. She details her search in books that particularly enlarged her vision of this world, readings that appealed to her developing intellect. Elena recalled the book by Henryk Sienkiewicz, *Kamo griadeshi* (*Quo vadis?*), which was a popular reconstruction of the lives of the early Christians that, she said, "thrilled me as I read it."[44] She fondly remembered

Frederic William Farrar's *Na rassvete khristianstva* (The dawn of Christian-ity), a book on the same subject. As Elena Semenovna later wrote, somewhat sarcastically, "Such books could still be found in the library." These works gave her a connection to others who had persevered in their own course, and her readings presented her with a first look at the social and political pressures that such converts had to accept and endure.[45]

Precocious, intelligent, and strong-willed, Elena Semenovna grew up physically attached to her family but mentally apart from it. In 1924, at the age of sixteen, she finished her course of study in Khar'kov, although the conflicts with her immediate family continued. Partly in response to these tensions, but more specifically to continue her schooling, Elena left Khar'kov for Moscow. She followed her grandmother, who had gone there in 1920 to live with Elena's uncle Iakov, whose wife had died earlier the same year and had needed her help with his two children, a son, Venia, and daughter, Vera. They lived in a large apartment in Moscow, and Elena's uncle warmly welcomed her into their family, thinking that her arrival would help with his children, who continued to mourn deeply the death of their mother. This move to Moscow had several fortuitous outcomes: it would prove decisive in Elena Semenovna's life, and, as will be seen, it would later play a significant role in shaping the life of Aleksandr Men.

A World Turned Upside Down

Although Elena Semenovna could find no one in Khar'kov with whom to confide, her situation changed in Moscow. Elena's cousin, Vera Iakovlevna Vasilevskaia, immediately grew attached to her. The two young women were kindred spirits who became close to each other not only through family connections but also because of disposition and temperament. "We felt that our souls had some kind of attachment, some kind of close relationship to each other, although our character was sharply different," Elena wrote.[46] In coming into the household, she brought a youthful, energetic spirit whose presence its members needed and found immediately helpful.

"I was a lively, joyful young woman, and was at the age of sixteen exu-berant about life, thankful that I was surrounded by love and care," Elena Semenovna noted.[47] Having come to the capital to broaden her education beyond what Khar'kov offered, she found a course of study that appealed to her. In Moscow, she developed an interest in construction engineering, dis-covering that she had a natural talent for architectural drawing, a field that fit not only her creative proclivities, but also the practical needs of a rapidly growing city. Elena's first few years in the city did not always go smoothly. Near the end of the school term in the spring of her second year, she fell ill with typhoid, accompanied by pleurisy. Bedridden for three months with an extremely high temperature, unable to move about, and forbidden by her doctors from reading or engaging in any physical or intellectual activity, Elena suffered greatly, her body at times racked with pain. During these difficult months, her cousin Vera often sat by her bedside, trying to give her comfort and, in the evenings, reading to her Tolstoy's novel *War and Peace*.[48] At the end of that three-month period, Elena finally managed to leave her sickbed and completed the assignments enabling her to finish her course of study.

During the mid-1920s, Moscow became a booming metropolis. As the Russian economy began to recover following the civil war and the introduction of Lenin's New Economic Policy in 1921, the city's population rapidly expanded, growing from 1,028,000 in 1920, its lowest level in twenty years, to 2,026,087 in December 1926, soon after Elena Semenovna's arrival.[49] In 1926, ethnic Russians comprised 87.8 percent of Moscow's population, as people from the countryside, looking for work or trying to escape the famine that engulfed southern Russia, flooded into the city. The number of Jews among the city's population had also significantly increased, making up 6.5 percent of Moscow's population in 1926, with most of the newcomers arriving after the revolution abolished the former Pale of Settlement.

Elena Semenovna arrived in Moscow at a time when the face of the city was undergoing a wholesale makeover, its economic pulse sharply escalating and its physical appearance quickly changing. As trade between the countryside and the city swiftly increased, stimulated by the New Economic Policy, Moscow came to life again. In early 1921, it had been a dying city, but by the mid-1920s, it had once more become a thriving metropolis. Its cabbies, trade establishments, and nightclubs returned, as the opportunities for immediate profits abounded.[50] The boarded-up windows of retail establishments were replaced, the windows repaired, and the plastering refinished.[51] American businessman Armand Hammer described his surprise when he returned to Moscow in August 1921, after an absence of only a few weeks: "I had been away little more than a month, but short as the time was, I rubbed my eyes in astonishment. Was this Moscow, the city of squalor and sadness that I had left? Now the streets that had been so deserted were thronged with people. Everyone seemed in a hurry, full of purpose, with eager faces."[52] Peasants could be seen everywhere in the city "selling fruit, vegetables and other produce, or transporting bricks, lumber and building materials in their clumsy, creaking carts."[53]

By the mid-1920s, such activity had given rise to a thriving market, as goods ranging from clothes and household items to sugar, tea, cocoa, perfume, narcotics, and vegetable oil could be found in plentiful supply in the city's shops and trade stalls. After a decade of hardship and severe economic restraint, the new energy produced by this national recovery could be seen in many parts of the city, as well as the excesses, rampant speculation, and greed. Along the Moscow River, near the Kremlin, food markets catered to nearby restaurants and cafés, where business and professional men and women could be seen enjoying sumptuous banquets of fresh caviar, salmon, peaches and cream, and imported wines.[54] In nearly every quarter, Moscow became a beehive of market activity, a vibrant colorful city that would have been difficult to imagine a few years earlier.

The city's expanding population and thriving economic activity created an escalating demand for new housing and social services. Elena Semenovna's specialization and drawing talents fit right into that market need. During her years in school, she had little trouble finding employment as a blueprint-detailer for construction projects in a Moscow corporation. Elena became part of a new working generation, serving the economic needs of a city being transformed by commercial enterprise and revitalization projects that transformed this socialist metropolis.

Busy with her schooling and adjusting to life in Moscow, Elena Semenovna rarely attended Orthodox church services during her first two years in the city. She ventured into a church only a few times, but found the services impenetrable. The use of the ancient Church Slavonic liturgical language and the confusing order of the services left her disappointed, and she became impatient and frustrated by her inability to understand the meaning of the service: "I wanted to incorporate all of it, every word. I could not comprehend in my youth why this understanding did not occur immediately."[55]

The search for spiritual nourishment led Elena Semenovna in a new direction. Near the end of her second year, she saw on the Petrovskii gate in the city's center a small, crudely written note with the words "Society of Christian-Baptists." The society, the note explained, "is built on the example of Christian socialism during the first centuries of Christianity."[56] Curious about the group and anxious to learn about the community, Elena began to attend their meetings. She found them much different from what she had experienced the few times she attended Orthodox services in Moscow. The structure of the service was easy to follow and there was no language barrier since services were conducted in contemporary Russian. Moreover, as she later recalled, she found what she described as the "Christ-centered focus" of the meetings radically different from her experiences elsewhere. This small gathering of individuals warmly received her into their community. Elena Semenovna did not reveal much about the people who attended or details about the content of the meetings, only that she invited Vera to accompany her, but her cousin found the meetings "distasteful, undistinguished and of a low order."[57]

After completing her studies, Elena Semenovna returned to Khar'kov, which she had planned all along to do, hoping that she could resolve the conflicts with her family. This decision, however, turned out to be misguided and one she soon regretted. Once again, Elena had sharp conflicts with her mother over her beliefs and her behavior, particularly after she attended several gatherings of a local society of Baptists, where she found a community similar to the one she experienced in Moscow. Her presence at these meetings horrified her relatives. Critical of Baptist religious practices, they also called the Baptists' beliefs primitive and poked fun at their practice of baptizing converts in the river. Elena's behavior drove her mother "into a frenzy, resulting in beatings and then throwing [Elena's] books and journals onto the fire."[58]

This time, Elena Semenovna's father also turned against her; he tore down the pictures she had posted on the wall over her bed. Unable to endure the conflict and crushed by the continued disdain of her mother and father, Elena left their home in deep personal crisis. She had no permanent place to go. She was estranged from her family and had a scar on her face, which her mother's repeated beatings had given her. Alone in the city, cast aside by her immediate family, Elena was also ashamed to appear at her workplace, she said, because her colleagues asked a lot of questions about the cut on her face. Even though she "tried to make a joke of it," they easily saw that she faced an unusually difficult, tormented situation.[59]

Once again, in acute distress, Elena Semenovna was uncertain about her future. She understood the impossibility of reconciliation with her family and the difficult personal circumstances in which she found herself. Her mother wrote to Vera Iakovlevna, telling her that Elena had "run away from home to the Baptists."[60] Vera Iakovlevna immediately took the train to Khar'kov and brought Elena Semenovna back with her to Moscow. Vera offered her despondent relative a place to stay and personal support until Elena could find her own way. Reaching out to Elena during her time of need and rescuing her cousin from her difficult situation cemented the bond between them, a bond that had long-term consequences.

Elena Semenovna sought a different path from the world in which she grew up. At a time when it would have been comfortable and convenient simply to have given in and followed the prevailing sentiments that surrounded her, she stubbornly refused to accommodate herself to this milieu. Instead, she navigated her own path, adhering to convictions derived from her own reading of the Gospels. Such behavior took courage, but even more than this, it came from a belief that her act of swimming against the current had to be followed, despite the consequences that she inevitably had to suffer.

In seeking her own way, however, Elena Semenovna did not stand alone. The support and friendship of her cousin buttressed her courage and sustained her during moments of personal crisis. Her cousin proved essential to her endeavor. Vera Iakovlevna grew up in a different family environment, had a much different education, and faced challenges dissimilar from those of her younger cousin. She, too, would ultimately have a large influence on Aleksandr Men. Her own story thus warrants a closer look, particularly in terms of the formative events in her life. Who was this person who later played a key role in the upbringing and development of the future priest? What significant experiences shaped her own perspectives, which brought her to this moment and to convergence with the life of Elena Semenovna?

In the Company of Children

Vera Iakovlevna Vasilevskaia (1902–1975) was seven years older than her cousin. Born and raised in Moscow, she had what Aleksandr Men would later describe as a "brilliant humanitarian education at a pre-revolutionary private gymnasium" before her admission to Moscow University and its Institute of Foreign Languages.[61] While her parents had only a mild interest in religion, they both read widely and encouraged their daughter in her studies of philosophy and languages, fields of study she intended to pursue at the university.

In 1918, the year Vera entered Moscow University, Russia was in the midst of a profound cultural upheaval, although the full scope of that upheaval had not yet penetrated deeply into the faculty. The philosophy faculty, into which Vera Iakovlevna matriculated, had the reputation of being among the most distinguished in the university and had a large number of world-class scholars. Among them were two renowned professors, I. A. Il'in, a philosopher of law, and G. I. Chelpanov, an experimental psychologist, both of whom were then at the peak of their teaching careers.[62] These two professors attracted large numbers of university students to their lectures, which they presented in lively, engaging form in the university's assembly hall. The questions both professors raised in their fields and their ability to cross the boundaries of their disciplines into issues related to religion and culture captivated many students. Il'in especially attracted a huge following, and students flocked to his lectures on state, law, and religion in such numbers, Vera Iakovlevna wrote, that the auditorium could not contain all of them, and those unable to find seats stood outside in the hallway and listened.[63]

Such students included many who were known as *maroseiskie*. They were the spiritual children of Fr. Aleksei Mechev, the distinguished and widely popular priest who served in the church of Saint Nicholas the Wonder-worker on Maroseika Street in central Moscow, which drew many people, young and old, members of the intelligentsia and the uneducated, believers and non-believers.[64] As will be discussed in greater detail later in this study, Mechev's pastoral care emphasized compassion and openness and was modeled after the famous elders of the Optina Pustyn' Monastery, with whom he had a close personal and spiritual relationship. Mechev had numerous devotees among Moscow University's student population. They greatly enlivened discussions in Il'in's classes, Vera Iakovlevna said, since they were passionately interested in the questions Il'in raised about law and religion, which she, too, found compelling and planned to explore further in her studies. [65]

In 1920, however, the sudden death of Vera's mother changed everything in her life. Reflective, deeply introverted, and disposed to melancholy, Vera was heartsick, her world having changed irrevocably, and she found that her emotional needs at that point had scant relevance to the theoretical issues raised in the classroom. The lectures she attended did not speak to the personal void caused by her grief: "After the death of my mother, I lost interest in this [philosophical] world; it lost its attractions, as well as its connections to reality," she said. "The occupations of philosophy and psychology remained interesting, but they did not provide me with the nourishment, for which my soul cried out."[66] She suffered from a depression that made her listless, and the theoretical interests in which she had immersed herself suddenly seemed irrelevant, in such stark contrast to the immediate concerns that engulfed her. Vera Iakovlevna's melancholy, however, resulted in circumstances that had a significant bearing on her future vocation, and, as will be shown later, on the upbringing of Aleksandr Men.

Shortly after her mother's death, as she continued her university studies, Vera Iakovlevna began to work in a children's kindergarten. For her, this was a fortunate experience, because being in the company of children had a cathartic effect during this painful, grief-stricken time in her life. The work with children gave her not only direction, but also connection at a time when she felt isolated from everything. In her memoir, she described those days of pain and deliverance movingly:

Among the children (in the preschool colony as it was called then), I immediately felt differently. The children seemed to grasp my most secret throughts and emotions, which I wasn't willing to share with anyone. One evening, when my soul felt especially heavy, one of the older boys called out to me, saying, 'Come sit with us, we are scared.' My personal fear and melancholy as if disappeared. From that time on, every evening I sat with the children, and watched them until they fell into a peaceful sleep.[67]

The political and economic dislocation of these years, marked by revolution and civil war, had a devastating effect on the structure of Russian families. From 1918 to 1920, death and destruction ravaged both city and countryside, leaving large numbers of orphaned children and severely affecting the security of those fortunate children whose families remained intact. In 1921–1922, government sources placed the number of orphaned and abandoned children in the country at four-and-one-half to five million.[68] By 1922 and the onset of famine in South Russia, their numbers reached seven million children, overwhelming state-sponsored boarding schools, orphanages, and government agencies designed to deal with displaced children.[69]

As Vera Iakovlevna walked among the sleeping children in the middle of the night in the kindergarten where she worked, they seemed to her to be completely at peace, in stark contrast to the violent, chaotic world outside. At such times, when she looked at their faces, she wrote, it seemed that "they were undisturbed by the evil surrounding them—these children of the terrible years of Russia, which succeeded in transforming the lives of many."[70]

In addition to the relationships she cultivated with the children, Vera developed a close relationship with a fellow worker, who, as it turned out, had a large influence on her future direction. When Vera first met Tonia (Antonina Zaitseva) in the kindergarten, Vera was eighteen years of age, and Tonia, nineteen. The two young women felt an immediate kinship, because Tonia as well had recently suffered the unanticipated death of her own mother. Struggling with melancholy, Tonia, too, "felt herself a stranger among her surroundings" and experienced a sense of personal isolation that she managed to overcome only by finding "comfort and consolation among children."[71] The two women worked with different age groups of children, Tonia with three- and four-year-olds and Vera with five- and six-year-olds, and in different parts of the kindergarten. Both women, however, were brought together in late evening, since both preferred nighttime responsibilities. Finding sleep difficult, they spent the night hours softly talking to each other while standing watch over the sleeping children. They discussed their lives, their interests, their recent experiences with death, and Vera confided in her friend her sadness, and Tonia "did the same to me."[72] They discovered they shared mutual views on many subjects, including a shared set of personal values that transcended their everyday concerns.

In her descriptions of these evening conversations with her new friend, Vera mentioned a growing feeling of strangeness about Tonia, a quality she did not understand but increasingly noticed. She sensed Tonia to be different from many of her other acquaintances. "I felt in her an equal light, which penetrated her soul and life, and shone through the borders of her personality," Vera wrote, but, at the same time, "I did not have the capacity and decided not to ask her about this, and she did not talk about it."[73] Yet it became obvious to Vera Iakovlevna that her friend came from a different world and lived a different life than other people she encountered, a world to which Vera was instinctively attracted but found impenetrable.[74]

In retrospect, these were years of transformation for Vera Iakovlevna, as they were for Russia as a whole. Vera's work experience in the kindergarten set her on her future course, leading to her decision to become a child psychologist. She went on to receive additional training and to specialize in childhood disorders. The social trauma of those years made her specialty a field in which there was high demand. Later, she wrote many books on the subject of childhood disorders, which enjoyed wide circulation and brought her national respect as a child psychologist.[75] Vera remained fascinated by the special mystery and unfathomable quality that her young friend Tonia had projected.

In the late 1920s, when Elena Semenovna came to live in Moscow, Vera introduced her cousin to her friend. The three of them spent time together, added other people to their numbers, and formed a small group of kindred spirits, bound together by common interests in children, literature, and spiritual matters. On one evening, Tonia invited her two friends to dinner. It was near the end of the 1920s, when Joseph Stalin had ascended to power and the Soviet government's campaign against traditional Russian culture and especially against religion had moved into high gear. That evening, as the two young women entered Tonia's apartment, they saw icons standing and candles burning on a table in the entrance. Tonia confessed to being devoutly Orthodox, telling them that despite the dangers this presented, she intended to continue to practice her faith. She told her two friends that she had a father superior, a priest named Fr. Serafim whom she visited regularly in the nearby town of Sergiev Posad.

Elena Semenovna and Vera Iakolevna each sought a meaningful place in a society in the midst of rapid social change, a world in which nearly all the traditional social moorings came under ferocious assault. Both young women came from families that highly valued learning and wanted their children to gain an education that would serve them well, professionally and personally. Both young women were rootless, shaken at different times in their lives and by different circumstances from the family background they had earlier known. Having to struggle with loss and with painful personal circumstances, Elena Semenovna and Vera Iakovlevna sought community, the kind of community that spoke to personal needs that went beyond the new society the Bolshevik government had begun to construct in the late 1920s and early 1930s. Resourceful, intelligent, and persistent, each of them tried to fashion a personal identity that provided meaning and purpose, but how this identity would turn out they did not know. They would soon take a dangerous and uncertain step, which their visit that evening to Tonia's apartment precipitated.

3

"The Stalinism That Entered Into All of Us"

The two most widely known pieces of memoir literature from the Stalin era are Eugeniia Ginzburg's *Journey into the Whirlwind* and Nadezhda Mandelstam's *Hope against Hope*. Beautifully written, widely cited, and deeply moving, their accounts portray individual struggles to maintain personal freedom in the face of nearly overwhelming political forces that sought to suppress individual rights and initiatives. Both memoirs are set in the context of political and police actions, which the authors reference throughout. Readers might come away from them, as they often have, believing that beneath the surface of the totalitarian state lived a wide array of individuals who mightily resisted its dominating influence and also harbored the desire for the state's destruction.[1]

In the last two decades, as many Soviet memoirs have surfaced following the end of the Soviet Union, historians have found in these published accounts a much different set of attitudes. Rather than resist the state, Soviet citizens generally internalized its value systems, and, whether consciously or not, conformed their feelings and opinions to them. Believing and collaborating offered ways of dealing with the intense political pressures that confronted a person from every quarter.[2] They enabled the citizen to repress fear. Politics and ideology provided the framework for most of a person's thoughts. As the Russian historian Mikhail Gefter has noted, "The real power and lasting legacy of the Stalinist system were neither in the structures of the state, nor in the cult of the leader, but in the Stalinism that entered into all of us."[3]

The writings of Elena Semenovna and Vera Iakovlevna conform to neither of these analyses. Both women lived most of their lives during the Stalin period. Vera Iakovlevna began her memoir in 1939 and worked on it for the next two decades, completing it in 1959.[4] The precise dates of Elena Men's "Moi put'" (My path) are uncertain, but she most likely wrote the large part of her memoir during the same years. State politics and ideology do not dominate either woman's story; neither relates the defining periods in their lives to the major events and turning points in the turbulent history of the Soviet era, as did many other memoirists. Instead, the decisive moments represent turning points in their own self-discovery. The relationships they sought were not to the state, which they rarely mentioned, but neither were they in overt opposition to the political order, except when the holding of private thoughts might be considered to be such opposition. There is a great deal in their writings about the family, the household, and the attempts of both women to nourish certain ideals that gave their lives meaning and purpose. In such endeavors, it was not so much freedom they sought, but the opportunity to live independently and build connections with friends, children, work, and, ultimately, what became known as the "catacomb church."

How did they develop these connections, under such great danger to their well-being, especially during a time when social and political pressures mitigated against such actions? What were the defining characteristics of the world into which Aleksandr Men was born in 1935 and how did he develop, in his early years, perspectives that counteracted the ideological pressures exerted by the state? What elements led not only to Aleksandr Men's survival, but also to his discovery of major sources of Orthodox tradition, while growing up in Moscow during some of the most turbulent years of the twentieth century?

A Gifted Teacher

Tonia's revelation of Fr. Serafim as her spiritual mentor, as mentioned earlier, came as a surprise to Vera Iakovlevna. Cautious, and unsure of where this knowledge would lead, Vera at that point did not inquire further. But once, while spending the night at Tonia's apartment, she saw Tonia, as she prepared for bed, approach the icon in the corner and kiss it, then proceed to pray. Later that summer, when the two young women lived and worked apart, they corresponded. Vera soon noticed that the letters she sent were being answered by Fr. Serafim, with Tonia serving as the intermediary.[5] The three of them established a relationship, although for Vera Iakovlevna the relationship with the priest remained half-hearted.

Fr. Serafim (Sergei Mikhailovich Bitiukov) was born in Moscow in 1880, where he later received a technical education. Although he worked in one of the large technical enterprises in Moscow, he had for many years had a strong desire to enter the priesthood and eventually acted on that calling.

He left his job and went to live in the famous hermitage at Optina Pustyn', near monks whose service to many people, including some of Russia's greatest writers, was legendary. There he assimilated the Optina Elders' strong belief in connecting the church to society, in moving beyond the monastery and seeking to serve the people. He read deeply in theological literature and the writings of the Church Fathers. He attended lectures in the Moscow Theological Academy, where he gained a superb education, both formally and informally.[6] A man of wide-ranging interests, with intellectual gifts and a deeply rooted commitment to his vocation, Sergei Bitiukov rapidly gained a reputation as a priest of uncommon ability and spiritual warmth.

Fr. Serafim's service to the Russian Orthodox Church took place during extremely difficult times, years that were marked by intense struggle between religion and atheism after the Russian Revolution. This battle, however, did not slow his ascendancy within the ranks of the church nor did it impede a rapidly growing reputation as a priest. In 1920, Patriarch Tikhon appointed Sergei Batiukov to the Church of the Sacred Martyrs Kir and Ioann in Moscow, which although small, was one of the most active parishes in the city. In 1922, he was given the sacred name Serafim after the revered priest Serafim of Sarov. In late 1926, the church elevated him to the rank of archimandrite, perhaps, as it was widely rumored, in preparation for an appointment among the upper hierarchy of the church. The parish he served in Moscow became known for attracting members of the Russian intelligentsia, whose attractions to Marxism-Leninism had waned in the 1920s and who came to his church on Solianka Street seeking other ways of finding meaning in their lives.[7]

Fr. Serafim was known as a gifted teacher and confessor. He had an openness and sincerity about him that individuals, brought to meet him for the first time, found immediately attractive. Vera Alekseevna Korneeva, one of his spiritual children, and eighteen years old in 1925, when she first met Fr. Serafim, remembered that meeting with the priest as bringing such "peace, joy, and lightness" into her whole being. "Not at any time since then," Vera Alekseevna wrote many years later, "have I failed to remember the experience of that day."[8] In 1928, Fr. Serafim was arrested and charged with hiding the church's valuables, which many priests did to protect such precious resources against the government's requisition.

His incarceration was only temporary. He was allowed to return to his church, although his stay was short-lived; in the summer of 1928 he was dismissed from church service for his refusal to sign the agreement, concluded in 1927, in which Metropolitan Sergii pledged that the Orthodox Church would support the Soviet government.[9] Miraculously avoiding arrest the next few years, moving from place to place, and hiding from the authorities, he eventually settled in Zagorsk (presently Sergiev Posad), where he lived secretly in the small wooden house of two nuns.[10] There, in the early 1930s, Fr. Serafim became one of the most activist priests in what is known as the "catacomb church," which soon came to play a large role in the lives of Vera Iakovlevna and Elena Semenovna and, eventually, in the upbringing of Aleksandr Men.

The Catacomb Church

In 1922, in response to his opposition to Bolshevik power, the government placed the patriarch of the Russian Orthodox Church, Tikhon (Belavin), under house arrest, where he remained until June 1923. At that time, the Bolshevik government offered Tikhon a compromise: if he maintained his staunch opposition to the new Soviet government, the government planned to continue its investigation into what it called his "criminal activities." If he were to make "a special statement in which he repents of his crimes committed against Soviet power and the toiling masses of workers and peasants and expresses a loyal current attitude to Soviet power," the Soviet government offered to reinstate him as patriarch.[11] Tikhon agreed to make that statement, as well as consent to other church reforms, and he was released from confinement and returned to his patriarchal position. Shortly after his release, he changed his mind about his agreement with the Soviet government, but before he could renounce his decision, on April 7, 1925, he died.

Tikhon's successor, Metropolitan Sergii, under enormous pressure both from within and outside the church, tried to find a way to retain the church's independence. He spoke of Christianity's vision as opposed to Marxism-Leninism and of the wide gulf separating the Marxists' materialistic understanding of history and Christianity's interpretation; he wanted the differences between them clearly articulated in any declaration of loyalty he was asked to sign. Such statements were unacceptable to the Bolshevik government, and they did not appear in the final draft, which Metropolitan Sergii (Stragarodskii) signed on behalf of the church. The "Letter to the Clergy and Faithful of the Patriarchate of Moscow" denied the Soviet government's persecution of the church. It expressed gratitude for the government's care for religious institutions. It accommodated the church to the Bolshevik regime: "We want to be Orthodox and at the same time recognize the Soviet Union as our civic motherland. Her joys and successes are our joys and successes, her misfortunes our misfortunes."[12]

The declaration of loyalty left little room for further compromise. It testified, as a leading scholar maintained, that the "Soviet stranglehold on the Church was getting stronger."[13]

The Soviet government required priests to sign the declaration of loyalty and summarily dismissed those who refused from their positions. Multiple arrests of parish members who protested the declaration followed. Churches that continued to function without cooperating with state requirements developed an illegal status, as did such priests as Fr. Serafim at the Sacred Church of Kir and Ioann. These were extremely chaotic years for a church that had thrived under its previous leadership. Parish members who had earlier resisted Metropolitan Sergii's declaration and did not succeed in hiding from the police were arrested.[14] In 1932, the Soviet government closed the Church of Kir and Ioann entirely and abolished the parish attached to it.

The abolition of the parish was a microcosm of a much larger picture in which the Soviet government struck against a foundational part of the Orthodox Church. Beginning in January 1929, a Party resolution "on measures to intensify anti-religious work" aimed at striking directly against the "power of the parish."[15] A priest might well inspire the parish's formation and define its ground rules, but the parish, in reality, had its own dynamic. In the countryside especially, it constituted the grassroots building block of the church.[16] Stalin's Great Turn, from 1929 to 1932, whose policies emphasized collectivization and industrialization, featured a wholesale assault on the parish, as a recent study has well shown.[17] This assault, accompanied by the government's insistence on the church's allegiance and support, the destruction of icons, the changes in the church calendar, the abolition of Easter as a holiday, and the closure of churches, aimed at obliterating religious belief. In the late 1920s and 1930s, the desire of some priests and nuns to preserve the church and its independence led to the emergence of the "catacomb church."

By the early 1930s, catacomb churches had spread all over the country, including Siberia, and even into the prison camps, where incarcerated priests heard confessions from fellow prisoners.[18] Illegitimate in the eyes of the government and the Soviet Orthodox Church, catacomb churches had no communication with the Moscow Patriarchate and operated totally outside it.[19] Participants in the underground church, if caught by the police, were subject to persecution, imprisonment, and excommunication. But they remained steadfast in their claims that they represented the true Orthodox Church and the spirit of that Church, with its belief in the internal freedom of the Church. Even during the most oppressive years, believers continued to practice their faith.[20] In Zagorsk, where he secretly served as a priest in the catacomb church, Fr. Serafim exemplified this belief.

Fr. Serafim's house resembled a typical, modest residence in the worker's district of Zagorsk. Unpainted, its wooden siding turned black with age, the windows had a white facing which gave them some protection from the cold and the wind. Heavy curtains covered the windows, preventing passersby from seeing movement in the house's interior. Fr. Serafim lived in a small room at the back of the house, rarely venturing outside on the street, and kept well hidden, as mentioned earlier, by the two nuns who lived there and remained devoted to the church. Upon entering the house, the visitor came upon a sparsely furnished room, whose interior door opened up into a second room. In it were an altar, a small table that held several icons, and a second table on which candles were placed. Here, at regular intervals during the week, and always under the constant threat of arrest, Fr. Serafim conducted services, attended by a small but devoted group of catacomb believers who came secretly to this house.

Mariia Sergeevna Zhelnavakova, the young daughter of two well-known parents, went to school in Zagorsk and participated in the services in the late 1930s. As she describes the scene inside the house:

> As a child, I stood and prayed in a tiny room in which the service proceeded in whispered tones. The windows were tightly sealed, and the light barely flickered. The service was done almost from memory. How could it have been otherwise? An archimandrite, Hieromonk Fr. Serafim Bitiukov, conducted the service. The choir was composed of nuns who had been expelled from their monasteries; among our parents stood our nanny (the nun Matrona). Sometimes they would get carried away and raise their voices to above a whisper. Their singing was very beautiful. Then, someone would suddenly realize what they were doing, and would stop the others; again it [the singing] would become a whisper. From time to time, someone would go listen at the outer door, return and signal that all was quiet, and the service would resume.[21]

It was a time of the "most-cruel persecution," of what Zhelnavakova described as "stoicism and courage," of "faith and endurance," on the part of those committed to holding on to their beliefs. Among them stood Fr. Serafim, in his "black mantiya, an epitrachilion, and his cascade of snow-white hair." He always conducted the service "at a slow pace, very calmly, with solemnity."[22]

Zhelnavakova makes clear that she was aware that their actions held much significance, not only for their present circumstances, but also as a means of keeping alive certain memories and traditions:

We were children of the Catacomb Church of those times, a Church to all external appearances seemingly weak and persecuted, but in practice powerful and victorious. . . . During that period of general darkness—I know no other way of characterizing it—it was an assembly of people who at the cost of their own lives were preserving the foundations of Christianity. . . . Their own fate, i.e., the death of the body, was a matter of no consequence to them.[23]

This was the community to which Tonia belonged and had slowly, using great caution, introduced to Vera Iakovlevna. Still, despite the desire to bring her close friend into her circle, she also knew of Vera's misgivings and timidity.[24] As circumstances developed, it would not be Vera Iakovlevna who became the first to take such a step.

"I Did Not Know Where They Were Going"

Living and working in Moscow, Elena Semenovna always assumed that someday she would marry and have a family. She had an interest in several young men, but she began to develop an attraction to one, in particular, in the early 1930s, although for some time she did not consider this relationship to be other than a friendship. He was an engineer named Vladimir, a technical specialist in the textile industry and an acquaintance of her cousin Venia, an electrical engineer who worked in the same town of Orekhovo-Zuevo, an industrial city fifty-three miles east of Moscow. The two young men had become friends, and on weekends they traveled to Moscow to see Venia's family and enjoy the city. Vladimir Grigor'evich, as Elena called him, was six years older than she, and she first met him in 1927, although for several years they had little more than a casual acquaintance. But by 1932, Vladimir could be found at the family apartment on Sunday afternoons, often with theater tickets, in hopes that Elena would accompany him. After several months of such activities, it became clear to Elena that he intended to pursue her.

In her account of their relationship, Elena Semenovna wrote that she did not plan to marry until later, since she had other aspirations. Eventually, she hoped to marry a man who shared the same religious values as she. Elena did not conceal her disappointment that Vladimir confessed to being an atheist, although he did not express the militant views of many others his age. Despite the frequent urgings of her grandmother that she find a husband, Elena was extremely reluctant to make this match, and although Vladimir several times broached the subject of marriage to her, Elena quickly excused herself from the conversation. But slowly, almost reluctantly, she began to soften toward him.

In the fall of 1933, Vladimir went away for a long time, as his job required, and, upon his return, moved to Moscow. Elena Semenovna noted that he had quit smoking, a habit she had always found distasteful. Early in 1934, he told Elena of his love and asked her directly why, despite his attraction and the many pleasurable times they had spent together, she refused to consider the possibility of marriage. Elena recalled that for some time she did not respond, but then she said to him, "It is because I confess a Christian faith." Vladimir sat there in silence for several minutes, clearly stunned by this statement, and likely, in Elena's mind, by the recognition of the unbridgeable gap separating them. Finally, Vladimir replied in a voice that expressed both amazement and hope: "You have become even higher in my eyes. All the time I have thought that you loved someone else."[25] On these words, Elena noted, their meeting concluded.

Such confessions, however, did not end their conversation. They had obviously grown in their relationship to each other, and although Elena's memoir does not reveal her thoughts or struggles in the ensuing days, what happened next suggests a great deal of consideration—on the part of both persons. The next time they met, Vladimir said to her, "Since you are a believer, it will not interfere with our life together. You can go to church and listen to some hierarch; I will go to the lectures, and then we will share with each other what we find to be the most interesting."[26] In her own way, prayerfully, Elena noted that she felt it to be "God's will" that she accept Vladimir Grigor'evich's proposal of marriage. She set the wedding date for two months later, April 15, the Sunday after Easter, the day of the Wedding after the Great Feast (Matthew 22:1–14).[27]

The marriage on April 15, 1934, resulted in several major changes in Elena Semenovna's life. Living in a small thirty-foot room on Derbinevskaia Street, she and Vladimir Grigor'evich Men began family life ostensibly as a young Soviet couple engaged in building a new industrial society in Stalinist Russia. As an engineer and a draftsperson living in a small communal flat in the middle of a dynamic city, they represented the future: Soviet citizens whose diligence and devotion promised to transform their society. The year 1934 witnessed the revival of the word *rodina*, the concept of the country as motherland and the state as a large family.[28] But this external picture does not begin to capture the values of Elena Semenovna in her role as a young wife. She aspired to have a family, but it was not the model of the family envisioned in the Soviet media. Her religious identity, which she largely kept to herself in those crowded living quarters, gave her a different sense of being than the people around her.

Shortly after her marriage, Elena became pregnant with her first child. News of the impending birth filled her and Vladimir with joy, since having a family was something both of them strongly desired. The birth was to occur in late January 1935. Long before that happy event, however, she selected the name Aleksandr should the child be male, in honor of one of Russia's most revered saints, Aleksandr Nevskii, the legendary twelfth-century prince of Novgorod, whose expansive vision of the world had been much larger than his immediate circumstances.

The birth of Aleksandr Men took place on January 22, 1935. His arrival came on the eve of Stalin's Great Terror, when political struggles inside the Soviet Union entered a white-hot period of purge within the Communist Party and led to the arrests of massive numbers of Soviet citizens. But within the family of Elena and Vladimir Men, this period represented something else. The birth of the child, Elena remembered, gave them a renewed sense of purpose, as well as new responsibilities. She and Vladimir briefly moved out of their cramped living space into the larger apartment of Vera Iakovlevna and her father, a move that united again the two women and proved to be a positive event for all of them. According to Elena, little Alik (diminutive form of Aleksandr), as they called him, "became the center of our family life," in which she included Vera Iakovlevna, and she remembered that Vera "sat for hours rocking the child and composing poems, which she recited to him while she rocked."[29]

At the beginning of the summer, they went to the family's dacha outside the city, in Tomilino, in the suburbs of Moscow, where they planned to spend several months. Toward the end of their stay, Vera's friend Tonia came to visit, and she had the opportunity to meet the child for the first time. Here, far from the city and eavesdropping neighbors, Tonia inquired of Elena whether she wished Aleksandr to be baptized.

> I said that I very much wanted to baptize him, but I did not know how this could be done. Tonia volunteered to help me with that. She then asked whether I myself wished to be baptized. Then, suddenly, there came over me some kind of fear, and I refused. "That means," she said, "that we will baptize Alik alone. . . ." On the way home, a strong upsurge of thoughts and feelings came over me. Since my ninth year, I had prepared to be baptized. And now eighteen years had passed, and when there was put to me this question, I was frightened, showed my poverty of spirit, and refused. Why? How could this be? Right away, I sat down and wrote Tonia a letter of repentance, and, of course, I said that I would accept baptism with joy.[30]

Tonia made the necessary arrangements, and they set the date of September 3. The timing of the event was deliberate: on the previous evening, Vladimir had left Moscow for the Caucasus. Elena had not told her husband of her plans; she had kept this information to the narrowest possible network of people, and she also did not expose him to the dangerous event in which she would soon participate.

On the evening of September 3, Tonia came to the apartment for Elena and Alik. Elena had packed a suitcase filled with swaddling clothes, and Tonia had brought with her three fish and several loaves of bread, and together they set out for Moscow's Northern Station. Vera went with them to the station, and although she had been told the general purpose of the trip, she did not know the precise details. "I did not know where they were going, and I did not ask anything," she said. When they arrived at the station, Tonia invited her to go along, but Vera refused. "This I could not do," she said.[31]

After they boarded the train, Elena Semenovna still had not been told their destination, and when she asked, Tonia did not answer.[32] It was only when they stepped down from the wagon of the train that Elena Semenovna learned that they had arrived in Zagorsk. As they walked along in the night on a deserted street, "Tonia took Alik in her arms, and I carried the suitcase," Elena recalled. She knew then she was going to Fr. Serafim and although she understood the purpose of the visit, she admitted to becoming increasingly anxious, even fearful. Tonia, carrying Alik, walked quickly in front of her, as if afraid that Elena at any minute "would reconsider and not return."[33] Eventually, they arrived at the house of their destination. Tonia rang the bell, and after several minutes passed, a middle-aged woman dressed in monastery clothing admitted them and led them into a well-lit room in which there were many icons. Elena recalled the evening in detail:

> The priest was not there and for a long time he did not appear. I understood that he was praying before he received us. Finally, he came to us. Tonia, holding Alik, approached him for his blessing, and I followed behind. Unknowingly, I placed my left hand over my right; the priest noticed it right away and repositioned them. Then, he said, "Sit down." If he had not said this, I would have collapsed to the floor from anxiety and tension. For some time we sat in silence. Finally, the priest asked me, "Do you know Russian literature?" I was surprised by this question, but recalled the "Brothers Karamazov" and the Elder Zosima, and I understood why he had asked me about that. He asked me several more questions about everyday life in general. Then we sat to eat. The food was simple, and the priest emphasized that this act had an immediate relationship to our baptism.

Afterwards, the woman who had opened the door for us earlier took Alik into her arms. Alik was quiet and peaceful, as if he understood that this was a serious proceeding. The priest led me into another room and asked me to tell him all my life. I told him everything, as I could. Then we lay down to sleep. Alik slept soundly, but I did not sleep the whole night, and, as I could, I prayed.[34]

Given the momentous step she was taking, Elena's anxiety is understandable. The history of her own life's circumstances and the extreme trust she placed in Tonia and Fr. Serafim brought her to this moment and its dangerous circumstances. She also saw the moment as crucial for her child and how she intended to raise him, connecting him to a sacred tradition radically different from the Soviet Orthodox Church. The event the following morning, which Elena had planned, signified that connection:

The next morning, at daybreak, the secret baptism took place. The baptism was entirely by immersion. And each time, when the priest immersed me, I felt as though I would die. After me, the priest baptized Alik. Tonia became his godmother. The day before, Fr. Serafim had shown me three crosses. The first, the long one, was silver, inscribed with the words, "Blessed by God and Grow in Him," and he told me this one was for Vera; the second, smaller, was gold and was for me; and the third, silver, with blue enamel and a crucifix, was for Alik. But my soul extended itself to the cross of the Crucified Savior. Suddenly, the priest, as though he had earlier made a mistake, put this cross on me. He seemed to see this as the will of God, and, therefore, he left it there. On Alik he put the golden cross. . . . After this, the priest began to bless all of life, and then he began the liturgy. We sang with low voices so that we would not be heard on the street. The baptism songs we sang well, with all our soul, although our voices were not loud and not strong.[35]

Elena Semenovna thus became a spiritual daughter of Fr. Serafim in the catacomb church and traveled often to the services in Zagorsk. Vera Iakovlevna soon joined her cousin. Aleksandr, little more than seven months old at the time of his baptism, spent his early years in that church, and these years would have a significant impact on his spiritual development.

Childhood

The early childhood years of Aleksandr Men contained both joyous and stimulating experiences. He had a loving family that took pleasure in his mental and physical growth and relished the considerable time they devoted to him. In 1937, Elena gave birth to a second son, Pavel, an event that added to the family's happiness. Surrounded by a close-knit, caring household, the young Aleksandr Men thrived. Aleksandr did not see much of his father during the day or even in the early evening. Vladimir worked long hours at his job. He was man of integrity and a highly capable person who, on the whole, "gave himself to his work."[36]

The secure, relatively peaceful existence that Aleksandr had known, however, did not last long. In 1940, authorities in the factory where Vladimir worked as chief engineer questioned him about funds that he, without proper authorization, had taken from the factory's accounts, securing them for his own private use. The security police came to the family's apartment in the evening to interrogate him further. Then, in early 1941, the police arrested Aleksandr's father, charging him not with a political crime, but with improper use of his signature on his company's financial documents. Although the courts soon freed Vladimir, exonerating him of the charges, he was no longer permitted to reside in Moscow, but required to live in another city. He chose Sverdlovsk (Ekaterinburg) as his place of residence, where he had relatives, including a married sister; he hoped he could eventually convince Elena and their children to move there with him.[37]

Vladimir's arrest left Elena with two small children and no means of support. Thus began an extremely difficult time for the whole family—a time of uncertainty, meager resources, and struggle to maintain their equanimity. In such challenging circumstances, Elena relied on her cousin for material and emotional support, and the two of them drew even closer, with Vera taking on part of the family responsibilities in the absence of the father. But Elena also demonstrated extraordinary personal strength in such frightening circumstances. Resourceful and strong-willed, she was determined to persevere, both then and in the future.

In the early morning hours of June 22, 1941, German armies crossed into Soviet Russia, catching the Soviet Union unprepared and nearly defenseless. That morning, Sunday, had promised to be a sunny, beautiful day as Vera Iakovlevna left her apartment for Zagorsk, where she planned to attend the All-Saints'-Day ceremonies with Fr. Serafim. When she arrived in Zagorsk, a light rain had begun to fall. As she made her way forward to her destination, she had no idea of the invasion, and neither did Fr. Serafim. But later that morning, as other members of the church arrived, rumor of war had begun to circulate among them, and when they listened anxiously at noon to the radio and heard Foreign Secretary Viacheslav Molotov's announcement of the German invasion, they understood the reality of what they had feared.

Fr. Serafim went to each person present and spoke to each one. Coming to Vera Iakovlevna, he walked outside with her and told her to convey to Elena his advice: she must leave Moscow immediately with her children and find a place to live in the environs of Zagorsk. He told Vera that many children left there are going to be killed; Zagorsk would offer a much safer place for Elena and her children, since they would be protected by Saint Sergii of Radonezh, Russia's greatest patron saint.[38]

Elena's decision to move her family to the environs of Zagorsk entailed great risk, but she trusted Fr. Serafim's advice and did not hesitate. After packing their goods, the next day she and Vera left Moscow with her children, going in an opposite direction from most Muscovite parents who evacuated their children to the east. She found a small, available room in the village of Glinkovo, only a mile and three-quarters from Zagorsk. There, she and her children settled, uncertain of what lay immediately ahead, how deeply German armies would advance into the region, or how they would find enough food to survive during the time they were there. She had complete trust in Fr. Serafim, said Pavel Men, who, although only a child, vividly recalled those years: "Fr. Serafim told her that not a single hair would fall from our head, and had given my mother complete confidence that it would be so."[39]

The years 1942 and 1943, the most crucial period of what the Soviet Union called the "Great Fatherland War," turned out to be years of enormous chaos and challenge for Elena Semenova. In 1941, Hitler planned to strike directly at Moscow, thinking that capturing the Russian capital, the heart of the country, would thus force the nation's surrender. The ferocious fighting in the Battle of Moscow and its surroundings between early October 1941 and January 1942 had turned back the German army. But the Russian victory did not mean the subjugation of the Nazi power. Rather, it meant its retrenchment, and the German army under General Fedor von Bock pulled back and dug in thirty-two to forty-three miles from Moscow, both in the north and the south. Russian supply lines were cut and the transportation network disrupted. When the spring of 1942 arrived, food would be in short supply, making this a year of hunger for all Russians in Moscow and its surrounding areas. Hunger severely tested Elena Semenovna, living alone near Zagorsk with her two children. By early 1942, the market in Glinkovo no longer existed, and Elena lacked a ration card. In March, heeding the earlier advice of Fr. Serafim, she moved directly into Zagorsk.

It was not only food that presented a challenge; so, too, did housing for her young family. Elena had no permanent residence in Zagorsk, and she had to move five times during the year, packing up her children and their things and shuttling from place to place, finally ending up in a house where the owner allowed her to stay provided she supply firewood for the household. Throughout these multiple trials, Elena demonstrated extraordinary resilience as she faced one severe challenge after another. All the while, parts of the German army were located thirteen miles way, threatening at any moment to enter the town and massacre its local inhabitants. At least once, Elena broke down, and, walking into a local church, she got down on her knees and cried before the icon of the Mother of God.

To her children, however, Elena Semenovna always exhibited "such a confidence, because she believed Fr. Serafim when he said that the Germans would not be able to enter Zagorsk. He said it, and it was enough for our mother," Pavel Men said.[40] In the winter of 1941–1942, with Moscow under enormous military pressure, Elena's husband wrote her many letters from Sverdlovsk, where he worked in a munitions factory, imploring her to move there with their children and expressing great fear for their safety due to her close proximity to the front lines. Elena chose, instead, to remain in Zagorsk, thinking it the safest place for all of them and bewildering Vladimir Grigor'evich and their friends, most of whom had evacuated Moscow and moved into the country's interior.

Elena Semenovna's story during these terrible wartime years exhibits inner resourcefulness and fortitude when annihilation threatened from all sides. Her account pays homage to an elderly priest who cared for his people in times of their need, despite his having to move secretly from place to place, because of wartime checks by police of the inhabitants of each house in the town. Fr. Serafim looked after Elena Semenovna and her children as though they were members of his own family.[41] She recounts the heroism and self-giving love of Vera Iakovlevna, who, continuing to work in Moscow, took a job as a librarian in a factory after colleagues in her institute evacuated Moscow. Despite the difficulties of travel from Moscow to Zagorsk, Vera did so each weekend, carrying food and other supplies. Her father and brother gave up part of their meager rations, instructing Vera to give their food "to the children."[42] Later in the war, both men died from starvation.

During the terrible winter of 1941–1942, Fr. Serafim, on whom for the past seven years Elena Semenovna had so much relied, died at the home of one of his spiritual children on February 19. His death was not unexpected, since his physical condition had considerably weakened in the first month of 1942, although he largely kept his deteriorating physical condition from many members of his church. Following his vigil and funeral, held secretly, he was buried in the basement of the house where he died, leaving Elena and others without his guiding voice; he did not, however, leave them as spiritual orphans.

Knowing that his final days were approaching, Fr. Serafim asked to hear Aleksandr's first confession shortly before he died. After the confession, he praised the seven-year-old boy, telling his mother of the child's unusual future promise.[43] Fr. Serafim also planned the transfer of his spiritual children to the care of three priests, all of whom lived in or near Zagorsk. He entrusted the future spiritual guidance of Elena's family to Fr. Petr Shipkov.[44] Fr. Shipkov had long been a priest in the Orthodox Church. After his ordination by Patriarch Tikhon in 1920, he served as the patriarch's secretary. Unwilling to accept the 1927 declaration of allegiance to the Soviet government, Fr. Petr had gone into the catacomb church. He moved to Zagorsk, finding employment as a bookkeeper in a local factory while simultaneously continuing his activity as a priest in a small underground church on the outskirts of the town.

Elena and her children quickly became attached to Fr. Petr. A kindly, generous person, fifty-two years old in 1942, Fr. Petr devoted himself fully to the care of his spiritual children. He had a great love for people in "all their weakness and helplessness."[45] He understood the church as a large family, in which no one should be isolated from the whole, but should rather exist as part of a larger body. His ideal of the church, which he repeatedly emphasized, was "a society of people, united by the spirit," who, "with a clear spirit," could say, "Christ is among us."[46] Throughout the year 1942 and the first half of 1943, which was a period of destitution, when hunger bit in deeply, as it did in many Russian families, this ideal became a practical reality. Several times during those months, Elena had no food for Aleksandr and Pavel, and, in desperation, went into the forest to search for mushrooms with varying degrees of success. On multiple occasions, Fr. Shipkov and members of his community, despite their own needs, shared their food with Elena and her children, as if they were bound together in communal acts of survival. "During this period," neither Aleksandr nor Pavel "fell ill, although their food supply was very meagre," a worry constantly on Elena's mind.[47] Despite the violence of the war surrounding them, Elena later recalled the many acts of kindness: "The children grew in a beneficent atmosphere, blessed by the prayers of Saint Sergii, among good believing people. This atmosphere contributed to their spiritual growth."[48]

Changing Relationships

The year 1943 marked a fundamental change in the relationship between the Soviet government and the Russian Orthodox Church. As the war shifted in favor of the Red Army early in the year, Stalin began to reconsider the government's policies toward the church, which had changed little since the 1920s. From the beginning of the fighting, the church had strongly supported the war effort. On June 22, 1941, the day of the German invasion, when Stalin had disappeared from sight, Metropolitan Sergii Stragorodskii, the guardian of the vacant patriarchal throne, had conferred "the Church's blessing on all Orthodox believers in defending the holy borders of our Motherland."[49] By defining the struggle against the "hostile forces of fascism" as a "holy war" and raising funds of 300 million rubles to support the military effort, the church provided significant "patriotic service" to the defense of the country.[50] But it was not, as historian Dimitry Pospielovsky has written, to display his gratitude for this service that Stalin changed the policy.[51] Neither were the reasons ideological; they were entirely pragmatic, and aimed to turn the church's "patriotic activity" toward his own political use, both internally and externally.

On September 4, 1943, late in the evening, Stalin convened a meeting in the Kremlin with Metropolitan Sergii and his two associates, metropolitans Aleksii and Nikolai. The purpose of the meeting was to discuss the needs of the church and to respond to any questions they might have. Stalin had prepared this session carefully: earlier that day, he had met at his dacha at Kuntsevo with Georgii Karpov, a colonel in the state security police, as well as Georgii Malenkov and Lavrentii Beria, members of the Politburo. Stalin told them of his desire to normalize relations between the Soviet government and the Orthodox Church. He revealed to the three of them his intentions to restore the patriarch of the Russian Orthodox Church and to create a special government body with executive authority, the Council for Russian Orthodox Church Affairs, to connect the government directly with the patriarch. He wanted to appoint Karpov as the council's chairman. He talked at length with Karpov about Metropolitan Sergii's personal qualities, especially his popularity in comparison with former Patriarch Tikhon. Stalin also discussed the importance of establishing good relations with the leaders of Orthodox churches in Czechoslovakia, Bulgaria, Yugoslavia, Romania, and other territories still under German occupation. He expressed his desire to move quickly in seeking normalization of relations with the church. He would be meeting in Teheran with Prime Minister Winston Churchill and President Franklin Roosevelt in November, and he had obvious desires to go to that first wartime conference having concluded the concordat with the church.

The three church leaders represented all the metropolitans remaining in the Russian Orthodox Church. The three of them had conveniently been present in Moscow on September 4, and had expectantly awaited Karpov's afternoon telephone call requesting the meeting.[52] Stalin knew they would respond immediately and not postpone the chance to discuss their needs, although the three metropolitans had to have approached this opportunity "uncertain of the sincerity of Stalin's intentions."[53] The meeting between Stalin and the three metropolitans, with Karpov also present, lasted nearly two hours and resulted in concrete changes in church-state relations.[54] Metropolitan Sergii requested permission to convene a bishops' *sobor* (assembly) for the election of a Holy Synod and patriarch.

Stalin immediately granted this request, asking that the *sobor* be convened quickly. As a result, on September 8, the bishops' *sobor* met and unanimously elected Metropolitan Sergii as patriarch. The metropolitan next requested permission to offer theological courses, and, again, after some hesitation, Stalin relented, adding that to provide teachers, he would permit the church to open theological academies and seminaries. Metropolitan Sergii then asked to resume publication of the *Journal of the Moscow Patriarchate*, which, in 1935, the government had suspended; this request Stalin granted as well. The metropolitan proposed that the church be allowed to reopen churches, because few were presently in operation. Although the Soviet leader did not give permission to reopen such houses of worship freely, he agreed that the church might open them "where they are few or do not exist at all."[55] The metropolitans had one other issue that troubled them a great deal, but which they hesitated to bring up for fear it would provoke Stalin's anger. Expressing some reluctance to broach the question, Metropolitan Aleksii finally raised the politically sensitive issue of freeing members of the Orthodox hierarchy from labor camps, prisons, and exile "in order that they might return to their religious service." Without hesitating or expressing any sign of displeasure, Stalin invited the metropolitans to "draw up a list and we will take a look at it."[56]

Near the end of their meeting, the Soviet leader told the three church leaders of his intentions to create a special Council for Russian Orthodox Church Affairs and name Karpov as the chairman. He asked them for their reaction to this appointment, and the bishops responded, "We are very grateful," which suggests, as historian Tatiana Chumachenko has pointed out, "that they knew Comrade Karpov and respected his appointment."[57] As its functions were subsequently defined, the council served as a bridge between "the government of the USSR and the Patriarch of Moscow and All Russia on issues related to the Orthodox Church."[58] Among its chief tasks were the responsibility to review issues raised by the patriarch, to draft legal acts and decrees on matters concerning the church, and to implement these legal acts and decrees. Thus, while the Soviet government negotiated a concordat with the Russian Orthodox Church and allowed the church greater operational latitude, the Soviet government concurrently set in place a means for regulating the church's activities and controlling that latitude.

The loosening of restrictions on religious activities applied only to the Orthodox Church and not to other faiths operating in the Soviet Union. Ironically, at the same time as the Soviet government negotiated with Orthodox Church leaders in Moscow, local police struck hard at the catacomb church in Zagorsk. On October 14, 1943, the police arrested Fr. Petr Shipkov, and for the next five years, his followers would learn nothing about his location. On the same day as the arrest, the police exhumed the body of Fr. Serafim and reburied it in an unmarked grave.[59] By striking at the leadership, these actions aimed to devastate the catacomb church in Zagorsk. But Fr. Petr had prepared for such actions. Anticipating his arrest, Fr. Petr earlier had introduced Elena to a nun who served in a small, active underground organization that had formerly been under the care of Fr. Serafim and that continued to uphold his teachings. After the arrest of Fr. Petr, this nun, Mother Mariia, reached out to the young Aleksandr. They immediately formed a close relationship, and that relationship proved to be fortuitous for the future development of Aleksandr Men.

Elena Semenovna and her children left Zagorsk and returned to Moscow on September 8, 1943. The war had not ended, but by then Moscow was out of danger, and they, like many other residents of the city, moved back. Spectacular advances by the Red Army in August and September 1943 had retaken large amounts of territory from German control in Ukraine and soon in Belorussia, and although complete victory lay far ahead, the war's final outcome became increasingly clear. By then, Muscovites had many reasons to be optimistic, but as a first-hand observer reported, "to individual Russians, the war, with its fearful casualties, continued to be a very grim reality. More and more young men were being drafted daily into the Red Army, and it was only too common to meet elderly men and women who had already lost several or all of their sons in the war."[60] Large parts of the territory surrounding Moscow lay devastated with nearly all the towns to the north and south, with the exception of Zagorsk, having suffered a similar fate. Shortages of nearly everything continued to be a daily challenge, and the rationing of food would continue for another year. Still, when Elena and her children returned to their apartment, they found it available and in good order, much the same as they had left it more than two years ago. Many families who returned to Moscow after the evacuation were not so fortunate, and found their former living quarters either ransacked or occupied by other tenants.[61]

During the next several years, as the war came to an end and the Soviet Union sought to rebuild from the devastating effects of the fighting on its soil, Elena Semenova and her family tried to reestablish their own lives. Shortly after returning to Moscow, she enrolled Aleksandr in a school that accepted eight-year-olds in the first form. She placed five-year-old Pavel in a kindergarten, took a job in the laboratory of a pedagogical institute, and enrolled in courses in the institute. In 1944, her husband Vladimir returned from Sverdlovsk, and while he wanted to play more of a leading role with their children, she clearly occupied this central place. After the war, on Saturdays and Sundays, as well as on holidays, she, Vera Iakovlevna, and the children walked to the church, now open, near their home. She read from the Gospels daily to her children. Usually, about once a month and still under dangerous conditions, they went to Zagorsk to see Mother Mariia.[62]

The changes in church-state relations during and at the end of the Second World War offer two different ways of viewing the Russian Orthodox Church. In early 1941, Stalin said, "We are living in the last days of the existence of the Russian Orthodox Church."[63] In September 1943, however, for multiple reasons, and primarily to serve his own political agenda, he allowed the Orthodox Church to get back on its feet. Following the Soviet leader's negotiations with metropolitans Sergii, Aleksii, and Nikolai, the church managed to rebuild its internal structure, with each diocese having a bishop at its head. Sergii, recently elected patriarch, held the office for only a few months, until his death in May 1944. In a large and elaborate ceremony in February 1945, attended by the patriarchs of Antioch and Alexandria, representatives of Balkan and Near Eastern patriarchs, and the patriarch of North America, Aleksii, metropolitan of Leningrad and Novgorod, was elected Patriarch of Moscow and All Russia.

In addition to electing the patriarch, the church council passed a law designating priests as the principal leaders of church parishes, an important administrative change contradicting the 1929 civil law that had placed a three-person executive board at the head of individual parishes. Under the previous arrangement, priests had little authority within their parishes; the 1945 law defined a much different structure, and it was destined to create a great deal of confusion at the local level.[64] Catacomb church leaders accepted Patriarch Aleksii's election as legitimate and the law on parishes as corresponding to church tradition, although in later years some of these leaders would again question the legitimacy of the council's actions.[65]

In parts of the country formerly controlled by the German Army, the Soviet government left churches alone that had reopened during the occupation. In other regions, however, the process of reopening churches proved much more erratic. Between 1944 and 1947, the Council of Religious Affairs reviewed 4,418 petitions from religious believers wanting local churches reopened, and approved 1,270, a little more than one-fourth of the requests.[66] In order to educate candidates for the priesthood, the church received permission to reopen the Theological Academy and its seminary, which first held classes on the grounds of the Novodevichy Monastery, and then, in 1948, relocated to the Trinity-Sergius Lavra at Zagorsk (Sergiev Posad).

Other seminaries soon followed in Leningrad, Lutsk, Minsk, Stavropol, Odessa, Saratov, and Kiev, giving the Soviet Union, at the end of 1947, eight functioning seminaries.[67] The country had two theological academies, in Moscow and Leningrad, where seminary graduates could go for advanced work, and in the 1950s both academies offered "evening courses for priests or deacons living within commuting distance."[68] The newly opened churches had the freedom to celebrate religious services within their own physical structures, but they did not have the right to move outside them or to engage the society as a whole. The importance of restoring certain church practices and reclaiming liturgical traditions in the Soviet Union spoke directly to the spiritual needs of a population ravaged by the experience of war. Yet state restrictions limited the church's ability to develop a broader presence within society.

The catacomb church did not face these limitations, although the need for secrecy and the dangerous conditions under which it existed curtailed its freedom of movement. But the beneficent atmosphere that Elena Semenovna experienced within the community of believers, the compassion for people in need, and the freedom to move outside narrow boundaries were qualities that deeply marked the catacomb church in Zagorsk. In her own way of being, Elena Semenovna exemplified these qualities, and from an early age they were strongly imprinted on Aleksandr's mind. He recalled memories of Fr. Serafim and his mother many years later:

> Fr. Serafim was a disciple of the Elders of Optina and a friend of Fr. Alexei Mechev. He baptized my mother and me, and for many years undertook the spiritual direction of our whole family. After his death, his successors took charge; they were people of great spiritual power, with the wisdom and illumination of the Elders. My childhood and my teenage years were spent near them and under the shadow of St. Sergii. I lived there with my mother, who is now dead, and she had a great deal to do with determining my spiritual life and orientation. She lived an ascetic and prayerful life, completely free of hypocrisy, bigotry, and narrowness: traits often present in people in her state. She was always filled with paschal joy, a deep dedication to the will of

God, and a feeling of closeness to the spiritual world, in a certain way, like St. Serafim or St. Francis of Assisi.[69]

After the war, as a schoolboy, Aleksandr Men became part of a school system that ostensibly inculcated Marxist-Leninist principles in its students. But in the unofficial world in which he also lived, he encountered a different reality that was diametrically opposed to the formulaic principles taught in his school. In those opposing settings, one emphasizing closed boundaries, the other open ones, how might the qualities he associated with his mother and the Optina Elders have been developed? What intellectual resources and perspectives enabled the young Aleksandr Men to exist outside the dominant paradigm of thought conveyed in the media and by the educational system?

4

. . . .

A Different Education

Afterrising to leadership of the Communist Party in 1928, Stalin began transforming the Soviet Union from a rural to an industrial society, as he re-forged the country's culture and identity. Waging war on Russia's past, customs, and traditional ways of thinking, the Communist Party repressed large segments of the population. By the mid-1930s, labor camps and "special settlements" had mushroomed in size, and the population interned in them increased to over 2.4 million, a prelude to the years of unbridled terror that touched nearly every family in the Soviet Union.[1] The policies of the Party affected not only the external life of the family, they also sought to refashion the internal life of the Soviet citizen, remake the personality, and reshape a person's mentality. The individual was expected to subordinate all aspects of private life and belief to the larger good of liberating humanity. In this endeavor, the Party became the fount of truth. The Party required loyalty. It proclaimed service to a new conception of family—that is, the whole of Soviet society—and it expected the individual to conform and "fit into" this new model.

Consequently, in the 1930s it became difficult to think or to speak outside the boundaries of the system imposed by the Communist Party. Fearful of being accused of being an "enemy of the people," people refrained from public dissent. A careless remark or a misinterpreted statement could easily lead to arrest. "We were taught to keep our mouths shut," recalled a Soviet citizen. "You'll get into trouble with your tongue—that's what people said to children all the time. We went through life afraid to talk."[2]

After World War II, facing a huge rebuilding task, the Communist Party continued along the same lines as before of constructing a strong industrial society. The experience of the war, in which Germany's occupation of large swaths of territory and its retreat, as well as the scorched-earth policy of the Red Army, destroyed towns and farms, resulted in massive amounts of industrial and agricultural capacity that needed to be rebuilt and farmlands that needed to be restored. The war had devastated approximately one-fourth of the country's material assets—its roads, railroads, buildings, factories, apartments, and houses—and all of them required immediate reconstruction.[3] Stalin had no doubt that this could be quickly done. National pride had never been higher than in the wake of the victory over Nazi Germany. Patriotic fervor, mixed with the ideology of Marxism-Leninism, could be seen everywhere, in street banners, throughout the media, and in school textbooks. Stalin announced that victory in the war proved "the superiority of the Soviet system," and demonstrated "its unconquerable strength. . . . By defeating the German and Japanese aggressors, the Soviet people saved the peoples of Europe and Asia from fascist tyranny, and that great service to humanity inspires in the hearts of Soviet people a legitimate feeling of national pride."[4]

In the years immediately after the war, Stalin's popularity reached its zenith, and the Great Leader promised to do still more to elevate the Soviet Union to a position of world leadership. Given the presence of foreign troops on Russian soil and Soviet troops outside the country's borders, the leadership saw imperative the removal of all elements of foreign contamination, particularly where they could most readily be found: in the cultural sphere. Following the expulsion of the poet Anna Akhmatova and the satirist Mikhail Zoshchenko from the Union of Soviet Writers in 1946, the doctrine of "socialist realism" became firmly entrenched in literature. Writers were to participate fully in the "building of socialism"; they were to be, in Stalin's terms, "engineers of human souls," and to be guided by unambiguous and clearly expressed "correct principles," as defined by the Party.[5] Under such prescriptions, works of imagination that fell outside narrowly drawn literary and artistic boundaries were branded as anti-Soviet. This political and cultural environment would provide the general framework in which the young Aleksandr Men attended school in postwar Moscow in the late 1940s and early 1950s.

Despite the meager circumstances of their existence both before and after World War II, Aleksandr's mother and aunt nourished a home environment in which books and ideas were a primary focus. When he was four years of age, his mother placed him in a French language study group and he learned to read Russian books before he reached the age of five. The two women knew that he learned easily, and they took much delight in observing his curiosity about the world around him, particularly his facility with words, which he appeared with little effort to incorporate into his memory.

Aleksandr Men's mother and aunt gave him an upbringing that encouraged the exploration of difficult religious and philosophical issues about humanity. The child was, his mother confided, "so intelligent and serious that she often talked with him about the most complex questions."[6] Marked with a lively imagination that constantly probed beyond the physical facts of life, he early on became interested in the animal kingdom and in art, subjects given minimal attention in his neighborhood school. By the age of ten he had advanced far beyond the educational level of his classmates, who were still learning simple reading skills. In his early teenage years, as his teachers focused largely on Marxist-Leninist interpretations of the world, Aleksandr had begun reading European philosophers, including Immanuel Kant, whose perspectives differed from those taught in school.[7]

Two individuals played an especially prominent role in Aleksandr Men's intellectual development as a child. The first of these, Vera Iakovlevna Vasilevskaia, whom he called his "aunt," remained extremely close to the family after the war. Broadly educated in both the sciences and humanities, unmarried, and on the faculty of the Institute for Childhood Disorders at Moscow University, Vasilevkaia, as mentioned earlier, had a special love for children, and she developed an extremely close relationship with Aleksandr. She became to him like a "second mother," teaching him to draw and later to read, and exposing him early on to a large variety of subjects.[8] Vasilevskaia nourished what she saw as his capacity for imagination, the capacity, as Wendell Berry has succinctly put it, to see things "clear and whole in the mind's eye."[9]

From childhood, Aleksandr Men had a curious and lively mind. A precocious child, he displayed proclivities that went in several directions, from art and literature to the animal world, all of which Vasilevskaia cultivated, gently pushing him to explore different parts of the universe. Despite the narrow strictures of his living environment in the close, physically confining space of his family's communal apartment, his intellectual world occupied broader, unrestricted spaces. His mental world transcended those enclosed structures, moving beyond them and incorporating other ways of seeing and being. Not insignificantly, Aleksandr's brother recalled, Vasilevskaia generously offered him a means of escaping the confines of the family's crowded apartment in postwar Moscow:

> My aunt had moved into a flat near ours, in a building directly across the courtyard. She lived on the fifth floor, and we were on the second floor; we could see through the windows whether she was home or not. Her apartment was about the same size as ours, and Vera Iakovlevna, who so much adored Aleksandr, allowed him to spend time there; it [her flat] served as

a refuge for him: he could go there and read his books and study. She dedicated a lot of her life, finances, and other resources to Aleksandr's education. . . . Aunt played an unparalleled role in his interest in the humanities.[10]

The generous and compassionate spirit Elena Semenovna had described in the "catacomb church" in Zagorsk during the war characterized Vasilevskaia's life. These qualities of *miloserdie* (compassion), which the Soviet state attempted to appropriate from family life, operated in the world of Aleksandr Men's family, a heritage that his aunt and mother passed on to their children. Pavel Men described this spirit of compassion as follows:

> Auntie's flat was only nine square meters, but she took in this old woman who had nowhere to go; the state had taken away her flat. This elderly woman, Mariia Markova, was a total stranger, who had nobody to look after her. Aunt Vera took her in, as one of her own, and tended her. Auntie, my parents, and the church cultivated in us a very important value system of mutual aid, of helping people who were either in the camps or had just returned from them. Raised in this environment, Aleksandr found it natural to minister and to serve people.[11]

Vasilevskaia had friends with close connections to members of the old intelligentsia, whose personal values and cultural attachments predated the Soviet period and who preserved remnants of Russia's traditional culture. Vera Iakovlevna did not engage in politics, and her memoir exhibits little interest in or mention of political subjects; her position as a psychology professor, however, gave her a multitude of diverse contacts who continued to nurture ways of thinking outside those fostered by the Soviet state.

When he was eleven years of age, Aleksandr became sickly, most likely because of the lack of nourishment that he, like many other children in Moscow, experienced in the immediate aftermath of World War II. Fearing for his health, which continued to worsen over several months, his aunt enrolled him in the children's sanatorium where she worked. Aleksandr went there after school, where he was given a hot meal, took physical exercise, and prepared his school lessons, after which he went home for the evening.

A close friend and former classmate of Vasilevskaia's, a speech therapist named Tat'iana Ivanovna Kupriianova (1900–1954), worked in the sanatorium. She, like Vasilevskaia, was extremely well educated, interested in ideas, and committed to the preservation of certain ways of thinking. Later, after his physical condition improved, she invited Aleksandr to her home to participate in a seminar she regularly held there.[12]

Tat'iana Ivanovna was married to Boris Aleksandrovich Vasil'ev (1899–1976), a graduate of Moscow University and its biological division of the physics-mathematical faculty. Boris Aleksandrovich specialized in ethnography, and his earlier work on two Siberian expeditions had produced original research.[13] In 1946, Vasil'ev completed his candidate's dissertation at Moscow University and received an appointment to work in the Institute of Ethnography of the Academy of Sciences of the USSR. Aleksandr Men remarked that his encounters with Boris Aleksandrovich, which began during the evenings he spent in his home, had a large influence on his youthful development.[14] Tall, slender, and with a deep, resounding voice, as Aleksandr Men recalled him, Boris Aleksandrovich easily commanded attention and respect. As Aleksandr soon learned, Boris Aleksandrovich was "not only a person of deep faith but also of original learning." His mannerisms in public discourse, as well as in private conversations, displayed the model of a scientist: he deeply researched the subjects that interested him, discussed them from several points of view, weighed the evidence from all angles, and then drawing on the most important facts to support his position, presented his conclusions. "I was then only a schoolboy," Aleksandr Men recalled, and he "often discussed with me the cultures of Egypt and Babylon," whose histories he knew well, and he would draw connections between the Ancient Near East and the Bible.[15] Aleksandr found such conversations fascinating, particularly as Boris Aleksandrovich set the Bible in historical context, pointing out the similarities and differences between the Biblical and historical accounts. Aleksandr's interest in such subjects (which he would later expand extensively in his multivolume *History of Religion*) began with his conversations with Boris Aleksandrovich.

Boris Aleksandrovich and Tat'iana Ivanovna lived and worked during the most dangerous years of the Soviet Union. Both of them were well-respected teachers whose interests spanned several fields of study and who had extensive knowledge of their specialties. But both of them also had other interests, which they clandestinely pursued, and which connected them to Russia's prerevolutionary traditions and culture. Boris Aleksandrovich spent several years in exile, moving from city to city in provincial Russia, serving as a teacher in various pedagogical institutes before finally returning to Moscow after Stalin's death in 1953. He held a position of leadership in the anthropology museum at Moscow University, and taught in the *kafedra* (department) of ethnography.[16] Not one of his colleagues knew that he was also a priest in the catacomb church.[17] He adored Aleksandr Pushkin, a love he harbored all his life, and he privately worked on a manuscript on spirituality in Pushkin's poetry.[18] He also revered the giants of Russia's late nineteenth- and early twentieth-century philosopher-theologians. In his written account of Boris Aleksandrovich, Aleksandr Men emphasized that "he especially implanted in me the love of Vladimir Solov'ev, Sergei Bulgakov, and Nikolai Berdiaev," bringing these three seminal thinkers into his consciousness "in those remote years when almost no one knew anything about them."[19]

In 1946 and for part of 1947, the household of Boris Aleksandrovich and Tat'iana Ivanovna became a cultural oasis for the young Aleksandr Men during a time when cultural and educational norms disparaged many earlier religious writers and traditions. A slightly built, courageous woman, Tat'iana Ivanovna taught young people in her home near the Old Arbat district in Moscow, and she regularly held a seminar on religion in the evenings.[20] Tat'iana Ivanovna instructed her youthful participants in the rituals, doctrines, and laws of Russian Orthodoxy, thus carrying on traditions that could not be freely and legally taught outside the structures of the church. Upon her invitation, Aleksandr attended these sessions, although he was considerably younger than the other participants. Tat'iana Ivanovna organized the readings and discussions around "questions of spiritual culture for children," which occasionally drifted into discussions of Pushkin, Anton Chekhov, early Christianity, and the writings of other Russian authors, which were connected to Russia's traditional culture, but were also among its greatest works of imagination.[21] Operating clandestinely, Tat'iana Ivanovna Kupriianova's evening seminar existed as a closed circle, a "world within another world," as Zoia Maslenikova described it: "In the terrible Stalinist time, this solitary woman fearlessly gave many years to the seminar she conducted, knowing that a single betrayal of confidence from any one of the participants would have brought an end to her career."[22]

The existence of such groups despite the tight controls imposed by the police suggests that the Stalin government's attempts to obliterate the past were never fully successful. In his upbringing, Aleksandr encountered people who held on dearly to Russia's rich religious heritage, and risked their lives in doing so. Like Kupriianova, such individuals gave Aleksandr Men a first-hand introduction to writers and philosophers whose works, thereafter, he deeply absorbed.

Mother Mariia

In addition to his "aunt," the second individual who played a large part in Aleksandr's early intellectual development was the remarkable Mother Mariia. Like Fr. Serafim, she viewed the 1927 accommodation with the government as a betrayal of Christianity, and joined the catacomb church in opposition, committing herself to preserving Orthodoxy's principles from a power aimed at destroying them. As a child, Aleksandr had known Fr. Serafim only briefly; he had limited personal contacts with the renowned priest, but his encounters with Mother Mariia were more direct and longer lasting. Like Fr. Serafim, under whom she had served, constantly under threat of arrest, Mother Mariia "moved in the shadows" of the Stalinist period.[23] But in her the young Aleksandr found a woman whose impact on him was inspirational and influential, and he remembered her teaching and the model of Christianity she offered for the rest of his life.[24] It was she who first exposed him to the beauty of the liturgy and to the Gospels, displaying a passionate dedication to protecting the "pure spirit of Orthodox Christianity" from violence and from compromises with the government.[25] She connected the young Aleksandr directly to the traditional Orthodox Church and its spiritual teachings.

Mother Mariia (1879–1961) became a leader in the "catacomb church" in Zagorsk shortly after the arrest of Fr. Petr Shipkov in December 1943. Like nearly all such catacomb church leaders, Mother Mariia had an extremely difficult, multifaceted, and circuitous earlier life before she arrived in Zagorsk. Having become a nun at an early age, she had slowly risen within the ranks of the Orthodox Church until her appointment as the head of a women's monastery near the town of Vol'sk in the Saratov region, on the right bank of the Volga River. Largely under her direction, this women's monastery had grown rapidly, expanding to include some five hundred nuns who lived there or nearby. During her years of service, she had known many hardships and experienced a great deal of personal suffering, especially after the Bolsheviks came to power, dispersed the nuns attached to the monastery, and persecuted Mother Mariia, the mother superior. The years following were extremely challenging for her. She witnessed a lot of violence, and she had a difficult time surviving, especially after 1927. Mother Mariia eventually settled in Zagorsk, where she was told that the spirit of Saint Sergii would protect her and where she knew and greatly respected Fr. Serafim. She secretly ran a small women's monastery in a house, then on the outskirts of the city, and it was there that Fr. Petr Shipkov brought Aleksandr's mother and her two children shortly before his arrest.

Early in her life, Mother Mariia had been deeply influenced by the elders of the Optina Pustyn' Monastery, and, during her long years of service to the church, she had lived out the principles taught by these famous elders. In the nineteenth century, Optina became the spiritual center of Russian Orthodoxy, and its influence and reputation spread all over the country. Despite the closure of the monastery, the destruction of several of its buildings, and the execution of many of its elders, the monastery's spirit continued to live on in such people as Mother Mariia.[26] She exposed the young Aleksandr Men to that spirit; thanks to her, it would be among the most significant influences on him. While many readers may be familiar with the monastery, a brief review should be helpful to the further discussion of Mother Mariia and the lessons he took from her.

Founded in the sixteenth century near the town of Kozel'sk in central Russia, Optina Pustyn' took its name from the legendary former brigand named Opta, who assumed the monastic name Makarii, a transfigured man following his conversion to Orthodoxy, and *pustynia*, or desert, denoting the "desert fathers," who conceived the remote desert communities where monasticism originated.[27] Like other monasteries, Optina Pustyn' fell into disuse in the eighteenth century, and by the end of the century had little significance in Russia's cultural life. This changed in the 1830s and 1840s when the monastery came under the leadership of several great religious leaders. They were part of a monastic revival and the development of a new model of monastic life. This new model moved the monastery out from under the domination of the court and powerful members of the nobility and toward a religious mission focusing on the society as a whole. Influenced by hesychasm and its vision that spiritual knowledge was best acquired through silence, as the desert fathers had maintained, the Optina Elders also reached outward, communicating their knowledge to those who came seeking advice and guidance.

The Optina Elders, beginning with the great Elder Leonid (Nagolkin, 1768–1841) in the nineteenth century, functioned differently from the monks in Russia's traditional monasteries. At Optina Pustyn,' elders held no formal office in the church hierarchy. They operated outside the church's institutional framework and related to people on a personal, rather than an institutional, level. As a result, they heard confessions more often and in greater detail than did other priests, offering advice and guidance on all kinds of issues, ranging from public morality to such private matters as marriage, illness, and what a person should do with one's life. By the 1840s, under the able leadership of Fr. Makarii, the monastery's spiritual director from 1836 to 1860, and the work of philosopher Ivan Kireevskii, the contemplative tradition of Optina developed a network of educated followers that linked Optina, a famous Moscow salon, Moscow University, and the Moscow Theological Academy.[28] Makarii conducted a wide-ranging correspondence with Russian clergy and laymen that led to personal visits by some of Russia's leading cultural figures, including Nikolai Gogol, Ivan Turgenev, and Vladimir Solov'ev.[29]

In 1865, when Fr. Amvrosii became the spiritual director of the monastery, Optina's reputation would spread all over Russia. During this time, people traveled from afar to speak with the famous *starets* (elder) and the other elders. In June 1878, after the death of his three-year-old son Aleksei, Dostoevsky made a pilgrimage to Optina Pustyn' to consult with Fr. Amvrosii, and he set the first book of his novel, *The Brothers Karamazov*, in the Optina Monastery.[30]

A *starets*, Vladimir Lossky writes, "by virtue of a special gift" is able to see "each being as God sees him, and he searches for a way to help him, opening his interior sense without doing violence to his will, so that the human person, freed from all hidden fetters, can bloom forth in Grace."[31] Fr. Amvrosii had those qualities, and despite continual illness that plagued him for much of his adult life, he exhibited a remarkable energy, a clairvoyance that enabled him to see into a person's inner being, and compassion for each individual he encountered. Whether a government official, a university student, or a poor, uneducated peasant, the Elder Amvrosii considered them the same. All were equal in his eyes, and "all required attention, kindness, and spiritual help."[32] The monks and nuns at Optina Pustyn' and the nearby Shamordino Convent were educated to be open to the world, to be humble before all of creation, and to have heartfelt concern for people from all walks of life. Their personal, physical presence and availability created a close bond between them and people from all walks of life who came seeking their counsel. They served as a bridge over the deep gulf that existed between the "church and the social and cultural life of the country."[33]

What also distinguished Optina Pustyn' was the rich conversation it stimulated between the church and the world. The Optina Elders were not hermits who withdrew from society in order to contemplate a different life, recluses removed from the concrete problems surrounding them. Dostoevsky's wife Anna attributed her husband's visit to Optina and his conversations with Fr. Amvrosii as having a "profound and lasting effect on him."[34] The Optina Elders' relationships and the form of their communications created a kind of fellowship, a covenant that united them with those who came to the monastery. Free from dogma and strict adherence to ritual, Optina Elders' concerns transcended the boundaries of the parish and diocese. In their words and their actions, they were strong believers in the unity of humankind and love of one's neighbors. They not only turned inward through strict obedience and prayer, but also looked outward, engaging constantly in a rich dialogue with all of humanity. Their concern with humanity and their emphasis on the importance of dialogue were strongly imprinted on Mother Mariia and the community she established in Zagorsk.

Short in stature, energetic, and a person of breadth and "deep wisdom," as another nun described her, Mother Mariia had a strong commitment to serving people, particularly the downtrodden.[35] In the early 1940s, her tiny house became a beehive of activity, despite the covert nature of its operations. The nun Dosifeia, who lived for several years with Mother Mariia, remarked that the first time she entered this small house, "I immediately felt myself in another world. It seemed to me that I was in one of the novels written by Mel'nikov Pecherskii: a tiny house, with several extremely narrow rooms, and, throughout, there was the special smell of a mixture of honey, beeswax, and a hot icon lamp."[36]

Soon after her move to Zagorsk, Mother Mariia attracted a small number of similarly persecuted nuns who either lived with her or in the neighborhood. Three or four normally lived in the house for a short period of five to six weeks, or occasionally for several years. But "factually, in her small house were many people, whom she hid," said the nun Dosifeia. "They came to her for advice, support, and to run away" from whatever intolerable trouble they faced; Mother Mariia created an "extraordinary place to which many persecuted people fled."[37] Despite her forced departure from the previous women's monastery, she received many people from that area who came wanting her advice or seeking the spiritual guidance she had once given them and bringing products from the Volga region, which they left to help support the nuns.[38] The Soviet government had closed the Optina Pustyn' Monastery more than twenty years earlier, but its spirit and worldview remained very much alive in such people as Mother Mariia.

Among her most salient qualities was the lack of force she embodied in her approach. It was this quality, so much a characteristic of the Optina Elders, that remained in Aleksandr's memory. He never forgot, he said, her advice to him as a child about the Orthodox service. He confessed to her that he did not like the long service. She told him simply to go in and stay only as long as he wished. "She never said, 'Stay through the whole service.'" If she had told him he should remain for all of it, he would have found it agonizing. "But most often I stood through the full service, because she gave me the possibility of leaving whenever I wished."[39] Aleksandr Men never forgot the personal qualities Mother Mariia exemplified in her daily behavior and in her spiritual guidance: her unwillingness to impose a rigid structure, her unwillingness to see the world through narrowly prescribed standards of conduct or belief, and her openness to all kinds of possibilities.

Mother Mariia became a mentor to Aleksandr. "In many ways [she] defined my life's course and spiritual framework."[40] She taught him how to read the scriptures. She handed him the Bible when he was seven years old, telling him, after he asked her for guidance, that she would give him no directions. He had only the instructions to open the book, begin on the first page, and "simply read," letting the words speak directly to him.[41] In this process, she spoke to him about mystery, wonder, and their importance in reading the text. She never attempted to be authoritative. Like his mother and aunt, Mother Mariia nourished his imagination. She encouraged him always to open his mind and his eyes and to see differently from what the formal structures operating in his society sought to impose on him. The teaching methods she employed were designed to stimulate the imagination in still another way: she rarely, if ever, moralized. Whenever they were together, Aleksandr Men recounted, she "always told me some kind of unending story—fantasy or reality, having taken place formerly or going on presently. These stories were like parables, from which it was possible to draw a lesson," usually with multiple meanings.[42]

In her personality and relationships with people, Mother Mariia offered a concrete example of her approach to life and her beliefs in her attempt to bring together several different worlds. She was "full of humor, of life, of the humor of the common people, rich and robust," wrote the nun Dosifeia. It was as if in her small house two worlds existed and "ran parallel to each other: on one side, life, filled with humor and craftiness, funny and sometimes childish, and on the other side—prayers and mystical connection with an invisible world, which, through the mother, we experienced as especially close."[43]

Mother Mariia never turned away anyone who sought her out, regardless of the person's need, social class, or education. She went to extraordinary lengths to help those who came to her in extremely dire circumstances. In her account of living with Mother Mariia, the nun Dosifeia recounted the arrival at the house of an elderly nun whom Mother Mariia had never seen before. Accompanied by a lay sister, the elderly nun, in extreme physical pain, sick with cancer and near death, had nowhere else to go and was in need of a place to rest. Despite the cramped space in the house, Mother Mariia gave them a room. One night, during the Paschal cycle at Easter, Mother Mariia, accompanied by other sisters in her house, went into the room where the old nun lay dying. "I remember how she looked at us," Dosifeia said. "We stood near her, singing 'Christ is risen,' and she smiled at us, and large tears fell from her eyes onto her cheeks."[44] After the elderly nun died, Mother Mariia continued to provide shelter to the nun's lay companion, blessing her and saying, "That is how we must always relate to one another."[45]

Such beneficence did not consist of single acts but rather were a common feature of Mother Mariia's approach to people. She was vulnerable and had multiple health problems, but you "could always see that spark in her eyes," said Pavel Men. He recalled the "appalling living conditions" in her house: the absence of running water, the need to haul water from a well, the ancient stove, which poorly heated the entire facility—"but you would hardly if ever hear a complaint from any of the nuns."[46] But it was Mother Mariia's generosity that to him stood out most and singularly expressed her character:

> Sometimes I would be in her cell and see a priest or two, who had come to visit with her. I remember a priest who came to her from Saratov, I believe; and he told her how difficult it was to live with three children, and he asked her to pray for him and his family. She took out, from somewhere she had hidden, some 200 rubles and gave them to him. That was a lot of money in those days, but she willingly gave it. Her act serves to illustrate how open hearted she was toward people who were in need, and I remember myself being utterly struck by her expression of kindness. She understood human need.[47]

Endowed with "unusual spiritual gifts, well-educated, and extremely humble in demeanor," as Fr. Aleksandr later described her, Mother Mariia had personal qualities that he greatly admired. For many years, her image loomed large in his mind, this small, delicate woman who had "borne many heavy burdens in her life," but preserved "in full a clear mind, a total absence of sanctimonious behavior . . . a lively sense of humor, and—what is especially important—a strong belief in the importance of freedom [*svoboda*]."[48] These characteristics Aleksandr himself carried with him throughout his life. As he reflected on what she had taught him at such an early age, he identified the qualities that the Optina Elders had ingrained in her, and she in him: "openness to people, their problems, their searchings—openness to the world," the same qualities that attracted so many of Russia's greatest writers to Optina Pustyn'.[49]

The Optina Elders contributed another perspective that Aleksandr Men never forgot. Despite the opposition of the political authorities, after a long period of silence, they renewed "the dialogue between the church and society."[50] Through Mother Mariia and Fr. Serafim, he saw a "living continuation of that dialogue," one of the defining themes of Orthodox Christianity.[51] The importance of "dialogue with the world" remained with him. It would mark his later ministry as a priest. Such a perspective was radically different from other aspects of his education. The lessons he derived from Mother Mariia in the "catacomb church" in Zagorsk stood in stark contrast to the teachings he encountered during his formative years in school.

The Little Red Schoolhouse

Aleksandr Men's early education in Soviet schools failed to add much of anything to the rich experiences he had at home with friends of his family and in the "catacomb church." He describes his school years as an unhappy period and, as mentioned above, his teachers did little to stimulate his imagination or broaden his desire to learn.[52] In some ways, they should not be blamed for shortcomings over which they had little control. The hunger that characterized much of the war in Moscow continued in the immediate postwar years, and Aleksandr knew many teachers who collected crusts of bread and classmates who came to school perpetually hungry. Moscow's schools had a shortage of teachers. The classes were large, most of them overcrowded, and filled with unruly children, more than half of whom had lost one or both parents during the war.[53] The school on Serpukhov Street existed in a rough neighborhood, a dingy, crowded place, where street fights often occurred and personal conflicts spilled over into the school. As Aleksandr described them, the students were not prepared to learn, and neither were the teachers, with their meager training, prepared to teach.[54]

But the most oppressive aspect of the school Men attended from 1943 to 1953 consisted of the atmosphere and the methods of instruction. These were, as he described them, non-productive school years, marked by uninspiring classes and listless teachers who ruled by using the rod and expected total compliance from their students. Aleksandr's references to his instructors are extremely harsh, even biting, as, for example, his description of the teachers of literature, whom the students called "fascists" for their ready use of corporal punishment and their rigid approach to literary texts. By his fourth year, Aleksandr was already in rebellion. "Everything I heard in school, I took the opposite" as nearer the truth; he revolted against what he perceived as the school's "mindnumbing system," beginning with the director—who he said resembled Karabas-Barabas, the evil puppeteer in Carlo Collodi's *Adventures of Pinocchio*, who tried to control the marionettes on strings—and ending with the lowest grade teachers, who feared to dispute anything.[55] By the fourth level of his schooling, Aleksandr had decided that everything "being taught was a lie."[56]

Teaching based on rote memorization, his instructors could not address the questions he had begun to raise. As Anastasiia Iakovlevna Andreeva, a childhood friend, recalled, his drawings and watercolors of "darkening brick Moscow houses, church cupolas standing out in the winter sky, white flakes of snow slipping off the roof onto a large fir tree in the courtyard, did not portray Moscow from a Stalinist point of view."[57] He saw "something else, some other kind of reality," different from the flat, one-dimensional world surrounding him, more lively and dynamic than the routine, preapproved forms promoted by the state. In 1947, on a holiday, Andreeva said, she stood with Aleksandr on Red Square in the evening, where the "Party had placed, shining splendidly, a gigantic portrait of Stalin, lighted at night with a projector—an idol expecting enthusiasm and submission from his slaves." She recalled that Aleksandr turned to her and said that "when he saw the portrait in the dark sky, it was precisely then that he understood that he had to become a priest."[58]

It is difficult to say what conditions in such schooling allow some students to thrive and others to reject their pedagogical framework. In the 1940s and early 1950s, the school on Serpukhov Street likely produced graduates who benefitted from the system of learning it established. Others, however, were able to rise above the rote learning approaches it fostered. In the class ahead of Aleksandr's were individuals who later became luminaries in their fields: Andrei Tarkovsky, one of Russia's greatest filmmakers and writers; Andrei Vosnesensky, the internationally acclaimed poet; and G. I. Seregin, a cardiologist in the Vishnevskii Institute of Surgery. Aleksandr Borisov, several years younger and a childhood friend of Aleksandr's brother, later became the head priest of the Church of the Sacred Martyrs Kosma and Damian in central Moscow, one of the most progressive parishes in the city.[59]

In secondary school, as in his earlier schooling, Aleksandr did not excel as a student. He went through the motions, studying only enough to satisfy the requirements, but little more. He hated those years, and could not wait to escape the narrow, unimaginative experiences they offered. His real schooling, however, took place outside the formal school environment—in his reading, his visits to the bookstalls of Moscow, and as discussed below, in an accidental meeting.

Throughout his school years, Aleksandr read voraciously, having already gained access to a wide variety of books. For him, books played a large part in creating a parallel existence to the political and ideological world surrounding him, a pathway into a world much different from the one to which his schooling exposed him. During a time when the state assaulted ways of thinking that lay outside the Marxist-Leninist mainstream, books kept alive older traditions and perspectives. Literature served as one of the primary vehicles for transmitting such traditions and perspectives, and Aleksandr Men tells us that books helped insulate him from the cult of Stalin.[60] The act of reading—in philosophy and poetry—further stimulated his imagination, taking him back to a time when words were less abstract and less ideological and weaving a richer tapestry of ideas than those confronting him in school and on the street.

Encouraged by his aunt, who put into his hands many texts, both classical and contemporary, Aleksandr found inspiration in them at an unusually
young age. Before his teenage years, he had absorbed Johann Wolfgang von
Goethe's *Faust*, Dante Alighieri's *Divine Comedy*, large parts of which he
memorized and all his life could recite, and Ernest Renan's *Life of Jesus*.[61]
As a teenager, he read many of the classics of European literature and philosophy and of world religions.[62] He rose before the other members of his
household awakened and read in the early morning hours. In some respects,
he educated himself, stimulated by a lively interest in ideas—philosophy, literature, history, and religion—that he could not get in his formal schooling.
Russia's own religious and philosophical writers especially intrigued him,
and he scanned the old bookstores of Moscow in search of their writings.[63]

Here, in Aleksandr Men's own words, is his recounting of these pleasures
and their importance:

> Precisely in the Stalin era, among the nails and guinea pigs at a market, I
> found the old books of Vladimir Solov'ev and Sergei Bulgakov, and I read
> them ... with trembling hands. During a time when there was neither
> "samizdat" [self-publishing] nor "*tamizdat*" [publishing abroad,] when in
> the sphere of philosophy only nonsense was published that was impossible
> even to hold in one's hands, I entered into the world of great thinkers. . . .
> In our youth, we searched for books. I worked during my schoolboy years,
> traveling to the Crimean national park reserve, in order to earn enough
> money to buy books. I began to collect a library, when I was still in the
> fifth class. At this time, when almost all the cathedrals, as well as the [Trin-
> ity-Saint Sergius] Lavra, were closed (except for two churches), I derived
> my vision of an internal church from literature and from poetry, from what
> the artist [Mikhail] Nesterov created, from everything surrounding them.[64]

But one field in school he did pursue avidly: the sciences, particularly biology and zoology. Aleksandr had long been attracted to all kinds of animals,
to the structure of the animal kingdom, the diverse characteristics of its
members, and to embryology. As a teenager, he often visited the zoological
museum operated by Moscow University on Herzen Street, where he studied the models of wild animals, birds, and reptiles on display and sketched
them on his drawing pad. Such drawings, as his notebooks reveal, included
an unusual amount of detail, as if their primary focus was on the bone structures and the internal organs of the animals, many of them coming from the
distant north or east of the country. These animals captivated his interest
from the beginning, and his frequent visits also attracted the attention of

the museum's director, Vasilii Alekseevich Vatagin, who observed the young student sitting before the animal models and intently studying them. Vatagin took an interest in the teenager, and invited him into the room where he drew and constructed models of the wild creatures.

This man, Russia's most prominent animal artist of the twentieth century, was a man "with a sparse beard and a rattling voice," as Aleksandr Men later portrayed him, who possessed an inner, "elemental power that he transferred to his creations."[65] Observing the teenager's drawings, Vatagin encouraged Aleksandr to continue to look beyond the external appearances of phenomena and to seek the inner life, the deeper reality that lay within. The artist and the student soon became fast friends; for more than a year they met regularly to talk about art and science and their underlying connections. At their meetings, which usually took place on Friday afternoons, Vatagin took long walks with his young protégé, instructing Aleksandr in his own artistic philosophy and telling stories about the natural world, about what attracted him to that world, and what he saw as the inner connections and beauty within all of nature. Aleksandr was captivated by these talks. He especially enjoyed the inquisitive, open approach to learning exemplified by this prominent scholar, which contrasted starkly with the teachings in the school on Serpukhov Street.

As their friendship developed, the conversations between Vatagin and Aleksandr encompassed other subjects, including religion. Vatagin related to Aleksandr his attraction to India and its mystical philosophies, which he spent considerable time studying. He confessed to Aleksandr that he embraced "theosophy"—the synthesis of philosophy, science, and religion, a system of knowledge derived from the Alexandrian philosophers of the third century. Theosophists maintain that knowledge of the universe is derived both from external and internal sources and requires acknowledgment of scientific and internal divine realms, which interact with each other. Nature and the spiritual world are in constant interplay with each sphere intermingling with the other.[66]

Aleksandr Men found these conversations with Vatagin fascinating. They opened up to him a new way of thinking about the world and its metaphysical components, and while he appreciated his elder friend's theosophical perspectives and thought about them at length, he could not accept such views; he found their mystical elements bordered on the occult. But Vatagin had opened his mind to his young companion, trusting him with ideas and speculations that the senior artist secretly incorporated into his work as an animal artist, productions that are considered among Russia's finest of the twentieth century.[67]

Vatagin's conversations with his young protégé took place in the early 1950s, the last years of the Stalin era and a time of ideological rigidity, when the confession of such private beliefs was very dangerous. Yet Vatagin "was extremely open and expressed his thoughts freely [to me]," Aleksandr recalled, even at this time when fear and distrust pervaded nearly everything.[68] Vatagin especially impressed upon the young Aleksandr the beauty and the mystery of the natural world; he thus opened up for Aleksandr a natural world to be explored whose inner connections required an imaginative mind.

These conversations with Vatagin and his studies in biology inspired Aleksandr to pursue further his interest in the sciences. Upon his graduation from secondary school in the spring of 1953, a few months after Stalin's death, Aleksandr elected the sciences as the next step in his future career. Since his Jewish background prevented him from admittance to Moscow University, he could not expect to attend Moscow's most prestigious university. Instead, with the encouragement of a childhood friend who enjoyed studying there and enthusiastically recommended it, he enrolled in the Institute of Fur. In the fall of 1953, he entered this well-regarded institute, located then in a large park on the outskirts of Moscow.

By the time he graduated from secondary school, Aleksandr Men fully opposed many aspects of the Soviet system, from the Young Pioneers to the glorification of Stalin. But his cynical attitude toward what he saw in Soviet life did not encompass all his relationships and his general attitude toward life. He had developed friendships with people who projected a much different view of reality than the official encounters he experienced. However, he had not yet channeled his rebellion into a concrete plan of action. He did not see his own way clearly, but as he entered the next stage of his education, that plan took on a sharper focus.

Significantly, the education Aleksandr received outside the official structures of power went far beyond opposition to the state-imposed structures. What he learned essentially involved a new way of seeing, of looking beyond the physical appearances of reality, and of seeing connections between seemingly disparate phenomena. This new way of seeing required freedom, as Mother Mariia had taught him, and the other individuals discussed in this chapter—the child psychologist Vera Iakovlevna, the ethnographer Boris Vasil'ev, the speech therapist Tat'iana Kapriianova, and the artist Vasilii Vatagin—enhanced this need to see differently. At the Institute of Fur, Aleksandr Men encountered people and circumstances that both gave him future direction and encouraged him still further to imagine his surroundings anew.

5

. . . .

Aleksandr Men in Siberia

The Formation of a Priest

Siberia seems an unlikely training ground for the priesthood. It is the home of the vast Siberian Gulag that, in Stalin's time, endeavored to break the human soul. Long before then, Siberia served as a place of exile for many thousands of Russians charged with "political crimes," whom the Tsarist government forced to "live apart." Siberia lay outside the European zone of civilization, the land of the Russian frontier, a place of resettlement where, in the twentieth century, Stalin moved whole peoples around like pieces on a chessboard. On the surface, Siberia would not be a place conducive to the education of individuals aspiring to leadership in the Russian Orthodox Church.

But physical obstacles did not present the only challenges to those who wished to enter the priesthood in Stalinist Russia. In a society priding itself on having already achieved "the complete victory of the socialist system," as Joseph Stalin proclaimed in 1936, such a desire diametrically opposed the Communist Party's aspirations.[1] Those courageous individuals who took this path understood that the years ahead promised severe hardship in service to a cause opposed to the Party's primary goals. In the late 1950s, when the Communist Party, under the leadership of Nikita Khrushchev, renewed its brutal war against religion, those who resisted or who had an opposing set of priorities faced a perilous, uncertain future.

In Aleksandr Men's path to the priesthood, several turning points in his future course took place in Siberia, during his student years, from 1955 to 1958. At that time, Aleksandr Men was a biology student in the Institute of Fur, which the government, in 1955, resettled from Moscow to the Siberian city of Irkutsk. In Irkutsk, Men cultivated personal relationships that shaped his entire life, encountered a world much different from what he had known earlier in Moscow, and raised questions that remained with him throughout his later service as an Orthodox priest. There, in Irkutsk, Aleksandr Men spent several decisive years, to which most studies of his life have given scant attention.[2] His years in Siberia, he wrote, "helped form many of my views."[3] How, then, did his student years there play such a formative role? How did they shape his perspectives on the world? In what ways did these years set the stage for the priesthood that followed?

Life on the Russian Frontier

Siberia is, in many ways, an imaginary place. It is a "figment of speech," since a physical, geographical entity called Siberia does not exist; it stands alone, as Ian Frazier has written, as though disconnected from any place, a geographical zone unto itself.[4] It evokes multiple, sometimes contradictory images of long, cold winters, of short, hot summers, of extreme distances, rich natural resources, exile and prison camps, of dense forests and powerful rivers, exotic wildlife, and the romance of the frontier.

Beginning from the west at the Ural Mountains and extending eastward to the Pacific Ocean, Siberia is a vast expanse of land, encompassing eight time zones. This expanse stretches from the Arctic Ocean in the north across an immense steppe land in the south. The width of this landmass from the Urals to Kamchatka Peninsula is about 3,700 miles, longer by 900 miles than the distance from San Francisco to New York.[5] Explored by the Russian adventurer Ermak Timofeevich, whose expedition across it began in 1581, Siberia soon became the destination for waves of Russian settlers, who moved further and further eastward, aggressively pushing against and sometimes displacing Siberia's indigenous people, including Buryat Mongols, Tatars, Samoyeds, Chukchis, Yakuts, and many others, in encounters not unlike America's westward expansion.[6]

A dense coniferous forest, generally called taiga, after its Turkish name, covers much of Siberia, from the Ural Mountains to the Ob River. The taiga is the home of a multitude of wild animals—elk, reindeer, brown bear, wolf, lynx, and the prized ermine and sable, which Western travelers in the eighteenth and nineteenth centuries found singularly impressive.[7] Such travel accounts, as R. A. French has pointed out, produced two contradictory portrayals of this land, interpretations that very much depended on different ways of seeing and on individual circumstances.[8] The first portrait emphasized Siberia's remoteness, its extreme cold, its difficulties of travel, its dens of criminals, the poor living conditions of its native peoples, and its exotic features. The second picture focused on Siberia's extraordinary beauty, the hospitality and charms of its indigenous population, the wildlife havens, the impressive stores of minerals, the immense reserves of petroleum and natural gas, and the creativity and ingenuity of its peoples. Praising the region around Irkutsk in 1856–1857, the American entrepreneur Perry McDonough Collins's descriptions exemplify this second portrayal. "The rivers are flanked with fine forests," Collins enthusiastically wrote, "the banks yield iron and gold, silver and copper, while the waters and forests are abundantly stocked with fish, fowl and game, only awaiting the advance of population and the introduction of steamships and railroads."[9]

In this vast landscape, Irkutsk served as a special city almost from the beginning, from its founding in the early 1650s as a winter stockade built on the Angara River. Its location on the river, but also on the southern boundary of one of the world's greatest forests, gave Irkutsk significant advantages. Included among those who settled there were ambitious, forward-looking people, fur trappers and merchants, who used the wealth they accumulated from the prized furs that were then in large demand in the Islamic Middle East and the Byzantine Empire to build the city's infrastructure and lavishly decorated local homes.[10] In 1799, the Russian-American Company, which transported furs to Western Europe and other places, chose Irkutsk as its headquarters.[11] In 1805, Irkutsk opened the first secondary school in Siberia; even earlier, in 1782, it established a public library and, in 1838, added a second, which served as the home for a number of leading Decembrists in exile, including Sergei Volkonskii, whose wife Mariia, followed her husband into exile, built the first theater in Siberia, worked in local schools, and had a large influence on city government. In 1851, the Russian Geographical Society opened its Siberian branch in Irkutsk, bringing to the city a number of talented scientists, who explored the geography, nature, and natural resources of Siberia.[12] By the end of the nineteenth century, Irkutsk had become the economic, intellectual, and cultural center of Siberia.[13]

In Soviet times, Irkutsk and its surrounding area had special significance.[14] In the 1950s, a series of government decrees emphasized Siberia's vast potential, which had not been fully realized.[15] Nikita Khrushchev's program for economic development, of which the Virgin Lands Campaign represented only a part, envisioned Siberia as a key component of the state's goals.[16] Animal husbandry had already become an extremely profitable component of the national economy, and its further development offered a promising means of strengthening the Soviet Union's export trade in a precious commodity.[17] This is one of the main reasons the government, in 1955, moved the Institute of Fur from the outskirts of Moscow to Irkutsk and integrated it into the Agricultural Institute located there. The move took advantage of certain new measures for the proposed expansion of commercial game, especially of many nearly extinct species of fur-bearing animals, such as martens and sables.[18] Aleksandr Men was a student in the institute, and the move to Irkutsk promised to give him and other students first-hand experience with a biological project at the forefront of Soviet scientific and economic endeavors.

A New Friendship

Aleksandr Men's admission in the Institute of Fur took place in 1953, the same year as Stalin's death. His enrollment in the institute that fall came as the first impulses toward political reform had begun to take hold in the aftermath of the dictator's death. A new generation of young people was coming to the forefront, more articulate, better educated, less timid, and politically more secure than its predecessors, whose outlook remained mired in the suspicious, bureaucratically inert older generation that preceded it. The first few years following Stalin's death witnessed sharp clashes between the reform-minded desires of this young generation, with their expectations of reform and social change, and the conservative, less flexible predecessors, still well-entrenched in positions of power.[19]

Eighteen years old, passionately interested in both the sciences and theology, and unsure of what eventually lay ahead, Aleksandr Men knew that his immediate prospects lay in the sciences. That fall, he threw himself into his coursework; he found his classes much different, much more enjoyable, than his earlier schooling, and he felt himself "like a fish in the water," with only his course in physics presenting any difficulty.[20] Men thus entered an educational world significantly different from his previous experience; it was not only the classes that provided a new environment, but also relationships with the faculty. Unlike the stern disciplinarians of his secondary school, most of whom were long-time residents of Moscow, teachers in the institute had a much different approach and employed the custom of associating with their students on a personal level. Before the move to Siberia, faculty members in the institute created a camaraderie with their pupils that extended beyond the classroom, making their work together joint endeavors. They worked alongside the students, enjoyed associating with them, and in their free time went on excursions and planned social events together. Since the institute was located outside Moscow, teachers and students lived in close proximity to each other, which encouraged these relationships. Most importantly, a large number of the faculty members were "people of a special stamp," as Zoia Maslenikova pointed out. "Not a few of them came from the distant taiga country, from obscure, dense forest places, which placed a high value on comradeship and a sense of mutual dependence."[21] Like the students, they presented an extremely diverse picture, and developed shared bonds within this diversity, which Men, as a student, absorbed into his own consciousness.

One afternoon, in 1953, during the first weeks of his study in the institute, while still in Moscow, Men caught the train from the city, where he had gone earlier in the day on an excursion. Other students filled the compartment and Men, as he often did on such trips, took a seat in the corner, opened a book, and became absorbed in his reading. As usual, he used the train trip to read on subjects unconnected to his schoolwork. The train had gone some distance, moving through the Moscow suburbs and into the forestland just outside the city, when a fellow student, sitting nearby, leaned over to him and asked about the book he was reading. Startled, Men showed him the book, expecting that this brief encounter would end as soon as he had satisfied his schoolmate's curiosity. Redheaded and pleasant looking, the student moved closer, and asked in a low voice whether Men had any books on Eastern religions. Men immediately became suspicious, his wariness aroused by this provocative question from a person with whom he was unacquainted. In the autumn of 1953, only months after Stalin's death, when the political climate was in turmoil, such an unexpected inquiry could hardly be taken lightly. Cautious and uncertain as to how to respond, Men gave a perfunctory response, referencing only a standard textbook: "There is, of course, the *History of the Ancient East*," he said. "That is not what I asked you," exclaimed the other student. This bold exchange would open Men to a relationship that would have long-lasting consequences both for Russia and for him personally. The other student turned out not to be a provocateur, but someone with a probing intellect and a courageous and outgoing personality, whose future at several crucial junctures would be entwined with Men's. The fellow student was Gleb Yakunin, and his introduction to Men on the train that day set the stage for a long-lasting friendship.[22]

Precocious and, like Men, an avid reader, Yakunin was then a year ahead of Aleksandr Men in the institute. Their paths had many similar and different features, both of which would affect their relationship. Born in Moscow into a family of musicians, Yakunin too had developed an interest in the sciences. His mother was a practicing Orthodox believer, but Yakunin early on had become an avowed atheist, like many of his generation, and he saw Christianity as a belief system essentially for elderly women. Nevertheless, he continued to question the teachings in his school and to read deeply in philosophy, history, and, occasionally, in theology. He had an extremely lively, engaging mind. Like Men, particularly at the time of their first meeting, he was in the process of developing his own views on a variety of subjects and of finding his own way.

Shortly after his initial encounter with Aleksandr Men, Yakunin approached him and gave him a copy of a book by M. V. Lodyzhenskii, *Higher Consciousness*, advising him to read it.[23] As Men later recounted this event, his reading of Lodyzhenskii brought the two students more closely together. He read the book several times, primarily because he wanted to understand Yakunin better and to be able to talk with him on his own terms. Lodyzhenskii was a theosophist, a perspective Men did not share and had previously rejected in his conversations with Vatagin. The earlier conversations helped him to engage with Yakunin, whose interest in Lodyzhenskii sparked similar discussions. While he disagreed with Yakunin, their friendship continued to develop.

Aleksandr Men greatly enjoyed these institute years within this small, tightly bound community before the move to Siberia. On Sunday mornings, he took the train into Moscow, continuing his service in the church with Fr. Nikolai (Golubtsov). And while he studied and read extensively, he did not become an academic hermit; he fully enjoyed parties, hunting expeditions, and opportunities to date young women, with several of whom he formed close relationships. On two occasions he fell in love, only to be disappointed when these brief romances did not sustain themselves. In 1955, when the government made the decision to move the institute to Siberia and incorporate it into the Agricultural Institute of Irkutsk, the familiar existence that Aleksandr Men had known most of his life come to an end. He entered a world much different in climate, culture, and social challenges. In the next three years, Siberia exposed him to experiences that would have a significant impact on his evolving view of the world.

Irkutsk

As he boarded the train for the journey to Irkutsk, Aleksandr Men faced his future both with anticipation and uncertainty. After a night of heavy partying, Men and his fellow students boarded the train, where they were "packed together like sardines" on the benches for the six-day trip to Irkutsk.[24] Now, at the age of twenty years, Men planned to spend the next three years completing his studies there, then fulfilling the required three years of service working in a game preserve. Eventually, he aimed to study for the priesthood, but how such a plan would be fulfilled, as he thought about it in 1955, he did not know.

Despite its relatively high level of culture, Irkutsk, like Siberia as a whole, had much that remained pioneer, rough, and raw.[25] After arriving in Irkutsk after the long train journey, Men, like his fellow students, explored the city, walking its streets, experiencing its different folkways, and observing its architectural patterns. His initial impressions were unfavorable. He saw immediately not only Irkutsk's physical distance from Moscow, but also its cultural distance, its slower pace of life, and its less intense, less spontaneous demeanor displayed on the faces of its peoples. He found all of it distasteful. "He did not like Irkutsk," Zoia Maslenikova writes. "The atmosphere was heavy and gloomy, and the same endless taiga oppressed him. He disliked the wooden pavement, the thick, broad faces, the squat wooden houses, the soot from the factory chimneys, the objects hanging out over the streets."[26] In time, however, as he adjusted his vision and, probably most importantly, his expectations, his impressions changed, and he came to see the city differently, recognize its hospitality, and appreciate its charms. Most of all, he learned to appreciate the city's openness, the cultural opportunities that life here offered, and the sense of a newfound freedom this frontier city, far from Moscow, gave him.

After his arrival in Irkutsk, Men elected not to live with the other students, but instead to find a room some distance apart. He wanted a quiet place to study, read the books that he had brought with him in a large trunk, write, and pursue both his interests in biology and theology undisturbed by the questioning eyes of other students. He found living quarters with a family in the city with whom he had made contact through a local church.[27] He and Gleb Yakunin decided to live together, and they moved into an adjoining room in the family's apartment. The months they lived in this household, sharing the same space, benefitted both of them. The two students talked a lot, discussing ideas they could not have easily spoken of elsewhere, and their time together in Irkutsk created a close and long-lasting bond between them. The effect of their relationship on Yakunin, as he later explained, would be transformative:

> I wasn't a Christian back then, but, as the saying goes, "I was on the way." When I was a child, my mother often took me with her to church. She was a devout believer, but, as is often the case, also somewhat simple-minded, and, naturally, she could not answer the many questions that had already emerged in my mind. She was a traditionalist, who abided by all the church

traditions without questioning them, as she had been taught to do. But growing up in the general environment of the 1930s and '40s, in effect, I lost my childhood faith in God, and by the age of ten or eleven, I had become a diehard atheist. Later, though, primarily through my reading in philosophy, literature, and the humanities, I gradually became an idealist of sorts; I recognized the existence of God, but not as something concrete and real. . . . It was at that point that I met Fr. Aleksandr, and we became friends. In Irkutsk, we wanted to live separately from the other students, because we realized that by living in the dorms it would be impossible to devote ourselves seriously to studying some very important questions about belief and about life. So we rented a small room not far from the train station in Irkutsk, and lived there together for about two years. Under his influence, as well as the guidance of several very intelligent friends from Moscow, I converted to Christianity.[28]

The time he spent with Yakunin in Irkutsk also had a significant influence on Aleksandr Men. Like Yakunin, he too was engaged in questioning everything and searching for the means by which he could most effectively pursue ideals, which, he knew, contradicted the state's prevailing values and methods of thinking. Here was a contemporary, asking many of the same questions as he, pursuing some of the same interests, and seeking connections between the sciences he studied formally and the theology he read privately. Even later, when they lived separately, Men could always find a willing ear in the person of Gleb Yakunin, whom he often sought out, knowing that with Yakunin he could safely share his private thoughts.[29]

Living in this frontier city, apart from the institute and his fellow students, directly exposed Men to the life of a diverse and multidimensional community in a way that his previous existence in Moscow could not have done. He experienced Russia's wide-open spaces, its distant horizons, and its large, unsettled lands, visible right before him. As opposed to the closed, restricted nature of Moscow, Siberia offered the vision of unrestricted territory, not as something to be fenced off, but as space that flowed outward to the east. He could also see his society's social complexity. Irkutsk represented a cultural crossroads: the city contained a large Buryat population that had suffered greatly during the Stalin era and whose Buddhist religion and traditions the government had made special targets of state repression.[30] In the countryside, near Irkutsk, there were Old Believer communities. Tightly knit, committed to their beliefs, and conservative in their customs, they remained a strong and vibrant group despite the harsh measures taken against them during the Stalin era. The largest Old Believer communities were located in the Altai Mountains and just east of Lake Baikal.[31] In Irkutsk, Men had the opportunity to interact and converse with these groups and many more.

In addition, as mentioned before, Siberia had traditionally been a place of exile or imprisonment for those who criticized or stood in political opposition to the established structures of the state. Not far from the house where Men and Yakunin lived in 1955 stood one of the labor camps. At a distance, they could see the long columns of prisoners marching to and from their work, the barbed wire enclosing their barracks, and the searchlights moving overhead in the night darkness.[32] These scenes and the stories that filtered into the city gave Men and Yakunin an immediate view of the human suffering that autocratic power inflicted, and further provoked the questions about power, authority, and human relationships that they had already begun to consider.

During these years, Men's primary attention focused on two issues, both of which emerged from concrete experiences he had while living in Irkutsk. The first concerned the church's limited capacity to speak to the Russian people. Soviet society was, at its core, secular, and it considered the church to be anachronistic, an institution that promulgated superstition and irrational views of life. The second issue centered on the connection between the sciences and religion, reason and revelation, and how they intersected, if at all. This issue had arisen in his mind earlier, but here in Irkutsk, it achieved particular sharpness. It, too, related to Orthodoxy's role in Russian society, as well as the church's capacity to address fundamental problems that transcended national boundaries.

The Church and Russian Society

Shortly after their arrival in Irkutsk, Men and Gleb Yakunin began to explore the role of the Orthodox Church in Russian society. "In Irkutsk, shortly after I converted to Christianity," Yakunin said, "we began talking about the fate and purpose of the church."[33] Their exploration soon led them into contacts with religious circles then operating in the city, connections that broadened the experiences of both young students. Yakunin described the nature of their discussions and the common aspirations that had begun to take shape in their minds:

> There were two priests there who we learned we could trust. There was one very unique priest, Fr. Vladimir, a teacher by trade who formerly had been arrested in Ukraine. At the time we met him, many priests were being

released from prisons, and it was there, during our conversations, with Aleksandr present, that I learned for the first time that Aleksandr's mother and aunt were not connected with the Moscow Patriarchate churches, but with the underground church. Aleksandr and I had long conversations with Fr. Vladimir, and he educated us about the true history of the church. He said that the official church was not the real church; the true church is the one that operated underground. He had spent some time in the prison camps, was later pardoned and released, and had a deep knowledge of church history. Fr. Aleksandr knew much of this history already, but, to me, it was a revelation. In the wake of these conversations, Fr. Aleksandr and I talked a lot about how to reform the church; we dreamed back then about what a real church ought to look like, a church free of the control of the KGB and free of state control. These became our youthful aspirations, our common ideals and dreams.[34]

In the mid-1950s, non-Orthodox denominations operated in Irkutsk, and they gave variety to the city's religious institutions. Men became friends with a young Catholic priest, a well-read, intelligent cleric, who had studied in the Vatican and had recently arrived. Their many conversations, Men noted, "revealed a great deal that I found new and interesting" and stood in contrast with the one-sided tracts that the Soviet government published and widely circulated.[35] These conversations, he wrote, gave him a different, more sympathetic view of Catholic doctrine than he had held earlier, although he could not subscribe to it. In order to understand better Catholic practices, he, by invitation of the priest, attended several of the services. He found neither them nor the priest to be particularly inspiring. But one element that he observed in the services and in his dialogues with the priest he did appreciate and admire: the Catholic Church's openness to the world, and this, he said, served as a "turning point" in the development of his ecumenical convictions.[36] The priest helped him to see more clearly the advantages of an open mind and how it both challenged and strengthened one's own religious beliefs. He was already becoming convinced that the church must turn outward and that an exclusively inward-looking vision held many dangers, including the risk of becoming fossilized.

Men visited a Baptist gathering and was immediately struck by the people, nearly all of them young factory workers, who crowded into a large room. He found impressive the emotional energy and passionate interest of those gathered there. They listened attentively to the minister's sermon, which, as Men noted, demonstrated a kind of heartfelt sincerity that the people in attendance found appealing. But what impressed him most of all was the warm welcome he received in this community. Their members did not appear overly concerned when he told them of his devotion to the Orthodox faith, but still reached out to him with open arms.[37] He appreciated the human connections and mutual support that the gathering encouraged, elements that had obvious appeal to the young workers who congregated there. In several other Protestant services, he observed confessions of faith intermixed with biblical criticism, which he did not find impressive; such study of the scriptures, he thought, achieved a higher level in the Catholic Church.[38]

What did Aleksandr Men observe in the Orthodox Church? Since his arrival in Irkutsk, he had been active in the local diocesan administration and a regular participant in the services. His experiences there stood in vivid contrast to some of the other religious communities he visited. "The difference was striking," he wrote. "A half-empty church, a disorganized order of service, depressed, melancholy elderly ladies, [and] a very short sermon filled with political information (something about China)."[39]

Men stored these images in his mind. The multiple models and approaches he saw in Irkutsk provoked sharply defined questions about the church's relationship to the people. How might the Orthodox Church present itself more effectively than it had in the past or the present? How might it recover its sacred traditions as well as its imagination and creative spirit during a time when not only the government attempted to suppress that spirit, but the official church, under great duress itself, also contributed to that suppression? His notes from that period suggest three responses, and while he had not yet worked them out fully, they had begun to take shape.

First, Men knew that the church had to concern itself with society: it could not focus entirely on the spiritual world, far removed from the struggles that individuals encountered every day, the suffering—physical and spiritual—that cried out for healing. In Irkutsk, Men saw such suffering at close range in the men and women in the nearby labor camp who stumbled along each day to their backbreaking labor under heavy guard. He also witnessed the broken bodies of children, piled high on uncovered wagons, taken to be buried.[40] These children were the victims of the second wave of the collectivization campaign, in which farmers were moved from collectives to state farms in the mid-1950s. They were the children of families who had resisted the government's efforts or who had died from malnutrition because of such resistance.

Second, such direct observations of human suffering raised the whole issue of coercion in human affairs. State coercion had long been employed to further social and economic goals, and Soviet industrialization and collectivization had heavily relied on this approach to achieve national goals. But Christianity, too, had a history of violence, in which church and state had joined together in the killing of their enemies. The religious wars of the sixteenth and seventeenth centuries and the church's support of state violence in nineteenth-century England and France offered much evidence of such atrocities. In recent years, both in the Soviet Union and elsewhere, secular opponents of Christianity had repeatedly accused monotheistic religion of promoting violence, fostering fanatical devotion to singular causes, and inspiring hatred.[41] Some argued that by claiming exclusivity, Christianity divided the world between "us" and "them," and such notions could be said to legitimize violence.[42]

Aleksandr Men took a strong stand against these ways of thinking. He saw other kinds of evidence of violence on a massive scale right before his eyes. Russian revolutionaries maintained that "revolution cannot happen without sacrifices." They used such reasoning to justify the killings and suffering of their opposition, as well as to rationalize the so-called "excesses of revolution."[43] The Communist Party made these arguments, claiming that the creation of a just society required such violence. Yet, as Men understood Christianity, it took a diametrically opposite position: the teachings of Jesus proposed a much different way of looking at human life, violence, and power. They suggested to him that violence used in any form constituted a misunderstanding of these teachings and a perversion of Christianity. Men believed that the church had to make a much stronger effort to uncover the sources of peace within its traditions. A key element in the church's role ought to be bringing human conscience back to life, uncovering it from the layers of tissue under which this "inner conscience" was buried. The church saw its primary mission as spreading the faith; Men was developing a view that saw its role differently. Its central importance did not lie in its external features, but in its internal capacities, especially its efforts to raise human consciousness to a higher level—namely, to nourish compassion for others.[44] He believed the church had an evangelistic mission, and a strong part of that mission lay in forging "a different citizen consciousness, whose need he saw in its wild form" on the Russian frontier.[45]

Third, Men knew that if the Orthodox Church aimed to play a critical role in the country, it had to formulate a convincing means of speaking to the Soviet people. Heavily indoctrinated to see religion as otherworldly, and representing an insignificant force in contemporary life, Soviet people had little knowledge of the scriptures or the teachings of the Church Fathers; Men understood that in his future task as a priest, he faced monumental obstacles. He would have to change the mindset of his people, particularly the unwillingness, on the part of many of them, to raise certain fundamental questions and to reconsider the roots of their beliefs. Most importantly, he would need to encourage them to view their cultural and religious identity imaginatively.[46] These issues occupied his mind during his years of study in Siberia. But these years also witnessed a major change in his personal relationships: his engagement and marriage to a young woman, who became a lifelong partner on the dangerous, difficult road along which he soon embarked.

Nataliia Fedorovna Grigorenko

On holidays, Aleksandr Men took the train home to Moscow, anxious to return to the city that had been his home all his life. But it was not simply to see his family that he made these visits. He came also to see a young woman in whom he had become seriously interested. He first met her in the winter of 1954, when both studied in the Moscow Institute of Fur, she in the business-marketing department, and he fell immediately for her charm and the dignified, self-assured way she handled herself.[47] The daughter of an agronomist and a singer in one of the finest choirs in Moscow, Nataliia Fedorovna Grigorenko (Natasha), like Men, had a great interest in biology, and he had originally seen her in a gathering of biology students in Moscow.[48] Photographs of her reveal a slender, dark-eyed, attractive young woman of medium height, with a serious yet gentle look on her face and in her eyes.[49] Introduced to her by mutual acquaintances, she responded to his attentions, and they quickly found themselves becoming friends, drawn together not only by a common interest in the sciences, but also by certain intangible qualities related to the heart. She had a generous, welcoming spirit and an openness to people that drew them easily to her. Aleksandr Men was one of them, and over the course of the next year, their relationship developed beyond mere friendship.

Nataliia Fedorovna, as Maslenikova portrayed her, "was blessed with a sharp, natural intelligence, a life-giving presence, a strong work ethic, a peaceful demeanor, and a loyal, faithful spirit."[50] At first, however, her relationship with Aleksandr Men did not develop smoothly. Shortly after her relationship with Men had become more than friendship, she failed to show up for their meetings. Her absences troubled Men; he neither knew nor understood the reasons for them, and after several days passed in which he did not hear from her, he knew he had to discover why she avoided him. Despondent and concerned about Natasha's behavior, he took the train to the nearby village of Semkhoz, where she lived with her mother and father. There, meeting her parents for the first time, he learned that Natasha had been hospitalized with appendicitis. This encounter had several significant outcomes in Men's evolving relationship with the young woman who later became his wife. First, it introduced him directly to Natasha's family, which immediately had positive results; both parents took a liking to him, and he also found the closeness of the parents to each other to be impressive. Second, he could not have known that he had entered a house in Semkhoz that would eventually become his own home, a place where he would spend many years of his adult life, including the last third.

As his attachment to Natasha Grigorenko grew over the next year, Aleksandr Men clearly relished being in her company. He was always careful with her, always respectful of her feelings and views. They had many lengthy discussions about their individual aspirations and life goals. They discussed common interests and values and also discovered their differences. He learned that she, like nearly all of her friends, was not a religious person. He understood that a loving relationship should not be an all-consuming affair, which repudiated an individual's own personhood, but should allow for self-development. Christian love, as he understood it, would not allow power over another person; it did not mean rejection of the self, but was creative and, through connection to others, worked to fulfill the self. He told Natasha of his eventual plans to become an Orthodox priest and made her fully aware of the hardships and personal challenges such a path entailed. And while it cannot be ascertained whether he or she could have understood then the depth of those future challenges, they went forward, remaining open to the possibilities that they offered each other.

When the Institute of Fur reorganized and transferred many of its students to Irkutsk, Natasha remained in Moscow to complete her studies.[51] She and Aleksandr continued their relationship on holidays and through correspondence, and increasingly it became clear to each of them that they were meant for each other. In 1956, the same year Nikita Khrushchev made his famous speech to a closed session of the Twentieth Party Congress, in which he denounced Stalin as a bloodthirsty tyrant, the two of them married. Aleksandr was twenty-one years of age and Natasha a year younger. The wedding took place following the liturgy in the Church of John the Baptist under the Pine Forest (*Tserkov' Ioanna Predtecha pod Borom*) in central Moscow, the same church Aleksandr had attended since his early teenage years. To judge by the photographs of the wedding ceremony, it was a traditional Orthodox service, beginning with the Rite of Betrothal, in which, after the priest blessed the rings, the couple exchanged them, evidence of the couple's commitment to each other and in recognition of their desire to complement and enrich each other constantly.[52]

Following the brief Rite of Betrothal, the wedding service began. Both the bride and groom were given candles, which they continued to hold throughout the service, symbolizing the couple's openness to Christ, "who will bless them through this Mystery."[53] The Service of Crowning came next, the climax of the wedding, in which the couple was crowned "in the name of the Father and of the Son, and of the Holy Spirit," evoking the blessing of self-sacrifice that would be required of each partner. The service then proceeded through the traditional acts, moving from the sharing of the Common Cup, the Wedding Procession around the sacramental table, to the priest's blessing of the groom and bride. The Orthodox wedding is not, it must be emphasized, "simply an exchange of vows or a contract," to which a civil ceremony gives prominence, but a sacrament "uniting the couple and His Holy Christ." It is thus not a private event, but takes place before the church as the Body of Christ, bringing all those present into communion with each other. The photographs of Aleksandr and Natasha's wedding exhibit that spirit of communion, a devotion to Orthodox tradition, and the willingness to share the mutual path that lay ahead, although she planned to remain in Moscow while her husband finished his studies. Suggestive also of this future path are the two people standing at each end of the photograph: on the left side, Boris Aleksandrovich Vasil'ev, Men's old friend, who was a member of the intelligentsia and a priest in the catacomb church; and, on the right side, Kirill Vakhromeev, a close childhood friend, who later became Metropolitan Filaret.[54]

Science and Religion

Aleksandr Men had always been an avid reader, locating books that long ago had ceased to be published in the Soviet Union. The authors of many of these books connected him to the rich streams of thought in Russia's philosophical and religious traditions that Soviet political leaders, aspiring to create a "New Soviet Man," had disparaged. His love of reading and quest for knowledge intensified during his years in Irkutsk. As before, he combed the bookstores in the city searching for old texts, especially the books of out-of-print Russian philosophers and theologians whose writings he prized. On one occasion, as he recounted to Zoia Maslenikova, a cleaning woman in the church he served in Irkutsk led him high up into the bell tower. She showed him a stack of early twentieth-century texts, a treasure trove of rare books that someone had placed in the dusty corner of a closet, and she invited him to take any of them he wished.[55] He found works he had not seen before, adding them to his rapidly growing collection that served him well then and in his later years.

In Irkutsk, Men read voraciously on many subjects. In 1953–1954, during his first year in the institute, he discovered one of Russia's preeminent philosopher-theologians, Pavel Florensky, whose works had relevance to the sciences. In Irkutsk, he also spent a great deal of time studying the writings of Vladimir Solov'ev, whose work, like Florensky's, gave him insight into the relationship between science and theology.[56]

Possessing an imaginative mind, and generally considered Russia's first philosopher, Vladimir Sergeevich Solov'ev had a short but extremely productive life (1853–1900), and his writings had a large influence on some of Russia's leading luminaries of the twentieth century, including the novelist and poet Andrei Belyi, the poet Aleksandr Blok, who called Solov'ev a "knight-monk," Pavel Florensky, Nikolai Berdiaev, and most of the "brilliant thinkers of Russian religious philosophy."[57] It is difficult to tell precisely which of Solov'ev's ideas Men, as a student, found most relevant, since his notes do not reveal his thoughts on this subject. But Men greatly admired Solov'ev and considered the philosopher important to his own thinking.[58] Many years later, when he gave a series of public lectures on Russia's foremost philosophical thinkers, he began the series with Vladimir Solov'ev.

The son of Sergei Mikhailovich Solov'ev, one of Russia's preeminent nineteenth-century historians, Vladimir Solov'ev early on displayed unusual talent as an original thinker and person of intellectual gifts. Growing up during a time when atheism had become fashionable among Russia's youth, he fell in with this trend and rejected his parents' religion. After reading Ludwig Feuerbach's *The Essence of Christianity*, he told his father "he had given up on Christianity." His scornful attitude, however, turned out to be only temporary. After he entered Moscow University, he majored in philosophy, with a particular focus on the natural sciences as well as theology. By then, his interests ranged across multiple fields of knowledge, always attracted, as Men described him, "to the fundamental mysteries of the world, with natural science comprising one of the bricks in the large mental structure, which he constructed."[59]

A brilliant student, Solov'ev by the age of twenty-one (1874) completed his master's thesis at the University of Moscow. He titled it "The Crisis of Western Philosophy: Against the Positivists" (Krizis zapadnoi filosofii: Protiv positivistov). The heading suggests his central argument: the West's heavy reliance on positivism, which dominated philosophical thought in

Western Europe, had reached a dead end. He defended his thesis in a large auditorium filled with hostile students and rabid positivists, believers in a philosophical ideology that viewed all knowledge as based on "positive," measurable data derived from experience. In opposition to the positivists, Solov'ev explored what he called the descent of philosophy in the late nineteenth century into a state of crisis. The reason for the decline, he argued, was that knowledge had come to be seen fundamentally as an "instrument of reason," giving knowledge, over time, a "one-sided character."[60] He traced the beginnings of this movement to the medieval era, which had split reason off from theology, lodging reason in its own autonomous sphere. This movement had allowed reason to go beyond boundaries that had once moderated it. As a result, reason had become all-embracing, all-consuming, and existing in its own separate realm, without the safeguards that had heretofore kept it in balance.

Solov'ev viewed all of nature as unified, and this perspective guided his thinking. The term "all-unity" had several different meanings, but in Men's interpretation of Solov'ev, it signified that "everything is connected," everything is in relationship, thus underscoring the importance of synthesizing, of seeking the connections between seemingly disparate parts.[61] In taking this approach, Solov'ev thus moved in a diametrically opposite direction from positivism, which split everything into smaller and smaller fragments. Moreover, he sharply criticized those who viewed observable phenomena in nature as the sole reality and conceived of knowledge as based only on measureable data existing in the natural world. When reason is torn from a larger context, when it is disconnected from other parts of life, it suffers a great loss, Solov'ev maintained; in that process, the fragments reason seeks to measure become more and more abstracted from the rest of the world.

Solov'ev did not separate the natural world from a divine creator, the source of "divine wisdom" (Sophia), which acted not as a force dominating nature, but existed in relationship to it: "All hatred, all power, which divides, which breaks apart thought, feeling, the body, nature is opposed to God's creation."[62] Solov'ev sought the connections within all of nature; he viewed knowledge as consisting of much more than the data derived from direct observation, or bits of information isolated from other parts of the universe.

While a student, Aleksandr Men read Solov'ev's famous lecture "On the Decline of the Medieval Worldview," which Solov'ev presented at a meeting of the Moscow Philosophical Society on October 19, 1891, and which elicited an angry public response. In his lecture, Solov'ev described the Catholic Church as an institution towering above society in all its magnificence and power, casting its long shadow over the entire social order.[63] Despite the common understanding of the medieval period as a time honoring the Catholic Church, Solov'ev took the opposite view: "Do not think that the Middle Age stands as a time celebrating Christianity," he said. "The medieval structure and order represented a compromise, which united in itself Christian forms and pagan understanding."[64] Although the medieval church professed Christian principles, it acted primarily to preserve its power and glory. Then, toward the end of his lecture, Solov'ev introduced a provocative and rhetorical question, certain to produce outrage on the part of many people. In the late medieval period, he asked, "Who protested against the use of torture?" he asked. "Who abolished the Inquisition, Christians or some other group of people?" In other words, who were the true reformers? "They were not the Christians" who had courageously sought to end these heinous practices, but rather non-believers, who had "kept the Christian spirit alive and thus compensated for the negligence of the purely nominal believers."[65] Solov'ev's speech struck like a bombshell in Russian society, and public criticism rained down on him. "He came to be viewed," Jonathan Sutton has written, "as an isolated figure, the speaker of distinctly uncomfortable truths, rootless, and without an easily identifiable following either in the scholarly world or beyond it."[66]

In his student notes, Men referenced Solov'ev's lecture, because he raised an issue parallel to Solov'ev's criticism of positivism. As the positivists divorced the natural world from theology, the medieval church had separated spiritual and earthly matters. By reducing their vision to one dimension, they had both lost an essential connection to a larger framework that nourished both of them. Both failed to see the connections between different parts of the universe, and both disparaged the "all-unity" of nature, shortcomings that severely limited their vision and capability.

How might that unity be restored without losing the advantages that positivism, as well as the medieval church, had provided? How might the balance between disparate elements be regained? Solov'ev had raised issues that would command interest and discussion by Russian theologians and philosophers in the late nineteenth- and early twentieth century, whom Lenin disparaged. [67] These issues were also raised by another Russian writer Aleksandr Men admired. As mentioned above, Men had earlier read Pavel Florensky, and he would return to him again and again.

Pavel Aleksandrovich Florensky (1892–1937) was one of Russia's greatest intellectuals of the twentieth century. Like Solov'ev, he did not have a long life; unlike his predecessor, who died a natural death, Florensky died at the hands of an executioner in Stalin's prison camps. As Men's later public lecture on the philosopher revealed, Florensky, too, had a large influence on his earlier thinking.

Florensky was born in Azerbaijan to well-educated parents, a Russian father who was an engineer and an Armenian mother, both of whom came from clerical families but had renounced Christianity for the sciences. Growing up in a secular family, Florensky had little early exposure to religion. But shortly after his entrance to Moscow University, at the age of seventeen, he had a personal crisis of belief and direction, and it was at this time, primarily through his reading, which included the work of Solov'ev, that he found his way to Christianity.[68] At the university, he majored in mathematics, studying with the renowned mathematician Nikolai Bugaev.[69] Original in his thinking, dedicated to his scholarship, and imaginative in seeing the connections of mathematics to other fields, Florensky was a brilliant student; among the professors, he had the reputation of being among the finest students in the sciences that Moscow University had known in many years. But upon his graduation from the university in 1904, rather than continue his studies in mathematics, as many urged him to do, he entered the Ecclesiastical Academy at Sergiev Posad.

The first quarter of the twentieth century witnessed a revolution in scientific thought as new discoveries challenged assumptions long dominant in the sciences. The emergence of quantum physics questioned the core principles of Newtonian theory, which were deeply entrenched in Western mathematics. In mathematics, discontinuity represented a developing field that challenged "the cementing idea of continuity" that "brought everything together in one gigantic monolith."[70] Rather than assuming a smooth transition from one point to another, as the traditional continuity view in mathematics had held, discontinuity theory recognized the possibility of "leaps," of unpredictable changes that did not necessarily conform to a regular, predictable pattern. Critics of the continuity theory opposed its rigid determinism, which its supporters had often applied not only to mathematics but also to other fields, from mechanics to theology. In contrast, as Florensky's mentor Nikolai Bugaev pointed out in a groundbreaking paper at the First International Congress of Mathematicians in Zurich in 1897, discontinuity "is a manifestation of independent individuality and autonomy."[71] In his own scholarship, Florensky elaborated this view even further: as opposed to determinism, discontinuity theory opened the door to freedom, intuition, paradox, and the creative imagination. He had in mind not only mathematics but also other fields, including philosophy, biology, molecular physics, and theology.[72]

In 1909, at the age of twenty-six and as a teacher at Sergiev Posad, Florensky published an original work, *The Pillar and Ground of Truth* (*Stolp i utverzhdenie Istiny*), which inspired heated controversy both then and later. In reading Florensky's book, Aleksandr Men found it profoundly moving. He said that he "lost himself in it, as I also had in Solov'ev."[73] *Pillar and Ground of Truth* revealed to him the paradoxical nature of truth in Christian dogma:

> You immediately notice that paradoxes permeate everything: God is single, but He is in three persons; Christ is a man, but He is also God; he is an authentic human being, and the true God. We say that human beings are free, but at the same time are led by God. Paradoxes are built into everything. The truth is as paradoxical as the reality of being itself. The great contribution of Florensky is that, while still a young man, he succeeded in showing us that.[74]

Florensky came "to the conclusion that truth is intuitively known."[75] This is the paradox of how knowing takes place: to know something requires a combination of rationality and intuition. Thus, for Florensky, as Men explained, the "language of truth is intuition-discursive," and to grasp the whole of something, to comprehend the structural realities of the natural world, requires more than formal logic, which by itself is insufficient.[76] The natural world contains a mass of contradictions, and formal logic cannot explain such contradictions. Florensky derived this insight from his study of mathematics, anticipating the principle of complementarity, which Niels Bohr, in 1922, conceived in physics.[77] Discontinuity, in Florensky's conception, allowed natural phenomena to be analyzed as having contradictory properties. But this did not mean, as Men emphasized, that Florensky perceived a chaotic universe, composed of separate, disconnected elements. On the contrary, Florensky viewed these elements as parts of an overall, non-deterministic unity that could be understood only by intuition and the creative imagination, as his mentor, Nikolai Bugaev, had argued. This was an insight that Men found deeply meaningful.

The *Pillar and Ground of Truth* and its importance to Men is further illustrated by the considerable space he gave the work in his later address on Florensky. In his lecture, he cut right to the heart of Florensky's book. "What in that book is the most important, the central idea?" is the question he posed to his audience. It was, he said, Florensky's opposition to the deterministic view of nature that the materialists had advanced, a different approach than the Soviet schools promoted in teaching the sciences. Despite the instruction in the schools, Men had found through Florensky another way of looking at the natural world. In reading Florensky, Men maintained, one becomes "more and more convinced that his theory does not reside in the clouds, but that everything is interconnected and interdependent, that the Heavenly Spirit is inside everything, and usually in the smallest things."[78]

When Men presented Pavel Florensky to a Soviet audience in the late 1980s, he gave an account of Florensky's contributions in multiple fields ranging from mathematics and theology to aesthetics and philosophy. He pointed out that Florensky became a priest in 1911 and served at Sergiev Posad, but his true vocation, in Men's interpretation, was as a scholar, one of Russia's greatest scholars of the twentieth century, whom the Soviet establishment hounded and forced from his professorial position. He published *Imaginary Points in Geometry* (*Minimosti v geometrii*) in 1922, one of his last philosophical works in the sciences; after that, his publications mainly concerned the field of engineering. "My father," Men said, "studied at the Institute of Engineering in the late 1920s." He remembered this "strange, small man, with long hair, dressed in a cassock, who entered the lecture hall" to deliver talks on engineering problems.[79] The students and professors deeply respected him, Men's father remembered. Despite the interminable political pressures he continued to face, Florensky refused to compromise the values he held. He also never left his native land, remaining as true to his country as to himself and his vocation, the same qualities that would, in time, define Aleksandr Men. Florensky's painful final years and eventual execution in 1937 by the police, Men noted, robbed Russia of one of its greatest minds.

In their views of science and religion, neither Solov'ev nor Florensky established rigid boundaries between the two spheres. But neither did the two philosophers confuse the methodologies of science and religion; they understood that each entity represented a distinctive way of knowing that, while separate, ultimately related to the other, connected, as they were, to life and to concrete reality. When phenomena in nature are no longer seen in relationship to other phenomena, Solov'ev maintained, "they lead into a blind alley"; they become abstractions removed from real life.[80] Solov'ev and Florensky proposed a way of seeing different from the materialist philosophy that defined the Soviet approach. Men found the two writers' views appealing, and although he had encountered some of their ideas earlier, his student experiences in Siberia solidified them even further in his mind. Simultaneously a student of the sciences, a voracious reader, and an aspiring Orthodox priest, Men was also a seeker who became increasingly convinced of the importance of perceiving the divine mystery that penetrated all parts of nature and the universe.

The philosophies of Solov'ev and Florensky fit Men's understanding of the natural world, which he saw as God's creation and whose beauty and order reflected divine goodness. To him, looking through a microscope at nature revealed God's handiwork. He believed in evolution and had no difficulty with its teaching.[81] God revealed His divine presence in two significant ways: through the scriptures and through nature. "In moments of inner enlightenment, can we not sense his [God's] unseen presence in all nature, in the breath of the forest, the blossoming flower, the mysterious life of earth and sky?"[82] In his country's gently flowing rivers, its bountiful meadows, and in the structures of the animal kingdom, he observed that presence. Men's forays into the dense forests and open fields and his visits to Lake Baikal, only seventy kilometers south of the city, added to his sense of wonder and offered further evidence of Florensky's belief in the "unity within all of nature."[83]

Leaving Irkutsk

In the spring of 1958, as part of the larger campaign to strengthen the ideological base of Communism and promote the Communist Party's announced forward progression toward its goals, the Institute of Fur introduced a new course on "scientific atheism" and required it of all students in the last semester before their graduation. Students met the announcement with consternation and bewilderment. Displeased with the timing of the new requirement, his classmates entreated Men, whom they knew had read widely in philosophy, to engage the teacher of the course in debate. He agreed to do so and proceeded to question the teacher on many of the principles he presented to the class. On several occasions that spring, this exchange resulted in the defeat and embarrassment of the instructor, whose knowledge of philosophy lacked the same depth.[84]

In the days preceding the final exams for the spring term, graduates constantly talked about their future plans, their assignments to various locations in the countryside, and their ultimate hopes to be together again in the coming years.[85] These days were filled with expectations and hope, but also with sadness and a strong sense of nostalgia, as the community of students, who had begun studies together five years earlier, would soon be dissolved. Shortly before the state final exams began, the institute held a special assembly meeting, at which the rector presided. At one point in the meeting, the rector began to talk about the unsatisfactory behavior that spring of a student whose actions would not be tolerated and who would not be given admittance to the final exams. Aleksandr Men realized that the rector had him in mind. Following the convocation of the school's administrative council, only a few days before his anticipated graduation, he was dismissed from the institute.

The experience could easily have been a crippling blow. As mentioned earlier, Men had planned to complete his studies and then fulfill the required three years of service at a game preserve. But these plans now took a radically different turn, which he tried to view positively. As Maslenikova explains,

> At any rate, the experience thus was clearing the road for what he had long thought of doing. The education was received. He did not regret his years of study in the institute; biology had been his passion, and he was thankful for the knowledge his studies had given him. But the diploma of a game warden? Would that really be necessary for a priest?[86]

When he left Irkutsk to return to Moscow, Aleksandr Men departed a changed person from when he arrived three years earlier. Part of the change represented a wider vision of Orthodoxy than the one he had previously held. His personal encounters with multiple ethnic groups and exposure to other religious perspectives in Irkutsk significantly expanded his knowledge of their commonalities, as well as with their differences, from Orthodoxy's traditions and beliefs. Such encounters laid the early basis in his mind for the importance of dialogue, the need to learn from one another, and to grow from these experiences. Part of the change in his life resulted from the deepening personal relationships that took place during these years, above all, his marriage to Nataliia Grigorenko, who would share his future journey as a priest. Men's developing friendship with Gleb Yakunin sharpened his perspectives on the church. He became convinced that the church must not reflect the portrait painted in Nicholas Leskov's nineteenth-century novel *Cathedral Folk* of a slavish, inward-looking, deeply conservative institution, more devoted to external forms than to internal substance.[87]

One of Aleksandr Men's most outstanding characteristics was his ability to interact with a wide variety of people, and even though he had a superb education, he had the capacity to relate to others in all their diversity and ways of seeing the world. Part of this talent lay in his innate sensibilities, as well as his belief in the importance of every individual. But no small part of his ability to relate to people across social and educational boundaries derived from his student experiences in the institute, first in Moscow and then in Irkutsk. In these settings, he was thrown together with multiple groups—Buryats, Samoyeds, Cossacks, Ukrainians, Jews, Old Believers, traditional Russians, and others—of widely different ethnic and religious backgrounds. As a young man, he learned firsthand how to relate to them, to speak with them, and to share their friendship. Living in close quarters with these diverse individuals, at least part of the time, going to class with them, and encountering them on the streets and in the neighborhoods of Irkutsk, he had little difficulty seeing them as brothers and sisters and accepting them as part of a common humanity.[88] His style of communication crossed all of these boundaries.

Aleksandr Men knew that, despite the severe political obstacles the Orthodox Church faced, it had to connect with the fresh, creative voices within its tradition in order for it to become an effective voice within Russian society. Above all, it had to overcome what he would later call "the inner conflict within Christianity."[89] By inner conflict, he meant, only in part, the split between Eastern and Western religious denominations, the division that had existed for almost a thousand years. His studies and his readings in Siberia laid the groundwork for another interpretation of this "inner conflict" within Christianity. Fr. Mikhail Aksenov-Meerson, who served with Men and knew him well, interpreted Men's use of "inner conflict" to signify not only the division between Eastern Orthodoxy and Roman Catholicism, but also within them, as well as within Protestantism:

> He meant, I believe, religion's helplessness in the face of modern science and technology, in all ways of life. On the one hand, in Eastern Orthodoxy under Soviet conditions and in all forms of neo-fundamentalism, the church ignores the challenges of these two powerful forces. On the other hand, in nearly all mainstream Western denominations of today, religion surrenders itself easily to modern ways of life informed by science and technology.[90]

Men believed the church had to find a way to speak convincingly about science and technology without "surrendering itself to the world."[91] In his intensive reading of Solov'ev and Florensky, he had begun to formulate his approach.

As he prepared to leave Siberia, Men well understood that, as a future priest, he would have to develop a language, a manner of speaking, and a vision of the world that expanded the role of religion in the public square, rather than constrained it. As Siberia had widened his personal vision, so too did he come away believing that the church, in order to strengthen its capabilities, had to look deeply into its own traditions and sources. On the Siberian frontier, Aleksandr Men developed further an appreciation of the beauty of nature when it is seen whole, the indispensability of the imagination, and the need to look beneath the physical surface of things. His experiences there ingrained in him the importance of an open attitude that is free and compassionate, rather than closed and self-satisfied, an attitude that would mark his entire life and his ministry. He did not see Christianity as a means of soothing people, as a narcotic, in Karl Marx's interpretation, that encouraged the lower classes to accept their fate. On the contrary, the religion he sought served to awaken and to lead them toward respect for others and the recognition of human dignity.

In May 1958, having been dismissed from the institute without a degree, Aleksandr Men returned to Moscow and to his wife, Nataliia Fedorovna. He had many questions whirling in his mind about his future, as well as about the church and his role within it. How would he negotiate this role? How would he resolve the tensions between his faith and the society in which he lived, especially during a time of increased political pressure on the church? As will be seen, the intensity of these tensions would soon escalate.

6

. . . .

First Years as a Parish Priest

A leksandr Men's entrance into the Russian Orthodox priesthood came during the terrible years of Nikita Khrushchev's assault on religion in the Soviet Union, when the Communist Party carried out a full-scale attack on the clergy and what it considered the last vestiges of religious belief. At the end of the 1950s and the 1960s, particularly in the first half of that decade, this assault, which a close observer described as an "anti-religious war," continued unabated.[1] Thus, Men struggled at the beginning not only to survive, at first without any formal education for his chosen vocation, but also to develop his own identity in a political environment aimed at making that pursuit as treacherous as possible, and even destroying the framework supporting it. These experiences reveal a great deal about the constraints and the opportunities of a young parish priest during the tumultuous years from 1958 to 1968, the period spanning the era of Nikita Khrushchev and the first years of Leonid Brezhnev. In addition, Fr. Aleksandr would forge personal and intellectual relationships that, in large part, helped to define him through his service in the three parishes— Akulovo, Alabino, and Tarasovka—in which he lived and worked during this tempestuous decade.

The State's Assault

In the few months before and the years immediately following Stalin's death in March 1953, the church enjoyed a period of quiescence in its relationship with the state. Such quiescence did not mean the church's revival, nor did it suggest that the Soviet government began to look favorably on religious activity. But during this period, a few liturgical books were published, including the Bible, the church consecrated eight bishops in the year

Stalin died, and by 1957, their total number had increased to seventy-three.[2] The government also began to release prisoners from the Gulag, many of whom the police had incarcerated for their religious beliefs, and their return prompted a sense that the church would soon be given a freer hand to operate.

Still, Orthodox leaders lived in a state of constant anxiety. The power struggle in Soviet leadership, following Stalin's death, contained both hopeful and ominous signs. On the one hand, the years of cruel leadership had come to an end and a fresh beginning lay close at hand.[3] On the other hand, several leading participants in the power struggle, especially the Party's general secretary, N. S. Khrushchev, expressed strong antireligious views. Orthodox leaders were well aware that the favorable church-state relations over the last decade rested on fragile foundations.[4]

By the beginning of 1958, the period of quiescence ended, as the church's relationship to the Soviet government underwent a series of major changes. The heaviest and most decisive blow against religion fell on the Orthodox Church, "the most influential and most populated in the country," but all religious bodies in the Soviet Union suffered from the government's actions. Part of the changes, as M. I. Shkarovskii, the preeminent Russian scholar of church-state relations, has pointed out, came about because of "certain illusions" fostered by the death of Stalin, which led a significant component of the Russian intelligentsia, the so-called *shestidesiatniki* ("the people of the sixties"), to believe it possible to build a just socialist order.[5] Fired up by the hope for significant political reforms, they believed the road now lay open to recover earlier socialist ideals that Stalin's rule had perverted. Inspired by such aspirations, they expressed an indifference to religion, which they considered irrelevant to the social order they wished to build. As a result, they voiced little concern over government measures aimed at suppressing religious bodies.

In addition, changes in the leadership of the Communist Party now brought to the forefront those individuals who, as mentioned earlier, had strong antireligious views. In order to gain political ascendancy in the Presidium of the Central Committee and to seek wider support in other key government agencies, Khrushchev forged two main alliances: with a group of Party ideologues—M. A. Suslov, E. A. Furtseva, L. F. Il'ichev, and P. N. Pospelov—and with leaders of the Komsomol, the Soviet youth organization on whom Khrushchev heavily relied for political support.[6] Both groups favored a "decisive struggle with religion," a move aimed at removing what they described as the "surviving remnants of capitalism." The future Soviet state, Khrushchev asserted in an interview in 1957, "does not have a place for faith in God."[7]

In addressing the Twentieth Party Congress on the night of February 14, 1956, Khrushchev delivered has famous speech on the "Cult of Personality" that Joseph Stalin had created around himself. His speech featured revelations on the crimes of the Stalin era, shattering the beliefs held by most of the delegates present that evening. Khrushchev's speech also conveyed his belief that a promising road lay ahead for the Soviet state; the present marked a transition to constructing a Communist society. Such a transition presupposed liquidating the Stalinist heritage that heretofore had stood in the way. Allowing religion to survive had been part of that heritage, and now it had to be quickly obliterated. "Our party," he said, "is full of creative strength, powerful energy and unbending will to accomplish this great goal—the building of communism."[8] Khrushchev urged Party organizations to "protect the purity of Marxist theory" against Marxism's ideological enemies, remnants of the past that had to be left behind. He left little doubt that he intended to make a full-scale assault on religious belief in the Soviet Union. The following year, in an interview with a foreign correspondent, Khrushchev underscored his view that "the people's enlightenment, the expansion of scientific knowledge, and the study of the laws of nature" left no room for what he viewed as superstitious beliefs.[9]

The main centers of power shared the view that a powerful blow had to be inflicted on religion, because the Party's chief goal of building a Communist society could not allow the existence of any kind of ideological opposition.[10] But other, secondary reasons also underlay the government's assault. In 1957 and early 1958, church officials had increasingly asked for concessions, including the return of monasteries and the opening of a printing press, as well as the election of a representative to the governing authority, requests that increasingly annoyed the Party's leadership. Moreover, by 1958, the government needed new sources of revenue. Its ambitious economic program, especially in agriculture, required enhancing the state's treasury, and this need invited the government's temptation, in Shkarovskii's words, "to put its hand in the church's pocket."[11]

Khrushchev's "war against religion," beginning in 1958 and continuing until the end of his tenure in 1964, was massive and multifaceted. It included a secret resolution of the Central Committee in October 1958 that included an enormous expansion of scientific-atheistic propaganda by all Party and government organs throughout the country. A month later, the assault encompassed a "cleansing of church libraries" and the seizing of many books. It tasked local authorities to reduce severely the pilgrimages to "holy places" and to close unregistered churches and castigated these same authorities for taking "too passive" an approach to religious activities. Party resolutions levied heavy taxes on monasteries, and in January 1960, asked local organs of power to submit plans to reduce the number of religious educational establishments, churches, monasteries, and all other spiritual organizations in their districts. In March 1961, a government regulation permitted these same authorities to interfere directly in internal church activities, which enabled them to organize bands of youth to disrupt church assemblies, break out the windows, and conduct antireligious demonstrations on holidays.[12]

Then, on July 18, 1961, the government issued a regulation on "parish reform" that struck at the backbone of the church's organization and identity. The priest lost control over the parish, as leadership passed into the hands of the local soviet, including administrative authority over the parish's economic and financial activities. The regulation gave each local soviet power to appoint a *starosta* (elder), often an elderly person or nonbeliever, who served as the actual leader of church affairs in the local area.[13] The new regulations fostered an atmosphere of subservience and intimidation. The closure of churches, monasteries, and religious organizations and the arrests of priests continued. These losses dealt a devastating blow to the power of the Russian Orthodox Church to sustain its operations and its ability to reach out to the people. By the end of Khrushchev's rule in 1964, only three of the eight Orthodox seminaries operating in 1959 remained open; less than one-third of its convents continued to function; and 40 percent of the priests active in 1958 no longer served because of death, retirement, or dismissal.[14]

Khrushchev's fall from power in October 1964 and replacement by Leonid Brezhnev as first secretary of the Communist Party ushered in a long period of less erratic policies, slower economic growth, government corruption, and less fervent ideological claims. The ferocious assault on the church that marked the Khrushchev era ended, but the enmity between the government and the church continued, as suspicion combined with oppressive controls over religious bodies continued to dominate this political dynamic.[15] Priests came under pressure to compromise the ideals they may have once harbored and to collaborate with the KGB and local Party officials. Such intense pressure had psychological ramifications for priests and affected their ability to build trust. In this situation, as Nathaniel Davis writes, "It was difficult for a bishop, or even a parish priest, to know the boundary line between effectiveness in bringing the sacraments to the people and the faithlessness of lost personal integrity."[16]

This inability to build trust and the loss of effectiveness created a psychological climate that made it difficult for the church as a whole to act as creatively and energetically as it might have. Nevertheless, even during a time of "antireligious war" under Khrushchev and government hostility under Brezhnev, other cultural crosscurrents were brewing and moving in an opposite direction from what church officials expected and what state policy makers intended.

First Decade as a Parish Priest

When he returned to Moscow in the spring of 1958, Aleksandr Men had a young family to support, but he had no job and, lacking the appropriate credentials, he had no position in the church he aspired to serve. Without a degree from the institute in which he had spent the last five years, he could not engage in scientific work, not even the temporary employment that such a prospect might hold. He needed to get his feet on the ground, to establish a course of action, and to find a way, even in such uncertain times, to pursue the goals he had set for himself. Several months passed in which he could see no clear direction and searched, without success, to gain entry to the service of the church.

Later that same year, temporary help came from a person Men had encountered on several occasions earlier in his life, and knew of his talents and desire to restore the legacy of the Orthodox Church. Anatolii Vasil'evich Vedernikov served as editor of the *Journal of the Moscow Patriarchate*, the church's official publishing organ.[17]

Vedernikov had met Aleksandr Men several times, first in 1947, when Vedernikov worked as inspector of the Moscow Theological Academy, then located in Novodevichy Monastery. "I went to see him," Aleksandr Men said, "hoping to sort out whether I could go and study there (I was still at school then)."[18] The precocious youth walked into the office to find, sitting behind a desk, this young man "with a very handsome profile," accompanied by a black-and-white portrait of Stalin and a lectern on which was positioned "an antique Bible and various other books." Anatolii Vasil'evich responded to Aleksandr's inquiry, "You are still so young! You will be eighteen when you complete your studies ('I was then hardly fourteen'). Come back then." Aleksandr lamented that he could not take the course Vedernikov taught at that time on the history of Russian religious thought, and he recalled his chagrin upon learning of Vedernikov's later removal from the Academy and his transfer to the theological institution in Zagorsk.

Still, Anatolii Vasil'evich would play an important part in Aleksandr Men's life. Men had made a positive impression on Vedernikov, who did not forget the young man's aspirations, or his resolve. In 1956, shortly after Vedernikov's appointment to the *Journal of the Moscow Patriarchate*, Men went to see him again and discussed his future plans. It is likely that Vedernikov encouraged him and offered the young man direction, because he continued to visit Vedernikov during his student years in Irkutsk. Aleksandr's view of the older man was extremely positive and remained so; he described Vedernikov as lively, "rather conservative, healthily so, open to different views," and "very flexible, capable of accommodating himself anywhere; nevertheless, an intelligent man with a pure religious faith."[19] In 1958, when Men returned from Irkutsk, he learned that Vedernikov held frequent meetings in his office in Novodevichy Monastery to which he invited people from differing perspectives to discuss questions relating to his main concerns. These sessions, lively and wide ranging, lasted several hours and, for a short time, became an intellectual source from which Vedernikov drew contributors for the journal he edited. Vedernikov invited Aleksandr to attend the discussions. Soon thereafter, he offered Aleksandr part-time work writing articles for the *Journal of the Moscow Patriarchate*.[20]

Vedernikov supported Aleksandr Men in yet another way. Impressed with his young friend's knowledge and passion for the church, he went to see Nikolai, metropolitan of Krutitsy and Kolomna, and recommended that he consider Aleksandr for a church appointment. Vedernikov explained that Aleksandr had read and mastered all the texts prescribed in the three-year seminary curriculum, had extensive knowledge of theology and history that went far beyond the normal course of study, and all his life had engaged in service to the church. It is testimony to the church's weak position, having suffered such an assault on its institutions by the state, that Metropolitan Nikolai accepted Vedernikov's recommendation, without requiring a more formal process of ordination. On July 1, 1958, Pentecost Sunday, in Fr. Nikolai Golubstov's church on Donskaia Street, Aleksandr Men was ordained as a *diakon* (deacon, servant of the church). The church assigned him to the parish of Akulovo, an appointment that allowed Aleksandr, at the age of twenty-three, to take the first step toward fulfilling his long-term dream of becoming an Orthodox priest. His confirmation as *diakon* took place at the time as Khrushchev's assault on religion got underway.

The Moral Quest

The government's renewed assault on religion took place at a time of growing intellectual ferment, including an interest in spiritual themes. Khrushchev's 1956 speech, while aimed at examining Stalin's legacy, inadvertently opened a Pandora's Box of questions relating to morality, traditions, and Russian culture. Such issues are best seen in certain cultural themes, beginning with Boris Pasternak's *Doctor Zhivago*, published only in the West in 1958, which likened the disappearance of Russia's cultural heritage to "frozen music."[21] In 1962, the publication of Alexander Solzhenitsyn's novel *One Day in the Life of Ivan Denisovich* in the journal *Novyi mir* marked a further step in this cultural awakening. In this and in other early writings, Solzhenitsyn extolled Russia's traditional spirituality, creativity, and integrity, as well as the humanizing values they embodied. He wrote that

> When you travel the byroads of Central Russia you begin to understand the secret of the peaceful Russian countryside. It is in the churches . . . they lift their bell towers—graceful, shapely, all different—high over mundane timber and thatch . . . from villages that are cut off and invisible to each other they soar to the same heaven.
>
> People were always selfish and often unkind. But the evening chimes used to ring out, floating over the villages, fields, and woods. . . . These chimes, which only one old tune keeps alive for us, raised people up and prevented them from sinking down on all fours.[22]

The release of thousands of prisoners from the Gulag, which reached a steady stream in the late 1950s, unleashed a pent-up demand for conversation about cultural values, particularly about Russia's national heritage. The famous creation of samizdat (self-publishing) in the Moscow apartment of the poet Aleksandr Ginzburg in late 1959 served as the vehicle for this informal conversation that, in the next decade and afterward, spread underground throughout Russia's major cities. Samizdat published Pasternak's *Doctor Zhivago* in typewritten form; it circulated manuscripts formerly written only for the "desk drawer" and brought them into the public domain and became a primary means for supporting what a recent scholar has called a "community of imagination."[23]

The moral quest that characterized much of the 1960s in the Soviet Union took diverse forms. One of these was a deepening interest in religion. In a curious but decisive reversal of the historical pendulum, the intelligentsia, which had embraced atheism in opposition to the regime in the nineteenth century, turned now to the church again, partly in opposition to the policies of the authorities.[24] These shifting attitudes and priorities took place just as the young Aleksandr Men began his service to the church. They created for him both unusual opportunities and major challenges.

The moral quest and the deepening interest in religion raised an issue that lay at the core of Russia's cultural awakening: the question of freedom. One would hardly have been able to explore, to use the imagination, and to engage in serious dialogue without the freedom to speak. Freedom requires the courage to act without fear of reprisals. The 1960s in Russia witnessed many examples of individuals who expressed such courage in seeking greater freedom, two of whom intersected directly with Aleksandr Men.

The first was Anatolii Krasnov-Levitin, whom Men met in 1956 upon a visit to Vedernikov's editorial offices at the *Journal of the Moscow Patriarchate*. The two men hit it off immediately and spent the rest of the day talking as they walked from the editorial offices in Novodevichy Monastery to the Kremlin.[25] Lively, cheerfully optimistic, and a Christian intellectual, Krasnov-Levitin had served nearly a decade in the labor camps before his recent release.[26] He published articles under the pseudonym of A. Krasnov in samizdat, and he also had written, he told Aleksandr, some forty articles for the *Journal of the Moscow Patriarchate*. He claimed to be both a socialist and a Christian, and combined the two in his beliefs. The author of a series of fascinating articles on religious topics, Krasnov-Levitin was a staunch defender of freedom of conscience. His interchange with government and police officials in May 1965 is illustrative of his stand and his will "to carry on, using my right to freedom of speech." As he reminded the authorities,

> Russian literature has always defined the word "citizen" as someone who is fighting for and upholding the truth, not as someone who crawls on his belly before the authorities. I'm not afraid of anything and never have been. This is even more true now at fifty, as I approach the limit beyond which any kind of threats cease to be effective.[27]

The second example is Fr. Sergei Zheludkov, an Orthodox priest in Pskov, whom Aleksandr came to know well and admire for his personal integrity and his defense of freedom of belief. Aleksandr became acquainted with Zheludkov in 1964–1965, and it did not take long for them to become close friends. Zheludkov linked religion to freedom of expression; he believed their connection was essential to the creation of a just social order. In March 1968, he demonstrated that conviction by writing a letter in support of Pavel Litvinov who, together with his friends Aleksandr Ginzburg and Iuri Galanskov, was arrested for publicly disseminating the secret transcripts of the Sinyavsky-Daniel trial.[28] In his letter, Zheludkov called Litvinov the "conscience of the Russian intelligentsia" and he criticized the paralysis of social activism in the priesthood, which in large part resulted from fear and its control by the state. In his letter defending Litvinov, Zheludkov maintained that Christianity and creative freedom belonged together and were mutually reinforcing:

> Socialist society should . . . find a viable combination of public discipline and creative freedom. Together with the need to preserve peace, this is the central problem of our time. It is obvious that the absence of freedom is the death of creativity in all aspects of life. It is equally clear, however, that freedom without the other principles of Christianity would turn to anarchy and hooliganism. . . . In truth, "Without me, ye can do nothing."[29]

The desire for greater freedom of religious expression among the intelligentsia coincided with Aleksandr Men's beginning service to the church. Energetic and fully committed to his mission, he had to operate in a world in which the dragon always lurked at the door. There was always the temptation to compromise one's integrity and become paralyzed, as Zheludkov accused the Russian Church of doing in what he called these "indescribably difficult circumstances."[30] But these were also times of unusual opportunity; they offered to members of the intelligentsia a chance to address this moral quest and religious search. To raise again the question posed throughout this study, how would Aleksandr Men reach out to members of his society, particularly to the Russian intelligentsia, during such a tumultuous period? Most immediately, how might he carve out a position to pursue the ideals he had begun to formulate during his time in Siberia? A partial answer to these questions came from his encounters with a priest who served as a model for his future course.

Fr. Nikolai Golubtsov

Aleksandr Men's relationship with Fr. Nikolai Aleksandrovich Golubtsov (1900–1963) dated to 1957, when he, as a college student, found the priest to be a kindred spirit, a man with wide-ranging intellectual interests, kindly in disposition, humble, and self-sacrificing. Men asked him to be his spiritual mentor. "He gave me a lot," Men said, "and I did not lose my connection to him up until his death in 1963."[31] In 1960, Fr. Nikolai supported Aleksandr Men's appointment to the priesthood, convinced that the young man's depth of spirit and breadth of mind promised to serve people well in the years ahead.

Nikolai Golubtsov's role in shaping Aleksandr Men's future direction went further than recommending the young man's appointment. He was the living embodiment of much that Fr. Aleksandr aspired to be, a person whose family background, intellectual interests, and love of people prepared him for a life of service. The second child in a priestly family, his father, Aleksandr Petrovich Golubtsov (1860–1911), was a professor of liturgy and church archeology at the Moscow Spiritual Academy, who also lectured on painting, sculpture, and church architecture. He was, according to his biographer, "one of the best educated people of his times," and his educational perspectives were formed under the influence of several of Russia's foremost scholars—V. O. Kliuchevskii, N. F. Kapterev, and E. E. Golubinskii.[32] The father's love of learning and his deeply held religious views were passed on to his highly capable and inquisitive son.

But another set of strong characteristics appeared early on in Nikolai Aleksandrovich, characteristics that his mother, herself the daughter of a distinguished churchman, possessed: "the inclination to help others, the commitment to service."[33] Although attracted to the humanities, Nikolai Aleksandrovich selected the biological sciences as his course of study, choosing the discipline least affected by ideological pressures.[34] He graduated from the prestigious Timiriazov Agricultural Academy with a degree in agronomy. He spent most of his professional career as a scientist: in employment as an agronomist at a field station near Sergiev Posad (then Zagorsk), as a lecturer to peasant farmers during the winter months, and as a librarian in the All-Soviet Academy of the Agricultural Sciences in Moscow. Yet all the while, he privately engaged in pastoral activity, serving people in need, unofficially performing priestly duties, and engaging in many acts of compassion.[35] Such actions took place during the difficult 1930s and 1940s. Both he and his wife constantly reached out to people from their small home in the Izmailovskii section of Moscow. It was hardly surprising when, after the war, in 1949, Nikolai Alekandrovich entered the newly opened seminary and, although nearing fifty years of age, prepared for the priesthood.

After his appointment to the priesthood, Fr. Nikolai's parish near the historic Donskoi Monastery in Moscow attracted large numbers of people from all walks of life. They found this educated and compassionate priest to be special. Among those who came to him were members of the Moscow intelligentsia. Fr. Nikolai saw them as his special mission, a group of people whom the Orthodox Church generally regarded as unreachable. They included the famous pianist Mariia Veniaminovna Iudina, who later became a devoted follower of Aleksandr Men. He also attracted the young Svetlana Alliuevna, Stalin's daughter, whom he baptized.[36] Fr. Aleksandr, too, found Fr. Nikolai deeply inspiring. He impressed on Aleksandr Men the need to develop a language that spoke to the young and the educated, people who, believing that the Orthodox Church had nothing to offer, had broken from it.[37] Fr. Aleksandr saw Fr. Nikolai as learned but humble, devoted to the church but never arrogant or forceful, a bibliophile but also a lover of people, a priest who reached across social and educational boundaries to serve others, and who, lacking an automobile, traveled by subway, bus, and on foot to distant corners of Moscow to succor the lonely, the sick, and the dying.[38] He showed up in hospitals despite Soviet laws that strictly forbade such appearances.[39] "He was not a priest, but a pastor," recalled Fr. Aleksandr.[40] Serving always under challenging circumstances during some of the most difficult years in the history of the Soviet Union, Fr. Nikolai Golubtsov provided an example of courage and commitment that Aleksandr Men never forgot.

Akulovo (1958–1960)

The parish at Akulovo is located in the southwestern outskirts of Moscow, some thirty-five minutes by railway from the Belorussian station and near the factory town of Odintsovo. Aleksandr's assignment to the church of the Protection of the Virgin brought him much excitement, perhaps dimmed when he first saw the ramshackle house where he was appointed to live. Weather-beaten and falling apart, the house was hardly a comfortable place for him to bring a young wife and newborn child. Nevertheless, he went there with a spirit of resolve and joy, and he exhibited a quality to be repeated in later parishes. He set about remodeling and improving the physical setting in which he found himself. Aleksandr Men had no experience as a carpenter, but with the help of a close friend, he learned these skills and spent the summer and early fall turning the dilapidated structure into barely passable living quarters.[41] The two years he spent in Akulovo, however, were times of physical hardship. He had little money, and his salary of one hundred rubles a month did not suffice to provide adequate food, firewood, or clothing for his family and himself, and during the first winter, a thick coat of ice formed and stayed on the wall between the windows and the floor. His financial situation was made a bit easier by Anatolii Vedernikov, who offered him the opportunity to write articles for the *Journal of the Moscow Patriarchate* and paid a small honorarium for them.

Aleksandr served under a priest who had worked as an accountant for most of his career and who had a rigid approach to the liturgy and the order of service that went straight by the book. Formal and cool in his relationships with the parishioners, this priest attracted only a small group of people to the services. Aleksandr took a much different approach. In contrast to the senior priest, he was fully engaged, informal, and personal in his relationships, sometimes provoking the ire of the real power in the parish, an elderly woman who looked with disapproval upon his informality and his relationships with the parishioners. Taking exception to his approach, she sometimes scolded him and complained to the senior priest, who also became irritated by the young man's lack of restraint. Aleksandr must have felt the tension over these issues within the small parish, but there is no evidence that he backed down, and his behavior forecast a way of connecting the church to the world that later marked his service, an approach that repeatedly created tension between him and his superiors but endeared him to his parishioners. Moreover, at Akulovo, he had little time to reflect on such matters. In addition to his work in the parish, his writing projects, and the care of his young family, he began correspondence courses at the Leningrad Theological Academy. Aleksandr completed his studies in two years. In 1960, his graduation from the academy qualified him for the priesthood and reappointment to another parish.

Alabino (1960–1964)

Aleksandr Men was ordained a priest in a ceremony conducted by Bishop Stefan (Sergei Nikitin) in the Donskoi Monastery in Moscow. Following the ceremony, the church assigned him to the parish of Alabino, located also in the environs of Moscow, to the southwest. The four years he spent there were among the happiest of his priesthood, a time whose first months his biographer Zoia Maslenikova calls the "honeymoon years" of his service, when he enjoyed more independence and the opportunity for creativity than he subsequently possessed in the entire decade of the 1960s.[42] Officially, his appointment made him the parish's second priest, but he served under an elderly, sickly head priest, who gave Fr. Aleksandr nearly full rein. After a year, the elderly priest died, and Fr. Aleksandr became the pastor. In his first year at Alabino, his wife Nataliia gave birth to a second child, a son, Mikhail (Misha). In 1961, during his second year, Patriarch Aleksii I signed the abovementioned infamous "church reform," giving the rights and privileges of the parishes to executive bodies of lay people or church soviets, who governed under the authority of a *starosta*, usually a secular person. Ostensibly, the reform crippled the power of the parish priest and aimed at the destruction of parish life.

In Alabino, however, the reform had little immediate impact. Fr. Aleksandr promoted the election of a woman as *starosta* who "relied completely on him."[43] She fully supported him in his parish activities, allowing him wide scope in fostering changes and engaging in activities that he believed essential to the life of his parish. She permitted him to carry out, in his words, "an external revolution" in the appearance of the church, a project that occupied him for three years of his priesthood. He engaged professional Moscow artists to redo the crude, poorly conceived wall art of the church, supplanting the former paintings with frescoes depicting biblical scenes. He replaced the clear glass windows with stained glass, he ordered the icons to be restored and added new ones, and he followed each step of the process with much attention. During a time when many churches in the Moscow region were being plundered and, in some cases, destroyed, the church he served underwent reconstruction and beautification.

Fr. Aleksandr's work in restoring the icons involved central themes of his theological approach. Several reasons underlay these efforts. The relics reconnected parishioners to some of the deepest and most important traditions of the Russian Orthodox faith. By the 1960s, as Fr. Aleksandr wrote, these traditions had been nearly lost; in most Moscow churches, the clergy had redecorated and "daubed the interiors."[44] Fr. Aleksandr viewed reclaiming this nearly forgotten tradition as essential to reclaiming other important elements of the faith.

The emphasis on icons related to another important aspect of the tradition. In the prayerful traditions to which they relate, icons speak, without the use of spoken words, both to the mind and the spirit. Within the framework of Orthodoxy, they underscore the importance of creativity and the need always to look beyond the surface of things.[45] To a generation whose education had taken place entirely in Soviet schools, with their near total emphasis on the material world, icons offered an alternative view of reality. They illustrated the importance of search, struggle, and the continual quest for truth. This pursuit dovetailed almost exactly with the moral and religious quest among young members of the Russian intelligentsia that developed after the Twentieth Party Congress.

At Alabino, Fr. Aleksandr organized a small group of priests, most of whom served in Moscow or in nearby parishes. The members of this group were young, having grown up in the last years of the Stalin era, and represented a new generation, undeterred by the compromises made earlier by the church hierarchy. They raised questions about the meaning of Orthodox tradition, the relationship between church and state, and how to make the church more accessible and relevant to the Soviet population. They came together, said one of its leading members, because "in those times many young priests who had entered the church understood that church meant more than performing the liturgy, and were looking for ways to bring about a renaissance in the church, so that the Orthodox Church could compete and be viable in our society. This was the main reason behind our gatherings and discussions, but to do anything tangible was, of course, impossible without the backing of our episcopates."[46]

The priestly group included about a dozen members, many of whom were old Moscow friends thrown together by common experiences, trying to make their way in an unpredictable setting, but one that promised hope and possibility, although severely tempered by recent state policies. They wanted dialogue, both within the church community and with government officials who made state policy. Fr. Aleksandr had met many members of the group in Anatolii Vedernikov's office or at Vedernikov's dacha in the village of Peredelkino.

While bound by common interests, they represented a diverse group, different in background, personality, and perspectives. Gleb Yakunin, his old friend, was a member. Yakunin graduated from the Agricultural Institute the year after Men had been expelled, and returned to Moscow, where he enrolled in the Moscow Theological Seminary and studied to be a priest. He was dismissed from the seminary at the end of his first year, accused of appropriating from the seminary's library a book forbidden to students, *Philosophy of Freedom*, written by N. A. Berdiaev. Yakunin, however, had returned Berdiaev's book immediately upon receiving a request to do so. Recently ordained a deacon, he served as a sexton at the Moscow church of Saint Trifon the Martyr. By 1963–1964 he already felt strongly about the need to protect the civil liberties of believers. In 1965, as will be seen later, he played a large and active part in the defense of religious believers; his participation in this and other human rights movements would bring him much personal suffering.

Fr. Dmitrii Dudko (1922–2004) was a second member of the group. The son of a peasant who had suffered greatly in the collectivization campaign during the late 1920s and 1930s, Dudko had experienced Stalin's terror firsthand. In 1948, after writing a poem considered "anti-Soviet," Dudko spent eight and a half years in the prison camps. Released in 1956, he entered the seminary, and following graduation in 1961, he was ordained and served in the Moscow church of Peter and Paul, which the government closed in 1963 before destroying it.[47]

Fr. Dmitrii had already gained a reputation as a brilliant preacher, whose sermons conveyed a simplicity and depth appealing both to the educated and the uneducated. When he lost his church parish, Fr. Aleksandr invited him to serve with him. In these early years of their friendship, Fr. Dmitrii spoke admiringly of Aleksandr Men, calling him "truly an Orthodox priest" who "encounters people like the apostle Paul: with the Hellenist, he is a

Hellinist, with the Jew, he is a Jew, with the learned person, he is learned, and with simple people, he is a simple person."[48]

The third well-known member of Fr. Aleksandr's circle was Fr. Nikolai Eshliman (1928–1985), whom he first met in 1956, and whom he found extremely charming and engaging. During Fr. Aleksandr's service at Alabino, they became close friends. Married to the granddaughter of Count Sergei Witte, Russia's famous finance minister and premier at the end of the Tsarist era, Eshliman and his wife held an open house in their room on Pushkinskaia Street in the center of Moscow, where people came "to talk and to drink." He was, as Fr. Aleksandr described him, "exceptionally fascinating, adaptable, and attractive to everyone," a true man of the intelligentsia, whose talents ran in many directions; he was involved in multiple projects, which he never seemed to complete. He "played the piano a little," painted "just a little," although surprisingly well, "sang a little," and "decorated churches," captivating and charming everyone. He was a great storyteller. Eshliman's ordination into the priesthood, in 1961, transformed him completely, Fr. Aleksandr wrote, and he threw himself with total dedication into the services. "He celebrated the liturgy in an unforgettable way," he said beautiful prayers, and he was a powerful preacher. Eshliman was drawn to mysticism, which Aleksandr Men disdained. "I loved him," Fr. Aleksandr said. In those days, "there was no one with whom I was so close."[49]

Most members of the group saw a large gap between the clergy who performed their duties in the parishes and the episcopate, the "official church," which held the key positions of power. Members of the group were dismayed with the 1961 church reform and sought to change what they saw as an unacceptable situation developing in the country. Fr. Aleksandr explained the reasons for the group's formation: "Sometimes we meet at festivals or visit one another on our name days, so why don't we meet to discuss theological questions that particularly interest us, and also our pastoral experiences? We don't have an academy, but we can be an academy for each other."[50]

When he studied in Irkutsk, the young Aleksandr Men learned from visiting congregations of various religious faiths. He saw the beauty of reaching out to people and creating relationships that went beyond the formalism of the service. As a parish priest, he now had the opportunity to put his learning into practice; his earlier observations did not remain theoretical exercises. But given the restrictive policies of the government, he also had to be extremely careful to work within these guidelines. To violate the legal boundaries imposed by the state on the priest's activities meant to cross into dangerous ground. Fr. Aleksandr understood the legal limitations, and he well knew that reaching beyond the physical walls of the church required creativity. At Alabino, he used his parish's automobile to travel all over his parish, often conducting several funeral services in one day. He used these occasions to talk with families, sometimes in the cemetery, sometimes in the privacy of their homes, telling them about Orthodox traditions and beliefs, and offering these families succor and support. When local authorities questioned him about these activities, he showed them the number of signed official documents that granted him permission to conduct funeral services.[51]

Fr. Aleksandr established friendly relations with local authorities, including the police, and these relationships protected the parish from outside political harassment. He cultivated these relationships, seeking to integrate the parish into the local community, rather than creating a closed space that served only his parishioners. The parish had an automobile, and when the government ordered local authorities to confiscate all motor vehicles owned by parishes throughout the country, local officials overlooked the one belonging to Men's parish, an omission that gave Fr. Aleksandr a rare access to private transportation, enabling him to travel all over the large territory of his parish. These activities continued until the fourth year of his priesthood at Alabino, when Fr. Aleksandr became involved in a near disastrous scandal that forced him to leave the parish.

Fr. Aleksandr constantly faced a dangerous and unpredictable political context. He worked within a system that aimed to circumscribe as narrowly as possible a parish priest's activities. Faced with multiple restrictions, Fr. Aleksandr sought to manipulate the system's guidelines to his advantage. But each step he took brought great risks, any one of which could have ended his priesthood.

First, Fr. Aleksandr could never be certain that all the newcomers who arrived at his parish were people of integrity and good will. Given his attempts to expand the boundaries of his parish activities, his service required an instinctive sense about the character and motives of the people he encountered. Second, the authorities deliberately planted individuals in his parish to report on him and others within his group. At Alabino and the parishes he later served, he detected certain people who, as he said, appeared "strange."[52] He could not trust them, and he had constantly to be on guard in their company. The presence of such individuals made it extremely difficult for him to build trust within his community, a quality he considered essential to his mission.

The actions of one of the newcomers led to a scandal that severely threatened Fr. Aleksandr's role at Alabino.[53] The incident began with his willingness to accept a young man, brought to him by a friend of Nikolai Eshliman's, who aspired to serve the church by becoming a psalm singer. Educated as a historian, the young man worked on the academic staff of the nearby New Jerusalem Museum of History, Architecture, and Art, but recently had converted to Orthodoxy and wished to make a career change. Fr. Aleksandr agreed to assist the young man, named Lev Lebedev, and during the next months, he taught him to read music and to sing. Lebedev had, however, a major problem, which soon became evident: he was an alcoholic. Although Lebedev continued to live and work at the New Jerusalem Museum, he came often to Alabino, bringing with him small pieces of pottery and books, which he claimed to be superfluous pieces, and presented them as gifts to Fr. Aleksandr. Since the books lacked the stamp of any establishment, Fr. Aleksandr accepted both gifts and placed them in his library.

On July 1, 1964, the day of the Bogoliubskaia Mother of God festival, Fr. Aleksandr, Nikolai Eshliman, and Eshliman's wife traveled to the New Jerusalem Museum, which Fr. Aleksandr had never visited. One of Lebedev's colleagues at the museum, whom the group met, expressed strong antireligious views. This man had a reputation for making rude comments about priests and also for defacing icons, some of which he used as various household implements. As they toured the buildings and grounds of this famous religious site, Lebedev put some pieces of pottery in Fr. Aleksandr's bag, items, he said, that were soon going to be discarded and might be useful to his restoration of the Alabino church.

At the end of the day, as the group sat talking in Lebedev's office, the door opened and the police and Lebedev's colleague entered. He accused the two priests of stealing the museum's property and, throughout their visit, of behaving in an unruly manner. A confused scene followed, with Lebedev throwing several punches at his colleague and Lebedev's wife berating the police official, while Fr. Aleksandr and his friends quickly departed in their automobile. When he arrived home, Fr. Aleksandr destroyed all the items in his bag, but he knew that the whole incident was not at an end.

He was right. Accompanied by Lebedev's museum colleague, a police squad arrived at Fr. Aleksandr's home two days later, armed with a search warrant. They searched the books in his library, confiscating several extracts from Pasternak's *Doctor Zhivago*, two icons, pieces of pottery, and the books Lebedev had given him. Shortly thereafter, the local newspaper published an article, titled "Fal'shivy krest" ("The false cross"), reporting that two priests, Eshliman and Aleksandr, accompanied by "some girls," had arrived at the New Jerusalem Museum, stolen valuable objects, sung vulgar songs, and engaged in boisterous behavior.

The whole affair subsequently would get much worse. Fr. Aleksandr had to endure two lengthy police interrogations, an accusation of bribery of a police official, and the threat of imprisonment. While on holiday with his wife and children, he was recalled and made to respond to charges of criminal behavior. These accusations took place, he wrote, when "persecution was at full spate." "Everyone was fair game," and local newspapers "were full of slanders, insinuations, and scandal." And then, after being interrogated by a high-ranking member of the KGB and fearing arrest and imprisonment, inexplicably, in what he referred to as "a miracle," the investigation abruptly ended. Summoned to a meeting with the diocesan secretary, Fr. Aleksandr learned that he was being removed as priest at Alabino. You should "just keep your head down for a month or two," the church official said, "We'll find you a nice little place, don't worry, just keep quiet and all will be well."[54]

The scandal reveals, in microcosm, the arbitrary and hazardous personal interactions that characterized any attempt of a committed priest to strengthen parish life. Such unpredictable, capricious actions threatened every part of that life, especially in times when state policy deliberately aimed to limit the priest's role in society. In such a context, the importance of developing good personal relationships with local officials stands out as essential to developing any kind of stability. Fr. Aleksandr learned that during the crisis, government administrators in his district had stood by him, always making positive statements about him, when repeatedly questioned by the KGB.[55] The decision to remove him came from outside the local area. After officiating at a final service, the Feast of the Assumption, he was forced to leave behind the parish community where he had spent some of the most enjoyable years of his early priesthood.[56] The Alabino parish did not long endure. After his departure, local officials, on orders from above, closed the parish. Fr. Aleksandr found a vacancy in the parish of Tarasovka, and moved there in September 1964, one month before Khrushchev's fall from power.

Tarasovka (1964–1970)

The parish of Tarasovka lies about thirty miles north of Moscow near Zagorsk (Sergiev Posad). Fr. Aleksandr could not have known beforehand that the years he served there would be extremely difficult. In contrast to Alabino, with its comfortable living quarters, Tarasovka offered no parish residence for him. His salary of two hundred rubles a month, which the state heavily taxed, represented one-half of his previous earnings, and he had now to support his wife and two small children.[57] At Alabino, he had enjoyed a great deal of independence; in his new parish, he served under an elderly priest, Fr. Nikolai Morozov, an intractable, unpleasant, and pedantic person who assigned Fr. Aleksandr most of the work in the parish while criticizing every move that his younger subordinate made.[58]

In 1964, nearly destitute and with no place to live in the vicinity of the Tarasovka church, Fr. Aleksandr, his wife, and their two small children moved into the home of Nataliia's family in Semkhoz. They occupied the small, unheated attic of the house. Here, Nataliia Fedorovna proved herself a "genius at homemaking."[59] She, with her husband's help, created out of the attic two small rooms, prepared meals over an electric burner, and set aside a space, the size of a closet with a table, for Fr. Aleksandr to read and write. The Tarasovka parish offered no place for Fr. Aleksandr to meet parishioners outside the church service. But parishioners and visitors who came to his home in Semkhoz found there a welcoming, hospitable place, which was largely created by Nataliia Fedorovna. Soon after his move to Tarasovka, Fr. Aleksandr faced another challenge to his role as a priest, in circumstances that had long-lasting consequences for one of the groups that formed around him.

The group of young Orthodox priests that had convened in Fr. Aleksandr's former parish continued to meet at Tarasovka. But as the members discussed the revitalization of the church, their conversations took a new turn. They had talked earlier about common problems that the 1961 government reform of the parishes had created and the despair it had precipitated among many parish clergy. In the group with Fr. Aleksandr, several of the young priests believed it necessary to issue a public denunciation of the reform. As the closure of churches continued in the early 1960s, the desire among some members of the group to take a strong stand became even more compelling. Khrushchev's fall from power in October 1964, however, and Leonid Brezhnev's accession, changed the political context. In hopes that the new administration would bring immediate reform, most members of the group decided to take no further action. Nevertheless, two of them, Gleb Yakunin and Nikolai Eshliman, pressed on, believing that a determined stand would lead to needed dialogue between clergy and government authorities.

The immediate cause for their action came from the courageous stand taken by Bishop Yermogen of Kaluga, who, accompanied by eight Russian Orthodox bishops, in the summer of 1965, petitioned the Moscow patriarch to rectify what they called the "abnormal situation" caused by the 1961 parish regulations.[60] The Holy Synod dismissed Bishop Yermogen from his diocese and forced his retirement to a distant monastery. Given these unfortunate results, why did the two priests move forward? Gleb Yakunin offers at least a partial explanation: Bishop Yermogen encouraged the young priests to act. "We traveled often to see him," Yakunin said, and "he told us that Patriarch

Aleksii secretly supported the reform movement, and gave his blessings to initiatives calling for the church to have a greater voice."[61]

The two priests drew up two letters, one addressed to Patriarch Aleksii and the second to the chairman of the Presidium of the Supreme Soviet of the USSR, Nikolai Podgorny, dated December 13 and 15, 1965, and signed by Gleb Yakunin and Nikolai Eshliman. Other members of their group were reluctant to sign the two letters, but Yakunin and Eshliman believed they had to take a strong stand, particularly at this decisive moment. The letters made several significant arguments, among them that leaders of the Council of Ministers with "flagrant violation of the very principles of socialist justice and Soviet legislation on religion and the church," illegally closed churches and monasteries, and breached the separation of church and state that the Soviet Constitution had clearly established.[62] Second, Yakunin and Eshliman accused the ecclesiastical leadership with conniving with the government, thus deviating "from their sacred duty before Christ and the church" and violating "the apostolic command by 'compromising with this world.'"[63] Third, a civil authority headed by atheist officials had gained more authority over the church than the civil authority established by Peter the Great. The Council of Religious Affairs, they argued, had created an atmosphere of fear, intimidation, and arbitrary interference in church affairs, which made it impossible for parish priests to fulfill their responsibilities. Fourth, the two priests' letter to the patriarch severely criticized the silence of the supreme ecclesiastical authorities, whose refusal to speak out was evidence of a "spiritual sickness," a loss of vision, and a deafness to the voice of God. According to Yakunin and Eshliman, the ecclesiastical authorities maintained that their silence allowed the church to preserve itself, but in reality, this silence was destroying the church, undermining church unity, and permitting the "'wolves' to scatter and plunder the flock." Eshliman and Yakunin asked the patriarch to summon immediately a new General Church Council, with the widest possible representation, so that the voices of the church might freely speak and be heard, "for its soul is worn out from remaining silent."[64] The tone of the letter to the patriarch was insistent and uncompromising. Eshliman and Yakunin referred to a large and increasing group of "evil pastors" who were "now becoming the most dangerous threat to the Russian Church."[65] But the letter was also hopeful and expressed the belief that the patriarch would act decisively to set the church on a proper course.

The two letters, issued publicly, garnered worldwide attention and generated much support for believers inside the Soviet Union. But the letters did not produce the results their writers had hoped. church leaders came down hard on Yakunin and Eshliman and suspended both priests. The dialogue they had wanted did not take place, and the arbitrary actions and the constant interference in parish life continued.

Yakunin and Eshliman responded much differently to the retribution. "I am a fighter by nature," Yakunin said. "The persecutions did not frighten, but rather incited me, with the result that I went into the dissident movement, the human rights movement."[66] Despite the retribution he suffered, Yakunin recovered and went on to become a leading fighter for human and religious rights in the Soviet Union. Eshliman's life took a much different turn; psychologically crushed by the political response, he withdrew into himself, became a heavy drinker, and eventually suffered from severe depression.[67]

It is sometimes thought that Aleksandr Men wrote the two letters. There is no substance to these rumors. "We understood that we were like kamikazes, and that sooner or later the state would come crashing down on us," Yakunin said, referencing his and Eshliman's authorship.[68] Fr. Aleksandr did not approve of sending the letters, since he considered their timing and political maneuvering ill-advised: "I have always prized courage in people, but I have always been worried by chickens who cackle loudly but produce only one small egg. It was all too early."[69] Nevertheless, he agreed with the substance of the letters and sympathized with the two authors, whose ideas on the division between the church and state he supported in other ways, both then and later. The results of the letters did, however, influence his priesthood. They convinced him that he could be most influential by focusing on his work in the parish, where, he believed, the theological foundations for the future church might be built.[70]

Beyond the Parish

At Tarasovka, Fr. Aleksandr reached out constantly to people, and many responded to him and increasingly sought him out. Lacking the physical space in the church's buildings, he met with them on the street, on the train, or in his rooms in Semkhoz. He wanted to be accessible, as his mentors in the catacomb church had been to him earlier, and this was a practice that he continued throughout his priesthood. He also proved to be an adept listener. Even then, in his early thirties, a personal quality that characterized him throughout his life was discernable: he had an intrinsic ability to lend a sympathetic ear, extend himself to those who suffered, and encourage people in their lives. All of these qualities he based firmly on his understanding of the Gospels and the commission, which he took from Saint Paul, as well as the Church Fathers, to care for all of God's creation.[71]

In these early years of his priesthood, Aleksandr Men had not yet gained the wide reputation he later acquired; few Muscovites were aware of his existence, but some of them learned of a parish priest who exemplified unusual depth and commitment. Despite the lack of adequate facilities, Wednesday evenings he held a discussion in his home with people who wanted to learn more about the Gospels, theology, and Orthodox traditions. Each of these evenings, twenty-five to thirty people crammed into his narrow quarters and participated in a conversation on subjects that had not been part of their education elsewhere.[72] He began the conversation with a diverse group of people, some of whom came out from Moscow to engage in it, in part as a response to a moral quest that was slowly developing among certain segments of the young in Soviet society, particularly among members of the Russian intelligentsia.

Fr. Aleksandr had long prepared for such a role, which began in earnest during his years in the Alabino parish. He had a great capacity for relating his knowledge to the spiritual problems of his society as well as to the individuals who increasingly sought him out, people who raised fundamental questions about subjects seldom discussed in their formal education. As will be discussed later in more detail, Fr. Aleksandr had an unusual ability to build a bridge between the present and philosophical schools of thought that had nearly been forgotten, between current concerns and the Gospel and the Church Fathers of his own tradition, all of which were largely unknown among the Russian elite hungry for such subjects.

Fr. Aleksandr was the keeper of these cultural memories, a priest capable of making connections between widely disparate fields in a society where such affiliations between the sciences and the humanities, between the Gospels and the arts, were rarely drawn. These capacities made him highly attractive to the intelligentsia, who began to seek him out. They had rarely, if ever, encountered an Orthodox priest of such capacity and learning, a priest able to connect diverse subjects and make these associations so elegantly. Alabino and especially Tarasovka witnessed a steady stream of visitors, which grew wider and wider. The intelligentsia in the Tarasovka parish witnessed what Fr. Aleksandr called a "demographic explosion" during the years 1965 and 1966, foreshadowing a trend that would later become extremely prominent.[73]

In the 1960s, Fr. Aleksandr attracted a variety of leading people in the arts who came regularly to meet with him. He cultivated these relationships, knowing how seriously such individuals took their conversations with him and how their presence enriched the parish community. They included the Russian avant-garde artist Aleksandr Mikhailovich Iulikov; the art critic

Evgenii Viktorovich Barabanov, who later played a large part in the legal defense movement; Elena Aleksandrovna Ogneva, educated as a biologist, who became an icon-painter and also wrote a history of Russian religious thought; the artist Anatolii Rakuzin; and the pianist Mariia Veniaminovna Iudina, who was thirty-six years older than Fr. Aleksandr and a classmate and friend of the composer Dmitrii Shostakovich. Iudina was exceptionally gifted and her performances, as Fr. Aleksandr described them, "deeply affected even lay people."[74] He met her in 1965 at an art exhibition of his friend Vasilii Vatagin, and the two of them soon became close. Iudina came often to Tarasovka to take communion and also to walk with Fr. Aleksandr and talk with him about Pasternak and the writings of her other friends.[75] She sent many of her friends to him.

Fr. Aleksandr's interests in the arts and in literature are signature characteristics of his priesthood, qualities in him that became even more pronounced over time, as will be explored more fully in subsequent chapters. In the 1960s, these interests, as well as his desire to reach beyond his parish, were manifested in his relationship with Alexander Solzhenitsyn, the preeminent Russian writer of the decade, whom Fr. Aleksandr came to know in 1964.

At the time, Solzhenitsyn, a teacher of mathematics in the provincial city of Riazan', had recently published his novel *One Day in the Life of Ivan Denisovich*. He had completed other manuscripts, as yet unpublished, but which circulated in samizdat. Fr. Aleksandr read one of these manuscripts while on vacation in the Crimea, and he was deeply touched by the author's writing and discussion of current themes. Through a mutual friend, he arranged a meeting with Solzhenitsyn. Accompanied by Fr. Dmitrii Dudko, Fr. Aleksandr traveled to Solzhenitsyn's home. "I expected to find a small, frail, and downcast person," but instead encountered "a large, energetic, and curious-minded man," whom Fr. Aleksandr immediately saw as having "a strong personality."[76] They spent the day conversing about a variety of topics, including Solzhenitsyn's literary work, his ethical views, and his vision of Russia's future. The two men met on several other occasions, developing a friendship and even exchanging manuscripts, including a contraband copy of Solzhenitsyn's then unpublished novel *First Circle*. Solzhenitsyn revealed to Fr. Aleksandr that he had difficulty getting his manuscripts to the West for publication. The priest told Solzhenitsyn that he had a channel for sending his own manuscripts to a Western publisher, and he offered to help him.[77]

The two men were different in perspective as well as in temperament. Fr. Aleksandr portrayed Solzhenitsyn as a Tolstoyan whose views of Christianity were much different from his. According to Fr. Aleksandr, Solzhenitsyn understood Christianity primarily as an ethical system, which offered a code of how human beings should live, with Jesus Christ as the embodiment of this ethical system. Fr. Aleksandr professed admiration for Solzhenitsyn: he was a person of big ideas, a brilliant writer, and an artist of great depth. But his portrayal of him was not wholly positive. As Fr. Aleksandr described the Russian writer, he was also a person who recognized no barriers to his own personal desires, and who, like many brilliant people, "plunges serenely ahead without batting an eyelid even when he is creating havoc."[78]

Fr. Aleksandr's friendship with Solzhenitsyn, as well as his attractiveness to members of the Russian intelligentsia, carried great personal risk, particularly for a young priest trying to establish himself. His connections to members of the artistic and literary community could not have failed to attract the interest of the KGB, particularly as these relationships developed in the mid-and late1960s. After Khrushchev's fall from power in October 1964, the KGB targeted individuals critical of the political and social system of the Soviet state.[79] Alexander Solzhenitsyn became a special object of the KGB's suspicion.

On September 13, 1965, an automobile carrying officials of the KGB arrived unannounced at Fr. Aleksandr's Semkhoz home. Impeccably dressed, polite, and formal in their approach, they knocked on the front door, and inquired whether Fr. Aleksandr had any concealed weapons. They requested admission to the house, asking if he had any anti-Soviet literature, whose possession they considered a criminal offense. When Fr. Aleksandr responded that he did not have such literature, the KGB officials told him they needed to search the family's living quarters. "They locked my sister and me in the children's room," recalled Mikhail Men, then only five years old, and proceeded with their search of the premises. They were looking for manuscript copies of Solzhenitsyn's unpublished novels *First Circle* and *Cancer Ward*, works the KGB considered subversive.[80] Finding neither, the officials then told Fr. Aleksandr they needed to search his church. They asked him to ride with them in their automobile, then proceeded to drive to the church in Tarosovka, where they carefully examined all parts of the church, including a large wooden trunk filled with religious literature, in which they showed little interest.

The KGB officials returned to the house and continued to rummage through the family's belongings, convinced that there was a manuscript copy of Solzhenitsyn's works somewhere in the household. The search lasted eight hours, without turning up what they hoped to discover. They did uncover Fr. Aleksandr's personal diary and read parts of it before returning the diary to its proper place. "Why don't you look in the garbage dump?"

Nataliia Fedorovna asked. "Don't be sarcastic," the KGB official responded. "This could go badly for you."[81]

The one place the KGB officials failed to examine closely was a coal shed located adjacent to the house, recalled Fr. Aleksandr's son. "My family had a stove heated by coal, which they stored in the shed; my father brought a bucket of coal into the house each evening. Father had the manuscript of 'First Circle' hidden in the coal shed; when KGB officials began their search, he was afraid they might find the book."[82] They looked into the shed, but seeing how dirty it was, they closed the door, without going inside."[83]

KGB officials had come to Fr. Aleksandr's Semkhoz home hoping to implicate him in anti-Soviet activity. They discovered religious literature, some of which was brought in from abroad, but its possession did not constitute a crime. "They asked him," Mikhail Men said, "who sent him these books and what kind of connections he had. In the end, however, they were not able to charge him with anything."[84] Fr. Aleksandr managed to escape this frightful incident, but he did so by the narrowest of circumstances. The entire incident left him and his family physically unscathed, but it had a deep psychological impact as a first-hand reminder of the ominous presence of the KGB, whose threats to their personal relationships with the intelligentsia they could never afford to ignore.

Fr. Aleksandr Men's biographers have described his growing appeal to the Russian intelligentsia, but there is one aspect of his attraction that warrants more attention. This attribute comes out in Nadezhda Mandelstam's memoir, *Hope against Hope*, which is generally considered to be among the best accounts of the Russian intelligentsia in the twentieth century. Mandelstam, too, became a devoted "spiritual child" of Fr. Aleksandr. The widow of the great poet Osip Mandelstam, she provides a memorable account of the intelligentsia's struggles to maintain traditional cultural values in the face of furious government assaults that sought to obliterate cultural memories and replace them with newly conceived models. Mandelstam presents her husband's depiction of the intelligentsia as follows:

> M. once asked me (or himself, rather) what it was that made someone a member of the intelligentsia. He did not use the word itself—this was at a time when it was still a term of abuse, before it was taken over by bureaucratic elements in the so called liberal professions—but that was what he meant. Was it a university education, he wondered, or attendance in a pre-revolutionary grammar school? No, it was not this. Could it be your attitude toward literature? This, he thought was closer, but not quite it. Finally he decided that what really mattered was a person's feeling about

poetry. Poetry does indeed have a special place in this country. It arouses people and shapes their minds. No wonder the birth of our new intelligentsia is accompanied by a craving for poetry never seen before—it is the golden treasury in which our values are preserved; it brings people back to life, awakens their conscience and stirs them to thought. Why this should happen I do not know, but it is a fact.[85]

The reverence for poetry, in Mandelstam's husband's eyes, was peculiar to Russia, and this devotion was poorly understood in the West, which, on the whole, lacked such an appreciation. In Russia, poetry occupied a sacrosanct place, which the intelligentsia firmly embraced and which, despite the attempts to render it lifeless, perpetually called out to be reborn:

> My young friend who loves [Aleksandr] Blok and nourishes his own pessimism by reading him was for me the first sign of the intelligentsia's rebirth, and I find his pessimism unjustified. The new awakening is accompanied by the copying out and reading of poetry, which thus plays its part in setting things in motion again and reviving thought. The keepers of the flame hid in darkened corners, but the flame did not go out. It is there for all to see.[86]

Fr. Aleksandr had the poet's mind and the poet's mission. The qualities described above contributed to the values that he, too, embraced and sought to sustain. His appeal to the intelligentsia had many facets, and chief among them were the attributes similar to those that Mandelstam describes—attributes that ultimately attracted her to Fr. Aleksandr's parish. He spoke in the language of the poet, keeping the flame alive, connecting the past to the present, and summoning a new awakening in the midst of darkness.

7

. . . .

The First Decade

The Writer

The tumultuous decade of the 1960s and the near disastrous events that befell the young priest made daily existence extremely difficult. In such troubled times, when Fr. Aleksandr Men came under attack, creative activity appeared to be nearly impossible; the struggle to survive had to take top priority. The watchful eye of the KGB, constant interruptions of his work, and vicious attacks in the press all conspired to create an oppressive atmosphere and general climate of anxiety that, for Fr. Aleksandr, pervaded nearly everything. This anxiety seemed to restrict creative thought and activity to their narrowest possible limits and discouraged new ventures, especially those contradicting prevailing systems of belief.

Yet such generalizations would poorly describe the realities of Fr. Aleksandr's life. In the late 1950s, while facing conditions of near poverty with a wife and child to support, he was befriended by an editor, Anatolii Vasil'evich Vedernikov, who, as mentioned earlier, gave him the opportunity to supplement his small income. Throughout his tenure at Tarasovka, Fr. Aleksandr did his writing at home in the early mornings or at night. Yet all this time, he never divorced his work from his family. Shortly after the birth of his son, he could be seen at his writing table in the garden, steadying his child on his knee with one hand, holding his pen and writing with the other.[1]

During the 1960s, at the beginning of his priesthood, Fr. Aleksandr consistently wrote articles and books aimed at deepening the understanding of religion in his society. He saw such writing as a major part of his calling to service and as a way of strengthening connections to his parishioners, as well as to those preceding him, especially the late nineteenth- and early twentieth-century philosopher-theologians with whom he felt a close relationship.[2] In 1959, at the age of twenty-four and still a deacon, he began to publish articles in the *Journal of the Moscow Patriarchate*. These early writings, which he completed before moving to a project that occupied him throughout the entire decade and beyond, are examined in this chapter.[3]

Journal of the Moscow Patriarchate

Aleksandr Men's first article in the *Journal of the Moscow Patriarchate* focused on one of the great luminaries of the early church, Saint Gregory of Nazianzus (325–389), later known as Saint Gregory the Theologian.[4] Traditionally, Gregory, Basil of Caesarea, and John Chrysostom are venerated as the three great fathers of the Russian Orthodox Church. In selecting this topic, Fr. Aleksandr dealt with a church leader whose entire life was caught in conflict between differing visions of Christianity and who constantly struggled to follow the path he believed true to his understanding of Jesus's teachings. Gregory became the chief defender of the Holy Trinity in the struggle with Arian theology. As Paul Tillich has written, Gregory's eloquent support of his belief rightfully earned him a venerable place as the "creator of the definitive formulae for the doctrine of the Trinity."[5]

Born in Nazianzus in southwest Cappadocia, the son of the bishop of Nazianzus, Gregory received an excellent education in advanced rhetoric and philosophy in Nazianzus, Caesarea, and Alexandria, before going to Athens to study with several of the most renowned scholars of his times. While he preferred an aesthetic life, Gregory was brought, against his wishes, into the political-administrative service of the church, first, in 372, as Bishop of Susima, and, after returning home later that year to help his father, as an administrator of the diocese of Nazianzus. He soon wrote several episcopal orations that stand among the greatest of the patristic age.[6] Nearly a decade later, in 381, Gregory was selected to lead the Second Ecumenical Council in Constantinople, which he did until a dispute among the bishops, which threatened to tear apart the church, made him resign. His theological contributions in defense of the Trinity and his poetry earned him the reputation of being one of the greatest teachers and writers in the history of the church.

While Fr. Aleksandr's article treats the philosophical views of the ancient theologian, it is Gregory the person and his aesthetic creations that comprised Fr. Aleksandr's chief focus. He skillfully placed Gregory in the context of his times, an era marked by intense struggles between Christians and non-Christians, as well as bitter disputes within the church itself. In his depiction of Gregory, Fr. Aleksandr displayed an approach that would characterize his later writings: he made the person of his essay come alive as he described the personal qualities, the passions, and the internal battles that distinguished his subject. He discussed Gregory's early life and his commitment to a purpose larger than himself, which Fr. Aleksandr attributed to two main circumstances: a mother who was convinced that her son would be a special servant of God and a voyage on the Mediterranean Sea that carried him to Athens to begin his university studies, in which, during a violent storm, he promised to devote himself to God's service, wherever that might lead.

Gregory's early life exemplified the qualities that later made him a superb leader and spokesperson of Eastern Orthodoxy. He had a brilliant, well-rounded education at the University of Athens and a love for the sciences as well as for rhetoric, grammar, history, and poetry. "In all of his productions," Fr. Aleksandr writes, "he stands before us not only as an artist or as a priest of wise spiritual experiences, but also as a person of great culture and encyclopedic knowledge."[7] In Athens, Gregory became friends with Basil, a fellow student, who later became the revered Basil the Great in the Eastern Church. Their friendship would be lifelong, a relationship that Gregory recounted in his poetry. Both young men grew disillusioned with Athens and with the students who led an "idle and dissolute life, more resembling a spectacle than an academic existence." Eventually tiring of the city, the two friends retreated to the "desert," which became the home of what Fr. Aleksandr called their "second schooling."[8] Basil had built a shack by the cliffs of the Pontic coast near a waterfall, where Gregory soon joined him and where the two of them lived quietly, studying and praying. The two young men ultimately left their sheltered existence for active service in the hierarchical structure of the church.

As a church leader, Gregory carried within him both the love of a contemplative life and the call for leadership, a conflict found in his poetry, which Fr. Aleksandr liberally quoted. This conflict incessantly tormented Gregory and pulled him in directions he did not want to go but to which he felt called by God. He did not like the bustle and noise of the city, and neither did he like the social activities nor the false air of superiority that governed many of the people living there, which was personified by the Stoic philosophers, who were so revered in his times. Gregory greatly preferred the seclusion of the mountains. He had the temperament, Fr. Aleksandr wrote, similar to that of the book of Ecclesiastes, fearlessly "going down into the black fog of pessimism" and finding there the "light that in the darkness shines," a theme that Fr. Aleksandr says reaches its highest expression in Gregory's poem "On Human Nature."[9] As Fr. Aleksandr described him, Gregory was a seeker, a quality that caused some of his most intense suffering, but also served as a source of his greatest poetic achievements.

Aleksandr Men had more than just an academic interest in the life of Gregory the Theologian. Many of Gregory's challenges mirrored Fr. Aleksandr's own struggles, and the issues the ancient theologian faced were not unlike those he confronted. Gregory fought against the abuse of power, which was a major theme in Russian society during this time, given that only three years earlier, Nikita Khrushchev had given his speech criticizing Stalin's abuses of power. But Fr. Aleksandr's treatment of Gregory also had wider implications than abuses of power within the government. Similar abuses took place within the church. In Gregory's time, people had come into the church who only desired to please the emperor and align themselves with public opinion.

Gregory stood against these trends. His support for the "New Testament unity of heaven and earth, on the foundation of Jesus Christ" lay at the core of his belief.[10] He aspired, Fr. Aleksandr wrote, to give poetry to future generations of much greater power than pagan authors could offer. Like his friend Basil, Gregory believed poetry and music were "genuine vehicles for the good, reforming morals by way of melodies."[11] In elaborating on Gregory, Fr. Aleksandr essentially argued that Russian Orthodoxy needed to take a fresh look at the roots of its faith, including the relationship between religion and culture.

Fr. Aleksandr's articles in the *Journal of the Moscow Patriarchate* cover a wide variety of topics, but among them, several main themes stand out. They foreshadow the ideas he later continued to develop in his writings and teachings. The first is Fr. Aleksandr's perspective on the life of Jesus Christ. This is the focus of the second article he published, dealing with Jesus's upbringing and life as a young adult in the town of Nazareth.[12] As with many other topics in his publications, Fr. Aleksandr took an unusual and imaginative approach to this topic. He examined the part of Jesus's life that had received little attention: the thirty years before his subject left his native town to begin a mission that changed the history of the world. Most of the existing biblical materials elaborated on the following three years, when Jesus's prophetic teachings drew a large following and challenged the political and social structure of Rome. But the years preceding were also important in shaping the character of Jesus. While the surviving written records largely passed over them, leaving few details, Fr. Aleksandr devoted attention to those crucial times.

Why, Fr. Aleksandr asks, is the story set in the town of Nazareth, an insignificant and humble outpost "hidden among the hills of Galilee," a town known literally to no one beyond its local provincial borders?[13] Doubters of the town's creative capacities often asked the cynical question, "Can anything good come from Nazareth?" God did not elect either the magnificent cultural center of Babylon or the powerful city of Rome for what Fr. Aleksandr called the "completion of the greatest event in world history."[14] Yet this dusty, distant frontier outpost, neither an economic nor a political center, became the "cradle of Christianity" and the birthplace "from which came our redemption." Every detail one can uncover about this place, every artifact that might reveal the nature of its environment, has significance, Fr. Aleksandr noted, as he recreated the narrative of those years that shaped Jesus's preparation to serve the people.

In telling his story, Fr. Aleksandr followed closely the teaching of Saint Gregory of Nazianzus and, before him, the decisions of the First Council of Nicaea (325 CE), which had defined the tripartite nature of God's identity as God, Jesus Christ, and the Holy Spirit.[15] Fr. Aleksandr stood squarely in that tradition. He embraced Jesus's divinity and his crucial part in expressing God's love for humankind, but here Fr. Aleksandr's focus was mainly on the human aspects of Jesus's life and his interactions with the physical setting in which he grew up. Born to a humble mother and a carpenter father, Jesus walked the streets and surroundings of the small Jewish settlement, hidden in the mountains, whose hills he often ascended.

In these picturesque mountainous surroundings, the young Jesus felt an immediate connection. Transformed into a garden in the springtime, with the beauty of its open fields and within sight of mountain roses, lilacs, and red anemones, such a setting must have filled him with joy. Fr. Aleksandr had never visited this region, but this distant witness, gained largely from travel accounts, neither detracted from his ability to render precise details nor prevented him from capturing the artistic flavor of the environment. While the town of Nazareth had changed greatly over the course of two thousand years, the surrounding nature, he pointed out, "remained the same as it did in those days, when the Son of God walked here."[16] Fr. Aleksandr's words are lyrical in his descriptions of the "hot sun, the mountain air, and the green valley giving off a special freshness," the "sounds of the turtle doves," and the flowers, these "models of the soul," expressing the "joy of the Creator over everything."[17]

Fr. Aleksandr noted just how many of the concrete images Jesus used in his later parables are drawn from this location. The shepherd who risked his life to save a solitary sheep, the fig trees, the farmer scattering his seeds around the fields, and the vineyard with its ripe grapes were all common images drawn from everyday life. Above all, here lived the mother of Jesus, engaged in prayer and in her work; the father, a poor carpenter, in whose household the Redeemer of the World grew up; and farmers, dressed simply, their hands covered with calluses, humble laboring people who took pride in their work and whose wheat, grapes, and pomegranates nourished the town.

Fr. Aleksandr Men drew a significant lesson from this simple description, which, he claimed, was illustrated by Jesus's early life, and was a lesson reflected in his teachings. In this thirty-year period, the Savior taught us that truth lay less in miraculous occurrences and spectacular settings than in the very most ordinary circumstances. In these everyday conditions, it is "possible to live an authentic life in God." A person must search for his or her own well-being and identity, "not in some place far away, but here, in one's own living place, in one's own simple, everyday affairs."[18]

The second theme running through Fr. Aleksandr's essays concerned the problem of human brotherhood. In his article "On the Threshold of a New Year," published in January 1960, he addressed this issue.[19] He began by examining the historical forces that he saw emerging and shaping the present and future, pointing out the compression of time and the major events that characterized the twentieth century and distinguished it from earlier periods. The tempo of history had accelerated over time, which fostered new patterns of social interaction. Writing at a time when Khrushchev's revelations about Stalin and new breakthroughs in science and technology were forcing a redefinition of Soviet society, Fr. Aleksandr felt these winds of rapid historical change all around him. In the context of such change, his article at the beginning of the year took an optimistic approach to the church's future possibilities despite the heavy, oppressive hand of the state that had previously shackled it.[20] He called for the church to look deeply into its sources of tradition and to recover the vision of peace and brotherhood that had characterized the first generations of Christians.[21]

Aleksandr Men issued a clarion call to Christians everywhere, who, for complex reasons, had forgotten that Jesus Christ introduced a new law for humanity—the "law of brotherhood."[22] Over time, enthusiasm for his new law grew cool, and various kinds of antagonisms reappeared. Fr. Aleksandr attributed this reemergence to the heritage of paganism, which continued to exert a strong influence on human relationships. A pagan spirit had led to the separation of East and West, with each side claiming superiority. These views had produced their estrangement, which he also attributed to the rise of the theocratic state, a form of governance that, he said, lacked "any kind of Christian justification."[23]

If enmity deeply marked the past between East and West, extending well into the twentieth century, Fr. Aleksandr viewed ecumenism as an emergent theme for the future. The time had come to explore the causes separating East and West, he said, which he attributed to political interests prevailing "over the spirit of Christian love."[24] He saw evidence that Western churches no longer looked upon Eastern Orthodoxy with disparaging eyes and that the time had come for the Russian Orthodox Church "to reach out to these outstretched hands in the spirit of Christian love."[25]

The third theme of Fr. Aleksandr's writings involves a question about the historical significance of the twentieth century: why have we witnessed such horrible events of human cruelty and injustices on the world stage, including sufferings brought about by war, oppression, and human exploitation on a massive scale? These events put before all of humanity questions about the causes of this suffering and the reasons underlying the bloodshed and the fierce cruelty that have marked recent times.[26] Fr. Aleksandr understood the complexity of these issues, but he did not attempt to offer a comprehensive response. He explored what he considered to be a central cause of the violence and what he called "various delusions" of humanity.[27]

In discussing these difficult issues, Fr. Aleksandr singled out racism and its underlying assumptions about humanity. He defined racism as the belief that human beings emerged from diverse origins, "consequently not having a unified, common ancestry," and thus developing along different paths that produced dissimilar human capacities.[28] Promoting this viewpoint, racial theorists claim that human races come from diverse biological species, supporting a myth about the "unfulfilled value" of certain races and the "superiority" of other biological species.[29] Fr. Aleksandr traced the evolution of these theories on racial superiority to Old Testament times, when ancient peoples considered foreigners to be "people who were damned," and called them "wild people."[30] He examined thinking concerning people of different faiths, from pantheists, such as Giordano Bruno and Lucilii Vanini in the sixteenth century, to theorists on the colonization of North America in the seventeenth and eighteenth centuries, to the defenders of evolutionary polytheism, such as the German scientist Karl Vogt (1817–1895) and the biological naturalist Ernst Haeckel (1834–1919) in the nineteenth century, the latter, "in the name of science," blessing the excesses of the neocolonialism of German Kaiser Wilhelm II. "Reason," Haeckel wrote, "appears for the most part to be the capacity only of the superior races, and remains very incompletely or entirely undeveloped in the lower orders."[31] From there, in Fr. Aleksandr's mind, it was only a short distance to the racial theories of the Nazi regime and its claims of Aryan racial superiority, contentions that ultimately plunged the world into an unparalleled bloodbath.

In developing this line of thinking, proponents of racial superiority closed themselves off from empirical research that contradicted their views. They ignored such scientific research because it would have revealed their conclusions to be "entirely unfounded." Fr. Aleksandr cited the ground-breaking work of Nikolai Nikolaevich Miklukho-Maklai (1846–1888), the renowned Russian explorer, anthropologist, and ethnographer, whose first-hand studies of people living far from European civilization showed that the so-called superior mental capacities of "whites" had no basis in concrete reality.[32] Fr. Aleksandr also referenced the work of Wilhelm Schmidt (1880–1954), the German-Austrian linguist, anthropologist, ethnographer, and Roman Catholic priest, whose field research in New Guinea and Togo revealed that primitive cultures had a monotheistic religion that served as the foundation for a well-developed sense of morality.[33] Racial theorists claimed to be scientists; they based their views on what they called "rigorous science," supported by statistics and biochemical analysis. But, as Fr. Aleksandr argued, they did not possess the cardinal features of true scientists: openness to other points of view and research that did not confirm their predetermined convictions; they suffered from a lack of humility about their work. They were not true scientists, but rather proponents of an ideology.[34]

The church had an obligation to take a stand against this ideology of human hatred, Fr. Aleksandr maintained, pointing out that some of its deepest and most important teachings profoundly rejected a belief in human inequality. The ideas of human brotherhood, he noted, are expressed in three short but powerful forms: in the book of Ruth and its expression of love for all people; in the life of the prophet John the Baptist, which also demonstrated God's compassion for human beings everywhere, without exception; and most fully in Christ's parable of the Samaritan and his response to the lawyer's question, "Who is my neighbor?," which Men called "an unequivocal and unambiguous condemnation of all national and religious enemies, of all hatred and contempt toward people of other faiths and members of other tribes."[35]

Just as proponents of the "science" of racism excluded opposing scientific studies, Fr. Aleksandr noted, they also had refused to consider the teachings of Christianity. Claiming that their work involved rigorous scientific methods, they banished the church from their discussion, claiming it to be irrelevant. He expressed little sympathy for this approach, seeing it as a ruse that hid all kinds of weaknesses and untenable contentions. Such closed-mindedness, he maintained, had ultimately turned a large part of civilization into "smoke and ash."[36]

Fr. Aleksandr Men's article did not explore the underlying causes of the terror and violence in Russia, which had similarly brought enormous suffering. Even though he wrote at a time when the Communist Party had begun to explore the political aspects of such questions in its reexamination of Stalin's legacy, Fr. Aleksandr did not focus on the Soviet Union, because he could not hope to pass the state's censorship. But in writing about racism and Nazism, he indirectly applied his critique to Russia's own situation. The narrowly restricted views, the lack of openness, and the ideological approach to truth had immediate relevance to the present. "The propaganda of racism, in Nazi Germany as before, was indissolubly connected with the struggle against Christianity," he maintained.[37] Fr. Aleksandr cited the decree promoting the doctrine of racial superiority signed by Martin Bormann, Hitler's head of the Party's Chancellery, in June 1941, concurrent with Germany's invasion of the Soviet Union. To this end, the decree stated, "The influence of the church must be suppressed, completely and unequivocally." It was not science that called for the church's suppression, but ideology. The brotherhood of humankind and the equality of all people before a "Single Creator" stood, in Fr. Aleksandr's mind, as one of the cardinal teachings of Christianity.[38] It was a theme he would develop still further in his own work, both in his parish and in his other publications.

Between 1959 and 1966, Aleksandr Men published twenty-one articles in the *Journal of the Moscow Patriarchate*, nineteen of them between 1959 and 1962, while A. V. Vedernikov served as editor-in-chief. In 1962, Vedernikov was removed and replaced by Metropolitan Pitirim (Nechaev, 1926–2003), who remained the editor-in-chief for the next thirty-two years.[39] The move changed the entire focus of the journal. Pitirim encouraged Fr. Aleksandr to continue to make submissions, which he did. In the end, however, only two of them appeared in print, one in 1963 on the apostle Luke, the other in 1966 on the Roman pope Liberius (reigned 352–366), who was revered as a saint in Eastern Orthodoxy and was a leading defender of Orthodoxy against Arianism.[40] After that date, Fr. Aleksandr lost the one avenue in the Russian Church open to his writings.

But the closure of this major channel for his publications did not signal an end to Fr. Aleksandr's efforts as a writer. He continued to work on the themes to which he remained most committed. In terms of scholarship, the first decade stands among the most productive in his entire service as a priest.

Aleksandr Men's submissions to the *Journal of the Moscow Patriarchate* comprised selected parts of a manuscript he had conceived when he was fifteen. While still a schoolboy, he began work on a manuscript that he completed in 1958. He continued to work on it in the 1960s, circulating a copy in the underground press and, in 1968, published it abroad with the title *Son of Man* (*Syn chelovecheskii*).[41] The circumstances under which he wrote *Son of Man* offer a prelude to the text of one of his most widely read and influential works.

An Alternative Vision

"Father did nearly all of his writing at home in his study, in the quiet of the evening or early in the morning," recalled Mikhail Aleksandrovich Men, Fr. Aleksandr's son. "In summers, when the weather permitted, he moved outside into the garden," where he set up a table and went there with his writing pad and his typewriter.[42] He also wrote during his vacation times, which he and his family spent in the Crimea, and where he first had gone as a youth and learned to love the sea, the mountains nearby, and the opportunity to renew his inner resources.[43] Such times offered periods of solitude.

Aleksandr Men continued to work on *Son of Man* for much of his later life, revising it numerous times and sharpening its focus and deepening its content. Given the primary readership at whom the book was aimed and the setting in which it was written, such continual revision was essential. "This sharp, lively story about evangelistic experiences," wrote Fr. Mikhail Aksenov-Meerson, "responds to the questions of non-believers and to the prevailing atheistic theory" surrounding them on all sides.[44] At the time of its dissemination, possession of a copy was extremely dangerous as the police considered it to be anti-Soviet.[45]

Throughout his priesthood, Fr. Aleksandr extended himself to the people of his parish, nurturing them in their spiritual needs, reaching out to them in multiple ways, and relating the church to the community. While he gained energy through such active service, writes a close associate, he "by his very nature was even more a person of the study [*chelovek kabineta*]," who had, from time to time, to find solitude—to pray and to think. Fr. Aleksandr "felt himself most at home in the library or at his writing table."[46] This description applied to his later life, but also accurately characterized him in his earlier years—from his student days to his experiences as a young priest. Surrounded by a busy, demanding world, he had to find time to be alone. In this respect he resembled the legendary Serafim of Sarov, who had a great reputation for reaching out to people but often felt the desire to "hide in the forest" in order that "nature might strengthen and enlighten him."[47]

Syn chelovecheskii

Since making the decision to become a priest, but particularly during his actual service, Fr. Aleksandr Men had confronted a cardinal tenet of Soviet ideology: that Jesus Christ never existed. This belief had been a key element in Lenin's thinking, and it had featured in the early Soviet assault on religion.

In the late 1950s and 1960s, as the government resumed its attack, the view that Jesus existed only as a figment of the imagination again became a predominant claim, which was heavily emphasized in Soviet schools and in the press.

In *Son of Man*, Fr. Aleksandr had to deal with this prevailing interpretation, and he approached it head on. He appended to the book a lengthy essay titled "Myth or Reality?" ("Mif ili deistvitel'nost?").[48] Originally, Fr. Aleksandr intended the essay to serve as an introduction to *Son of Man*, but he changed his mind and inserted it as an appendix.[49] As such, it is a closely reasoned, well-documented, and powerfully written survey that stands apart from his book. "Myth or Reality?" is essential to contrasting Fr. Aleksandr's own view of Jesus, as presented in the Gospels, with interpretations provided by mainstream Soviet authors.

The Soviet interpretation of Jesus derived from the writings of the German philosopher and historian Arthur Drews (1865–1935). Drews, a professor of philosophy at the Technische Hochschule in Karlsruhe, Germany, is the author of multiple works on religion in the ancient world.[50] In 1909, he published *The Christ Myth*, his most widely distributed book, which generated immediate controversy. *The Christ Myth* denied the existence of Jesus Christ, maintaining that the image of Jesus was a product of the imagination and a concoction assembled by writers living several centuries later who put together various early myths about the coming of a divine savior of humankind. As Drews expressed the central premise of his work:

> [The name of Jesus] has never at any time been anything but such an empty vessel: Jesus Christ, the Deliverer, Saviour, Physician of oppressed souls, has been from first to last a figure borrowed from myth, to whom the desire for redemption and the naïve faith of the Western Asiatic peoples have transferred all their conceptions of the soul's welfare. The "history" of this Jesus in its general characteristics had been determined even before the evangelical Jesus.[51]

Drews's thesis appealed to V. I. Lenin, who found the logic of his presentation convincing. In a seminal article, "On the Significance of Militant Materialism," written in 1922, which elaborated on the new Soviet ideology, Lenin proposed an "'alliance' with the Drewses, in one form or another and in one degree or another," which, he said, was "essential for our struggle against the governing religious obscurantists."[52] The influence of Arthur Drews on Soviet thinking lasted well beyond the Second World War, and although later scholars turned more frequently to Friedrich Engels's ideas, put forward in his *Early History of Christianity*, the mythological aspects of the Christian story remained firmly entrenched in Soviet teachings about religion.[53] Major writers of the educational establishment stressed the harmful elements embedded in religion, specifically in Christianity, which created a "fantasy world" promoting a blissful future as a substitute for dealing with the harsh realities of this world.[54]

The argument denying the historicity of Jesus might be summarized as follows. The fiction of Christ took place gradually, over several centuries, and was spread by early church writers who sought to transform a mythological deity into a human being. Various ancient and eastern myths were woven into the story of Christ, producing an all-embracing narrative that had little basis in actual fact. The historical evidence for the gradual evolution of the Jesus myth is much stronger than the evidence for Jesus's actual existence because none of his non-Christian contemporaries say anything about him. In addition, the Gospels are filled with mistakes and contradictions; they cannot be considered trustworthy sources. What might be termed a "long silence" existed between the supposed life of Christ and the Gospel accounts of his existence, thereby allowing all kinds of factual inaccuracies and mythological events to enter the story. Consequently, faith in the historical reality of Christ is misguided. Further, it is a fiction that has resulted in the enslavement of human beings, preventing them from becoming fully human and achieving their full potential on this earth.[55]

Such arguments were brilliantly summarized in the opening pages of Mikhail Bulgakov's novel *The Master and Margarita*. First published in 1968–1969, in successive issues of the journal *Moskva* (Moscow), Bulgakov's work was well known to Fr. Aleksandr. In his essay "Myth or Reality?" Fr. Aleksandr referenced the scene near Patriarch's Pond in which the "enlightened," "self-satisfied" Berlioz instructed the poet Ivan, saying, "There is not one Eastern religion, in which, as a rule, the pure maiden did not proclaim the light of god. And Christians, not having thought of anything new, in exactly the same way created this Jesus, who, in reality, never lived."[56] Bulgakov's novel, Fr. Aleksandr noted, portrayed "a whole army of graduates and semi-literates" who were "heartily brainwashed like the naïve Ivan."[57] They readily accepted what passed for scientific testimony without having the means to explore contradictory evidence. Aleksandr Men saw as his task the exploration of such opposing evidence.

Fr. Aleksandr realized the enormity of the task he faced during a visit to the Leningrad Museum of the History of Religion and Atheism. Established in 1931 in the transformed Kazan' Cathedral, the museum was designed to "examine the myth of Christ," thus exposing the essence of Christianity as an "anti-scientific, deeply reactionary ideology."[58] Prominently displayed at the center of the museum hung a large portrait of Christ, set against a "background of intersecting swords":

> To Him are stretched connecting threads to the figures of gods and myth-ological figures of the heroes of ancient Greece, Asia Minor, Egypt, Persia, and even India. The visitor to the museum may track how, from scraps of paganism, the myth of Christ was "formed." Here is the birth of Buddha, the flight of Isida with the infant Gurom, the crucifixion of Mithra and Marsyas, the weeping of Adonis and Attis, the resurrection of Osiris. Almost all the main episodes of the Gospel story. It is as if everything was foretold.[59]

In his essay "Myth or Reality?" Aleksandr Men offered an alternative view to these accounts. He based his work on extensive research in primary and secondary sources taken from a variety of fields, working to dispute the mythologists' claims about the paucity of sources that prevented a histor-ical reconstruction of Christ's life. He admitted that many facts remained obscure, but it was possible to draw a reasonably full picture, which he attempted to do. Spending many afternoons in the Patriarchal Library of the Moscow Spiritual Academy, pouring through multilingual collections of historical materials, he endeavored to present that picture.[60] His knowl-edge of Greek, Hebrew, and Latin enabled him to read the original texts of Greek and Roman writers; he studied the works of Jewish historians of the first and second centuries and that of archeologists whose recent discoveries provided concrete details about the physical setting in which Christ lived.[61] A look at the book's scholarly apparatus reveals vast, wide-ranging read-ing in biblical, historical, and archeological scholarship, both Russian and Western, which enabled Fr. Aleksandr to fill in physical and anthropological elements mostly disregarded by the mythological proponents.[62]

   A cardinal piece of the mythological school concerned the "centuries of silence," the long period between Jesus's existence and most of the accounts of his life. In addressing this issue, the core of Fr. Aleksandr's reading cen-tered on the Gospels: "If we want to know the truth about Christ, then we should seek it first in the Gospels."[63] Their significance in creating an intimate, immediate picture was unmatched. "[The Gospels,] having been written by those who are neither chroniclers nor historians, contain a testi-mony coming from the first century of the church, when eyewitnesses of the mortal ministry of Christ were still alive."[64] Fr. Aleksandr did not concern himself with trying to rectify certain apparent contradictions, but instead focused on the larger story the Gospels told.

But in presenting this larger story, he had first to dispel the mythologists' account of Jesus. *Son of Man* recognized the common elements Jesus shared with earlier prophets who had achieved a sacred place in other religious traditions. He paid respect to the similarities that existed between Israel's prophets and other great teachers of the West and East who believed in an "absolute Source of Existence," a God of the "perfect Light and Good," or, like Plato and Anaxagoras, "spoke of Him as creation's Rationality, or Wisdom." Nearly everywhere, from India to Italy, these great teachers had broken through old world beliefs in the power of magic, ritual, and incantations and had sought answers to the "burning questions of life and faith."[65]

The mythologists, however, either ignored or did not understand the fundamental differences between these other religious and philosophical traditions and the Hebrew prophets who preceded Jesus. Unlike these other traditions, the prophets did not construct any speculative systems; they did not create hypotheses, and they did not view God as separate from the world, existing in another sphere.[66] According to Fr. Aleksandr, the Hebrew prophets saw themselves as messengers, voices of a Divine Being who had never departed from the world, but related to people in the "very depths of their being." "This revelation," he pointed out, "was unique among other religions."[67]

In telling the story of Jesus, Aleksandr Men approached his task as an icon artist deals with painting an icon.[68] He spent a great deal of time each day in prayerful reflection, striving for personal humility and seeking the inspiration to depict truthfully and deeply the subjects of his art. He wanted to encourage the reader to think, a principal goal he stated in the introduction to *Son of Man*: he hoped to "awaken," as the icon painter aspired to open a window into a large, sacred world.[69] The icon painter works within a certain canon, but this canon provides "only a general, directive value," wrote Sergei Bulgakov; "[it] leaves room for personal inspiration and for the creative spirit . . . [and] even presupposes such creativeness."[70]

In writing, Fr. Aleksandr worked within a framework and canon, but he never saw that framework as either rigidly prescribed or fully prefigured. He kept his mind open to countervailing pieces of evidence, which, as he claimed in his earlier piece in *Journal of the Moscow Patriarchate*, ideological writers never did.[71] The Gospels offered personal inspiration; they never provided a closed system of thought and belief, and Fr. Aleksandr did not see Christianity as an ideology.[72] The Gospels allowed plenty of space for creativity, encouraged new thinking, and, in the process, offered hope, even in the darkest times.[73] These fundamental beliefs were well understood by

Aleksandr Pushkin, Russia's greatest poet, whom Aleksandr quoted on the
first page of *Son of Man*:

> There is a book . . . whose every word is interpreted, explained, preached in
> all corners of the earth, applied to all possible circumstances of life. . . . This
> book is called the Gospel, and such is its eternally new treasure, that if we,
> satiated by the world and overwhelmed with depression, accidentally open
> it, we do not have the power to resist its sweet calling and are spiritually
> immersed in its divine eloquence.[74]

The mythologists argued emphatically that the Gospels belonged to the past
and were vestiges of a dying prescientific order. Fr. Aleksandr aspired to
show that they belonged not only to the past, but also to the present and to
the future.

As *Son of Man* presented him, Jesus affirmed and yet changed the message of the Hebrew prophets. Unlike other great religious teachers, he did
not wait for people to gather around him, but went directly to the people.
He was, Fr. Aleksandr wrote, "profoundly human," never shying away from
the world," never displaying a sense of gloom or dogmatism, and constantly
loving simple things, among them flowers, plain speech, and children.
There was an "inexplicable attractiveness about him," partly a result of the
atmosphere of "love, joy, and faith" that emanated from his whole being.
He encouraged a sense of wonder, which he consistently modeled in his
behavior, and he always remained open to new possibilities. As distinct
from pagan priests, there was nothing bombastic in his demeanor or
speech. His hands were calloused; they belonged to a person who had
done hard physical labor. His words and actions were addressed not to
one part, but to the whole of a person's being. Whereas the prophets of the
Old Testament referred to God and the people, Jesus spoke of God and the
person, "God and the individual soul." He was the "good shepherd," who
"calls each person by name."[75]

The question Jesus posed to his disciples, "Who do you say that I am?,"
Fr. Aleksandr wrote, is as relevant today as it was two thousand years ago.[76]
Son of Man presents the response to that question as key to understanding
the uniqueness of Jesus. Both then and now, a common response continues to be that Jesus served as a prophet or a great moral teacher, similar to
Jeremiah, Buddha, and Socrates.[77] But to reduce the Gospel to this level is
to misrepresent the essence of its meaning, as well as to miss fundamentally
the evidence provided in the historical sources "of those who walked with
Him through the cities and villages of Galilee."[78]

Simon Peter's answer to Jesus's question, "You are the Christ, the Son of the Living God," underscored that he is far more than a prophet or a great moral teacher. Here, in Fr. Aleksandr's words, "an abyss suddenly opens wide between the Son of Man and all other philosophers, moralists and founders of religions."[79] The paradox of Jesus as God and man, "of this improbability and historical reality," Fr. Aleksandr maintained, cannot be explained, as the mythologists attempted to do, by "flat 'Euclidean' intellect": there is much in history that remains beyond logical explanation.[80]

The mythologists denied the biblical account of the Resurrection. They argued that such an event had no basis in reality, its logic defying even the most fertile imagination. In their view, the image of a savior-god who died and rose again was a concocted story that evolved from Eastern cults, with whom the ancient Jews were well acquainted.[81] But to Fr. Aleksandr, the Resurrection lay at the core of Christianity, and he devoted a great deal of attention to the death and resurrection of Christ, events he told with much passion and skill. In doing so, he also criticized Western theologians such as Rudolf Bultmann, who cast "doubt on the trustworthiness of everything we know about the earthly life of Christ."[82] Like the apostle Paul, whom he freely quoted, Fr. Aleksandr believed that without the Resurrection, there would be little hope for humankind; meaninglessness, death, and the forces of darkness would triumph.[83] The Resurrection signified the coming transformation awaiting each individual, which Christ represented, when he no longer appeared as the teacher but as the "Incarnation of the Living God." In Fr. Aleksandr's terms, the Resurrection connects the truths of reason and faith: in it, they were no longer separated.

The mythologists, Fr. Aleksandr pointed out, had no explanation for the abiding power of this vision, how it became a core belief that extended from Roman slaves and African shepherds to Dante and Dostoevsky, or how and why the image of the God-man had "illuminated the thinking of [St.] Augustine and [Blaise] Pascal . . . inspired poets and sculptors, called to life the powerful sounds of symphonies and chorales," and stimulated the art of Andrei Rublev, Michelangelo Buonarroti, and Rembrandt van Rijn.[84] The mythologists had not convincingly shown why, despite many attempts to erase the story of Christ from memory and suppress it, the story had always revived, in some cases more powerfully and authentically than ever.[85]

In his presentation of Jesus, Fr. Aleksandr focused on what he considered a key passage in the Gospels: "I am the truth and the truth will make you free." The mythologists paid little attention to this statement in the Gospel of John. The leading scholar of the mythological school, Iosef Aronovich Kryvelev, discussed the term "freedom" only in his brief analysis of Dostoevsky's chapter "The Grand Inquisitor" from his novel *The Brothers Karamazov*.[86] In contrast, Fr. Aleksandr's *Son of Man* portrayed Jesus as giving human beings "freedom." He is the "Liberator."[87] He frees people from slavery of all kinds, most especially from the domination by other human beings. For example, he completely transformed the status of women and freed human beings from a narrow, unhealthy devotion to material goods. He stood firmly in opposition to an "enslavement of the heart" as he sought to replace the emphasis on ritual and sacrifice with compassion and charity. Liberating human beings from dependence on external objects, Christ created a new way of looking at the self and at other people. This different way of seeing uprooted the old law, based on rigid prescriptions, and introduced a new, organic law, based on love.[88]

The Christ whom Fr. Aleksandr described in *Son of Man* did not appear as people had expected, that is, as a judgmental and extraordinarily violent figure who would destroy his enemies. Instead, they were presented with a carpenter, born in a stable, "Who called to Himself, 'all who labor and are heavy laden.'"[89] He was an outcast, a wanderer, and a "homeless stranger" who eschewed authoritarian power and the use of force. Most of all, he was highly critical of closed-mindedness, dogmatism, and those unwilling to accept a sense of mystery. He required striving, not certainty, and those who could not recognize him were unable to do so because of "their fixed views and wounded class pride."[90]

Fr. Aleksandr's writing on all of these topics is vivid and colorful. He thought in specific, concrete forms in the language of poetry and pictures, which gave precise meaning to his ideas. Rather than dealing in abstractions, he rendered physical facts with a dynamism that opened the way to these abstractions, cutting to their core, putting them in the context of a larger story, and intimately connecting them to life's events and circumstances. Fr. Aleksandr followed Saint John Chrysostom's recommendation that, when reading the Gospels, one should imagine oneself in the "concrete situation that served as a background to those sacred events."[91] *Son of Man* heeded that advice. The pictures he painted in his mind are transferred to the text and then to the reader, who finds himself drawn in, seeing before him the scene or the person Fr. Aleksandr depicted. In his descriptions of the natural world, the reader experiences not only nature's outline, but also its colors and smells. Men draws a close connection between Jesus and the earth, as in his portrayal of Nazareth:

> If we were somehow able to visit the Nazareth of those years, we would see about a hundred white homes with flat roofs scattered about the mountain

framed by vineyards and olive groves. From the gently sloping peaks unfolds a picturesque panorama upon which Jesus must have rested His gaze, likely more than once: chains of blue mountains, green valleys, and sown fields. Much has changed since then, but the natural environment has remained almost the same these two thousand years. Travelers, with one voice, maintain that Nazareth and its surroundings are a unique pocket of sacred land; they call it 'the mountain rose,' 'the terrestrial paradise.' The air atop the mountains is pure and clear. After winter rains, Nazarene slopes turn into gardens, covered with variegated flowers of the tenderest hues: lilies, mountain tulips, and anemones. Jesus loved flowers. He said that not even King Solomon's adornments could be compared with them.[92]

A Developing Network

An artist and a member of the Russian intelligentsia, Zoia Afanas'evna Maslenikova became acquainted with Fr. Aleksandr at the end of 1967 while he served in the parish at Tarasovka.[93] Having worked also as a professional editor, she offered her editorial services to him after he showed her the manuscripts on which he was currently working. Until then, he had not used an editor, but, in 1968, he accepted her help, and she remained his editor for the next twenty-two years.[94] Thereafter, each week she traveled to his home in Semkhoz, returning his written work with her editorial comments. "I saw how he worked," she said. Sitting at a wooden table, he had a large number of books "arranged around the table's periphery," and each week he had "replaced them with new ones."[95] The relentless research and the pursuit of knowledge Aleksandr Men had developed as a young student never abated, and it characterized his entire life as a parish priest. "He always had a book in his hand," remarked his son Mikhail, "even when he was caring for us as young children."[96]

When he first began to write *Son of Man*, Fr. Aleksandr had no expectation that it would ever be published, much less reach a wide readership. The several chapters he published in the *Journal of the Moscow Patriarchate* had a very limited distribution and readership. The book, however, despite the politically charged time in which it was completed, came to be widely known because of two major circumstances.

The first means of distributing *Son of Man* came through samizdat, the unofficial self-publishing enterprise that constituted a major source of information for significant groups of people. Originating with the poet Nikolai Glazkov in the late 1940s, who coined the term "samo-sebia-izdat" to signify a "self-published" book of his poems, in the late 1960s, samizdat became an increasingly prominent method of circulating monographs that could not pass the government censor.[97] Samizdat, as literary scholar Ann Komaromi has pointed out, represented an "un-standardized, spontaneously disseminated, unfixed oral culture," which she likens to the post-Gutenberg, "global internet culture of today."[98] While such texts are often depicted as a means of political opposition to the government, this is misleading.[99] Samizdat had a much broader purpose than political dissent. The inclusion of artistic, literary, and religious works ranged far beyond politics. An author typed or made several copies of a manuscript and distributed them to close friends who, in turn, reproduced from six to ten additional copies and passed them on.[100] This process brought together social networks that might otherwise not have existed, organizing these networks around specific interests that ranged over a wide terrain. The dissemination of *Son of Man* in the late 1960s and 1970s forged one of the networks.

Samizdat's growth signified a path different from what one of its creators called the "ideological somnambulism" of Soviet society; it served as part of a social awakening and a desire to reclaim personal judgment, rather than delegate this right to the collective.[101] Samizdat developed alternative means of expression parallel to the official monologue of the party-government.[102] *Son of Man* had wide distribution among those members of the intelligentsia searching for a spiritual alternative to the monolithic nature of Soviet ideology. According to Anatolii Krasnov-Levitin, by 1975, Fr. Aleksandr was "already widely read in samizdat," and had become a "popular figure" among the Moscow intelligentsia.[103]

The second means of distribution involved publication of the manuscript abroad (*tamizdat*, as distinct from samizdat), followed by its reentry into Russia. In Aleksandr Men's case, this course was facilitated by a courageous woman, Anastasia Durova, who worked in the French Embassy in Moscow. The daughter of Russian émigré parents who left with their young child for France during the Russian Revolution, Durova retained her love of her native country, its culture, and Russian Orthodoxy.[104] Offered a position in the French Embassy in Moscow in 1964, she was delighted to accept. She returned to Russia full of curiosity and intent not only on fulfilling her official assignments, but also on reconnecting with Russia's cultural heritage.

Warm-spirited, fluent in the Russian language, and knowledgeable about Russian culture, Durova quickly became a valued embassy employee, who served in Moscow for the next fifteen years. She also had an adventurous spirit. Not content to work all day, then go home to the embassy compound, where she lived with other embassy personnel, Durova, on her own, experienced the city. According to Yves Hamant, then a young student of Slavic languages and cultures, who lived for a brief time in her apartment, Anastasia left the compound each evening, walking past the guard stationed at the entrance, and disappeared into the city's population. "Thanks to her typically Russian appearance," Hamant wrote, "her mastery of the language—her mother tongue—and with the aid of a scarf hastily thrown over her head, she had no trouble losing herself among the crowd, and was thus able to visit her many Russian friends she had gotten to know as times and circumstances permitted."[105] They included a group of young people who had formed around Fr. Aleksandr and with whom she developed close friendships.[106]

In July 1966, these friends introduced Anastasia Durova to Aleksandr Men. In their first meeting, they "talked about the tragic situation of the church." They soon became friends, she inquiring about his parish and his needs, and he, in response to her questions, telling her about his writing, his vision of the church, and the "pressing need for religious books."[107] Over the next several years, Durova became an important secret conduit for bringing religious books into the Soviet Union, supplying Fr. Aleksandr with foreign texts and others in her circle with books published abroad. She also took his manuscript *Son of Man* with her to Belgium, where she had contact with another Russian émigré, Irina Posnova, who had established a small publishing house called "La Vie avec Dieu" (*Zhizn' s Bogom*).[108]

In 1968, La Vie avec Dieu published Fr. Aleksandr's book under the pen name of Andrei Bogoliubov. Through Durova and other intermediaries, the publication came back into Russia and was distributed among people hungry for a fresh and engaging account of the Gospels, a work much different from the mythological perspectives favored by the educational establishment. The Belgian press, operating on a shoestring budget, went on to publish many of Fr. Aleksandr's subsequent books among the more than one hundred titles it printed over the next decade.[109]

The books published by this small printing press in Brussels had a "significant impact on the spiritual awakening of this country," Hamant wrote. Passed from person to person and read by others, such books had an impact far beyond their original issue. *Son of Man* became one of the books that increasingly had a wide circulation, and it would soon be followed by others.[110]

It is difficult to gauge precisely the responses of readers to *Syn chelovecheskii* or the depth of this early awakening. Undoubtedly, some readers responded critically, as did two persons who, having read one of Fr. Aleksandr's articles in the *Journal of the Moscow Patriarchate* in the early 1960s, criticized its "unscientific" approach.[111] Another, writing at about the same time, called the young priest a "falsifier" of history.[112] Without mentioning his name, historian Dmitrii Modestovich Ugrinovich cited one of Fr. Aleksandr's articles as an example of the "irrational, mystical," thinking that occupied the mainstream of Orthodoxy, which Ugrinovich went on to disparage as "inaccessible to human reason" and thus "beyond understanding."[113] In a 1971 letter to Fr. Aleksandr, an Orthodox believer and respected Shakespeare scholar took offense at *Son of Man*'s use of contemporary language, which, she said, revealed Aleksandr Men as a "modernist" and "neophyte" who must have "come to faith not long ago and is a stranger to church tradition."[114]

Other readers, however, responded differently. Fr. Aleksandr did not retain most of the letters he received, but he quoted from two of them in his correspondence with a critic. The first came from a "well-educated woman who for many years had lived outside the church," who wrote, after reading *Son of Man*:

> I drank in page after page, as though I found a second wind. For the doubters, searchers, non-believers—but those weighed down by their disbelief, and these are the majority—Your book offers a great deal. It speaks to the mind and to the soul. The uniqueness of Your account lies in its realistic approach (if such an expression is appropriate) to Christ and His circumstances and surroundings. The reader is neither required to look beneath the surface nor rise into the sky. This is the strength of Your book, because it confirms the reality of Christ. Until now everything has been foggy to me. And it was if you took me by the hand, led, and showed me. From this came a sense of trust in what had happened. And when you came to the main subject, speaking about what is most important and majestic, in the process of reading, a feeling of the reality of what had taken place continued to act upon me, and undermined my earlier certainty about the impossibility and incredulity of these happenings. And what joy entered my soul from this change.[115]

Reading Fr. Aleksandr's book taught her to see differently. The connection to the story he recounted elicited in this woman a sense of wonder that lay buried in her consciousness, awakening in her a response that she had not anticipated.

The second reader, who identified himself as a person from within the church, spoke of how he came to a similar conclusion. "Everything is narration," he wrote, and "procedes slowly, building to the end, containing separate waves of passages, sounding like poems, like sermons, and like prayers."[116] This reader praised Fr. Aleksandr's method of moving "from a simple and clear description of historical facts, through events, to the most difficult mysteries." Such a gradual process "you to go to the heart of the matter," allowing a reader to "overcome many obstacles" that previously had obstructed the view.[117]

The letters of appreciation, Zoia Maslenikova said, greatly exceeded the few negative responses Aleksandr Men received from readers.[118] These positive communications encouraged him to continue his writing and to move further along the path he had set for himself earlier.[119] They underscored the need to connect his writing to his parish work and the importance of awakening the members of his parish to sources that had long been neglected and nearly forgotten, sources that aimed to open up the world, rather than close it off.

In the first decade of his priesthood, Fr. Aleksandr Men's writings in the *Journal of the Moscow Patriarchate* and his *Son of Man* elaborated several themes that, since his youth, had germinated in his mind. His talents as a parish priest were not limited to his service in the three parishes he served from 1958 to 1968, but, through his publications, reached outward, speaking to issues he saw as essential to the Russian Orthodox Church and to his society. In each of the parishes he served, Fr. Aleksandr confronted extremely challenging political and religious conditions, but they did not undermine his creative responses to the needs of his parishioners, large numbers of whom belonged to the Russian intelligentsia.

Reflecting on his writings in the 1960s, particularly on his book *Son of Man*, Aleksandr Men spoke of the widespread ignorance about Christianity prevalent in Soviet society. Unable to read the Bible, the writings of the Church Fathers, and the books written by Russia's brilliant philosophers and theologians of the late nineteenth and early twentieth century, the Russian people lacked access to the sources they needed to gain a clear understanding of Christianity.[120] The perceptions they had of Jesus came largely from antireligious propaganda or from certain literary masterpieces. Among the latter, Mikhail Bulgakov's *Master and Margarita* stood out as a widely popular novel among the intelligentsia, as well as among the general reading public. Yeshua, one of the book's main characters, who represents Jesus, is a weak and solitary figure, incapable of commanding a following.[121] Fr. Aleksandr's *Son of Man* offered a much different picture, depicting a person whose message of freedom and human dignity provided a sharp contrast to the image found in Bulgakov's novel or, more broadly, in Soviet textbooks.

Through his writings in this first decade, Fr. Aleksandr encouraged people to think and to see differently. He fought against the common practice of isolating the mind from other parts of the human being; as a writer, he addressed the mind and the heart. He struggled against the walls of separation that divided people, internally and externally. He challenged the mindset that produced these divisions and forced thinking into ideological categories. He continued to struggle against dogmatic, rigid views and beliefs, both within the church and in his society. That struggle shaped the future development of his service to the church and another significant work he completed later, his *History of Religion: In Search of the Way, the Truth and the Life*.

Vladimir Grigor'evich and Elena Semenovna Men on their wedding day, April 15, 1934. Courtesy Fond imeni Aleksandra Menia, Moscow.

Fr. Aleksandr Men with his wife Nataliia Fedorovna and their children Elena and Mikhail. Courtesy Fond imeni Aleksandra Menia, Moscow.

Fr. Aleksandr's home in Semkhoz, where he lived during most of his priesthood.

The icon wall inside the front of the house in Semkhoz. The Icon of the Transfiguration is at top, in center.

Fr. Aleksandr's writing desk and office in his home in Semkhoz.

Sretenskii church at Novaia Derevnia, where Fr. Aleksandr served from 1970 to 1990.

Fr. Aleksandr at Novaia Derevnia, Easter, 1982. Courtesy Fond imeni Aleksandra Menia, Moscow.

Icon of Saint John the Baptist, painted by Fr. Aleksandr. Courtesy Fond imeni Aleksandra Menia, Moscow.

Gleb Yakunin, 1959. Courtesy Fond imeni Aleksandra Menia, Moscow.

Alexander Solzhenitsyn, Iurii Titov (song writer), and Fr. Aleksandr. Courtesy Fond imeni Aleksandra Menia, Moscow.

Fr. Aleksandr with Nadezhda Mandelstam at Semkhoz. Courtesy Fond imeni Aleksandra Menia, Moscow.

Fr. Aleksandr lecturing in the auditorium of the factory "Krasnaia Presnia," autumn, 1988. Courtesy Fond imeni Aleksandra Menia, Moscow.

The Sunday school in the Sretenskii church at Novaia Derevnia, which Fr. Aleksandr began in 1990. Courtesy Fond imeni Aleksandra Menia, Moscow.

Communion in the Sretenskii church at Novaia Derevnia. Vladimir Arkhipov is attending. Courtesy Fond imeni Aleksandra Menia, Moscow.

Dr. Ekaterina Iur'evna Genieva, the late director-general of the Library of Foreign Literature in Moscow.

Pavel Vol'fovich Men, younger brother of Fr. Aleksandr, in the main office of the Aleksandr Men' fond in Moscow.

Mikhail Aleksandrovich Men, son of Fr. Aleksandr (on left), in the governor's office in Ivanovo, with author.

Location of the place of Fr. Aleksandr's death outside his house in
Semkhoz, September 9, 1990.

The pathway to the train station in Semkhoz, on which Fr. Aleksandr walked on Sunday morning, September 9, 1990.

Commemorative statue of Fr. Aleksandr in the courtyard of the Library of Foreign Literature in Moscow.

8

. . . .

The Transition to Novaia Derevnia

The long period of Leonid Brezhnev's rule, from 1964 to his death in 1982, is commonly described as the "era of stagnation." The term came from Mikhail Gorbachev, shortly after his accession to power in 1985, to distinguish his plan for reform from the slow decline the Soviet Union had experienced during the Brezhnev years. "Stagnation" called up a host of negative associations with the policies of his lethargic predecessor: the rampant cronyism, the swelling size of the bureaucratic system, the widespread corruption, the slowing rates of economic growth, the cynicism, the lack of energy, and the collapse of morality. These were qualities exemplified by Brezhnev himself and his lethargic leadership, which was characterized by his unwillingness to undertake needed economic and social reforms and his growing reliance on the KGB to suppress dissent. Reaching maturity during the Stalin years, Brezhnev (b. 1906) incorporated some of the principal attributes of those times, with their emphasis on great power status, social conformism, and collective responsibility. Among his major initiatives, Brezhnev sought to force educational and economic institutes to adopt mutual policing policies to create what he called "healthy collectives" focused on joint responsibility in order to keep uncooperative people in line. These policies created a stifling intellectual atmosphere.

The "era of stagnation" also described the Russian Orthodox Church and its relations with the state. In 1970, Patriarch Aleksii I died, after having held the position of leadership throughout an extremely turbulent period. In 1971 the *sobor* elected Pimen (Izvekov) to the patriarchal throne, passing over a much younger, reform-minded rival, Metropolitan Nikodim, for the patriarchal position. Perceived as a weak leader, passive, and middle-of-the-road, Pimen possessed attributes that commended him to the Council of Religious Affairs and members of the Church *Sobor*. In the 1970s, Patriarch

Pimen did not press the government to reopen churches it had formerly closed, and a further weakening of the institutional church marked the decade. In the Brezhnev era, the number of open churches fell from about 8,000 in 1965 to fewer than 6,800 in 1982.[1]

This weakening of the institutional church at its center was also seen in governmental policy. A 1975 state law gave ultimate power over the opening and closing of churches to the Council of Religious Affairs, removing authority from local administrators and placing it in this central body. This action transformed the council from an organ connecting the state and church to one having final authority over church matters. Article 52 of the 1977 Constitution reaffirmed the separation of church and state but gave the government the privilege of issuing antireligious propaganda; the article did not extend to the church the privilege of issuing anti-atheistic propaganda. The constitution expressed the right of prelates to perform the rituals and liturgy in church services but confined these activities to church services only, and made it legally impermissible for prelates to extend them beyond the walls of their churches.[2]

The education of the Soviet population, however, represented a signal achievement during Brezhnev's rule. He continued, and even accelerated, a trend that began earlier and ranks among the Soviet government's most important accomplishments. In 1939, only 1.3 percent of the population had completed a higher education, and 11 percent a secondary education; in 1959, these numbers increased to 3.37 percent for higher education and 40 percent for secondary education; in 1979, 10 percent of the population had earned a higher education degree and 70.5 percent a secondary degree. The total numbers of students attending Soviet institutions of higher education show even more rapid growth: in 1940–1941, 800,000 students enrolled in higher education; in 1970–1971, they numbered 4.6 million; and in 1980–1981, they increased to 5.2 million. While many of these students enrolled in technical institutions, growth in the numbers of students in universities also greatly expanded, a trend that significantly changed the social and educational composition of the entire Soviet population.[3]

The general depiction of the Brezhnev years as an "era of stagnation" presents only a partial picture. While several political and religious elements of the picture are certainly representative, they neither convey the full story of that period nor speak to the struggles of individuals—in local parishes, in educational institutions, and in certain groups—who, often courageously, endeavored to act on their ideals. For Fr. Aleksandr Men, the 1970s were an extremely active, even decisive, period in his parish.

From Tarasovka to Novaia Derevnia

As a parish priest, some of the most difficult challenges Fr. Aleksandr faced came from within the Orthodox Church and often even closer to home within his own church administration. A great deal depended on the nature and character of the senior priest under whom he served. The willingness of such priests to give him latitude to strengthen the parish and to reach out to people, both within and outside its immediate boundaries, deeply affected the scope of his work. Whether the senior priest resented a youthful, well-educated, and energetic subordinate or welcomed the advantages he might bring had a great deal to do with the openness of the church at the parish level. As described earlier, the difficult conditions Fr. Aleksandr faced at Akulino changed dramatically at Alabino, despite passage of the repressive parish reform act of 1961. The congenial atmosphere he experienced at Alabino made this one of the most enjoyable and creative periods of his life and explained why his forced resignation from there in 1964 brought him such pain.

Fr. Aleksandr Men's encounters with the church administration in his Tarasovka parish proved entirely different. His relationship with the head priest, Fr. Serafim Golubtsov, whom the church appointed to Tarasovka six months after Fr. Aleksandr's arrival, was contentious from the beginning. Ironically, Fr. Serafim was the brother of Fr. Nikolai Golubtsov, Aleksandr Men's earlier spiritual mentor in Moscow, but the two priests had opposite dispositions. They related to Fr. Aleksandr in diametrically different ways. Unlike his more compassionate and magnanimous brother, Fr. Serafim was mean-spirited and closed-minded, "an inveterate Stalinist," in Zoia Maslenikova's words. "[He was] devoted with his whole soul and body to security, and he possessed an extremely quarrelsome personality, often flying into a rage." By nature, she said, "he possessed the quality of a shark."[4]

At Tarasovka in the late 1960s, Aleksandr Men found his situation extremely difficult to endure. Repeatedly reprimanded by Fr. Serafim, who closely watched him and several times wrote denunciations to the police, he suffered personal attacks from his superior, and the weight of these attempts to undermine his position severely circumscribed his activities and his personal sense of well-being. Men explains that in one of these denunciations Fr. Serafim "wrote that he did not have any complaints with my conduct of the services, and everything there went very well, but that it was the conversations I had with people, the books I read and gave to others to read and so on," to which he objected.[5] Fr. Aleksandr responded to Patriarch Pimen, denying that these allegations lay outside the responsibilities of his priesthood and requesting a transfer to another parish. After receiving a petition from parishioners requesting that Fr. Aleksandr not be transferred and holding a tense meeting in his office with the two priests, Pimen left him in place. "Everyone calmed down" for a while, Fr. Aleksandr Men wrote. But as Men also pointed out, personally, "I was in an oppressive situation, because it was difficult to serve with my superior at the altar; on one occasion, we did not speak with each other. . . . In general, everything was unpleasant. For nearly a whole year, I had to serve under these conditions."[6]

Another, less obvious reason contributed to their conflict. Fr. Serafim had two children, both nearly grown, who became alienated from their father and left the church, believing that it had little to offer. Fr. Aleksandr reached out to them, and in the sensitive, nonthreatening manner that characterized his pastoral approach, formed a close relationship with the two young people. He brought them back into the church, succeeding where their father had failed, but Fr. Aleksandr's success only led to resentment on Fr. Serafim's part, perhaps also to jealousy.[7]

At Tarasovka, journalist Sergei Bychkov observed, two worlds came sharply into conflict. On the one hand, Fr. Aleksandr represented an open approach to Orthodoxy that was characterized by wide-ranging discussion, in which newcomers were warmly welcomed and controversial social and religious issues were given extensive treatment.[8] According to Bychkov, who joined the parish in 1967, "It seemed that nothing could be used to keep Fr. Aleksandr from associating with the parishioners, to keep separate his joy of life from them."[9] Aleksandr Men cultivated personal relationships with people who sought him out. He encouraged an atmosphere of freedom, in which both personal and intellectual matters were openly explored.

On the other hand, there was the closed, restrictive world represented by the head priest. Here, mistrust and suspicion reigned. The tightly constructed performance of ritual and the close observance of rules characterized the religious service; conversations, relationships, and meetings outside these formal observances were discouraged. The contrast manifested here on a personal level forecast a much larger conflict over a closed and open model of the church that would later take place on a national level.

Fr. Grigorii Kryzhanovskii, the senior priest at the nearby Novaia Derevnia parish, suffered from illness, and several times Fr. Aleksandr filled in when he was physically unable to conduct the services. As these illnesses became increasingly severe, Fr. Aleksandr began to go there more frequently, although he did so secretly, without telling Fr. Serafim. Early in 1970, needing the younger priest on a regular basis and dissatisfied with his own assistant, Fr. Grigorii formally requested Fr. Aleksandr's transfer to

Novaia Derevnia. This time, the church administration accepted the request, despite the displeasure of his former superior. Fr. Grigorii made a special trip to Aleksandr Men's home in Semkhoz to "fetch" him and bring him to Novaia Dervenia, a transfer, Fr. Aleksandr wrote, that he "had dreamed would take place."[10]

In February 1970, Fr. Aleksandr began his formal service in the Novaia Derevnia parish, where he remained for the next twenty years, until the end of his life. He was extremely pleased. "It has been a long time since I had experienced such a light-hearted feeling," he wrote to Maslenikova. "It is as if a millstone had fallen from my neck."[11]

At the time of Fr. Aleksandr's transfer, Fr. Grigorii Kryzhanovskii (1890–1977) was seventy-six years old and had spent most of his life abroad, having lived until 1929 in Czechoslovakia before serving in the Orthodox Church in Bulgaria and, from 1950, in Albania. He returned to Russia in 1962, and Fr. Aleksandr met him in the mid-1960s, when both of them annually attended the name-day services for Archbishop Kiprian (Zernov) in Moscow.[12] A photograph of Fr. Grigorii in 1976 shows him with a full white beard, slightly stooped, and frail in appearance.[13] Kindly and good-natured, he exhibited a loving attitude toward his parishioners, although his mental faculties had declined and he sometimes became confused during the services.[14] Fr. Grigorii suffered from multiple sclerosis, which made it difficult for him to stand for long periods at the altar. He needed a younger and more energetic priest whom he could trust, and Fr. Aleksandr fit this description well.

The Novaia Derevnia parish lay a sturdy walking distance from the railway stop at the town of Pushkino, northeast of Moscow. The brightly painted wooden church could hold about two hundred people, primarily consisting of elderly women, when Fr. Aleksandr arrived in 1970. Beside the church stood a wooden building consisting of rooms for the priest and the *starosta* and, beyond them, a small room with a stove, bed, and writing table, which Fr. Aleksandr used as an office and where he spent the night on special church holidays. Here, too, he received visitors and members of the parish, who waited for him to seek personal counsel after the services.

Gradually, Aleksandr Men settled in to his new responsibilities. Fr. Grigorii was not reluctant to delegate most of the church and parish activities to his youthful assistant, and chose to appear only sporadically and for a short period at the altar during the services. In contrast to Fr. Aleksandr's experience of a rigid, tightly controlled environment at his previous parish, at Novaia Derevnia he had wide scope to engage with parishioners, with the senior priest rarely interfering and never making objections. Fr. Aleksandr devoted himself to this work. He created a much livelier atmosphere than had existed earlier, which often incurred the displeasure of some of the elderly local parishioners, who regarded this newcomer of Jewish heritage with suspicion.[15] In time, though, he won most of them over, patiently building relationships that cut across the large differences in age and temperament.

Lost Connections

Everything, however, did not always go well, and there is a note of despondency in Fr. Aleksandr's writings about these early years at Novaia Derevnia. He lost the personal connections to some of his closest friends, people whom he had earlier mentored and who were among his confidants:

> I have stopped traveling about, stopped going to Moscow, and all my con-nections have begun to fade away and break. Many have emigrated—what they call a "big wave" of emigration has started. . . . All these have now receded into the past: the night walks along Beliaev-Bogorodskii and along Leningradskii Prospekt, the apostolic ventures around Moscow, sometimes accompanied by [Sergei] Zheludkov—he remembers it all very well. All this has receded into the past, because I understood that it pro-duced nothing special, except for weariness. God himself sends the people who are needed.[16]

There were several reasons for the loss of connections that contributed to this sense of melancholy. The internal demands of his new parish required a great deal of his attention and consumed a large amount of his time. He had to earn the trust of his new parishioners, a task that required immediate, continual care. But perhaps the chief cause of his despondency related to the actions of the government: in the early 1970s, facing increasing public unrest and resistance, the government placed even greater limitations on the discussion of human rights, religion, and alternative ways of looking at liter-ature, art, and politics. In 1971, the Kremlin created a new policy encourag-ing those most active in the human rights movement to emigrate, and since Russian-Jewish intellectuals were among the movement's leadership, they comprised the group the government had foremost in mind.

Iurii Andropov, head of the KGB, allegedly conceived of this idea of relieving political pressure caused by such groups by allowing them to leave the country without the possibility of return.[17] Between 1972 and 1974, more than 75,000 educated Jews left the Soviet Union, most of them from

Moscow, Leningrad, and Kiev, as well as from the Baltic States and Georgia.[18] They included Mikhail Aksenov-Meerson, a young, talented cleric who had joined Fr. Aleksandr's parish in Alabino more than a decade before and remained extremely close to him. Fr. Aleksandr had tried to dissuade Aksenov-Meerson from emigrating, but was unsuccessful, given some personal difficulties that the younger cleric faced.[19] In 1972, the gifted civil rights activist Iurii Iakovlevich Glazov also departed, ultimately finding teaching positions in universities in the United States and Canada.[20]

The arm of the police reached close to Fr. Aleksandr through the people with whom he had close relationships. In 1973, the KGB interrogated Evgenii Viktorovich Barabanov (b. 1944) about his role in helping transmit Alexander Solzhenitsyn's manuscripts to the West. An art historian and an active member of Fr. Aleksandr's parish since the early 1960s, Barabanov readily admitted to these allegations. He had played a major role in smuggling these materials and asserted that such actions were justifiable and did not contradict state laws.[21] A year later, in February 1974, the Kremlin formally expelled Alexander Solzhenitsyn from the Soviet Union, charging him with treason. In exposing in detail the horrors of the Soviet labor camps, his manuscript, *The Gulag Archipelago*, overnight created an international sensation. Smuggled back into the Soviet Union, his work further stimulated human rights activists in that country. Both Barabanov's interrogation and Solzhenitsyn's arrest and expulsion led Fr. Aleksandr to believe that he, too, soon would face criminal charges.[22]

Despite these threats, other circumstances soon extended the scope of his activities and his reputation among the intelligentsia. In late 1975, a second wave of young members of the intelligentsia began to frequent his parish at Novaia Derevnia. Coming mainly from Moscow but also from several nearby towns, such people were seeking alternative ways of viewing the world, and they saw Fr. Aleksandr Men as a potential source of knowledge, instead of the official church hierarchs whose political connections to the Soviet government they mistrusted.

Why did this second wave occur just as the Soviet government was making serious efforts to counteract it? Specifically, what inner dynamics fostered among Russia's "best and brightest" the search for alternative means of understanding life and of appreciating human connections? Why did so many of them come here to this small parish, somewhat off the beaten path?

First, the process that began a decade earlier, when Fr. Aleksandr served the Alabino parish, expanded at Tarasovka and continued to develop at Novaia Derevnia. Word of Fr. Aleksandr's openness, ability to communicate, and knowledge of many subjects spread among young, searching members

of the intelligentsia. Aleksandr Borisov, a former classmate and close friend
of Fr. Aleksandr's brother, Pavel, who was with Fr. Aleksandr at Alabino and
remained with him at Novaia Derevnia, witnessed firsthand the gradual,
then rapid, development of interest in religion. Among older generations,
he observed, such interest usually began with excursions in the 1960s and
'70s to the medieval cities of Vladimir and Suzdal'. There, viewing their
ancient treasures, the magnificent churches and resplendent icons, visitors
came away with many questions about the beginnings and evolution of
Orthodox Christianity in Russia, as well as its role in the country's cultural heritage. This interest was sparked by the artistic creations they saw
in Vladimir and Suzdal'.[23] But among Russian youth, their pursuits traveled
along a different trajectory.

The mid- and late 1960s witnessed a flowering of interest in science fiction, mystical religions, and the occult, as occurred in Western Europe and
the United States. Learning of the existence of a priest whose openness to
such issues distinguished him from most others, young members of the
intelligentsia went to see him. They raised questions about the role of science
in society, engaged in speculation about the future, and explored the power
of imagination in their lives. These young people had read books on science
fiction.[24] But there, at Tarasovka and later at Novaia Derevnia, they were
surprised to find a priest whose reading in the same subjects far surpassed
their own, a person able to discuss current popular writers in depth. Such
young members commonly viewed Jesus as an extraterrestial being and the
appearance on earth of this Man-God as a supernatural event. From their
own readings of the limited materials available to them, they concocted a
view of Christ that belonged to the cosmos.[25]

"Speaking about the unique spiritual nature of human beings, Fr. Aleksandr
conducted conversations [with them] in clear, understandable language," Fr.
Borisov recalled from these meetings. "He always underscored that human
beings exhibit the reality of another plane of existence," and he used the
model employed by the English writer G. K. Chesterton of never attempting
to build a large, complete philosophical system, but rather tried "to hit his
target indirectly," drawing images from biology, poetry, and art to make his
points obliquely and to draw people into further exploration.[26]

This second wave of interest among the intelligentsia resulted from an
evolving process of rediscovering cultural and religious connections lost
from view since the early 1920s. To some, the involvement in religious activities represented an act of rebellion, a protest against state policies and the foundations on which the Soviet state was built, and a rejection of the established
political order.[27] But the intellectual ferment also had wider implications as a

quest for new ways of seeing the world and understanding cultural relationships. For many, this quest had appeal. It manifested itself in multiple forms,
among them in the classroom of the philologist Sergei Averintsev at the University of Moscow. In the early 1970s, Averintsev lectured on the history
of ancient and Byzantine culture in an auditorium designed to hold two
hundred students, but which, for his class, expanded to nearly four hundred,
with people sitting "in the windows, on the floor, and in the entrance way,
crowded together shoulder to shoulder, listening to this still young professor, dressed in a sweater and jacket, of slim build, speaking in an almost
monotonous voice . . . [who] cast a spell over the listeners" as he explored
the spiritual relationships between "two worlds, the ancient Greek and
Biblical-Christian."[28] According to this testimony, in his lectures Averintsev
moved across cultures and from the past to the present, transitioning from
Saint Francis of Assisi to Carl Jung and Oswald Spengler, never speaking
in abstractions and bringing to life materials usually found on museum
shelves. His teaching and scholarship made intercultural connections and
opened the door to spiritual subjects that had long remained closed.[29]

Years later, reflecting on those times, Averintsev described the young
intelligentsia's attraction to Fr. Aleksandr in much the same way Averintsev's
students had portrayed him: as a unique voice speaking during a time when
government propaganda built a powerful ideological wall around him, a
voice able to move across different fields of knowledge and "converse with
people of art and literature on themes close to their heart" with the capacity
to relate controversial issues in the past to the present. Fr. Aleksandr had, as
Averintsev characterized him, a "missionary voice" that incorporated secular and religious culture in addressing what the philologist called the "wild
tribe of the intelligentsia," and who "wrote and spoke in the language of
present times, in order that they might hear him."[30]

Third, in the mid-1970s, Soviet science and its ideological foundations
reached a crossroads. Lenin's emphasis on the materialist underpinnings of
human existence had shaped education in the Soviet Union, and he had
criticized other philosophical approaches, which, he maintained, "must
always be met with skepticism."[31] Since the late 1920s and the enormous
challenges of building an industrial economy, Soviet education had focused
on applied science and engineering. The government divided the world
into two groups of scientists: Marxist and bourgeois, and enhancing the
former, it had turned its back on "bourgeois" science, proclaiming it to be
dominated by class interests and weakened by metaphysical speculation.[32]
This ideological division cost Soviet science dearly in some fields, especially
genetics, and constrained the creativity of many top scientists. By dividing

the world into two camps and isolating Soviet scientists from their Western counterparts, the government had cut them off from the wide dissemination of new discoveries in genetics, quantum mechanics, and mathematics. The Soviet Union aspired to become a dominant world economic power, but by the 1970s it had become increasingly clear, at least to some, that it could not reach its ultimate goals by continuing to reject advances in thinking and revolutionary discoveries taking place outside its boundaries.

These trends in science raised questions about whether scientific discoveries could be confined to class interests and labor productivity, as traditional Marxist theory had claimed. Did creative thinking take place outside these class structures, transcend them, and have universal significance and application? As historian Dimitry Pospielovsky has pointed out, questions suggesting that intellectual thought may have preceded and may even lay outside material processes began to appear in the late 1960s and early 1970s.[33] An editorial in the journal *Voprosy filosofii*, in 1969, maintained that human consciousness came before the development of labor, rather than following it.[34] Such thoughts did not dominate Soviet philosophical writing, which remained strongly wedded to traditional Marxist theory, but they cast doubt on the division of the world into two opposing camps. They invited a whole host of other questions about the role of intuition and the imagination in fostering new discoveries.

It was within this wider context that Fr. Aleksandr reached out to the second wave of the Russian intelligentsia, and they to him. He understood their search, and he could speak to their desires and their dissatisfaction with the confined intellectual space constructed by the Soviet state. His love of poetry and other literary forms only enhanced his attraction, and made him even more relevant and appealing.

Within the broad framework of the Russian Orthodox Church in the 1970s and '80s, among its priests and laypersons, not everyone appreciated Fr. Aleksandr. Critics thought he did not operate inside the lines of Orthodoxy's main traditions. The opposition included a group of priests at the Orthodox theological center at Zagorsk, who considered him too liberal in his interpretations of the Gospels and too flexible in his views of other religious denominations. These critics labeled him a "rationalist," a parish priest overly enamored with the use of the mind and with human reason, relegating faith and church tradition to the background. They resented his foreign contacts and his broad knowledge of Western theologians and philosophers, which they viewed as trendy, and as contaminating the essential teachings of Orthodoxy's rich, timeless heritage. Primarily self-taught, a priest who had received his formal training through correspondence courses, Men had not advanced through the rigorous theological academies. His critics did not fail to point out what they viewed as his academic deficiencies.

Most of all, they resented his work with the Russian intelligentsia and the attraction of educated young men and women, large numbers of whom were Jewish, to his small parish. He aroused the ire of some people within the church because of his Jewish heritage, who "accused him of turning the Orthodox Church into some sort of Jewish church, a 'synagogue from within.'"[35] Still others disliked his approach, which threatened the established religious order, and his disparagement of the church hierarchy as too enamored with ritual and too satisfied with the status quo. Opposing what he called the "closed form of Christianity," he had little regard for priests who idealized the past, the "chauvinists and obscurantists," who stood in sharp contrast to what he believed to be the essence of Christianity.[36] The Orthodox Church had clerics who admired Fr. Aleksandr's work and greatly appreciated his emphasis on love and freedom, but they "did not define the spiritual and psychological climate inside the church."[37]

"I think the main thing he resurrected is his understanding of Christianity as a family, which was firmly understood in the Christianity of early centuries," said Fr. Georgii Chistiakov. "I think that this is the centerpiece of his thinking."[38] But others held a much different view of Men. Sergei Lezov, who claimed to have read Fr. Aleksandr's *Son of Man* while a student at Moscow State University in the late 1960s, maintained that, as a parish priest, Fr. Aleksandr "fostered an illusion."[39] Those attracted to his parish at Novaia Derevnia dreamed of a "politically free Russia," and were drawn to Fr. Aleksandr principally to pursue this dream.[40] Men created at Novaia Derevnia what Lezov called "an alternative reality" to the Soviet state, a "liberal sub-culture inside the church," which only marginally related to how the church traditionally defined itself.[41] These criticisms of Fr. Aleksandr's deviation from Orthodoxy were often repeated among his opposition. They speak to the developing tensions within Orthodox circles in an ongoing debate about the church's identity and purpose.

"My Father Was Not Afraid"

Just as the previous decade had been, these early years at Novaia Derevnia were both difficult and exhilarating. The increasing numbers of talented people searching for alternative ways of looking at life and attempting to satisfy the emptiness they felt in their own personal circumstances made these years a time of extraordinary opportunity for Fr. Aleksandr as a parish priest. He met large numbers of new arrivals, many of whom came seeking him out, wanting to speak with him personally, and standing in a long line of people after the services asking for his counsel.[42] Not all new arrivals, however, were satisfied by these encounters. Many of them came looking for immediate answers to the questions they had; they were impatient with doubt and unwilling to live with ambiguity. Such individuals did not remain for long and left disappointed, occasionally even angry.[43] In his approach to faith, Fr. Aleksandr was neither forceful nor dogmatic; one question led to another, often to still another, and he encouraged exploration, which some individuals disdained.

Fr. Aleksandr's personal circumstances also greatly changed. The supportive groups of young, ambitious priests who, at the beginning of their careers, had formed around him, by now had dissipated. In 1976, Fr. Gleb Yakunin became a leading voice in the human rights movement and, in 1979, suffered arrest and, later, imprisonment. Dispirited by his forced removal from his former parish, Fr. Nikolai Eshliman no longer showed interest in pursuing reform. By the mid-1970s, the church had transferred Fr. Dmitrii Dudko to a remote province and he, too, soon suffered imprisonment. Other former members of Fr. Aleksandr's circle, threatened by similar reprisals from the church administration, went their separate ways. He had little support from his senior priest. The tasks he faced in pursuing the mission he had earlier set for himself, by necessity, had to be accomplished in a sea of opposition.

During these years the members of Fr. Aleksandr's family also faced challenging social circumstances. As the wife of a cleric whose vocation large segments of the population scorned, Nataliia Fedorovna felt these pressures acutely. It is likely, said his brother, that Fr. Aleksandr confided in her the conflicts he experienced as well as the ideas he had for strengthening his work in the parish.[44] But he also tried to shield her from the political dangers that inevitably resulted from being the spouse of a priest. The wives of priests in Russia, as elsewhere, often played active roles in the operation of the parish and in relationships with certain members. Largely for her protection, Fr. Aleksandr deliberately kept Nataliia Fedorovna from fulfilling such a role.[45] He kept her apart, particularly when he expanded his operations beyond the traditional boundaries. Nataliia Fedorovna attended services in the church and took communion, but she limited her participation to these formal settings; members of Fr. Aleksandr's parish hardly knew her. She occasionally showed up in services at other churches.[46]

Nataliia Fedorovna was chiefly responsible for maintaining the household and raising the children. Aided also by her mother and father, who, by the late 1970s, had retired, she engaged in remodeling parts of the house in Semkhoz as well as working in the garden, a task her own mother especially loved.[47] Nataliia Fedorovna also had a profession, working as an accountant in an educational institute attached to the forestry industry, in the nearby town of Pushkino. She used her maiden name, and for many years her colleagues did not know of her priestly connection. By keeping this fact a secret, she thereby avoided harassment from them, and it was only a decade later, in the mid-1980s, that her work colleagues learned of her marriage to Fr. Aleksandr, a revelation that resulted, for her, in some painful experiences.[48]

When Fr. Aleksandr moved to the parish of Novaia Derevnia, his son, Mikhail Aleksandrovich, was only ten years old. The 1970s thus represented his adolescent years, which he vividly remembers, including his father's life at home.[49] He warmly recalled Fr. Aleksandr's relationship with his children. Although he did not spend a lot of time at home, "he always found time for me and my sister; he scheduled time to be with us." Always busy and in demand, "he taught me when I was still a child that time is like a racehorse that runs ahead, and a watch is like a bridle that you must control."[50] Mikhail Aleksandrovich spoke highly of his father's care for his children, a concern that burns brightly in his memory.

Growing up in the home of a priest, however, had its own set of challenges, which created a sharp disparity between the two worlds Mikhail Aleksandrovich encountered. His life at home and his life at school offered diametrically opposite ways of seeing and interpreting nearly everything. "It was very difficult both for my sister and me to study at school," he remembered, "because there they taught one interpretation, and in our family we heard another." Mikhail Aleksandrovich grimaced as he spoke of those years.

When asked how he negotiated the abyss between his home and his school and how he reconciled both worlds, Mikhail Aleksandrovich credited several of his teachers. "They, as well as my school friends, understood my situation; they allowed me to explain my own views, which would have been impossible in some other places. We lived in the country, in a little township, and life there was softer, calmer, and with less pressure than we would have had to endure in a large city."[51] In addition, Mikhail Aleksandrovich praised his father. He was never forceful and never dogmatic in sharing his point of view. "When we asked him any question, he always recommended that we read this or that journal or book. He definitely wanted us to come to the same conclusion as he, but he wanted us to discover the answers for ourselves."[52] Fr. Aleksandr's son expressed admiration for his father's method of teaching, an approach he wished could be adopted more widely in Russia as a path to a less rigid and more creative means of discovery. His father, he said, had little fear of being open and truthful with him and his sister:

> When I reached sixteen years of age, my father talked to me about the situation in the country. He was unafraid that I would say anything to anyone about our conversations. He placed himself at risk for doing so, because a young man of fifteen or sixteen years old can use this information in a careless way. . . . But my father was not afraid, because he understood that a normal, open relationship between us was impossible without the truth.[53]

Mikhail Aleksandrovich discussed his father's attempts to find new, fresh ways of speaking to people who remained closed to the Gospels. His father had a great interest in technology as a means of presenting ideas in different forms than they had heretofore been conveyed. During a time when many other priests looked askance at new, unaccustomed approaches, Fr. Aleksandr began to experiment with the use of media. "My father had three aspects to his preaching that he used to reach out to people: his sermons, his writings, and a third component, which he developed in the mid-1970s. He learned to reproduce slides of certain carefully selected biblical scenes, slides sent to him by someone in Europe." At that time in the parish, video recordings were nonexistent. Fr. Aleksandr wanted his own words, as well as music, to accompany the slides, and his son, then a student in the school of music, learned how to make the recordings. "From the age of fourteen or fifteen," said Mikhail Aleksandrovich, "I became his helper in this enterprise, although I well understood that it must have been a difficult decision to involve me, because some people went to prison for these movies."[54]

The equipment they used was primitive by current standards: two tape recorders and a vinyl record player. Son and father locked the door to the son's room at home, and they worked together on the production, a shared activity that, Mikhail Aleksandrovich confessed, he found deeply enjoyable. His father also recognized that he courted danger in undertaking such a process; the involvement of his teenage son as his accomplice "could well have resulted in a serious accusation," a fear Fr. Aleksandr disregarded. Working collaboratively, the two of them brought words, pictures, and music together. Mikhail Aleksandrovich usually selected the music, always the instrumental parts of songs and popular songs, but also classical music, including Nikolai Rimsky-Korsakov, and "they served as background for our slides." "We used a tea glass and a spoon to coordinate his words with the music and pictures," Mikhail Aleksandrovich said, with his father tapping the tea glass with the spoon when he wanted the next picture.[55]

A primitive, but powerful combination of visual images and sounds, Fr. Aleksandr passed these productions—a box of slides with a cassette—from person to person, and they were widely distributed. On a different level, such productions functioned in a similar way to samizdat publications. They offered a means of communication outside official channels. Lively, engaging, and multidimensional, they also served as part of a social awakening that characterized the Russian intelligentsia in the mid- to late 1970s. "I know many people," Mikhail Aleksandrovich said, "who came to hold a different understanding of Christianity from watching these films."[56]

Like his samizdat publications, Aleksandr Men's visual productions extended and deepened the network of individuals he developed after his move to Novaia Derevnia. It was here, too, that he published his six-volume work on the history of religion, which placed Christianity in a world context. It also addressed a fundamental issue: whether religious belief represent a desire to escape the hard, concrete realities of this world, or represent something else entirely, a paradoxical way of seeing, which simultaneously venerated reason as well as mystery.

9

. . . .

Fr. Aleksandr and the History of Religion

During his student years in Irkutsk, Aleksandr Men began work on a comprehensive study of world religions. In this large, ambitious project, he explored the question of the relationship between Christianity and other great religious traditions that had developed some of the highest forms of human wisdom. As a young priest in the 1960s, during the challenging years of his early priesthood, he continued his research and writing on this issue. By the end of the decade, he had completed the initial drafts of the first four volumes of the anticipated six-volume *History of Religion: In Search of the Way, the Truth, and the Life (Istoriia religii: V poiskakh puti, istiny i zhizni).*[1] At the time he began the study, wrote Sergei Sergeevich Averintsev, the distinguished Russian philologist, Fr. Aleksandr "set out on his work alone," researching a subject by himself, a solitary figure exploring a topic in depth, which few others in his society had managed to complete.[2]

Fr. Aleksandr continued to revise and update each volume for many years, particularly during his time at Novaia Derevnia. Under the pseudonym Emmanuil Svetlov, he published the first volume, *Sources of Religion (Istoki religii)*, with the Brussels publisher La Vie avec Dieu in 1970, volumes two through five with the same publisher in 1971–1972, and the last, volume six, in 1982.[3] Why did he feel compelled to write this multivolume work, which required such extensive research over many years? Why did he place this study near the top of his life's goals and view it as essential to his service as a priest? What does his work on this project tell us about Aleksandr Men as a person, his interests and commitments, and, above all, his response to the oft-repeated contention that religion represented an illusion that had to be rejected in order for human beings to realize their full potential?[4]

History of Religion

In writing his *History of Religion*, Fr. Aleksandr entered a debate begun more than a century earlier in European intellectual history. Reviewing Fr. Aleksandr's works shortly after the priest's death, Fr. Mikhail Aksenov-Meerson placed Men's *History* within a long-standing controversy. The debate centered on the contributions religion had made to world civilization, both positively and negatively.[5]

According to Aksenov-Meerson, the German philosopher G. W. F. Hegel (1770–1831) formulated the parameters within which the discussion took place.[6] In two influential essays, the first in 1795, titled "The Positivity of the Christian Religion," and the second, probably completed in 1799, titled "In the Spirit of Christianity and Its Fate," Hegel examined the similarities and differences in the major world religions and found in them a common theme: that the first characteristic of God is his power. In all these religions, God is the almighty, the infinite, and the creator, who brought the world out of nothing into being.[7] In Christianity, Hegel maintained, Jesus located God within human beings; he taught them they had the capacity to "kindle higher hopes."[8] According to Hegel,

> The sole task, a hard one indeed, was to give them a sense of their selfhood, to make them believe that they, like the carpenter's son, despite the miserable existence they actually led, were capable of becoming members of the kingdom of God; freedom from the yoke of the law was the negative element in this belief. Hence what Jesus attacked above everything else was the dead mechanism of their religious life.[9]

But Christianity as it developed following his death misrepresented Jesus's teachings. Jesus renounced trivialities, but his successors "soon fashioned rules and moral commands, and free emulation of their teacher soon passed over into slavish service of their Lord."[10] As it became institutionalized, Christianity overlooked the most dynamic features of Christ's teaching, turning it into a "religion for slaves" (of dependency) and reducing human beings to weak creatures who possessed a limited capacity to reach for the stars.[11] The church had separated the "being of God and the being of man." In Hegel's words,

> How were *they* [human beings] to recognize divinity in a man, poor things that they were, possessing only a consciousness of their misery,

of the depth of their servitude, of their opposition to the divine, of an impassable gulf between the being of God and the being of man? Spirit alone recognizes spirit.[12]

What, then, Hegel asked, had allowed Christianity to gain prominence over other religions? The philosopher saw Christianity's main strengths as its capacity to incorporate basic beliefs taken from other religious traditions and to find a resolution to their most glaring contradictions. Christianity stood side by side with these different religious traditions, "absorbing within itself all their postulates" about the human condition, which the teachings of Jesus Christ had originally elevated over them.[13]

Hegel's writings on these matters, Aksenov-Meerson maintained, contained several important shortcomings. Preeminent among them was the failure to show convincingly how Christianity represented a synthesis of other religious traditions. This weakness opened him up to strong criticism by those who came afterward, whose efforts to fill the gaps he left characterized a major part of European intellectual history in the years following Hegel's death in 1831. How Christianity related to other religious traditions and the features that gave it prominence continued to be a subject of heated discussion.[14]

Late in the nineteenth century, the Russian philosopher Vladimir Sergeevich Solov'ev attempted to speak to the same issues Hegel had addressed. "On a philosophical level," Aksenov-Meerson wrote, "Solov'ev showed how the existence of all religions, each of which he perceived as revealing a part of the truth, found its fulfillment and completion in Christianity, which expressed a synthesis of the full truth."[15] Solov'ev focused on the question of Christianity's uniqueness, and he sought to elucidate its defining qualities in many of his essays. He aimed to set Christianity in the framework of other great world religions and wanted to write a large, comprehensive study of the relationships between all of them that would ultimately show Christianity's unique qualities and the reasons why it had achieved such prominence. Solov'ev, however, never brought such a study to completion, although he had set this task as an ultimate goal.

At the beginning of the twentieth century, other Russian historians and philosophers attempted to write a similar, comprehensive history without success.[16] Fr. Aleksandr aspired to fill that gap. He well understood the difficulties he faced in achieving a goal his predecessors had not succeeded in finishing. As if to give himself guidance, he placed a large, framed portrait of Vladimir Solov'ev on the wall to the immediate left of the writing table in his study, and he dedicated his *History of Religion* to him. He called the Russian philosopher his chief inspiration, the person who had taken this subject and "opened it up to wide investigation."[17]

What did Fr. Aleksandr mean by "opening up" the history of religion "to wide investigation?" Other than pursuing the task his predecessor had wished to complete, but had not, what was Aleksandr Men's purpose in writing such a history, and defining it as one of the chief goals of his life? In part, he felt engaged by this long-standing, controversial issue in European thought. But, in addition, as he stated in the introduction to volume one, "The goal of [my] work is the exploration of ancient religions, essential because, without this, it is impossible either to gain an understanding of world history, in general, or of Christianity, in particular."[18] The religious believer, whether a member of Fr. Aleksandr's parish or not, could not understand the unique vision Christianity offered unless he or she saw it in the wider context, as the culmination of human striving to approach "the way, the truth, and the life." This quest, as the history of such striving showed, represented a never-ending process, an ongoing struggle in which the divine and the earthly are united. The great religions served as the preceding chapters to the New Testament and the life of Jesus, preparing the soil and raising the essential life-giving questions to which the New Testament responds:

> In the same way that white absorbs all the colors of the spectrum, so the Gospel encompasses the faith of the prophets, the thirst for salvation in Buddhism, the dynamism of Zarathustra, and the humanity of Confucius. It consecrates the best in the ethics of the philosophers of Antiquity and the mysticism of the sages of India. In doing this, Christianity is not a new doctrine, but rather the *announcement of a real fact*, an event accomplished on two planes, the terrestrial and the celestial. Limited by place and time, it transcends temporal boundaries. All roads lead to it. By its light the past, present, and future are evaluated and judged. Every movement towards the light of communication with God, even if accomplished often and unconsciously, is a movement towards Christ.[19]

In his *History of Religion*, Fr. Aleksandr endeavored to trace this "movement towards the light of communication with God." The five volumes preceding the culminating sixth represent a closely researched, well-written examination of the human story, the quest for meaning, the diverse forms in which the great religious traditions viewed the world, and the men and women who participated in this drama, their hopes and dreams (or the ideals they expressed) on their long historical journey.

In the process, Aleksandr Men reveals himself to be in many ways a product of his times and circumstances. He responds to the view, deeply embedded in Soviet education and culture, that religion represents an illusion, a fantasy divorced from actual reality. In other ways, however, his study extends beyond his own times and concerns issues that go far beyond those circumstances. The *History of Religion* is the story of world religions leading up to the coming of Jesus Christ, the God-manhood, in the language of the philosopher Vladimir Solov'ev. In telling the story, Aleksandr Men covers a multiplicity of subjects, all of them relating to this central theme.

Those diverse subjects are outlined in the present chapter, but then the focus returns mainly to the first volume and to issues that concerned Men throughout his priesthood; that is, the problem of seeing the world as a whole, of seeking the connections between its disparate parts. Several primary intellectual influences on Aleksandr Men's writing are examined in the chapter before his perspectives on the relationship between reason and faith, science and religion, and whether Christianity has enhanced or limited the progression of humankind are addressed.

History of Religion: An Overview

The *History of Religion* begins with an introductory volume that examines the sources of religious belief. Fr. Aleksandr took a close look at the "essence and origins of religion" and the assumptions underlying religious thinking.[20] He established the framework for the volumes to follow by carefully defining his terms and exploring diverse forms of interpreting the universe. These topics led him to a discussion of the theory of evolution, in which he demonstrated his belief in human and biological progress. In this process, he examined a large number of topics, among them religion and social ideals, human consciousness of the world, matter and materialism, and the question of evil. His bibliographic citations are impressive, evidence of extensive reading in Russian and Western sources, as well as in ancient manuscripts and archaeology.

Aleksandr Men compared two major, opposing world perspectives, both of them emerging at the dawn of human history and continuing to play out, even within Christianity: "On one side, a creative, always searching movement," which revealed itself in a "dynamic spirituality" and a "reverence for the Almighty." On the other side, a spiritual tendency that had its foundation in static, repressive attitudes toward the world, perspectives that flatten out everything and seek comfort in static ways of thinking. In Fr.

Aleksandr's mind, the latter approach represented a perversion of the quest for truth.[21] He threaded the conflict between these two opposing viewpoints throughout the succeeding volumes of his study.

In the second volume, *Magic and Monotheism: The Religious Path of Humanity up to the Epoch of the Great Teachers* (*Magizm i Edinobozhie: Religioznyi put' chelovechestva do epokhi velikikh Uchitelei*), Fr. Aleksandr distinguished between magic and faith, and he painted a vast panorama of the historic struggle between these two entities. Magic, as he used this term, denoted the desire "to be like God"; it was the aspiration to "acquire the power of God" and to remake the world to fit one's own image. A magical worldview dominated the long pagan prehistory of humanity: there was a lengthy period in which shamans and witch doctors held sway over local populations, casting magical spells and claiming charismatic powers. The era of what Fr. Aleksandr called "religious magism" introduced a rigid attachment to rituals and sacrifices, which served as a means to appease the gods. These practices expressed humanity's relationship to the gods and the desire to manipulate them, thereby controlling their actions.[22] Such control could be accomplished, Aleksandr Men wrote, if one could "find the key, the word, or the activity." Then "everything would be in the hands of human beings."[23]

Magism provided stability in a world characterized by constant danger and unpredictability. Fr. Aleksandr found that similar beliefs expressed themselves universally in primitive societies, despite the large geographical separation of different cultures that had little interaction with each other. His second volume moved from India to Egypt, Greece, Sumeria, and Mesopotamia, extending throughout the history of the ancient world. He argued that magism suppressed creativity since its commitment to ritual had a negative influence on the spiritual development of human beings.

Among Aleksandr Men's strongest attributes in writing these volumes was his ability to connect the past to the present, even the distant past to contemporary practices and patterns of thought. He related the aspiration "to be like God" to the Tree of Knowledge in Genesis and the fall of man. The fall marked the beginning of a "spiritual sickness" that extended all through history, a sickness that had given birth to patrimonial social structures, rule by force, and, most recently, to the absorption of the individual into "the masses" and control by a dominating authority.[24] Reading this volume, Andrei Eremin, the Russian psychotherapist and Fr. Aleksandr's associate, pointed out that "we should not forget that the book was written at the very epicenter of a contemporary magical, collective civilization . . . which revealed itself to the whole world as a leading example of spiritual, cultural, and economic stagnation."[25]

"Magic expects only gifts from Heaven," Fr. Aleksandr wrote. "It wishes to dominate Nature, including its invisible powers; it governs society through force."[26] The magical approach might be seen in the collective thoughts and actions over which an authoritarian leader, a "Grand Inquisitor," rules. In such a state of being, a person became dissolved into the whole, which was much easier to control than the individual acting alone. The individual gave up his own quest, finding comfort in what the leader, whom Fr. Aleksandr called the "true magician," prescribed.[27] The religious search was thus subsumed into a powerful, dominant collective, although Fr. Aleksandr argued that this quest of the individual could never be fully extinguished. It would find a way of expressing itself, sometimes in unanticipated forms.

In volumes three and four, Aleksandr Men focused on the great prophetic leaders who brought about a "spiritual and philosophical revolution" in the first millennium BCE.[28] The third volume, *At the Gates of Silence* (*U vrat molchaniia*), moved from Israel to Indian and Chinese religion and philosophy and the emergence in both countries of great spiritual leaders who struggled against the predominant pagan views of the world. Fr. Aleksandr devoted most of the volume to Buddhism and Confucianism, discussing the personal characteristics of their founders, the appeals of their teachings, and their influences on civilization. In writing about these two great spiritual traditions, he provided an extremely positive picture of the Buddha, especially his "humanity, patience, and love of the world."[29] The Buddha belongs, Fr. Aleksandr wrote, "in the family of the greatest Teachers of the pre-Christian era. Many of his teachings will survive forever as lucid expressions of human wisdom."[30] They speak of higher life, a path to eternity, and a deep-rooted respect, even reverence, for the natural world, its beauty, and its "intimate connection to humanity."[31] But Fr. Aleksandr also distinguished Christianity from both Buddhism and Confucianism, and he placed its emergence alongside these other great traditions. All of them represented different attempts to find purpose in human existence, although only Christianity represented a religion of incarnation.

The fourth volume, *Dionysos, Logos, and Destiny: Greek Religion and Philosophy from the Epoch of Colonization to Alexander* (*Dionis, Logos, Sud'ba: Grecheskaia religiia i filosofiia ot epokhi kolonizatsii do Aleksandra*), focused on the Hellenistic era, particularly the brilliant philosophers whose ideas had such a significant influence on Western Civilization and on Christianity. "The Fathers of the Church, in the majority, were the sons of the Greco-Roman world," Fr. Aleksandr stated at the beginning of the volume. He then proceeded to elaborate on their connections.[32] The story he developed takes the reader through Plato, the Stoics, the Greek mystics, Heraclitus, Aristotle, and various other philosophers and schools of thought and their social and spiritual ideals. He traced the close cultural contacts with their Near Eastern contemporaries and the cross-fertilization of their ideals.

Aleksandr Men's portrait of the Greek world, for the most part, was positive. He admired its achievements in science, philosophy, and political theory, and he gave them salutary treatment.[33] But the legacy of ancient Greek civilization was not wholly favorable: he recognized the negative experiences—the abuses of power, persecutions, and despotic rulers that also characterized Greek civilization.[34] These shortcomings, and many others, came under withering examination by Socrates, whom Fr. Aleksandr venerated and whose courage and "indefatigable quest for truth" made him one of his heroes. Socrates remained, to the end, "committed to a celestial freedom," which Fr. Aleksandr described as the "source of his courage and peaceful joy, which was so striking to his students."[35] "It is not accidental," he wrote, "that the Fathers of the Church considered Socrates among the 'Christians before Christ.'"[36]

The fifth volume in the series, titled *The Messengers of the Kingdom of God: Biblical Prophets from Amos to the Restoration (8th to 4th century BCE)*, (*Vestniki tsarstva Bozhiia: Bibleiskie proroki ot Amosa do Restavratsiia [VIII-IV vv. do n.e.]*), was written in a different style than the preceding works. In place of the analytical presentations of the earlier books, Aleksandr Men moved to a more dramatic approach that forms a compelling narrative depicting the movements of people, the construction and destruction of cities, and the clashes of warriors, interwoven with personal portraits of political leaders, philosophers, mystics, and, above all, preacher-prophets.[37] He described the birth of a new religious teaching that emerged with the children of Israel. The prophets of this new teaching—Amos, Jeremiah, Ezekiel, Isaiah, and Samuel—believed they lived in "the presence of the Divine," a universal First Cause. The absolute, "Yahweh, was for them a flaming abyss, a blinding sun, shining far above comprehension and attainability."[38]

Following a divine call, the ancient prophets struggled against tyranny and injustice and "the cult of power and nationalistic arrogance, god-building and hypocrisy"—these mass enemies that "oppress the human being in our times not less than in the era of Amos and Isaiah."[39] Responding to the call of God, Aleksandr Men observed, each prophet never became simply a follower, a mere "automaton," but always, in the end, a "free participant." Here, Fr. Aleksandr revealed his view of history as something very different from succumbing to fate or following deterministic patterns, but rather as something unpredictable, in which there is "always an alternative and a choice of the road."[40]

Aleksandr Men's narrative skills are impressive, especially in the sixth volume, which he titled *On the Threshold of the New Testament: From Alexander of Macedonia to the Preaching of John the Baptist* (*Na poroge Novogo Zaveta: Ot epokhi Aleksandra Makedonskogo do propovedi Ioanna Krestitelia*).[41] He considered this work, the culmination of his six-volume series, to be of particular importance.[42] He took special care with it, working on it throughout the 1970s.[43] It is by far the longest volume, amounting to more than eight hundred pages, and Fr. Aleksandr appended a bibliography of nearly twelve hundred works to it, which he hoped would encourage his readers to go more deeply into the topics he examined.

Aleksandr Men's purpose in volume six was to place the Gospels in historical context. In it, he described the religious world on the eve of Christ's birth, carefully setting the stage for the arrival of the God-Man.[44] He reiterated the central theme of the conflict between two ways of looking at the world; that is, the antagonism between the view that was hostile to foreigners, elevated ritualism to the highest order, and was deterministic in its world outlook versus the view that was universalist, free from narrowness and excessive reliance on ritual, and open to the Spirit of God, in which fate and determinism were absent.[45]

Because of his universalist viewpoint, Fr. Aleksandr was particularly drawn to the writings of Philo of Alexandria, the Hellenistic Jewish philosopher who lived during the Roman Empire and to whom he devoted some of the most sympathetic writing in the book. Philo "placed at the center of his attention not the path of the people of God and not the path of humanity, but the fate of the individual soul, aspiring to a higher sensibility."[46] It was here, Fr. Aleksandr wrote, in Philo's teachings, that "the core of the philosophy of the Bible unexpectedly appears: He understood 'Knowledge of God' not as a rationalistic comprehension, but as an achievement of love," a position Fr. Aleksandr saw as unique among the ancient thinkers he examined.[47]

Aleksandr Men found many features of Philo's thought compelling, as Andrei Eremin has noted, including Philo's emphasis on the grace of God, his view of reason not as an enemy of faith but as a partner, his understanding of the relationship between divine inspiration and creativity, and his respect for other religions.[48] As Eremin observed, Fr. Aleksandr's chapters on Philo of Alexandria and on John the Baptist are especially lyrical and reverential. Significantly, he devoted the last chapter of the volume to John the Baptist, the immediate forerunner of Christ, who prepared the way for him.[49] John the Baptist recognized Jesus as the Messiah, and, before his tragic end, brought thousands of people to his faith. Ironically, the funeral of Fr. Aleksandr took place on the day of the anniversary of the beheading of

John the Baptist. But this coincidence, as Andrei Eremin has written, is not the important point; rather it is that both the prophet and the village priest brought large numbers of people to the gateway to Christ "and then moved away to the side."[50]

Aleksandr Men's *History of Religion* is a product of prodigious research that incorporated ancient texts, Russian sources, and Western publications. While some of these materials were readily available to him, many others were not, since their accessibility was limited by government restrictions and ideological constraints. Fr. Aleksandr did not have at his disposal the full range of materials available on his subject, a limitation that he constantly had to confront. Still, he managed to acquire a plethora of books and other materials that were rarely available and distributed. How was this possible?

As mentioned earlier, since his teenage years, Aleksandr Men had scoured Moscow flea markets for books their owners had discarded, fearing possession of these books in case of a police search. He had also used his summer earnings to build a small personal library of historical and philosophical books, many of which were no longer published in Russia, and he had access to collections in the possession of friends among the Moscow intelligentsia. Books had long fired his imagination, connecting him to a larger world beyond his immediate circumstances.

Aleksandr Men's family supported these endeavors. His mother encouraged his explorations, especially in theological and artistic subjects, and gave these pursuits high priority in his upbringing. After World War II, as his brother recounted, people living in hungry Moscow often sold their possessions in order to buy food. "Once we were walking through the Danilevskii market [in Moscow], when Aleksandr saw an illustrated Bible, with Gustave Doré's illustrations. I remember it clearly: it cost 700 rubles, an enormous sum back then." Aleksandr, according to his brother, "nearly made himself sick over that book":

> He would run to the market to check whether or not the book had been sold, and he would turn slowly through the pages and study the illustrations. That is how he was introduced to Doré's works, his drawings on the Old Testament masters. After that, my parents somehow managed to exchange some of the things they had at home for him to be able to buy that book. Ever since then, he had this special attitude to Doré's work. He came to love Doré as an artist.[51]

Fr. Aleksandr's appetite for books did not dissipate during his priesthood. He read constantly—on the train, at home, in his garden, in the library, and on the road—in fields ranging from the sciences to literature, philosophy, and the arts. Both close friends and foreign guests brought him books; at Novaia Derevnia, he developed a network of people who supplied him with these literary riches, sources not readily available in the Soviet Union, and many of which they brought from abroad. According to a parishioner,

> I saw that every Sunday and every holiday, when Muscovites came to the church, they brought him books published in the West. Also, every Sunday, they brought Fr. Aleksandr mimeographed pages. The typist, who was named Nellia, typed them, and Andrei Eremin, Sergei Bychkov, and Fr. Vladimir [Arkhipov] edited them, and this was a constant practice. In various combinations, during and before the service, in the church and in the office, or on a bench under a bush, they corrected the pages, edited them, made comments, and worked through these printed materials.[52]

The term "search" in the title of the series on religion is significant to Aleksandr Men's underlying theme: the importance of the quest for truth, which in multiple ways is an unending, dynamic pursuit. In telling the story, Fr. Aleksandr's images and words are concrete; rarely are they abstract. His work is "similar to an historical novel," says one writer. "Fr. Aleksandr does not repeat the traditional scheme," writes another, "but provides a captivating spectacle of religious searches for universal meaning . . . the pinnacle of which appears in the coming of God incarnate."[53]

Primary Intellectual Influences

The first volume of Aleksandr Men's *History of Religion* contained a large number of primary sources. These sources included the writings of the Church Fathers, the Gospels, philosophers, historians, and contemporary authors in multiple fields. In addition to the sacred texts of the Orthodox tradition and the philosopher Vladimir Solov'ev, three more recent writers played a significant role in establishing the framework of the introductory volume. They warrant a brief look as a prelude to examining more closely the relationship between reason and faith, a central theme in volume one, as well as in Fr. Aleksandr's life. These seminal intellectual influences were Nikolai Berdiaev, Christopher Dawson, and Pierre Teilhard de Chardin.

Nikolai Aleksandrovich Berdiaev (1874–1948) played a leading role among the philosopher-theologians who revitalized Russian religious thought at the beginning of the twentieth century. Born in Kiev into an aristocratic family, Berdiaev studied law at Kiev University before joining the Social Democratic Labor Party, which resulted later in his removal from the university for engaging in illegal political activities. His move from Marxism to Christianity marked a major turning point in his life, which led to a long and distinguished career as a teacher, philosopher, and author. Berdiaev's first significant works were *The Philosophy of Freedom* (1911) and *The Meaning of Creativity* (1916), books containing central themes on which he elaborated in many of his later publications.[54] Berdiaev had a large influence on Fr. Aleksandr; his picture hangs beside Vladimir Solov'ev's on the wall next to Fr. Aleksandr's writing desk in his study.

In *The Philosophy of Freedom* and *The Meaning of Creativity*, Berdiaev articulated the importance of a free human personality, which he contrasted to collectivism and the mentality of the crowd. This personal foundation, which the Creator gives to every individual, must be allowed to develop freely, to act and to think, unrestricted by outside pressures to conform. The free human personality, he maintained, is "one of the highest features of spirituality": it is the "image of God" that lives in each person. It is a person's "I."[55]

Berdiaev's philosophy of personalism, creativity, and freedom were among his signature contributions to Russian religious thought, and Fr. Aleksandr included much of this philosophy into his own thinking. Like Berdiaev, Aleksandr Men conceived of spirit as the essence of creativity, which manifested itself not only in religion but also in art and in human relationships. Creativity flourished where it had the chance to develop freely, whether in the world or within the individual. Freedom also characterized the Absolute, which created the world in the spirit of freedom. After the act of creation, God did not become an "agent in control," but left to each individual the freedom to choose between good and evil and the freedom to decide how to act and to be in the world. This view of the Absolute, however, did not mean that God remained powerless. It meant instead that power is manifested not through force and domination, but through God's grace and through love.[56]

The two opposing principles—freedom and attempts to suppress it—existed throughout history, Aleksandr Men wrote. The personal basis of freedom marks the relationship between God and human beings, and Fr. Aleksandr, borrowing from Berdiaev, saw this relationship as a continuous dialogue:

> [The essence of] the Old Testament religion is living man in the presence of the living God that does not mean any dissolution in ecstasy or any retreat into some kind of mystical silence. In this religion, man is neither a

speechless slave nor a bodiless visionary. Instead, he is a rebellious and conflicting creature of strong will and with a clearly expressed personality. And
it is this wholeness of personality and his passionate soul that is brought by
man to God's feet.[57]

Freedom for the human being is a critical component of such dialogue. The
historical account, as Fr. Aleksandr elaborated it, is a forward movement,
not a record of fortuitous, accidental circumstances, and this forward movement was a distinctive characteristic of Christianity.

Second, in writing his historical account of religion, Aleksandr Men was
influenced by the model formulated by the distinguished English historian
Christopher Dawson (1889–1970). While still a secondary school student,
Men read Dawson's *Religion and Progress*, and Dawson's historical insights
remained with him.[58] Dawson's vision of history offered a diametrically different approach than the Leninist account ingrained in Soviet textbooks,
which connected human beliefs and actions to the economic structure of
societies. In contrast, the English historian viewed religious beliefs and aspirations as the bedrock of human consciousness. They gave societies stability, core sets of values, and the foundation for the development of arts and
science. Dawson never divorced culture from its religious context, and Fr.
Aleksandr adopted this approach throughout his *History of Religion*.[59]

Writing between the two world wars, Dawson believed European civilization had lost its moral underpinnings; he did not want to return to some
golden age of the past, but he was convinced that Europe needed to recover
the spiritual traditions that had given it moral strength and social cohesion.
"This does not, however, mean that the material and spiritual aspects of
life must become fused in a single political order which would have all the
power and rigidity of a theocratic state," he wrote:

> Since a culture is essentially a spiritual community, it transcends the eco-
> nomic and political orders. It finds its appropriate organ not in a state, but
> in a church, that is to say a society which is the embodiment of a purely
> spiritual tradition and which rests, not on material power, but on the free
> adhesion of the individual mind.[60]

Aleksandr Men incorporated this theme into his own thinking. Religious
aspirations served as a stimulus to social progress. He maintained that powerful "social forces, which combine to destroy the old and create the new,
emanated from religious beliefs," although he did not envision religion as
the only motivating element underlying society.[61] But it was a powerful, and

often neglected, impulse, which he contrasted to the positivist and nihilist trends that cast a long shadow over the whole age. He also repudiated the "God is dead" phenomenon, then popular in Western Europe and also among some segments of the Russian intelligentsia. Those who held this view overlooked the parts of the world, including Russia, where Christianity exhibited remarkable vitality.[62] "Even the struggle against religion," which marked European civilization over the last two centuries, Fr. Aleksandr pointed out, "is indirect recognition of its significance."[63]

His views on Christianity and history led Aleksandr Men to the third major intellectual influence on his writing: Pierre Teilhard de Chardin (1881–1955), the prominent Jesuit geologist and paleontologist. Translated into Russian in 1965, shortly after the Khrushchev era, but still during the antireligious campaign, Teilhard's *The Human Phenomenon* served as a source of enduring importance to Fr. Aleksandr Men.[64] Likely published in a small number of copies, *The Human Phenomenon* had a very limited Russian readership, but Fr. Aleksandr was one of those readers who valued the book "when no one in Russia had read or even knew" of Pierre Teilhard de Chardin.[65] He found Teilhard's work illuminating, a gem that opened new pathways into thinking about the sciences, human evolution, and the "continual transformation of the world."[66]

Fr. Aleksandr Men referred often to Teilhard and appended an essay to *Sources of Religion* on the French scholar's "new way of thinking." Multiple times he emphasized the importance of Teilhard for contemporary Christianity.[67] Teilhard, as Fr. Aleksandr pointed out, underscored "the unity of all the sciences," an interdependence that, over time, would become even clearer than at present. Fr. Aleksandr believed it was important for the future of Christianity for it to embrace this new way of thinking and to stand at the forefront of its development. Moreover, the scientific synthesis that Teilhard envisioned opened up new opportunities for dialogue between Christians and non-Christians, possibilities that the church should not let pass.[68]

In Teilhard's *Human Phenomenon*, matter and spirit did not exist as two distinct, separate entities, but were interdependent parts of the natural world. Matter, to Teilhard, was not an abstract, lifeless substance, but a living, active substance connected to humanity. Connecting spirit and matter, Teilhard saw revelation as existing in nature, part of its own processes and evolution from simple to more complex forms:

> Now, in the degree to which a more precise and penetrating study of the facts becomes possible, the ordering of the parts of the universe is found to be more and more astonishing every day. The farther and deeper we

penetrate into matter with our increasingly powerful methods, the more
dumbfounded we are by the interconnection of its parts. Each element of
the cosmos is woven positively from all the others; from below itself by the
mysterious phenomenon of "composition" that gives it substance in the point
of an organized whole, and from above by being subjected to the influence
of unities of a higher order that encompass and dominate it for their own
ends. It is impossible to cut into this network, to isolate a piece, without all
its borders fraying and coming undone.[69]

In contrast to the gloomy, pessimistic, and dispirited view offered by Albert
Camus, Jean-Paul Sartre, and many other contemporary writers, Pierre
Teilhard de Chardin provided a positive outlook on the natural world. The
possibilities of a regression into darkness did not trouble him. His was a
hopeful vision; he believed old ideals about human life and the future needed
to be recovered, reworked and held up before all of humanity. Seeing science and religion as tightly interdependent aspects of human consciousness,
Teilhard conceived of a unified and interconnected world united through
love. He did not fear the future, as Fr. Aleksandr noted, but embraced it,
showing clearly the need for new ideals that pointed the way forward.

Aleksandr Men found such thinking extremely compatible with his own
beliefs and his understanding of the Gospels, and very different from the
foreboding outlook held by many prominent figures, both Russian and
foreign.[70] Teilhard's experience, Fr. Aleksandr stated, provided "a priceless
jewel for Christianity."[71] It provided a way to respond to the contention that
religious belief represented weakness, a flight of fantasy that offered human
beings an escape from the harsh realities of their existence.

Science and Religion Revisited

In the first lines of an appendix to *Sources of Religion*, Fr. Aleksandr Men
cited a statement commonly repeated in Russian textbooks: "Religion has
always been and remains presently an enemy of science."[72] This is a conviction, he said, that we Russians were accustomed to hearing "during our
school days," a supposition that "to many of us, has seemed not subject to
doubt and examination." To be fair, as he went on to write, in recent years,
atheistic propaganda had refrained from stating as forcefully that religion
stood in opposition to science; nevertheless, the teaching of science usually
assumed that a "condition of war" continued to operate, if not directly, then
in "hidden form." In this conflict, religion had to be obliterated, because it

hindered social progress and stood in the way of solving "the mysteries of the universe."[73]

The materialist philosophy that was dominant in the Soviet Union at the time Aleksandr Men was writing rejected a "Divine Being" and believed that scientific progress required a wholesale rejection of religion. The materialists conceived of human beings as "thinking machines" that originated from a material substratum that generated thought.[74] Human beings were intimately connected to this material substratum, which conditioned their ways of looking at the world, including their ideas about life and perspectives on culture. None of these processes existed apart from the socioeconomic and political bases from which they emerged and with which they continued to be related. The materialists insisted on the primacy of matter; they maintained that the world is knowable and that everything in it could be understood by scientific reasoning. Mystery, miracles, and the spiritual realm were highly questionable assertions; they could not be verified by hard science and lay in the realm of fantasy and deception. Science and religion thus were contradictory ways of seeing. They were incompatible approaches to understanding life, and religion detracted from the human capacity to reach one's full potential.[75]

The first volume of the *History of Religion* challenged the premises of these predominant ways of viewing the world. First, Fr. Aleksandr went back to the origins of science and its foundational principles. He showed that the sciences came into existence in close connection to the church and to priests in ancient Egypt and Babylon, who were the creators of medicine, astronomy, and mathematics.[76] The temples were the "real cradles of science," for it was in them, championed by priests, that the first mathematical formulas, the first maps, and the first anatomical atlases originated.[77] It is too often overlooked, Fr. Aleksandr noted, that the "creators of classical science were at the same time religious thinkers" who did not see the two spheres of thought and creativity in opposition.

Aleksandr Men then went on to point out their relationship in later times, citing the society of Pythagoreans, members of a religious order who advanced progress in mathematics, and Aristotle, whose philosophical principles entered religious thought. He recalled that the church, during the long medieval centuries, existed as the "sole cultural hearth" and the preserver of classical science. He mentioned Saint Albert and Saint Thomas Aquinas, those encyclopedic minds who "attributed to science great significance and taught diverse fields of it." And he cited the contributions to science of Roger Bacon, who was also a theologian.[78] None of these leaders in the development and preservation of science considered theology and science to be in conflict. They aspired to expand as fully as possible the mental and spiritual capabilities of humankind, and not one of them sought to limit either way of seeing and knowing the world.

Second, Fr. Aleksandr explored the contention that reason and faith had come directly into opposition with the explosion of scientific thought and discovery during the scientific revolution, when scientific knowledge began to have a large impact on human consciousness. He discussed the leading and most creative minds in the sciences who viewed God as the author of two fundamental books: nature and the scriptures. Isaac Newton and René Descartes, Blaise Pascal and Johannes Kepler had not seen science and religion in opposition; Men argued that these two ways of interpreting the world had important things to say to each other.[79] Because they raised different questions, they needed to be in dialogue.[80] Neither science nor religion could answer questions arising outside its own sphere. They emanated from two different sources of knowledge, but such distinctively different spheres did not require ironclad boundaries of separation. Science and religion, he maintained, were not ideological opponents.

In what came to be known as the "free-thinking eighteenth century," the eminent Russian scholar Mikhail Vasil'evich Lomonosov (1711–1765) valued the contributions that each of these spheres made to understanding the universe. Lomonosov was particularly important to Fr. Aleksandr, because within the Soviet pantheon of scientists he was considered a linchpin of the materialist worldview. This "encyclopedic mind," founder of Moscow University in 1755, and the creator of many diverse fields of science in Russia, held an esteemed place in the Russian Enlightenment. Given his original work in such developing fields as physics, astronomy, chemistry, geology, and linguistics, as well as poetry, it was little wonder that the materialists claimed him as one of their own. The standard Soviet text, published by the Academy of Sciences, described Lomonosov as the "forefather of Russian materialism," a scientific genius whose "brilliant works in the natural sciences provided firm ground for his materialism." Lomonosov, the author of this text claimed, "played a leading role in the history of atheistic thought."[81] Another prominent historian identified Lomonosov as the "forerunner of Russia's philosophy of materialism, the founder of the materialistic tradition of Russian philosophy."[82]

In *Sources of Religion*, Fr. Aleksandr challenged the predominant interpretation of Lomonosov. A close reading of Lomonosov's writings, he showed, revealed that such assertions, universally incorporated into school textbooks, had little basis in reality. Fr. Aleksandr could not find "one atheistic statement, either in [Lomonosov's] prose or poetry" that supported his supposed materialistic philosophy. So on what basis, he asked, did historians of science make such claims? Men argued that "they only wished to make Lomonosov into a scholar of materialism" in order to advance their views, regardless of whether these contentions had any basis in reality.[83]

The great scientist's true views needed to be rediscovered, a task that required a reading of the original texts. "Truth and faith," Fr. Aleksandr quoted Lomonosov, "are two native sisters, emanating from one Great Father." The Russian scientist well understood that science and religion operated in two separate spheres, one that was visible and measurable and another that called for a much different way of seeing.[84] Science had great power to comprehend the world, as Lomonosov well knew; yet he also understood that science did not have the capacity to answer certain great questions.

Third, science and religion ought to be understood as allies, rather than as competing worldviews.[85] Fr. Aleksandr Men challenged the widely held perspective that "man is the measure of all things."[86] The reader will recall his critique, in *Magic and Monotheism*, of the desire to acquire "god-like powers"—the essence of magic—which held a central place in human consciousness during the long prehistoric evolution of humankind. Believing they had such supernatural capabilities, human beings had decoupled themselves from their covenant with God. Fr. Aleksandr called the breaking of this linkage "original sin," the desire to remake the world in one's own image. This belief, which held human beings "captive to magical powers," he maintained, "paralyzed human creativity."[87]

On this point, Aleksandr Men's admiration for the ancient Greeks stood out. As previously noted, he considered the development of science to be among the Greeks' greatest achievements. Unlike the Egyptians and cultures elsewhere, where theology and science were interwoven and science remained the property of priests, the ancient Greeks separated science from theology and made each a distinct field of inquiry. Did the Greeks' actions represent a step forward for humankind, he asked? Over time, might this separation truly be considered a landmark event in history?

Fr. Aleksandr Men answered clearly in the affirmative, pointing out that their separation had to take place so that both science and theology could advance and mature without "obstructing each other." "Empirical knowledge, the study of nature, and abstract thought required their own 'rules of play,' without intrusion by the other."[88] Likewise, theology was not science: it operated by its own set of standards. Fr. Aleksandr considered theology a higher form of knowledge than science, a deeper and more all-embracing means of understanding. By emancipating science and philosophy "from the tutelage of theological theory," the Greeks "cleared the way" for advancement in each of these fields.[89]

But Aleksandr Men was extremely critical of attempts to make each field totally autonomous, to close off each of them from other ways of seeing. When either scientists or theologians looked upon the other with contempt and viewed the others' methodologies with disdain, both of them suffered. But opportunities for dialogue were also lost when either scientists or theologians attempted to inject their own discipline into the territory of the other, losing sight of the boundaries and projecting them onto the other. The "rationalists," Fr. Aleksandr noted, had made empiricism and direct observation into "the highest court" of knowledge. Fr. Aleksandr called this the "original sin of thought," whose limitations some of the greatest scientists in recent times had recognized.[90]

Fourth, science and religion employed entirely different methodologies. Science relied on the experimental method, a powerful tool whose development during the scientific revolution, in the words of T. H. Huxley, became "simply the mode at which all phenomena are reasoned about, rendered precise and exact."[91] The experimental method did not support any specific epistemological position; rather, it was a method of examination, which was used in the physical and natural sciences, but also extended beyond them to many other fields of study.

Religion, and more specifically Christianity, employed a much different approach to knowledge. Its equivalent of the experimental method was trust. Trust comprised the framework in which Christianity operated and from which it took both its starting and ending points. Trust conveyed the mystery inherent in the relationship between God and humanity. It suggested that "Divine Nature" cannot be known entirely through reason nor proved with absolute certainty. Trust was a term that Fr. Aleksandr Men used repeatedly to express God's love for humanity, and humanity's ideal relationship to the Creator.[92] Trust elicited reverence and mystery, which were qualities that religion and science, ultimately, had in common. In this sense, Fr. Aleksandr's perspective was similar to what Albert Einstein's most recent biographer describes as the great scientist's distinguishing characteristic: "a profound reverence for the harmony and beauty of what he called the mind of God as it was expressed in the creation of the universe and its laws."[93]

Fifth, the desire to make science into an ideology, in Fr. Aleksandr's view, exhibited a remnant of magical thinking, which continued to reside deeply in contemporary life. The ideological blinders within Marxism-Leninism, the need to force ideas and beliefs into narrowly defined, predetermined categories, or to ignore competing views, deprived the scientific imagination of its most essential powers. In support of this argument, Fr. Aleksandr referred to Ernst Haeckle's racial theories as examples of narrow-minded tendencies that hindered scholarship.[94] As an open-ended, experiential approach to knowledge that recognized contradictory claims, science could not be made into ideology without impeding its development.

But Fr. Aleksandr also addressed the other side of this argument. By the mid-1980s, certain voices within the church, as well as among the political elite, had begun to see the Orthodox Church as a bulwark against the West. To these groups, which included ultranationalists, the Russian Orthodox Church represented a core element in Russia's national identity; it needed to be restored to its rightful place of honor in the state. Such voices, by the end of the 1980s, has become even stronger, particularly as the ideological strength of Marxism-Leninism weakened. Ultranationalists, including some within the church, saw in Russian Orthodoxy the linchpin of a new Russian ideology.[95]

Such trends greatly troubled Fr. Aleksandr. He made no attempt, nor could he have, to speak about individuals who advocated such uses of the Orthodox Church. But his writings served as a constant reminder of the church's proper role. When Christianity is made into an ideology—an always powerful temptation—it loses its purpose and its creativity.[96] Men wrote that "the Good News entered the world as a dynamic force, encompassing all sides of life, open to everything created by God in nature and in human beings. It is not just a religion which has existed for the last twenty centuries, but a Way focused on the future (John 14:6; Acts 16:17, 18:26)."[97] It always had to be open to new and diverse ways of seeing the world. This, according to Fr. Aleksandr, was the perspective of the Church Fathers, especially those he most admired, such as the Christian Apologists, Saint Gregory the Theologian, and Saint Clement of Alexandria.[98]

The teachings of the Church Fathers offered Fr. Aleksandr what he believed was the proper approach to the relationship between science and religion. The Church Fathers constantly remained open to the world and to new discoveries. Neither the Church Fathers nor the Gospels restricted knowledge; neither did they confine it to fit narrow, dogmatic ends. They rejected a static paradigm of belief. In Fr. Aleksandr's view, therefore, efforts to find in such writings "statements about natural science held to be valid for all times" greatly misunderstood the dynamic nature of their thought.[99]

Fr. Aleksandr urged his followers to pay attention to science. Science provided insights into the material world, and he greatly valued its powers, while recognizing its limitations. Educated as a biologist, Aleksandr

Men retained throughout his life a love for science and an appreciation of its methods of discovery. But he also appreciated the relationship between science and religion; in his *Sources of Religion*, he expressed the paradoxical nature of these two ways of seeing and knowing as follows:

> Religious thought quite often uses scientific methods for uncovering and analyzing intuitive religious experience, but it can also function without these methods. Exactly in the same way, science can develop under the banner of a religious worldview or can remain outside of it.[100]

The contentions that science offered a "unique world view" and "all of life lends itself to scientific analysis" seemed shortsighted to Fr. Aleksandr. Behind such views lay harmful, potentially destructive presumptions:

> There is something tragic and moving about the atheists' attempt to take shelter from the abyss of an indifferent universe, from an empty dark sky. It is not simply fear and dread, but an unconscious attraction to those things which dogmatic materialism denies: to meaning, purpose, and to a rational origin of the universe. This mysterious attraction, which is inherent in human beings, cannot be eradicated by any doctrine. . . . Where does this need originate? . . . If through the ages, the human spirit had longed for beauty, goodness, or something higher, something worthy of worship, is it right to see this as self-deception? Is it not more natural to recognize that just as the body is connected to the objective world of nature, so also the spirit is drawn to the invisible reality which is kindred to it and beyond it? Is it not significant that when human beings turn away from this reality, superstitions and secular "cults" spring up in its place? In other words, if people turn away from God they inevitably turn to idols.[101]

Human beings, then, long for meaning beyond the material facts of existence, and this longing has throughout history expressed itself deeply and irrevocably. Following Pierre Teilhard de Chardin, as well as his own concrete experiences as a parish priest, Fr. Aleksandr knew that study of the material world could not provide answers to questions that went beyond the process of experimentation, questions relating to such categories as "meaning and value, compassion and evil."[102] These questions exceeded the limits of science, yet they did not stand in opposition to it. As Teilhard de Chardin observed when discussing the particles of the universe, each part contributes to the whole of the organism. Further, Fr. Aleksandr cited physicist Max Planck's conclusions about the creative mind and its underlying spirit:

"science and religion do not exclude each other; rather, for each thinking person, they are complementary and mutually reinforce each other."[103] Denial of this search for something that transcends the natural world, rejection of this quest for a higher order of reality, is "to deny one of the primary needs of humanity."[104]

When writing about Fr. Aleksandr, Sergei Bychkov, a Russian journalist and a member of his parish, claimed that "the principle value of his theology consists of his [successful] attempts to create a synthesis of contemporary science and the Christian worldview."[105] Fr. Aleksandr based many of his ideas on concrete observations, founded on "scientific data." As he explained in the opening pages of *History of Religion*, he drew on the rich heritage of scientific thought and discovery.[106] Concurrently, he attempted to show that throughout human history, one would be hard pressed to find a single factor that had played a greater creative role in world culture than religion:

> The Egyptian temples and Babylonian hymns, the Bible and Parthenon, Gothic stained-glass windows and Russian icons, "The Divine Comedy" of Dante and the creations of Dostoevsky, the thought of Plato and [Søren] Kierkegaard, the music of [Johann Sebastian] Bach and [Benjamin] Britten, the social ideas of [Girolamo] Savonarola and [Thomas] Müntzer—all these have their roots in religion, which gives earthly life a higher meaning, connecting it with the Transcendent.[107]

While science conceives of one unity operating within the natural world, Fr. Aleksandr conceived of two: one existing within nature, the other between human beings and the Creator. The first of these, in his words, focuses "on the visible world. . . . Even if science seems to explain freely the entire material world, the sphere of the non-material world remains closed to it."[108] The second is the source of creativity and the sense of wonder. In the evocative language of an unnamed contemporary theologian, to whom Fr. Aleksandr referred, this creative source resembles a spring "which does not produce a river, but endlessly supplies it with water."[109]

Surveying the history of leading twentieth-century scientists, Fr. Aleksandr recognized the presence of those who adhered to materialist philosophy. But in contrast to the assertions found in Soviet textbooks, many of the most distinguished did not fall within that framework. Among the scientists who also embraced religion were George Cantor, in mathematics; Werner Heisenberg, in physics; Sir John Eccles, in neurophysiology; Theodore Schwann, in biology; Pierre Teilhard de Chardin, in geology; the Abbé Breuil, in ethnography; and P. W. Schmidt, in paleontology.[110] History,

Fr. Aleksandr pointed out, did not support the view of religious belief as dying, and many of the greatest scientists of the twentieth century bore witness to the opposite view.

"He offered us hope, even in moments of our deepest despair," said Fr. Georgii Chistiakov of Fr. Men.[111] Chistiakov, now deceased, recalled the moment, in 1969, soon after the Soviet army reoccupied Czechoslovakia, when he encountered Fr. Aleksandr on the street in Moscow. Like so many of his friends, Chistiakov spoke of his moments of depression after the "Prague Spring" was crushed by armed force. "Many of us experienced an overwhelming sadness," he said. But Fr. Aleksandr expressed a different point of view. He told Chistiakov that the tragic events they had witnessed "must not be seen as the end of a process but as the beginning."[112] Fr. Aleksandr's belief in an evolving universe, his appreciation of the beauty of creation, his understanding of the Gospels, and his innate humility fostered hope. Like Teilhard de Chardin, he thought the potential for good was stronger than the potential for destruction. Human beings had an inherent, internal capacity to create a coherent world. He believed it was as important to cultivate this internal being and to nourish the creative spirit living inside each individual as it was to plan and construct the physical, objective exterior. Human beings possessed a psychological need for an ideal; they longed for a unified world, a longing that was found within, as it existed in nature.

The Public Reception

Aleksandr Men had little confidence that his books would ever be issued in his native country. Nevertheless, he did not engage in the time-consuming, arduous task of scholarship in order for his works to remain confined to his desk drawer, as manuscripts written to satisfy his own personal predilection for writing. Due to government censorship, he could only publish his works abroad with the knowledge that they might one day reenter Russia, where he knew his primary readership would be. But how widely did his six-volume *History of Religion* come to be known? And was it recognized for what he intended it to be: a fundamental work that set the story of Christianity in a global context, showing its unique qualities and its compelling message?

Aleksandr Men's first and most immediate purpose aimed at providing the members of his parish with written material rarely available elsewhere, books they needed to strengthen their understanding of Orthodox Christianity. He distributed books from his library, as well as his own writings, still in manuscript form, to newcomers to his parish. Iurii Tabak, a member of the Moscow intelligentsia, who joined Aleksandr's parish in Novaia Derevnia in the early 1970s, attested to this common practice. "Fr. Aleksandr would often give you a book, saying, 'Here is something that you might find interesting and helpful.' When you returned the book, he then handed you another."[113] He was neither intrusive nor forceful, but he always encouraged the curious mind to explore further.[114]

As in the case of his *Son of Man*, his multivolume *History of Religion* came back into Russia through various carriers. Once there, the volumes were either spread among friends or copied and distributed through samizdat. By the late 1970s, Fr. Aleksandr's reputation both as a parish priest and as a writer of interesting, provocative books had gained widespread attention among members of the Russian intelligentsia, including the writers Nadezhda Mandelstam and Ludmilla Ulitskaia. Mandelstam considered Fr. Aleksandr to be her spiritual father.[115] Ulitskaia, in her twenties when she first met him in the late 1960s, described him as the first well-educated person she had ever encountered who believed in Christ.[116] "At that time, this was extremely rare: culture and belief seldom came together." He was like a "fresh wind blowing in the desert."[117] Her account of him and what he meant to her is extremely moving.[118]

Anatolii Krasnov-Levitin, a leading voice among Russia's young intelligentsia, described Aleksandr Men as among Russia's freshest and most compelling voices.[119] "One could write a whole book about him!" Levitin said, in 1975. "[He is] one of the best Russian priests today . . . already he is widely read in samizdat, [and has become] a very popular figure in Moscow."[120]

Fr. Aleksandr Men's reputation, thanks to the underground chain of samizdat, had also begun to spread beyond Moscow. Although the number of readers cannot be accurately ascertained, the distribution of certain publications was often spontaneous, with local people taking it upon themselves to copy and then pass around his manuscript. Mikhail Aksenov-Meerson, who served with Fr. Aleksandr in the early 1970s at Novaia Derevnia, recounts the following episode:

A priest came to me from another town, which has fewer books than Moscow, and asked to read something new in religious apologetics. I gave him a book written in Russia, *The Origins of Religion* (*Istoki religii*), which made the rounds in typed copies for several years. It reached the West, where it was published, and in that form returned to Russia. He took it away and in one month brought back the book and twenty-five exact Xerox copies that were neatly bound. It turned out that local readers liked the book so much

that they decided to spread it. They came out with 100 copies, the majority of which they distributed. They asked that the remaining twenty-five
be taken to Moscow, this as a percentage or so as not to waste the extras.[121]

Naturally, the police kept close watch on these proceedings. When police
officials searched the residence of a person suspected of engaging in illegal activities, they usually confiscated books and other materials published
outside the state's control. But such confiscations were not always a means
of incriminating an individual who possessed such printed materials. Party
members also seized the materials to gather information and gain knowledge of subjects they could not otherwise obtain. The following incident,
reported by a provincial priest about Aleksandr Men's *Sources of Religion*
and a local Party organization, is illustrative:

> A provincial priest who once took a good samizdat book on the origins of
> religion, began to apologize to me later that he could not return it to me.
> The book had gotten into the hands of the party *obkom* [regional committee
> of the CPSU] and was being read by the whole staff. Finally, it reached the
> secretary himself who, utilizing his power, was 'engrossed' in it.[122]

Such behavior, as Aksenov-Meerson pointed out, took place in a country
and at a time that lacked consistent guidelines about what was forbidden.[123]
The action taken by authorities depended a great deal on circumstances,
personal relationships, the temperaments of local authorities, and whether
a certain act threatened an official's authority. While the unofficial and often
secretive nature of book distribution issued in samizdat or *tamizdat* format
prevents a precise account of the readership, there is enough evidence to
suggest this readership was substantial. Moreover, the people interested in
the subject matter of Fr. Aleksandr's books were drawn from various social
groups, who, for many different reasons, found that his *History of Religion*
made for compelling reading. According to Andrei Eremin, *History of Religion* and *Son of Man* served as "guiding stars" to Christianity in a society
dominated by an atheistic political and educational structure.[124]

Fr. Aleksandr's *History of Religion* went through two editions in the 1970s
and '80s, both of which he published in Brussels. As mentioned before, he
constantly reworked his major books, and he completed a third edition
shortly before his death in 1990. This third edition, published in Moscow in
1991, marked the first time *History of Religion* was issued in Moscow, where
the large public interest in the book was demonstrated by the printing of
100,000 copies of the work. An abridged version of the book appeared in

1992, and 11,000 copies of a two-volume condensed edition were published in 1997, 1999, and again in 2000.[125] The demand for the book has continued long after Aleksandr Men first broached the subject of the origins and early setting of Christianity.

Not all the responses to *History of Religion*, however, have been positive. In January 1990, the Soviet journal *Peoples of Asia and Africa* (*Narody Azii i Afriki*) published an excerpt from the second volume of *History*, to which the editorial staff attached a note saying that its members could not agree with the article's contents. The staff strongly took issue with Fr. Aleksandr's contention that the ultimate unification of world religions was to be found in Christianity, the views of the philosopher Nikolai Berdiaev, and Aleksandr Men's statements about the equality of world cultures.[126]

Other voices were much more critical, even deeply demeaning. In the early 1990s, Deacon Andrei Kuraev, who later wrote similar, strongly worded attacks against Aleksandr Men, published an article in which he denied Fr. Aleksandr's Orthodox identity. According to Deacon Kuraev, Fr. Aleksandr failed to draw fully from Orthodox texts, instead preferring Western historians and theologians and transmitting them to Russians because he did not accept the "true Orthodox pathway to God." Kuraev attacked Fr. Aleksandr's books as "carelessly written" and "filled with mistakes," although he failed to mention specific errors.[127] Such claims expressed either a near total misreading of Aleksandr Men's *History of Religion* or a deliberate attempt to denigrate him as an Orthodox priest. They also ignored his upbringing in the bosom of the Orthodox Church and the Orthodox traditions on which he drew so deeply.

10

. . . .

Novaia Derevnia

Reaching Out to a Diverse World

In the second half of the 1970s, Fr. Aleksandr suffered the loss of people who, heretofore, had been among the pillars in his life. In 1975, Vera Iakovlevna, his aunt, who had been such a major influence on his childhood, died. Then, three years later, the head priest at Novaia Derevnia, the elderly, infirm Fr. Grigorii Kryzhanovskii, who had welcomed him to the parish and had allowed him latitude to set his own course in the parish, also died. While not unexpected, his departure required the diocesan bishop to name a replacement, which, given Fr. Aleksandr's previous experiences, could not have given him much comfort.

In the late fall of 1977, Fr. Alekandr's mother, Elena Semenovna, became ill, took to bed, and could not seem to recover. Medical attention did not help, and even medicines brought from abroad gave her little relief.[1] On some days, Elena Semenovna appeared better, her spirits became brighter, and she managed to walk around in the open air. But such times were sporadic; on the following days her condition worsened.[2] Gradually, her strength ebbed, and with Fr. Aleksandr at her bedside, in January 1979, she died. The effect of her death on Fr. Aleksandr was one of both extreme sorrow and gratitude. He confessed to spending several days crying, as well as remembering: "Her life was uncommonly full, everything [she had] she devoted to Christ. It is difficult even to evaluate how much I am indebted to her. We shared a common life and a common spirit."[3] He traveled to see his brother Pavel, who was in the Russian army and stationed near Saint Petersburg (then Leningrad); they wept together and shared stories about their mother's service to the church and her great influence on them.[4] Elena Semenovna was buried near Fr. Aleksandr's church at Novaia Derevnia.

Meanwhile, the Novaia Derevnia parish was undergoing transition. The new senior priest assigned to the parish following Fr. Georgii's death was Fr. Stefan Sredi, a person previously unknown to the parishioners. What kinds of internal changes would he bring to the parish, and how would he relate to its members, and especially the people who came from Moscow and nearby towns to meet with Fr. Aleksandr? Would he set obstacles in the way, even forbid, perhaps, the lines of people who waited for Fr. Aleksandr, hoping to seek counsel from him? These questions caused Fr. Aleksandr anxious moments as he awaited the arrival of the new superior.[5]

Born in Ukraine, Fr. Stefan had finished the Moscow Spiritual Academy and then served the church in Khimki, an industrial center in the suburban region of Moscow, northwest of the city. He lived with his family in Zagorsk, which made travel to his Khimki parish difficult. Fr. Stefan had earlier asked for a transfer to a more accessible parish, and, when the nearby Novaia Derevnia became a possibility, he likely greeted it with pleasure.[6]

At first, the relationship between Fr. Stefan and Fr. Aleksandr was cordial and respectful as Fr. Stefan became accustomed to the formalities and routines of his new parish. He kept a watchful eye on the proceedings and treated Fr. Aleksandr in much the same way as his predecessor, allowing him wide range to conduct his affairs as he had earlier. After the first few years in his position, he began to take a different approach, becoming suspicious of any kind of innovation and deviation from the prescribed order, either in the service or the relationship to the parish community. "It was not easy," Zoia Maslenikova, Fr. Aleksandr's long-time editor, wrote, "for him to serve side-by-side with such a well-known priest, learned theologian, and matchless pastor."[7] Fr. Stefan's relationship with his subordinate became increasingly strained, and he soon gave Fr. Aleksandr the smallest possible part of the service.

The Start of the House Groups

In 1977, Fr. Aleksandr began to experiment with the boundaries and the nature of the parish. He was a priest, his associate and friend Andrei Eremin said, whose whole being identified with the parish, a priest who thought continually about the needs of his people.[8] In that year, Fr. Aleksandr began to organize several small groups, first at Novaia Derevnia outside the formal services of the church. The chief purpose of these small groups was to engage in prayer and read the Gospels. But the small groups also had another purpose: they bound together their participants, forming over time personal relationships that otherwise might not have developed.

Gradually, these small groups expanded beyond the immediate boundaries of Novaia Derevnia into Moscow. Members met in individual apartments and included mainly young people and their families, who explored the Gospels, as well as various components of the Orthodox tradition. Nearly all the participants were members of the Moscow intelligentsia and were composed of people who had traveled to the services at Novaia Derevnia (or even earlier, at Tarasovka), had engaged in conversation with Fr. Aleksandr, and had found compelling both his distinctive way of relating to people and his explication of the Gospels.[9] These meetings in Moscow were illegal and involved a high degree of risk to those who attended. But they also formed part of Fr. Aleksandr's larger vision of the church and its role in the world. Moreover, he well knew that the interest of the young people who came to him could not be sustained without additional means of instruction and personal connection. The countervailing winds blowing powerfully in the media, the educational system, and the political structure acted to ensure conformity to a very different worldview.[10]

The question of the church's role and purpose in Russian society had concerned Fr. Aleksandr almost from the moment he decided to become a priest. It had occupied his attention during his student days in Irkutsk, when he and Gleb Yakunin, living in a multicultural city, had together explored this issue. In the late 1970s, in his responsibilities as a priest in a diverse, rapidly changing parish and society, the question of how Orthodoxy might flourish became a central concern for him.

In dealing with this issue, Fr. Aleksandr had an earlier, dynamic model on which he could draw for instruction and inspiration. Multiple times in his life, he recalled the example of Aleksei and Sergii Mechev, father and son, as primary influences on his life's course and his views of the parish community.[11] "My mentors," Fr. Aleksandr wrote, "(except for my relatives) were people connected to Optina Pustyn' and the Maroseika Community [*Maroseiskie obshchina*] of the Fathers Mechev."[12] In the first three decades of the twentieth century, Fr. Aleksei and Fr. Sergei Mechev successfully served one of the most influential parishes in Moscow before the Bolsheviks shut it down in 1931. Several of Fr. Aleksandr's mentors had come from that parish and carried its memories with them.[13]

The Mechevs

The Mechevs had been among the few Russian priests in the early twentieth century who had attracted the intelligentsia and who had the ability to speak to them. As a consequence, their parish on Maroseika Street in the heart of Moscow became the central home of a large, talented, and diverse group of men and women.[14] Their example provided Fr. Aleksandr with an early model of how the church might relate more effectively to a religiously diverse community, and how it might inspire dialogue among its members and between the church and the society. Historians have given little attention to the Mechevs, the offspring of their parish, or their influence on Fr. Aleksandr Men. Yet the model they created warrants a closer look, particularly in terms of the dialogue that developed there and its relationship to Fr. Aleksandr.

The stories of Aleksei and Sergei Mechev are unusual on several different counts. How the father, Aleksei Mechev, arose from extremely meager circumstances to become the spiritual leader of one of Russia's largest parishes in central Moscow is in itself remarkable. The steady, at times rapid, growth of the parish during years of revolutionary change, when the predominant cultural and political trends in Russia moved in an opposite direction, is also a tale of surprising durability and strength. It is impressive that the parish produced individuals, who, decades after the parish closed, carried on its legacy and established it in others during some of the darkest years for the Orthodox Church in the Soviet Union.

Sergei Alekseevich Mechev was born on September 17, 1892, in Moscow, the fourth of five children in the family of Fr. Aleksei Mechev and his wife Anna Petrovna. He had two older sisters, Aleksandra and Anna; a brother, Aleksei, who died in infancy; and a younger sister, Ol'ga, with whom Sergei had an especially close relationship throughout his childhood and youth. All the children grew up under extremely harsh material conditions, in a family that struggled to make ends meet and often suffered shortages of food and fuel.

Sergei's father, Aleksei Alekseevich Mechev, had graduated from the Moscow Spiritual Academy, then, in 1893, was appointed priest in one of Moscow's smallest churches, the Church of Saint Nikolai the Wonderworker, on Maroseika Street. Located in the city's center, it had few parishioners, and since its location was in a district where many churches competed with it, the parish had meager prospects for increasing its prominence. It was among the poorest parishes in Moscow. During these first years in the parish, Fr. Aleksei served in a nearly vacant church and lived with his family in a dilapidated rectory, constructed over a large pit, into which water flowed from the entire courtyard and gave the interior of the building a damp, unhealthy atmosphere.[15]

Nevertheless, despite these unfavorable conditions, Fr. Aleksei took his responsibilities seriously and served with unflagging commitment.

He joined the People's Reading Society (*Obshchestvo narodnogo chteniia*), whose members read in prisons and in the dining rooms of the poor, and he opened a church school in his home that served the poorest children in his parish.[16] Each day he diligently performed the liturgy before an empty church, which people passed by. He became the brunt of jokes by other clergy in the district. As one of them chided him, "Whenever I walk by your church, the bells are ringing for people to enter. Then I go inside to see, and the church is empty. No one comes; you ring the bells in vain."[17]

The challenges of his parish, however, were not the only difficulties Fr. Aleksei faced in the first eight years of his priesthood. His wife, Anna Petrovna, a beauty in her youth, suffered from a serious heart ailment, a condition that ran in her family and severely affected her. The windy and damp circumstances in the rectory made her illnesses even worse.[18] Her suffering affected the whole family, especially her son, Sergei, who was also in poor health and deeply attached to his mother. As her condition worsened, the burden on the family became nearly unbearable. In the months after her death in 1901, the family managed to reorganize itself, but Fr. Andrei remained "disconsolate in his grief, which seemed to him beyond his human strength to bear."[19]

Having reached nearly the end of his ability to cope, Fr. Aleksei's life at this point took a sudden turn. Desperate and seemingly unable to find within himself the resources to continue, he turned to one of Russia's great charismatic priests for help, Father (later Saint) John of Kronstadt (St. Ioann Kronstadtskii), whose service among the poor of Saint Petersburg and workers in the dockyards of Kronstadt was renowned. Friends of Fr. Aleksei asked him, while on a visit to Moscow, to talk with the grieving priest. He counseled Fr. Aleksei to listen to people and open himself up to them: "You complain and think there is no greater grief in the world than yours, but I advise you to go to some distant place and listen to people; you will hear things that are much more than what you are bearing and will see that your unhappiness is little compared to what some others are dealing with. In comparison with theirs, yours will seem easier to bear."[20]

Fr. Aleksei followed this counsel. Some time afterward, he went to the Chudov Monastery and began to work in the nearby Khitrov market, where he conducted readings and began to listen carefully to the people who talked with him and sought his support. The numbers of people began to grow and, perhaps to his surprise, he discovered a new and more powerful approach to his ministry. He uncovered new and fundamental aspects of his priesthood and how he must serve, how he must reach out to people, and how to rebuild his pastoral activity.[21]

These experiences totally changed Fr. Aleksei's approach to his parish. After returning to Moscow, he gave himself to his parishioners, and, from morning to evening, extended to them the lessons he had learned, putting into practice what Fr. John had taught him, never refusing to see anyone who sought him out. His "empty church," according to Pavel Florensky, a direct observer, soon "was transformed and filled with worshippers."[22] Throughout the day and into the evening, "crowds of people clustered around the home where Fr. Aleksei lived, with people sitting on the stairs and standing in the courtyard. On reception days, people came and spent the night by the gate, in order to lose no chance at being able to see Fr. Aleksei." Some came "in deep melancholy," unable to gain a sense of direction and purpose, "tormented by innumerable punishments and afflictions"; others, after Fr. Aleksei's reputation began to spread, arrived out of curiosity, wishing to see for themselves what had drawn such large crowds of people, and a few came out of enmity, with the intent to harm him.[23] All these people left very different from how they were when they had arrived, even those who came with malicious intent. Fr. Aleksei had a "special sensitivity," said another prominent observer, a "capacity to penetrate all kinds of another's suffering" and take on himself their grief, transferring to them, in some mysterious way through his prayers, his own good will.[24]

Fr. Aleksei's son, Sergei Alekseevich, had had a special bond with his father since childhood. As a graduate of the Moscow Theological Seminary, Fr. Aleksei knew well the advantages and the deficiencies of a religious education, and he wanted his son to have a first-rate secular education. He believed a "free and liberating" education to be essential to carrying out one's responsibilities to the priesthood, and while he wanted nothing more than for his son to follow him into that vocation, he strongly believed that such a decision had to be his son's alone.[25] Sergei Alekseevich, as it turned out, had a brilliant intellectual capacity and a curious mind, and, in 1910, after finishing the gymnasium, he told his father that he wished to travel to Western Europe before entering the university. His ordination was to come later.

After going first to Switzerland and several towns in Italy, where he spent a lot of time visiting the churches and art galleries and being deeply impressed, Sergei Alekseevich went on to Rome. He fell in love with the city, the beauty of the Sistine Chapel, the rooms filled with the paintings of Raphael, and the sights and the beauty of the city itself. He wrote his father about the city's enchantment, its charms, and its classical traditions and their impact on him, letters that contained, as well, statements of tender love for his father.[26]

Sergei Alekseevich's decision to follow his father into the priesthood and a turning point in his life took place during his journey to Optina Pustyn' in the fall of 1918, shortly after his marriage. The elders there, especially two of them, Fr. Anatolii and Fr. Nektarii, developed a relationship with him that was similar to the one they had with his father. To Fr. Anatolii and Fr. Fedosii, and later the elder Fr. Nektarii in particular he felt a special kinship, and he turned to them for counsel.[27] As Elder Fr. Nektarii said to someone who had traveled to Optina from Moscow, "Why do you come to us, when you have Fr. Aleksei?"[28] In his approach to Orthodoxy, "Fr. Aleksei brought Optina Pustyn' to Moscow." Sergei Alekseevich had already for many years served at the altar with his father, been moved by his father's prayers, and identified with the beauty and depth of the Orthodox service.[29] On March 30, 1919, Palm Sunday, he was ordained a deacon.[30] This action, and his ensuing placement in the church on Maroseika Street with his father, gave the parish of Saint Nikolai the Wonderworker two of the most powerful and respected clergy in the city. Nikolai Berdiaev, shortly before his forced exile in 1922, described his visit to the parish and his encounter with the parish's leader, Fr. Aleksei: "There was indeed something about him reminiscent of Dostoevsky's Starets Zosima. He seemed to belong to a wholly different spiritual world from that of the majority of the Russian clergy. . . . Through him I came to feel a new bond with the historical Orthodox Church, which has in fact never been completely broken, despite all my non-conformity and protestations against it."[31]

Several foundational beliefs and practices underlay all the activities of the parish throughout the lives of Fr. Aleksei and Fr. Sergei Mechev. Both priests saw concrete experience and active service, grounded in the Gospels, as fundamental to their faith. They did not see religious belief as providing a temporary boost of energy or a calming sedative, but as a way of living and a manner of viewing the world.[32] At the core of Fr. Aleksei's faith was love—"the strongest love," Pavel Florensky said, "for everything around him," and his lips breathed "only peace, love, and comfort."[33] Christ gave us the model and the instruction: "to love God, to love our neighbors; to live not for oneself, but for the benefit of those who are our neighbors."[34] This was the "Divine Law," which was "higher than liturgical regulations."[35] In both their beliefs and actions, he and Fr. Sergei exemplified another principle: spiritual freedom. It was, in N. A. Struve's words, among Fr. Aleksei's "special gifts," and distinguished him and the Maroseika parish from many others in Moscow.[36]

In 1922, by a personal order of V. I. Lenin, both Mechevs were imprisoned, but were soon released. Fr. Aleksei did not long survive: he died on

June 9, 1923. In 1929, the Soviet government again arrested Fr. Sergei, and, as mentioned earlier, two years later closed the Maroseika church. Fr. Sergei Mechev died in a Iaroslavl' prison in 1942.[37] Nevertheless, their teachings would later be transmitted to very different political and social circumstances, and the core principles and the lived experiences of the Mechevs would be reinterpreted and applied in Russia's social setting at the end of the twentieth century.

Connecting Sacred and Secular

In the late 1970s and 1980s at Novaia Derevnia, Fr. Aleksandr faced challenges similar to those that the Mechevs had faced earlier in the twentieth century, although the social and political settings were very different. Men spoke to a broadly diverse group of people, whose interests and needs ranged across a wide spectrum. Like the Mechevs, he sought to recover and emphasize the foundations of the Orthodox tradition, but under circumstances in which those foundations had either been repressed or severely misinterpreted. In three ways, Fr. Aleksandr followed the Mechevs' teaching.

First, Fr. Aleksei Mechev never imposed his own views on the people he encountered and never employed threats or force in an effort to encourage Orthodox belief. In taking this approach, he learned not only from Fr. John of Kronstadt, but also from the elders of the Optina Pustyn' Monastery, with whom he had close relationships. Whether a believer or nonbeliever, Orthodox or non-Orthodox, a Jew or member of another faith, he never offered to convert or baptize them nor did he "make even an oblique allusion" to these actions, but instead, in the same spirit as the Optina Elders, he "warm[ed] them by his love."[38]

In his relationships with his parishioners at Novaia Derevnia, Fr. Aleksandr Men followed the same course, never attempting to coerce, but only to affirm the dignity of the person, regardless of his or her religious affiliation. This positive affirmation of each individual, this attempt to draw out the best in a person, was a hallmark of his priesthood, said Fr. Vladimir Arkhipov, who served at Novaia Derevnia.[39] Fr. Aleksandr affirmed the dignity of each person who came to him, and, in reaching out to each individual, he looked beyond the external appearance to the inner being, to the "I", which he tried to nourish and which he considered one of the primary responsibilities of a priest.[40]

Second, in the early twentieth century, the Mechevs had built relationships with parishioners that extended far beyond the physical structures on Maroseika Street. The two priests developed what came to be known as the "Maroseika Community" (*Maroseiskaia obshchina*), composed of both men and women, a "free-standing society of people," convened by Fr. Sergei Mechev and blessed by Patriarch Tikhon in 1919. The "brotherhood" described itself as an "open society" and explored certain topics—peace, reason, conscience, the family, sacred literature—and read excerpts from the Holy Fathers. The sessions, or "conversations," as they were commonly called, were led by the parish's "young priests"—Sergei Mechev and Sergei Durylin.[41] In creating this spiritual community, Pavel Florensky argued, the Maroseika community became the "daughter of Optina Pustyn."[42]

The small groups of people Fr. Aleksandr created in 1977 and thereafter, meeting all over Moscow and elsewhere, served a similar purpose. These groups connected their participants to the primary sources of their tradition: sacred texts and teachings that had been lost and needed to be rediscovered. By emphasizing prayer for the vulnerable and weak, underscoring the importance of compassion and care, and nurturing people in historic Orthodox beliefs about peaceful living, these groups struck against the violence in their society, spoke against imposing one's views on others, and cultivated peace and hope for the world.[43]

The Mechevs served during a period of great social change in Russia marked by war, revolution, and civil strife. "In Moscow," as one close observer recalled, "came hunger, after it, sickness; each day came new anxieties, fear, and dangers."[44] In the years 1917 to 1921, more and more people showed up at Fr. Aleksei's small church, seeking the council and prayers of the Mechevs, having "lost their property, their means of subsistence, and the ground under their feet, broken down by heavy circumstances, mutual hostility, and desperation." These individuals were looking for compassion and a sense of direction and hope, which, according to multiple sources, they found at the Mechevs.'[45] A similar spirit characterized the parish at Novaia Derevnia, where Men used an approach that connected him to Optina Pustyn' and the Mechevs.

Fr. Aleksei Mechev had appealed to the Russian intelligentsia, and they became his special mission. They found his humility, his lack of pretension, and his openness inviting, often compelling, and distinctively different from many other priests.[46] When someone began to talk to him in abstract language or in terms drawn from some publication, he replied, laughing and rolling his eyes, "I am an illiterate. I don't understand." But this response, as Florensky notes, was deceiving, because "in reality he had an enlightened and penetrating mind," and members of the intelligentsia did not come to him only about matters of everyday life, but they also "received advice about the plans of their work in various fields of culture, and departed from him satisfied."[47] He, like Fr. Aleksandr Men later, did not turn his back on secular culture. When Sergei Alekseevich joined his father in the work of the parish, his knowledge of ancient Russian literature, art, and contemporary writers expanded the parish's scope and capacity to connect with both the secular and spiritual worlds.

Similarly, in his parish activities and his writings, Fr. Aleksandr did not draw a firm line between the secular and the sacred. Christianity, in his understanding, is the unity of God and human beings. "In our Orthodox tradition," said Yves Hamant, "we have a wrong understanding when we say that anything of the world is not to be embraced." As Fr. Aleksandr interpreted the New Testament, "the task of a life in Christ is the search for the harmony between these two dimensions of life. People who come to Christ should not leave behind their previous life; they should not leave the world."[48] In the late 1960s and 1970s, Hamant saw many young people who gathered around Fr. Aleksandr and became his followers and who questioned whether service to God meant they should leave their previous life. Fr. Aleksandr's response always encouraged them to "continue their activities. The writer must continue to write books, the artist must continue to paint. It is very important that all these activities—the secular and the sacred—be joined."[49]

Lastly, the practice of hospitality marked the service of both Fr. Andrei and Fr. Sergei Mechev and characterized the atmosphere of their entire parish. A wide variety of people—professors, doctors, students, workers, Sisters of Mercy, and impoverished people, even those in the most difficult circumstances—"met here a heartfelt welcome."[50] In the bitterly cold winter of 1918–1919,

> In the cold church, Father [Fr. Andrei] often is sick with a cold, and lies in bed, but those thirsty for his help and his words come as before and, in long lines, stand on the stairs. By twos, they are allowed into the small hallway in order to get warm; by ones, they enter the dining room. In the middle of the room, is an iron stove with a pipe extending through the ventilation window—wet firewood emitting more puffs, then heat: the room is filled with smoke. The priest lying in bed, his eyes red, tears up from the smoke. But he has the same love, the same light and smile. "You rarely come to see me." "Yes, Father; you have grown old and sick. How could one possibly disturb you? . . ." "What do you mean old? This insults me, I am offended, I am still young. . . . No, no, you must come to me."[51]

At Novaia Derevnia, Fr. Aleksandr demonstrated hospitality similar to that of Fr. Aleksei Mechev. A young woman described her first visit with a friend to the parish:

> When she saw how the priest came forward, embraced her, kissed her friend, she for the first time in her life saw that there existed such a father. In his demeanor, he was not a guru or severe elder. He was a man, who imparted to us on a human level the meaning of the spiritual life. Most of all, the relationship of Fr. Aleksandr with his parishioners illustrates the parable of the prodigal son. A true spiritual father is one who relates to his children with tenderness and without pressure, who is able, without quarreling, to set free the lost child from the "distant country."[52]

Repeatedly, individuals who came to speak with Fr. Aleksandr described his generosity, his extension of himself to them, and his total absorption in their problems and sufferings, all while others stood in line to recount similar misfortunes.[53] This generosity, and its accompanying compassionate spirit, knew neither religious nor ethnic boundaries.

Reaching across the Boundaries

Neither Fr. Aleksei nor Fr. Sergei Mechev saw Orthodoxy as an exclusively Russian religious faith, nor did they expressly attempt to convert individuals to their own perspectives. They "generously distributed" to parishioners the values they understood lay at the core of their tradition: humility, compassion, joy, and love.[54] The Maroseika parish consisted of Orthodox and non-Orthodox believers, including many Muslims, Jews, Armenians, Lutherans, Communists, and nonbelievers.[55] These diverse groups coexisted, and their presence in this ethnically diverse community enriched the entire parish.

At Novaia Derevnia, Fr. Aleksandr Men also appealed to a broad spectrum of individuals, who held widely different perspectives on life, faith, and religious traditions. These individuals were drawn to him for a variety of reasons, not least of which was his capacity to see each person who came to him as unique, a "child of God," despite the personal differences separating them from each other. Through the doors of his office, wrote a fellow priest, "came thousands of diverse people: guests and his spiritual children, friends, strangers, Orthodox, Catholics, educated, and illiterate people." Anyone entered "who was interested in the Truth and the road to it, everyone who had questions and doubts about faith and wished to resolve them, everyone who searched for the meaning of life and answers to the burning questions of good and evil, injustice and what lay beyond their strength—all these were welcomed as friends."[56]

These circumstances raised a question that would become even more important in the future, given the demographic trends in his society: How could Orthodoxy flourish in an increasingly diverse and religiously divided world? What could Orthodoxy's tradition contribute to the development of a pluralistic and peaceful world, when historical trends drew strong lines of separation between different religious groups, pitting one set of religious beliefs against another, often leading to violent confrontations?

Aleksandr Men, according to his friend and colleague Fr. Aleksandr Borisov, maintained that "knowledge of God is a process"; it is neither complete nor fixed in time. When a person makes a claim to complete truth, he suffers from an illusion, and history is replete with examples of the tragic and violent consequences of such an illusion. Fr. Aleksandr did not look down on people of different faiths, but rather viewed individuals who had even a vague sense of the Divine with appreciation. The same appreciation applied to people with divergent views of truth. The Muslim who "believes in a single God as sovereign of history and humanity," Fr. Aleksandr said, "also confesses a truthful faith."[57]

What he rejected was a static, dogmatic assertion of faith. Such a mind-set disregarded faith as a process, a constant act of becoming. From the beginning, biblical revelation opened up to humankind "a non-static model of world history," a dynamic model in which the "whole cosmos is in movement," evolving toward something different from what had appeared earlier.[58] Thus, the world is incomplete, and human attempts to profess a complete version of truth, as the high priests of the Catholic Inquisition during the Middle Ages did, betray Christianity. They were arrogant holdovers, in Fr. Aleksandr's view, of paganism.[59]

The Divine Spark: Creativity and Freedom

While God's revelation in Christ had already taken place, Christianity, Fr. Aleksandr maintained, was still in its infancy.[60] Theologians and priests "usually don't speak in this way," said Yves Hamant.[61] Aleksandr Men, however, pointed out that humanity needed a lot of time to understand the fullness of Christianity in all its dimensions, and this was a lengthy, evolving process in which each member of the parish community was called to participate. Such participation called for creativity. This was the "divine spark" that God had placed in each individual, in the expectation that the person would remain open to the world, respect it in all its beauty, and strive constantly to use all one's faculties to serve and improve the common good. It was when a person ceased to create and explore, falling into a static, dogmatic view of truth, that an individual betrayed God's purpose.

It requires freedom to hear the call of this creative element, which is one of humankind's greatest and most fundamental gifts. It is each person's responsibility to nourish the divine source, this internal icon; without the struggle of the mind and soul, this nourishment could not take place. Christ had come into the world in order to stimulate the mind and the heart and to heal, not to stifle the spirit, reward complacency, or break things asunder. When the followers of Christianity act in ways that run counter to the creative spirit and to fresh ways of seeing, their behavior contradicts the most essential teachings of Christ. They reveal their weakness and their inability to see and hear clearly as Christ had taught and as he had lived.[62] At Novaia Derevnia, Fr. Aleksandr's goal for his parishioners was similar to that of Fr. Aleksei Mechev earlier at Maroseika: "to strengthen in them freedom and a sense of responsibility" to others and to the world, both of which nourish the creative spirit.[63]

Creativity requires the struggle of the soul with itself, a process that lies beyond the boundaries imposed by an external authority. Thus, in Fr. Aleksandr's view, a person has to break free from the absolutist teachings of the state, and the church, in order to speak effectively, also has to renounce its alliance with the Russian government. The connection to state power twists the Orthodox Church into something it was never meant to be, detaching the church from its original teachings.[64] To discover its proper role and to connect to what he called the "divine flow" in each person, creation must remain free.[65]

Aleksandr Men's conception of freedom had several correlates. The Russian Orthodox Church had repeatedly misrepresented its call to freedom and offered something else. It confused freedom with power. It had enshrined certain tendencies that suppressed freedom and supported its opposite. As Fr. Aleksandr stated, "Gazing sometimes under the cupolas of the ancient cathedrals and seeing there the face of Christ presented in the image of the Pantocrator, the giant with terrifying eyes, looking down on the crowd with frightful eyes, I thought how little the representation depicts Christ."[66] Such an image scarcely "resembles the Christ who came into the world and who said: 'You shall know the truth and the truth will set you free."' Living up to this ideal requires seeing through new eyes, liberating oneself from indoctrination, both political and religious.

The freedom Fr. Aleksandr had in mind required openness to the world. In his teachings, this unencumbered view was an essential feature of authentic Christianity. He called for the Orthodox Church to embrace the spirit of the Church Fathers—to be open to adventure, to the beauty of the world in its multiple forms, and to different ways of seeing.[67] When the church had exposed itself to new voices within its tradition and welcomed diverse ways of seeing, it had been most creative and constructive. But when the church had closed itself off and turned into an instrument of power, as it had done multiple times in Russian history, it lost its integrity and betrayed its primary mission of speaking effectively and healing a fragmented world.[68]

It must always be kept in mind, in the words of Andrei Eremin, that Fr. Aleksandr grew up in the "bosom of the church in the years of ideological dictatorship."[69] This ideological dictatorship deeply affected the inner workings of the church, including its approach to Christianity, an approach that also had authoritarian characteristics. Never succumbing to these autocratic structures and reading and interpreting the Gospels through his own mind, Aleksandr Men never had the impulse to impose his will on others. "Never did he attempt to predetermine our steps or intrude upon our views," Eremin said, and "never did he try forcibly to open the petals with his hands before the flower bloomed, but nourished the flower with its own juices, warming it with love."[70]

Fr. Aleksandr sharply criticized the dangers of religious rigidity, the unwillingness to see beyond narrowly constructed boundaries. He had emphasized this danger in his book *Syn chelovecheskii*, particularly the Pharisees' attempts to make "external exhibitions" the center of religious life.[71] When Christ said, "Mercy is more pleasing to God than ordinances," the Pharisees attitude took his words as attempts to subvert the religious order.[72] Such an attitude could not fulfill the church's proper mission: it fostered pride, and often promoted violence on the part of religious zealots who sought to defend the rituals from outsiders.[73]

A dogmatic, narrow, and coercive interpretation of Orthodoxy, in Fr. Aleksandr's view, undermined the church and misrepresented the teachings of Christ.[74] Fr. Aleksandr labeled the uncompromising attachment to external forms a "sickness" similar to an "obtrusive neurosis" that "has not infrequently taken hold of Christians, who forget that, for Christ, love for God and other people is incomparably greater than all external prescriptions."[75]

Humanity and Unity Based on Compassion

The importance of human relationships was the subject of one of Fr. Aleksandr's most significant talks, which he presented in the form of a "household conversation" in one of his informal gatherings. Titled "To Love God and to Love Humankind" ("Liubit' Boga i liubit' cheloveka"), his talk examined the nature of human flourishing, how it originates, and how it becomes part of God's plan for the world.[76] Fr. Aleksandr began his "household conversation" with a reference to the parable of the division of the sheep and goats, taken from the Gospels of Matthew and Mark. Fr. Aleksandr maintained that the genetic divisions between the two animals are rarely pure, since each species contains part of the genetic structure of the other. His use of this example suggested that the lines that are often drawn between different groups, animal or human, are often artificial constructs.

Fr. Aleksandr developed his argument skillfully by looking at nature, drawing a portrait of the natural world from biology and focusing on how nature's parts operate together to form a particular movement or object. A leaf or a blade of grass, for example, is composed of cells, which, in forming inner connections with each other, comprise the whole organism. A similar process defined the human body, which is constructed according to the same principle. Fr. Aleksandr asked what would result if the cells in the body lost connection with their surrounding cells and broke away from them. When cells break away from the control of the whole organism and develop in places where they are not needed, they produce cancer, whose ultimate outcome is often death.

Human beings had a need for unity similar to these cellular organisms, but with one major difference. Humans are conscious of what is taking place; they have an ingrained need for unity with other human beings and for service to them. This need is well expressed in the biblical injunction: "It is more blessed to give than to receive." Fr. Aleksandr maintained that a willful withdrawal into the self—a desire to close oneself off and to look wholly inward—contradicted this biblical teaching and produced "melancholy and pessimism." Work that focused on the self and aimed only to satisfy a person's own needs undermined a fully productive life and usually hastened illness and death. In Genesis, Cain's punishment was separation from the rest of humankind: "He was banished into the desert." Fr. Aleksandr pointed out that is was not an accident that this ancient, primordial form of punishment served as his sentence.[77]

What is required, therefore, for human beings to flourish, and how, in practice, might that be accomplished? These questions, Fr. Aleksandr asserted, were among the most important in a person's life. He was adamant about what flourishing is not, taking an position opposite from the common view of how persons are fulfilled, both in the West and increasingly in Russia, that is, by the ethic of consumption. In his household conversation, he painted a critical picture of the person who accumulates great monetary wealth and is showered with praises and high honors, but who also expresses a cynical view and demonstrates little regard for other people. These material satisfactions, Fr. Aleksandr said, are temporary and have to be replenished again and again in order to be sustained. A social order based on material consumption ultimately degrades the individual.

What, then, is essential for an individual, as well as a culture, to be fulfilled and to live well? The common answer to that question is "to love," but, as theologian Miroslav Volf has emphasized, the choice a person makes is "*what* to love but not *whether* to love."[78] Fr. Aleksandr's response to the question evokes an ancient Orthodox and biblical understanding of human flourishing centered on love for God, and, by extension, love for one's neighbors. Human beings find joy when they love God with their heart and mind and show this love to other people. Fr. Aleksandr, like Aleksei Mechev in the early twentieth century, maintained that compassion for the less fortunate members of society, for the sick, the infirm, and those who suffer, exemplifies this love. This meaning of human flourishing calls for interdependence among human beings. The "cosmic dance of existence," present from the creation of the world, connects all of life, Fr. Aleksandr said.[79]

This means that when humans "open [themselves] to good relations with other people, overcoming their sense of exclusivity, and move in a natural direction," a movement inherent in creation itself, they flourish.[80] The openness he had in mind requires a willingness to see beyond the narrow boundaries that the political and religious order has constructed. The "openness" Fr. Aleksandr advocated entails extending the self to other people, "being prepared to help each other."[81]

In his presentation, Fr. Aleksandr never used abstract language, but consistently expressed his ideas on a concrete level, using the same approach as the novelist or the poet and focusing on the everyday world. Near the end of his talk, he followed a method he commonly employed, referencing an individual whom he admired. He recounted his perspective on life of Dmitrii Evgen'evich Melekhov (1899–1979), one of the Soviet Union's most prominent scientists and a leading doctor of medicine at Moscow's Ganushkin Medical Center. A psychiatrist and author of more than 170 scientific publications and four monographs, Melekhov had a long and distinguished career of service, working at full capacity until his death at the age of eighty.

Shortly after he died, Melekhov's widow sent Fr. Aleksandr a letter, reminiscing about her late husband and recalling a question someone asked him when he was a young doctor, inquiring why he chose to specialize in psychiatry. He responded, "Because I love people."[82] Aleksandr Men knew Melekhov well; he had joined Fr. Aleksandr's parish, and, many years earlier, Fr. Aleksandr had asked Melekhov the same question about the choice of his profession, with its constant stress and the mental fatigue it provoked. Melekhov responded, "[It is because] I simply love people."[83] The psychiatrist's life had not been without physical difficulties. While still in his fifties, he had developed cancer of the throat and had undergone major surgery during which, except for part of his esophagus, his throat was removed. Yet despite this severe affliction, Melekhov had moved beyond it, serving at the highest level, his fortitude coming from an inner strength, Fr. Aleksandr pointed out, that derived from his care for other people.

During the dark years of the 1970s, when the government accused many religious dissidents of violations of the law and placed them in psychiatric institutions, Melekhov refused to become involved in politics. He had kept his balance, Fr. Aleksandr said, always retaining uppermost in his mind his commitment to the integrity of his vocation.[84] Early in his life, Melekhov had been a member of the Mechevs' Maroseika parish.[85] A secretary of the student-run Russian Christian Movement (*Russkoe khristianskoe dvizhenie*) in the 1920s, Melekhov had kept its ideals after the government suppressed the organization, turning these ideals inward and living them out through his work.[86] It was in that work, his service to others, and his love for people that he professed his Christianity, not unlike the way Aleksandr Men expressed his own commitments during his most difficult years. Melekhov's life offered an instructive and inspiring example. It is for these reasons that Fr. Aleksandr kept a framed picture of the psychiatrist on the wall of his church office at Novaia Derevnia.[87]

Several years after Melekhov's death, Fr. Aleksandr addressed employees and residents at a home for the elderly and invalids. He knew well the sense of hopelessness that pervaded this institution, and he neither tried to identify nor sympathize with the individuals he saw there, many in the final stages of life, suffering from terminal illness, with amputated limbs, or living in despair. Instead, he talked about Mother Teresa and her work in the streets of Calcutta and her recent visit to the Soviet Union, using her service to other people, to whom few paid any attention, as a means of talking about love, God, and the need to reach out to others, regardless of one's status in life or condition. For God, Aleksandr Men told them, "There are no people of a second [lower] order."[88] He encouraged them, regardless of their age or physical condition, to reach out to others, to care for them, and to bring them peace. It did not matter, he emphasized, whether a person was Orthodox, Catholic, Muslim, Lutheran, or atheist; what mattered was love for God and love for each other. "When you love, you live in eternity," he said, "when you believe, you live in eternity, when you hope, you live in eternity."[89]

Fr. Aleksandr lived in a multinational and multiethnic country in which violence had, in the past, characterized the relationships between its diverse religious identities. He made frequent statements about openness and about the need to remove the boundaries separating different people, and he often spoke about how Russian Orthodoxy should relate to other religions in this respect, preserving and even strengthening its own identity in the face of the challenges it confronted from all sides. The position Aleksandr Men took did not mean that he advocated the blending together or the absorption into a single unified body of all religious traditions, in an attempt to overcome their separate identities. He firmly argued against such notions. This idea had failed in the past and would not work in the present, and he illustrated his point by using a simple example from painting, asking what happened when individual styles of icon painting, rococo, the Renaissance, Cubism, and the art of antiquity were intermingled.[90] The results would not produce greater creativity, but rather a "pitiful eclecticism."

How, then, should diverse religious traditions learn to live peacefully together, when they each aspired to gain as large a share of the public square as possible, restrained only by a powerful government that kept their aspirations in check? A large, although not exclusive, part of the discussion of this issue was directed to the Muslim population, which, by the mid-1980s, comprised the second largest religious body in the Soviet Union. Muslims made up 19.2 percent of the Soviet population in the late 1980s, with a growth rate five times higher than any non-Muslim group at that time.[91] A first priority for the church, Aleksandr Men argued, was to refuse "to be fed by rumors, myths, and the hatred literature of other humans," which corrupted the mind and the spirit.[92]

A second priority for the Orthodox Church entailed refocusing on Christianity's emergence in the world, conveying its foundational principles.[93] During a period of intense strife, hatred, and suppression of dissent, the apostle Paul proclaimed that in Christ, "there is neither Greek, nor Jew, nor barbarian, nor Scythian, nor slave, nor free." This is not to negate, Fr. Aleksandr said, the national forms of Christianity or the imprint of culture on particular practices and expressions of belief, but these influences did not diminish the principles that lay at the core of that religious tradition.[94]

Aleksandr Men recalled the long, tragic history of the relationship between Christianity and Islam, a history marked by conquests, violent crusades, and bloodshed. This history had created a framework characterized by suspicion and the expectation of conflict. It was crucial, Fr. Aleksandr insisted, to break out of this narrow framework; if they did not, the future would be replete with "never ending hatred and bloodshed."[95] Fr. Aleksandr believed this was a task in which the church must lead, since it was the sole institution capable of such leadership. He pointed out the similarities between Orthodox Christianity and Islam, beginning with the shared belief in a single, transcendent God, the prophetic traditions the two cultures had in common, and other shared beliefs. It was essential to rediscover the commonalities and to build bridges between these two great religious traditions. He well understood that a peaceful world in the future greatly depended on such an effort.[96]

The Vital Importance of Dialogue

The most promising, as well as challenging, means of dealing with the threat of violence involved the use of dialogue. Dialogue serves as a means of narrowing the deep chasm lying between differing world visions. Aleksandr Men found support in the writings of the British novelist Graham Greene. Fr. Aleksandr had great respect for Greene and when young had begun to read his work.[97] He admired Greene's humor, his use of paradox, and his subtle ability to unmask the arrogance and hypocrisy of political and religious figures in positions of power. He particularly appreciated Greene's approach, including the setting of his heroes usually in some distant, extreme situation, where they confronted some of the most formidable, contentious problems of their times, as well as the eternal questions of "good and evil, duty and compromise, and the choices made along life's road."[98] Such situations cried out for dialogue between people with widely differing perspectives, as Greene emphasized in *The Power and the Glory*, a novel Fr. Aleksandr began to translate into Russian in 1980.[99]

The Power and the Glory takes place in Mexico in the 1930s, when the book's main character, a nameless "whisky priest," living in a provincial town, confronts what he sees as his shortcomings, both present and past. He is one of the last remaining Catholic priests in a country that is determined to abolish religion and had executed many of its priests. He loves strong drink and has fathered a child with a woman in the parish he previously served. The priest is relentlessly pursued by a young lieutenant who is committed to an atheistic state and is convinced that the church has always been an ally of wealthy landowners and a corrupt governing order; he is not opposed to violence as a means of exterminating the enemy. The lieutenant leads the priest into a trap, but in the process, as they get to know each other, they discover that the distance between them is not as great as they had previously imagined.

Dialogue, as Greene showed, and as Fr. Aleksandr reiterated, required not only a look outward, but also inward, a reexamination of the self. The priest in Greene's novel learns in jail, when everything is stripped away, that he has to confront what cannot be taken away from him and is most essential: his internal freedom and his compassion. When he is captured by the fanatical Communist lieutenant, he learns that they have much in common: a longing for justice, a desire to help the poor, and a common humanity. As they talk together at night on the road to the priest's imprisonment, the two antagonists discover the doctrinaire images they had held of each other begin to melt away.

Similarly, in Aleksandr Men's view, the Orthodox Church has to open itself up to dialogue with other faiths and traditions. This dialogue would expand the church's capacity for imagination, and encourage it to rethink its role in the world. It would also nurture the church's ability to speak to people longing for meaning and relevance. Such a dialogue offered a means to prevent the "spectre of apocalyptic catastrophe," of which *The Power and the Glory* had subtly and brilliantly given warning. "The spirit that permeates Greene's novel," Fr. Aleksandr wrote, "is characteristic of our stormy and contradictory century, which is marked not only by violence and cruelty, but by the passionate desire among people for peace and mutual understanding. It is now, as the twentieth century comes to a close, that we must begin to think seriously about the direction to which the inflated 'image of an enemy' leads."[100]

As Fr. Aleksandr interpreted it, the church's role was to look to those spiritual and intellectual sources that had not isolated the church from the world but rather had engaged it in dialogue. He also felt that the church needed to stress the use of reason and imagination in faith and that there was a need for reconciliation both with the Russian past and with other faith traditions. At the core of these convictions was God's love for humankind and for the world, whose extension entails loving one's neighbor, seeing the connections between all human beings, and acting on these connections with compassion.

One might assume that such teachings inspired little enmity, but that assumption would prove dangerously wrong, as will be shown in the following chapter. Aleksandr Men's efforts to articulate these principles were met with suspicion, particularly on the part of the security organs. They had a very different view of what the Soviet state needed and how it might be protected from what were called "unbridled elements."[101]

11

. . . .

Under Siege

Since the formation of the Soviet Union in 1922, the security police had kept close watch on all religious activities. In 1954, the year after Stalin's death and the execution of Lavrentii Beria, head of the secret police (the NKVD, or People's Commissariat of Internal Affairs [*Narodnyi komissariat vnutrennikh del*]), the Soviet party-government reorganized the state security apparatus, bringing its various branches together into one large body, the Committee for State Security, or KGB (*Komitet gosudarstvennoi bezopasnosti*). This reorganization gave the party-government greater supervision over the police and its various functions. In 1968, Iurii Andropov, director of the KGB, reformed the departments within the organization on the heels of the "Prague Spring" in Czechoslovakia, which was a movement for political liberalization that inspired hope for change throughout the Eastern Bloc. Within the KGB, the Fifth Directorate was assigned to monitor internal dissension in the Soviet Union. In this directorate, a special section, the Fourth Department, had responsibility for religious groups. The Fourth Department was charged with making reports, monthly and annually, to the Central Committee of the Communist Party detailing the activities and providing the names of individuals and groups the department believed threatened to subvert the Soviet state.

During the years of Men's priesthood, the relationship between the KGB and the Orthodox Church underwent several significant changes. After Khrushchev's fall from power in October 1964, the mass closures of churches and the heavy-handed incarceration of priests slackened. A different, more sophisticated approach was employed to achieve the Party's goal of developing a thoroughly secular society in the Soviet Union. In preparation for this new approach, in 1965, the Soviet government merged the Council for Russian Orthodox Church Affairs with the Council for the Affairs of Religious Cults, the latter covering all non-Orthodox religious denominations. The head of the new council was a KGB official, Vladimir Alekseevich Kuroedov, who was charged with coordinating police and legal actions against religious believers. The Council for Religious Affairs thus had KGB personnel both at the top and throughout its ranks, overseeing and reporting on religious activity throughout the country.[1]

But if the KGB had supervisory role in relation to all religious activity, the pressure to conform to its wishes fell with heaviest weight upon the hierarchy of the Orthodox Church.[2] From the late 1960s through the 1980s, the patriarch and leading bishops repeatedly carried out the commands of KGB officials, acted in concert with police objectives, and served as emissaries of government policies, although these policies ran counter to the church's integrity. The Council for Religious Affairs reported to the Council of Ministers; the Council of Religious Affairs was directly connected to the government's ideological struggle with political and human rights dissidents.[3] In this battle, the patriarch, leading church hierarchs, and the government joined forces.

In the late 1960s, while Fr. Aleksandr was experiencing difficulties in his Tarasovka parish, the leadership of the KGB was undergoing a significant change. In 1967, Iurii Vladimirovich Andropov became director of the KGB. His appointment coincided with increasing anxiety about Western attempts to undermine the Soviet Union by threatening the core principles on which the Soviet state was founded. This fear of "ideological subversion" particularly characterized Iurii Andropov. Earlier, in October–November 1956, while serving as ambassador to Hungary, he had experienced firsthand the spontaneous, popular uprising against the government of the Hungarian People's Republic. Looking down from a window in the Soviet embassy, he witnessed, to his horror, the lynching of members of the security police. He saw how quickly a government, believed to be invincible, had nearly collapsed.[4] Such memories remained deeply imprinted in his mind, and they again came to the surface during the "Prague Spring" in 1968, and, later, during the nationwide strike in Poland in the spring of 1981. He saw conspiracies everywhere, which he believed had to be met with constant vigilance and an aggressive response.

As a priest whose activities in the 1960s and '70s spread beyond the boundaries of his parish, Fr. Aleksandr could not have avoided the attention of the Fourth Department of the KGB. As noted earlier, during the 1960s the police suspected him of concealing an unpublished manuscript copy of Alexander Solzhenitsyn's novel *First Circle*, and searched his home and his church for it. Additionally, Aleksandr Men had close relationships with several known, prominent religious dissidents, including Gleb Yakunin,

Nikolai Eshliman, Dmitrii Dudko, and Sergei Zheludkov, and his friendship with Solzhenitsyn before the famous writer's exile in 1974 must have been cause for suspicion. His writings on the Gospels, the history of religion, and multiple other topics offered views radically different from the dialectical and historical materialism that comprised the core of Soviet ideology.

The first known reference to Aleksandr Men in the files of the KGB is found in a 1974 report to the Central Committee of the Communist Party of the Soviet Union (CPSU). Written by KGB head Iurii Andropov and labeled "state secret," the report concerns groups within the Russian Orthodox Church described by Andropov as having come under Catholic influences and as seeking to become more independent from desired ways of thinking and believing.[5] Andropov accused Fr. Aleksandr of being the leader of this group of independent-minded people, and he also pointed out Fr. Aleksandr's relationship with a so-called "Catholic press" in Belgium, with whom Aleksandr Men published his books. As Andropov's report charged,

> A group of pro-Catholic minded priests, led by A. MEN (Moscow region), propound the idea in their theological works that the ideal of church life is represented by Catholicism. The works mentioned, illegally taken abroad, are published by the Catholic publisher "Life with God" (Belgium) and are then sent for distribution in the USSR [and elsewhere].[6]

Andropov referenced an "ideological battle against the USSR," spearheaded in the Vatican, which aimed to this ideological conflict by seeking connections with the Russian Orthodox Church. The KGB director cited a series of conferences sponsored by the Vatican, which were held in Leningrad in 1967, in Bari, Italy, in 1970, and most recently, in Zagorsk, in 1973, the latter on the theme of "Justice, Peace, and Religious Freedom." He believed these dialogues to be extremely dangerous for the Soviet Union, since their ultimate motive, he maintained, was to undermine the Soviet state.[7]

Several aspects of Andropov's report relating to Fr. Aleksandr bear mention. The first concerned the KGB director's suspicion of the Catholic Church and what he claimed was its desire to seek greater influence in the Soviet Union, to "draw the Russian Orthodox Church into its orbit." Sinister goals, he asserted, underlay efforts to reach out to Orthodox parishes. By implication, Fr. Aleksandr's activities, which aimed at crossing certain religious boundaries, had to be curtailed. Andropov was particularly critical of Pope Paul VI's attempts to heal the divide between Catholic and Orthodox churches and his portrayal of these churches as "sisters, between which

exists an almost complete relationship."[8] Andropov's projection of an ideological war revealed either what he firmly believed or what, in his mind,
members of the Central Committee wanted to hear. His report exaggerated
the coherence of a group of young, like-minded priests whose attraction to
Catholicism brought them together. They were not at all a unified group, as
journalist Sergei Bychkov noted, but a loose collection of individuals who
occasionally came together to talk about common problems and how to
make the Orthodox Church more dynamic.[9]

Second, the KGB director's warned the Party about the political consequences of such dialogue. His assertion that the Catholic Church blamed
the "leadership of the Russian Orthodox Church for excessive loyalty to the
state" suggested his own firm support for that relationship and opposition
to anything that might suggest independence.[10] Equally, he argued that dialogue pointed to attempts to revive religious life and that it threatened the
official policy of the state.

Third, Andropov cited Fr. Aleksandr's writings, but it is obvious that the
KGB director had not read any of them. Nowhere did these pages support
Catholic positions; nowhere did Fr. Aleksandr express the view "that the
ideal of church life is represented by Catholicism." Moreover, Andropov's
claim that a Catholic press published Men's books abroad and shipped them
into the Soviet Union was a total misreading and misinterpretation of the
Belgian publisher. There was no evidence of the Vatican's involvement in the
work of the press or with the editor, Irina Posnova.[11] While she had joined
a Catholic parish in Brussels, she was the daughter of a Russian immigrant,
retained a passionate interest in Russia, and had a strong commitment to
the Orthodox tradition, in whose spirit she began her publishing house. It
served the interests of the police and Party establishment in the war against
religion to theorize about the exaggerated projection of a Catholic network,
established by the Vatican, whose long arm stretched from Rome to a small
printing press in Brussels and then to a group of young clerics led by a
well-educated priest in a small parish. The KGB director's report called for
close watch over Fr. Aleksandr Men and his activities.

In the KGB's documents, the security police gave Fr. Aleksandr the code
name of "Missionary." The police assigned such appellations to police victims as well as to their own agents, and subsequent communications often
referred to Fr. Aleksandr only by his code name.[12] This action confirms that
he had become a target of KGB observations. The shadowing of Aleksandr
Men included the placement of informants in his parish, most of whom
he easily identified and then notified his closest associates about.[13] The
police stationed observers near the transit lines leading to Novaia Derevnia,

assigned them to record the people who entered the parish, listen to their conversations, and report on foreigners who came to visit.[14] In January 1977, a report prepared by the Fourth Department and sent to the Central Committee referred to "information received by agents," which disclosed "the hostile activity of Yakunin, Dudko, Men and others," and asserted that "many believers and church people have begun to speak negatively" about them.[15] The individuals cited in the report were to be observed with even greater vigilance.

But it was not only these suspicions that warranted the KGB's attention. Aleksandr Men's relationships with his parishioners, his personal integrity, and his commitment to crossing the boundaries that separated people threatened the political interests of organizations that had a stake in preserving, even strengthening, these boundaries. He constantly professed a lack of interest in politics, and he eschewed actions that opposed the political and religious establishments. He insisted his chief obligation lay in serving his parishioners and teaching and living through the Gospels. But these commitments, which appealed to people searching for alternative ways of viewing the universe, challenged the closed structure established by the government on many different levels.[16]

The KGB and Ideological Warfare

In her study of the KGB and its relationship to the Russian Orthodox Church, Russian historian Irina Ivanovna Maslova examined diverse archival materials relating to the Committee for State Security and the Central Committee of the Communist Party. Her impressive study revealed the primary concerns of the security police and how, in the last decades of the Soviet era, the agency communicated its concerns to the Party's leadership. She found that beginning in May 1964, KGB documents informed the Central Committee about a supposed new tactic engineered by the Vatican: the search for "fresh methods to improve and secure the influence of the Catholic Church more broadly among the masses."[17] According to the deputy director of the KGB, S. Bunnikov, these initiatives consisted of exchanging blessings with leaders of other religions throughout the socialist countries and rapprochement with all Christian denominations, with the ultimate goal of creating "a united front against countries in the socialist camp and the communist movement in the whole world." In his report, Bunnikov warned of the need to guard firmly against such ostensibly congenial, but ominous, tactics. "Under the warm, inviting cloak of friendship," Pope Paul

VI, elected in 1963, was "engaged in a flexible, well-camouflaged struggle with communism."[18]

From the perspective of KGB officials, political motivations underlay the ecumenical movement spearheaded by the Catholic Church, and recent efforts to engage in dialogue and form relationships with other faith traditions concealed destructive elements. According to the KGB in later communications to the Central Committee, in 1971 the Vatican prepared a decisive offensive against atheism, setting out three geographical zones on which the ecumenical movement intended to concentrate: Moscow, the Baltic region, and the Caucasus. Under the cover of tourist organizations and educational programs, according to Filipp Bobkov, director of the KGB's Fifth Directorate, these oppositional forces aimed at establishing contacts with three specific groups, whom he thought especially susceptible to Western influence: members of the Orthodox priesthood, representatives of the intelligentsia, and the young.[19]

The plan aimed to establish contacts with Orthodox priests and also to focus on certain specific groups of the population—the intelligentsia, religious believers, and students— engaging them by encouraging them "in ideological activity of the first order and expanding religious propagandistic literature."[20]

In the late 1960 and '70s, the KGB and the governing apparatus of the Soviet Union perceived that ideological warfare between the Soviet Union and Western countries was taking a qualitatively different turn. Religious believers and church institutions became central battlefields in that struggle. This was particularly well illustrated in 1968 in Czechoslovakia when, as KGB intelligence and the reports of the Central Committee pointed out, large numbers of letters containing thousands of signatures from Czech citizens were written demanding reform and support for democratization, both in the state and the church, processes that the letter writers saw as going hand-in-hand. The predominant signatures on those letters, according to KGB reports, belonged to members of Roman Catholic, Greek Catholic, and Czech Brotherhood evangelical churches.[21]

In describing the conflict between the Soviet Union and Western European countries, most scholarship has focused on economics, foreign policy, and politics, relegating religion to the periphery. But Maslova's research, as well as other recent studies, convincingly shows that religion lay not at the margins, but at the center of the conflict.[22] Under Iurii Andropov's leadership, the KGB, which Maslova calls the "vanguard of the Party," increased its emphasis on controlling religious beliefs and practices, keeping them within the narrowest possible limits, and subjecting priests who operated outside such narrow boundaries to constant surveillance and harassment.

In the 1970s and '80s, cooperating with the KGB, the hierarchs of the Russian Orthodox Church played a large role in enforcing these restrictions. The KGB's relationship to the church hierarchy fulfilled two main purposes. The first related to the need to control perceived internal threats. Through the Council of Religious Affairs, the Moscow Patriarchate channeled information to the KGB, filing reports on parish activities, coordinating information on the work of scholars and graduate students in leading theological institutions, and providing accounts of individual priests. Cooperation with the KGB brought large material and political rewards. It is difficult to know, in some cases, whether church leaders' greater loyalty was to the government or to the Orthodox Church.[23]

The second reason concerned the international image of the Soviet Union. Patriarch Aleksii II and his successor Pimen, directed by the KGB, fostered a positive picture of the Soviet Union abroad. At international meetings they attended, both patriarchs strongly affirmed the peace initiatives of the government. Hierarchs were planted on various committees of the World Council of Churches to promote the actions of the government, and their contributions, according to KGB documents, "proved politically advantageous."[24] In June 1977, in Zagorsk, the Moscow Patriarchate hosted an international conference on "Lasting Peace, Disarmament, and Just Relations among Nations," attended by 663 representatives of all major world religions from 107 countries. The conference, organized behind the scenes by the KGB, featured an address by Patriarch Pimen, in which he trumpeted the Soviet Union's "long history of effort in the cause of peace, justice and social progress."[25] In December 1976, Pimen paid homage to what he called President Leonid Brezhnev's "titantic work in the cause of international peace" and his "efforts to secure a peaceful sky over the planets."[26]

The KGB and the government recognized the diversity within the priesthood and the presence of those who wanted the Orthodox Church to divorce itself from the government and function independently.[27] Government agencies could not tolerate that independence; neither could they accept the need for dialogue between different religious faiths and traditions, seeing open-ended dialogue as a threat to the unified political and social order these agencies aspired to create. The kinds of dialogue that Fr. Aleksandr Men believed to be essential to the Orthodox Church challenged these political controls and, most importantly, they were diametrically opposed to a uniform, one-dimensional, and static view of the Russian Orthodox faith.

"Dark Clouds Were Forming over Fr. Aleksandr's Head"

Given the Communist Party's unrelenting campaign against religion and religious believers, it may appear that conflict with the church ensued only between state authorities and Orthodox priests. The policy documents of the government and the actions of KGB agents certainly lend themselves to this interpretation. But, as a close look at the parishes Fr. Aleksandr previously served suggests, conflict also took place within the church itself, even within the parish, where personal relationships could easily turn to resentment and sometimes to outright hostility. Such enmity occurred in the Novaia Derevnia parish in the early 1980s, and it dovetailed with the ongoing KGB interrogations of Fr. Aleksandr. The conflict intensified the pressures he faced, which came not only from outside, but also inside his parish.

These early KGB investigations came at a time when "dark clouds were forming over Fr. Aleksandr's head" inside the Novaia Derevnia parish.[28] Such ominous concerns came about largely through the machinations of the new head priest, Fr. Stefan Sredi, who became head priest in January 1978. Fr. Stefan's dislike for Fr. Aleksandr soon fueled a campaign to disparage his younger, more popular colleague.

In 1979, Fr. Stefan obtained a copy of the notorious anti-Semitic *Protocols of the Learned Elders of Zion*, a forgery that allegedly represented the minutes of an 1897 meeting of Zionist leaders in Basel, Switzerland, to plot the development of a world government run by Jewish leaders. This sensational document warned against Jews disguising themselves as members of the clergy and secretly working for this Zionist cause. Given a copy of the *Protocols* by his relatives, who lived in nearby Zagorsk, Fr. Stefan distributed it among members of the parish. Surreptitiously, Fr. Stefan also encouraged two long-time members of the parish, who resented some of the changes the junior priest had initiated in the church service, to begin a petition against Fr. Aleksandr, accusing him of trying to develop in Novaia Derevnia "a half Greek and half Jewish church." The two parishioners distributed the petition throughout neighboring communities, collecting signatures. With Fr. Stefan's encouragement, they sent a letter of denunciation about Fr. Aleksandr to the authorities, recommending that he be made to answer for his "indiscretions" to the diocesan administration and the Council of Religious Affairs.[29]

Fr. Stefan, again behind the scenes and with the help of two female associates, worked to undermine Fr. Aleksandr. The senior priest dismissed the churchwarden, a woman who had long supported Fr. Aleksandr. By standing

as a buffer between him and local administrative authorities, she had protected him from criticism. In February 1980, Fr. Aleksandr reached the tenth
years of his service at Novaia Derevnia, and as customary on such occasions,
the local church governing board (*dvadtsatki*) convened to review his work.
At this meeting, the board appointed a person known to be an enemy of Fr.
Aleksandr, a woman who resented his parish work and the newcomers he
attracted. Fr. Aleksandr left the meeting, fearful that his dismissal from
the priesthood was about to take place. Although his removal did not occur,
he began to inquire in nearby communities about a possible transfer.[30]

Escalating the Ideological Battle

Meanwhile, the storm clouds thickened outside the parish. In a special
plenum held in May 1979, the Central Committee of the Communist Party
announced plans for "intensification of the ideological assault on religious
believers."[31] The announcement came as part of a larger overall effort to
expand atheistic teaching in the ideological war against religion. A revised
1977 Constitution had made clear the Party's belief in the need for a new,
more vigorous campaign. The constitution guaranteed the right to "conduct
atheistic propaganda," but denied religious believers the right to propagate
their beliefs.[32] Priests could perform religious rites, but the constitution limited their responsibilities only to those activities. Children attended schools
in which only atheistic points of view could be taught, and countervailing
ideas were prohibited, thus creating, as historian Jane Ellis has written, "an
atmosphere where atheism is all-pervasive."[33] Other government directives
were introduced, the first of which, in 1975, strictly forbade bookstores
from selling literature published by religious organizations, and the second
of which, in 1977, expressly aimed at prohibiting second-hand bookstores
from reselling books written by two philosophers, Nikolai Berdiaev and
Sergei Bulgakov, whom Lenin had expelled from the Soviet Union in 1922.[34]

In 1978, the stakes in the battle escalated still further with the election of
Karol Józef Wojtyla as Pope John Paul II (1978–2005). Born in Wadowice,
Poland, the first non-Italian pope in more than four hundred years, his election signified what the Central Committee in the Soviet Union viewed as
an especially dangerous trend in relation to Eastern European countries, as
well as to the Soviet Union. The new pope's support for an alliance between
Judaism, Islam, and Christianity and for religious pluralism represented
an immediate threat. Scholars in the Polish Institute in Moscow, Maslova
wrote, concluded in a document produced for the Central Committee that

"the existing ideals of pluralism inside the church and in society entail a softening of ideological contrasts, and this will be the means to multiply the numbers of supporters of Christian ideas."[35]

For Fr. Aleksandr, the late 1970s and early 1980s were a time of intense anxiety and concern about the future as well as a time of uncertainty about the well-being of the cause to which he had devoted himself. While he rarely displayed his anxiety in public, privately he was greatly troubled by the threatening circumstances that surrounded him.[36] He well understood that the political atmosphere had changed and every step he made required the utmost circumspection. The plenum announcement in May 1979 about the Party's intention to intensify its ideological assault served to him as a warning, possibly even a threat. "This will not end well for us," he confided to the French diplomat Yves Hamant.[37]

Fr. Aleksandr's premonition was not the first time he had sensed the perils that lay immediately ahead, but his anxiety suggests one of his most fundamental political strengths: the ability to gauge accurately the larger framework in which he lived and the subtle changes in the political atmosphere that either restricted or offered opportunities. He had "a special sense and intuition about politics," Hamant observed, knowing when he needed to curtail or shift his activities, or even to "entirely disappear for a time from the field of sight."[38]

Several additional reasons underlay the renewed hard-line approach to religion and dissent, including the Soviet Union's invasion of Afghanistan in December 1979, which precipitated worldwide protest; the planned opening of the Olympic Games in Moscow in the summer of 1980, with the opportunity for much greater contact between religious believers, political dissidents, and large numbers of foreign guests; and sociological evidence of a declining commitment among the population to Marxist-Leninist ideology and a growing interest in the Orthodox Church. Political authorities decided to draw a firm and resolute line in response to the spread of samizdat literature, the emergence of a human rights movement in the mid-1970s, and the widespread attraction to religion, especially among the young. On November 1, 1979, the KGB arrested Fr. Gleb Yakunin and incarcerated him in the Lefortovo prison. In January 1980, the government sent Academician Andrei Sakharov, the outspoken advocate of human rights, into forcible exile in the city of Gorky. On January 15, 1980, the KGB arrested the popular Orthodox priest Fr. Dmitrii Dudko, whom the church had already removed from his parish in Pskov. In January 1980, the KGB also arrested the leaders of The Christian Seminar, one of several seminar groups that had emerged to study the Orthodox tradition.[39] Given these ominous events, it had to be a matter of grave concern to Aleksandr Men when he received, in the same month, orders to report to KGB headquarters in the Lubianka prison for interrogation.

Anticipating Arrest

Facing an ever-deepening KGB presence in his parish, Fr. Aleksandr had long anticipated his summons to KGB headquarters. In preparation for it, several years earlier he gave a private interview, giving instructions for its publication only in event of his arrest.[40] Knowing that rumors might be spread about his background, he attempted to clarify certain facts about his past.

The interview mainly covered the biographical details of his upbringing, education, and publications, the latter point countering the frequent claims that he published only in foreign countries, thereby catering primarily to a Western public. Fr. Aleksandr cited the large number of chapters, comprising major parts of two of his books, which first appeared, from 1959 to 1966, in the main journal of the Moscow Patriarchate. He sent his books abroad, he said, only because Russian publishers issued a very small number of theological books.

Why, then, had he published these books under a pseudonym, not under his own name? Putting his own name on them, he pointed out, would have produced an "undesirable reaction, and could be incorrectly interpreted." What Fr. Aleksandr likely meant is that, within the church, certain factions would have disapproved of his interpretations. He had not written for officials in the Orthodox hierarchy. "For me it is more important that people could read my books. I did not look to make sensations and personal problems."[41] He wrote, he said, as a parish priest, who aspired to speak to his parishioners and to others, who searched in vain for accessible accounts of Christianity.

Aleksandr Men knew well that accusers would charge him with taking a narrowly superficial view of the church, its contributions to humanity, and its contemporary relevance. As a counter argument to such claims, he discussed the primary influences on his spiritual education, as well as the Church fathers and both Russian and Western authors who had significantly shaped his world view. Among these many authors, he cited the representatives of Russian religious philosophy at the end of the nineteenth and beginning of the twentieth century. His presentation made a strong case for him as standing in one of the most significant streams of Russian religious thought. In addition, as a priest, he had not restricted himself to a national framework, but had drawn widely on the leading theological writers of his times.

But Fr. Aleksandr's perspectives on certain controversial subjects troubling both the Russian government and society also stands out in this interview. These issues concerned Alexander Solzhenitsyn, recently expelled from the Soviet Union, Fr. Sergei Zheludkov, who had harshly criticized the Soviet government, and the future role of the Orthodox Church. Fr. Aleksandr knew he would be charged with holding views similar to these controversial figures and their opposition to the Soviet government. Seeking to set forth clearly his own position, he expressed sympathy for each of these well-known personalities, but he also set himself apart from them on many issues. He was convinced that Solzhenitsyn's "enormous role" in exposing the horrors of these times would ultimately be valued, even by his present opponents.[42] He did not, however, agree with the writer's political ideas or his strong nationalistic views.

Fr. Aleksandr spoke of his admiration for Fr. Sergei Zheludkov's desire to examine Orthodoxy's heritage through critical eyes, but he confessed that his friend had often held extreme views, which he disliked. Fr. Sergei correctly emphasized that the Orthodox could not simply "swim downstream," but had to engage contemporary issues seriously, despite the "complex situation" in which the church presently found itself. Fr. Aleksandr shared Fr. Sergei's belief, he said, that the church had to take a close look at itself internally: its canons and theology needed to be "reexamined and deepened," but this need, Fr. Aleksandr pointed out, was recognized not only by him, but by many other people in the church, at every level.[43] Such expressions are revealing of Fr. Aleksandr's ultimate commitments: in times of personal danger he was not primarily concerned with exonerating or promoting himself, but conceived of the issues as much larger than self-preservation. His main interests focused on the long-term well-being of the parish community and the Orthodox Church.

In mid-March 1980, Fr. Aleksandr believed that his arrest and possible death lay near at hand. Still, as he had during other periods of stress, he continued to write. He worked on commentaries on the Old Testament and completed his *How to Read the Bible* (*Kak chitat' Bibliiu*), the volume that was published the following year in Brussels.[44] He also gave instructions that should he be arrested, his parishioners should neither hold demonstrations, engage in public protests of any kind, nor write letters on his behalf to the patriarch. If he were to die, what then should they do? He asked that his closest friends simply carry on as before. They served, he said, a much larger purpose than concern for him.[45]

Fr. Aleksandr's summons to KGB headquarters took place on April 1, 1980. Except for members of his household, he told no one about the meeting.[46] Early that morning, he went to Novaia Derevnia, cleared his office of papers and any correspondence that, in case of a search, might be of interest to the police. He then delivered some of these materials to his editor, Zoia Maslenikova, for safekeeping and, as she recorded, he gave her instructions in the event he did not return. Before leaving, Maslenikova noted, he "asked that I pray for him at 3:00 p.m., the hour of his scheduled appointment at KGB headquarters."[47] Judging from the context in which this event took place, Aleksandr Men's arrest and incarceration appeared to be a likely outcome.

Maslenikova learned the details of what happened on that day the following week. She telephoned Fr. Aleksandr's home at 11:00 that evening, hoping that somehow the KGB had questioned and released him. To her surprise, Fr. Aleksandr answered the phone: he had arrived home a few minutes earlier. "Everything," he told her, "had gone fairly well."[48] But, as she learned later from Fr. Aleksandr, KGB officials had begun the interrogation with threats and intimidations, and this process lasted for several hours. The verbal assault and the nature of the assertions made by the police became increasingly intense, and, Fr. Aleksandr said he felt that the danger had reached a high level. But then, two hours later, the interrogation took what Fr. Aleksandr called "an inexplicable turn and change of direction." The tension in the room subsided, even became "peaceful."[49]

Whether because of his skill at responding to his interrogators' questions, the lack of concrete evidence against him, or some unknown reason, the KGB officers eventually told Fr. Aleksandr he could leave. But the decision to release him did not mean the end of the KGB's close watch over his activities or its efforts to intimidate him. On April 17, he was again summoned to the Lubianka prison for questioning about his activities and relationships with his parishioners. A year later, on June 10, 1981, KGB officers arrived at his home in the evening and questioned him again. While little information exists on the nature of this discussion or the length of the meeting, the entire episode dispirited Fr. Aleksandr. Maslenikova noted that when she met with him the following day he seemed exhausted, agitated by the atmosphere of suspicion, and unable to find peace. It seemed to her, she wrote, that his work "does not bring him joy."[50] That same summer, in August, the Fourth Department of the KGB's Fifth Directorate again summoned him for interrogation at police headquarters, questioning him about the *Protocols of Zion* and the disputes within the parish that the circulation of this incendiary document had aroused.[51] Despite the intimidation, the security police did not have sufficient evidence for his arrest. These actions, however, were only preliminary steps to the assault soon to follow.

Parish Work "Does Not Bring Him Joy"

The death of Leonid Brezhnev in November 1982 and his succession by Iurii Andropov (12 November 1982–February 1984) as leader of the Soviet Union placed supreme power in the hands of the former chairman of the KGB. Andropov brought with him into office the suspicion of dialogue and openness that characterized his leadership of the state security police. Andropov had long viewed Fr. Aleksandr as a priest requiring close surveillance, and he now intensified the pressure on Fr. Aleksandr and his activities. In the fall of 1982, while still KGB chief, Andropov announced that religion had become the main field for political dissidents, and, therefore, it was essential to cleanse the church of those voices who dissented from the established order.[52] After his accession, the new Soviet leader extended that policy to the whole of society, tightening the screws on any opposition and causing renewed fear among those who continued to have contacts with foreigners. In 1983, Fr. Aleksandr was subjected to constant close surveillance; whenever he met with her, his editor Maslenikova noted, an automobile always pulled up and parked across the street from her house.[53]

This began a nearly four-year period, from the end of 1983 to 1987, when KGB harassment of Fr. Aleksandr was most intense. The noose the police placed around him tightened in earnest in the autumn of 1983, when the police arrested Vladimir Nikifor, a former member of Fr. Aleksandr's parish, for his association with foreigners and conversion to Catholicism. Nikifor's conversion took place during a trip to Czechoslovakia, after which he returned home and allegedly began an underground Catholic organization, which met regularly in his Moscow apartment for purposes of prayer, Bible study, and the education of children. Unfortunately for Nikifor, the group included a KGB informer. Following his arrest and imprisonment in the Lefortovo prison, Nikifor confessed to the charges of state subversion, and in his testimony, he implicated several members of the Novaia Derevnia parish, including Fr. Aleksandr, who, Nikifor said, had encouraged him on this path. In January 1984, likely in exchange for his testimony, the KGB released Nikifor from incarceration, although he remained under police guard at his residence.[54]

Shortly thereafter, the KGB arrested another of Men's parishioners, Sergei Markus, who had been careless with several statements he made in public. Fr. Aleksandr had earlier broken his connections with Markus, although he knew, after learning of the arrest, that Markus could be a danger to some of his parishioners, and he cautioned them to act with extreme care. During his interrogation and trial, Markus kept his composure and stood firm against the accusations of his prosecutors; in the end, however, he broke down and appeared on television, "his head shaved and his face emaciated," and confessed to having "been involved in political activity criminal under the State and harmful to the church."[55]

During these proceedings, Fr. Aleksandr faced intensive interrogation by the KGB. In December, after Vladimir Nikifor's arrest, the police summoned him almost daily to its headquarters, so often, he told a close friend, that "he went as if to work."[56] In January 1984, as the KGB pursued the Markus case, at the conclusion of the morning service in Fr. Aleksandr's church, KGB officers arrived in a black Volga automobile and took him away, action that immediately fostered rumors of his arrest.[57] Again, the police questioned and released him, but not without intensifying the atmosphere of intimidation and harassment.

The death of Iurii Andropov on February 9, 1984, brought lavish praise of the Soviet leader from the patriarch. Paying tribute to the man who had consistently and mercilessly persecuted the church, Pimen spoke of the "great loss suffered by our Motherland" on this day. "Our people knew and respected Yuri Vladimirovich," the patriarch said, "as a man of high personal qualities, sensitive and attentive to the needs and hopes of people, who had dedicated himself wholly to the work for the good of the whole nation, to promote its prosperity and spiritual growth."[58]

Andropov's death, among those who wanted reform, fueled speculation that the regime's tight hold over the church had reached its apogee and soon would be greatly reduced. But these hopes soon proved to be unfounded. Under Andropov's successor, the septuagenarian Konstantin Chernenko (1911–1985), the Soviet government intensified still further its pressure on the Orthodox Church. To support its ideological agenda, the Communist Party again heavily relied on the KGB. During Chernenko's short-lived tenure as general secretary (February 1984–March 1985), the government passed four resolutions to strengthen atheistic education and decrease the number of church registrations.[59] These actions set the stage for still another attempt to incriminate Fr. Aleksandr.

A Carefully Laid Plot

In March 1985, the political leadership of the Soviet Union passed to Mikhail Gorbachev (b. 1931), Chernenko's much younger colleague, who immediately pledged to continue the policies of his predecessors. The Twenty-Seventh Party Congress of the Communist Party of the Soviet Union, held from February 25, 1986 to March 6, 1986, the first under Gorbachev's leadership, replaced many of the old guard who had shown resistance to change, but the new regime continued to express the same atheistic spirit as in the past.[60] Gorbachev criticized past members for their "deafness to the new"; in his political speech to the Congress, however, he showed little conciliation toward the Orthodox Church. The KGB's dominating presence in enforcing the Communist Party's guidelines on religion and harassing creative activities continued on, just as they had since Andropov. Fr. Aleksandr Men became a special target of that investigation and concern.

Looking back at the interrogations of Fr. Aleksandr from the early 1980s to 1986, it is apparent that the KGB was steadily building evidence against him and making a case designed to discredit him as a religious leader. Repeatedly, Fr. Aleksandr insisted that he represented only the priest of a small parish in the countryside. But his increasing popularity, his growing reputation as a visionary pastor and writer, and his attraction to the Russian intelligentsia made him, in the eyes of the KGB, less a simple parish priest and much more a political figure whose activities had to be stopped. The best and most effective approach to that end, police authorities believed, was to undermine his credibility and show him to be disloyal both to the Orthodox Church and to the state.

In the mid-1980s, the focus on Aleksandr Men developed under the direction of Colonel Vladimir Sychev of the Fourth Department of the KGB. Among the large numbers of people who participated in the services at Novaia Derevnia were investigators who reported to Sychev. Soon after the sentencing of Sergei Markus for state subversion, in 1985, the police arrested Sandr Riga, the Latvian leader of an ecumenical group of Christians living in Moscow. At this time, Riga counseled young people disillusioned with the practices of the Communist Party, many of whom had become alcoholics and drug addicts. Sandr Riga could often be seen at Novaia Derevnia.[61]

Once more, interrogations of Fr. Aleksandr began, but this time, given the events of the last year, they took another direction, aimed at portraying him as a sinister political figure. Col. Sychev played a large role in this carefully planned effort to portray Fr. Aleksandr as someone whose positive public image concealed disloyalty to the Soviet state. On September 9, 1985, Sychev summoned Fr. Aleksandr to a meeting in the offices of the Council of Religious Affairs, where he and Genrikh Mikhailov, the council's deputy director, interrogated the priest. Their conversation, in which both officials took an active part, lasted five hours and signified the beginning of an investigation and an attempted public assault that lasted over the next year.[62] In attendance at the meeting, sitting silently but listening attentively, taking notes, and recording the conversation, was Nikolai Dombkovskii, chief political correspondent for *Trud* (Labor), one of Russia's largest daily mass-circulation newspapers.

In the interrogation, Sychev and Mikhailov asked Fr. Aleksandr to provide them with the names of his parishioners who had most actively engaged in missionary activity to convert others to a religious worldview. In addition, they demanded that Fr. Aleksandr write a "heartfelt statement of repentance" admitting his wrongdoing in meeting with foreigners and professing his allegiance to the Soviet system, which, they said, he should submit for publication to a popular newspaper like *Izvestiia* (News). The aim of his interrogators, as Fr. Aleksandr readily understood, "was to make a Dudko out of me," a reference to the once popular priest Dmitrii Dudko, whose arrest in 1980 led to a stunning reversal of his professed views and an expression of admiration for Joseph Stalin.[63] Dudko's act of "repentance" resulted in a near total loss of respect for this once venerated priest. Aleksandr Men's interrogators desired a similar outcome for him.

The following weeks were times of anger, inner conflict, and resolve for Fr. Aleksandr Men. Failure to do what the police authorities demanded would, without doubt, result in his arrest and the loss of his parish. Compliance with the orders, on the other hand, meant the betrayal of his beliefs, as well as of those who looked to him for guidance in their lives. He wrote the letter as suggested by the KGB, first forwarding a copy to Metropolitan Iuvenalii, his supervising bishop. Then, as the police had directed, he published the letter, only he did not send it to a mass-circulation newspaper, but to a church publication.

The letter he wrote represented a cleverly composed, double-edged piece of writing that walked a narrow line between acquiescence and refutation. In his letter, he dispelled rumors, which, he said, were "widely circulated" in the Western press about his arrest and impending emigration. He also denied that the police had subjected him to seizures and to searches of his home.[64] Such false information, he wrote, served only the interests of Western political propaganda. He wished, he said, to clarify certain matters:

I have served the Russian Church for twenty-eight years now, and have suffered no repression, either by secular authorities or by church leaders. . . . I wish to register a strong protest, because my position is, and always has been, unchanged: always to be an honest citizen of my homeland, a Christian and faithful son and servant of our Russian Orthodox Church.[65]

In making these statements, which exonerated the authorities of any wrongdoing and of carrying out illegal searches, Fr. Aleksandr was not being entirely truthful. But his words also contained little of the contrition for his actions that Sychev and Mikhailov had hoped for, thinking that such an admission of guilt would demean him in the eyes of his followers. His use of standard Soviet newspeak about Western propaganda may have also been a clever ploy to appease the authorities and yet place his "statement of repentance" in a different context from that which they originally had sought. He issued the letter in a journal of the Moscow Patriarchate's Department of External Relations, a publication read mainly by top officials of the Orthodox Church hierarchy and by church leaders abroad, with little readership inside the Soviet Union. Fr. Aleksandr's letter did him scant harm. It did not produce the desired outcome that the leaders of the KGB and Council of Religious Affairs had intended.

Sychev and Mikhailov soon learned that their plan had not succeeded, after which they conceived of a wider, more inflammatory plot aimed at Fr. Aleksandr's arrest and public humiliation.[66] Their scheme involved the aforementioned Moscow newspaper *Trud* and its journalist Nikolai Dombkovskii. For many years, Dombkovskii had worked in connection with the KGB and published information passed on to him by Vladimir Sychev.[67] In the winter months of 1985–1986, Dombkovskii was given access to KGB files on Fr. Aleksandr. The plan the KGB conceived involved one Boris Razveev, a prisoner serving a sentence in one of the KGB's prison camps for "slandering the Soviet state." In the winter months, Dombkovskii, carrying a television recorder, traveled to the camp where Razveev served his term and interviewed him at length. Then, in March 1986, the Central Committee of the Communist Party directed the preparation of an article titled "Krest na sovesti" ("Cross on One's Conscience") for publication in *Trud*.[68]

Early in the evening on April 9, 1986, Dombkovskii's interview with the prisoner Boris Razveev showed on Soviet television. Appearing contrite and repentant, Razveev admitted his "anti-Soviet" activity. He proclaimed his naiveté and gullibility in listening to views harmful to his native country. When asked about his "anti-Soviet" actions, he pointed to two people who had led him "on his ruinous path"—the priest Aleksandr Men and the journalist Sergei Bychkov.[69] These accusations set the stage for the more detailed articles that soon followed.

"Krest na sovesti" appeared in two installments, on April 10 and 11, 1986, and they were bombshells.[70] The article began by recounting Boris Razveev's confession that his earlier "anti-Soviet" behavior had been a serious mistake, for which he asked the forgiveness of the Soviet people. He discussed his background, upbringing, war experience, and occupation before going on to mention his attraction to the latest fashions, from Western "hippies" to rock music. Having invested himself in Western popular culture, soon he could listen only to radio transmissions from the West—"Voice of America" and "Freedom"—gradually beginning to look at life mainly through these perspectives and allowing what he called their "ideological poison" to seep "slowly but eternally into him." Imbibing this poison, he developed a self-love and nearly unquenchable thirst for comfort that made him critical of nearly everything in his own country.

What is most interesting in the article is Razveev's account of his falling in with certain individuals, who seduced him into direct opposition to the political order in the Soviet Union. This seduction took place following his move to Moscow, after he had taken and failed the state examinations in Bashkir University, a failure he had blamed on his professors, whom he labeled "obstructionists," that is to say people who disliked students who thought differently from them. After moving to Moscow, Razveev said that he had fallen under the influence of Aleksandr Ogorodnikov, a religious dissident. Ogorodnikov convinced him that "Soviet citizens 'do not have the right to their own views,'" and turned him toward religion, but not the religion of the official church, but rather of what Ogorodnikov called the "free church."[71]

Razveev described a particularly salient moment in his Moscow experiences, a moment whose significance far transcended his own story and had political implications for the country as a whole. The meeting he described—and which he attended—took place in a private apartment, located near the metro station Rechnoi Vokzal. In addition to Razveev, participants at the meeting included Sergei Bychkov, Fr. Aleksandr's friend and a leading member of his inner circle; the political dissident Gleb Yakunin; John Stepanchik, political officer of the US Embassy in Moscow; and a special guest, Professor John Meyendorff, who had come from abroad and whom Razveev identified as a "son of the Russian White emigration, grandson of the tsar's courtier," and a person who had, for "many years, actively collaborated with anti-Soviet circles in the USA, France, and other Western countries."[72] In the meeting in Bychkov's apartment, the goal was to establish an underground network of religious believers, an organization distinctly different from the official church, persecuted and tied to the government as it was.

Razveev portrayed Fr. Aleksandr as a leading figure in this movement, which aimed to unite secret parishes and connect them to the West to be supported by Western radio transmissions, literature, and funds. The plan proposed opening in the Soviet Union a correspondence division of the Saint Vladimir Seminary in New York, whose task would be to prepare underground priests who could spread information about the "oppression of faith" in the Soviet state. These purposes explained Professor Meyendorff's presence at the meeting.

In both style and substance, "Krest na sovesti" followed the pattern often found in Soviet literature of writing a narrative that portrayed, in good and evil in concrete terms, and depicted the life of a person who has been led astray but ultimately comes to his senses and is led back onto the path of redemption.[73] Razveev's attachment to Western fashions and his gullibility brought about his downfall and the near betrayal of his country, facts his biography neatly wove into a story of sin, confession, and request for forgiveness. The narrative he concocted brought Fr. Aleksandr into this framework. Razveev presented the priest as a former aspiring scientist whose ambitions were diverted when his institute was transferred from Moscow to Irkutsk, Siberia, and he and his friend Gleb Yakunin learned that, after graduation, their future assignments were to be in a remote corner of Siberia. According to Razveev, Fr. Aleksandr's disappointment precipitated his return to Moscow and his entrance into the priesthood.

"Krest na sovesti" spoke of Fr. Aleksandr's publications in Western Europe, his personal connections with Western political and religious officials, and his attraction to Western literature: "A crooked road had led him from a normal life's path, directed him in turn to the ranks of the 'oppositionists.'"[74] Readers of the articles were led to the conclusion that a poison aimed at fostering social discontent had seeped into Soviet society under the guise of religion. By using the "church as a subversive instrument against the socialist order," the West, namely Great Britain and the United States, conducted an ideological war against the Soviet Union, and Fr. Aleksandr Men served as a leading figure in that campaign.[75]

The articles in Trud placed Fr. Aleksandr in a precarious situation, both inside church circles and, more broadly, outside, in Russian society. Personally, given the public campaign and the crude, but carefully laid plot against him, he faced being discredited as a parish priest. The circulation of this story on television and in a mass circulation newspaper severely hurt the members of his family. Until this time, Nataliia Fedorovna, Fr. Aleksandr's wife, had managed to conceal the identity of her husband as a priest, but when the news story appeared she became the subject of ridicule at the institute at which she worked.[76] Until then, she had escaped identification by her coworkers as the wife of an Orthodox priest. But in April 1986, she, too, faced public recrimination.

Shortly after the articles' publication, Fr. Aleksandr had to deal with further intensive interrogation by the KGB.[77] The state security police again demanded from him a confession of wrongdoing for conducting illegal meetings and distributing materials of a "religious-propagandistic character." Fr. Aleksandr was also summoned to the offices of Metropolitan Iuvenalii, chief supervisor of the Moscow diocese.

The dangers, political and personal, that Fr. Aleksandr confronted at this moment had escalated to a precipitously high level, and his anguish, as well as dilemma, over how to respond to the KGB's demands tormented him deeply. On May 20, he telephoned Zoia Maslenikova and asked her to meet him later that day. He walked with her along the tree-shaded pathways of Novodevichy Monastery as he, still "wearing his cassock" and "attracting the glances of the curious," searched for an appropriate means of responding to his "delicate and dangerous situation."[78]

Maslenikova's diary notes relate Fr. Aleksandr's inner turmoil about the dangerous position in which he found himself. According to her, Fr. Aleksandr asked for her help in drafting the formal "letter of confession" the KGB demanded. In her notes, she described his struggles with the wording of his statement, his efforts to preserve his integrity, and his dilemma of finding the right words to appease the authorities. When he took the first version of his letter to Maslenikova for editing, she found it "unacceptable," his wording too harsh and uncompromising, demonstrating little regret for wrongdoing. The present version of the letter, she told Fr. Aleksandr, "would send him straight to the camps."[79] He was "frustrated and angry," and he refused any recantation, indignantly exclaiming that he "will not apologize, and will not repent of anything." "All this," he said, "is dog's rubbish" (chush' sobach'ia).[80] Eventually, he calmed down, but not without further expressions of resentment at having to respond to charges for which there was little evidence. He worked for several hours revising and refining the wording, before finally finishing the "confession," which he then delivered to Metropolitan Iuvenalii.[81]

Fr. Aleksandr's letter went through at least two additional significant revisions. Each time, after receiving the letter, Metropolitan Iuvenalii submitted it to the higher authorities, as required, and each time a demand for changes came back. The Council of Religious Affairs, which reviewed Fr. Aleksandr's submissions, continued to press for a letter of repentance for publication in *Trud*. After repeated drafts, delays, and negotiations, he delivered what would be the final version, written, Maslenikova says, as he expected his imminent arrest.[82]

Fr. Aleksandr's "Confession"

On September 21, 1986, *Trud* returned to the subject of "Krest na sovesti." The newspaper account in September began by reminding readers of the "creation of an anti-Soviet underground under the cover of religion," whose purpose was to sow dissent and disunity in the Soviet Union.[83] The article featured the repentance of Boris Razveev, who remained in prison for his "slanderous" actions against his homeland.

Since the publication in April, the newspaper editorial staff had received, they said, "many responses" from readers throughout the Soviet Union voicing disappointment and indignation at the actions of those individuals cited in the earlier articles. The resentment expressed by a producers' collective in the Kazakhstan town of Temirtau is typical of the responses: "How could they [the individuals cited], educated in the Soviet Union, in our society, have fallen so low? Our country raised them, gave them an education, and they sold out everything for foreign finery. For such conduct there is no forgiveness."[84]

The article also contained Fr. Aleksandr's "letter of confession," which was addressed to the editor of *Trud*, only part of which the newspaper published. *Trud* omitted several sections in which Fr. Aleksandr denied certain allegations. He elected to refute the accusation claiming a connection between the American autocephalous Orthodox Church and the individuals cited in the original article. He had also denied participation in a clandestine meeting with Fr. John Meyendorff in his friend Sergei Bychkov's apartment, as the earlier article had charged. These and other statements were not included in *Trud's* article. In his confession, which the newspaper printed, Fr. Aleksandr stated: "In the twenty-eight years in which I have freely carried out my church service, I have always considered intolerable all activities that are antagonistic to the church and to our society, and caused them harm."[85] He knew, however, that he had violated certain Soviet laws, although such violations had not been his desire. "Thus, several of my unfinished manuscripts and recordings left my control and are in circulation." In such a way, Fr. Aleksandr admitted complicity in these actions, but he did so expressing his own devotion to the church and to his society, never consciously intending to bring harm to either of them. In writing these statements, he again was not completely truthful. The members of his parish and others familiar with him well knew that he never freely carried out his service to the church, but had suffered severe restrictions, including his recent painful experiences with the KGB.

In his statement, Fr. Aleksandr admitted several unfortunate instances that he wished had happened otherwise:

> My association with the parishioners of the church, despite my intentions, had led to what to me were regrettable ends. Several of my parishioners were found guilty of anti-social behavior or were on the verge of breaking the law. In my view, I bear a definite moral responsibility for these [acts]. In addition, the Western press used the publications of my theological works issued by the Western Catholic press "La Vie avec Dieu" against me with the purpose of placing me among the "oppositionists." At the present time, I am weighing my actions more strictly.[86]

In his "confession," Fr. Aleksandr contended that he did not foresee, and perhaps could not have predicted, where the results either of his activities or his publications might lead. It is this line of thinking that the editor of *Trud* accepted, concluding the article with a quotation from a reader's letter about the many citizens, who "close their eyes to how, under the appearance of 'sacred faith,' Western enemy propaganda catches in its snares the unthinking, the unprincipled, and also those people who fall outside the sphere of the trustworthy."[87]

But another, closer reading of Fr. Aleksandr's words yield a different meaning. They suggest a carefully considered, deliberately conceived effort to find a middle ground between preserving his integrity and giving the authorities what they demanded. Nowhere in his letter did he confess to breaking Soviet laws, an admission of guilt that would have resulted in his arrest. Moreover, he correctly pointed to several former parishioners whose subsequent actions might have crossed legal boundaries and for which they were morally responsible. Finally, and most importantly, Fr. Aleksandr's followers could easily have read between the lines of his letter and could readily see that they contained a great deal of "double-speak." His statements about "unfinished manuscripts," about the absence of obstacles to his services, about activities "antagonistic to the church and society," among others, had double meanings. This wording conveyed much more than its literal meaning, and sympathetic readers of these lines understood precisely the more expansive, deeper implications they communicated.

The KGB's carefully planned case against Fr. Aleksandr did not produce the results they desired, which was to silence his voice and ruin his attractiveness to the Russian intelligentsia. The newspaper campaign in *Trud* had little impact on the parishioners at Novaia Derevnia. But the lack of success in this case did not bring to an end the KGB's efforts to find a pretext for his arrest.[88]

The dangerous circumstances in which Fr. Aleksandr found himself during these years raises a major question, both about the Orthodox Church and his own inner resources. How did he manage to survive these repeated challenges, both politically and personally? Several times during this period he came perilously close either to arrest or the loss of his parish. Fortuitous circumstances on several occasions, as well as a lack of fear, played a partial role in these circumstances, but this was not all that was at work. Other elements were also involved in these complex situations.

First, Metropolitan Iuvenalii's (Poiarkov) actions in several instances, particularly Fr. Aleksandr's encounters with the Council of Religious Affairs and the KGB, had a significant bearing on the outcome. The metropolitan of Krutitsy and Kolomna, a position he had held since 1972, and a permanent member of the Holy Synod, the church's highest ecclesiastical council, Iuvenalii had served during the difficult Brezhnev years, when the KGB put intense pressure on the clergy and recruited a large number of its members. As later revelations would demonstrate, Iuvenalii had connections to the KGB. The same revelations also show that the nature of the clergy's relationship to the security police varied greatly, with much depending on an individual's personal qualities and level of commitment to the KGB's goals.[89] As head of the Moscow diocese, Metropolitan Iuvenalii had long been aware of Fr. Aleksandr, had met him on several occasions, and had great respect for him as a parish priest.

During this dangerous period, while facing public assault in the press and repeated interrogations by the KGB, Fr. Aleksandr had many meetings with Metropolitan Iuvenalii. In the spring and summer of 1986, he could be found several times at Iuvanalii's residence in Novodevichy Monastery, where Fr. Aleksandr went to discuss his situation, mainly at Iuvenalii's behest.[90] At these meetings, Iuvenalii questioned Fr. Aleksandr about the allegations made against him, but he also offered the priest counsel. Through Iuvenalii's office, Fr. Aleksandr submitted drafts of his "letter of confession" to the Council of Religious Affairs. While the metropolitan did not have ultimate authority to determine the outcome, Maslenikova's diary notes make clear that Iuvenalii "became the protector of Fr. Aleksandr." On him, she writes, "the priest's fate much depended."[91] After a lengthy meeting with the metropolitan in late August 1986, Iuvenalii invited Fr. Aleksandr to have supper, a gesture signifying a "mark of special disposition" toward the beleaguered priest.[92] That summer and fall, the friendship between the church hierarch and the priest deepened. Personal support from a high-ranking church official was important and helpful when the external pressure on Fr. Aleksandr reached its most intense level.

Second, Aleksandr Men's ability to withstand the near constant pressure in the late 1970s and a large part of the 1980s, both from within and outside his parish, demonstrate his remarkable resources of internal fortitude and endurance. The attacks on his integrity, assaults on his identity, suspicion of his loyalty to the country, interruptions of his parish activities, and nearly constant interrogations conspired against nearly every aspect of his existence. Perhaps most dispiriting were the attacks coming from inside the church, particularly from within his own parish, where he had worked hard to build relationships centered on the teachings of the Gospels. In the most difficult times, and fearing for his life, several of his friends encouraged him to emigrate, but he refused, saying that his place of service remained in his home country.

The capacity to withstand these attacks reveals a great deal about his inner resources, his unwavering devotion to the road he had chosen, and the strong support of his family and closest associates. Nevertheless, at the darkest moments of despair, moments when he experienced descent into the inner circles of hell—alone, assaulted from many sides, threatened with imprisonment—inspiration came from the depths of his faith. During one of these dark moments, he told a friend, Christ's words suddenly came to him:

> But before all these things, they will lay hands on you and persecute *you*, delivering *you* up to the synagogues and prisons. You will be brought before kings and rulers for My name's sake. But it will turn out for you as an occasion for testimony. Therefore settle *it* in your hearts not to meditate beforehand on what you will answer; for I will give you a mouth and wisdom which all your adversaries will not be able to contradict or resist.[93]

Fr. Aleksandr could not have known that the intensive scrutiny of his activities, two years into the Gorbachev era and the beginning of perestroika, was nearing an end. Soon, far-reaching changes in the Soviet Union would greatly alter the entire political and social landscape, recasting the public space in which he operated. These changes projected Aleksandr Men far beyond his parish, and they brought to the forefront large and contentious issues that had occupied him for years in his parish: the rebuilding of Russia's culture and the rediscovering of its connections with its religious roots. As with all major changes of direction, such issues were fraught both with opportunities and dangers.

12

Religion and Culture (I)

In Fr. Aleksandr Men's home in Semkhoz, an icon occupied a central place, visible to all who entered the main passageway of his house. It was the Icon of the Transfiguration, commemorating Christ's metamorphosis on Mount Tabor, in which Christ appeared with Moses standing on his left side, and the prophet Elijah on his right. Christ is the predominant figure, and, having ascended to the mountaintop, he is transfigured, his face "shining like the sun," his "garments becoming glistening white." Jesus has taken three of the apostles with him to the mountain—Peter, James, and John, who are depicted as having fallen down, overcome with awe. Jesus reaches out to them and tells them not to be afraid; when the apostles look up, according to the biblical account, their vision is also transfigured.

As one of his parishioners eloquently said, the Icon of the Transfiguration might well represent "Fr. Aleksandr's hopes for the spiritual transfiguration of Russia, the path to which he devoted his entire ministry."[1] This path, he believed, had been conceived too narrowly during the last several centuries, separating the church from society and leading the church to turn inward, away from the spiritual needs of the people. The church had broken its intimate relationship with Russian culture. As the icon portrays the connection between the divine and earthly ministry of Jesus, one of Fr. Aleksandr's key goals was the restoration of the relationship between religion and culture, a connection broken by various attempts to destroy it, including the Bolshevik assault on both religion and traditional Russian culture.

Beginning in late 1987, the political and religious life of the people of the Soviet Union underwent a major change, which dramatically changed Fr. Aleksandr's public role. While unfortunate circumstances later put an end to that public role, for several highly creative, productive years, he played a significant part in Russia's transformation, particularly in expanding its vision of future possibilities. In the process, he resumed the dialogue between religion, culture, and society—a dialogue that had earlier been curtailed, then restarted by the famous Optina Elders in the nineteenth century and the religious philosophers in the late nineteenth and early twentieth century, only to be extinguished again in Russia for most of the twentieth century. In restoring that dialogue, Fr. Aleksandr's efforts encountered opposition, sometimes violent, both in society and within the Orthodox Church.

A Changing Era

On April 29, 1988, President Gorbachev met with Patriarch Pimen and five members of the Holy Synod in the Moscow Kremlin, an event marking the first meeting between the leader of the Soviet government and the head of the Russian Orthodox Church since the 1950s. At this historic meeting, Gorbachev formally rescinded a central goal of Marxism-Leninism, the obliteration of religious beliefs and practices from Soviet life. He affirmed that "believers are Soviet people, workers, and patriots, and they have the full right to express their convictions with dignity."[2] This event and the ensuing celebrations of the millennium of Russian Orthodox Christianity are usually described as the milestones that ushered in a new era in the relationship between church and state in Russia and the rehabilitation of the church as a social institution.

In reality, however, changes in these relationships had begun earlier, before President Gorbachev's meeting with Patriarch Pimen. New perspectives had broader support than from the president alone. All through 1987, popular reformist publications such as *Ogonek* (The flame), *Literaturnaia gazeta* (The literary gazette), and *Moskovskie novosti* (Moscow news) had issued calls for civil liberties and freedom of speech, which included religious liberties and their protection under the law.[3] A series of international conferences sponsored by the Orthodox Church—the first held in Kiev in July 1986, the second in Moscow in May 1987, and the third in Leningrad in January 1988—discussed a wide variety of topics, ranging from the history of the church to theology, mission, liturgy, and church art. The conferences were not limited only to church representatives, but brought them together with Soviet scholars and members of the government.[4] These sessions fostered a dialogue between religious and secular scholars, the type in which, for many decades, neither the government nor the church had engaged.[5] In the closing months of 1987, Gorbachev announced the government's return to the church of two famous monasteries: the Tolga Presentation of Mary Monastery near Iaroslavl' and the Optina Presentation men's hermitage near Kostroma. The Soviet government had closed both monasteries in the 1920s; both were renowned for their outreach to society and the attraction felt for them by many of Russia's greatest cultural figures.

A whole series of diverse reasons underlay the historic reversal of the Soviet government's approach to religion and the Russian Orthodox Church. Poor harvests in 1986 and, as projected, in 1987 signaled a crisis in agricultural productivity and the need for different policies in much of rural Russia. The nuclear catastrophe at Chernobyl' in late April 1986 exposed the lack of a public safety network, including charity relief organizations, capable of responding to social needs. The policies of democratization, announced at the Twenty-Seventh Party Congress, were logically extended to the Orthodox Church and other religious organizations, given the support for this measure by individuals both inside and outside the Soviet government.

President Gorbachev based his political program on the need to reawaken Russian society, improve its work ethic, and combat alcoholism, all of which made the church a potential ally in his campaign. As the Russian historian Mikhail Shkarovskii has pointed out, the head of the Council of Religious Affairs, Konstantin Kharchev, played a significant role in convincing the Soviet leader of the church's possibilities. His reports to President Gorbachev made clear the failure of restrictive government policies in the face of the rapidly growing interest in religion among the population. Gorbachev's meeting with Patriarch Pimen in the Kremlin in April 1988 took place with Kharchev's encouragement.[6]

The millennial celebrations, which began in June 1988, became, as President Gorbachev told Patriarch Pimen in April, not only a religious celebration, but also "a socially significant jubilee." It marked a landmark "in the centuries-old development of the country's history, culture, and state."[7] In the summer of 1988, concurrent with the millennium celebrations, and throughout the next year, multiple significant events symbolized the changing status of the Russian Orthodox Church. In June 1988, the Church Council, convened during the celebrations, canonized nine people whose achievements from the fourteenth through the nineteenth century represented the church's contributions to Russia's history. They included Grand Duke Dmitrii Donskoi (1350–1389), the Moscow prince and military leader, who occupied first place on the list of newly canonized saints; Andrei Rublev (1360–first half of fifteenth century), Russia's greatest icon painter; Maksim the Greek (1470–1556), the venerated medieval icon painter, translator, and philosopher; Amvrosii (1812–1894), the famous elder of the Optina Pustyn' Monastery, and five others.[8]

More than a year later, October 9–11, 1989, the Bishops' Council made what Shkarovskii called one of its most important decisions: to canonize Patriarch Tikhon (Belavin). With this act, the church began to glorify the "martyrs of the Soviet period."[9] Elected patriarch in November 1917, Tikhon had a distinguished ecclesiastical career. Known for his humility, approachability, compassion, and love for people, he served as head of the church when the Bolsheviks came to power, and he originally defied them, courageously calling Bolshevik repression "the work of Satan" and entreating the faithful "not to enter [into] any communion with such dark monsters of the human race."[10] In his long years of service, he exemplified many of the virtues of the prerevolutionary Orthodox Church and its devotion to the people. Aleksandr Men had great respect for him; he paid visits to Tikhon's tomb, and he was ordained as a priest in the same little church on the grounds of the Donskoi Monastery in which Patriarch Tikhon is buried.[11]

As previously mentioned, the transformative events of 1987–1988 also produced a major change in Fr. Aleksandr's life and ministry. It would have been nearly impossible to predict, given the constant questioning he had to endure from the KGB and the scandalous circumstances he faced in late 1986, that such a dramatic shift lay on the horizon. In May 1988, as the millennium celebrations approached, Fr. Aleksandr spoke to a large audience in one of Moscow's educational institutes. Shortly afterward, he received numerous invitations to appear on television and on the radio. He lectured frequently in institutes, cultural centers, clubs, and to scientific organizations, nearly always before overflow audiences, anxious to hear this learned priest talk about subjects that had, for many decades, not been a part of their members' educational experiences.[12] He tried not to deny any invitation to speak, and the response was nearly overwhelming.

By 1989, Fr. Aleksandr was giving six to seven talks each week. He presented a long series of lectures on the history of the church, a series on the Bible, a series on Russian religious thinkers, and on the Orthodox liturgy and principles. He also accepted a large number of interviews for newspapers and journals, all the while keeping up his responsibilities to his parishioners: meeting with them constantly, responding to their solicitations for advice, and hearing their confessions. These were whirlwind years, in which he returned, by train, from Moscow to his Semkhoz home late at night. They were years for which he had long prepared, and now he was determined to seize the opportunity fully. He liked to quote his friend and colleague Fr. Sergei Zheludkov about giving everything he had to his work: "It isn't easy to understand someone who for years has been tied up on a leash," Fr.

Aleksandr said. "I am not complaining for myself, because God has given me the possibility of doing something, even on the end of this leash."[13]

The historic events in the spring and summer of 1988 started a wide-ranging debate about Russian history and culture. The contributions of the Orthodox Church to that history and culture lay at the core of the debate. During most of the twentieth century, the Soviet Union had defined itself as a secular state; its political structures, educational institutions, and the ways of thinking of its citizens aspired to be totally secular. Now, facing the future, how would each of these elements be conceived? How would the interplay between the secular and sacred be worked out and defined? The tension between the secular and sacred, these two historic forces, became a central part of the debate in the final years of the Soviet era and has yet to subside.

In 1988 and 1989, these issues came to the forefront as the task of recovering Russia's historical memory—and its cultural identity—became key subjects of discussion. Simultaneously dealing with a dying ideology and entering a dynamic global environment, the major participants in these discussions faced a daunting problem: what parts of Russia's heritage had greatest relevance to its cultural reconstruction? From what experiences should it learn?[14] During this time of difficult transformation, would Russians turn their attention outward, as they had done many times before, seeking external enemies as the causes of the country's internal problems? Or would Russians look inward, in an effort to rediscover in their own rich culture the resources to build a dynamic new structure?[15]

The Orthodox Church is not, as it is sometimes conceived, a one-dimensional body, expressing a united voice on major issues. In dealing with the questions posed above, three different groups, each with its own perspectives, can be identified: fundamentalist, statist, and ecumenical. These terms capture more precisely the views of their advocates than do the common, amorphous and often misleading labels "conservative" and "liberal." Each of these groups played a significant role in the discussion of religion and culture. On many issues, they took distinctively different positions, although, at times, their views somewhat overlap.

The fundamentalist wing publicly proclaimed Orthodoxy to be synonymous with Russia. "We are Russian," one spokesperson boasted, "to the extent that we are Orthodox. This is the central theme! It is the key to understanding our 'historical Golgotha,' our present crossroads and the future road of our people."[16] Metropolitan Ioann of Saint Petersburg and Lake Ladoga, whom many considered to be the founder of the fundamentalist group in the late 1980s, wrote well-publicized articles proclaiming Orthodoxy as the core of Russia's national identity.[17] To Metropolitan Ioann, as well as to other fundamentalist adherents, the church served as a bulwark for protecting the country against what they perceived as destructive Western influences—democracy, pluralism, and ecumenism.

To the members of this group, which included many Communist Party members, Orthodoxy offered a means of rebuilding Russia's national identity. Church bells, which began to ring again after decades of silence, did not hold an ecumenical, but rather an ultranationalist message, signifying Holy Russia, national unity, and authoritarian conceptions of power. While the fundamentalists exhibited a range of views on current problems, in general they displayed hostility to national minorities and Jews, saw ecumenism as a betrayal of Russia, and railed against such conceptions as freedom of conscience. "Russian people," a fundamentalist priest wrote, "must not be assembled under these alien banners that undermine for us the eternal words of 'Orthodoxy, Motherland, and national resurrection.'"[18] The fundamentalists praised the historical connection between church and state, an alliance that, in the past, had saved Russia many times from destruction.

The "statists" refer to the broad, middle group within Orthodoxy representing the large majority of the official church's bishops, priests, and other members of the clergy. Having endured for decades under the oppression of the Soviet government, the majority of clergy in this group went diligently about the tasks to which they had been called—conducting services, ministering to parishioners, christening infants, and performing funerals. In contrast to the fundamentalists, they did not want a close alliance with the government, but favored *symphonia*, an older, time-honored relationship between church and state. The concept of *symphonia* represented a partnership of church and state, based on equality; it rested on an equilibrium between these two partners that dated to the sixth century and the Byzantine emperor Justinian. While historians dispute its actual practice in early Russia, *symphonia* stood for a cherished ideal, in which the church exercised dominion over spiritual affairs, the government over human affairs.[19]

But the church also wanted the return of the property the state had earlier confiscated in its assaults on the church's wealth and power. The church's landholdings, buildings, icons, relics, and other sacred objects represented a treasure trove that had been illicitly taken away and, now, they needed to be returned in order for the church to rebuild itself. Moreover, the church needed state financing: educational institutions had to be rebuilt, church schools restored, and theological academies and seminaries greatly expanded in order to serve the spiritual needs of the country. These needs, to members of the statist group, became the top priorities. The financial support for such essentials could only come from the state, so the church increasingly became committed to the new government, fostering a political relationship of dependence.

The third group within the Orthodox Church, the ecumenicists, was led by Fr. Aleksandr Men and took a much different position on the immediate steps needed to restore the church. While Fr. Aleksandr enjoyed only limited support within the Orthodox hierarchy, the size of his following in Russian society grew rapidly in the late 1980s, for a variety of reasons, which played out over the succeeding decade and beyond. Fr. Aleksandr sharply criticized the arrogance and power-seeking he observed all around him. He disagreed with those who wanted simply to restore the church to its prerevolutionary position of wealth and authority, which, he argued, had significantly contributed to precipitating the Bolshevik's rise to power and to Russia's catastrophe in the twentieth century. He took issue with what he called the simplistic and dangerous "nostalgia for the past" that defined the mind-set of conservative clerical groups.[20]

Aleksandr Men's criticism of the behavior of these clerical circles had a sharp tone: "When we believers celebrated the millennium of Christianity [1988], there was not a single word of repentance, not a single word about the tragedy of the Russian Church, only triumphalism and self-congratulation."[21] This sense of victory held disastrous consequences for the future, he suggested, because it implied that the church had regained its social status, whereas the struggle to speak with an effective voice had only just begun.

In Fr. Aleksandr's mind, the church's first act should be the call for repentance. He turned to an ancient Orthodox teaching that repentance preceded any significant action. He recalled Jesus's teaching, with its first word: "Repent."[22] This teaching in the Greek text, as Men pointed out, meant "to rethink your life," and it had profound meaning for the present: "Repentance is not a sterile 'grabbing around in one's soul,' not some masochistic self-humiliation, but a reevaluation leading to action, the action John the Baptist called 'the fruits of repentance.'"[23] Thus, before the church could have any hope of recovering its mission and purpose, it had to reexamine its recent history and rethink the actions that had contributed to Russia's spiritual sickness. "Unless the abscess is lanced," he reiterated, "there will be no cure."[24]

Such statements contradicted the frequent claims in the final years of the Soviet Union that Russia must look to the future. At that time, economic and social problems moved to the forefront, becoming the central issues of importance occupying the minds of policy makers, who sought to rebuild the country from within. Aleksandr Men took issue with their order of priority. The Russian Orthodox Church could neither function creatively nor act imaginatively unless it first rethought and cleansed its own history. "It's always a risky business to make the future into a tranquillizer, an 'opiate,'" he maintained. "Contemporary civilization may have no future unless it looks truth in the eye, unless it finds a firm foundation for moral principles."[25] He stated these convictions with ironic reference to the views that had predominated earlier in the Soviet Union and still had many adherents: "It wasn't so long ago that it was thought axiomatic that social and economic measures are all that are needed to transform the world. That illusion cost us dear."[26] To Fr. Aleksandr, before material problems could be solved, certain nonmaterial issues had to be addressed.

The premise at the core of these statements emphasized the need for healing. Fr. Aleksandr's approach to this need did not lie in idealizing the church, but in looking deeply into its past, both in examining the church's culpability and seeking its sources of reconciliation. Orthodox believers should locate again the sources of beauty, of compassion, of love, and of what was most vital in Orthodoxy's rich inheritance. Fr. Aleksandr's words called for reconciliation, and he made that case powerfully.

But the ecumenicists did not differ from members of the "statists" on all issues. They shared the belief that the renewal of parish life was essential to the church's role in the future. Given that the parish was the grassroots building block of the institutional church and the fundamental point of contact with the community, the level of its vitality would greatly determine the strength of the Orthodox Church and its ability to speak to the people. In his writings on this subject, Metropolitan Kirill (Gundiaev) of Smolensk and Kaliningrad (the future patriarch) emphasized the importance of the parish to the revitalization of the Orthodox Church: "The church is separated from the government," he wrote in 1990, "but it is not separated, and by the nature of its task cannot be separated or cut off from the society or the people."[27] In the eyes of church leaders, the parish offered that connection, and it had to be strengthened for the church to thrive.

The importance of education offered another subject on which the views of the second and third groups overlapped. In his first pronouncement as patriarch, Aleksii II, enthroned on June 10, 1990, as the new patriarch of Moscow and All Russia, identified the religious education of the Russian people as among the country's most daunting challenges. The Communist Party's violent assault on the church's educational institutions and on Russia's cultural foundations over seventy years had exacted a heavy toll on traditional ways of thought and the teaching that supported them. "The greatest wrong wreaked on our society by the Soviet government," the patriarch said, "was its moral and spiritual assault. This attack on the base of our humanity was the deepest wound inflicted by the Communist dictatorship." And further, he said, "All other evils were the result of the systematic and total eradication from the souls and consciousness of the people of the very notion of spirituality."[28] The church, therefore, had to reconstruct the foundation of biblical knowledge, Orthodox rituals, and its central beliefs. The role of education, as described by the patriarch, was not just to uncover the past, this "old tree," but also recover what was vital in that past.[29]

At Novaia Derevnia, Aleksandr Men, too, faced the task of educating his parishioners and of moving them away from an all-encompassing ideology to a less circumscribed view of the world. Throughout his writings and teachings in the late 1980s, Fr. Aleksandr talked about a persistent thirst and need for spiritual values that could be found throughout Russian society.[30] In his exploration of Russian history, he sought to elaborate why the church had responded poorly to this need. The cultural gap between educated society and large parts of the population was exacerbated, in his mind, because the church had looked inward, rather than outward; it spoke a language and developed an inward focus far removed from the life and needs of the people.

The church had failed to fulfill its mission to preach, to be a witness, to educate, and to be present in the world, purposes that were meant to be accomplished "not by bearing witness to some kind of ideology, but by bearing witness to the divine presence in all of us."[31] While the church had the capacity to be the instrument of Christ in the world, it had drawn away from this mission. It had little interest in spreading the faith, but this failure was not simply because Russia lacked theological education:

> In the eighteenth century, the Moscow Spiritual Academy was already in existence, albeit under a different name; there were already those people who studied Eastern languages and ancient philosophy. The instruction in the academy was in Latin; people knew Greek, but they could not genuinely bear witness about faith in Russian. If one examines teaching in the academies in the eighteenth and early nineteenth centuries, one will find that this teaching was conducted in foreign languages, however, and not even in conversational French spoken in the salons, but in antiquated Latin. And when the best preachers of that time addressed the people from the pulpits of the church in Russian, they spoke in a heavy, poorly understood language that sounded as if it required translation again. One of our theologians, a church historian, emphasized that, in the Nikolaevian epoch [1825–1855], the language of theological literature became antiquated as soon as it was published. Such theology was already dead at its birth.[32]

As an example of this antiquated thinking, Fr. Aleksandr cited the highly respected Metropolitan Filaret (Drozdov), a church leader whose life spanned the reign of three tsars—Alexander I, Nicholas I, and Alexander II. Among the best-educated churchmen of the century, Metropolitan Filaret was "an extremely capable man of deep thought and impressive intellect." But he spoke in the stodgy, little understood language of antiquity. During his long life, he published many volumes of theology, but few people read these volumes, because "neither the people, nor the church leadership, nor even the theologians considered them relevant to much of anything. His sermons seemed to those who heard them like rocks 'overgrown with moss.'"[33] The nineteenth century resurrected the tradition of preaching. But this preaching had an extremely restricted scope, and elsewhere, Fr. Aleksandr said, "in this vast land clergymen were silent." Consequently, the large majority of the Russian people, most of whom were illiterate, had little exposure to the word of God.[34]

In Aleksandr Men's view, one of the primary problems facing the church consisted of healing the schism between the church and society. Men offered a contrasting view of reconciliation to the fundamentalists, who also wanted to unify the people and saw such unity as a key element in rebuilding Russia's strength. To him, reconciliation meant recognizing and overcoming the distorted features of the church's history, especially the church's inability to address spiritual needs. It meant reacquainting Russians with the foundations of the Christian culture of Russia, the older voices who expressed love for all people and spoke out against violence in all its forms. It meant recovering the voices of the Russian philosopher-theologians writing at the end of the nineteenth and early twentieth centuries, people who understood brilliantly Russia's cultural ideals and tried to build on them.

Christianity and Russia's Cultural Ideals

"Culture serves as that which distinguishes a human being from the animal kingdom. Therefore, for us it is always important to know what culture is and from where it comes. When we look closely at the fruit of any culture—its ethics, its art, its science, its vision of nature—we in the end always come to a certain primary source."[35] Aleksandr Men's statement, which began his October 22, 1988, lecture at the Moscow club *Laterna magika*, identified the primary source as religion, or, more precisely, "faith." "This is the view of the world," he said, "a deep, intuitive view of the world, which expresses the forms of social life, the forms of art, and all the remaining manifestations of culture."[36] Such a way of seeing, he maintained, needed to be recovered in order to heal the long-standing breach between the Orthodox Church and society.

Several main themes in Fr. Aleksandr's public statements and writings stand out in his attempt to recover this tradition. First, in his view, Russian culture had deep roots in Christianity from its beginnings. In the introduction to his lecture on the Christian culture of Russia ("Khristianskaia kul'tura na Rusi"), Men cited Academician Dmitrii Sergeevich Likhachev, the pre-eminent twentieth-century historian of early Russia: "The appearance of the Russian Church marked the beginning of the history of Russian culture."[37] Drawing from Likhachev's works, those of the nineteenth-century historian V. O. Kliuchevskii, and other sources, Fr. Aleksandr described a religion that did not fall on barren soil when it came to the medieval state of Kievan Rus', but, as elsewhere, mixed with local customs and beliefs to create a rich literature, art, and spiritual culture. By accepting Christianity, Russia also entered the family of European nations, becoming part of a larger network, reflecting a framework that was more complex and more interdependent than it had known previously. The resulting exchange of cultural and spiritual ideas greatly stimulated Russia's growth.

In contrast to the fundamentalists, who saw this relationship much differently, Fr. Aleksandr viewed the connection with European countries as extremely positive: "Culture cannot develop in isolation." To advance, it required what he called a "constant going in and going out," an exchange of ideas with diverse people and beliefs.[38] According to Men, such interactions promoted the flowering of spiritual culture and ideas, as they had during the time of Prince Vladimir in the tenth century and for two centuries afterward. Cultural stagnation occurs when a country looks inward, becoming isolated from others and cutting itself off from the stimulation that cultural encounters provide. Russia had suffered from such isolation. The Mongol invasion at the beginning of the thirteenth century had isolated Russia and had undermined the social ideals and the shared notions of political power that Kievan Rus' had developed.[39]

A second theme in Fr. Aleksandr's work was his criticism of the church-state alliance that emerged in the fifteenth and sixteenth centuries, which later became even more entrenched. Together with Russia's cultural isolation, this church-state alliance created a deep divide between the official church and the Russian people. "The church leadership, having lost its capacity and the possibility to act and speak to the people ... seemed to hurl itself backward, to cut itself off from the culture of educated society," as well as the rest of the population, Fr. Aleksandr argued.[40] He described the church schism of the seventeenth century; Peter the Great's hastily prepared reforms, including his 1721 Ecclesiastical Regulation; the dominating power of the imperial bureaucratic system; and the cultural gap that resulted from separating educated society from the majority of the Russian people as all having had unfortunate consequences.[41]

Aleksandr Men had a lively imagination and a humility, both of which he displayed in his teaching and his parish activities. These qualities made him a severe critic of actions that stifled the imagination and flattened out the capacity for creativity. Having such a perspective, he criticized the church's close relationship to the government. The church's connection with political power robbed it of the creative spirit, and the quest for social justice, because the alliance with the government had made the church captive to political interests.[42]

Fr. Aleksandr argued that this problem had roots that went much deeper than the Bolshevik era. He traced the relationship to tsarist times, to its formalization during the time of Peter the Great. His analysis of this relationship between the church and the state is insightful: he located this process in the worship of the emperor and in the human will to power.[43] By confusing the divine emperor and the divine Christ, the church, he claimed, had limited its independent voice and its creative spirit, both of which he now hoped to reclaim.

Aleksandr Men's discussion of imagination and religion comprises some of the most fascinating pages of his writings. His analyses also distinguish him from many other church officials of his time, whose interpretations of the church's needs and of Orthodox theology moved in a different direction. Fr. Aleksandr did not want to close Russia off from other religions and diverse kinds of experiences, interactions he saw as healthy for the Orthodox Church. He promoted open dialogue with other faiths as essential to rebuilding the church and strengthening its theological base. This dialogue would open up the church's capacity for imagination; it would encourage the church to rethink its role in the world. For much too long, he maintained, the Orthodox Church had existed behind closed doors, cut off from the world, and isolated from perspectives that might challenge its thinking. The church's unwillingness to engage in this dialogue stemmed from a lack of confidence in its own theological perspectives. This lack of confidence, he believed, was unwarranted and hindered the church's ability to change and to engage the modern world.[44]

To Fr. Aleksandr Men, therefore, Russia's recovery of its cultural ideals and the church's ability to engage the modern world were inextricably linked processes in Russia's transformation. How might Russia regain these cultural ideals, and how might the church become more dynamic and more actively relate to the modern world? Great art, the highest creative expressions of human beings, embodied the spiritual; this was true in Old Testament times, Fr. Aleksandr said, and remained true in the present.[45] He believed Russia needed to rediscover such connections and that they were essential elements in its transformation. Russia's late nineteenth- and early twentieth-century philosopher-theologians were an accessible place to begin that rediscovery.

A Living Tradition

In 1988–1989, Fr. Aleksandr gave a cycle of lectures in Moscow on Russian philosophical thought. In these lectures, he focused on seminal thinkers from what is often called the "Russian Renaissance," the glorious period in philosophical thought at the end of the nineteenth and beginning of the twentieth century. He presented these thinkers at a time when the Russian public, cut off from their writings for nearly seventy years, knew little about them, but were hungry to learn about their ideas.

Under the new conditions of openness, Russian journals hastened to include excerpts from these long-disallowed thinkers, and publishing houses began to issue volumes of their writings. Fr. Aleksandr's lectures became part of this process when, in Vladimir Illiushenko's words, "the old was crumbling, but the new had yet to appear: the vacuum needed to be filled, and Fr. Aleksandr began filling this vacuum."[46] Proclaiming that Christianity was not an acceptance of certain moral postulates, dogmas, and theories, Fr. Aleksandr argued that it was first of all a transformation of the self, which in turn transformed the environment.[47] Fr. Aleksandr's lectures on some of Russia's most creative thinkers focused on that transformation, especially as he tried to relate them to the present.

In the winter of 1988 and early 1989, Fr. Aleksandr presented twelve of these lectures, which fill an entire volume.[48] His subjects included Vladimir Solov'ev, whom, as the reader will recall, Fr. Aleksandr once called his mentor and whose works he had discovered as a youth. Solov'ev viewed Christianity as a "life-giving force, not as an abstract ideal."[49] Fr. Aleksandr bemoaned the loss of this earlier voice to several generations of Russians; he argued that Solov'ev had much relevance to the present, and urged listeners to become acquainted with his writings.[50]

In addition, Aleksandr Men emphasized the importance of the collection of essays published in Vekhi (Landmarks), in 1909. Written by Nikolai Berdiaev, Sergei Bulgakov, Semen Frank, and other philosophers and theologians, the essays offered perspectives relevant to Russia's present moral situation. Although they differed on many points, the *Vekhi* authors shared a common view of the importance of spiritual life: they believed that "the individual's inner life is the sole creative force in human existence, and that this inner life, and not the self-sufficient principles of the political realm, constitutes the only solid basis on which a society can be built."[51]

Fr. Aleksandr also discussed Nikolai Berdiaev, whose writings continued to be a source of inspiration to him. As the icon restorer cleansed discolored elements from the physical surface of the icon to find the true representation underneath, so the individual, Berdiaev believed, had to look inward to uncover the icon lying beneath the exterior. As Fr. Aleksandr interpreted Berdiaev, the spirit is "like the flowing waters of a river, and objectifying it is like taking this same water and freezing it in place."[52] Fr. Aleksandr strongly recommended this writer to his audience. Berdiaev, he said, "is a brilliant stylist, a publicist, who writes colorfully, aphoristically, and there is exhibited his fiery temperament, his spirit, which constantly boils up like a volcano and which he captures in words; he can repeat the same word fifty times on the same page."[53]

Fr. Aleksandr believed that the writers he discussed in his lectures needed to be rediscovered, but three of them, in particular, are most relevant to the subject of this chapter. In addition to Solov'ev and Berdiaev, Men felt especially close to these three individuals, both personally and intellectually. The three of them grew up and matured under different circumstances, had diverse interests, and had very different final outcomes, but Fr. Aleksandr believed all of them—Sergei Nikolaevich Bulgakov (1871–1944), and two brothers Sergei Nikolaevich (1862–1905) and Evgenii Nikolaevich Trubetskoi (1863–1920)—had much to say about Russia's present circumstances.

Sergei Nikolaevich Bulgakov

In his public lecture on Bulgakov, Aleksandr Men began with a scene in a Dresden museum, where Bulgakov, in his early twenties, had gone to study with the Marxist economist Karl Kautsky. Men described a young man standing before a painting of the Madonna. Absorbed in contemplating the details, the young man moved from side to side of the painting, lost in reverence, as if he were seeing the artist's themes for the first time. It would be, Bulgakov would tell us later, a revelatory moment in his life. It was as if something spoke to him from the depths of his being, opening up a world of ideas that engaged him for the rest of his life.[54]

Bulgakov, Fr. Aleksandr reminded his audience, grew up on the boundaries of the nineteenth and twentieth centuries, a time filled with exuberant hopes, fortified by strong beliefs in science, social progress, and the innate capacity of human beings to construct a world different from the past. Such a future based on reason and human improvement seemed assured by the physical progress visible all around—in the marvels of construction, the energy of city life, and in the vast new networks of transportation. People were only dimly conscious that the coming age might have an outcome much different than they expected, that war and violence on a scale hitherto unseen might offer a more accurate characterization than these rosy, optimistic expectations.

Fr. Aleksandr told his audience about Bulgakov's seminary education in Orel, his early attraction to Russia's radical writers—Dmitrii Pisarev, Nikolai Dobroliubov, and Nikolai Chernyshevskii—and his adoption of atheism, which seemed to him a more vibrant, truthful way of thinking than the dull, flat, seemingly irrelevant teachings offered by his seminary instructors.[55] He was convinced "that conservative power, including church power, held the people in perpetual stagnation and immobility."[56] In the end, he became a Marxist, a member of the enlightened activists known as Legal Marxists, who found in Marx's *Das Kapital* the inexorable laws that would lead society to economic progress and social enlightenment. As a young adult, Bulgakov dedicated himself to the study of political economy, believing that it would enable him to understand the economic base of reality and thus the means of human betterment.[57] As a student he spoke "of the poetry of his childhood being displaced by the prose of the academy."[58] But poetry only lay submerged in his consciousness, to be reawakened at a later time.

Tracing Bulgakov's subsequent development as a scholar and his slow evolution away from Marxism to Christianity, Fr. Aleksandr impressively interwove Bulgakov's life and his thought.[59] He described Bulgakov's graduation from Moscow University's School of Law, his increasing attraction to history and philosophy, his ordination as a priest, and his growing stature within church circles. Exiled with other non-Marxist intellectuals by Lenin in 1922, Bulgakov went first to Berlin and then to Paris, where he later founded the Saint Sergius Institute. The institute became one of the leading Orthodox theological centers in the world, and many students were attracted to his lectures, seminars, and the gatherings in his home. "I have had the occasion to know many of them," Men testified, "people who have told me about his unusual warmth, his depth of thought and wisdom, and his extraordinary erudition."[60]

But what is most impressive in Fr. Aleksandr's treatment of him is Bulgakov's connection of Orthodoxy with his intellectual pursuits. The Byzantine spiritual tradition, for Bulgakov, did not exist apart from modernity. It was not a closed system with little relevance to a rapidly changing world, as its critics often maintained; it was a living tradition, whose sources expanded the conversation about contemporary issues. His collected works comprise twenty-eight volumes of material; he wrote several hundred articles, and his creative papers run to twenty thousand pages. He was not a professor who isolated himself in his study, keeping his distance from the world and the problems surrounding him. Those problems "troubled him to the depths of his soul; they were his life, and he gave himself to them."[61]

Like the elders at Optina Pustyn', Sergei Nikolaevich Bulgakov connected the church to the world. He was an intellectual who did not see Orthodoxy and philosophy as antithetical pursuits, but rather as parts of an overarching creative vision. Bulgakov was, Aleksandr Men said, a monumental figure, a person with a "gigantic intellect and religious faith," who struggled all his life with issues of universal importance.[62]

The Trubetskoi Brothers

Unlike Bulgakov, Sergei Nikolaevich Trubetskoi and Evgenii Nikolaevich Trubetskoi belonged to an ancient noble family of princes and aristocrats with a long and distinguished record of service to the Russian state. Born only one year apart on a country estate near Moscow, they "received a brilliant education" with tutors at home before entering secondary school in Kaluga, growing up in "an atmosphere of music, poetry, love for culture, and love of native traditions."[63] Like many others in their generation, they went through identification with materialist philosophy, populism, positivism, and rejection of all spiritual values before moving on to study classical philosophy and, later, metaphysics. Fr. Aleksandr noted that they also had another important experience: a close friendship with Vladimir Sergeevich Solov'ev, which lasted to the end of Solov'ev's life. As Fr. Aleksandr reminded his audience, Solov'ev died in 1890 in the arms of Sergei Nikolaevich on the Trubetskoi estate.

Sergei Nikolaevich, Fr. Aleksandr pointed out, became one of Russia's finest biblical scholars, and, until recent years, "perhaps the best at expounding the fundamentals of biblical theology."[64] Fr. Aleksandr described Trubetskoi's doctoral dissertation at Moscow University, "A Study of the Logos" ("Uchenie o Logose"), as a unique, brilliant exposition of the New Testament world and the conflicting ideas that dominated that world. Trubetskoi's largest and most impressive work, "A History of Ancient Philosophy" ("Istoriia drevnei filosofii"), is a detailed exposition of the forerunners of Christianity.[65] While his roots remained firmly embedded in Russian soil, Sergei Nikolaevich never considered Western and Russian ideas to lie in opposition.

Sergei Nikolaevich believed human culture developed as an organic, living whole, which should always be considered in "continual interdependence and interaction, in dialogue, with other cultures."[66] Such interaction was what stimulated the growth of cultures and made them healthy. But these developments depended on "freedom of speech, freedom of conscience, and freedom of the press," to which Trubetskoi gave his wholehearted support. Yet that support cost him dearly. Beloved by faculty and students at Moscow University, where he served as rector, his outspoken stand for these freedoms aroused the enmity of political and clerical authorities. His short-lived tenure as rector ended with his removal in 1905.

Evgenii Nikolaevich Trubetskoi was cut from a different cloth than his brother. He did not share the same interest in metaphysics, but rather focused on the social and religious ideals of Western Christianity. Deeply influenced, like his brother, by Vladimir Solov'ev, he had to struggle to separate himself and to seek his own intellectual independence, a struggle Fr. Aleksandr described. A professor at Moscow and Kiev universities, Evgenii Nikolaevich wrote a two-volume biography of Solov'ev, a detailed study of his life and thought, which Men praised; a two-volume, richly factual account of Western Christianity and its socioreligious ideals; and several other works.[67]

But among his most interesting, enduring works were his smaller, extremely rich studies of ancient Russian icons, which, Fr. Aleksandr pointed out, introduced a "new understanding of the icon."[68] Written during a time when icons were being rediscovered as a major artistic form, three essays, written by Evgenii Nikolaevich, deserve emphasis: "Speculations in Colors" ("Umozrenie v kraskakh," 1915), "Two Worlds of Ancient Russian Iconography" ("Dva mira v drevne-russkoi ikonopisi," 1916), and "Russia through her Icons" ("Rossiia v ee ikone, "1917).[69] In these essays, Trubetskoi argued that ancient Russian icons portrayed the organic unity of the world, a vision that had been lost, but that needed to be recovered.[70] It was not the dark face on the icon that, to Trubetskoi, revealed its message, but the icon's brightness, joy, and reflection of a harmonious world.

In his lecture on the Trubetskoi brothers, Fr. Aleksandr called the members of his audience—and by extension the church—back to the eternal message contained in ancient Russian icons. Artists painted these sacred images during some of the darkest years of Russian history, the fourteenth century, when the entire land lay dispirited under the Mongol yoke. Fr. Aleksandr recalled Evgenii Trubetskoi's essay "Two Worlds of Ancient Russian Iconography," which depicted a world of cruelty, violent struggle, and loss of hope—"a world of death."[71] Suspicion and enmity reigned supreme; they were a constant feature of daily life. But ancient icons opened up before people a different world, in stark contrast to the prevailing darkness: they presented a world of light and beauty, in opposition to death and the enemies that seemed to be everywhere. Icons captured and kept alive a spirit of unity—a collective unity, or *sobornost'*—which Evgenii Trubetskoi emphasized. In Russia's ancient churches, which preserved the original paintings, there existed this spirit of unity, this vision of the organic unity of the entire world.[72]

The years at the beginning of the twentieth century, Fr. Aleksandr reminded his audience, saw a surge of interest in Russian icons fostered by the discovery of new techniques in restoration that removed chemical deposits accumulated over centuries; this discovery gave new meaning to these precious artworks. Until then, icons were considered to be dark, the faces on the wooden panels blackened by the oils layered on them. When the original paintings were restored, their brilliant colors showed through, each color having special significance, the lines representing "notes of mysterious vision." As Trubetskoi showed in his "Speculations in Color," the "notes of mysterious vision" were then transferred to the observer.[73]

Aleksandr Men's lecture on the Trubetskoi brothers also featured another remarkable individual, who played an important role in Moscow's intellectual life. Discussing the city's cultural atmosphere at the beginning of the twentieth century, he attributed to this individual, Margarita Kirillovna Morozova, a large part in raising the consciousness of educated Russians about questions of long-lasting significance. Morozova was wealthy, owned several homes in the Arbat district of Moscow, and had a deep interest in culture and religion.[74] She also loved Evgenii Nikolaevich Trubetskoi, a relationship Fr. Aleksandr described as platonic.[75]

In one of her elaborately furnished homes in a corner of the Arbat, Morozova assembled the most talented, young "representatives of Russian religious thought, and a mass of listeners."[76] Her home on those evenings was decorated beautifully, its halls containing tables laden with refreshments for her guests, the walls covered with icons, many of which recently had been restored. Her home had large spaces for lectures and smaller, special rooms for discussions, a setting, as Men noted, where papers were presented and discussed, ideas formulated, and the subjects of many articles originated.

In addition to the evenings she hosted, Morozova offered Evgenii Nikolaevich the financing for a religious-philosophical press. The publishing house took the name "Put'" (The Way); it issued a large number of significant religious-philosophical books, including Evgenii Trubetskoi's biography of Solov'ev, Pavel Florensky's *Stolp i utverzhdenie Istiny* (*The Pillar and the Ground of the Truth*), the works of the Slavophile Petr Kireevskii, the long unpublished manuscripts of Petr Chaadaev, and many more.[77] With the leadership and financial support of Margarita Morozova, there "was forged that unique religious-philosophical movement, physically obliterated by the Revolution, but part of which succeeded in going to the West, and whose literary and spiritual legacy is now being returned to us."[78]

Sergei Nikolaevich Trubetskoi died in 1905 at the young age of fifty-two, at the end of his service as rector of Moscow University. During the Russian Revolution, his brother Evgenii Nikolaevich Trubetskoi refused to emigrate, despite encouragement from many of his friends, saying that he always intended to die in his native country. In 1920, during the Russian Civil War, he left Moscow for southern Russia, where he joined the White Army fighting against the Bolshevik government. He contracted typhus and died that same year.

Since the early 1920s, as Fr. Aleksandr pointed out, the writings of Sergei and Evgenii Trubetskoi had not been published, the names of the two brothers "rubbed out of the history of Russian culture."[79] They needed to be reclaimed, their works made available again after such a long period of silence, and their vision of the organic unity of culture embraced by the Orthodox Church.

"Is creativity necessary? Are literature, poetry, and the other arts necessary?" Fr. Aleksandr asked in his Moscow lectures. How relevant were they to building a civilized, dynamic order in Russia? How important were they to the Orthodox Church? The Church Fathers, Men said, responded to the same questions with a resounding affirmative.[80] These sacred leaders themselves had been outstanding writers, poets, and social activists, who had modeled creativity and imagination in their own lives.[81] They showed us, he pointed out, that Christianity must be open to the world; it should not consider any question outside its interests or alien to its concerns. Human beings must exhibit a similar creative spirit. "Christ said that each person carries within himself his own treasure," Fr. Aleksandr said.[82] Such a treasure is not to be viewed as a function of the body, but as a sacred aspect of being that requires a constant willingness to see and to imagine what may not be visible on the surface of things.

Raised in the bosom of the Orthodox Church, Aleksandr Men understood the Orthodox tradition as encouraging, rather than restricting, the imagination. In an environment that placed such emphasis on materialism, the imagination enabled the discovery of another, deeper reality, one that went beyond the material world. The creative spirit recognized the importance of mystery. It underscored the connection between religion and artistic quest, both of which constantly aspired to see the world through fresh eyes. Cultivating the creative spirit, Fr. Aleksandr claimed, was among the primary responsibilities of the church.

13

Religion and Culture (II)

In the eighteen months between the end of 1988 and the summer of 1990, Fr. Aleksandr Men was engaged in a whirlwind of activity. He, along with several others, including the distinguished philologist Sergei Averintsev, recreated the Russian Bible Society, which had not existed since 1813. He also led the founding of the Cultural Renaissance Society, dedicated to recovering seminal aspects of culture that the Bolshevik government had nearly destroyed. In his Novaia Derevnia parish, he began a Sunday school for children, and taught in it regularly. He helped organize a new Orthodox university, the Aleksandr Men Open University in Moscow, whose curriculum included both religious and secular subjects. In collaboration with Saints Kosmos and Damian Church in Moscow, he founded a Christian charitable organization to raise money for children of poor families to pay for their hospital treatment; many of the children he helped suffered from incurable illness, and he also regularly visited them during this period. He not only talked about the Orthodox Church's role in society, but demonstrated through his own actions his commitments to that active service. He built a bridge from the church to the world.[1]

The recovery of what he understood as disparaged, even forgotten, verities became, for him, a driving force. The essential goal, in Fr. Aleksandr's view, had a larger framework than the task of gaining the church's independence from the government. The fundamental issue concerned how to make the church more dynamic, how it might fulfill its mission, and how it might construct the necessary life-giving connections to the treasures of Russia's rich culture. In the final years of Fr. Aleksandr's life, his activities spoke to much more than Bolshevik policies on religion. His statements on religion and culture addressed the problem of mob rule and of how the person might nourish one's creative being. In dealing with such issues, Aleksandr Men turned to a subject rarely addressed in the Soviet Union: the connections between the Bible and Russian literature.

Two Understandings of Christianity

In January 1989, Fr. Aleksandr gave a lecture in Moscow that attracted a great deal of attention and that remains one of his seminal statements on Orthodoxy and society.[2] Titled "Two Understandings of Christianity," the topic he addressed dealt with the church and the world on one level and with the practices that make for the vitality of Christianity on another. He explored the approaches that distorted Orthodoxy in hopes that the church might free itself from these distortions. The lecture came six months after the celebrated millennium of Orthodoxy in Russia in the summer of 1988, an event that marked the return of the church as a national institution.

At the beginning of his lecture, Fr. Aleksandr recalled the portraits of two famous monks from Dostoevsky's *The Brothers Karamazov*, polar opposites in their approach to Christianity. He told his audience that he had not chosen the topic "idly or casually," but because it had "deep relevance to the history of spiritual culture, to the history of literature and the history of Christianity in Russia and in other Christian countries."[3] One of these central characters was the *starets* Zosima, who, some scholars maintained, Dostoevsky modeled on the *starets* Amvrosii at Optina Pustyn', the holy man who had befriended Dostoevsky when the writer suffered the loss of his young son.[4]

Dostoevsky described the *starets* Zosima as a "radiant personality," who drew people to him easily, exhibiting a kind of magnetism clearly evident to everyone who came to the monastery. Zosima's compassion for human beings and ability to reach out to them, allowing them to unburden themselves in his presence, was evident in the constant stream of visitors who lined up to see him every morning. Zosima always stood ready to assist those in need, whether their suffering was physical or psychological; his humility, insights, and wisdom convinced those who came to see him that they were in the presence of a person near to God. This openness and reverence for all of creation attracted people from all over Russia, including Dostoevsky, Lev Tolstoy, Aleksei Khomiakov, Ivan Kireevskii, Konstantin Leontiev, Vladimir Solov'ev, and Sergei Bulgakov. "They didn't stream off to any other monastery," Fr. Aleksandr noted, "but specifically to this one," whose monks could discuss not only an individual's problems, but also broader cultural topics.[5] "That was why Dostoevsky created his Zosima with Optina Pustyn' in mind, for he found there a kind of open variant, an open understanding of Orthodoxy and an open understanding of Christianity."[6]

But in addition to Zosima, another *starets* lived in the monastery: the famous ascetic Ferapont, the extreme opposite of the outgoing Zosima. Ferapont, as Dostoevsky depicted him, was a solitary figure, who walked around barefoot and dressed simply, in a dark, belted overcoat. As an ascetic, he was turned inward on himself, apathetic to the social and cultural concerns of the world, and focused primarily on salvation and care of the soul. He had an intense dislike of Zosima and his attraction to people. When the sickly Zosima died, Ferapont denounced him over his grave, severely criticizing the life Zosima had led and what Ferapont believed was his excessive attention to worldly matters. Ferapont, too, was a representative of the church, a powerful element within Orthodoxy who showed, Fr. Aleksandr said, that not everything in Christianity fit into one framework of belief.

The clash between different interpretations of Christianity, Fr. Aleksandr argued, had dominated the Christian world for twenty centuries, beginning with the first church councils and continuing throughout the Great Schism that divided Catholicism and Orthodoxy. Despite sharing many of the same core beliefs, different interpretations had arisen over doctrine and particularly over the understanding of Christianity. These different interpretations had also emerged within the same faith traditions, making the creation of a unified structure of religious belief nearly impossible. As these different interpretations had characterized the story of Christianity in Western Europe, they had also described Orthodoxy, a subject to which Fr. Aleksandr then gave particular attention.

Aleksandr Men's "Two Understandings of Christianity" offered a reflection on Russian history, although the implications of his lecture went far beyond that national context. The ascetic ideal, which he pointed out originated in India and Greece, is necessary for spiritual growth. Within Russian Orthodoxy, however, this ideal had become narrowly defined and distorted. Certain biblical passages—for example, "He who hates his life in this world will keep it for eternal life" (John 12:25)—had been taken out of context and reinterpreted, a process that had severely limited the church's ability to speak effectively to the world.[7] It had all too often represented the only ideal, leading to a turning inward and hiding behind the stout walls of the monastery in the desire to escape having to deal with concrete social problems. In the eighteenth and even more deeply in the nineteenth century, asceticism had become a dominant theme in Russian Orthodoxy. Consequently, the church had practiced an "otherworldly type of Christianity," which "shunned the life surrounding it, shunned history, creativity, and culture, and developed along its own lines."[8] Focused only on salvation, the church "set Christianity outside the world and above it," producing a total indifference to things of the world—poverty, serfdom, and issues of social justice.[9] The results had been disastrous for Orthodoxy and for society.

In the early nineteenth century, educated Russians came to identify Orthodoxy with the ascetic ideal, a perception that remained in their minds for a long time. But Russian Orthodoxy contained other voices, different lines of thought that clashed with this otherworldly indifference to the things of the world. "There grew up two languages," Fr. Aleksandr said, a "church language and a secular language"; they were poles apart, each of them existing in separate spheres, whose division became greater with the passage of time. Focused only on salvation, the ascetic ideal dominated religious thinking. Operating in its own special world, the church had driven out voices that spoke differently, people who believed Christianity ought to address the world, including social problems, moral questions, and even art.[10]

Russian Orthodoxy did have courageous, learned theologians who sought to bring together the two separate spheres of thought. The primary example Fr. Aleksandr used concerned the renowned writer Archimandrite Fedor Bukharev, a monk at the Trinity-Saint Sergius Monastery during the time of Tsar Nicholas I (1825–1855). The gifted, scholarly Bukharev wrote *Orthodoxy and Its Relationship with the Contemporary World*, the first attempt to overcome the breach between the two different understandings of Christianity. Bukharev's book, Fr. Aleksandr said, "pointed out the problems that concern everyone—culture, creativity, social justice and many more. They were not matters of indifference to Christianity; rather the contrary, that in the resolution of these problems, the spiritual ideals of the Gospel could be important and might be an inner resource for their solution."[11]

Abused in the press for these ideas and slighted by the church, Bukharev was driven from his position and publicly humiliated. He represented one of the first in a line of creative theologians and biblical scholars toward whom the church expressed indifference. Others Fr. Aleksandr discussed included Vladimir Solov'ev and Nikolai Berdiaev, who also tried to heal the divide separating the two approaches to Christianity. They, too, believed Orthodoxy needed both the ascetic and the creative ideals.[12] In Fr. Aleksandr's mind, the church needed more humility, willingness to accept other points of view, and openness to different perspectives. It had to overcome the pride that hears only one voice.[13] When it became folded in on itself, tolerating only a single point of view, the church lost the richness of the differing perspectives found within Christianity.

Above all, the Orthodox Church must not foster a uniform, one-dimensional way of thinking. When it behaved in such a way, it lost its vitality, its capacity to speak effectively to large numbers of people. The dynamism of the church greatly depended on pluralism, accepting diverse points of view, looking both inward and outward, and seeking the eternal in all the disparate parts of the universe. Pluralism meant understanding that life expressed itself in contradictory forms, as Christianity, too, appeared contradictory between different denominations.[14] Such perspectives required that the person must never engage in "group think," a uniform, flattened way of thinking that robbed individuals—and the church—of their vitality.

In a world that is unfinished, constantly evolving, and open to conflicting possibilities, humans are creative beings. As God is the creator, so human beings, having within themselves a divine presence, are asked to participate in the world's creation. They are endowed with creative capacities, which historically have been displayed in diverse forms, ranging from everyday acts of kindness to the highest, most resplendent artistic creations. "Creativity—this is the dialogue with Eternity"—is how the poet Vladimir Iliushenko recalled Fr. Aleksandr's words; "it is not for nothing that two understandings of the world—art and religion—stand side by side."[15] "The artist," Iliushenko elaborated, "does not imitate the world, but creates the world," and he cites the twentieth-century Russian poet Marina Tsvetaeva: "By its relationship to the spiritual world, art is a kind of physical world of the spiritual."[16]

Part of Fr. Aleksandr's significance as a spiritual leader lay in the importance he gave to the arts, which he saw as fundamental to Orthodox Christianity. In his lecture "Christianity and Creativity," he interpreted the Incarnation as a calling to the creative act, an invitation not to deny or reject the material world but to reach out and embrace it. Some within the church viewed creativity as a form of sin, an aspect of man's fallen state. But to Fr. Aleksandr, culture and religion, including secular works of art, arising from the spiritual world are "indissolubly connected . . . [and] . . . feed off each other."[17] Creativity expressed a "spontaneous movement within the person . . . some kind of ringing in the soul, a desire for transformation coming from the depths of one's being," representing the opposite of the slavish dependence on external authority that characterized the "ant-hill of civilization."[18]

Aleksandr Men's thinking about this "slavish dependence" related to an author whose work he believed had immediate relevance to Russia, the French writer Henri Bergson. Bergson's work is too large and complex to receive full attention in this study, but several of his ideas, particularly in his last book, need to be highlighted, because they relate to Fr. Aleksandr's views on freeing the individual from the crowd, the thread that runs through his talks on Russian literature.

The Society of the Anthill

Henri Bergson (1859–1941), the renowned French scientist and philosopher, won the Nobel Prize for Literature in 1927. The author of original studies on free will, the relation between body and mind, evolution and memory, and biology and creativity, Bergson offered new perspectives on nearly every subject he studied. He had the rare ability to speak effectively not only to specialists in his field, but also to general audiences everywhere. By the 1930s, most of his major books had been translated into Russian. His works had a significant influence on several of Russia's most creative minds, including Mikhail Bakhtin (1895–1975), one of Russia's most influential literary critics and theorists of social discourse in the twentieth century.[19] Fr. Aleksandr was familiar with Bergson, admired several of his major works, and considered him among the chief European writers educated Russians should read.[20]

In the last book he wrote before his death, *The Two Sources of Morality and Religion* (1932), Bergson posed the question of how societies had originated and the religious and moral characteristics they developed as they matured. He distinguished between two kinds of social orders: closed and open societies. The closed society he defined as having a purpose akin to a biological function: it seeks to maintain social unity by upholding a clan mentality, in which the actions of its members are intended to support the common good. Among its highest commitments are love for family, the community, and the nation, which it attempts to preserve by setting boundaries around morality and religion and excluding members of the clan from much interaction with others.[21] The closed society is one "whose members hold together, caring nothing for the rest of humanity, on the alert for attack or defence, bound in fact to a perpetual readiness for battle. Such is human society fresh from the hands of nature. Man was made for this society, as the ant was made for the ant heap."[22] The closed society, like its counterpart, exists at the "end of one of the two principal lines of animal evolution," comparable to human societies at the other end of the evolutionary spectrum. The members of the closed society abide by their instinct, the open society by their intelligence.[23]

Bergson discussed how the closed society lives, how it communicates and retains its confidence, and how it responds to creative activities. The closed society is primarily concerned with self-preservation, stability, and reproduction. Individuals have well-defined, specific tasks, and adherence to tradition becomes the main governing principle. In the closed society, religion and morality evolved out of that framework: they are essentially static forms, determinate, and geared to promoting group solidarity and to subordinating the person to the whole; morality is ingrained in custom. The closed society also practices a static form of religion that is focused on rituals, seeks to hold everything in proper order, and functions largely through myth-making.[24]

In contrast to its bounded and exclusive counterpart, the open society is indeterminate and inclusive. It is not enclosed or restricted within narrowly defined rules of behavior; rather, its main focus is on creativity and it is, therefore, accepting of continuous, unpredictable change. The open society values tradition but does not see it as immutable, frozen in time, or beyond adaptation to new circumstances:

> The open society is the society which is deemed in principle to embrace all of humanity. A dream dreamt, now and again, by chosen souls it embodies on every occasion something of itself in creations, each of which, through a more or less far-reaching transformation of man, conquers difficulties hitherto unconquerable. But after each occasion, the circle that has momentarily opened closes again. Part of the new has flowed into the mould of the old; individual aspiration has become social pressure; and obligation covers the whole.[25]

The open society is less concerned with rigid obligations and more with creativity and progress. It derives its religion and morality from sources different than the closed society; the religion of the open society is mystical, and it is not so much concerned with a central set of prescribed doctrines or rituals as it is with expressions of love and grace. Reality is always in a state of becoming. The individual is much more than one part of a disciplined, tightly structured, cohesive social order; each person is a creative participant in an expanding, dynamic community.

Bergson's analysis of the open society was important for Aleksandr Men. He found in Bergson similarities to Berdiaev's concept of the free human personality. But even more than this, Bergson offered him a means to critique the static, restrictive, and inward-looking mentalities that had characterized so much of Russia's past, including the church's inability to speak to the social world. Bergson further opened up for him the dangers that came from the tyranny of the masses, which continued to afflict the Russian people during this period of transformation. [26] Fr. Aleksandr spoke to the connection between Christianity and creativity. The spirit represented a paramount quality in the individual; it expressed one of a person's chief properties. In it lay the uniqueness of each human being, not "in the mob, where people lose control of their identities and are thrust backwards," becoming something else.[27]

In 1989 and 1990, Fr. Aleksandr imagined the outcome should Russia become like the mass society of the anthill. He referred to the kind of society described by the science-fiction writer Herbert George Wells (1866–1946) in his futuristic novel *The First Men in the Moon* (1901), in which Wells predicted the complete "subordination of the person into the whole."[28] Speaking openly and frequently in 1989 and 1990, Fr. Aleksandr, more than ever before, emphasized the opposition between individual personality and mass consciousness, between spiritual freedom and the mechanistic structures that had dominated Russian society for most of the twentieth century.

The present time offered a unique opportunity to speak to the creation of a different kind of social order. He threw himself wholeheartedly into that process, as though there were not much time to make the case. He believed that the human resources existed to create a different, more dynamic, and pluralistic society. As in Russia's religious and philosophical heritage, he saw in its literary culture the moral and spiritual capital to support an open society.

The Bible and Literature

All his life, Aleksandr Men had loved and taken inspiration from Russian literature. But now, in the late 1980s, he had the opportunity to speak publicly about Russian literature as he had never done before. The subject fit well into his contention that Russia's cultural heritage derived from its religious roots, which shaped and sustained its literary heritage. Moreover, as the social framework had eroded, the connections between religion and literature offered moral guidelines for reconceiving that structure, but also for counteracting the "crowd mentalities" that Aleksandr Men feared.

Fr. Aleksandr gave a series of talks focusing on the Bible and Russian literature.[29] Open to the public and held in various places in Moscow, they attracted both young and old, mostly well-educated people. His primary interest in these talks concerned how the stories told in the Bible and in the four canonical Gospels were reinterpreted by writers and poets in different ages, according to the moral problems that writers and their contemporaries faced in these successive periods. Russian literature, he emphasized, is preoccupied with eternal questions, which brings readers of this literature closer to "the beautiful, the sacred, and the divine."[30]

Fr. Aleksandr built his lectures using a chronological framework, beginning with the origins of Russian literature in the early years of his country's foundation. Soviet scholars generally had portrayed the emergence and development of early Russian literature as evidence of an emerging national consciousness, which had its roots in Byzantine civilization, but slowly took a different direction, mingling with multiethnic people in the Russian interior to form a distinctive national culture. This process took place as the center of Russian civilization moved northward, interacting with the material culture of the forest around Novgorod, Tver', and Iaroslavl-Pskov.[31]

By contrast, Aleksandr Men was concerned with the development of Russia's spiritual consciousness, specifically with the spread of Christianity on Russian soil. He pointed out that Christian ideals were quickly incorporated, and argued that this rapid integration occurred because the ground had already been well prepared: "The seed fell on fertile soil, as Biblical passages were translated into the Old Slavonic language a hundred years before" the arrival of the Bible.[32] He credited the educational work of Greek missionaries Cyril and Methodius, the importance of the Cyrillic alphabet they brought to Slavic cultures, and the contributions of Yaroslav the Wise (grand prince of Kiev, 1019–1054), who built a cathedral in Kiev, rivaling the finest in Eastern Europe, and collected a huge library. But Fr. Aleksandr had also researched the question of what made the scriptures appealing to the people of ancient Russia; the attractions, he believed, lay in their "special, spiritual, mystical historicism—the perception of human life as a kind of drama, a whole drama that has plot and direction."[33] The storytelling nature of the scriptures is what gave them, in this case, power and resonance.

Aleksandr Men did not aspire to discuss all of early Russian literature, but rather was selective in his choice of works. He began with treatment of the "Tale of Bygone Years" ("Povest' vremennykh let"), the famous revision of the Primary Chronicle, written in the early twelfth century by the monk Nestor of the Kievan Caves Lavra, the first historiographer to place Russia in the mainstream of world civilization. Fr. Aleksandr next discussed other early writers and their contributions: Metropolitan Ilarion's "Sermon on Law and Grace" ("Slovo o zakone i blagodati"), written between 1037 and 1051, the famous sermon about regeneration and rebirth; and the "Instruction [*pouchenie*] of Vladimir Monomakh [*Monomachus*]," written at the end of the Kievan grand prince's life in 1125, for his children.

Fr. Aleksandr then briefly surveyed Russia's period of feudal disintegration, the Tatar yoke, and Moscow's ascendency to connect his story with two great seventeenth-century writers: Archpriest Avvakum Petrov, the famous schismatic and Old Believer, and author of the first full literary autobiography in Russia, who was burned at the stake in 1681; and his ideological opponent, Simeon of Polotsk (1629–1680), whose poems and plays on biblical themes were celebrated at the court of tsars Aleksei Mikhailovich (1645–1676) and Fedor Alekseevich (1676–1682), both of whom he served.

The literary creations of these writers, which Fr. Aleksandr admired, contained themes he believed were part of Russia's cultural identity. The oneness of humanity he saw as an ancient and extremely bold idea, which the "Tale of Bygone Years" had presented; it closely paralleled the teachings of the scriptures, which offered "a unique example of the unity of humanity." Fr. Aleksandr believed that vision to be especially important in the present era of selective internationalism, the division of the world into our people and others, the "people of the tribe" and the "outsiders."[34]

In his lectures, Aleksandr Men gave a sacred meaning to the vision of freedom presented in the "Tale of Bygone Years" and also in the Biblical account of Christ's entrance into the world, without the use of any external force, armed only with the gift of free choice. Moving to a later time, Fr. Aleksandr emphasized the rich literary language and the vivid style exhibited in the texts of Archpriest Avvakum, including his ability to express himself in simple, understandable words accessible to ordinary people, his passionate condemnation of the sin of alcoholism, and his brilliant sense of humor.[35] In his brief treatment of these literary masterpieces, Fr. Aleksandr spoke to certain aspects he believed needed to be recovered and reemphasized. In each case, he addressed the present and the future, and, from the depths of his own reading, aimed to offer direction to his people and to the church.

The special nature of early Christianity for Russia is examined in Metropolitan Ilarion's "Sermon on Law and Grace." For Fr. Aleksandr, the sacred ideas contained in this ancient text had great relevance to the present and to Russian Orthodoxy. Delivered shortly after the Feast of the Annunciation in Kiev, the "Sermon on Law and Grace" spoke of two opposing forces, law and grace, which the apostle Paul originally articulated as principle antipodes within Christianity. Written in two parts, the "Sermon on Law and Grace" affirms the God of the Old and New Testaments, which Fr. Aleksandr maintained were identical; neither in Metropolitan Ilarion's presentation nor in the biblical text did God have a bifurcated, dual nature. To Metropolitan Ilarion, the law established by God in the Old Testament served as a forerunner and a servant to grace and truth—that is, to Christ. With the appearance of Christ, the law recedes to make room for grace.[36] It is grace, the concept of God's love and compassion, which Christ brought into the world; Christ's message of love and compassion for one's neighbors—for all one's neighbors—gave rise to moral order. This was, to Aleksandr Men, a fundamental belief in Christianity, and when fully grasped fully, it transformed the person. When the message became a distant memory, scarcely recognized or obscured, he emphasized, "it leads to an ecological disaster of the spirit."[37] Such a conception, already present in ancient Russian writing, served as a major theme that threaded throughout nearly all of Russian literature.

In other public lectures, Men surveyed the seventeenth and eighteenth centuries. But to the nineteenth and twentieth centuries, when Russian literature fully blossomed, he gave most of his attention. Turning to writers of the golden age of Russian literature, the nineteenth century, he made a sharp distinction between Russian and European literary works. In this century of global transformation, "spiritual problems and biblical themes entered in the fabric of European, Russian, and world literature," but whereas much of European literature pushed eternal moral problems into the background, Russian authors made such burning issues the central focus of their works, although they approached them from many different points of view.[38]

Fr. Aleksandr underscored the connection between the literature of the nineteenth century and ancient Russian literature, both of which were characterized by their authors' inquiring minds and openness to the world. He cited an additional distinctive feature of these nineteenth-century works of art: writers dealt in detail with the problems of social life and the immediate controversies that swirled around them, but they invariably kept readers focused on deeper, eternal themes transcending this existence.

Fr. Aleksandr's lectures on nineteenth-century writers focused on the integration of biblical themes in their works. On this subject, he turned to a whole series of Russia's outstanding authors: V. A. Zhukovskii, Aleksandr Pushkin, Mikhail Lermontov, Aleksei Khomiakov, Ivan Turgenev, Fedor Dostoevsky, Lev Tolstoy, Aleksei Tolstoy, and Vladimir Solov'ev. Fr. Aleksandr did not claim to be a literary scholar; neither was his concern with literary theory, but in a rapid excursion through a complex, multifaceted subject, he wished to bring to light for the members of his audience several major moral themes that attracted the minds of these creative people.

Fr. Aleksandr portrayed the efforts of Aleksandr Pushkin, Russia's greatest nineteenth century poet, to break free of traditional social constraints and ceremonies that hindered the development of his creativity. At first, making a mockery of these conventional customs as he matured, Pushkin came to realize a deeper, more fulfilling approach; exploring biblical teachings about humanity, he underwent a personal transformation that enabled him to see the world differently than he had earlier. Fr. Aleksandr described this transformation in Pushkin's poem "The Prophet" ("Prorok"). Saying that the poem is usually "interpreted only in its poetic sense," Fr. Aleksandr elucidated it in another manner that was often ignored: the poem is "almost a literal reiteration of the beginning of the sixth chapter of the book of the prophet Isaiah."[39] The biblical passage recounts how the prophet Isaiah, facing mortality, his own sinfulness, and dissatisfaction with life, has an internal experience in which he begins to understand the world differently. The biblical passage concerns the need for seeing the world anew, looking beneath the superficial exterior of things, and learning how to imagine reality in depth. Visible reality is turned upside down. In their encounter with the divine, Fr. Aleksandr said, "God directed Isaiah and other prophets to set the hearts of people on fire, leading them to repentance and God-consciousness."[40] The reader finds, Fr. Aleksandr said, a direct connection from the passage in Isaiah to the experience recounted in Pushkin's poem about his transformation, in which the poet discovered his true creative gifts and how they must be used, showing people how to see the world differently from what social convention sought to impose.[41]

A similar line of thinking might be found in the works of Aleksei Stepanovich Khomiakov (1804–1860), although he took the theme of personhood and mass society in a different direction. A talented artist, historian, theologian, philosopher, publicist, and cofounder of the Slavophiles, Khomiakov, according to Fr. Aleksandr, is often misunderstood and misinterpreted.[42] Esteemed by his contemporaries, Khomiakov was highly respected even by his opponents, including Aleksandr Herzen, who spoke with admiration of Khomiakov's engaging personality and sharp, evocative essays. Many of Khomiakov's theological writings, Fr. Aleksandr pointed out, did not pass the church's censorship; they could only be published in Western Europe.

Fr. Aleksandr argued that Khomiakov needed to be recovered in Russia's memory. Some of the philosopher's finest poems, once included in Russian literary anthologies, had not been republished in the Soviet period, and they remained largely forgotten.[43] Fr. Aleksandr focused on only three, each of which displayed strong biblical themes, which, while set in a distant, bygone era, Fr. Aleksandr believed related to contemporary times. Khomiakov's poem "Zvezdy" ("Stars"), devoted to the New Testament, is essentially about the strength of the spirit in its confrontation with power and violence. This is the theme, Fr. Aleksandr says, to which Khomiakov devoted a great deal of his writing. He kept at the forefront of his mind how Christ is represented in the Gospels:

He is the victor in the New Testament, but a victor who does not humiliate, who does not destroy, and who preserves human freedom. The greatest gift that distinguishes us from animals is freedom, and God treats it carefully. Therefore, the appearance of Christ took place without violating the personality and conscience of the human being. Christ always allowed a person the opportunity to turn one's back on Him.[44]

Fr. Aleksandr emphasized that it is the same today as in biblical times, and it is this freedom of choice, this freedom which is opposed to violence, that runs through Khomiakov's poetry. Written during the period of Tsar Nicholas I (1825–1855), when military glory and the power of the Orthodox Church were at the center of state interests, Khomiakov's poetry illustrated the conflict between freedom and power. By underscoring these conflicting forces, Fr. Aleksandr suggested their relevance also to Russia as it considered the direction of its present and future.

The themes of the individual against the crowd and the ability to hear one's own inner voice are carried throughout Fr. Aleksandr's discussion of the second half of the nineteenth century, the period of some of Russia's greatest masterpieces. These themes are depicted first in the context of a heated debate that took place beginning in the middle of the century about the creation of the "new person" (*novyi chelovek*) who sought to rise above the prevailing social order, exposing its conventional beliefs as shallow, unexamined sentiments. Fr. Aleksandr referred to the portraits of the "new person" in Rakhmetov, a character in N. G. Chernyshevskii's novel *What Is to be Done?* (1863); in Bazarov, from I. S. Turgenev's *Fathers and Sons* (1862); and in Prince Myshkin, in F. M. Dostoevsky's *The Idiot* (1869). The latter is a Christlike character whom Fr. Aleksandr considered an inaccurate and unsuccessful portrayal of Christ's qualities.[45]

Fr. Aleksandr believed, however, that the image of Christ served as the centerpiece of all of Dostoevsky's work, so he gave special attention to that depiction. Again, it is important to note that Fr. Aleksandr is speaking to a generation whose views were shaped in a cultural context in which such themes had received meager treatment. Fr. Aleksandr focused on the "Legend of the Grand Inquisitor" in Dostoevsky's novel *The Brothers Karamazov*, and the confrontation between the Grand Inquisitor and Christ. The passage presented a juxtaposition of material needs and desires and the freedom of the soul, which Fr. Aleksandr related to the present, given that similar issues confronted the country, as well as the Orthodox Church, as it sought its way forward. Fr. Aleksandr also saw the Grand Inquisitor's arguments as parallel to the popular slogan of the 1920s and '30s: "With an iron hand we will bring humanity to happiness."[46] Fr. Aleksandr was speaking to the disparity between freedom and power.

The biblical ideal of freedom was also conveyed in the work of the poet and historical dramatist Aleksei Konstantinovich Tolstoy (1817–1875), whose poems "Sinner" ("Greshnitsa") and "Against the Current" ("Protiv techeniia") Fr. Aleksandr briefly discussed. Tolstoy's poetry expressed opposition to the philosophy of utilitarianism that was embraced by certain radical members of the intelligentsia, who viewed art as useless unless it served social needs.[47] Tolstoy fought against the crowd and courageously stood against the social currents of his times, remaining true to his own vision in the service of art and the quest for truth.

In his discussion of the Bible and Russian literature, Aleksandr Men singled out Dostoevsky, Lev Tolstoy, and Vladimir Solov'ev for special treatment. While the first two are obviously among Russia's greatest literary minds, his inclusion of Solov'ev in the group is curious, because the philosopher is not often viewed as a literary figure. Fr. Aleksandr disagreed with Tolstoy's theological views, his explication of selected parts of the New Testament, and his lack of belief in the power of human personality to shape historical events, which Tolstoy articulated in his novel *War and Peace*. Neither did Fr. Aleksandr agree with Tolstoy's efforts to rewrite the Bible, to lift from it certain teachings while dispensing with what Fr. Aleksandr considered some of its most essential qualities, namely the divinity of Christ.

Despite his disagreement with Tolstoy, Fr. Aleksandr greatly respected him; he expressed regret that the Soviet government had not published Tolstoy's writings on religion earlier, and he urged people to read them.[48] His treatment of Tolstoy exemplified, in practice, the kind of civil discourse Fr. Aleksandr advocated elsewhere, in that he showed his respect for a person's views with whom, on many issues, he disagreed. His approach differed from the practice that characterized much of Russia's public discourse, in which one could not disagree and respect the views of an opponent, but must eviscerate those views and envision their presenter as an enemy.[49] Tolstoy's essays on religion, as Fr. Aleksandr described them, raised significant questions that needed to be seriously considered.

Vladimir Solov'ev is known mainly for his philosophical writings. But Fr. Aleksandr called attention to Solov'ev's poetry, which, on several different levels, stood in opposition to Tolstoy's views on the Bible. Solov'ev, who was born later and died earlier than Tolstoy, offered a picture of the Old and New Testaments that contrasted with that of his contemporary. Unlike Tolstoy, he appreciated all of the Bible, interpreted the Old and New Testaments using the original Greek and Hebrew texts, and, according to Fr. Aleksandr, used the Bible as the "foundation for all his creative work."[50]

Fr. Aleksandr recommended that his audience take a close look at several of Solov'ev's poems, particularly at "Fireplace of Nebuchadnezzar" ("Kamir Nebukudnera") and "Light from the East" ("Orienta lux"), both of which Fr. Aleksandr believed had much relevance to Russia's present. He saw in them a single theme, which, for Solov'ev, had become extremely important: in contrast to the church, which envisioned a deep divide between East and West, Solov'ev saw in the Bible their unity. The East contained two opposing elements: cruel despotism and also "the light of the Star of Bethlehem, the Star of Christ."[51] The West represented the revolt against tyranny, which nourished individual initiative, citizenship, democracy, and freedom. Asiatic despotism had too often shut out the light of Bethlehem and, over the last five centuries—from the time of the Persian ruler Xerxes and his mercenary warriors—these two major forces, tyranny and freedom, had collided. They confronted each other in Solov'ev's time, and they did so again, as Fr. Aleksandr said, in the present.

This confrontation, which Solov'ev's poetry elaborated, allowed Aleksandr Men to raise the question he believed to be central to Russia's future. He viewed his country as standing at a historical crossroads. Would it choose the tyranny of Xerxes or the Star of Bethlehem? Solov'ev believed that biblical history had not yet been completed; for Fr. Aleksandr, the story also remained unfinished. If Russians elected to follow the Star of Bethlehem, it required them "to take part in the struggle against enslavement, stagnation, indifference, the lack of spirituality, and darkness."[52] This was the path away from the "rule of the mob," and he believed that the Star of Bethlehem pointed the way.

The portrait of Christ in twentieth-century literature is a subject to which Aleksandr Men gave a lot of attention in these lectures. The fascination with Christ among nineteenth-century poets and prose writers continued in this later period. In the radically different circumstances of the succeeding century, how did the image of Christ change?

As before, the literary portraits were extremely diverse. In Aleksandr Blok's famous poem "The Twelve" ("Dvenadtsat'") (1918), Christ is the Other, marching in the streets of Petrograd at the head of twelve apostles and wearing not the martyr's crown of thorns, but a "crown of white roses," leading Fr. Aleksandr to question whether he is Christ at all.[53] To the lyrical poet Sergei Esenin, in his poem "Ionia" (1918), Christ is a "warrior for justice," who enters the New Nazareth on a mare; Esenin leaves no doubt, Fr. Aleksandr said, that Old Russia will not survive.[54] In Andrei Belyi's poem

"Christ Is Risen" ("Khristos voskres," 1918), Christ is a real man, but also the "Spirit of the Sun," who came to Earth to change its aura. In the poetic compilation *Temple of the Sun* (*Khram solntsa*, 1917), by Ivan Bunin, who loved and carefully studied the scriptures, Christ is the son of Galilee and Jerusalem and exemplifies love and beauty. To Maximilian Voloshin, whom Fr. Aleksandr called the most perspicacious poet of the times, the Revolution did not represent a new apocalyptic world, but was a catastrophe, and the poet likened Russia to Christ on Golgotha.[55]

Later, in the poetry of Boris Pasternak (1890–1960), the image of Christ is taken to a new level. Pasternak makes connections between nature, life, the sacred, and human beings that transform the Gospels' story and invite the reader to participate in it. In his discussion of Pasternak, Fr. Aleksandr recalled Evgenii Trubetskoi's essay "Two Worlds in Ancient Russian Iconography," in which Trubetskoi emphasized how icons portray the entire range of human emotions. "The sunny lyrical motif of joy inevitably interweaves with that of the greatest sorrow on earth, the drama of two worlds colliding with each other," Trubetskoi wrote.[56] Fr. Aleksandr likened Pasternak's poems on the Gospels to ancient Russian icons.

In Pasternak's poems in his *Doctor Zhivago* cycle, nature fuses with human beings in the celebration of holy events, particularly in "The Star of the Nativity" ("Rozhdestvenskaia zvezda") and in "Holy Week" ("Na strastnoi"). In the latter, which Fr. Aleksandr called "one of the most beautiful presentations on the Orthodox liturgy," birch trees at the church gate participate in the prayer service: they "step aside" to allow "tear-stained faces to enter."[57] Elsewhere, in "Rift in the Clouds" (1956), Pasternak described a church that Fr. Aleksandr said is the "church in his soul," and nature is an icon, made by an icon-painter.[58] Here, as in the *Zhivago* cycle, nature, the liturgy, and human beings are interwoven, expressing sorrow but also proclaiming the joy of creation and the promise of Resurrection. As in ancient Russian icons, Christ, in the last poem in the *Zhivago* cycle, looks to the future and calls for human beings to awaken:

> I shall go to the grave, and on the third day rise,
> And, just as the rafts float down a river,
> To me for judgment, like a caravan of barges,
> The centuries will come floating from the darkness.[59]

The passion and humanistic values exhibited in Pasternak's poetry form a connecting link to a more recent Russian writer, Iurii Osipovich Dombrovskii (1909–1978). Aleksandr Men spent only a short amount of time on Dombrovskii, but it is clear from his words that he considered him to be extremely significant, a person he greatly admired. Fr. Aleksandr called Dombrovskii a "true hero of our time"; he is, Fr. Aleksandr said, a "real human being, courageous, a shocking mischief-maker, bearing a little resemblance to Solzhenitsyn, but whose work contains more humor, more mischief."[60]

Dombrovskii's novel *The Faculty of Unnecessary Things* (*Fakul'tet nenuzhnykh veshchei*), which he completed in 1978 and published in Paris, did not appear in Russia until 1988, when the journal *Novyi mir* printed it. Dombrovskii was beaten in the streets of Moscow in 1978 soon after the publication of his novel and died soon thereafter, his death precipitated by the beating.[61] His tragic death would later parallel the end of Fr. Aleksandr's life, forming an unforeseen but close bond between these two men.

The Faculty of Unnecessary Things is, in part, autobiographical. Set in the Central Asian republic of Kazakhstan in 1937, it is about a young archeologist who is asked to help the Cheka's investigation as the security agency attempted to organize a show trial, similar to the one taking place in Moscow. The novel contains a wide range of interesting characters, including an ex-priest who is writing a book about Christ, and the excerpts from it, which figured prominently in the novel, formed the center of Fr. Aleksandr's attention. The ex-priest is convinced that there were two betrayers of Christ, someone else, in addition to Judas. Dombrovskii's main character posed the question, "There was a second; who might this have been?"[62] The novelist explored the question through the twelve disciples, closely looking for evidence of the betrayal among each of them. But Dombrovskii also related this deeply significant issue to his own period and to the culture of betrayal that it created, and it was the lasting effects of this culture that Fr. Aleksandr emphasized and that had to be overcome for Russia to move forward.

In Aleksandr Men's account, Dombrovskii stood for integrity and humanistic ideals; he was, as Fr. Aleksandr described him, the embodiment of these ideals in the face of fear and denunciation, "the disease of our time."[63] While Fr. Aleksandr did not spell out the consequences of such fear, they are implicit in the context of all his lectures on literature. The culture of denunciation, endemic to the Stalinist system, had long-lasting effects on the human psyche. The system had deliberately fostered a lack of trust in other people; it had promoted the social isolation of the individual from others, forging a reliance on the state as the sole agent of social cohesion.[64]

This intention was the precise opposite of a main idea expressed in ancient Russian icons, especially in those of Andrei Rublev and other artists during the most creative periods of icon painting. These ancient icons conveyed the "idea of the unity of all creation," not discord and enmity, but peace and communality.[65] The icons exhibited bright rainbow colors, in the words of Evgenii Trubetskoi, the "hope of restoring the lost order and harmony . . . opposed to the howling of beasts" and the wolves that hovered nearby.[66] Fear and denunciation undermined this spirit of communality, of *sobor*, Fr. Aleksandr claimed; they had fostered a spiritual sickness, which had "reached its apotheosis in the Soviet interpretation of the Gospel story."[67]

Near the end of one of his public lectures, Fr. Aleksandr turned to Mikhail Afanas'evich Bulgakov's masterpiece, *The Master and Margarita*. He recounted that immediately following the novel's publication in the journal *Moskva*, his parishioners besieged him with questions, specifically about the meaning of Woland and his sudden, mysterious appearance in Moscow. Beginning with these questions, Fr. Aleksandr elucidated several main themes, which differed from how many others had interpreted the novel.

While readers had commonly approached *The Master and Margarita* through the lens of the Gospels, in Fr. Aleksandr's view, the novel's chief similarities lay with the book of Genesis. Woland did not represent Satan; he is not the perpetrator of evil, the agent of destruction. As an outsider, he paid a purposeful, "miraculous visit to Moscow," and this "miraculous visit" parallels a similar appearance in Genesis, when the three visitors suddenly appear before Abraham "while he was sitting at the entrance of his tent in the heat of the day" (Genesis 18).[68] God has arrived to deliver a "miraculous" message to Abraham and his wife, Sarah; he has also come to confirm the condition of the world, in this instance, Sodom and Gomorrah.

A similar theme evolved in classical literature. Closer to our own times, Fr. Aleksandr said, "the miraculous visit" was incorporated into Goethe's *Faust*, and, later, in the work of Herbert Wills, in which a mysterious visitor appears to examine conditions of life in Victorian England. "Still closer" to the present is Woland's sudden appearance in Moscow, in which he arrives to check up on Muscovites, and then sets everything in motion. Through him, Fr. Aleksandr pointed out, the reader sees all the "gamma rays" of life—the "love of Margarita, the dream of Ivan Homeless, the tragedy of the Master, and the vile actions" of so many different people.[69] A major subject in the novel is also human betrayal, a common practice at the time Bulgakov was writing, and a theme Fr. Aleksandr explored in some detail.[70]

As in his other lectures, Aleksandr Men's interest was in the portrayal of Christ. He mentioned two models found in ancient Rus', as described by Sergei Sergeevich Averintsev: one with a stern countenance and knitted brow; the second with a warm and compassionate expression, the Christ depicted in the icon painting of Andrei Rublev.[71] In *The Master and*

Margarita, Bulgakov added a third model, Fr. Aleksandr said, the image of a "gentle and kind man, a wondering philosopher."[72] He was not the Christ of the Gospels, but something else, some new creation. Christ was neither a philosopher nor a hapless wonderer. Fr. Aleksandr speculated that Bulgakov left the novel unfinished and, given time, he might have portrayed Christ differently, in what otherwise Fr. Aleksandr considered a thought-provoking, powerful, and profound work.

Fr. Aleksandr's treatment of major twentieth-century Russian writers did not aim to be comprehensive. Missing from his discussion were two poets, Anna Akhmatova and Marina Tsvetaeva, whose poetry might have contributed to the themes he explored. The reasons for their omission are difficult to discern, and the failure to include them weakened his presentations. But the attention he gave, both to poetry and prose, related the Gospels to many of Russia's greatest literary creations, placing the eternal themes of those creations squarely within the interests of the church.

Aleksandr Men's cycle of lectures on Russian literature, particularly given the time in which he delivered them, addressed issues and made connections that were given little attention in Soviet literary circles and educational institutions. He spoke largely to the Russian intelligentsia, who were already familiar with these writers and who had read the works he discussed, but most likely had not approached them in the way that he did. Even more significantly, in his discussions, Fr. Aleksandr made no distinction between secular and sacred themes, but instead crossed over such boundaries, blending them together without acknowledging the categories that had often separated these different ways of looking at culture. As a priest, his vision was not turned inward to the interior of the monastery's walls, but rather he looked outward to the world and to creative works of the imagination. He did this with grace and skill, exhibiting wide-ranging knowledge of his literary sources, shattering, as his son Mikhail Aleksandrovich said, a then prevalent image of "a Russian cleric as dark, uneducated, and mired in tradition."[73] In making connections between literature and religion and drawing parallels between his own times and earlier literary achievements, Aleksandr Men also spoke to Russia's cultural heritage and its recovery at a time when this subject was a matter of passionate concern. However, his interpretations, as well as public activities, could not fail to provoke passionate opposition.

14

. . . .

Freedom and Its Discontents

The elegant wooden church at Novaia Derevnia has a different shape than the circular form of most other Orthodox churches in the central region of Russia. Fr. Aleksandr's church resembles a ship, a vessel set well within the forest, where it was moved by villagers in 1920 to escape destruction by the Bolsheviks.[1] The building to the church's immediate left, whose blueprint Fr. Aleksandr drafted to serve as a Sunday school and to host other meetings, was constructed in the architectural style of the northern city of Novgorod. Both structures speak of openness to the world and, in reaching out and welcoming people, of light in the midst of darkness. As an early twentieth-century author wrote, "Like the icon lamps glimmering in the monastery cloisters whither the people thronged through the centuries in search of moral support and instruction, these ideals, this light of Christ, illuminated Rus."[2] Novaia Derevnia is a modest village parish. But to the large numbers of people who came here in the late 1980s, it represented these ideals, and chief among them was spiritual freedom.

Aleksandr Men's son, Mikhail Aleksandrovich, lived with his parents until 1978, when, at the age of seventeen, he left to enter the Institute of Culture in Moscow. However, on weekends for the next twelve years, he always came home to spend time with his family. In the late 1980s, he devoted a lot of time talking with his father, conversations, he recalled, that became more and more intense in 1989 and 1990. At that time, at the age of twenty-nine and thirty, he had already begun to follow his own course in life: from the art world, where he had originally begun, he had moved into business, where he encountered what he described as a "lot of negative issues" that had developed with perestroika.[3] On his visits home, he and his father went into Fr. Aleksandr's office and talked about those issues.

The extended conversations Mikhail Aleksandrovich had with his father often turned to politics. They talked about the merits and deficiencies of perestroika and the direction the country needed to go. They often argued, Mikhail Aleksandrovich said. To Fr. Aleksandr, perestroika represented a "breath of fresh air"; it heralded democratic changes, which promised a better future. "He was more romantic than I," said his son; "I was not as idealistic. I had run into several new problems with our free-wheeling bureaucracy, and I had seen, at first hand, some criminal elements, which undermined my optimism about the road on which we were traveling."[4]

During their discussions, father and son argued about the prospects for Russia's political transformation. In order for Russia to develop a democracy, popular mentalities needed to undergo a significant change, which Fr. Aleksandr saw as a more promising possibility than did his son. Fr. Aleksandr believed that the movement away from a slavish dependency on authority toward a more independent, personal, and spiritually based and responsible view of the self held an important key to this transformation, and the church had to play a large role in that development.

Mikhail Aleksandrovich expressed grave concerns about his own generation. "I have gone through a difficult period, a difficult change, as have many people my age," he said. "Until I was nearly thirty years of age, I lived in one country; then, I found myself in a different country, with different ideals."[5] He noted that his father helped him "understand the negative elements of the Soviet system, particularly its injustices," but the psychological transformation for him, and for other members of his generation, remained extremely difficult.[6] In 1990, as the ideological and social foundations of the old order continued to crumble, he had little assurance of what the future might hold.

Rising Tensions

The winter months of 1989–1990 witnessed a whole series of internal tensions in the Soviet Union. These months, from December to early spring, began what Jack F. Matlock, the American ambassador, called the "winter of discontent," a sense of foreboding stimulated by uncertainty, rising prices for food and clothing, the end of the Communist Party's political monopoly, and sharp disagreements between reformers and "traditionalists" over the future course of the Soviet Union.[7]

On January 13, 1990, two days after President Gorbachev arrived in Vilnius to conduct talks with the Lithuanian prime minister Kazimiera Prunskiene, violence erupted in Baku, the capital of Azerbaijan, as well as in Ganja, Azerbaijan's second largest city. In the bloody riots, launched by the Azerbaijani Popular Front against Armenians living in Baku, the entire structure of public order in Azerbaijan came under assault. The Popular Front threatened to seize control of the government. The Soviet Army was sent in to secure the border between Azerbaijan and Iran and to reestablish the Communist Party's control.[8] Threats of violence in other locations in the country continued to be an ongoing concern.

Nearly everywhere in the country, the late winter and early spring saw a period of increasing rage, accompanied by a sense that the Communist order needed to go and the whole political structure needed to be swept clean. In early February, in Moscow, a crowd of several hundred thousand people marched toward the Kremlin, clamoring for political change and a multiparty government. It was the largest crowd demonstration, journalist David Remnick reported, "since the rise of Soviet power, and there was nothing polite about it."[9] Facing such popular pressure, the Central Committee, on February 7, issued resolutions essentially proclaiming an end to the one-party monopoly on political power.

The spring of 1990 witnessed several significant additional challenges to the old order, including the emergence of a powerful new leader, Boris Yeltsin, in the Russian Supreme Soviet. The political order that had existed for the last seventy years came under attack on multiple fronts. The formation earlier that year of a new political organization, Democratic Russia, brought together a large number of former groups under one umbrella, whose ostensible purpose was to promote the democratic ideals of the famous physicist and human rights activist Andrei Sakharov, who had died in December 1989. Democratic Russia became the vehicle that championed Yeltsin's rise to power.

In its name alone, Democratic Russia signified a challenge to the Soviet Union, because the name itself connected the democratic movement with the Russian Federation. It was the first time these labels had been placed together, thus defining an awakened Russia apart from the larger confederation. In the March elections to the Congress of the Russian Federation, Democratic Russia gained a majority of seats and immediately demanded that power in the Russian Soviet Federative Socialist Republic (RSFSR), including authority over the military and police, should pass to the Congress of People's Deputies. Democratic Russia emerged in direct opposition to the Communist Party of the Soviet Union.[10]

The centrifugal pressures within the Soviet Union grew steadily throughout the spring of 1990. In March, Lithuania declared independence, and despite attempts to force its retreat, its separation from the USSR became a reality. The other two Baltic states, Estonia and Latvia, soon followed suit. But these movements toward independence and democratization also brought powerful counterforces into the political arena. Strong oppositional groups created National Salvation committees within a year; such organizations were already beginning to form by the summer of 1990. Made up of Communist Party members and nationalists, they quickly began to assert their own antidemocratic views.

The emergence of these competing voices raised the debate over the role of the Orthodox Church in Russian society to an even more intensive level. The controversy was not new, because its legacy reached back to the seventeenth century.[11] But the sharpness of the debate, as well as the stakes in its resolution, bore heavily on both the present and the future, especially after the death of Patriarch Pimen (Izvekov), who had served as head of the Russian Church since 1971, on May 3, 1990. His replacement by the younger, more energetic Aleksii II (Ridiger), who was enthroned as patriarch of Moscow and All Russia on June 10, signaled the church's resurgence and the prospect of an accelerated recovery of its property and status.[12] The debate over the church as a key element in Russia's identity touched all the major political parties and organizations—from the left to the far right on the political spectrum.[13] The significance of this issue was evidenced by national surveys, which showed, in 1990, that among the Russian population, the church was the most highly respected institution in Russian society.[14]

Because the main questions raised in the debate concerned Russia's future direction, they quickly became extremely contentious. In 1989 and 1990, discussion of the Orthodox Church received extensive coverage in all the major newspapers and journals, from *Literaturnaia gazeta* to *Izvestiia*, *Pravda* (Truth), *Ogonek*, and *Znamia* (The banner), to mention only a few, and continued long into the summer and fall of 1990, as the Congress of People's Deputies worked on the new Soviet Law on Freedom of Conscience and Religious Organizations.[15] The issues involved education, property rights, social reforms, the relationship between Orthodoxy and other religious faiths, and ownership of the artistic treasures of the Soviet Union. Most importantly, to Fr. Aleksandr, who frequently appeared on television, on the radio, and in Moscow lecture halls, the main question concerned the spiritual freedom of the individual as a child of God.

The Individual and the Crowd

As emphasized throughout the preceding chapters, the relationship between religion, culture, and personal freedom became a central theme for Aleksandr Men. The subject previously had been a concern, but he now saw the chance to enlarge on it, given Russia's changing political directions. Hitherto, Fr. Aleksandr had refrained from engaging in the political arena, but in the charged political environment of the spring and summer of 1990, he could hardly have avoided it. His participation in two events connected him to the conflicts taking place over Russia's future direction.

The first event took place in May 1990, when Fr. Aleksandr traveled to Germany, leaving his native land for only the second time in his life. He accepted an invitation to take part in an international symposium, cosponsored by the Catholic Academy of the episcopate of Rottenburg-Stuttgart and the Russian journal *Foreign Literature* (*Inostrannaia literatura*) that was being held in the historic West German town of Weingarten, in Baden-Württemburg. Convened by the well-known Kyrgyz novelist Chinghiz Aitmatov, the symposium featured leading writers, literary specialists, and theologians from the Federal Republic of Germany, the USSR, Switzerland, and Austria. These prominent cultural figures gathered to discuss a subject that cut across national boundaries, but, given the timing of the symposium, had immediate relevance to Russia: the relationship between the "power of politics and the power of the spirit."[16] The May symposium represented the last of three similar meetings, the first two having dealt with the relationship between "Communism and Christianity," and "The Artist and Power."[17] All three topics focused on what the chief spokesperson for the symposia called among the most significant of those problems confronting the Soviet Union and Eastern Europe.[18]

The third symposium, titled "Individual and Mass Consciousness," opened with a keynote address by the distinguished German theologian Hans Kung. Kung spoke to what he described as the "new ecumenism," an emerging international spirit of cooperation, which he deemed to be threatened by old but still powerful ideological points of view. Kung's speech set the stage for the dialogue that followed. As a prelude to this dialogue, Chinghiz Aitmatov posed what he called a "large and important question" about current trends and where they might lead. He referred specifically to the Soviet Union: "We are going through a difficult period, a time of troubles, of internal danger, which is assaulting our self-image, and many in our society want to put an end to this discourse, wishing to revert to an earlier period of mass consciousness," where group thought and state control offered them greater comfort.[19]

This issue, Aitmatov emphasized, had been a serious problem in the Soviet Union, as it had earlier in Germany, where Nazism rested on the foundation of submerging the individual into the crowd. In Germany and the Soviet Union, he maintained, mass consciousness had fostered extreme forms of nationalism. This misguided form of nationalism encouraged the search for scapegoats on which to blame social problems, thereby producing some of the greatest human atrocities in the twentieth century. How might such a trend be prevented, when the danger of its reemergence seemed a large possibility, especially in "our country, tormented by anxiety that has accompanied the recent changes?"[20]

Aleksandr Men's contributions to the symposium came near the end. In addressing a subject to which he had recently given a lot of attention, his words expressed conviction and passion. He well understood, he said, that the present represented a crucial moment not only in his own country, but also in Europe. In that spirit, he focused on human dignity and its impor-tance to the development of a civilized, peaceful world order. If govern-ments did not seek to build this kind of order, separately and universally, he claimed, humankind is destined "to suffer the same fate as the dinosaurs."[21] It is critical, he emphasized, that we find our universal connections, which have always existed but repeatedly have been brushed aside.

Fr. Aleksandr pointed out that such shallow thinking has invariably led to human degradation and to a general impoverishment, which always comes from separating the "part from the whole, from amputating the foot or hand from the body, and sinking the limb into a biological liquid, so that it might go on living."[22] The dignity of the individual, Fr. Aleksandr said, cannot be divorced from a person's spiritual being. A reciprocal rela-tionship existed between them: they nourished each other, and on the rec-ognition and enhancement of this relationship, he argued, "we can build a new paradigm."[23]

Fr. Aleksandr's remarks at the Weingarten symposium were closely related to his recent concerns about attempts to suppress the spiritual quest. His comments signaled the dangers that ensued when this quest was diverted into other pursuits, or when political and religious institutions sought to close off this spiritual quest. Elsewhere, in a recent article, he referenced the nineteenth-century Russian tsar Nicholas I's efforts to "freeze Russia."

[W]ith all his strength [he] opposed the translation of the Bible into the Russian language: copies of the translation were burned in the factory fires, and the translators were imprisoned. And in place of [the Gospel], he put the slogan Orthodoxy, Autocracy, and Nationality. It is easy to understand, why his opposition became so strong, when "Orthodoxy" meant the Fourth Section, "Autocracy," the cult of personality, and "Nationalism," conform-ism and the exaggerated enthusiasm of the intimidated masses.[24]

These statements about an intimidated, manipulated mass society had strong political overtones. In his remarks at the symposium, he underscored the importance of Henri Bergson's distinction between the open and the closed society. The latter degraded the individual.

Earlier in the symposium, Fr. Aleksandr's Russian colleague Nikolai Anastas'ev cited the Spanish philosopher José Ortega y Gasset's classic work, *The Revolt of the Masses*. Ortega's work on "mass society" is extremely relevant to the theme of the symposium, Fr. Aleksandr said, because Ortega showed how the crowd is easily manipulated and is far easier to control than the person acting alone. "Christ said that the road to God is in each soul, not in the mass or the people."[25] To Fr. Aleksandr, this principle confirmed the absolute value of each person, a principle that writers and other cultural leaders everywhere had the responsibility to uphold. It was a spiritual principle, which mass consciousness did not recognize. Coming at the end of the Weingarten symposium, Fr. Aleksandr's comments represented a clarion call to the symposium's participants. Although he spoke from a Russian context, his words had universal relevance. "Concentrated efforts are needed at present more than ever," he said, "if humanity as a whole is going to survive."[26]

As has been emphasized in this chapter, in the last year of his life, the theme of freedom occupied Aleksandr Men's mind, particularly with regard to the internal freedom of the person to decide which path to follow. This, to him, represented a core principle of Christianity and a central part of Christ's teachings. This theme surfaced at the second event connecting Fr. Aleksandr to the current conflicts in his society: a series of lectures he delivered in the spring and summer of 1990 at the Moscow State Historical and Archival Institute. Titled originally "The World of the Bible," Fr. Aleksandr's talks in this series that spring and summer presented far more than a dry compendium of historical facts about the ancient world. They related the past to the present and included subjects that ranged from the dilemmas confronting people in the world preceding the birth of Christ to the difficult choices facing his own countrymen in these years of declining Soviet power.

The lectures comprised part of a special project planned by the institute's well-known director, the historian Iurii Nikolaevich Afanas'ev. Afanas'ev believed that the humanities, in their power and richness, had degenerated and had been nearly lost during the Soviet period. They needed to be renewed and revitalized. He planned lectures for students in order to present to them "at the highest possible level, the power of the humanitarian thought of individuals who had kept this thought alive in the face of Stalinist dogmatism."[27] Fr. Aleksandr represented one of these people invited to speak, not to convert students to Christianity, but to portray, in a scholarly format, the world of the ancient east from which the Bible, one of the seminal books in world history, had emerged.[28]

Fr. Aleksandr turned down any compensation for his lectures. According to one of the professors and organizers of the series, Fr. Aleksandr dazzled the students, who packed into the auditorium to hear his presentations, which gave them a different historical account from what they had previously studied.[29] Even the youngest of those in the largely student audience had grown up during a time when their educational background remained dominated by a Marxist-Leninist interpretation, with its view that material underpinnings and class relationships had produced the slave society of the ancient world.

Aleksandr Men's account of ancient history began with the Exodus, the movement of the Israelites from ancient Egypt, which he portrayed as a movement from slavery to freedom. He developed this narrative in ten succeeding sessions, bringing the story up to the era of the New Testament world, portraying a progressive story, which he told on several different levels and from diverse points of view. He included in his talks a large array of scholars, as well as recent historical discoveries. Most impressively, he wove into his narratives numerous literary references, many of which the students were well acquainted and with which they personally identified, including a variety of nineteenth and twentieth century authors—Pushkin and Goethe, Dostoevsky and Chaadaev, Belyi and Iskander, and others. [30]

In these lectures, Fr. Aleksandr also took a much different approach to slavery than what the members of his audience had been accustomed to hearing. He depicted the fundamental character of slavery in ancient Egypt as psychological, not material. While in Egyptian bondage, the Israelites satisfied their physical needs; they had plenty of food and they lived in relative security. Their movement toward freedom did not involve an escape from physical deprivation, but something far less tangible—a desire to think, to be less dependent, and to make one's own moral choices. Such freedom, as Fr. Aleksandr emphasized, is difficult: it is embraced only by the few, it is internal, and it is where the teachings of Christ ultimately lead. True freedom is not what most people desire; they want something else: they wish to be controlled and to be given the answers. Freedom, in contrast, encapsulated a conscious moral choice that every human being must freely make, although they might wish to assign that choice to others.[31]

In the public presentations he made in 1989–1990, two distinctive qualities stood out. First, Fr. Aleksandr, spoke in a conversational voice, holding a microphone and moving about the stage, using concrete, specific terms and eschewing the abstract language many of his predecessors had used. He made a lasting impression. He had the ability to address people personally, despite the size of his audience. It was a gift he had cultivated over many years, beginning with the small household talks that he had earlier created. Now, projected on a much larger stage, his message, as well as his method, remained the same. Before audiences numbering in the hundreds, sometimes thousands of people, "he always spoke as if he were talking to each person."[32]

At the end of each presentation, Fr. Aleksandr usually asked for questions, which members of the audience wrote on thin scraps of paper and brought to the front of the auditorium. He thus opened up a dialogue, exploring with his audiences issues that had not been publicly raised for a long time. This kind of open exchange of ideas, Yves Hamant noted, had not been seen since the 1920s, when atheist speakers engaged members of the church in public debate.[33] At clubs, schools, and academic institutions, to which he was often invited, Fr. Aleksandr again made a striking contrast to how many members of the public traditionally conceived of Orthodox priests. But his mannerisms, openness, interpretations of Orthodoxy's heritage, and the importance he ascribed to freedom did not sit well with certain other groups, both within the church and elsewhere in Russian society.

The Opposition

In his presentations and publications in the late 1980s, as well as in his public appearances, Aleksandr Men wished for the Orthodox Church to become more dynamic. This aspiration led him to criticize the church as an agent of the status quo that had frequently played a negative role in Russia's past. He disapproved of what he saw as the Orthodox Church's rigid conservatism and its bureaucratic mentality, which hindered it from speaking out effectively to the Russian population, who had, in times of need, hungered for its leadership. Unless the church became more flexible and more open, unless it was willing to reach across its own narrow boundaries and truly engage current concerns in language comprehensible and engaging to the population, it would again lose a historic chance to provide leadership.[34]

Fr. Aleksandr took issue with what he called the simplistic, rigid mindset of certain clerical groups, who wanted to recreate the past and to restore the church to its prerevolutionary position of wealth and authority. In 1989, he worried that the church again was surrendering to a narrow, restrictive conservatism and nostalgia for the past; its bishops were failing "to speak of the essentials of what we believe."[35]

In 1990, Aleksandr Men's anxiety about these clerical circles took a sharper tone as he expressed disappointment with the church's failure to pray for repentance for its previous complicity with the government.[36] In recovering from the Communist assault and regaining its properties, the church exuded a sense of victory. This triumphant attitude, in addition to the church's affiliation with the Russian government, he maintained, foretold disastrous consequences for the future.

If Fr. Aleksandr achieved increasing popularity among the public, in other circles, he incurred resentment. A large, growing segment of the clergy found his television and radio appearances contrary to what they conceived to be the church's proper role. At the time, these members of the clergy perceived the media as pernicious, and a priest's involvement with them as wrongful collusion with a secular instrument of power that was inherently corrupting of the priesthood's sacred mission.[37] While there were notable exceptions, members of the church elite were suspicious of priests who acted independently of the collective wisdom of the hierarchy.[38] These members were focused on the church's internal problems, rather than on the larger religious and social questions that Fr. Aleksandr raised.

Fr. Aleksandr's criticism of the church as an agent of the status quo and its role in Russian history also provoked opposition within the established theological academies. Fr. Aleksandr appeared as a rebel whose challenges to tradition, proposals for greater openness, and desires for dialogue between Orthodoxy and different faiths were unacceptable. Aleksei Il'ich Osipov (b. 1938), professor of systematic theology and the director of graduate studies at the Spiritual Academy of the Moscow Patriarchy at Sergiev Posad, was one of those critics. Osipov did not see Fr. Aleksandr as acting within the mainstream of Orthodox tradition. To him, the priest held a Western perspective on church and state relations, and he categorized Men as a "liberal" whose interpretations of classical texts were misrepresentations.

Professor Osipov taught (and continues to teach) graduate courses on the Russian theologian-philosophers who lived at the end of the nineteenth and early twentieth centuries. He disagreed with Fr. Aleksandr's interpretation of them as ecumenical writers who held ecumenical perspectives. He was convinced that the public fascination with Fr. Aleksandr would soon pass. "He is, in my view," Osipov said, "a marginal religious figure, whose place in our history will soon be forgotten."[39]

Other writers accused Fr. Aleksandr of heresy. A study issued in 1991 in the series *Troitskii blagovestnik* (Trinity blessed messenger), a publication of the Trinity-Saint Sergius Lavra, parts of which were reprinted in the secular press, sought to denigrate Fr. Aleksandr as a biblical scholar.[40] The author attacked Fr. Aleksandr's interpretation of the Bible, particularly his writings on Christ, labeling him a proponent of Arianism, a follower of the arch-heretic Arias (250–336), the desert father who had viewed Jesus as only an earthly being. The Church Council of Nicaea, in 325, had rejected this belief, affirming that the word of God was "personally incarnate in the Lord Jesus," thus branding Arianism as heretical.[41]

The opposition to Fr. Aleksandr had several faces, ranging across the political and religious spectrum. In mid-1989, national-patriotic organizations, which had emerged during perestroika, aspired to fill the ideological void that opened up with the declining influence of Communism. These groups became an immediate threat to political and religious leaders who advocated for a more open society. In the tense atmosphere of 1990, the political voices of these ultranationalist organizations became increasingly strident. They also cultivated connections with fundamentalists within the church and with the KGB, both of whom encouraged their activism.[42]

Looking for the causes of what they viewed as Russia's internal chaos, ultranationalist organizations proclaimed "international imperialism" and "rootless cosmopolitanism" as among the main causes of Russia's weaknesses. These arguments targeted Jews as agents of the "diseases" that had penetrated Russia, undermining its national unity and moral fiber. These were old charges that had been used before to paint Jews as the culprits.[43]

Aleksandr Men's Jewish background, ecumenical perspectives, and critique of the Orthodox Church and its relationship to the state made him an obvious target. On this level, the opposition to Fr. Aleksandr became more than a theological dispute. Nationalist-patriotic groups perceived his views as symbolic of the problems afflicting Russia—its attachment to Western perspectives, openness to non-Orthodox religious denominations, decline of military strength, and weak political institutions. Among the extremist groups, Pamiat' (Memory) quickly became one of the most outspoken and the most dangerous.

Pamiat' had its roots in Moscow's Aviation Ministry, part of Moscow's city organization. When it first emerged in the late 1970s, Pamiat' called itself "a society of film lovers," whose original goal was to celebrate the six-hundred-year anniversary of Moscow's military victory over the Tatars at Kulikovo Field in 1380. Soon afterward, the film society split, and one of its most active factions assumed the name of Pamiat'. Under the leadership of Dmitrii Dmitrievich Vasil'ev, a photographer, artist, and sometime actor, Pamiat' became an extremist, ultranationalist organization.[44]

During perestroika, Pamiat' sharpened its rhetoric, boldly proclaiming its message of defending the motherland against an encroaching Western culture. On May 1, 1987, it issued a manifesto on Manezh Square, by the Moscow Kremlin, in which the group labeled itself an "historical-patriotic organization" aimed at preserving the memory of the sacred Russian people. The manifesto demanded a meeting with Gorbachev and Boris Yeltsin, then first secretary of the Moscow Communist Party.[45]

Dressed in black shirts reminiscent of Russia's prerevolutionary anti-Semitic organization the Black Hundreds, Pamiat' members espoused foundational principles that loudly embraced an extremely aggressive form of both anti-Semitism and anti-Americanism. The organization supported the Orthodox Church, calling it Russia's "Mother Church," and arguing that Western-leaning liberals were attempting to silence its authoritative voice.

The protocols and resolutions issued by Pamiat' claimed evidence of internal infiltration of Russia by Jewish organizations connected to the West. Russia, the group's leaders maintained, faced no less a crisis than it had in World War II: its survival and future identity depended on its capacity to rid itself of these internal enemies dressed as "wolves in sheep's clothing."[46] Jewish agents, pretending to be Orthodox, might be found within the Orthodox Church, arguing for universal government, open borders, and Western ways of thought. As support, Pamiat' members distributed copies of the *Protocols of Zion*.[47]

In an interview he gave on September 5, 1990, Fr. Aleksandr cited the personal attacks against him emanating from anti-Semitic and xenophobic organizations. These organizations were "harmful and dangerous," he said; their followers "are sprouting like mushrooms."[48] The demise of Communist ideology had opened up a formerly closed Russian society, but rather than welcome such openness and the opportunity for a creative recovery of national traditions, the members of these organizations wanted to narrow the range of possibilities. They did not appreciate Fr. Aleksandr's desire to examine the past critically, nor did they support his emphasis on a key principle in Orthodox tradition: the need both for repentance and reconciliation.[49]

In the past, Aleksandr Men had managed to deflect the periodic anti-Semitic threats he faced, but in 1990, such dangers became omnipresent. He described the ultranationalists as individuals with a deep-seated hatred and fear, and he likened their mentalities to the Cossacks in Nikolai Gogol's story *Taras Bulba* who campaigned against the Catholic Poles. Asked whether he found himself to be a similar target, Fr. Aleksandr gave the following revealing response, which bears witness to the increasing pressure of the personal attacks he experienced in the summer months of 1990: "I have been a priest for a long time, more than thirty years, but this [hatred] has started to happen now. I feel it in the way people behave towards me, in the way they talk to me, in everything."[50]

Years earlier, Fr. Aleksandr had received an anonymous letter, one of the few unsigned among the many venomous messages sent to him. He had a long-standing habit of discarding such anonymous letters, not allowing them to divert him from the mission he viewed as divinely inspired, but this one he kept. The tone and content of the letter exemplified the resentment he stirred among his opposition:

> For a long time, Fr. Aleksandr, I have been observing your activity. You do not know me, and up to now I have not met you, although I have heard about you for many years. I know that you appear as a Christianized Jew and serve as an Orthodox priest. Such a combination neither embarrasses me in the least, nor does it embarrass any Orthodox person, because antisemitism does not exist in the nature of Orthodoxy. . . . The matter is not only in you, as a God-created person, but in those visible and invisible forces that rule you. Let's call those collected forces under which you serve Zionism. . . . Under the disguise of the Old Testament, under the disguise of a Single true God, they [Jewish people] succeeded in creating a secret worship of the devil, Satan, or "Lucifer," as they sometimes call him. . . . You are a fountainhead of Zionism within the Orthodox Church. . . . During recent years a very tight bond has been formed between Zionism and the leaders of the Catholic Church, and this can be explained not only by the "double game" that they play, but also by their common spiritual heritage.[51]

Fr. Aleksandr was not in the habit of displaying anxiety about his life, and he did not normally talk about his own personal circumstances. He faced the present as he always had, accepting the difficulties, but aware that he served a much larger purpose than his own willful desires might have dictated. He saw himself as an instrument, rather than the main designer or the solitary person acting independently. It was this sense of service that had always given him the courage to be and to act, often in the face of unpleasant, sometimes dangerous circumstances.[52]

Meanwhile, in the late summer of 1990, he had a sense of urgency, as well as a sense of foreboding, which in hindsight suggests awareness that his life was nearing an end. Whether he became acutely aware of the dangers he faced from multiple political quarters, or came to some inner understanding, cannot be known with certainty. As mentioned above, he did not change his schedule; he went about his business, even intensifying his activities. He did his parish work, he visited hospitals, he continued to give a series of lectures in Moscow, he met with school groups and with members of his parish, and he worked on another manuscript.

On the evening of September 8, 1990, Aleksandr Men gave what would be his last lecture. Some members of his circle later interpreted the lecture as his presentiment of his impending death. But the significance of the talk goes beyond such speculations; it represented his testament, a summation of the theological beliefs he had expressed for many years. It completed the cycle of talks on world religions he gave that summer at the House of Culture in Moscow. He looked both to the past and to the future. He went back to the Gospel, which, he believed, represented a crowning achievement in world history, and yet he believed that the story the Gospel told was not yet finished.

In his lecture, Fr. Aleksandr affirmed Christianity as the penultimate faith tradition: "And so together, we have reached the end of our journey, which has taken us through the ages, around the world philosophies, and we have come to the summit, to that sparkling mountain spring wherein the sun is reflected, which is called Christianity."[53] As in his other works, he did not present Christianity in opposition to other faith traditions, but as completing them, rising above them, and also adding something that is extraordinarily powerful. He spelled out clearly what this is: in Christianity, God and humanity are joined together. Despite the bloodshed, the violence, and the apparent chaos of events, Christianity asks human beings to trust in the existence of the good. Christianity teaches human beings to see differently than before, to view the world differently; it brings an internal transformation and a new life that prompts us to reach out to other people, loving them, in Christ's words, as "I have loved you." Fr. Aleksandr's message was optimistic: with Christ, the good news has already come into being. Christianity, he again maintained, is only in its infancy.[54]

Where is the kingdom of God, he asked? It is not in some futuristic possibility, some distant hope, but exists in the present: "When you do good, when you love, when you contemplate beauty, when you feel the fullness of life, the kingdom of God is already touching you."[55] It is easy to deny the world, he said, and to see it as meaningless, chaotic, and absurd, views that are expressed by many significant contemporary writers. Aleksandr Men, however, stood for the opposite approach. He spoke from what he referred to as the "strongest impulse in Christian spirituality," which is "not to deny, but to affirm, to include and to complete."[56] Near the end of his last lecture, Fr. Aleksandr spoke words that rang out memorably in the tragic days that lay ahead:

So if we again ask ourselves the question, what is the essence of Christianity, then we must answer: it is God-manhood, the joining of the finite and temporal human spirit with the eternal Divinity, it is the sanctification of the flesh, for from that moment when the Son of Man took on our joys and our sufferings, our love, our labors, from that moment, nature, the world, everything in which he was, in which he rejoiced, as a man and as God-man, no longer is rejected, no longer is degraded but is raised up to a new level, and is sanctified.[57]

Having given this lecture, Fr. Aleksandr went to the Iaroslavskaia railway station to take the train for the hour-and-a half journey to his Semkhoz home. It was late that evening when he arrived, weary after an event-filled day. Some time later, Fr. Aleksandr's assassins, probably two of them, entered the woods near the path he always walked, preparing to wait and to strike in the autumn dawn.

15

. . . .

"This Was Not a Common Murder"

I
n the summer months of 1990, Aleksandr Men, either directly or indirectly, talked about "not having enough time left to complete his work"
and expressed the belief that his life was soon coming to the end.[1] Political changes in the Soviet Union had opened up many positive benefits, but
these changes also had taken the lid off antagonistic, dangerous elements
that rapidly came to the surface, forces that Fr. Aleksandr recognized.[2] His
frequent presence on television and radio made him an easy target for certain political interests who saw him as an enemy of everything they valued.
Rarely had he ever before expressed anxiety about his safety, but in recent
months he had begun to be concerned. Often arriving late at night on the
train from Moscow, he had to walk along the dark, wooded pathway to his
home. In early September, Fr. Aleksandr asked one of his associates to look
for a place in the city where he might, on occasion, spend the night.[3]

Ekaterina Genieva, a close friend of Fr. Aleksandr, wrote an assessment that is remarkable for its detailed personal observations, as well as its
remembrance of his last days. The general director of the M. I. Rudomino
State Library of Foreign Literature in Moscow, one of Russia's most impressive ecumenical research centers, Genieva had for many years been close to
Fr. Aleksandr; he had performed the wedding ceremony for Genieva and
her husband.[4] A large photograph of Fr. Aleksandr hangs on the wall in
Genieva's office; the library's guidebook notes that his "ideas inspired the
library's concept of humanity as an ecumenical whole."[5] He lectured there
often, presenting a course on biblical history to a large audience in the main
auditorium of the library not long before his death. On Friday evening,
September 7, 1990, he went there to lecture. Genieva's assessment focused
on this "last meeting" and the details of their discussion.

Scheduled to begin his address at 6:00 p. m., Fr. Aleksandr arrived a few
minutes early, after an extremely busy day, having performed the liturgy,

fulfilled his other parish responsibilities, and participated in several other afternoon meetings in Moscow. Genieva asked him whether he would like some tea. He responded affirmatively, and then told her that he was terribly hungry and had not had much to eat the last three days. When she questioned him about his activities, he explained that he had spent most of this time writing. Genieva later regretted that she had not asked him about his project, especially since the authorities had not located his briefcase, which he always carried with him.[6]

Busy processing a large shipment of books for an upcoming exhibition, Genieva did not attend Fr. Aleksandr's lecture. But afterward, he returned to her office, and together they left the library for the train station. Genieva's reminiscences at this point have a sense of foreboding. As she, her daughter, and Fr. Aleksandr departed the building that evening, Genieva saw an automobile, in which several large men were sitting, parked directly across from the library's entrance. As she recalled, the scene aroused her suspicions; she called the automobile to the attention of the library's security officer, and she recorded the license number. The next morning, upon arriving at the library, she asked the policeman about the automobile, and he told her it had driven away a few minutes after she, her daughter, and Fr. Aleksandr left the premises. While she later reported this information and the license number to the investigating committee, it was her impression that the committee ignored them.

Genieva did not know for certain whether "Fr. Aleksandr knew his life was nearing the end," although she believed he had such a premonition. As their train reached the Pushkino station and mother and daughter left to transfer to another line, Fr. Aleksandr suddenly gripped her daughter's hand tightly and said, "Be glad, have joy, Dasha." They had taken this route many times before but Fr. Aleksandr had never acted this way. "I didn't understand then, what had just taken place," she said, and it was only later that she realized the significance of his parting words. Then, as she stepped away from the platform of the station, Genieva looked through the window and saw him for the last time. He had taken a seat, "opened his briefcase, taken out some papers, and began to write."[7] These images, Genieva recalled, were etched in her mind: his reaching out to her daughter, his sense of gratitude and joy, and his bending over his papers. To the end, the power of the word continued to play a central part in Fr. Aleksandr's thoughts and in his actions. As director of a major library, Genieva is a caretaker of written words. As a creator and transmitter of language, Aleksandr Men symbolized to her the power of the word to shape and transform the ways human beings relate to each other.

As the reader will recall, on September 8, the night before his murder, Fr. Aleksandr presented the last of a series of lectures on the history of Christianity. One part of his lecture bears further mention, because he addressed Russia's present situation and hopes for its future. Those who heard his talk recalled the passion in his voice, its unusual cadence, and how, in this last lecture especially, his words came from the heart.[8]

In his lecture, he spoke of faith not as it is often defined as a conviction, but as trust, reemphasizing a theme that marked his entire ministry. He talked about Russian Orthodoxy as much more than ritual, which is only the outer shell of the faith, but Christianity in its creative aspect is perpetually generative, and "grows like a tree, out of a little acorn."[9] His talk was laden with words underscoring his central Christian beliefs, words that he had so many times discussed throughout his years. He now accentuated what, in his view, people most needed to hear and to remember: trust, which he mentioned three times in the lecture; freedom; grace; faithfulness; mystery; Christ-centeredness; a New Covenant; and love, which he underscored multiple times, a self-giving love that represented faith in action, transcended all human boundaries, and considered human beings everywhere as brothers and sisters. All of these words were interrelated, were parts of a whole, and, together, led to an internal transformation that, in turn, reached outward to the world.

Christ did not leave us with a "single line of writing," a single system or set of rules, Fr. Aleksandr said. He uttered to us, instead, some prophetic words: "I do not leave you orphaned, but I will come back to you," and he constantly says this, even today. Fr. Aleksandr asked his audience to trust these words, to take comfort in them, and to use them as guideposts for ordering their lives. As they reflected upon his statements in the next several days, those present that evening must have been mindful of their irony, of the sense of loss and hope.

Fr. Aleksandr's murder on Sunday morning, September 9, 1990, shocked and dismayed his many followers, from the members of his parish, who were the first to appear at his church that morning, to the international community, who saw in him the promise of a reformed, enlightened Russia. Anastasiia Iakovlevna Andreeva, Aleksandr Men's childhood friend, recalled being stunned at the news.[10] Andreeva described him as a "prophet in his homeland," whose healing words had spoken to the oppressed and the persecuted and had brought hope where it had been nearly nonexistent. The murder, "accomplished with an axe and on a calculated day," had physically taken away this prophetic voice.[11]

The outpouring of grief, as well as bewilderment, quickly spread abroad, where people who had visited Fr. Aleksandr's church or had met privately with him similarly expressed profound sorrow. "Russia has lost one of its greatest citizens," said the French diplomat Yves Hamant, who had known Fr. Aleksandr since the late 1970s and had only recently visited him at Novaia Derevnia. The murder, in the lingering days of late summer, wrote the Russian journalist Aleksandr Minkin, was a defining moment: "Humanization and democratization exist on one side of our system. On the other side is murder."[12]

At the funeral, two days later on a clear Tuesday morning, more than a thousand people crowded into the small church and the courtyard. They were men and women, mostly young or middle-aged, among the thousands Fr. Aleksandr had baptized in his service as a pastor, many of them members of the Moscow intelligentsia. Patriarch Aleksii II did not attend, but he sent a letter, read before the burial service, in which he called Fr. Aleksandr a "talented preacher of the Word of God" and praised his reconstruction of the parish at Novaia Derevnia, particularly his ability "to bring it to life in all its fullness."[13] In words that exhibited a bit of caution, displaying an awareness of controversies swirling within the Orthodox Church, the patriarch tempered his praise: "In his theological daring, Fr. Aleksandr expressed opinions which, without close examination, may not be unconditionally held by the whole [Russian Orthodox] Church. Yet, it is necessary to have diverse opinions among us, to ensure that the best [views] will rise to the top."

After the reading of the patriarch's letter, Iuvenalii, metropolitan of Krutitsy and Kolomna, made a statement. Fr. Aleksandr's friend and protector during difficult years, when KBG investigations threatened his life, Metropolitan Iuvenalii expressed his appreciation for the life of the deceased priest. He called Fr. Aleksandr an "authentic pastor, who loved the church, from his earliest to his last days, and who gave to it all his strength and his knowledge."[14]

> I remember one of the conversations I had with Fr. Aleksandr, when he, with deep enthusiasm, spoke about the possibilities that have opened up for the [Russian Orthodox] Church. And I asked him: "You are a popular person. Why did you not put your name on the ballot as a people's deputy?" And he replied to me with all his sincerity and childlike simplicity: "My Superior! When do we have time to engage in politics? Today we have the opportunity to preach the word of God, and I give myself fully to it." He did so in the schools, in the factories, in large workers' auditoria, and among the intelligentsia. Preaching the teachings of the Lord Jesus Christ, who saved the world, Fr. Aleksandr found the words understandable to all of these people.[15]

By September 23, 1990, major international and Russian newspapers carried extensive coverage of Fr. Aleksandr's death and its significance. "Men's death hangs like a shadow over the progressive trends in Soviet life," wrote Stephen Handleman on the front page of the *Toronto Star*: "Men symbolized the church's rebirth as a force in Russian life."[16] The national outpouring of grief following Fr. Aleksandr's murder suggested much more was at stake than the killing of a popular priest.[17] Writing in *The Independent* (London), Michael Bourdeaux described Fr. Aleksandr as the unofficial patriarch, whose significance went beyond that office and who, "more than almost anyone else, stood for *perestroika* in the church, preaching the Gospel through the media and taking it into schools and other areas from which it had been excluded throughout Soviet history."[18]

The Paris newspaper *Russkaia mysl'* (Russian thought) carried news of Fr. Aleksandr's death at the top of its first page. *Russkaia mysl'* published several lengthy articles, including an eloquent piece by the Russian writer Irina Ilovaiskaia, in which she lamented the losses, in less than a year, of the two leaders of freedom and democracy, Andrei Sakharov and Aleksandr Men.[19] Fr. Aleksandr's sudden disappearance, she maintained, had no less significance for Russia: like Sakharov, he conveyed the message of "human dignity and respect for individual truth."[20]

Leading Moscow newspapers voiced a similar perspective. "It's as though some evil force has broken through forbidden boundaries," maintained *Izvestiia*. "Just as Russia was stepping on the path of purification, straightening itself out, thanks to the efforts of our nation's healthier forces, this happens."[21] Writing in the Russian popular magazine *Ogonek* a week after the murder, the aforementioned young Russian journalist Aleksandr Minkin penned a moving eulogy to Fr. Aleksandr that captured well the pathos of the moment: "In the beginning was the Word," Minkin cited the Gospels. "The Word became Eternal. His whole life 'only' the Word was the weapon of Fr. Aleksandr." His opponents employed a different weapon. Minkin did not believe Fr. Aleksandr's murder was an accident, carried out randomly by a drunk or a robber waiting in the woods for any passerby on that early September morning. "This death was on purpose, planned by a black soul wielding an axe, and whose selection of this instrument was intentional."[22]

Many questions were raised about the meaning and significance of Men's death. But the most immediate issues concerned the identity of the murderers and the reasons behind the act. President Gorbachev promised a full-scale investigation into the case and ordered the police expeditiously to bring the culprits to justice, a commitment that Boris Yeltsin, a year later, also made. Given these resolutions at the highest levels, it was expected that the answers to the questions posed above would soon be forthcoming. Since the murder had taken place only a short distance from Moscow and near a major route of transportation, such a presumption seemed reasonable.

At the same time, Fr. Aleksandr's murder presented several troubling aspects. His attackers did not leave footprints or any other pieces of evidence that might yield clues to the killers' identity. Fr. Aleksandr's briefcase, which he always carried on his way to the Sunday service, disappeared, as did the weapon the killers used in the attack, and a search nearby turned up neither the briefcase nor the weapon; only Fr. Aleksandr's broken reading glasses and his hat were left at the scene. The attack took place early on a Sunday morning and at an isolated place on the footpath, where witnesses to the crime appeared unlikely. With the exception of two women walking further down the pathway to the train station and reporting having seen Fr. Aleksandr minutes before his death, no other people admitted being nearby. Clues suggesting possible investigative directions seemed to have vanished into the early morning mist.

The formal investigation into the murder of Aleksandr Men began immediately. The first investigative team, created in the criminal division of the Moscow oblast procurator (prosecutor), was composed of two KGB officers and detectives in the procurator's office. On the third day after the murder, the group identified the alleged assassin, a neighbor of Fr. Aleksandr's, one Gennadi Bobkov, who confessed to the crime: "The motive was robbery," the police report read. "The weapon of the murder—an axe."[23]

Bobkov had previously been in trouble with the police, and he had a criminal record, but his confession proved unconvincing, particularly after he changed his story, maintaining that a local priest hired him to kill Fr. Aleksandr. When it turned out this priest, a friend of Fr. Aleksandr's, had never met Bobkov, the account proved without merit. The police, nevertheless, retained Bobkov in custody. Many days passed without substantive leads, and although the procurator's office was besieged with anonymous, sometimes strange, telephone calls, nothing the investigating group pursued yielded promising results.[24]

Robbery or Political Motivation?

What were the possible political motivations for the assault on Aleksandr Men? Why had the murder of a popular priest taken place precisely at that moment and place, on a Sunday morning, when Fr. Aleksandr was on his way to church? These were the questions that lay heavily on the public perception of the tragic case. The circumstances recalled the memorable last lines in Tenghiz Abuladze's popular 1988 film *Repentance*: "All roads lead to a church." What kind of church and what role would it play in Russia's future? During the last two years, they had become major questions, and with Fr. Aleksandr's murder, they became even more disputatious.

Describing these processes, Larisa Kislinskaia, a correspondent from the Soviet news agency TASS, writing in *Leninskoe znamia* (The Lenin banner), lucidly presented both the specific facts and the larger issues.[25] Kislinskaia spoke about the significant contribution of religion to the Soviet Union's social transformation and the role the church needed to play in dealing with some of the country's most intractable problems—alcoholism, narcotics, and the internal conflicts that threatened to tear the country apart. She spoke too of Fr. Aleksandr's personal integrity, large following, and his leadership, which had already become evident in these efforts. Her article succinctly framed the questions behind his death. What were the motives underlying the murder, particularly at that moment? Whose interests did the assault serve? What implications did his death have for the Soviet Union's social and religious transformation? These were the issues Kislinskaia believed had to be kept firmly in view.

The fall of 1990 and early 1991 saw a whole series of attacks on Orthodox priests. Since the 1930s, priests had not generally suffered physical assaults by the government or by private citizens. Other methods of intimidation, including threats of arrest, incarceration, and public ridicule had served as instruments of repression. But in 1990, the narrative changed: priests became objects of brutal physical assault. From that perspective, Fr. Aleksandr's murder represented the first of these attacks, in a rising wave of violence that appeared to target certain priests.

In addition to the assault on Fr. Aleksandr, three other murders of well-known priests came in rapid succession. On November 6, Fr. Ivan Kuz', a parish priest serving in the village of Repuzhits, in western Ukraine, was shot three times and killed. Fr. Ivan's assailants took nothing from his apartment, including the large amount of money in his possession, leading the Ukrainian newspaper *Pravda Ukrainy* to conclude that a political or religious motive lay behind the murder. The newspaper also reported that the police had arrested the alleged killer, who had confessed, but gave no information on his motive.[26]

On December 26, 1990, a third priest, Fr. Lazar (Viacheslav Solnyshko) was killed in his flat in central Moscow. A secretary to Bishop Grigorii of Mozhaisk, Fr. Lazar was found beaten to death, a victim, according to the police, of an attempted robbery. A popular priest, active among charitable organizations in the capital, he had devoted a lot of his time to work in hospitals and orphanages. Some accounts suggested that a political motive may have prompted the assault, although *Izvestiia*, in January, published a police report alleging that Fr. Lazar, a homosexual, had been careless about some of the people he brought home with him.[27] Fr. Lazar's colleagues and relatives, however, strongly rejected that explanation. They claimed that several assassins had planned and carried out the murder, found the priest alone in his apartment, and ruthlessly beat him to death. These colleagues and relatives deemed improbable the police's explanation of robbery as the motive because Fr. Lazar had nothing valuable in his apartment.[28]

On February 4, 1991, neighbors discovered the body of a fourth priest in a Moscow apartment, where he lived temporarily following his recent move to the city. Fr. Serafim Shlykov was found bound, gagged, and beaten to death, struck repeatedly with a blunt instrument on the head. Only thirty-two years old, and recently appointed dean of a church in central Moscow, Fr. Serafim had spent the last year serving in a monastery in Jerusalem. The police again attributed the motive of his murder to robbery, since money, a radio, a video recorder, and several other objects were missing. But like the other three murders, robbery might have been a quick, convenient explanation; political motivations could not be dismissed.[29]

None of the other three priests had either the large following or the same national significance as Aleksandr Men.[30] Public pressure, particularly coming from his spiritual children and other groups, mounted on the authorities to identify his killers and discover their motives. The urgency is perhaps best exemplified by a letter written by a member of the Russian parliament and addressed to President Mikhail Gorbachev.[31] Writing during the first days after Fr. Aleksandr's death, the deputy reminded the officials that "on September 9 took place the brutal murder of the prominent Orthodox theologian, preacher, and teacher of life for a hundred thousand Russian people, who knew him personally, heard his sermons, and read his books."[32] The deputy called for construction of a carefully crafted plan to bring quickly the culprits to justice or risk destabilization of the country. "In these days in Moscow," he said, "everyone recalls the name of the Polish priest [Jerzy Popieluszko], [who was] killed under analogous circumstances."[33]

Whether the murder of Aleksandr Men represented the beginning of a series of similar intentional acts by undetermined agencies is a matter of conjecture.[34] The widely different circumstances in which each of these murders took place suggest that they were disconnected criminal acts. Nearly all of them, however, involved socially active priests whose activities might easily have threatened certain political interests. The rapid succession of the murders, as well as the uncertainty of the motives, brought back chilling memories from the past, in which murder had been used to silence certain leading figures. As Aleksandr Minkin wrote, Aleksandr Men's death had brought Russia to a crucial juncture: "We had only begun to free ourselves from the power of fear. The ax is a very good means of conveying the feeling of everyone becoming deaf to freedom. Sober up and remember. They remind us that we are defenseless."[35]

The Investigation Widens

Within a week and a half of Fr. Aleksandr's murder, the Russian government committee widened its inquiry into the circumstances of the case. Detectives from the agency of internal affairs, local and regional officials, the KGB, and the procurator's office were joined by special criminal investigators, prominent medical experts, and forensic specialists.[36]

During the following eight months, as internal political pressures continued to escalate, the police investigation of the murder continued. The police interviewed scores of people, constructed and reconstructed the known facts in the case, and searched for further clues about events on the morning of September 9. In May 1991, expressing frustration with the inability of the police to solve the case, Russian news sources reported that the large number of police assigned to the case had nevertheless produced other benefits: the widening investigation "helped solve more than one hundred other crimes" that had formerly been unresolved.[37]

As the months passed, the trail grew colder, making it more and more unlikely that the police inquiry into the case would ever yield satisfactory results. But public interest in the identity and motives of Fr. Aleksandr's killers did not diminish, particularly because of the political ramifications. On May 16, 1991, TASS reported an interview with the chief investigator, Ivan Leshchenko, in which Leshchenko expressed dissatisfaction with the results, stating that the police, during the last nine months, had conducted background checks on more than five hundred individuals and completed more than two thousand interviews. The results did not match the intensity of the process. Explaining the failure to solve Fr. Aleksandr's case, Leshchenko noted, "Someone clearly needed to throw investigators off the track." When he took over the inquiry, the case seemed to have been "artificially concentrating on evidence that might give a wrong explanation of the motives of the crime."[38]

Leshchenko's appointment to head the investigation, in February 1991, brought to the forefront an experienced police official, who spoke forthrightly about the government's purpose in solving the case. But the reshuffling of the original investigating committee also signaled that the resolution of the case remained far from completion. As a representative of the regional procurator's office, Leshchenko carefully followed procedural guidelines, continuing to interview people and pursuing every conceivable lead, most of which proved fruitless. At one point, Leshchenko's committee believed its work was nearing culmination, only to learn that again they had been led along a false trail.[39] It became difficult to disentangle fact from fiction and hard evidence from misinformation. As in Mikhail Bulgakov's novel *The Master and Margarita*, concrete reality blended with what appeared to be the surreal.

By the late summer of 1991, Russia's "white hot summer," when political passions reached what James H. Billington called "fever pitch," the widespread public interest in Fr. Aleksandr's murder temporarily receded into the background.[40] The transformative political events of that time, including the abortive August coup of authoritarian forces within the government, the demise of the Communist Party's influence, and the restructuring of the government, dominated public concerns. Later in the year, Russian newspapers devoted nearly all their attention to the end of the Soviet state. During the next several years, political and economic issues—the formation and evolution of the new Russian government, the parliamentary clash with President Boris Yeltsin in 1993, and economic crises—became the central stories. By 1995, Leshchenko's investigative committee had amassed thirty-four volumes of materials and had still not solved the murder.

The official inquiry's failure, however, offers the opportunity to refocus several questions in Fr. Aleksandr's case and to take another look at certain facts leading to his murder. A primary issue, raised earlier, might be pursued further: who had an interest in seeing Aleksandr Men murdered? Related to this issue is the question of whose perspectives on Russia's future direction were most threatened by Fr. Aleksandr's activities and views. When the question is posed in this form, the evidence points in a particular direction.

Violent Opposition

Not everyone in Russian society found Fr. Aleksandr's interpretation of the scriptures appealing, with its emphasis on a "self-giving love," an ecumenical vision, and the unqualified importance he ascribed to trust. Chief among them were two groups who regarded him with hatred and could be considered among the most likely assassins: fundamentalists and anti-Semites. Both groups fell under the umbrella of national-patriotic organizations, and both existed within the diverse framework of the Russian Orthodox Church. Beginning with the fundamentalists, each warrants a closer look.

Fr. Aleksandr's ecumenical views, belief in the separation of church and state, and interpretations of Russian cultural history stood in sharp contrast to the fundamentalists' convictions. The fundamentalists did not see Fr. Aleksandr as a Russian patriot, but as a priest who wanted to undermine everything they held as sacred and wished to preserve. In reading the Holy Scriptures for political guidance, Russian fundamentalists divided the world between the forces of light and darkness, "good" and "evil." These forces were engaged in constant battle, a spiritual struggle in which the Russian state currently participated. The fundamentalists accepted no compromise between these warring factions: fundamentalists disparaged their opponents, described them as "satanic," and proclaimed them to be false emissaries whose goal was to enslave. Orthodoxy thus had to defend itself against these evil forces, particularly as they attempted to corrupt and eventually to destroy it from within. Politically, Russian fundamentalists shared the vision of national-patriotic organizations, which identified Russia as the sole protector of Orthodoxy.[41] They looked to the past as a "golden age" in which authoritarian rule had dominated, a past built on a firm "moral-ethical foundation," which had driven out what they called the "liberal elements from Christianity."[42]

The authoritarian political and religious order that fundamentalists embraced sharply contrasted with the openness that Fr. Aleksandr viewed as a principal feature of Christianity. Protecting Russia from what they saw as the poisonous influences emanating from Western Europe and the United States, they wanted to close off Russia from what they perceived as secular values—human rights, freedom of conscience, democracy, and dialogue with different religious traditions—which they believed weakened Russia. The fundamentalists wanted religious and social unity and a powerful, unified state capable of thwarting what they maintained their Western enemies wanted; that is, to make Russia an economic appendage and to enslave its people.[43]

Fr. Aleksandr's public presentations and writings blatantly offended and deeply challenged fundamentalists. His participation in the recent symposium in West Germany, as well as the criticisms of mass consciousness that he made there, offered concrete evidence of the threats he posed to everything the fundamentalists cherished. They wanted to silence his voice, and his death served well the authoritarian voices in Russian society.

The fundamentalists sought to disparage Fr. Aleksandr, both before and after his death, as a priest and as a person.[44] The infamous Ioann, metropolitan of Saint Petersburg and Ladoga, offers an example; his 1992 denunciation belittled every aspect of Fr. Aleksandr's priesthood:

> The priest A. Men was an ordinary, common, dull, average servant of the church. He had no musical talent, no ear for music, a strong, deep, but unpleasant voice. His speeches and conversations were very satisfying to Muscovites and people from other cities. Local people (from the town of Pushkino and the village of Novaia Derevnia) paid no attention to him. . . . And if one looks, from the point of view of the nationalities, then his attention was directed almost exclusively to those of Jewish nationality and to those parishioners who had one Jewish parent.[45]

The second group, the anti-Semites within the structure of the church, likewise resented Fr. Aleksandr's influence. Sergei Bychkov, an investigative journalist, editor of a popular Moscow newspaper, and friend and parishioner of Fr. Aleksandr Men, identified anti-Semitic groups as among the most plausible culprits in the murder. Despite its exposure as a forgery, the *Protocols of the Elders of Zion*, wrote Bychkov, "inculcated themselves into the consciousness of our citizenry."[46] The *Protocols* spoke to a kind of paranoia, the existence of a "Masonic-Jewish plot," whose masterminds lived in New York and London and wanted to destroy the Soviet state. The key components of their plot included ecumenism in religion, globalization in economics, and world government in politics. Anti-Semites connected Fr. Aleksandr to each of these movements; they could be seen in the previously mentioned anonymous "Letter to the Priest Aleksandr Men," written in the mid-1970s and widely circulated in Orthodox and samizdat publications over the next fifteen years.[47]

In 1989–1990, as Fr. Aleksandr's popularity grew sharply, Bychkov pointed out that Aleksandr Men came to represent much more than a parish priest. To anti-Semitic groups and individuals, Fr. Aleksandr's presence in the public media and his charismatic, learned presentations, which addressed a broad audience, made him an unofficial spokesperson for Russian Orthodoxy.[48] In anti-Semitic circles within the church, Fr. Aleksandr's increasing popularity fed suspicions they already harbored. He had led the Russian intelligentsia astray and, in the eyes of anti-Semitic ultranationalists, he was now leading the country down a destructive path.

Aleksandr Men well understood the enmity he provoked within certain Orthodox groups. He felt the rising tensions that produced hatred, some of which was directed against him. In an interview with the Italian jour-nalist Pilar Bonet, on September 5, three days before his murder, he spoke candidly about the threatening circumstances in which he found himself. Bonet asked him whether he had "witnessed any kind of disturbing con-crete symptoms recently," and Fr. Aleksandr responded that he had seen the emergence of what he called "Russian fascism," which "many church activ-ists energetically support." He elaborated:

> There has taken place a unification of Russian fascism with Russian cler-icalism and [also] with church nostalgia. This, of course, is a disgrace for us, for believers, because society looks to us for support, and the support they receive is for fascism. Of course, not everyone is so oriented, but the numbers of these fascists are not a small percentage.[49]

They have taken various forms, he said—"this person is a monarchist, this one's an anti-Semite, that one's an anti-ecumenicist, and so forth." In previ-ous years, such people had not been like this but, at present, they gravitated toward extremist views, which had become "characteristic of our epoch."[50] Fr. Aleksandr's enemies had charged him with being not only a Jew, but also, secretly, a Catholic, whose interest in ecumenism exhibited anti-Orthodox and anti-Russian commitments.[51]

Both of the two groups mentioned above had sufficient motives for the murder of Aleksandr Men. Both identified him as an enemy whose death removed one of the leading opponents of the ideological platform they wanted. Neither group was hesitant to use violence to further their goal of a unified, inward-looking, and authoritarian Russia, with the Orthodox Church as its moral and spiritual foundation.

But these possibilities left unanswered several questions that cast doubt on their involvement, either in concert or alone. Both groups were amateur-ish operations, easily infiltrated by the security police. Why was the evidence surrounding the murder so meager, both in quantity and substance? Why did the hundreds of interviews that the police conducted fail to produce reli-able leads, which might easily have led to any of these groups? Why were the investigators, early in the proceedings, to use Leshchenko's terms, "thrown off the track," provoking a comedy of errors and mysterious happenings?[52] Most importantly, why didn't the political authorities—the Russian parlia-ment, President Gorbachev, and, later, President Yeltsin—who expressed commitment to bringing the culprits to justice, demand more accountabil-ity from the investigating committees, particularly since solving the murder served the national interest? While the above-named groups had sufficient reasons to murder Aleksandr Men, focusing exclusively on them omits a crucial part of the story.

In the summer of 1990, two countervailing political forces and perspectives in the Soviet Union began to solidify. The issues separating them concerned not only the restructuring of the Russian state, but also the Russian Orthodox Church. To authoritarian groups, ranging over a wide assortment of organizations and views, the need to rebuild Russia, the geographical center of the state, and to construct a national ideology based on traditional principles became a paramount objective. Viewing the Orthodox Church as a cornerstone of this ideology, the leaders of the movement strongly favored a closed religious order, linking the authoritarian state to a tightly controlled church. These leaders, maintained historian and poet Vladimir Il'ich Iliushenko, had "enormous resources under their command" and wanted "to change the communist ideology in which they had long ceased to believe, into a new ideology, a superpower-state Orthodoxy—in short, a chauvinistic merger of sorts."[53]

The reason for such trends, as Fr. Aleksandr understood them, had not suddenly appeared within the Orthodox Church. They resulted from many years in which the church, in combination with the government, had mercilessly suppressed every living impulse, every experimental attempt to enliven itself. "If a bishop breathed the spirit of freedom, independence, or experimentation, he was immediately sent to the provinces, or forced into retirement—that is, placed on pension," he said.[54] As Fr. Aleksandr had argued that spring in the conference in West Germany, the "future ecumenism," which he supported, greatly depended on breaking free from all forms of "spiritual authoritarianism, paternalism, and state religiosity."[55] These forms, which the Orthodox Church had long supported, suppressed the human spirit, preventing it from growing and reaching out to others.

The patrimonial attitudes that the church had cultivated had political consequences. In the spring and summer of 1990, Fr. Aleksandr did not refrain from pointing out the relationship between these two spheres of national life. The patrimonial attitudes found within the church had parallel views in society in the desire for authoritarian leadership, nostalgia for the past, and xenophobia. When the individual gave up his internal creative powers, he transferred them to certain outside persons and glorified them. That is why, Fr. Aleksandr said, the political powers love the church, why state bureaucrats and the KGB love the church, seeing it as a nonthreatening "grey-haired old person, as a museum."[56]

The full spiritual and creative development of the person is what Fr. Aleksandr advocated. Such a possibility required the freedom to choose one's future course of belief; it also demanded rejection of the perverted forms of religious life, including the transfer of a person's spiritual freedom to certain idols, including the state, which absolved the individual of personal responsibility.

The Assassins

To the authorities, whose power depended on control of the population, Aleksandr Men's public statements on Orthodoxy and freedom undermined their views of the church and the state. Fr. Aleksandr's teachings and influence "posed a grave danger to those authorities," who were also trying to fill the moral and spiritual vacuum that had "opened up with the weakening of Communist ideology."[57] The internal freedom that he saw as a central tenet of Orthodoxy challenged the whole framework of control on which authoritarian groups, inside and outside the church, heavily depended. Reflecting on the last years of his father's life, Mikhail Men spoke of the many times Fr. Aleksandr had talked about the freedom of Christianity. "I do not know precisely what happened and who gave the order to murder my father," said Mikhail Aleksandrovich, "but I believe the answers to these questions lie in that sphere."[58]

Many times, in concert with other political authorities, KGB agents sought incriminating evidence to be used against Fr. Aleksandr. The use of legal means had neither succeeded nor frightened him into submission. The planned intimidation, surveillance of his parish, the political controls, and the crudely designed provocations had not produced the desired result and led to his silence. It is likely that the repeated failures of these legal efforts led to another, final attempt.

Although the precise facts relating to what took place in the early morning of September 9, 1990, await the opening of KGB archives, enough evidence exists that fits the circumstances of the murder and points in the direction of the responsible party. This evidence responds to many of the questions raised above, particularly the political motives underlying the case.

Fr. Aleksandr's son recalled a meeting he had with an experienced investigator of his father's murder, a reliable person whom Mikhail Aleksandrovich trusted. The police official had worked on the case for a year and a half. "He told me," Mikhail Aleksandrovich said, "that this was not a common murder." Usually, in similar locations where an attack had taken place, "we find at least some evidence, but, in this case, we found nothing. . . . The murder," the police official concluded, "was accomplished by skilled professionals."[59]

By the summer of 1990, Vladimir Sychev, the KGB official who had relentlessly interrogated Fr. Aleksandr in the mid-1980s, no longer occupied his former position. He now worked as a teacher in the Higher School of the KGB. Sychev told investigators that he had not spoken to Fr. Aleksandr since his interrogation ended in 1986, but other evidence suggests that he lied. In the summer of 1990, Fr. Aleksandr related to the journalist Sergei Bychkov that Sychev paid him a visit at Novaia Derevnia.[60] The KGB official came to the church and, standing near the front, had a personal conversation with Fr. Aleksandr. The priest did not divulge the content of their conversation. Given their previous adversarial relationship, it is highly unlikely that his intentions were friendly. Whether Sychev warned Fr. Aleksandr of an impending attack or threatened him, as he had done in previous years, must remain a matter of conjecture. But the unusual visit, particularly at such a politically sensitive moment, had ominous implications.

The official investigators failed to solve the murder, but, unofficially, Aleksandr Men's closest associates continued to raise questions and posit different possibilities. Sergei Bychkov's investigations yielded valuable information as he vigorously pursued leads related to the causes of the murder. But the most important contributions in the unofficial inquiry come from Pavel Men, Fr. Aleksandr's brother, who has refused to let the murder pass from his memory. Pavel Men has a wide circle of acquaintances in various government ministries and among the intelligentsia from whom he sought information. A friend, a high-ranking official in the Ministry of Education who had multiple contacts within the KGB, told Pavel Men that the "KGB hated Aleksandr Men."[61] Pavel Men's source told him "about the atmosphere within KGB circles at the time, and how police officials responded to the name of Aleksandr Men." Their ideas of the Russian Orthodox Church sharply differed from what Fr. Aleksandr believed. "They wanted a Byzantine-like church, an institution represented by the traditional imperial two-headed eagle." They had in mind an absolutist government, Pavel Men was told, supported by an absolutist, compliant Orthodox Church.[62]

Control of the population constituted one of the KGB's main objectives. Like the government it served, the KGB tolerated the church as long as it operated as a ritualistic, ceremonial, and bureaucratic institution whose primary activities remained limited to those functions. Fr. Aleksandr's vision of the Orthodox Church, as this study has emphasized, transcended those narrow boundaries. Repeatedly using traditional tactics of intimidation, the "church section" of the KGB sought to control his actions and confine their scope to the smallest space possible. In those efforts, fear became a principal instrument of control. "[But] my brother," recounted Pavel Men, "could not be controlled by the use of fear. He feared neither incarceration nor death; their threat had no effect on him."[63] And this total lack of fear, Fr. Aleksandr's brother believed, "the KGB could never accept."[64]

The fundamental issues, as Pavel Men saw them, concerned government power and control. They had always been the main issues. In 1990, with reformers on the ascendency within the Russian government, promoting a liberal political and economic order and enacting legislation on the rights of religious believers, absolutist political structures of the past appeared on the decline. The "open model" of Orthodox Christianity represented by Aleksandr Men gained a lot of support, even among some members of the church hierarchy, which was a reversal of earlier trends.[65] Unable to find legal reasons to imprison Fr. Aleksandr, the KGB resorted to "other means" to silence him. "I have absolutely no doubt," Pavel Men said, "[that] the KGB planned and executed his death."[66] The security police had the motive and the means to carry out the act, and they had the support within the official investigating agencies to cover it up effectively.

Standing firmly for his beliefs and the principles he found sacred in the Russian Orthodox tradition, Aleksandr Men refused to submit to or be intimidated by the agencies arrayed against him. Rather than receding in the period of perestroika, these forces became increasingly threatening. He received letters from multiple sources calling themselves "Russian patriots" who threw horrible insults at him, calling him a subversive Jew, a Catholic sympathizer, a Protestant admirer, a person bent on the destruction of Orthodoxy, and much more. He withstood all of these insults, only rarely attempting to respond, refusing to give up a calling he felt compelled to pursue unto his death, to fight evil with good in the belief that good would ultimately prevail. "I do not think it is important who killed him," said Fr. Viktor Grigorenko, who presently serves in the church dedicated to Fr. Aleksandr's memory. "What is important is how we move forward, instilling Fr. Aleksandr's hope, his love for people, and his faith into the living."[67]

In his reflections on Aleksandr Men's death, the Russian philosopher Iurii Petrovich Senokosov has written that Fr. Aleksandr saw Orthodox tradition "not as something dead, but as living truth, as did the Church fathers."[68] Senokosov, who knew Fr. Aleksandr for more than twenty-five years, described him as a priest with an extremely wide horizon, who believed in the breadth of Christianity and claimed it had the capacity to incorporate unto itself other traditions and perspectives. He had a broad vision of Russian culture that opposed xenophobic trends in Russian society, and he was killed because of that vision.[69]

On the wall above the desk in his church office, Fr. Aleksandr placed a
replica of Andrei Rublev's famous icon "The Trinity." He had always loved
the icon and had it situated where he and the visitors to his office could
draw from it both inspiration and guidance. Several weeks before his death,
speaking about Russia's present situation, Fr. Aleksandr made the following
reference to this sacred icon:

> You know that Andrei Rublev painted his icon "The Trinity" in a bleak
> time, when hatred raged all over the world (however, when has it not raged
> everywhere?).... He painted it in honor of Saint Sergii [of Radonezh]
> who named his small wooden church in honor of the Trinity. This was not
> accidental, because, as the *Chronicle* tells us about his life, the venerable
> Sergii wanted Divine love to teach people, so that the people, seeing this
> Divine love, might overcome evil divisions in the world. That is what is
> most important.[70]

All his life Fr. Aleksandr Men represented the same ideal. As a parish priest,
he used all the gifts he had, struggling to overcome the hatreds that spawned
these dangerous and destructive divisions, wherever they existed. This effort,
to cite his words again, may be "what is most important."

. . . .

Epilogue

Strategically placed throughout the courtyard of Moscow's Library of Foreign Literature are seventeen statues of leading world figures. Invariably, these marble images depict men and women of courage, whose bold actions, often in the face of danger, challenged prevailing views; in so doing, they lifted up humanity and encouraged people everywhere to look beyond the narrow lenses through which they viewed the world.

Mohandas Gandhi dominates the setting near the courtyard's entrance. But as one moves to the center, other people come into view: Charles Dickens, English novelist; Heinrich Heine, German poet and essayist; Abulkasim Nizami Ganjevi, Iranian poet; Gabriela Mistral, Chilean poet and laureate of the Nobel Prize for Literature in 1945. One American is found here: a relatively small statue of Abraham Lincoln stands near the library's entrance. The one Russian to appear among this coterie of leaders is not who one would commonly associate with individuals whose bold actions undermined the Soviet state—Mikhail Gorbachev or Boris Yel'tsin. The lone Russian is Fr. Aleksandr Men. His bust stands on the left side of the library's entrance in a far corner of the courtyard, under the overhanging limbs of young maple and fir trees. The sculpture captures well his lively, penetrating eyes and his elegant bearded face; the inscription on the statue, in addition to the dates of Fr. Aleksandr's life—22 January 1935 to 9 September 1990— has only three words: Priest, Writer, Philosopher.[1] Embodying these roles in his life and actions, Fr. Aleksandr challenged the Communist state to its core, and his teachings, like many of those represented in the courtyard, extend far beyond his own isolated moment in time.

Fr. Aleksandr's killers, on September 9, 1990, physically silenced a chief critic of nationalist trends within the Russian Orthodox Church. Within certain circles, the next steps required besmirching his reputation as an Orthodox priest and undermining his views of the Orthodox Church and his perspectives on Russia's present and future. These moves aimed to attack the ecumenical principles that he had advanced in his public presentations, but they also aspired to portray Fr. Aleksandr's theological interpretations as misguided, even dangerously misleading, and as following a path not toward Orthodox teachings, but away from them. Having welcomed his physical demise, Men's opponents sought "to finish him off as a writer."[2]

The first wave of attacks came from extremist "national-patriots," who earlier had repeatedly criticized him as an enemy of Russia and as a priest who undermined the country's national unity. Valerii Nikolaevich Emelianov, a Pamiat' activist, who for many years had fought against what he considered the Masonic infiltration of Russia, interpreted Fr. Aleksandr's death as divine retribution. In the weeks after September 9, Emelianov and other "national-patriots" attacked him, asserting that his murder was a lesson to those people who held views similar to Fr. Aleksandr's. As one periodical warned, "May his death be a lesson to all those in the church, who flirt with Satanic forces."[3]

The most prolonged, serious attacks, however, came from within the Orthodox Church itself. Individuals claiming to have great support from certain groups within the church voiced some of these criticisms. The most widely distributed critical analyses of Fr. Aleksandr's writings consisted of essays in a small book, published first in 1993 and, then, in expanded format, reissued in 1999. Titled *On the Theology of Archpriest Aleksandr Men* (*O bogoslovii protoiereia Aleksandra Menia*), the book featured three Orthodox authors: Archpriest Sergii Antiminsov, Feliks Karelin, and Deacon Andrei Kuraev, each of whom dealt with a different aspect of Fr. Aleksandr's writings.[4] Although they refrained from branding his theological views as heretical, the three writers maintained that Fr. Aleksandr had severely misinterpreted, even perverted, the Orthodox faith.[5]

On the Theology of Archpriest Aleksandr Men did not universally condemn his writings. The authors commented favorably on several aspects of his writings and their seductive nature, especially to people with little knowledge of the Gospels. Fr. Aleksandr's books, the three authors pointed out, were well-researched and their narrative content made for interesting reading. They noted that Fr. Aleksandr's descriptions of personalities and events, drawn from Biblical sources, were especially well crafted and that he had a lively, often compelling, literary style. Yet they pointed out Fr. Aleksandr's weaknesses in failing to ground his work in a strong ideological foundation and completely falsifying the relationship between reason and faith.

An Orthodox layman, Feliks Karelin (1929–1992) had known Aleksandr Men since the 1970s, when Fr. Gleb Yakunin first brought him to Novaia

Derevnia.[6] Well-spoken, charismatic, and intellectual, Karelin had recently been released from a prison camp; he quickly gained acceptance in the parish, attracting some young members into his orbit. It also soon became known, however, that he had once been a provocateur and perhaps also a murderer. A person of extreme views and apocalyptic in his thinking, Karelin eventually became estranged from Fr. Aleksandr and left the parish. His essay is the most personally degrading of those in the volume.[7] He accused Fr. Aleksandr of twisting the scriptures to fit his own views of the Jewish people as a special elite, called by God to serve a uniquely divine mission. According to Karelin, Fr. Aleksandr ignored Jesus's words that he "came not to repudiate the law or the prophets, but to fulfill them."[8] He alleged that Fr. Aleksandr proclaimed that the Jewish people enjoyed sovereignty over all others. Karelin accused Fr. Aleksandr of "religious racism," which "has no place in God's church."[9]

According to the author of the second essay, Archpriest Sergii Antiminsov, Fr. Aleksandr's study of the Bible "gave the decisive role to human knowledge— philology, history, and archeology," thereby viewing the Bible as essentially a human production, rather than as the divine revelation of God.[10] Fr. Aleksandr examined the scriptures on the same human level as Dante's *Divine Comedy* or "Tale of Igor's Campaign" and employed similar literary techniques to analyze all of them. Thus, Fr. Aleksandr missed what Antiminsov called the "truthfulness of the Sacred Scriptures," because the word of God is the whole truth, which cannot be broken down, divided, or analyzed without losing its singular truth. As a rationalist, Fr. Aleksandr's excessive reliance on the sciences led him to deny the Bible's authorship, as well as the historical existence of Christ. He used secular reasoning to explain biblical events in an effort to distinguish fact from fiction, reality from mythical explanations. Antiminsov claimed that Fr. Aleksandr had fallen under the influence of Arianism, Pelagianism, Nestorianism, and Manichaeism, which the church condemned as heretical.[11] His books, Antiminsov asserted, were full of errors, distortions, and false premises, which came close to heresy.[12]

The least personally degrading but still highly critical essay came from Deacon Andrei Kuraev, whose contribution is titled "Aleksandr Men: poteriavshiisia missioner" (Aleksandr Men: The Lost Missionary).[13] Kuraev found Fr. Aleksandr's books to be worthy of reading and seriously studied; they contributed to what Kuraev believed to be an essential need, a thorough revision of the history of religion in Russia and the role of Christianity in the story of civilization. But he also saw Fr. Aleksandr's views as strange, off-centered interpretations that were not truly Russian Orthodoxy, but something else. He strongly objected to Fr. Aleksandr's alleged universalism, contending that Fr. Aleksandr understood Christianity as only one religion among many others, each of equal value. He accused Fr. Aleksandr of having an open attitude toward parapsychology, astrology, and UFOs, which, Kuraev said, was characteristic of his liberal, progressive attitude, and which fell outside the Orthodox tradition.[14] Kuraev returned to the argument he made earlier, in a 1993 interview published in *Nezavisimaia gazeta* (Independent newspaper), in which he said that Fr. Aleksandr's theology did not belong to the Orthodox Church. Both here, and in a book he published concurrently, Kuraev maintained that Fr. Aleksandr's views departed from Russian Orthodoxy, and he identified Fr. Aleksandr as a Uniate, or Catholic of the Eastern Rite. According to Kuraev, Fr. Aleksandr preached Catholic doctrines and followed Catholic rites.[15] As a priest and a writer, Kuraev said, Fr. Aleksandr essentially functioned as a Catholic.

The book *The Theology of Archpriest Aleksandr Men*, as well as Deacon Andrei Kuraev's many publications, were widely distributed in Orthodox bookstores and kiosks maintained by the church. In large part, these publications attempted to expose Fr. Aleksandr as a non-Orthodox priest whose writings fell outside the mainstream of the church's sacred traditions. The prevalence of such writings and the disparaging picture of Fr. Aleksandr they created were aimed at overwhelming the opposite point of view. In contrast to the widespread availability of such publications, Fr. Aleksandr's books, until recently, could only be found in two or three church bookstores in Moscow.[16]

Despite the campaign to denigrate his contributions, Aleksandr Men's former parishioners did not succumb to the campaign directed against him. Accustomed to such attacks, the crudest of which resembled KGB tactics used in the past, Fr. Aleksandr's followers fought to keep alive the deceased priest's memory and the vision of Orthodoxy he believed represented the core of its sacred heritage. In many thoughtful, well-reasoned articles, Fr. Aleksandr's colleagues responded to claims that his writings fell outside Russian Orthodoxy.

Among many such responses, those written by two scholars, Leonid Vasilenko and Aleksandr Ermolin, stand out for their detailed, analytical content. Vasilenko dissected the arguments made against Fr. Aleksandr, showing them to be based largely on faulty reasoning, misattributions, and selective use of statements, while ignoring more conclusive evidence to the contrary.[17] Vasilenko showed that the charges that Fr. Aleksandr disputed Christ's divinity, based his views solely on scientific reasoning, and distorted Orthodox teachings were built on inaccurate readings of Fr. Aleksandr's books. In their false, unsubstantiated claims, Vasilenko maintained, the authors of *The Theology of Archpriest Aleksandr Men* repeatedly "bore witness to hatred, slander, ignorance, and envy, presented in the name of the Gospel."[18]

In an incisive, eloquently written paper on "The Place of Fr. Aleksandr in Orthodox Tradition," philosopher Aleksandr Ermolin offered a strong defense of Fr. Aleksandr as an Orthodox priest.[19] In his paper, Ermolin raised what he called the "simple but complex question": "Who was Fr. Aleksandr Men?" Ermolin maintained that Fr. Aleksandr was not a theologian, nor did he ever see himself in such a way. In its hagiography, the Russian Church gave the name theologian to three sacred Church Fathers: Ioann the Theologian, Gregory the Theologian, and Simeon the New Theologian.[20] According to Ermolin, Fr. Aleksandr saw himself as a missionary, whose principal goal was to lead people to Christ. He created neither a theological nor a philosophical system; he was essentially a systematizer, whom Ermolin characterized as a person of "encyclopedic knowledge," whose sermons drew from the sciences and the works of the Sacred Fathers of the Church. Finally, Fr. Aleksandr was a priest and confessor, a "village priest," as he defined himself, and, in the Orthodox tradition, the spiritual father to a large number of people who sought his guidance and spiritual advice.[21]

Drawing on a wide range of Fr. Aleksandr's writings, Ermolin disputed the claims of critics who placed him outside Russian Orthodoxy. Fr. Aleksandr read in multiple fields, expanding his knowledge as broadly as possible, but Ermolin pointed out that the numbers of Catholic and Protestant authors he read represented only a small fraction of these sources. Fr. Aleksandr respected the other major religious traditions and the great teachers who brought them into being. They were part of a universal search for meaning, whose ultimate path led to the highest expression and the resolution of that search, which he believed to be Christianity. Russian Orthodoxy needed to reach out to those other religious faiths. They had been driven apart because of several reasons: human sinfulness and political, cultural, and economic conflicts. The ecumenical vision that Fr. Aleksandr had, according to Ermolin, was based solidly in the teachings of the sacred Church Fathers and the apostle Paul.[22] "Fr. Aleksandr keenly felt that Christianity is a living and dynamic religion, which [had been] intricately squeezed into rigid boundaries with a single standard."[23]

Ermolin's discussion raises a fundamental question underlying the debate between Fr. Aleksandr and his opposition. How dynamic does one (or the church) believe Christianity to be? Is it capable of existing boldly within a cacophony of competing voices and perspectives, or must it be narrowly preserved and zealously protected within rigidly defined boundaries? Aleksandr Men represented the former belief, his opponents the latter. His enemies found his dedication to reconciliation deeply threatening to the future of Orthodoxy and, ultimately, to the identity of Russia. But to Fr. Aleksandr Men, the creation of rigid boundaries sapped Russian Orthodoxy of one of its greatest strengths—and might well open the pathway to its eventual demise.

Given his untimely death in 1990 and the efforts to erase his memory, how influential was Fr. Aleksandr Men? Because the church provided political as well as ideological support for the Russian government throughout the 1990s and thereafter, it appeared to many observers that his role within the broader framework of Russian Orthodoxy had meager significance. To such analysts, the flame, which burned brightly in the late 1980s, left only a small mark on Russia's national consciousness in ensuing decades, making scarcely an imprint on its thoughts and activities.[24] Dmitrii Furman, the distinguished sociologist of religion and scholar in the Russian Academy of Sciences, whose studies of religious attitudes rank among the most comprehensive in the former Soviet Union, is among those who consider Fr. Aleksandr's influence to be extremely limited. "Aleksandr Men and his circle of followers represent only a marginal group of people within the Russian Orthodox Church; they are more important to the Americans than they are to the Russians," he said. "They always had little support, and existed mainly as a fringe group, with hardly any actual impact, either then or now."[25]

Yet these observations do not take into account other facts, which support a much different picture. Such evidence suggests that Fr. Aleksandr's legacy may have more significant ramifications than some might believe. The ferocity and length of the campaign directed against him after his murder is testimony to the perceived challenges he presented. These challenges went far beyond the capacity of a marginal group of people to exert influence. Fr. Aleksandr's enemies wished to silence his voice and instill fear in his followers, motives the Russian journalist Aleksandr Minkin ascribed as the main reasons underlying his murder. But if his enemies wanted to silence him, their violent act "did not achieve their goal, but had the opposite effect." Public interest in the deceased priest dramatically increased after Fr. Aleksandr's death, and, according to his son, his father began "to be taken more seriously not only in Moscow, but around the country."[26]

Until the early 1990s, Aleksandr Men's books could only be published abroad in extremely limited editions and brought illegally into the Soviet Union, where they were recopied and distributed through samizdat. Only in 1990, at the end of the period of perestroika, was his first book published in Russia.[27] His television, radio, and public lectures during the short time they became available gave him exposure to a public that found his ideas increasingly appealing. As a bridge builder into nearly forgotten parts of Russia's cultural and religious memory, a "systematizer" of the teachings of the Church Fathers, and an apostle of freedom, Fr. Aleksandr spoke as a teacher precisely at a time when Russians were searching for meaning and identity. In terms of public appearances, the window for his teachings opened only briefly, but in the years immediately following his death, in many parts of Russia, public demand for his writings escalated. In the 1990s, the Russian publication of *Son of Man* sold 440,000 copies; a small book of Fr. Aleksandr's lectures, *To Be a Christian (Byt' khristianin)*, sold two million copies; his *Orthodox Liturgy: Mystery, Word, and Image (Pravoslavnoe bogosluzhenie: Tainstvo, Slovo, i Obraz)* was issued in 500,000 copies and his six-volume *History of Religion* in 220,000 copies.[28] In the two decades following Fr. Aleksandr's death, the Russian public bought more than five million copies of his books, sermons, and lectures. The demand for *Son of Man* has never ceased, and more than one million copies have been published, an additional seven thousand in 2014.[29]

Lucidly written, easily accessible, and presented in narrative format, *Son of Man* bears witness to a biblical account that readers continue to find compelling. Fr. Aleksandr's additional books, including collections of his sermons and instructional manuals on various aspects of worship, have appealed to a wide range of individuals and groups of people. Another highly respected scholar of religion and society in Russia, Sergei Borisovich Filatov, has a different interpretation of Fr. Aleksandr than Furman: "I consider Fr. Aleksandr to have been and still to be significant," Filatov said. "While some people regard Fr. Aleksandr as a marginal figure within Russian Orthodoxy, I look at the numbers of his books Russians have bought, his large appeal to the intelligentsia, and also his attraction to the broad middle of our intelligentsia, and find his influence to be much greater than some would have us believe."[30]

As a spokesman from the Orthodox Church to the world, Fr. Aleksandr was a priest whose vision may be seen in full display at several places in Moscow: in the superb, skillfully maintained reading room dedicated to him in the Library of Foreign Literature; in the Church of the Assumption of God (*Khram Uspeniia Bogoroditsy na Uspenskom Vrazhke*), whose head priest is Fr. Vladimir Lapshin; and especially in the Church of the Sacred Martyrs Kosma and Damian, in central Moscow, whose head priest is Fr. Aleksandr Borisov.

A childhood friend of Pavel Men and close associate of Fr. Aleksandr Men, Fr. Aleksandr Borisov became the church's head priest during Gorbachev's perestroika. During the economic crises of the late 1990s, few churches played as large a role in feeding the hungry in Moscow as the Church of Kosma and Damian, and its strong outreach to the community is one of its central social missions.[31] To these institutions should be added the Orthodox community headed by Fr. Georgii Kochetkov, with its home on Petrushka Street, also in central Moscow. Fr. Georgii holds Sunday services in Moscow's Novodevichy Monastery that attract large numbers of Moscow's intelligentsia, as do those at the Church of Kosma and Damian.[32]

The distribution of books and the attraction of certain religious services, however, do not fully represent the legacy of Aleksandr Men. In the last two years of his life, Fr. Aleksandr began additional activities that had lasting significance. The "Cultural Renaissance Society," which he founded in the summer of 1988, aimed to stimulate the rebirth of Russia's cultural heritage. "Having lived through the most difficult crises in history," the society's charter statement read, "[and] finding itself [on] the verge of extinction, of its physical or spiritual disappearance, [Russia's cultural heritage] is in the process of resurrection."[33] The society's leadership officially registered the organization in March 1991, renaming it the "Cultural Renaissance Society, in honor of Aleksandr Men" (Obshchestvo "Kul'turnoe Vozrozhdenie" imeni Aleksandra Menia) in May 1992, and expanding its responsibilities.[34] It had a clearly defined identity: the society was "conceived as a center of spiritual-cultural enlightenment and aspired to bring together the followers of Fr. Aleksandr, his spiritual children, and people who understand and hold dear the tasks of cultural rebirth."[35]

The society committed itself to spreading Fr. Aleksandr's writings widely, particularly his ideas about the relationship between religion and culture. As the group's charter explained, the October 1917 Revolution had fostered the dismemberment of this relationship, a course of action that had disastrous results. Members of the society believed the breach had to be healed for Russia to move forward, and they committed themselves to rediscover the "rich cultural heritage of the country, work for its preservation, and promote the development of Russian cultural thought."[36] Society members had no illusions that these goals could be accomplished quickly; such complex and difficult tasks would require many years.[37] But the journey had to begin, and it had to start in the schools, with the education of children.[38]

Fr. Aleksandr's death represented a "spiritual catastrophe," wrote the historian and poet Vladimir Iliushenko, but "Fr. Aleksandr Men's mission—the spiritual rebirth, the resurrection of Russia's rich cultural heritage, went beyond his physical presence."[39] Committed to carrying on his work, members of the society pledged themselves to promote open dialogue between all religions, to nourish spiritual freedom, to strengthen Russia's cultural heritage, to encourage tolerance of "foreign points of view," and "to oppose nationalistic and chauvinistic" perspectives that undermined the "peace and capability of the country."[40] The society agreed to hold a commemorative meeting in honor of Fr. Aleksandr on September 9, 1992, which eventually became a common practice on the anniversary of his death. This event evolved over the next five years into annual lectures on various subjects relating to Fr. Aleksandr, commemorative meetings that served educational purposes.

Aleksandr Men did not draw a dividing line between the church and the rest of society. He eschewed the sharp divisions that characterized much of Russian society, and believed that the church had the obligation to reach out beyond physical boundaries and to address suffering humanity, particularly where such needs were most desperate. In 1989, in partnership with the Church of the Sacred Martyrs Kosma and Damian, Fr. Aleksandr created a Help and Charity Service at the Russian Children's Clinical Hospital in Moscow (*Rossiiskaia detskaia klinicheskaia bol'nitsa*), which offered support for families whose children faced life-threatening illnesses. The charity group looked for sponsors to pay for operations, hospital equipment, and medical treatment for poor families who were unable to bear the costs of these expensive services.[41] The group he established had a special concern for orphan children, who had no means of financial or emotional support, and who faced extremely dire circumstances.[42] Fr. Aleksandr's group tried to find families to adopt these children, thereby attempting to respond to one of Russia's greatest social problems. He became personally involved in the project, and despite his demanding speaking schedule and parish responsibilities, each week he visited the children's pediatric hospital.[43]

The charity group rapidly grew far beyond its original scope. Fr. Georgii Chistiakov played a major role in the project. He had been a longtime, close friend of Fr. Aleksandr, and his energy and his compassion for children provided the charity group the guidance and structure it needed to expand. After Fr. Aleksandr's death, Fr. Georgii "became the charity group's spiritual leader," and he brought outstanding personal gifts to this project. As a priest who wrote elsewhere about society's "responsibility for the fate of its children," he felt "their fate imprinted on his heart."[44] Fr. Georgii engaged hundreds of volunteers in the group's work—artists, philologists, art therapists, circus performers, and musicians, who gave themselves wholeheartedly to serving children in Moscow's leading pediatric hospital. Describing himself as heavily influenced by Fr. Aleksandr, who brought him back to the church after he left it as a young man, Fr. Georgii lived out the connection between the arts and Christianity.[45] He passionately believed that the arts, as well as laughter, provided invaluable treatment in situations where children faced life-threatening circumstances. The collaboration between doctors and the volunteers he and Fr. Aleksandr recruited made the children's hospital a unique medical facility in Russia: it became "a pioneer in art therapy."[46] Fr. Georgii Chistiakov himself was no stranger to personal hardship: diagnosed with leukemia earlier in his life, he suffered greatly in the last years of his life. But before his premature death on June 22, 2007, at the age of fifty-three, he brought color and a spirit of optimism into the cheerless world of the children's hospital. The work he and Fr. Aleksandr began in 1990 continues into the present.

Despite repeated efforts to stifle Fr. Aleksandr's voice, interest in his writings has also continued, and, in some quarters, has expanded. In the Baltic countries, Fr. Aleksandr's publications are widely distributed, largely by the work of an international center headquartered in Riga, Latvia. Named the Aleksandr Men International Charity Center (*Mezhdunarodnoe Blagot-voritel'noe Obshchestvo imeni Aleksandra Menia*), the center is engaged in multiple charitable activities; it also publishes annually an almanac of high quality, devoted to the work of Fr. Aleksandr Men.[47] Internationally, Fr. Aleksandr's work has been translated into fourteen languages, including all major European languages. Most recently, his books have made significant inroads in South America: by the summer of 2013, Men's *Son of Man* had sold 22,000 copies in Brazil alone.[48]

Meanwhile, in Russia, Fr. Aleksandr's books have become available at some, although not all, bookstores operated by the Orthodox Church. Shortly after the church elected Kirill (Gundiaev) patriarch of Moscow and All Russia, in February 2009, the new patriarch changed the church's official position on Fr. Aleksandr's writings. On September 9, 2010, the annual scholarly conference (*Menevskie chteniia*), dedicated to the memory of Fr. Aleksandr, opened in a building not far from the priest's home, with about two hundred people in attendance. The conference began with two events of long-lasting significance: first, the dedication of a newly constructed, beautiful church, built on the place of Fr. Aleksandr's death and sanctified as the Church of Saint Sergii of Radonezh, in honor of Russia's greatest saint. Second, the conference was highlighted by Patriarch Kirill's official greeting, which he sent to be read by Metropolitan Iuvenalii. In his greeting, the patriarch blessed Fr. Aleksandr's books. "It is important for us to keep in mind," said the patriarch, that Fr. Aleksandr is "a well-known apologist, preacher, and missionary . . . who . . . lived and worked in entirely different conditions [than the present]."[49] Patriarch Kirill expressed gratitude "for Fr. Aleksandr's educational and catechismal works," and his devotion to the "living and inspirational word, through which many people had come to faith and had become active members of the Holy Church." In his greeting, Patriarch Kirill left little doubt of the church's official position on the significant service Fr. Aleksandr had rendered in times of great spiritual need.

In the summer of 2009, I went back to Fr. Aleksandr's parish at Novaia Derevnia. It was a sunny, nearly cloudless July day, and the flowers in the gardens around the fence of the churchyard were in full bloom. Upon entering the church, at the beginning of the weekday service, I saw a small group of people inside, whose numbers steadily grew during the next hour, amounting to forty or fifty people by the time everyone had arrived. A few elderly people stood among them, but most of those gathered here were young to middle-aged men and women, some with children in hand. They were mainly village people, who had arrived on foot; only a few had come by automobile.

The head priest was Fr. Vladimir Arkhipov, who served here with Fr. Aleksandr at Novaia Derevnia during the priest's last years. Fr. Vladimir had once joined one of Fr. Aleksandr's small groups, had attended the Moscow Theological Seminary, and later had come back to Novaia Derevnia. He bears little physical resemblance to the young man with a thick beard and full head of hair reflected in his earlier photographs. Tall, slender, clean-shaven, and totally bald, Fr. Vladimir has a dignified, impressive presence that fits nicely into the presumptions one might have of Fr. Aleksandr's successor at Novaia Derevnia—that of a well-educated, unpretentious, and warm-spirited person.

I wanted to find out what had been Fr. Aleksandr's lasting influence on the parish and how, over the course of the last twenty tumultuous years, the parish had changed. Fr. Vladimir said that his understanding of Fr. Aleksandr's "gifts [were] not the talents of a philosopher, but his main gift lay in his perception and understanding of God as creator. I perceived him this way. So I offer this understanding of Fr. Aleksandr to the people of our parish. His books are a source for his way of thinking."[50] Fr. Vladimir considers one of his main tasks to be "to awaken people to an independent, personal understanding and thinking. I try to awaken in them the will to serve others, to serve the church; from this position, we are trying to build life here." This is a task, he emphasized, that goes beyond studying Fr. Aleksandr's books. "We do not wish to glorify him; nor do we envision him as a hero, but as a servant of God. The main thing is that people, with the help of his writings, will respect themselves, love themselves, trust themselves, and they should understand that each person is called to fulfill such high intentions. This, as I see it, is Fr. Aleksandr's influence."[51]

Gone from Novaia Dervenia are the large numbers of the Moscow intelligentsia who traveled here in the 1980s. Presently, about fifty people from Moscow and other cities regularly come to Novaia Derevnia, retaining contact with a place that transformed their lives. In total, parish members number approximately two hundred, of which one hundred and fifty are local people. The parish has retained the small groups that Fr. Aleksandr created, fifteen to twenty of them, each having five to ten participants who meet regularly. Similarly, the parish has continued other activities Fr. Aleksandr began: the seminars devoted to specific topics—human dignity, the meaning of humility, love of self and neighbor—usually attract about one hundred people; a large group that works in a nearby children's hospital and in an orphanage; a Sunday school for children and one also for adults.[52]

"This is a modest village parish," said Fr. Vladimir. It does not attract the famous people, who once came here, nor are the parishioners, on the whole, well educated. But the primary mission has remained the same, and he paraphrased what he called one of Fr. Aleksandr's favorite lines: "God gives the glory to us, but not to thy name." Fr. Aleksandr taught us "to give ourselves to God. He taught us humility, and the need to hear the person who has another point of view. He taught us that faith is not a set of rituals, not blind following of something one does not understand, but trust in God. He taught us that every human being is a child of God."[53]

Acknowledgments

This book rests on the shoulders of many people without whom it could not have been accomplished. First and foremost, Pavel Vol'fovich Men, Fr. Aleksandr's younger brother, has been a constant source of new information, ranging from details about family life to Fr. Aleksandr's parish and his contributions to the national discussion of Russia's future. As director of the Aleksandr Men Foundation in Moscow, the central repository of his brother's papers, Pavel Vol'fovich allowed me many hours of conversation, patiently answered my questions, and shared materials that comprise the core of my work. He also offered encouragement at every stage of this study.

The same is true of Fr. Georgii Chistiakov, now deceased, who opened up several important doors that gave me access to individuals who knew Fr. Aleksandr. Fr. Georgii's kindness and generosity and his impressive knowledge of Russian culture inspired a great deal of my work on Fr. Aleksandr. Similarly, the late Ekaterina Iur'evna Genieva, director-general of the impressive All-Russian Library of Foreign Literature in Moscow, offered strong support at key junctures in my research. In several hours of interviews with Dr. Genieva in her Moscow office, she provided important details about Fr. Aleksandr's writings and talks.

I owe a large debt of gratitude to Fr. Viktor Grigorenko, who, in the summer of 2013, received me in Semkhoz and gave me an extensive personal tour of Fr. Aleksandr's former home, including his study. Despite a very busy schedule as governor-general of Ivanovo province, Mikhail Aleksandrovich Men, Fr. Aleksandr's son, permitted me a lengthy interview in which he responded in detail to many aspects of my research that had previously been obscure, including Fr. Aleksandr's family life. I am grateful to many others who were willing to talk openly about Fr. Aleksandr, especially Vladimir Il'ich Iliushenko, Fr. Aleksandr Borisov, Fr. Mikhail Aksenov-Meerson, Fr. Gleb Yakunin, Elena Volkova, Iurii Mikhailovich Tabak, Fr. Vladimir Arkhipov, Sergei Borisovich Filatov, Fr. Georgii Kochetkov, Larisa Musina, and Yves Hamant.

Libraries have played a large part in this work, and their librarians went to extraordinary lengths to provide access to materials relevant to Fr. Aleksandr. One cannot ask for a more pleasant environment in which to work than the special reading room dedicated to Aleksandr Men in the Library of Foreign Literature. Since the library's founding in 1921 by the young Margarita Ivanovna Rudomino, it has devoted itself to maintaining

Russia's international cultural connections, its capacity to hear humanitarian voices that reach beyond politics. The skilled, devoted staff of the reading room honors that tradition. I wish also to thank research librarians at Emory University, Duke University, the University of North Carolina at Chapel Hill, Mercer University, and Baylor University. Linda Daniel, research librarian at Duke University, and Cecilia Williams, supervisor of the Interlibrary Loan Division at Mercer University, aided me throughout my research, and I am especially grateful to them.

The Keston Archive, housed at Baylor University, contains a rich trove of primary documents relating to religion and society in Russia and the former Soviet Union. While its holdings are still being catalogued, I have been privileged to work in the archive, both in Waco, Texas, and earlier, in Oxford. The vision of Michael Bourdeaux, Keston's founder, is evident throughout the archive. I am grateful to Xenia Dennen for her encouragement and support, and to Dean Pattie Orr, Kathy Hillman, and Larisa Seago for enhancing the archive and making its vast holdings so accessible.

Mercer University is a special place to work. The university's commitment to interdisciplinary study and research has played an instrumental role in this project, as has the university's president, William Underwood. I owe a special word of thanks to him for his long-standing support. I also thank my colleagues in the Department of History for fostering research that crosses interdisciplinary boundaries.

I owe a large debt of gratitude to my Russian colleague and friend Grigorii Kliucharev of the Institute of Sociology, Russian Academy of Sciences, for his assistance throughout this project and for making my many research trips to Moscow more productive than I could ever have managed on my own.

I have presented various parts of the book in several different venues, and I am grateful for the invitations offered by their organizers and the stimulating conversations with participants in each of these settings. I particularly thank George Munro, Andrew Crislip, William E. Blake, Theofanis Stavrou, Podraic Kenney, Ekaterina Genieva, Elizabeth Roberts, Ann Shukman, Donald Smith, and Fr. Viktor Grigorenko. The presentations are listed in the order in which they were given: Moscow, commemorative conference on Aleksandr Men (January 21, 2010); Virginia Commonwealth University, Nineteenth Annual William E. and Miriam S. Blake Lecture in the History of Christianity (February 23, 2012); Moffat, Scotland, international conference on "Aleksander Men—His Life and Legacy" (September 14–17, 2012); Indiana University, conference on "Ready for Democracy? Religion and Political Culture in the Orthodox and Islamic Worlds" (February 28–March 2, 2013).

Some of the materials in chapters 12 and 13 appeared in articles published earlier: "Father Aleksandr Men and the Struggle to Recover Russia's Heritage," in *Demokratizatsiya, The Journal of Post-Soviet Democratization* 17, no. 1 (Winter 2009): 73–91; and "Aleksander Men, Intellectual Freedom, and the Russian Orthodox Church," in *Kirchliche Zeitgeschichte, Internationale Zeitschrift für Theologie und Geschichtswissenschaft* 24, no. 1 (2011): 92–119. Both chapters, however, are considerably expanded beyond their original format.

Several colleagues read and commented on various parts of the book. They are Ann Shukman, Michael Bourdeaux, Jonathan Sutton, Charles Twombly, Patrick Michelson, and April French. Their critiques and suggestions contributed a great deal to this study and saved me from many errors in the final drafting of the manuscript. Mary Pearson read the entire work, and I have benefitted from her editorial skills and stylistic comments. Diana de Gratigny (Kovaleva) assisted with translations, and Tanya Clark reviewed my Russian translations. Jerome Gratigny and Matt Harper provided important technological assistance. I thank all of them. I am fully responsible for any shortcomings that remain.

I wish to express my appreciation to the reviewers of the manuscript for their careful readings and their helpful suggestions. I also thank Northern Illinois University Press and its editor, Amy Farranto, for encouragement of this project from its early stages and superb guidance throughout. I am grateful for the editorial skills of Nathan Holmes, managing editor of the press and other members of a first-rate editorial staff who helped make this a better book than when the manuscript was first submitted.

Lastly, I owe a large debt of gratitude to my wife, Karol, who in multiple ways has lived this book with me, shared in my thinking through several difficult parts, and offered sustained support throughout the entire process. To her this book is dedicated.

Notes

Notes to Preface

1. James H. Billington, *Russia in Search of Itself* (Washington, DC: Woodrow Wilson Center Press, 2004), esp. ch. 5.
2. Wallace L. Daniel, *The Orthodox Church and Civil Society in Russia* (College Station, TX: Texas A&M University Press, 2006).
3. Yves Hamant, *Alexandre Men, un témoin pour la Russie de ce Temps*, preface by J. M. Lustiger (Paris: Mame, 1993).
4. Zoia Afanas'evna Maslenikova, *Zhizn' ottsa Aleksandra Menia* (Moscow: Pristsel's, 1995); Andrei Alekseevich Eremin, *Otets Aleksandr Men': Pastyr' na rubezhe vekov*, 2nd ed. (Moscow: Carte Blanche, 2001). Maslenikova was a poet, sculptor, and a spiritual daughter of Fr. Aleksandr. Her diary, included in her biography, is a valuable source for descriptions of their relationship, with first-hand observations of his activities and struggles. Andrei Alekseevich Eremin is a psychotherapist who currently continues to practice his profession. He served for ten years as an acolyte at Novaia Derevnia, Fr. Aleksandr's last parish, before becoming his unofficial secretary. Intimately connected with the daily operations of the Novaia Derevnia parish, he provides a detailed description of Fr. Aleksandr's activities and teachings.

To these works should be added two other recently published accounts, although, strictly speaking, neither is a biography: Andrei Mikhailovich Tavrov, *Syn chelovecheskii: Ob ottse Aleksandre Mene* (Moscow: Eksmo, 2014), and Michel Evdokimov, *Father Alexander Men: Martyr of Atheism*, trans. Margaret Parry, foreword by Neville Kyrke-Smith, intro. Metropolitan Kallistos of Diokleia (Leominster, Herefordshire, England: Gracewing, 2011). Tavrov's book offers a close observation of Fr. Aleksandr as a parish priest from 1983 to 1990, the years that Tavrov was a member of the parish. He shows, in detail, both the dangers and the joys of venturing to the Novaia Derevnia parish. Michel Evdokimov, an Orthodox priest and emeritus professor of literature at the University of Poitiers, provides a deeply reflective account of Fr. Aleksandr's teachings. Evdokimov's small book places Fr. Aleksandr firmly in the Orthodox tradition and testifies to his ability to reach out to the Russian intelligentsia.

5. Michael Meerson, "The Life and Work of Father Aleksandr Men," in *Seeking God: The Recovery of Religious Identity in Orthodox Russia, Ukraine, and Georgia*, ed. Stephen K. Batalden (DeKalb: Northern Illinois University Press, 1993), 19.

Notes to Chapter One

1. James H. Billington, *Russia Transformed: Breakthrough to Hope; Moscow, August 1991* (New York: The Free Press, 1992), 136.
2. Sergei Bychkov, *Khronika neraskrytogo ubiistva* (Moscow: Russkoe reklamnoe izdatel'stvo, 1996), 7–8.
3. Fazil' Iskander, "Svetiashchiisia chelovek," *Znamia*, no. 9 (1991): 205.
4. Ibid.
5. Ibid., 206.
6. Ibid.

Notes to Chapter Two

1. Fr. Georgii Chistiakov, interview by author, Moscow, May 30, 2006.
2. Mark Weiner, "Foreword" [to the Russian Edition], in *About Christ and the Church* by Aleksandr Men, trans. Alexis Vinogradov (Torrance, CA: Oakwood, 1996), 8.

3. *Nauka i religiia*, founded in 1959, near the beginning of Nikita Khrushchev's campaign against religion, played a major role in the ideological assault upon what the government proclaimed as "religious superstition" for nearly thirty years. The journal served as the counterpart to the Museum of Religion and Atheism in Saint Petersburg, where instruments of the Inquisition and other artifacts were featured, graphically attempting to show the human misery inflicted by the church. Changes in the journal's editorial policy toward religion are discussed in greater detail in Victoria Smokin-Rothrock, "The Ticket to the Soviet Soul: Science, Religion, and the Spiritual Crisis of Late Soviet Atheism," *Russian Review* 73, no. 2 (April 2014), 171-197; Wallace L. Daniel, "Religion and Science: The Evolution of Soviet Debate," *Christian Century*, January 29, 1992, 98–100, and "The New Religious Press in Russia," in *Christianity after Communism: Social, Political, and Cultural Struggle in Russia*, ed. Niels C. Nielsen, Jr. (Boulder, CO: Westview Press, 1994), 54–60.

4. "Russia in Crisis," in *Christianity for the Twenty-First Century: The Life and Work of Alexander Men*, ed. Elizabeth Roberts and Ann Shukman (London: SCM Press, 1996), 147.

5. Yves Hamant, interview by author, Moscow, January 20, 2010. In these "gatherings," as Bishop Seraphim Sigrist has so well pointed out, Aleksandr Men sought to resurrect the conception of community that the Soviet state had "assiduously sought to destroy." Built on the principle of "sharing and exchange" among their participants, they followed Jesus's command to "bear one another's burden." Seraphim Sigrist, *A Life Together: Wisdom of Community from the Christian East* (Brewster, MA: Paraclete Press, 2011), 9, 14.

6. Yves Hamant, *Alexander Men: A Witness for Contemporary Russia (A Man for Our Time)*, trans. Steven Bigham, introduction by Maxym Lysack (Torrance, CA: Oakwood, 1995), 119, 223n151. Paul VI established these principles in the apostolic exhortation of 1975.

7. Aleksandr Men, "The Role of the Church in the Modern World," in *About Christ*, 64.

8. Alexis Vinogradov, Preface to Men, *About Christ*, 10.

9. John Doyle Klier, *Russia Gathers Her Jews: The Origins of the "Jewish Question" in Russia, 1772-1825* (Dekalb: Northern Illinois University Press, 2011), 17–19.

10. Ibid., 19. According to Klier, Russia received approximately 45,000 Jews during the first partition (1772).

11. Ibid., 76, 81–82, 154–56. Klier notes, however, that embryonic elements of the later residential and occupational restrictions on Jews had their origins in decisions made in the period between 1772 and 1825.

12. Eugene M. Avrutin, *Jews and the Imperial State: Identification Policies in Tsarist Russia* (Ithaca, NY: Cornell University Press, 2010), 5; Klier, *Russia Gathers Her Jews*, 75.

13. Mikhail Ignat'evich Mysh, *Rukovodstvo k russkim zakonam o evreiakh*, 2nd ed. (St. Petersburg: Tipo-litografiia M. P. Frolovoi, 1898), 132–35; Avrutin, *Jews and the Imperial State*, 5–6.

14. The specific causes and distinctive features of these pogroms are analyzed by John Doyle Klier, *Russians, Jews, and the Pogrom Crisis of 1881-1882* (New York: Cambridge University Press, 2011); Hans Rogger, "Conclusion and Overview," in *Pogroms: Anti-Jewish Violence in Modern Russian History*, ed. John D. Klier and Shlomo Lambroza (Cambridge: Cambridge University Press, 1992), 314–72; and Heinz-Dietrich Löwe, "Pogroms in Russia: Explanations, Comparisons, Suggestions," *Jewish Social Studies* 11, no. 1 (2004): 16–23; Louis Greenberg, *The Jews in Russia*, vol. 2, *The Struggle for Emancipation: 1881-1917*, ed. Mark Wischnitzer (1951; repr., New York: Schocken Books, 1976), 19–25, 47–48.

15. Anna Osipovna Vasilevskaia was the widow of Veniiamin Vasilevskii. I am grateful to April French for this information.

16. Elena Semenovna Men, "Moi put'," in *Katakomby XX veka: Vospominaniia*, ed. Roza Adamiants et al, comp. Nataliia Grigorenko and Pavel Men (Moscow: Fond imeni Aleksandra Menia, 2001), 231.

17. Ibid.

18. Aleksandr Men, *O sebe: Vospominaniia, interv'iu, besedy, pis'ma* (Moscow: Zhizn' s bogom, 2007), 11. One of her sons, Il'ia, got into a lot of trouble. Engaged in a skirmish with an officer who

had insulted him, he was arrested. It was only Anna Osipovna Vasilevskaia's pleas for mercy with the magistrate that prevented him from corporal punishment. He was sentenced to exile in Siberia.

19. Men, *O sebe*, 11.

20. Ibid., 13.

21. Vladimir Danilenko, "The Beilis Case Papers": Documents on the Beilis Case from the State Archive of the Kiev Oblast," Fonds 2, 183, 864, http://www.eastview.com/docs/IntroductionEng.pdf.

22. Robert Service, *Lenin: A Political Life*, vol. 1, *The Strengths of Contradiction* (Bloomington: Indiana University Press, 1985), 143–44.

23. Dmitrii Volkogonov, *Lenin: A New Biography*, trans. and ed. Harold Shukman (New York: The Free Press, 1994), 74.

24. Lenin responded to Bogdanov's contention that ideas offer a powerful, all-embracing organizing force and that the materialist view was limited and out-moded: "Acceptance or rejection of the concept matter is a question of the confidence man places in the evidence of his sense-organs, a question of the source of our knowledge, a question which has been asked and debated from the very inception of philosophy which may be disguised in a thousand different garbs by professional clowns, but which can no more become antiquated than the question whether the source of human knowledge is sight and touch, hearing and smell. To regard our sensations as images of the external world, to recognize objective truth, to hold a materialist theory of knowledge—these are all one and the same thing." Vladimir Il'ich Lenin, *Materialism and Empirio-Criticism: Critical Comments on a Reactionary Philosophy*, https://www.marxists.org/archive/lenin/works/1908/mec/two4.htm.

25. Men, *O sebe*, 18.

26. Ibid.

27. "Kharkiv," *Encyclopedia of Ukraine*, http://www.encyclopediaofukraine.com/pages%5CK%5CH%5CKharkiv.htm.

28. Walter Benjamin, *Moscow Diary*, ed. Gary Smith, trans. Richard Sieburth (Cambridge, MA: Harvard University Press, 1986), 85. See also Evgenii Bershtein, "'The Withering of Private Life': Walter Benjamin in Moscow," in *Everyday Life in Early Soviet Russia: Taking the Revolution Inside*, ed. Christina Kiaer and Eric Naiman (Bloomington: Indiana University Press, 2006), 220–21.

29. Walter Benjamin, letter to Jula Radt, December 26, 1926, in *Moscow Diary*, 127.

30. Benjamin, *Moscow Diary*, 26; Bershtein, "Withering of Private Life," 220–21.

31. Jochen Hellbeck, "Fashioning the Stalinist Soul: The Diary of Stepan Podlubnyi (1931–1939)," *Jahrbücher für Geschichte Osteuropus* 44, no. 3 (1996): 345–73; *Revolution on My Mind: Writing a Diary Under Stalin* (Cambridge, MA: Harvard University Press, 2006); "Self-Realization in the Stalinist System: Two Soviet Diaries of the 1930s," in *Stalinismus vor dem Zweiten Weltkrieg: Neue Wage der Forschung*, ed. Manfred Hildermeier and Elisabeth Müller-Luckner (Munich: Oldenbourg, 1998), 275–90; Jochen Hellbeck and Klaus Heller, *Autobiographical Practices in Russia/Autobiographische Praktiken in Russland* (Göttingen: V and R Unipress, 2004); Igal Halfin and Jochen Hellbeck, "Rethinking the Stalinist Subject: Stephen Kotkin's 'Magnetic Mountain' and the State of Soviet Historical Studies," *Jahrbücher für Geschichte Osteuropus* 44, no. 3 (1996): 456–63; Igal Halfin, *Terror in My Soul: Communist Autobiographies on Trial* (Cambridge, MA: Harvard University Press, 2003). See also Alexander Etkind's critical review of Hellbeck's interpretations, in "Soviet Subjectivity: Torture for the Sake of Salvation?" in *Kritika: Explorations in Russian and Eurasian History* 6, no. 1 (Winter 2005): 171–86.

32. Elena's maiden name was Elena Semenovna Vasilevskaia. She changed her patronymic to sound more Russian, a common practice among Jewish families.

33. Halfin, *Terror in My Soul*, x, 43–95; Halfin and Hellbeck, "Rethinking the Stalinist Subject," 456; Hellbeck, "Fashioning the Stalinist Soul," 344.

34. Halfin, *Terror in My Soul*, 45; Hellbeck "Fashioning the Stalinist Soul," 355.

35. Elena Men, "Moi put'," 217, 220.

36. Ibid., 217.

37. Ibid., 220.

38. Ibid., 208.

39. Ibid., 209.

40. Ibid., 211.

41. Ibid.

42. Ibid.

43. Ibid., 212.

44. Ibid.

45. Ibid. Henryk Sienkiewicz (1846–1916), Polish writer, satirist, historian, and novelist, published *Quo vadis?* (Where are you going?) in 1895, the work that brought him his greatest success. The novel focused on Christian persecution during the era of the Roman emperor Nero. Sienkiewicz wrote many other works that earned him acclaim across Eastern and Western Europe, and he is considered to be the greatest Polish writer of the second half of the nineteenth century. He was awarded the Nobel Prize in Literature in 1905.

"Na rassvete khristianstva" is likely a reference to the Russian translation of Frederic William Farrar's *The Early Days of Christianity* (London: Cassell, 1882). Born in India as the son of an English missionary, Farrar (1831–1903) was educated at King's College, London, and went on to be dean of Westminster Abbey, rector and then arch-deacon of Westminster, and dean of Canterbury. He enjoyed a wide reputation as a preacher and writer; included in his large number of publications were several books of popular fiction in which he combined fiction and history. The work cited above is likely F. V. F., *Skvoz mrak k svetu, ili, na rassvete khristianstva (povest' iz vremen Neronovskogo goneniia na khristian)*, originally published in Russian in 1897, reissued in 1995, in Saint Petersburg by Satis' Press.

46. Elena Men, "Moi put," 212.

47. Ibid., 213.

48. Ibid., 214.

49. For these population figures and the ethnic breakdown of Moscow's inhabitants cited here, see Timothy J. Colton, *Moscow: Governing the Socialist Metropolis* (Cambridge, MA: Harvard University Press, 1995), 157, appendix A, 757–58; Diane Koenker, "Urbanization and Deurbanization in the Russian Revolution and Civil War," *The Journal of Modern History* 57, no. 3 (September 1985): 424–25.

50. Alan M. Ball, *Russia's Last Capitalists: The Nepmen, 1921–1929* (Berkeley: University of California Press, 1987), 41–42, 86–87, 93, 179; Orlando Figes, *The Whisperers: Private Life in Stalin's Russia* (New York: Henry Holt, 2007), 9, 65; Negley Farson, *Black Bread and Red Coffins* (New York: Century, 1930), 41–45.

51. Allan Monkhouse, *Moscow, 1911–1933* (Boston: Little, Brown, 1934), 134–35.

52. Armand Hammer, quoted in Ball, *Russia's Last Capitalists*, 85–86.

53. Walter Duranty, *I Write as I Please* (New York: Simon and Schuster, 1935), 138.

54. Monkhouse, *Moscow*, 134–35; Duranty, *I Write as I Please*, 140–49. Duranty described how the N. E. P. for a time "took the lid off" as gambling halls and nightclubs flourished. The largest gambling establishment opened on the corner of Arbat Square. Named Praga, this gambling facility attracted all kinds of people, from "low-class jackals and hangers-on of any form," to men of a different social class, including former nobles in formal clothing and Red Army soldiers "in uniform, back from fighting Moslem rebels in Central Asia," as well as women "of all sorts, in an amazing variety of costumes." "A strange sight, this Praga," Duranty noted, "in the center of the world's first Proletarian Republic." Duranty, *I Write as I Please*, 145–46.

55. Elena Men, "Moi put," 214.

56. Ibid., 215.

57. Ibid.

58. Ibid., 215–16.

59. Ibid., 216.

60. Ibid.

61. Men, *O sebe*, 18.

62. Ivan Aleksandrovich Il'in (1883–1954) was a religious philosopher, jurist, and publicist. Politically, he was conservative, a monarchist, and a specialist in the philosophy of law. He lectured and wrote on the state, law, and religion. He emphasized the special responsibility of educated Russia to the uneducated and its spiritual mission to enhance law and justice, or what he called the "conscience of law." He was among the intellectuals forced by Lenin into exile in 1922.

Georgii Ivanovich Chelpanov (1862–1936) was a psychologist, philosopher, and founder (1912) of the Moscow Institute of Psychology, a center of experimental psychology in Russia. Chelpanov served as the institute's director until 1923. He is the author of *Brain and the Soul* (*Mozg i dusha: Kritika materializma i ocherk sovremennykh uchenii o dushie: Publichnyia lektsii, chitannyia v Kieve v 1898-1899 godu* [Kiev: Sklad izd. v knizhnom magazine V. A. Prosianichenko, 1906]), a critique of materialism that enjoyed wide circulation. A strong defender of the freedom of science, he maintained that science and philosophy could flourish only when they were allowed to operate unconstrained by outside political forces.

63. Vera Iakovlevna Vasilevskaia, *Katakomby XX veka: Vospominaniia*, ed. Roza Adamiants, comp. Nataliia Grigorenko and Pavel Men (Moscow: Fond imeni Aleksandra Menia, 2001), 23.

64. Fr. Aleksei Mechev (1859–1923) was named parish priest of the church of Saint Nikolas the Wonderworker in 1895 and served his church as a *starets* in the world. Fr. Aleksei was confessor to many prominent people, including Nikolai Berdiaev. After Fr. Aleksei's death, his son Sergei succeeded him as priest. See Sergei Sergeevich Bychkov, comp., *Maroseika: Zhizneopisanie ottsa Sergiia Mecheva, pis'ma, propovedi, vospominaniia o nem* (Moscow: Martis, Sam and Sam, 2001). Aleksei and Sergei Mechev are discussed in greater detail in chapter 10 of the present study.

65. Vasilevskaia, *Katakomby XX veka*, 23.

66. Ibid.

67. Ibid., 24.

68. Allen Ball, "The Roots of *Bezprizornost'* in Soviet Russia's First Decade," *Slavic Review* 51, no. 2 (Summer 1992): 247–48. While a decade of war, revolution, and civil war partly caused the high number of orphaned and abandoned children, the reasons lay much deeper than these cataclysmic events, as Ball shows in his important study. He discovered other significant causes, including the wartime mobilization of adult males, which forced mothers to find work outside the home; the famine of 1922–1923; starvation and disease; the parental sense of helplessness; the high Soviet divorce rate; and, in 1918–1919, the Bolshevik's ideological campaign against the family.

69. Ball, "Roots of *Bezprizornost'*," 247–49, 255–56, 267; Jennie A. Stevens, "Children of the Revolution: Soviet Russia's Homeless Children (*Besprizorniki*) in the 1920s," *Russian History* 9, nos. 2–3 (1982): 246–47; Margaret K. Stolee, "Homeless Children in the USSR, 1917–1957," *Soviet Studies* 40, no. 1 (January 1998): 65, 69–70.

70. Vasilevskaia, *Katakomby XX veka*, 24.

71. Ibid., 25.

72. Ibid.

73. Ibid.

74. Ibid., 25–26. "One time, when I was especially sad, Tonia said to me, 'There are people with whom it is possible to talk the same as to my mother.'" Such words, Vera Iakovlevna wrote, "went deeply into my heart, but I do not desire to speak about this."

75. Only a portion of her manuscripts have been published, but among them are: *Ponimanie uchebnogo materiala uchashchimisia vspomogatel'noi shkoly* (Moscow: Akademiia pedagogicheskikh nauk RSFSR, 1960), and "N. I. Pirogov i voprosy zhizni," in *Psikhiatriia i aktual'nye problemy dukhovnoi zhizni: Sbornik pamiati professora D. E. Melekhova*, ed. V. Ia. Vasilevskaia, Georgii Kochetkov, and M. G. Gal'chenko (Moscow: SF MVPKhSh, 1997), 62–79. She is the translator into Russian of the following works: E. Kheisserman, *Potentsial'nye vozmozhnosti psikhicheskogo razvitiia normal'nogo i nenormal'nogo rebenka* (Moscow: Nauka, 1964); Frantsisk Sal'skii, *Vvedenie v blagochestivuiu zhizn'* (Moscow: Stella Aeterna, 1999). Another translation of hers remains unpublished: K. De Griunval'd, "Kogda Rossiia imela svoikh sviatykh," as well as two of her own manuscripts: "Emotsial'naia zhizn'

malen'kogo rebenka" and "Chto takoe Liturgiia." See Fr. Aleksandr Men's introduction to Vasilevskaia, *Katakomby XX veka*, 16.

Notes to Chapter Three

1. Orlando Figes, *The Whisperers: Private Life in Stalin's Russia* (New York: Henry Holt, 2007), xxxiii.

2. Such issues of social identity and the millennial undercurrents present in Soviet citizens' dreams and aspirations during the first decades of Soviet rule are examined by Igal Halfin, *Terror in My Soul: Communist Autobiographies on Trial* (Cambridge, MA: Harvard University Press, 2003). "It is time for us to read what is actually written in the lines of the Communist text, not only what is between them," Halfin writes (p. x). Halfin maintains that spiritual development and the attempt to rewrite the self, demonstrating a new political consciousness and emphasizing how the individual overcame religious superstitions, became central aspects of the Communist autobiography. See also Jochen Hellbeck, "Fashioning the Stalinist Soul: The Diary of Stepan Podlubnyi (1931–1939)," *Jahrbücher für Geschichte Osteuropas* 44, no. 3 (1996): 345–73; "Self-Realization in the Stalinist System: Two Soviet Diaries of the 1930s," in *Stalinismus vor dem Zweiten Weltkrieg: Neue Wege der Forschung*, ed. Manfred Hildermeier and Elisabeth Müller-Luckner (Munich: Oldenbourg, 1998), 275–90; and "Russian Autobiographical Practice," in *Autobiographical Practices in Russia/ Autobiographische Praktiken in Russland*, ed. Jochen Hellbeck and Klaus Heller (Göttingen: V and R Unipress, 2004), 279–98.

3. Mikhail Gefter, "V predchuvstvii proshlogo," *Vek XX i mir*, no. 9 (1990): 29, quoted by Figes, *The Whisperers*, xxxii.

4. Aleksandr Men, "Predislovie," in *Katakomby XIX: Vospominaniia*, by Vera Iakovlevna Vasilevskaia, ed. Roza Adamiants, comp. Nataliia Grigorenko and Pavel Men (Moscow: Fond imeni Aleksandra Menia, 2001), 16.

5. Vera Iakovlevna Vasilevskaia, *Katakomby XIX: Vospominaniia*, ed. Roza Adamiants, comp. Nataliia Grigorenko and Pavel Men (Moscow: Fond imeni Aleksandra Menia, 2001), 28.

6. Men, "Predislovie," 13.

7. Ibid.; Mariia Vital'evna Tepnina, "Iz vospominanii-interv'iu," in Vasilevskaia, *Katakomby XX veka*, 264–65; Viktor Grigorenko, "Zhiznennyi put' Arkhimandrita Serafima (Bitiukova)," in *Tserkovnaia zhizn' XX veka: Protoierei Aleksandr Men' i ego dukhovnye nastavniki; Sbornik materialov Pervoi nauchnoi konferentsii "Menevskie chenteniia" (9–11 Sentiabria 2006 g.)* (Sergiev Posad: Izdanie prikhoda Sergievskoi tserkvi v Semkhoze, 2007), 110–11.

8. Vera Alekseevna Korneeva, "Vospominaniia o khrame Svv. Bessrebrenikov Kira i Ioanna na Solianke," in Vasilevskaia, *Katakomby XX veka*, 252. See Vasilevskaia's beautiful memoir and description of Fr. Serafim, in her *Katakomby XX veka*, 21–125.

9. Metropolitan in the Russian Orthodox Church designates the bishop of the capital of a province. The 1927 agreement is elaborated later in this chapter.

10. Men, "Predislovie," 14.

11. "Protocol No. 24, June 12, 1923," in Felix Corley, ed. and trans., *Religion in the Soviet Union: An Archival Reader* (New York: New York University Press, 1996), 54.

12. "Letter from his Grace, Sergius, Metropolitan of Nijny Novgorod, *locum tenens* of the Keeper of the Patriarchal Throne to the clergy and faithful of the Patriarchate of Moscow; Moscow, 16th /29th June 1927," in *Christians in Contemporary Russia*, by Nikita Struve, trans. Lancelot Sheppard and A. Manson, 2nd ed. (New York: Scribner, 1967), 363–64.

13. Dimitry V. Pospielovsky, *The Orthodox Church in the History of Russia* (Crestwood, NY: St. Vladimir's Seminary Press, 1998), 251.

14. Men, "Predislovie," 14; Nina Vladimirovna Trapani, "Iz vospominanii ob ottse Petre Shipkove," in Vasilevskaia, *Katakomby XX veka*, 272–73.

15. See especially the study by Gregory L. Freeze, which examines closely this large and important issue and reconsiders Stalinist religious policy: "The Stalinist Assault on the Parish," in

Stalinismus vor dem Zweiten Weltkrieg: Neue Wege der Forschung, ed. Manfred Hildermeier and Elisabeth Müller-Luckner (Munich: Oldenbourg, 1998), 209–32.

16. The literature on the parish as this essential grassroots organization of the church is immense, but its foundational importance is emphasized both in earlier and much more recent accounts. See, in particular, Serafim (Leonid Mikhailovich Chichagov), *Obrashchenie Preosviashchennogo Serafima, Episkopa Kininevskogo k dukhovenstvu eparkhii po voprosy o vozrozhdenii prikhodskoi zhizhni* (Kishinev: Eparkhial'naia tipografiia, 1909); Kirill (Gundiaev), "Tserkov' v otnoshenii k obshchestvu v usloviiakh perestroiki," *Zhurnal Moskovskoi Patriarkhii* 47, no. 2 (February 1990): 32–38; Wallace L. Daniel, "The Church and the Struggle for Renewal: The Experience of Three Moscow Parishes," in *Burden or Blessing? Russian Orthodoxy and the Construction of Civil Society and Democracy*, ed. Christopher Marsh (Boston: Boston University, Institute on Culture, Religion, and World Affairs, 2004), 61–68.

17. Freeze, "Stalinist Assault," 215–16.

18. See the rich collection of archival documents compiled and published by Irina Ivanovna Osipova, the historian of the catacomb church, "Dokumenty po regionam i godam: Iz istorii gonenii Istinno-Pravoslavnnoi (Katakombnoi Tserkvi): Konets 1920-kh–nachalo 1970-kh godov." *Mezhdunarodnoe istoriko-prosvetitel'skoe pravozashchnoe i blagotvoritel'noe obshchestvo MEMORIAL*, http://www.histor-ipt-kt.org/doc.html, and "Kniga Pamiati po regionam i alfavitu: Iz istorii gonenii Istinno-Pravoslavnnoi (Katakombnoi Tserkvi), konets 1920-kh–nachalo 1970-kh godov." *Mezhdunarodnoe istoriko-prosvetitel'skoe pravozashchnoe i blagotvoritel'noe obshchestvo MEMORIAL*, http://www.histor-ipt-kt.org/KNIGA/moskva.html.

19. The catacomb churches' canonical foundation rested on the decree issued on November 20, 1920, by Patriarch Tikhon, the head of the church elected by the last All-Russian Council: Decree No. 362, "Regarding diocesan self-rule."

20. Irina Ivanovna Osipova, "*O, Premiloserdyi . . . Budi s nami neotstupno . . .*": *Vospominaniia veruiushchikh Istinno-Pravoslavnoi (Katakombnoi) Tserkvi: Konets 1920-kh–nachalo 1970-kh godov* (St. Petersburg: Kifa, 2011), 24–25, 191–92, 204, 205–7, 214–17, 222, 249–56, 358–69, 374–79.

21. Mariia Sergeevna Zhelnavakova, "Iz pisem," in Vasilevskaia, *Katakomby XX veka*, 309.

22. Ibid.

23. Ibid., 308.

24. Vasilevskaia, *Katakomby XX veka*, 28.

25. Elena Semenovna Men, "Moi put'," in Vasilevskaia, *Katakomby XX veka*, 223.

26. Ibid.

27. The Wedding Feast is a parable told by Jesus in Matthew 22: 1-14. In the parable, Jesus likens heaven to a wedding feast that the king has prepared to honor his son. Yet when the table was set and the guests invited, few came, and the king's messengers, who had gone out to spread word of the feast were treated harshly, some were killed. One of the guests, who appeared at the feast, "was not wearing wedding clothes." He was ordered outside "into the darkness, where there will be weeping and gnashing of teeth." Jesus concludes the parable by saying, "Many are invited, but few are chosen." The parable's main point concerns Jesus's entrance into the world to provide salvation for human beings. Many refuse to accept him and turn away, more drawn to temporal things. God's judgment will rain down on them. But the few who accept his invitation serve in a manner befitting their calling. By scheduling their wedding at this time, Elena affirmed her commitment to live in such a way.

28. James von Geldern, "The Center and the Periphery: Cultural and Social Geography in the Mass Culture of the 1930s," in *New Directions in Soviet History*, ed. Stephen White (Cambridge, MA: Cambridge University Press, 1992), 62–80.

29. Elena Men, "Moi put'," 225–26.

30. Ibid., 226.

31. Vasilevskaia, *Katakomby XX veka*, 33.

32. Elena Men, "Moi put'," 226.

33. Ibid., 227.

34. Ibid., 227–28.

35. Ibid., 228–29.

36. Aleksandr Men, *O sebe: Vospominaniia, interv'iu, besedy, pis'ma* (Moscow: Zhizn' s Bogom, 2007), 22.

37. Ibid.; Zoia Afanas'evna Maslenikova, *Zhizn' ottsa Aleksandra Menia* (Moscow: Pristsel's, 1995), 21.

38. The actions of June 22 are described in Vasilevskaia, *Katakomby XX veka*, 104–6. Saint Sergii of Radonezh was the founder of the Trinity-Saint Sergius Lavra (Monastery) at Zagorsk (Sergiev Posad). For more on him and the Holy Trinity Monastery, see Scott M. Kenworthy, *The Heart of Russia: Trinity-Sergius, Monasticism, and Society after 1825* (New York: Oxford University Press, 2010).

39. Pavel Vol'fovich Men, interview by author, Moscow, June 2, 2007.

40. Ibid.

41. Elena Men, "Moi put'," 238–39.

42. Vasilevskaia, *Katakomby XX veka*, 114.

43. Ibid., 107.

44. The other two priests were Fr. Ieraks (Bocherov, Ivan Matveevich, 1880–1959) and Fr. Dmitrii (Kriuchkov, Dmitrii Ivanovich, 1874–1952).

45. Vasilevskaia, *Katakomby XX veka*, 141.

46. Ibid., 134.

47. Elena Men, "Moi put'," 240–41.

48. Ibid., 244.

49. Sergii (Stragorodskii), "Pastyriam i pasomym khristovoi pravoslavnoi tserkvi," June 22, 1941, in *Russkaia pravoslavnaia tserkov' i Velikaia Otechestvennaia voina: Sbornik tserkovnykh dokumentov* (Moscow: 1-ia Obraztsovaia tipografiia Ogiza, 1943), 4–5.

50. Tatiana Aleksandrovna Chumachenko, *Church and State in Soviet Russia: Russian Orthodoxy from World War II to the Khrushchev Years*, ed. and trans. Edward E. Roslof (Armonk, NY: M. E. Sharpe, 2002), 5.

51. Dimitry Pospielovsky, *Russkaia pravoslavnaia tserkov' v XX veke* (Moscow: Respublika, 1995), 192; Chumachenko, *Church and State*, 7.

52. Olga Iur'evna Vasil'eva, *Russkaia pravoslavnaia tserkov' v politike sovetskogo gosudarstva v 1943-1948 gg.* (Moscow: Institut rossiiskoi istorii RAN, 1999), 108.

53. Ibid., 109.

54. "Zapiska G. G. Karpova o prieme I. V. Stalinym ierarkhov Russkoi Pravoslavnoi Tserkvi," September 1943, in Mikhail Ivanovich Odintsov, *Russkie patriarkhi XX veka: Sud'by Otechestva i Tserkvi na stranitsakh arkhivnykh dokumentov. Pt. 1: "Delo" patriarkha Tikhona; Krestnyi put' patriarkha Sergiia* (Moscow: Izd-vo RAGS, 1999), 283–91.

55. Vasil'eva, *Russkaia pravoslavnaia tserkov'*, 112.

56. "Zapiska G. G. Karpova," 287.

57. Chumachenko, *Church and State*, 55–56.

58. "The Regulations for the Council of Russian Orthodox Church Affairs," October 7, 1943, Decree No. 1095, *Zhurnal Moskovksoi Patriarkhii*, no. 4 (1945): 54.

59. Some of Fr. Serafim's followers identified the grave and placed a cross on it. Vasilievskaia, *Katakomby XX veka*, 136 (note at bottom of page).

60. Alexander Werth, *Russia at War, 1941-1945* (New York: Carroll and Graf, 1964), 761.

61. "None of our relatives who moved out of Moscow during the war were able to reclaim their living quarters in the city, and still have not managed to regain them," Pavel Men said in an interview with author, Moscow, June 2, 2007; Elena Men, "Moi put'," 245.

62. Elena Men, "Moi put'," 245–47.

63. Joseph Stalin, quoted in Vasil'eva, *Russkaia pravoslavnaia tserkov'*, 110.

64. Yves Hamant, *Alexander Men: A Witness for Contemporary Russia (A Man for Our Times)*, trans. Steven Bigham, intro. Maxym Lysack (Torrance, CA: Oakwood, 1995), 44.

65. Vasilevskaia, *Katakomby XX veka*, 136–37; John Anthony McGuckin, *The Orthodox Church: An Introduction to its History, Doctrine, and Spiritual Culture* (Malden, MA: Blackwell, 2008), 52.

66. Chumachenko, *Church and State*, 59.

67. Nathaniel Davis, *A Long Walk to Church: A Contemporary History of Russian Orthodoxy*, 2nd ed. (Boulder, CO: Westview Press, 2003), 179.

68. Ibid.

69. Aleksandr Men, "Pis'mo k E. N.," quoted by Hamant, *Alexander Men*, 40. *Startsy* are elders, venerated in the church. The most renowned were the elders at the Optina Pustyn' Monastery in central Russia, to which many famous Russian writers, including Gogol and Dostoevsky, made pilgrimages in the nineteenth century. The Optina Pustyn' Monastery will be discussed later in this study.

Notes to Chapter Four

1. Orlando Figes, *The Whisperers: Private Life in Stalin's Russia* (New York: Henry Holt, 2007), 208, 218; Catherine Merridale, *Night of Stone: Death and Memory in Twentieth-Century Russia* (New York: Viking, 2000), 192–210.

2. Razeda Taisuna, quoted in Figes, *The Whisperers*, 251.

3. John Erickson, "Soviet War Losses: Calculations and Controversies," in *Barbarossa: The Axis and Allies*, ed. John Erickson and David Dilks (Edinburgh: Edinburgh University Press, 1994), 265–66; V. A. Isupov, *Demograficheskie katastrofy i krizisy v Rossii v pervoi polovine XX veka: Istoriko-demograficheskie ocherki* (Novosibirsk: Sibirskii khronograf, 2000), 140–214.

4. Petr Nikolaevich Fedoseev, "Sotsializm i patriotizm," *Kommunist*, no. 9 (1953): 23–24, quoted in Geoffrey Hosking, *Rulers and Victims: The Russians in the Soviet Union* (Cambridge, MA: Belknap Press of Harvard University Press, 2006), 262.

5. See Abram Tertz [Andrei Sinyavsky], *The Trial Begins and On Socialist Realism* (New York: Vintage, 1965), 147–50; James H. Billington, *The Icon and the Axe: An Interpretive History of Russian Culture* (New York: Vintage Books, 1970), 535–36.

6. As referenced in Zoia Afanas'evna Maslenikova, *Zhizn' ottsa Aleksandra Menia* (Moscow: Pristsel's, 1995), 61.

7. Yves Hamant, *Alexander Men: A Witness for Contemporary Russia (A Man for Our Times)*, trans. Steven Bigham, introduction by Maxym Lysack (Torrance, CA: Oakwood, 1995), 48.

8. Maslenikova, *Zhizn' ottsa Aleksandra Menia*, 27, 60–61.

9. "Imagination in Place," in *Imagination in Place: Essays* by Wendell Berry (Berkeley, CA: Counterpoint, 2010), 4.

10. Pavel Vol'fovich Men, interview by author, Moscow, June 2, 2006.

11. Ibid.

12. In this paragraph, I have heavily relied on Maslenikova, *Zhizn' ottsa Aleksandra Menia*, 76.

13. See Pavel Vol'fovich Men, "Ierei Boris Vasil'ev. Ego zhizn', sluzhenie i tvorchestvo," in *Tserkovnaia zhizn' XX veka: Protoierei Aleksandr Men' i ego dukhovnye nastavniki; Sbornik materialov Pervoi nauchnoi konferentsii "Menevskie chenteniia" (9–11 Sentiabria 2006 g.)*, ed. M. V. Grigorenko (Sergiev Posad: Izdanie prikhoda Sergievskoi tserkvi v Semkhoze, 2007), 150.

14. Aleksandr Men, *O sebe: Vospominaniia, interv'iu, besedy, pis'ma* (Moscow: Zhizn' s bogom, 2007), 30.

15. Ibid.

16. Pavel Men, "Ierei Boris Vasil'ev," 152.

17. Men, *O sebe*, 30. Earlier, both Vasil'ev and Kupriianova were "Marioseiskie," parishioners of the Church of the Sacred Nikolai on Maroseika Street in central Moscow, led by the Orthodox priests Fr. Aleksei Mechev (1859–1923) and his son Fr. Sergei Mechev (1892–1941). After the church's closure by the Bolsheviks in the early 1920s, many members of the parish continued to remain in touch and supported each other; they had a significant influence on Aleksandr Men, as will be discussed later in this study.

18. Vasil'ev's manuscript was published in 1994: Boris Aleksandrovich Vasil'ev, *Dukhovnyi put' Pushkina* (Moscow: Sam and Sam, 1994). Vasil'ev also compiled the documents published in *Otets Aleksei Mechev: Propovedi, pis'ma, vospominaniia o nem*, 2nd ed., ed. Nikita Struve (Paris:

YMCA-Press, 1989). In 1970, Fr. Aleksandr Men sent these materials to Struve for publication; see Men, *O sebe*, 32n1.

19. Men, *O sebe*, 32.

20. The Old Arbat district is a section near the historical center of Moscow. In the eighteenth and part of the nineteenth century, it was a renowned location for the homes of the nobility.

21. Men, *O sebe*, 32.

22. Maslenikova, *Zhizn' ottsa Aleksandra Menia*, 76.

23. Ibid., 65.

24. Aleksandr Men, "Pis'mo k E. N.," in *"AEQUINOX": Sbornik pamiati o. Aleksandra Menia*, ed. I. G. Vishnevetskii and E. G. Rabinovich (Moscow: Carte Blanche, 1991), 185.

25. Aleksandr Men, quoted in Maslenikova, *Zhizn' ottsa Aleksandra Menia*, 44; Men, "Pis'mo k E. N.," 185.

26. The Bolsheviks executed the last of the Optina Elders, Archimandrite Issachlus II, on December 26, 1938. Fr. Serafim had also studied at the Optina Pustyn' Monastery and its elders had a major impact on his subsequent life and his understanding of Orthodox Christianity; Men, "Pis'mo k E. N.," 184–85; E. N. Mitrofanova, "Otets Aleksandr Men' i ego dukhovnye nastavniki," in Grigorenko, *Tserkovnaia zhizn'*, 156, 158.

27. Sergii Chetverikov, *Optina Pustyn'*, 2nd ed. (Paris: YMCA-Press, 1988), 31–32; Leonard J. Stanton, *The Optina Pustyn Monastery in the Russian Literary Imagination: Iconic Vision in the Works by Dostoevsky, Gogol, Tolstoy, and Others*, Middlebury Studies in Russian Language and Literature 3, ed. Thomas R. Beyer, Jr. (New York: Peter Lang, 1995), 47, 53. *Pustynia* also means "wilderness," both it and desert connoting a place set apart from the rest of society.

28. Stanton, *Optina Pustyn Monastery*, 92–93.

29. Chetverikov, *Optina Pustyn'*, 84–85; Stanton, *Optina Pustyn Monastery*, 81–82, 89, 101, 251.

30. Joseph Frank, *Dostoevsky: The Mantle of the Prophet, 1871–1881* (Princeton, NJ: Princeton University Press, 2002), 385–86.

31. Vladimir Lossky, quoted in John B. Dunlop, *Staretz Amvrosy: Model for Dostoevsky's Staretz Zossima* (Belmont, MA: Nordland, 1972), 27. Elders (*startsy*) occupied a unique and special place within Russian Orthodoxy. Originating in the ascetic communities of early Christianity and in Russian monasticism in the late thirteenth and fourteenth centuries, eldership (*starchestvo*) later gained widespread popularity in the nineteenth and twentieth centuries. There was never more than a small number of elders at any given time, and their popularity did not derive from the institutional church, but came from outside that position of authority. They were perceived as "holy men," who offered spiritual guidance to people who came to them seeking direction. As Irina Paert notes in her excellent study, elders fulfilled an unofficial ministry, earning their reputations "from below," from disciples, rather than from the church itself. Elders could be monks or priests, but this was not a sufficient condition, and many of them did not hold such sanctified positions. They were "healers of the spirit," teachers, counselors, and sometimes prophets, whose spiritual wisdom could transform how people who came to them looked at the world.

Startsy did not comprise a uniform group, as is often claimed, but were diverse and varied in their experiences, character, and ecclesiastical roles. The elders at Optina Pustyn' were widely known for their inner humility and service to others, including their service to society. But there were also other kinds of elders, some of whom practiced a "rigorously ascetic life" and strongly adhered to outward forms of piety. In post-Soviet Russia, certain self-appointed elders have emerged, who require strict obedience from their spiritual children and demand rigid adherence to church dogmas and decrees. Such diversity has created debate among church administrators and historians about the tradition of elders in Russian society, particularly about the division between the ascetics and the servants of society, those who withdrew from the world and those who gave themselves wholly, through the love of Christ, to service to the people. Sergei Sergeevich Khoruzhii, "Fenomen russkogo starchestva v ego dukhovnykh i antropologicheskikh osnovaniikh," *Tserkov' i vremia* 21, no. 2 (2002): 211–13, 223–26; Irina Paert, *Spiritual Elders: Charisma and Tradition in Russian Orthodoxy* (DeKalb: Northern Illinois University Press, 2010), 4, 214, 216; Kallistos (Ware), Bishop of Diocleia, *The Inner Kingdom*

(Crestwood, NY: St. Vladimir's Seminary Press, 2000), 129–30; Aleksei L'vovich. Beglov, "Starchestvo v trudakh russkikh tserkovnykh uchenykh i pisatelei," in *Put' k sovershennoi zhizni: O russkom starchestve*, ed. A. L. Beglov (Moscow: Pravoslavnyi Sviato-Tikhonovskii gumanitarnyi universitet, 2006), 5, 21–22, 25–26.

32. Chetverikov, *Optina Pustyn'*, 84–85.

33. Ann Shukman, Introduction to *Christianity for the Twenty-First Century: The Life and Work of Alexander Men*, ed. Elizabeth Roberts and Ann Shukman (London: SCM Press, 1996), 4.

34. Anna Grigor'evna Snitkina Dostoevsky, *Dostoevsky: Reminiscences*, trans. and ed. Beatrice Stillman, with an introduction by Helen Muchnic (New York: Liveright, 1975), 294. As Anna Dostoevsky wrote, "It was clear from my husband's stories about him what a profound seer and interpreter of the human heart this universally respected Elder was" (294). See also D. P. Bogdanov, "Optina pustyn' i palomnichestvo v nee russkikh pisatelei," *Istoricheskii vestnik*, no. 122 (October 1910): 327–39.

35. Dosifeia (Verzhblovskaia), "O Matyshke Marii," in Vasilevskaia, *Katakomby XX veka*, 279–306.

36. Ibid., 281.

37. Ibid., 280.

38. Ibid., 289.

39. Men, *O sebe*, 29.

40. Ibid., 27.

41. Ibid., 29.

42. Ibid., 30.

43. Dosifeia, "O Matyshke Marii," 281, 284.

44. Ibid., 293.

45. Ibid.

46. Pavel Vol'fovich Men, interview by author, Moscow, June 2, 2006.

47. Ibid.

48. Men, *O sebe*, 29.

49. Fr. Aleksandr's attribution of these qualities to Mother Mariia is taken from the earlier draft of his memoirs rather than from the published edition. The earlier draft is organized differently and part of the text differs as well. The reference above is not found in the published version, but is included in his discussion of Mother Mariia in the unpublished original text, "O moikh predkakh i roditeliakh," 4. I am grateful to Pavel Vol'fovich Men for access to the unpublished manuscript.

50. Men, "Pis'mo k E. N.," quoted by Hamant, *Alexander Men*, 40.

51. Men, "Pis'mo k E. N.," 185.

52. Hamant, *Alexander Men*, 41–42.

53. Alexander Werth, *Russia at War, 1941–1945* (New York: Carroll and Graf, 1964), 762.

54. Men, *O sebe*, 41–42; Maslenikova, *Zhizn' ottsa Aleksandra Menia*, 67–70.

55. Men, *O sebe*, 41–42.

56. Men recalled a history teacher, a "nice person" as a whole, who came to class, "pulled from his pocket a notebook and proceeded to read to us what was written in the textbook." The textbook was written after the Russian Revolution, and contained a large number of distortions, which Men easily recognized and which "we took as very funny." Ibid., 41.

Men did not join the Young Pioneers, the Soviet youth organization, as school officials encouraged the students to do, and his refusal caused a commotion. "I hoped to escape this degrading procedure, and when they dragged me violently before the class and made me stand there while everyone gave a 'seig heil' and pronounced the oath, I simply stood, held out my hand and prayed." He continued to resist, apparently without much retribution, although a school official called his mother. Men understood that many things to which the school paid homage existed only as a formality, representing an exercise devoid of all meaning. This, too, created opposition in him (Men, *O sebe*, 42).

57. Anastasiia Iakovlevna Andreeva, "V nem zhilo bessmertie . . . ," in *Taina zhizni i smerti*, ed. A. Ia. Andreeva (Moscow: Znanie, 1992), 4.

58. Ibid.

59. Men, *O sebe*, 43; Hamant, *Alexander Men*, 48.

60. Men, *O sebe*, 58.

61. Ibid., 63; Maslenikova, *Zhizn' ottsa Aleksandra Menia*, 69–70.

62. Men, *O sebe*, 65–69.

63. The standard bookstores did not carry these texts. In 1922, Lenin had declared leading members of Russia's philosophical and theological schools to be anti-Soviet. Lenin's campaign against "undesirable" intellectuals and his order that they be deported is lucidly recounted by Leslie Chamberlain in *The Philosophy Steamer: Lenin and the Exile of the Intelligentsia* (London: Atlantic Books, 2006).

64. Men, *O sebe*, 9.

65. Ibid., 34.

66. During the Enlightenment, theosophy attracted much interest from philosophers. German philosophers especially produced major works on theosophy as a speculative approach to understanding nature. Leading theosophists of the period include Johann George Gichtel (1638–1710), Friedrich Christoph Oetinger (1702–1782), and William Law (1686–1761), and, in France, Louis Claude de Saint-Martin (1743–1803). Later, in Russia, Vladimir Solov'ev incorporated certain aspects of traditional theosophy in his attempt to develop a comprehensive philosophical system: "In repudiating the false principles and absurd conclusions of empiricism and rationalism, genuine philosophy must contain the objective content of these currents as secondary, or subordinate elements. They are to be synthesized along with mystical knowledge to form the *basis* for genuine philosophy." Vladimir Sergeevich Solov'ev, *The Philosophical Principles of Integral Knowledge*, trans. Valeria Z. Nollan (Grand Rapids, MI: William B. Eerdmans, 2008), 71.

67. See L. Iu. Petrunina, ed., *Vasilii Alekseevich Vatagin: K 125-letiiu so dnia rozhdeniia: Materialy mezhdunarodnoi konferentsii, Moskva, 5–6 fevralia 2009 [s prilozheniiu: CD]* (Moscow: Ekspress 24, 2010).

68. Men, *O sebe*, 34.

Notes to Chapter Five

1. I. Stalin, "O proekte konstitutsii Soiuza SSR (Doklad na Chrezvychainom VIII Vsesoiuznom s'ezde Sovetov, 25 November 1936)," in *Voprosy Leninizma*, 11th ed. (Moscow: Gosudarstvennoe izd-vo politicheskoi literatury, 1947), 510.

2. An exception would be Zoia Afanas'evna Maslenikova, *Zhizn' ottsa Aleksandra Menia* (Moscow: Pristsel's, 1995), although Maslenikova's main interest is Men's student activities and not the primary influences and intellectual impact of these years on Fr. Aleksandr.

3. "Otvet na pros'bu Z. A. Maslenikovoi napisat' o svoem puti k Bogu, o svoem dukhovnom opyte," in *O sebe: Vospominaniia, interv'iu, besedy, pis'ma*, by Aleksandr Men (Moscow: Zhizn' s Bogom, 2007), 228.

4. Ian Frazier, *Travels in Siberia* (New York: Farrar, Straus and Giroux, 2010), 3.

5. A. J. Haywood, *Siberia: A Cultural History* (New York: Oxford University Press, 2010), xiii.

6. James Forsyth, *A History of the Peoples of Siberia: Russia's North Asian Colony, 1581–1900* (Cambridge: Cambridge University Press, 1992), 31–34, 40–41, 42–43, 110–11; Terence Armstrong, ed., *Yermak's Campaign in Siberia: A Selection of Documents*, trans. Tatiana Minorsky and David Wileman, Hakluyt Society Publications, 2nd ser., no. 146 (London: Hakluyt Society, 1975), 64–66, 70–72, 170–71.

7. Forsyth, *History*, 8; Maurice Auguste Benyowsky, *The Memoirs and Travels of Mauritius Augustus, count de Benyowsky: In Siberia, Kamchatka, Japan, the Liukiu Islands and Formosa*, trans. from the original manuscript (1741–1771) by William Nicholson, ed. Pasfield Oliver (New York: Macmillan, 1898), 137, 271, 278; Henry Norman, *All the Russias: Travels and Studies in Contemporary European Russia, Finland, Siberia, the Caucasus, and Central Asia* (New York: Charles Scribner's Sons, 1903), 97.

8. See the description of these contradictory reports, in R. A. French, Introduction to *The Development of Siberia: People and Resources*, ed. R. A. French and Alan Wood (Basingstoke: The Macmillan Press, 1989), 3–6.

9. P. McDonough Collins, *Siberian Journey: Down the Amur to the Pacific, 1856–1857* (Madison: University of Wisconsin Press, 1962), quoted by French and Wood, *Development of Siberia*, 4.

10. Forsyth, *History*, 38–40; Haywood, *Siberia*, 234. In 1799, the Russian-American Company, which transported furs to Western Europe and other places, chose Irkutsk as its headquarters. See Semen Bentsianovich Okun, *The Russian-American Company*, ed. and intro. B. D. Grekov, trans. Carl Ginsburg, preface by Robert J. Kerner (Cambridge, MA: Harvard University Press, 1951); Aleksandr Iur'evich Petrov, *Rossiisko-amerikanskaia kompaniia: Deiatel'nost' na otechestvennom i zarubezhnom rynkakh (1799–1867)* (Moscow: Institut vseobshchei istorii RAN, 2006).

11. Okun, *The Russian-American Company*, 234.

12. Maria Volkonsky's life is splendidly and movingly told by Christine Sutherland in *The Princess of Siberia: The Story of Maria Volkonsky and the Decembrist Exiles* (London: Metheun, 1984). See the accounts of expeditions and explorations of Siberia by members of the Russian Geographical Society and their resulting publications in Vera Fedorova Gnucheva, comp., *Materialy dlia istorii ekspeditsii Akademii nauk v XVIII i XIX vekakh: Khronologicheskie obzory i opisanie arkhivnykh materialov*, Trudy Arkhiva Akademii nauk SSSR 4 (Moscow: Izd-vo Akademii nauk SSSR, 1940), 230–31, 239, 242–44, 248–49, 252–53.

13. By the end of the nineteenth century, the population of Irkutsk had already reached 49,106, and by 1900, the Trans-Siberian railroad, which began construction in 1891, had been completed as far as Irkutsk. The railroad brought in a large number of immigrants into the region. In 1959, Irkutsk's population was approximately 366,000.

14. Stalin's first Five-Year Plan (1929–1933), whose main goal called for the industrialization of the Soviet Union, relied heavily on a large increase in Siberian grain production. See Maurice Dobb, *Soviet Economic Development since 1917*, rev. ed. (New York: International Publishers, 1968), 221, 252; Stanislav Gustavovich Strumilin, *O piatiletnem plane razvitiia narodnogo khoziaistva SSSR: Diskussiia v kommunisticheskoi akademii* (Moscow: Izd-vo kommunisticheskoi akademii, 1928), 28–29.

15. Akademiia nauk SSSR, *Istoriia sibiri s drevnikh vremen do nashikh dnei v piati tomakh*, vol. 5, *Sibir' v periode zaversheniia stroitel'stva sotsializma i perekhoda k kommunizmu* (Leningrad: Nauka, 1969), 231.

16. The Virgin Lands Campaign, introduced in 1954, began operation in 1957. In the Khrushchev years, more than ten million hectares of grassland came under cultivation, mostly in Western Siberia. Igor V. Naumov, *The History of Siberia*, ed. David N. Collins (New York: Routledge, 2006), 208.

17. M. G. Levin and L. O. Potapov, *The Peoples of Siberia* (Chicago, IL: University of Chicago Press, 1964), 198.

18. Ibid. Also in 1955, the Soviet government planned and the next year began to establish a whole new series of industries in Irkutsk—butter, milk, and airplane factories—the first two aimed at reviving parts of the national economy on which Stalin's policies of the late 1920s and 1930s had inflicted a heavy blow. All of these measures represented preliminary aspects of an ambitious agricultural plan for the Soviet Union that Nikita Khrushchev implemented more fully at the Twentieth Party Congress in 1956 and thereafter (Naumov, *History of Siberia*, 208).

19. Vladislav Zubok, *Zhivago's Children: The Last Russian Intelligentsia* (Cambridge, MA: Belknap Press of Harvard University Press, 2009), 44–59, 122.

20. Maslenikova, *Zhizn' ottsa Aleksandra Menia*, 117. Maslenikova, a spiritual daughter of Fr. Aleksandr's and someone who knew him well, writes that he had much interest in the philosophical problems and the general laws of physics but little interest in the mathematical details and formulaic aspects of the subject. He loved the study of biology, zoology, and geology, much less so physics and chemistry.

21. Ibid., 155.

22. This and the second paragraph following rely on Maslenikova's account, *Zhizn' ottsa Aleksandra Menia*, 117–19. Yakunin remembers this first encounter differently, although he agreed that their initial meeting took place in 1953, shortly before Men graduated from secondary school

and was in the process of applying to the institute. "He told me he was in the 10th form and would soon finish school." This meeting occurred, Yakunin said, on the train between Moscow and Bala-shikha (where the Institute of Fur was located). Gleb Yakunin, interview by author, Moscow, May 10, 2007.

23. Mitrofan Vasil'evich Lodyzhenskii (1852–1917), Russian theologian and theosophist, wrote a three-volume study of the Christian mystics and of mysticism in Western and Eastern religions at the beginning of the twentieth century. The first volume examines the mysticism of Eastern Christianity and its relationship to what he calls higher consciousness. In this work, Lodyzhenskii also explores the beliefs of Saints Francis of Assisi, Serafim of Sarov, and Simeon the New Theologian. Mitrofan Vasil'evich Lodyzhenskii, *Misticheskaia trilogiia*, vol. 1, *Sverkhsoznanie i puti ego dostizheniiu: Indusskaia radzhaioga i khristianskoe podrizhnichestvo; Opyt issledovaniia* (Petrograd: Ekaterininskaia tip., 1915).

24. Maslenikova, *Zhizn' ottsa Aleksandra Menia*, 129.

25. Richard E. Louterbach, *Through Russia's Back Door* (New York: Harper, 1950), 109.

26. Maslenikova, *Zhizn' ottsa Aleksandra Menia*, 129.

27. Ibid., 130.

28. Fr. Gleb Yakunin, interview by author, Moscow, May 10, 2007. I am grateful to Elena Volkova and Archpriest Viacheslav Tulupov for arranging the interview with Fr. Gleb. The interview revealed multiple aspects of Fr. Gleb's and Aleksandr Men's time in Irkutsk. Maslenikova's account states that the two men lived together for two months; Yakunin gives that time as two years.

29. Men had two other close friends, Viktor Andreev and Oleg Drobinskii, with whom he could discuss his thoughts about religion, but it was only with Gleb Yakunin that he shared everything, including his plans to become a priest. Maslenikova, *Zhizn' ottsa Aleksandra Menia*, 115, 119, 144.

30. Irkutsk province served as the western sector of Buryat territory in 1917–1918. The Buryats formerly were nomads who engaged in reindeer hunting and sable trapping, but who, after the Russian incorporation of their territory in the treaties of Nerchinsk in 1689 and Kiakhta in 1727, abandoned nomadism for agriculture. The Buryats comprised the largest minority ethnic group in Siberia.

Other indigenous people too had suffered under Soviet policies of the 1930s, when the Bolshevik's philanthropic activities of the 1920s were replaced by the coercive measures of the 1930s, including the five-year plans, industrialization, and collectivization. The Tungus, closely related to the Manchus and who lived northwest of Lake Baikal, and the Kets, a northern Asian people, whose small settlements were spread out along the Yenesei River, had also been uprooted by a Bolshevik social agenda that forced them to forsake their nomadism, tribal religion, and clan structure (Forsyth, *History*, 19, 21, 23, 250, 284).

31. Ibid., 44. See also Sergei Borisovich Filatov's account of the Old Believers in his monumental study of religious groups in Russia, *Sovremennaia religioznaia zhizn' Rossii: Opyt sistematicheskogo opisaniia*, ed. Michael Bourdeaux and Sergei Borisovich Filatov (Moscow: Logos, 2004), 1:169–254.

32. Maslenikova, *Zhizn' ottsa Aleksandra Menia*, 132.

33. Fr. Gleb Yakunin, interview by author, Moscow, May 10, 2007.

34. Ibid.

35. Men, *O sebe*, 87; Aleksandr Men, "Vospominaniia o studencheskikh godakh," in *Khronika neraskrytogo ubiistva*, by Sergei Bychkov (Moscow: Russkoe reklamnoe izd-vo, 1996), 146.

36. Ibid.

37. Men, *O sebe*, 88; Men, "Vospominaniia o studencheskikh godakh," 146–47.

38. Men, *O sebe*, 88. During his student years, Men read Adolph von Harnack's magisterial, seven-volume *Lehrbuch der Dogmengeschichte* (1885–1890), translated into English as *History of Dogma* (1894–1899). Harnack (1851–1930), a German Lutheran theologian and church historian, was one of the founders of the historical-critical method of biblical scholarship. In his *History of Dogma*, he interpreted Christian doctrine as a product of "Hellenization," in which Greek philosophical ideas became enmeshed in Christianity during the apostolic age. He had an especially critical view of Eastern Orthodoxy, proclaiming it a "perversion of the Christian religion." Men found Harnack's use of the historical method to interpret Christianity and his efforts to relate the synoptic gospels to the world to be interesting and important, but he did not accept Harnack's conclusions. Harnack has been severely

criticized by Karl Barth, Jaroslav Pelikan, and others, although his place as a major scholar of Christianity is firmly established.

39. Men, *O sebe*, 88.

40. Maslenikova, *Zhizn' ottsa Aleksandra Menia*, 132.

41. Concise summaries of these views are provided by Scott R. Appleby, *The Ambivalence of the Sacred: Religion, Violence, and Reconciliation* (Lanham, MD: Rowman and Littlefield, 2000); Gottfried Maron, "Frieden und Krieg: Ein Blick in die Theologie- und Kirchengeschichte," in *Glaubenskriege in Vergangenheit und Gegenwart*, ed. Peter Hermann (Göttingen: Vandenhoeck and Ruprecht, 1996), 17–35; and the discussion among Soviet academics in the late years of Soviet Union, in Viktor Garadzha, "Na urovne trebovanii zhizni," *Nauka i religiia*, no. 1 (January 1988): 10–12, and V. Pazlova, "Dialog? Poka tol'ko znakomstvo," *Nauka i religiia*, no. 6 (June 1988): 30–31.

42. See Miroslav Volf's discussion and critique of such claims in *A Public Faith: How Followers of Christ Should Serve the Common Good* (Grand Rapids, MI: Brazos Press, 2011), 40–43, and *Exclusion and Embrace: A Theological Exploration of Identity, Otherness, and Reconciliation* (Nashville, TN: Abingdon, 1996).

43. Maslenikova, *Zhizn' ottsa Aleksandra Menia*, 132.

44. Many of the church's former leaders, some of whom the church glorified, had done the opposite. They had supported institutions and social structures that had oppressed human beings and stifled freedom. Metropolitan Filaret (Drozdov), the revered church leader, represented a prime example of such egregious lack of compassion for people. Reading the historian Sergei Mikhailovich Solov'ev's autobiography, *Moi zapiski dlia detei moikh i esli mozhno i dlia drugikh*, Men learned that Metropolitan Filaret had been a chief defender of serfdom and autocratic power and policies supporting a strong national church, the opposite of the Christian ideals he represented. Men, *O sebe*, 88; Men, "Vospominaniia o studencheskikh godakh," 147.

45. Maslenikova, *Zhizn' ottsa Aleksandra Menia*, 133.

46. In this context, Men emphasized the close relationship between Orthodox Christianity and Russian culture, whose great works of art, literature, and music had flowered from the rich soil of Christianity, works that creatively addressed many of Christianity's major themes. These perspectives would be much more fully emphasized and elaborated, but their beginnings may be located in Men's student years in Irkutsk, as his notes on these years suggest. For their later development, see Alexander Men, "Faith and Its Enemies," in *Christianity for the Twenty-First Century: The Life and Work of Alexander Men*, ed. Elizabeth Roberts and Ann Shukman (London: SCM Press, 1996), 62–63, 66–67; Aleksandr Men, *Istoki religii*, vol. 1 of *Istoriia religii v semi tomakh: V poiskakh puti, istiny, i zhizni* (Moscow: Slovo, 1991), 13–24; "Two Understandings of Christianity," in Roberts and Shukman, *Christianity*, 159; "K problematike 'Osevogo vremeni' (O dialoge kul'tury i religii)," in *Trudnyi put' k dialogu: Sbornik*, ed. N. Matiash (Moscow: Raduga, 1992), 283–84, 286.

47. Pavel Vol'fovich Men, e-mail correspondence with author, July 8, 2012.

48. Angelina Petrovna Grigorenko sang in the choir directed by Nikolai Vasil'evich Matveev in the Church of the Icon of the Holy Mother Vsekh skorbiashchikh radost' (The Joy of All Who Sorrow), on Bol'shaia Ordynka Street in Moscow. Pavel Vol'fovich Men, e-mail correspondence with author, July 8, 2012.

49. *Put' chelovecheskii: K 75-letiiu so dnia rozhdeniia protoiereia Aleksandra Menia*, comp. Fr. V. A.Grigorenko (Moscow: Zhizn' s Bogom, 2010), 18; Men, *O sebe*, 73.

50. Maslenikova, *Zhizn' ottsa Aleksandra Menia*, 124. This and the following paragraph rely heavily on Maslenikova's account.

51. Pavel Vol'fovich Men, e-mail correspondence with author, July 8, 2012.

52. Men, *O sebe*, 73, and *Put' chelovecheskii*, 18. Fr. Dmitrii Delektorskii, assisted by Deacon Nikolai Sitnikov, conducted the wedding service.

53. See the description provided by the Korennaia (Kursk Root) Hermitage of the Birth of the Holy Theotokos, http://www.kurskroot.com/orthodox_wedding. html.

54. Men, *O sebe*, 73.

55. Maslenikova, *Zhizn' ottsa Aleksandra Menia*, 133–35.

56. Men, *O sebe*, 69, 72.

57. Aleksandr Men, "Vladimir Solov'ev," in *Russkaia religioznaia filosofiia: Lektsii*, ed. Marina Nasonova (Moscow: Khram sviatykh bessrebrenikov Kosmy i Damiana v Shubine, 2003), 47.

58. Ibid., 25; Men, *O sebe*, 58, 69. Men records his lifelong debt to Solov'ev in the dedication and introduction to his *Istoriia religii v semi tomakh: V poiskakh puti, istiny, i zhizni*, vol. 1: *Istokii religii*, ed. A. Z. Belorusets (Moscow: Izd-vo Sovetsko-Britanskogo sovmestnogo predpriiatiia Slovo, 1991), 5, 7-13.

59. Men, "Vladimir Solov'ev," 29.

60. Ibid., 30.

61. Ibid., 30-31.

62. Ibid., 37.

63. Vladimir Sergeevich Solov'ev, "Ob upadke srednevekovogo mirosozertsaniia," in *Sobranie sochinenii Vladimira Sergeevicha Soloveva* (Brussels: Zhizn' s Bogom, 1966), 6:381-93.

64. Men, "Vladimir Solov'ev," 43.

65. Ibid.; Solov'ev, "Ob upadke srednevekovogo mirosozertsaniia," 391.

66. Jonathan Sutton, *The Religious Philosophy of Vladimir Solovyov: Towards a Reassessment* (Basingstoke: Macmillan, 1988), 151.

67. See Lesley Chamberlain, *The Philosophy Steamer: Lenin and the Exile of the Intelligentsia* (London: Atlantic, 2006).

68. Aleksandr Men, "Otets Pavel Florenskii," in Men, *Russkaia religioznaia filosofiia*, 205.

69. Nikolai Ivanovich Bugaev (1837-1903), father of Andrei Belyi, the symbolist poet, spent his distinguished academic career at Moscow University, where he was an early proponent of the theory of discontinuous functions, which he also called "arithmology." He served as the professor and mentor of three star students who would later become major Russian mathematicians of the twentieth century: Dmitrii Fedorovich Egorov (1869-1931), Nikolai Nikolaevich Luzin (1883-1950), and Pavel Aleksandrovich Florensky. A recent study calls them "The Russian Trio." See Loren Graham and Jean-Michel Kantor, *Naming Infinity: A True Story of Religious Mysticism and Mathematical Creativity* (Cambridge, MA: Belknap Press of Harvard University Press, 2009), 66-90.

70. Quote by P. A. Florensky, ibid., 88.

71. Quote by Bugaev, ibid., 89.

72. Avril Pyman, *Pavel Florensky: A Quiet Genius; The Tragic and Extraordinary Life of Russia's Unknown da Vinci*, foreword by Geoffrey Hosking (New York: Continuum, 2010), 28, 32. Pyman's admirably lucid account and Hosking's excellent introduction set Florensky in the context of the controversies in politics and thought that circulated during this revolutionary period.

73. Men, "Otets Pavel Florenskii," 215. More than eight hundred pages long, with half of it devoted to source materials and learned commentaries, *The Pillar and the Ground of Truth* was in several ways revolutionary: it was beautifully produced; written in the form of twelve intimate letters to a friend; and the text contained illustrations, personal observations, and aphorisms, in contrast to the impersonal, stolid prose in which theological works, until then, were written. In addition, while *Pillar* included the latest scientific observations from Western Europe, it also had a solid grounding in Russia, especially in pre-Petrine Russia, with many examples drawn from Russian art, folklore, and religious symbols. See Nicholas Zernov, *The Russian Religious Renaissance of the Twentieth Century* (New York: Harper and Row, 1963), 101-103.

74. Men, "Otets Pavel Florenskii," 215-16.

75. Ibid., 211.

76. Ibid.

77. Ibid., 212.

78. Ibid., 213.

79. Ibid., 219.

80. Men, "Vladimir Solov'ev," 31.

81. Aleksandr Men, *Otvechaet na voprosy* (Moscow: Zhizn' s Bogom, 2008), 64-65.

82. Alexander Men, "Religion, Knowledge, and the Problem of Evil," in Roberts and Shukman, *Christianity*, 48.

83. Men, *Otvechaet na voprosy*, 182. Men, "Otets Pavel Florenskii," 217.

84. This episode is recounted by Sergei Bychkov in a list of errors he found in Maslenikova's *Zhizn' ottsa Aleksandr Menia*. Maslenikova erroneously maintains that the rector expelled him on a trumped-up charge of failure to attend a required class in military science, although in reality it was for his religious activities in a nearby church and his friendship with a local Catholic priest. See "Prilozhenie no. 6," in Bychkov, *Khronika neraskrytogo ubiistva*, 133–34n5.

85. Maslenikova, *Zhizn' ottsa Aleksandra Menia*, 149–50.

86. Ibid., 150.

87. Men, *O sebe*, 89.

88. Ibid., 142.

89. Ibid., 89.

90. Fr. Mikhail Aksenov-Meerson, e-mail correspondence with author, October 19, 2011.

91. Ibid.

Notes to Chapter Six

1. Irina Ivanovna Osipova, comp., *"O, Premiloserdyi . . . Budi s nami neotstupno . . .": Vospominaniia veruiushchikh Istinno-Pravoslavnoi (Katakombnoi) Tserkvi: Konets 1920-kh–nachalo 1970-kh godov* (St. Petersburg: Kifa, 2011), 32.

2. Nathaniel Davis, *A Long Walk to Church: A Contemporary History of Russian Orthodoxy*, 2nd ed. (Boulder, CO: Westview Press, 2003), 28–29.

3. Osipova, *"O, Premiloserdyi,"* 389–90.

4. Ibid., 31–32.

5. Mikhail Vital'evich Shkarovskii, *Russkaia Pravoslavnaia Tserkov' v XX veke* (Moscow: Veche, Lepta, 2010), 359.

6. Ibid., 359–60.

7. N. S. Khrushchev, quoted by Valerii Arkad'evich Alekseev, *"Shturm nebes" otmeniaetsia? Kriticheskie ocherki po istorii bor'by s religiei v SSSR* (Moscow: Rossiia molodaia, 1992), 221.

8. Ibid., 215.

9. Alekseev, *"Shturm nebes" otmeniaetsia?*, 221.

10. Shkarovskii, *Russkaia Pravoslavnaia Tserkov'*, 360.

11. These additional reasons are based on Shkarovskii, *Russkaia Pravoslavnaia Tserkov'*, 360–61. Shkarovskii's study, based on extensive research in state archives, offers much new information on the thinking underlying the government's actions.

12. Ibid., 362–67; Osipova, *"O, Premiloserdyi,"* 30–32. In addition, the KGB closely watched and reported the activities of members of the professional elite and the intelligentsia who attend religious services. See, for example, the report of KGB chairman A. Shelepin, who identified Professor N. V. Zvolinskii of the Kuibyshev Military Engineering Academy, who, "hiding his religious convictions at work, undertook a journey to the Odessa monastery"; G. P. Cherniavskii, a pensioner, who joined the Communist Party in 1920 and led a seminar on the history of the CPSU, but was "systematically present in the Yelokhovskii cathedral in Moscow"; and others. Such individuals, Shelepin pointed out, "are trying to spread religious convictions among those around them and to counter atheistic propaganda." He noted: "The Committee for state security considers it would be expedient to take appropriate measures through administration of the institutions and through party organizations to exert pressure on these individuals." A. Shelepin, Committee of State Security [KGB], Moscow, "To the CPSU CC," April 18, 1959, in Felix Corley, ed. and trans., *Religion in the Soviet Union: An Archival Reader* (New York: New York University Press, 1996), 210–11.

13. The July 18, 1961, regulation is published in Michael Bourdeaux, *Patriarch and Prophets: Persecution of the Russian Orthodox Church Today* (New York: Praeger, 1970), 44–46.

14. Davis, *Long Walk to Church*, 42.

15. Shkarovskii, *Russkaia Pravoslavnaia Tserkov'*, 384–85. In addition, the law on "parasitism," passed by the government on May 5, 1965, severely affected religious believers. Many of them who observed religious holidays refused to work on such days, and they became subject to the charges of "parasitism." Members of the catacomb church who had been arrested and served terms in the labor camps before their release in the mid-1950s were often re-arrested under this charge and sent back to the camps. See, for example, the cases of Hieromonk Filaret (Rusakov), Nadezhda Ershova, Ivan Vatkin, and others, in Osipova, *"O, Premiloserdyi,"* 102–4.

16. Davis, *Long Walk to Church*, 47.

17. As Fr. Aleksandr points out, Metropolitan Nikolai served as the journal's official editor, and Vedernikov's formal position was secretary, but, in reality, "that is practically the same thing." See Aleksandr Men, *O sebe: Vospominaniia, interv'iu, besedy, pis'ma* (Moscow: Zhizn' s Bogom, 2007), 119–20.

18. Ibid., 118–19.

19. Ibid., 119.

20. For greater detail, see the following chapter of this study.

21. See Vladislav Zubok, *Zhivago's Children: The Last Russian Intelligentsia* (Cambridge, MA: Belknap Press of Harvard University, 2009), 17.

22. A. Solzhenitsyn, "Along the Oka," *Encounter* (March 1965), 8–9, quoted in James H. Billington, *The Icon and the Axe: An Interpretive History of Russian Culture* (New York: Vintage Books, 1970), 581.

23. Zubok, *Zhivago's Children*, 192. In 1966, the well-publicized trial of the writers Andrei Sinyavsky and Iulii Daniel for publishing "anti-Soviet" works abroad brought to the forefront the disparity between constitutional rights and actual Soviet practices. Then, in 1968, the Soviet army brutally crushed what came to be known as the "Prague Spring" with its goal of providing "socialism with a human face"; such violence bore witness to the growing gap between Soviet ideals and its brutal actions.

24. See Dmitrii Efimovich Furman, "Nasha politicheskaia sistema i ee tsikly," *Svobodnaia mysl'*, no. 11 (2003), 9–30; Dmitrii Efimovich Furman and Kimmo Kääräinen, "Veruiushchie, ateisty i prochie: Novie issledovanie rossiiskoi religioznosti," *Voprosy filosofii*, no. 1 (January 1997), 79-91.

25. Men, *O sebe*, 120.

26. Anatolii Emmanuilovich Krasnov-Levitin was born in Baku, in 1915, to a justice of the peace father and an actress mother. His Jewish father was baptized a Christian, after which, in 1920, he moved the family to Leningrad (St. Petersburg). Anatolii Emmanuilovich grew up in Leningrad, was educated at the Herzen Pedagogical Institute in Leningrad, and did post-graduate work in literature. He taught literature in a secondary school before his arrest by the KGB in 1949, whereupon he was sentenced to ten years in a labor camp. The government released him after the Twentieth Party Congress in 1956. Following his release, he became what he termed a "church writer," and, as mentioned above, wrote a large number of articles for the *Journal of the Moscow Patriarchate* in the late 1950s and early 1960s.

Krasnov-Levitin was well-versed in both Russian and Western literature and blessed with a "prodigious memory" and brilliant conversational skills, and his Moscow apartment became a gathering spot for the Moscow intelligentsia. As Jane Ellis has described the meetings, they took place in "Anatolii Levitin's single, cramped, seven-foot square room," which served as a "mecca for the young, enquiring intelligentsia of all convictions and backgrounds, who were drawn there by the atmosphere of free, unfettered discussion and argument so rarely found in Soviet daily life. Talk went on endlessly, far into the night, accompanied by a meal of potatoes and onions, which were all the host could afford, and tea in chipped glasses" (Jane Ellis, introduction to "One Man's Witness: Selected Writings of Anatolii Krasnov-Levitin," in the Keston Archive, Krasnov-Levitin file, SU/Ort2/File 3). Continually under surveillance by the KGB, Krasnov-Levitin emigrated to Switzerland in 1974.

27. Anatolii Krasnov-Levitin, "Freedom of Belief and of Atheism: Face to Face," in Bourdeaux, *Patriarch and Prophets*, 266.

28. Pavel Mikhailovich Litvinov (b. 1940) is the grandson of Maksim Litvinov, who served as Joseph Stalin's people's commissar for foreign affairs from 1930 to 1939, and the Soviet Union's ambassador to the United States from November 1941 to August 1943. A physicist and writer, Pavel Litvinov in the late 1950s and 1960s became disaffected with Soviet ideology and policies. He published in samizdat and became a leader of the human rights movement in the Soviet Union, following closely the trial of Andrei Sinyavsky and Iulii Daniel in February 1966. Later, in April 1968, he and several associates participated in a demonstration on Red Square in protest of the Soviet invasion of Czechoslovakia and in support of Alexander Dubček, the leader of the Prague Spring.

29. Fr. Sergei Zheludkov's "Letter to Pavel Litvinov" of March 30, 1968, is published in Bourdeaux, *Patriarch and Prophets*, 339–41.

30. Ibid., 341.

31. Men, *O sebe*, 78.

32. I. K. Iazykova, "Dobryi pastyr'—Otets Nikolai Golubtsov," in *Tserkovnaia zhizn' XX veka: Protoierei Aleksandr Men' i ego dukhovnye nastavniki; Sbornik materialov Pervoi nauchnoi konferentsii "Menevskie chenteniia" (9–11 Sentiabria 2006 g.)*. (Sergiev Posad: Izdanie prikhoda Sergievskoi tserkvi v Semkhoze, 2007), 139.

33. The mother, Ol'ga Sergeevna Golubtsova (1864–1920), spent a great deal of time engaged in charity work. She died of smallpox contracted from "nursing children in Tambov province during the civil war." Ibid.

34. Ibid., 140–41.

35. Ibid., 143. Such acts of compassion were numerous, including the adoption by Fr. Nikolai and his wife, on two separate occasions, of four children whose parents had been sent into exile.

36. Ibid., 145.

37. Men, *O sebe*, 78.

38. See the personal testimonies included in O. N. Vysheslavtseva, *Pastyr' vo vremena bezbozhiia: Ob ottse Nikolae (Golubtsove)* (St. Petersburg: Satis', 1994).

39. Iazykov, "Dobryi pastyr'," 145.

40. Ibid.

41. Zoia Afanas'evna Maslenikova, *Zhizn' ottsa Aleksandra Menia* (Moscow: Pristsel's, 1995), 160.

42. Ibid., 179.

43. Men, *O sebe*, 103.

44. Ibid., 100.

45. Fr. Aleksandr Men, letters to Sister Ioanna (Iuliia Nikolaevna Reitlinger), September 2, 1974, n.d. 1974, n.d. 1974, n.d. 1975, in *Umnoe nebo: Perepiska protoiereia Aleksandra Menia s monarkhinei Ioannoi (Iu. N. Reitlinger)* (Moscow: Fond im. Aleksandra Menia, 2006), 37–40, 40–42, 67–68, 73–75.

46. Fr. Gleb Yakunin, interview by author, Moscow, May 10, 2007.

47. "Otets Dmitrii Dudko," in "Tri grusti siuzheta," Keston Archive, Fond Aleksandra Menia, 2. Following the closure of the church of Peter and Paul, Fr. Dmitrii found a position in the church of the Sacred Nikolai in Moscow.

48. "Iz interv'iu ottsa Dmitriia Dudko," in *Vokrug imeni ottsa Aleksandra*, comp. A. I. Zorin and V. I. Iliushenko (Moscow: Obshchestvo "Kul'turnoe Vozrozhdenie" imeni Aleksandra Menia, 1993), 44. Nataliia Solzhenitsyn, who met Fr. Dmitrii in the late 1960s, described his widespread influence among those who came to him searching for spiritual direction. "This was the time of the beginning of religious searching for many people, who had grown up under the yoke of communist ideology, which they had come to see as a total lie, with an inhuman essence. A large mass of people turned to the church and came under its influence. But it was not easy to find what they wanted: there were not many good pastors. But they discovered Fr. Dmitrii, and they came to him. One could find there many young mothers with their children, and grown men, and teenagers, well-known writers, artists, and entirely simple inhabitants of neighboring villages. Having been born into a peasant family, arrested, and having spent eight years in the gulag, he could identify with millions of people in our

multi-stratified society." Nataliia Solzhenitsyn, quoted in Jane Ellis, *The Russian Orthodox Church: A Contemporary History* (New York: Routledge, 1986), 309–10. See also Men, *O sebe*, 127. In 1973, Fr. Dmitrii began question-and-answer sessions on Saturday evenings after vespers, which were unique in that he was willing to respond openly to any question, including political ones; such sessions became widely popular. In 1980, primarily for his political activities, Fr. Dmitrii was arrested and, apparently under enormous pressure, broke down. After being freed, he recanted his previous views, praised the Soviet government, and turned on his earlier friends, including Fr. Aleksandr. His story is told in detail in Ellis, *Russian Orthodox Church*, 309–15, 313–17, 430–39; Ludmilla Alexeyeva, *Soviet Dissent: Contemporary Movements for National, Religious, and Human Rights*, trans. Carol Pearce and John Glad (Middletown, CT: Wesleyan University Press, 1985), 8, 66, 112–16, 251–53; Trevor Beeson, *Discretion and Valor* (1974; repr., Philadelphia: Fortress Press, 1982), 86–88, and, most recently, Oliver Bullough, *The Last Man in Russia: The Struggle to Save a Dying Nation* (New York: Basic Books, 2013).

49. Men, *O sebe*, 102n1, 112–16. Metropolitan Pimen ordained Eshliman, who served later in the Church of Pokrova Presviatoi Bogoroditsy, located in the Lyshchikovii Lane, in Moscow.

50. Ibid., 111.

51. Ibid., 105–8.

52. Ibid., 157.

53. The following account of the incident is based on Fr. Aleksandr's report, ibid., 129–40.

54. Ibid., 139.

55. Ibid., 134.

56. Ibid., 139.

57. Maslenikova, *Zhizn' ottsa Aleksandra Menia*, 201–2.

58. Ibid., 217–18.

59. Ibid., 201–2.

60. See the appendix to the letter of Nikolai Ivanovich Eshliman and Gleb Pavlovich Yakunin, "An Open Letter to His Holiness, the Most Holy Patriarch of Moscow and All Russia, Alexi," in Bourdeaux, *Patriarch and Prophets*, 221–23, and Bourdeaux's introduction to *Patriarch and Prophets*, 34.

61. Fr. Gleb Yakunin, interview by author, Moscow, May 10, 2007.

62. Nikolai Ivanovich Eshliman and Gleb Pavlovich Yakunin, "To the Chairman of the Presidium of the Supreme Soviet of the Union of Soviet Socialist Republics," in Bourdeaux, *Patriarch and Prophets*, 189–94.

63. Eshliman and Yakunin, "An Open Letter," 195–96.

64. Ibid., 218. Eshliman's and Yakunin's letter to the patriarch maintained that for the past forty years the church had operated within the framework created by Metropolitan Sergii in 1927, which has rendered the church leadership a "submissive tool in the hands of anti-ecclesiastical power" (220–21).

65. Ibid., 209.

66. Fr. Gleb Yakunin, interview by author, Moscow, May 10, 2007.

67. Men, *O sebe*, 172–73.

68. Fr. Gleb Yakunin, interview by author, Moscow, May 10, 2007.

69. Men, *O sebe*, 174.

70. This, too, is Yakunin's understanding of Fr. Aleksandr's role. "We never asked him to sign the letters," Yakunin said. "We also knew that even had we asked, he would not sign them." Fr. Gleb Yakunin, interview by author, Moscow, May 10, 2007.

71. Aleksandr Men, *Kniga Nadezhdy: Lektsii o Biblii* (Moscow: Zhizn' s Bogom, 2011), 160–64.

72. Men, *O sebe*, 161.

73. Ibid., 157.

74. See the superb description of Iudina provided by Fr. Georgii Chistiakov, "Mariia Iudina," in *V poiskakh vechnogo grada* (Moscow: Put', 2002), 63–66.

75. Men, *O sebe*, 139, 143, 158–59, 187–88; Maslenikova, *Zhizn' ottsa Aleksandra Menia*, 209–11; Christopher Vath, "Maria Yudina: The Pianist Who Moved Stalin," *Crossroads Cultural Center and*

the Siena Forum for Faith and Culture, September 17, 2011, http://www.crossroadsculturalcenter.org/
events/2011/9/17/maria-yudina-the-pianist-who-moved-stalin.html.

76. Men, *O sebe*, 162.

77. The channel Fr. Aleksandr had in mind will be discussed in the following chapter.

78. Men, *O sebe*, 163.

79. Alexeyeva, *Soviet Dissent*, 274–79; Zubok, *Zhivago's Children*, 259–61.

80. Mikhail Aleksandrovich Men, interview by author, Ivanovo, July 1, 2013.

81. Men, *O sebe*, 144.

82. Mikhail Aleksandrovich Men, interview by author, Ivanovo, July 1, 2013.

83. Maslenikova recounts this incident differently. She claims that, on the previous evening, a group of friends had gathered at Men's home to celebrate his nameday; he had taken the manuscripts the KGB had hoped to find and stored them under the downstairs terrace. Although they rummaged through Men's living quarters, the officials had not searched the first floor, where Natasha's parents lived and where the manuscript was located. See Maslenikova, *Zhizn' ottsa Aleksandra Menia*, 218.

84. Mikhail Aleksandrovich Men, interview by author, Ivanovo, July 1, 2013.

85. Nadezhda Mandelstam, *Hope against Hope: A Memoir*, trans. Max Hayward (New York: Atheneum, 1974), 333.

86. Ibid.

Notes to Chapter Seven

1. Ekaterina Iur'evna Genieva, interview by author, Moscow, July 3, 2009. Genieva, then director general of the Margarita Rudomino All-Russia State Library for Foreign Literature, had known Fr. Aleksandr's family since her childhood.

2. As mentioned earlier, Fr. Aleksandr read deeply in the works of these nineteenth- and early twentieth-century philosopher-theologians, especially Nikolai Berdiaev, Fr. Sergei Bulgakov, Vladimir Solov'ev, Semen Frank, and many others. He also believed that his parishioners needed to be acquainted with them, so he talked to them about the works of these writers. Andrei Cherniak, interview by author, Moscow, May 24, 2007; Vladimir Il'ich Iliushenko, interview by author, Moscow, June 5, 2006. Both Cherniak and Iliushenko were members of Men's parish. Fr. Georgii Chistiakov, interview by author, Moscow, May 30, 2006.

3. Andrei Alekseevich Eremin, *Otets Aleksandr Men': Pastyr' na rubezhe vekov*, 2nd ed. (Moscow: Carte Blanche, 2001), 480.

4. Aleksandr Men, "Poeziia sv. Grigoriia Bogoslova," in *Navstrechu khristu: Sbornik statei*, ed. Nataliia Grigorenko and Pavel Men (Moscow: Zhizn' s Bogom, 2009), 7–30, originally published in *Zhurnal Moskovskoi Patriarkhii*, no. 3 (1959): 62–67.

5. Paul Tillich, *A History of Christian Thought*, ed. Carl E. Braaten (New York: Harper and Row, 1968), 76.

6. As Fr. Aleksandr points out, many of the Christmas and Easter songs in the Eastern Church are based on Saint Gregory's holiday orations.

7. Men, "Poeziia sv. Grigoriia Bogoslova," 14.

8. Ibid., 15.

9. Ibid., 19.

10. Ibid., 9.

11. Peter Gilbert, Introduction to *On God and Man: The Theological Poetry of St. Gregory of Nazianzus*, trans. Peter Gilbert (Crestwood, NY: St. Vladimir's Seminary Press, 2001), 15.

12. Aleksandr Men, "Nazaret—kolybel' khristianstva," in Grigorenko and Men, *Navstrechu khristu*, 31–41, originally published in *Zhurnal Moskovskoi patriarkhii*, no. 9 (1959): 61–64.

13. Ibid., 31.

14. Ibid.

15. These perspectives on the Holy Trinity were also of great significance in the philosophy of Vladimir Solov'ev, who emphasized the Holy Trinity as an expression of the All-Unity, the

comprehensive and unifying nature of God. This subject is given detailed, extensive treatment in the sixth and seventh lectures in his series "Chteniia o bogochelovechestve," in *Sobranie sochineniia Vladimira Sergeevicha Solov'eva*, vol. 3 (Brussels: Zhizn' s Bogom, 1966), 3:79–102, 103–19; Vladimir Solov'ev, *Lectures on Divine Humanity*, trans. Peter Zouboff, revised and edited by Boris Jakim (Hudson, NY: Lindisfarne Press, 1995), 73–95, 96–111. For an excellent analysis of this central theme in Solov'ev, see Jonathan Sutton, *The Religious Philosophy of Vladimir Solovyov: Towards a Reassessment* (Basingstoke: Macmillan, 1988), 62–67, 88–95.

16. Men, "Nazaret—kolybel' khristianstva," 34.

17. Ibid., 35.

18. Ibid., 41.

19. Aleksandr Men, "Na poroge Novogo Goda," in Grigorenko and Men, *Navstrechu khristu*, 42–49, originally published in *Zhurnal Moskovskoi patriarkhii*, no. 1 (1960): 15–17.

20. Because of church closures from 1959 to 1960, the number of Russian Orthodox Church societies declined from 13,325 to 12,964; in 1961, they declined still further to 11,571, and in 1962, to 9,986. The figures were reported at the beginning of each year. Khrushchev's drive to close convents and hermitages took place even earlier than the closure of churches. The state closed nearly one-third of the convents and hermitages in 1959, leaving only forty-four still in operation in January 1960; in 1961, thirty-three remained. For these and other figures on church closures during Khrushchev's antireligious campaign, see Nathaniel Davis, *A Long Walk to Church: A Contemporary History of Russian Orthodoxy*, 2nd ed. (Boulder, CO: Westview Press, 2003), 38–42, 126, 164–66.

21. Men, "Na poroge Novogo Goda," 44. See also Aleksandr Men, "'Syn gromov' (ocherk zhizni i tvorenii apostola Ioanna Bogoslova)," in Grigorenko and Men, *Navstrechu khristu*, 244–45, originally published in *Zhurnal Moskovskoi patriarkhii*, no. 5 (1962): 49–60.

22. See also Aleksandr Men, "Svetochi pervokhristianstva," in Grigorenko and Men, *Navstrechu khristu*, 145–46, originally published in *Zhurnal Moskovskoi patriarkhii*, no. 7 (1961): 58–66.

23. Men, "Na poroge Novogo Goda," 44.

24. A recurring theme in Men's writings is his emphasis on Christian love as Jesus's greatest gift and the essence of his teachings. See Aleksandr Men, "Krest," in Grigorenko and Men, *Navstrechu khristu*, 89, originally published in *Zhurnal Moskovskoi patriarkhii*, no. 9 (1960): 36–38; "Svetochi pervokhristianstva," 145–46, and "Syn gromov," 297.

25. Men, "Na poroge novogo goda," 47; Fr. Aleksandr cites statements made by the Swedish pastor Christopher Klassen, Danish pastor Arne Bugge, Dutch pastor Hugo van Dalen, and the eminent German church historian and theologian Adolf von Harnack. As mentioned earlier, at the age of eighteen and still in secondary school, Men read the first volume of Harnack's multivolume *History of Dogma* (1885), which traced Christianity's doctrinal systems and the Hellenistic influences on them (Aleksandr Men, *O sebe: Vospominaniia, interv'iu, besedy, pis'ma* [Moscow: Zhizn' s Bogom, 2007], 67).

26. Aleksandr Men, "Rasizm pered sudom khristianstva," in Grigorenko and Men, *Navstrechu khristu* (Moscow: Zhizn' s Bogom, 2009), 198–216, originally published in *Zhurnal Moskovskoi patriarkhii*, no. 3 (1962): 22–27.

27. Ibid., 198.

28. Ibid., 200–211.

29. Ibid., 211.

30. Ibid., 200, 211.

31. Ernst Haeckel (1834–1919), *Chudesa zhizni*, 175, quoted in ibid., 205.

32. Nikolai Nikolaevich Miklukho-Maklai (1846–1888) is discussed by Men, ibid., 211. For more on the explorer, see his *Travels to New Guinea: Diaries, Letters, Documents* (Moscow: Progress, 1982), and Elsie May Webster, *The Moon Man: A Biography of N. N. Miklouho-Maclay* (Berkeley: University of California Press, 1984).

33. Men, "Rasizm," 211–12.

34. Ibid., 209, 215.

35. Ibid., 202.

36. Ibid., 208.

37. Ibid., 215.

38. Aleksandr Men, "Sviatiia sviatykh," in Grigorenko and Men, *Navstrechu khristu*, 97–98, originally published in *Zhurnal Moskovskoi patriarkhii*, no. 11 (1960): 51–52; "Taina Volkhov," in Grigorenko and Men, *Navstrechu khristu*, 176–77, 196–97, originally published in *Zhurnal Moskovskoi patriarkhii*, no. 1 (1962): 60–67; "Piatidesiatnitsu prazdnuem," in Grigorenko and Men, *Navstrechu khristu*, 145–46, originally published in *Zhurnal Moskovskoi patriarkhii*, no. 5 (1961): 55–58.

39. Men, *O sebe*, 119, 139n4. Men attributed part of the reason for the editor-in-chief's removal to Vedernikov's wife, Elena Iakovlevna Vedernikova, a talented icon painter, to whom Fr. Aleksandr and his wife, Nataliia Fedorovna, went for lessons on icon painting. According to Fr. Aleksandr, Elena Iakovlevna was a repatriate, which the Soviet government at the time viewed as a serious problem. He described her as extremely devoted to Moscow, even "pro-Soviet, in her orientation."

40. Aleksandr Men, "Sv. Apostol Luka kak deepisatel' Tserkvi," in Grigorenko and Men, *Navstrechu khristu*, 287–95, originally published in *Zhurnal Moskovskoi Patriarkhii*, no. 12 (1963): 50–52; "Sv. Liverii, papa Rimskii (K 1600-letiiu so dnia prestavleniia)," in Grigorenko and Men, *Navstrechu khristu*, 296–308, originally published in *Zhurnal Moskovskoi Patriarkhii*, no. 8 (1966): 52–57.

41. Aleksandr Men, "Pis'mo k E. N.," in *"AEQUINOX": Sbornik pamiati o. Aleksandra Menia*, ed. I. G. Vishnevetskii and E. G. Rabinovich (Moscow: Carte Blanche, 1991), 182; Sergei Zheludkov and Kronid Arkad'evich Liubarskii, "Katalog 1982: Izdatel'stvo Zhizn' s Bogom," in *Khristianstvo i ateizm* (Brussels: Zhizn' s Bogom, 1982), 244.

42. Mikhail Aleksandrovich Men, interview by author, Ivanovo, July 1, 2013.

43. Zoia Afanas'evna Maslenikova, "Moi dukhovnik," 20 August 1979, in *Zhizn' ottsa Aleksandra Menia* (Moscow: Pristsel's, 1995), 435–39; Vladimir Iliushenko, "Vospominaniia," in *Otets Aleksandr Men': Zhizn', Smert', Bessmertie*. 2nd ed. (Moscow: VGBIL im. M. I. Rudomino, 2010), 356–57.

44. Fr. Mikhail Aksenov-Meerson, "Zhizn' svoiu za drugu svoi," in *Pamiati protoiereia Aleksandra Menia*, ed. T. V. Gromova (Moscow: Rudomino, 1991), 117.

45. Zoia Afanas'evna Maslenikova, "K istorii knigi o. Aleksandra Menia 'Syn chelovecheskii,'" in Vishnevetskii and Rabinovich, *"AEQUINOX,"* 179.

46. Eremin, *Otets Aleksandr Men'*, 403.

47. Ibid.

48. Aleksandr Men, "Mif ili deistvitel'nost?," in *Syn chelovecheskii*, 4th ed. (Moscow: Izd-vo Sovetsko-Britanskogo sovmestnogo predpriiatiia Slovo, 1992), appendix 1:234–84. In the present edition, Fr. Aleksandr's *Syn chelovecheskii* is included as volume seven of his multivolume *Istoriia religii v semi tomak: V poiskakh puti, istiny, i zhizni*. There is strong, and convincing evidence, however, that *Syn chelovecheskii* should be considered a separate publication. Andrei Alekseevich Eremin does not include the book in his discussion of the individual volumes in Men's *Istoriia religii*. Eremin, *Otets Aleksandr Men'*, 442–80. See also Zoia Afanas'evna Maslenikova, "Otets Aleksandr—pisatel'," in Gromova, *Pamiati*, 136; Aksenov-Meerson, "Zhizn' svoiu," 117. Fr. Mikhail considers *Syn chelovecheskii* to be an introduction to the six-volume series. He writes: "The sharp, lively story about evangelistic experience is written for the contemporary reader, in which he [Fr. Aleksandr] offers answers to non-believers and to the prevailing governance of atheistic theory, down to the mythological school, which simply denied the existence of Jesus of Nazareth."

49. Men, "Pis'mo k E. N.," 182–202.

50. These works include *Religion and the Consciousness of God* (1906) and an edited volume on *Monism in Antiquity* (1908).

51. Arthur Drews, *The Christ Myth*, trans. C. Delisle Burns, Westminster College-Oxford Classics in the Study of Religion (Amherst, NY: Prometheus Books, 1998), 235. In 1911, Drews followed his book with a second part, in which he responded to his critics, carrying still further his argument that the "cult of Christ" came from myths already circulating before Christ supposedly lived; Arthur Drews, *Die Christusmythe*, part 2, *Die Zeugnisse für die Geschichtlichkeit Jesu, eine Antwort an die Schriftgelehrten mit besonderer Berücksichtugung die theologischen Methode* (Jena: Diederich, 1911).

52. Vladimir Il'ich Lenin, "O znachenii voinstvuiushchego materializma," in *Polnoe sobranie socheneniia* (Moscow: Izd-vo Politicheskoi Literatury, 1964), 45:28; James Thrower, *Marxist-Leninist "Scientific Atheism" and the Study of Religion and Atheism in the USSR* (Berlin: Mouton, 1983), 426.

53. Thrower, *Marxist-Leninist "Scientific Atheism,"* 426.

54. In the 1960s and '70s, the foremost Soviet historians on religion produced works that shaped the prevailing views, including Sergei Aleksandrovich Tokarev, *Religiia v istorii narodov mira*, 3rd ed. (Moscow: Polizdat, 1976), and *Rannie formy religii i ikh razvitiia* (Moscow: Nauka, 1964); Iosef Aronovich Kryvelev, *Istoriia religii: Ocherki*, 2 vols. (Moscow: Mysl', 1975–1976); and Iurii Ivanovich Semenev, "Razvitie obshchestvenno-ekonomicheskikh formatsii i ob'ektivnaia logika evolutsii religii," in *Voprosy nauchnogo ateizma* 20 (1976): 43–61. See Thrower, *Marxist-Leninist "Scientific Atheism,"* 216–19. Kryvelev's books remained influential until the end of the Soviet period. April French offers a detailed analysis of the works of these historians in "Spiritual Dissent: The Writings of Father Aleksandr Men as Dissent from Soviet Ideology" (MA thesis, Regent College, Vancouver, BC), 2011.

55. In addition to the sources mentioned above, see also the influential works of the popular historian Robert Iur'evich Vipper, *Vozniknovenie khristianskoi literatury* (Moscow: Nauka, 1946), and *Rim i rannee khristianstvo* (Moscow: Izd-vo Akademii nauk SSSR, 1954); Drews, *The Christ Myth*; and Aleksandr Men, "Mif ili deistvitel'nost," 235–37.

56. Men, "Mif ili deistvitel'nost'?," 241.

57. Ibid.

58. Mariia Sidorovna Butinova and Nikolai Petrovich Krasnikov, *Muzei istorii religii i ateizma: Spravochnik-putevoditel'* (Moscow: Nauka, 1965), 109.

59. Men, "Mif ili deistvitel'nost'?," 241–42; Butinova and Krasnikov, *Muzei istorii religii*, 107.

60. Maslenikova, "K istorii knigi," 180, and "Otets Aleksandr—pisatel'," 137.

61. Maslenikova, "K istorii knigi," 180.

62. In addition to these authors, Men's sources included the works of novelist François Mauriac, recipient of the Nobel Prize in Literature (1952); social anthropologist Sir James Frazer; Austrian prelate, author, and federal chancellor of Austria in the 1920s Ignaz Seipel; French archeological historian and theologian Pierre Benoit; Old Testament scholar and biblical archeologist George Ernest Wright; Russian philosopher and theologian Sergei Nikolaevich Bulgakov; Russian religious philosopher Sergei Nikolaevich Trubestskoi; Roman Catholic priest and one of America's preeminent biblical scholars Fr. Raymond E. Brown; Welsh New Testament scholar and theologian Charles H. Todd; English archeologist and director of the British School of Archeology Dame Kathleen Mary Kenyon; Polish biblical scholar and among the first to decipher the Dead Sea Scrolls Jósef Tadeusz Milik; German Lutheran theologian and scholar of Near Eastern studies Joachim Jeremias; Russian historian of theology Vasilii Vasilevich Bolotov; first-century Romano-Jewish scholar and historian Titus Flavius Josephus; archeologist and Catholic priest of the Franciscan Order in Jerusalem Bellarmino Bagetti; American archaeologist and philologist William Foxwell Albright; and many others.

63. Men, *Syn chelovecheskii*, 3.

64. Ibid., 6.

65. Ibid., 19.

66. Ibid., 20.

67. Ibid.

68. Maslenikova, "K istorii knigi," 180.

69. Such a window enabled the person to find the stillness at the center of life, which allows the individual to serve others with grace and love. See Fr. Aleksandr Men, letter to Sister Ioanna (Iuliia Nikolaevna Reitlinger, 1898–1988), September 2, 1974, undated letter (1974), undated letter (1974), and undated letter (1980), in *Umnoe nebo: Perepiska protoiereia Aleksandra Menia s monakhinei Ioannoi (Iu. N. Reitlinger)* (Moscow: Fond im. Aleksandra Menia, 2006), 37–40, 40–42, 106–7, 317; on the veneration of icons, see Sergei Nikolaevich Bulgakov, *The Orthodox Church*, foreword by Thomas Hopko, translation revised by Lydia Kesich (Crestwood, NY: St. Vladimir's Seminary Press, 1988), 139–44.

70. Bulgakov, *Orthodox Church*, 43.

71. See his discussion of "Na poroge novogo goda" earlier in this chapter.

72. When Christianity is made into an ideology, Fr. Aleksandr maintained, it becomes an enemy of faith. Such action poisons the church by suppressing its most creative minds and turning its living stream of thought into a rigid, dogmatic set of beliefs. He emphasized that "Christianity is not 'ideology,' an abstract doctrine, or an overstuffed system of rites." Aleksandr Men, "Osnovye cherty khristianskogo mirovozzreniia (Po ucheniiu Slova Bozhiia i opytu Tserkvi)," in *Kul'tura i dukhovnoe voskhozhdenie*, comp. R. I. Al'betkova and M. T. Rabotiaga (Moscow: Iskusstvo, 1992), 26. Later, at the end of the 1980s, when some political groups proposed to make Orthodoxy part of a "new Russian ideology," replacing Marxism-Leninism, Alexandr Men sharply criticized this approach. *Otets Aleksandr Men' otvechaet na voprosy*, comp. Anastasiia Andreeva, 2nd ed. (Moscow: Zhizn' s Bogom, 2008), 254; Aleksandr Men, "Rol' tserkvi v sovremennom mire," in *Mirovaia dukhovnaia kul'tura, khristianstvo, tserkov': Lektsii i besedy*, 2nd ed., ed. Anastasiia Andreeva et al., comp. A. Belavin (Moscow: Fond imeni Aleksandra Menia, 1997), 629–31.

73. See Fr. Aleksandr's depiction of the Pharisees, who cannot recognize Jesus because of their "settled views," in *Syn chelovecheskii*, 92–93, 104, 142.

74. Aleksandr Sergeevich Pushkin, quoted by Men, *Syn chelovecheskii*, 7.

75. Men, *Syn chelovecheskii*, 57–60; 66–67. Such a relationship between God and the individual, Fr. Aleksandr emphasized, thus changed the meaning of a "loving Creator."

76. Ibid., 127.

77. Ibid. "As evidence for the diverse and contradictory interpretations of Jesus's personality, in the past and present," Fr. Aleksandr writes, Soviet historians cite the many disagreements among scholars, which attest to the illusory nature of Jesus's existence. "Some consider Him a prophet or moralist, others—an advocate of powerlessness, still others—a rebel." In this case, "one might ask, can a truthful representation [ever be constructed] for such a contradictory person?" Men, "Mif ili deistvitel'nost'?," 258. A prime example of this viewpoint is Iosef Aronovich Kryvelev, *Chto znaet istoriia ob Iisuse Khriste?* (Moscow: Sovetskaia Rossiia, 1969), esp. 279–85.

78. Men, *Syn chelovecheskii*, 129.

79. Ibid., 127; Iosef Aronovich Kryvelev continued to draw on the mythological interpretation in his widely distributed textbook, *Christ: Myth or Reality*, trans. S. Galynsky, Religious Studies in the USSR, series 2 (Moscow: "Social Sciences Today" Editorial Board, 1987), 169–71. Simultaneously, Kryvelev describes Christ as "egocentric," and as combining megalomania "with a persecution mania and a feeling of doom; he was always speaking of his inevitable martyrdom. And this is reflected," Kryvelev said, "in his moods and his neuropsychological state which show a characteristic oscillation between elation and excitement and despair and dejection" (54–55).

80. Men, *Syn chelovecheskii*, 128, 218.

81. Kryvelev, *Christ*, 154–55, 165.

82. Men, "Mif ili deistvitel'nost'?," 280.

83. "'If Christ had not risen,' says the Apostle Paul, 'then our preaching is in vain and our faith is in vain,'" 1 Corinthians 15:14, quoted by Men, *Syn chelovecheskii*, 220–21.

84. Ibid., 231.

85. Ibid.

86. Kryvelev, *Christ*, 17–18.

87. Men, *Syn chelovecheskii*, 172.

88. Ibid., 71–72, 85–86, 87–88, 135–36, 144–45, 184–85, 220–21, 230–33. See also Fr. Aleksandr's "household conversations": "Tserkov' v istorii," in Men, *Mirovaia dukhovnaia kul'tura*, 593; "Beseda ob apostole Pavle," in *Tserkov' i my: Domashnie besedy* (Moscow: Zhizn' s Bogom, 2012), 99; "Fenomen cheloveka," in *Pravoslavnye vesti*, ed. Vladimir Erokhin (Moscow: Put', Istina, i Zhizn', 2005), 8; and especially his "Liubit' Boga i liubit' cheloveka," in *Liubit' Boga i liubit' cheloveka: Domashnie besedy*, ed. Roza Adamiants et al. (Moscow: Zhizn' s Bogom, 2012), 243, 245, 248–49.

89. Men, *Syn chelovecheskii*, 132–33.

90. Ibid., 142; see also 146, 150.

91. Ibid., 10.

92. Ibid., 42.

93. Maslenikova, "Moi dukhovnik," March 16, 1967, in *Zhizn' ottsa Aleksandra Menia*, 282–83.

94. Maslenikova, "Otets Aleksandr—pistatel'," 137. The manuscript Fr. Aleksandr gave her was *Magizm i Edinobozhie*, the second volume of his *Istoriia religii*. (Maslenikova became a believer in 1969, the year after she began to work with Fr. Aleksandr as his editor. She described her conversion in "Moi dukhovnik," January 23, 1969, 293).

95. Maslenikova, "Otets Aleksandr—pistatel'," 137.

96. Mikhail Aleksandrovich Men, interview by author, Ivanovo, July 1, 2013.

97. Olga Zaslavskaya, "From Dispersed to Distributed Archives: The Past and Present of Samizdat Material," *Poetics Today* 29, no. 4 (Winter 2008): 678.

98. Ann Komaromi, "Samizdat as Extra-Gutenberg Phenomenon," *Poetics Today* 29, no. 4 (Winter 2008): 632, 634–35, 666.

99. Ibid., 630, 631–32.

100. Julius Telesin, "Inside 'Samizdat,'" *Encounter* 40, no. 2 (February 1973): 25–33.

101. Michael Aksenov-Meerson, "The Dissident Movement and *Samizdat*," in *The Political, Social, and Religious Thought of Russian "Samizdat": An Anthology*, ed. Michael Aksenov-Meerson and Boris Shragin, trans. Nicholas Lupinin (Belmont, MA: Nordland, 1977), 25.

102. Ibid., 24, 32, 35.

103. "Conversation with A. Krasnov-Levitin," interview by Michael Bourdeaux, Moscow, December 3, 1975.

104. Her parents had sent Anastasia to a French Catholic school and, although she had formally converted to Catholicism, she remained deeply attached to Russian Orthodoxy. Douroff discusses her conversion and her interest and attachment to Russian culture in her memoir, Anastasia Douroff and Evgeniia Svin'ina, *Rossiia—ochishchenie ognem: Iz dnevnika khristianki, Moskva, 1964–1977* (Moscow: Rudomino, 1996), 25–28, 34–35, 38–52, 81–89.

105. Yves Hamant, *Alexander Men: A Witness for Contemporary Russia (A Man for Our Times)*, trans. Steven Bigham, intro. Maxym Lysack (Torrance, CA: Oakwood, 1995), 158.

106. Ibid., 158. In her memoir, Douroff recounts her discussions with young people: "We talked about everything that concerned us and that troubled our heart. We met in the home of my new friend," Evgenii Viktorovich Barabanov, then twenty-two years old, who "lived with his relatives in one small room in a communal apartment"; Douroff and Svin'ina, *Rossiia*, 121. Douroff writes about her interest in the elders of the Optina Pustyn' Monastery and her research in the archives on them, her discussions with an elderly woman about the monastery, her trip to Leningrad to visit the grave of the poet Anna Akhmatova, and many other interests.

107. Douroff and Svin'ina, *Rossiia*, 121. She often visited Fr. Aleksandr's church in Tarasovka. Hamant, *Alexander Men*, 158.

108. For these and other details on Posnova's background and service, see Hamant, *Alexander Men*, 158–59; Douroff and Svin'ina, *Rossiia*, 36. Since World War Two, Posnova had devoted her energies to working with former Russian soldiers who could not return home and with those who had been deported. She founded a charitable organization to serve their physical and spiritual needs; as part of this organization, she created the publishing house.

109. Zheludkov and Liubarskii, "Katalog 1982," 244, 247, 248.

110. Iv. Aman (Yves Hamant), "Razmatyvaia nit' vospominanii," in Gromova, *Pamiati*, 101; Maslenikova, "K istorii knigi," 179.

111. A. Sukhikh and L. Bondarenko, "Sovremennoe Pravoslavie i dvoistvennaia istina," *Nauka i religiia*, no. 3 (March 1964): 14.

112. A. Chertkov, "Sviatoi rozhdestvenskii obman," *Nauka i religiia*, no. 12 (1962): 24, 27.

113. Dmitrii Modestovich Ugrinovich, *Vvedenie v teoreticheskoe religiovedenie* (Moscow: Mysl', 1973), 24; French, "Spiritual Dissent," 84n30. The article Ugrinovich cites is Aleksandr Men, "'Gospod' moi i Bog moi,'" *Zhurnal Moskovskoi Patriarkhii*, no. 4 (1964): 54–57. Ugrinovich's reference is to Men's statements: "Faith does not prove, but shows, itself. Its reality enters into the essence of a person not as an external fact, but as a power, which penetrates all of one's internal life" (57).

114. Men, "Pis'mo k E. N.," 183.

115. Ibid., 191.

116. Ibid.

117. Ibid., 191–92.

118. Maslenikova, "K istorii knigii," 180.

119. Ibid.

120. Alexander Men, "Russia in Crisis," in *Christianity for the Twenty-First Century: The Life and Work of Alexander Men*, ed. Elizabeth Roberts and Ann Shukman (London: SCM Press, 1996), 147.

121. Men, "Mif ili deistvitel'nost'?," 241; and *Otets Aleksandr Men' otvechaet*, 167–70.

Notes to Chapter Eight

1. Mikhail Gorbachev, *Perestroika: New Thinking for Our Country and the World* (New York: Harper and Row, 1987), 18–25, 37; Mikhail Gorbachev and Zdeněk Mlynář, *Conversations with Gorbachev on Perestroika, the Prague Spring, and the Crossroads of Socialism*, trans. George Shriver (New York: Columbia University Press, 2002), 31–32, 48; Geoffrey Hosking, *Russia and the Russians: A History* (Cambridge, MA: Belknap Press of Harvard University Press, 2001), 541–43, 545–47, 557; Roy Aleksandrovich Medvedev, *Lichnost' i epokha: Politicheskii portret L. I. Brezhneva* (Moscow: Novosti, 1991), 166–93; Nathaniel Davis, *A Long Walk to Church: A Contemporary History of Russian Orthodoxy*, 2nd ed. (Boulder CO: Westview Press, 2003), 47–53, 57–59; Dimitry V. Pospielovsky, *The Orthodox Church in the History of Russia* (Crestwood, NY: St. Vladimir's Seminary Press, 1998), 331–40, 341–44.

2. Mikhail Vital'evich Shkarovskii, *Russkaia Pravoslavnaia Tserkov' v XX veke* (Moscow: Veche, Lepta, 2010), 392; Dimitry V. Pospielovsky, *Russkaia pravoslavnaia tserkov' v XX veka* (Moscow: Respublika, 1995), 337–38.

3. Hosking, *Russia and the Russians*, 550; Dietrich Beyrau, *Intelligenz und Dissens: Die russischen Bildungsschichten in der Sowjetunion 1917–1985* (Göttingen: Vandenhoeck and Ruprecht, 1999), 312; Basile H. Kerblay, *Modern Soviet Society*, trans. Rupert Sawyer (London: Methuen, 1983), 149, 158, 161.

4. Zoia Afanas'evna Maslenikova, *Zhizn' ottsa Aleksandra Menia* (Moscow: Pristsel's, 1995), 218.

5. Aleksandr Men, *O sebe: Vospominaniia, interv'iu, besedy, pis'ma* (Moscow: Zhizn' s Bogom, 2007), 175.

6. Ibid., 176.

7. These details are taken from testimony of Pavel Men, interview by author, Moscow, July 2, 2013.

8. Sergei Sergeevich Bychkov, "KGB protiv sviashchennika Aleksandra Menia," in *Vestnik Khristianskogo Dvizheniia*, n.s., no. 196 (2010): 108–9.

9. Ibid., 109.

10. Men, *O sebe*, 177.

11. Letter of Fr. Alexandr Men to Zoia Maslenikova, February 13, 1970. Maslenikova includes the latter in her "Moi Dukhovnik," in *Zhizn' ottsa Aleksandra Menia*, 307.

12. Men, *O sebe*, 177nn1–2.

13. Ibid., 179.

14. Maslenikova, *Zhizn' ottsa Aleksandra Menia*, 221.

15. Ibid., 222.

16. Men, *O sebe*, 177–78. Beliaev-Bogorodskii is a Moscow neighborhood where several of Fr. Aleksandr's close friends lived. Fr. Sergei Zheludkov had become an associate of Fr. Aleksandr's who often visited his Novaia Derevnia parish. Fr. Aleksandr considered him one of the most knowledgeable and creative minds on the "most difficult and controversial issues facing the Orthodox Church in the Soviet Union," and he often relied on Fr. Sergei for counsel. See Fr. Aleksandr's reminiscences of him in *O sebe*, 181–92.

17. Vladislav Zubok, *Zhivago's Children: The Last Russian Intelligentsia* (Cambridge, MA: Belknap Press of Harvard University Press, 2009), 310–11.

18. Boris Morozov, *Evreiskaia emigratsiia v svete novykh dokumentov* (Tel Aviv: Ivrus, 1998), 199, 201. Among the 75,000 people who emigrated, 60,000 were scientists (Zvi Gitelman, "Soviet Political Culture: Insights from Jewish Emigres," *Soviet Studies* 24, no. 4 [October 1977]: 546).

19. Men, *O sebe*, 177. Aksenov-Meerson left the Soviet Union in 1972. Today he is head priest of the Church of Christ the Savior in the American Orthodox Autocephalous Church in New York and a professor at Georgetown University in Washington, DC.

20. See Glazov's memoir, Iurii Iakovlevich Glazov, *V kraiu ottsov (Khronika nedavnego proshlogo)* (Moscow: Istina i Zhizn', 1998); and Men, *O sebe*, 177n6.

21. Alexander I. Solzhenitsyn, *The Oak and the Calf: Sketches of Literary Life in the Soviet Union*, trans. Harry Willetts (New York: Harper and Row, 1979), 356.

22. Aleksandr Men, "Interv'iu na sluchai aresta," in *Kul'tura i dukhovnoe voskhozhdenie*, comp. R. I. Al'betkova and M. T. Rabotiaga (Moscow: Iskusstvo, 1992), 356–63.

23. Aleksandr Borisov, "Dukhovnyi realizm ottsa Aleksandra Menia," in *Tserkovnaia zhizn' XX veka: Protoierei Aleksandr Men' i ego dukhovnye nastavniki; Sbornik materialov Pervoi nauchnoi konferentsii "Menevskie chteniia" (9–11 Sentiabria 2006 g.)*, ed. M. V. Grigorenko (Sergiev Posad: Izdanie prikhoda Sergievskoi tserkvi v Semkhoze, 2007), 164.

24. Ray Bradbury and Isaac Asimov were among the most widely read of these writers in the Soviet Union. Bradbury's novels *Fahrenheit 451*, *The Martian Chronicles*, and *Dandelion Wine*, as well as his short stories, had a large following. As former Leningrader Mikhail Iossel has written, "In the last three decades of the Soviet Union's existence, Ray Bradbury was the country's most famous and widely read American writer. Only Isaac Asimov, Ernest Hemingway, and J. D. Salinger enjoyed comparable degrees of popularity. The big Soviet cities boasted dozens of Ray Bradbury fan clubs. It was impossible, as well as extremely uncool, for any au courant Soviet teen-ager or intelligentsia-bound young engineer not to have read and be able to discuss, at a party or in a dentist's chair, 'Fahrenheit 451,' 'Martian Chronicles,' or 'Dandelion Wine,' and the iconic stories 'A Sound of Thunder' and 'There Will Come Soft Rains.' For broad swaths of the Soviet readership, it was literary love at its purest, one unencumbered by any extraneous political motivations." Mikhail Iossel, "Reading Ray Bradbury in the U.S.S.R.," *New Yorker*, June 8, 2012, http://www.newyorker.com/books/page-turner/ray-bradbury-in-the-u-s-s-r.

25. Borisov, "Dukhovnyi realizm," 164.

26. Ibid., 164–65.

27. Judith Deutsch Kornblatt, *Doubly Chosen: Jewish Identity, the Soviet Intelligentsia, and the Russian Orthodox Church* (Madison: University of Wisconsin Press, 2004), 80–83. See also the study of Dmitrii Furman, the distinguished Russian sociologist of religion, who argues that the intelligentsia's interest in religion paralleled the nineteenth-century Russian intelligentsia's adoption of atheism: Dmitrii Efimovich Furman and Kimmo Kääriänen, "Veruiushchie, ateisti i prochie: Novoe issledovanie rossiiskoi religioznost," *Voprosy filosofii*, no. 1 (January 1997): 79–91.

28. These statements are drawn from comments printed on the back cover of Sergei Sergeevich Averintsev, *Religiia i literatura: Sbornik statei* (Ann Arbor, MI: Hermitage, 1981). The book contains articles published by Averintsev in *Voprosy literatury* from 1968 to 1973.

29. Averintsev is the author of several stimulating articles in the fifth volume of the *Philosophical Encyclopedia* of 1970, whose publication historian Dimitry Pospielovsky describes as a "miracle of sorts." Averintsev's contributions included certain seminal pieces on theology, the Eucharist, the liturgy, and Orthodoxy that asserted the historical reality and significance of Christ and drew a connection between religion and the origins of freedom, in direct contradiction to the state's ideology. Akademiia nauk SSSR, Institut filosofii, *Filosofskaia entsiklopediia*, ed. Fedor Vasil'evich Konstantinov (Moscow: Sovetskskaia entsiklopediia, 1970): 5:59, 61–63, 107–8, 158–59, 182–83, 189–91, 198–99, 199–202, 225–26, 382–83, 435, 466, 491–92, 506, 517–19, 580–82, 600–602, 611–12, 615, 620–22,

624; Dimitry V. Pospielovsky, *Soviet Studies on the Church and the Believer's Response to Atheism*, vol. 3, *A History of Soviet Atheism in Theory and Practice, and the Believer* (New York: St. Martin's Press, 1988), 99.

30. Sergei Averintsev, "Vmesto nekrologa," in *Pamiati protoireia Aleksandra Menia*, ed. T. V. Gromova (Moscow: Rudomino, 1991), 40–41.

31. Vladimir Il'ich Lenin, "O znachenii voinstvuiushchego materializma," in *Polnoe sobranie sochinenii*, 5th ed. (Moscow: Izd-vo Politicheskoi Literatury, 1964), 45:23–33.

32. Pospielovsky, *Soviet Studies*, 85.

33. Ibid., 87.

34. "Filosofskie i sotsialogicheskie problemy nauchno-tekhnicheskoi revoliutsii," *Voprosy filosofii*, no. 4 (1969), 3–15; Pospielovsky, *Soviet Studies*, 87.

35. Vladimir Il'ich Iliushenko, interview by author, Moscow, June 5, 2006.

36. Ibid.

37. Ibid.; Fr. Vladimir Arkhipov, interview by author, Novaia Derevnia, July 1, 2009.

38. Fr. Georgii Chistiakov, interview by author, Moscow, May 30, 2006.

39. See Vladimir Il'ich Iliushenko's discussion of Sergei Lezov's "Pobeda i porazhenie. Mertvaia forma tiagoteet nad myshleniem," *Nezavisimaia gazeta*, February 25, 1993, in *Otets Aleksandr Men': Zhizn', Smert', Bessmertie*, 2nd ed. (Moscow: VGBIL im. M. I. Rudomino, 2010), 148–70.

40. Sergei Lezov, "Est' li u russkogo pravoslaviia budushchee? (Ocherki sovremennogo pravoslavnogo liberalizma)," *Znamia*, no. 3 (March 1994): 175.

41. Ibid., 173–74, 180–81.

42. Maslenikova, "Moi Dukhovnik," 1970 (only the year is given), 307.

43. Maslenikova, *Zhizn' ottsa Aleksandra Menia*, 242–43.

44. Pavel Vol'fovich Men, interview by author, Moscow, July 2, 2013.

45. Ibid.

46. Ibid.

47. Fr. Viktor Grigorenko, interview by author, Semkhoz, July 4, 2013. Fr. Viktor is the nephew of Nataliia Fedorovna. He grew up in the nearby town of Khotkovo and often could be found at his grandmother's house in Semkhoz, the same house that Men's family occupied.

48. Ibid.; Mikhail Aleksandrovich Men, interview by author, Ivanovo, July 1, 2013.

49. In his later life, Mikhail Aleksandrovich followed a course very different from his father's. Currently, he is a political leader; in the summer of 2013, he served as governor-general of the Russian textile province of Ivanovo. Sitting in a spacious, well-furnished office on the top floor of the central administrative building in the city of Ivanovo, his appearance made an impression. In the months following the interview, the Russian government changed his position, elevating him to minister of construction and municipal economy in the central administration.

50. Mikhail Aleksandrovich Men, interview by author, Ivanovo, July 1, 2013.

51. Ibid.

52. Ibid.

53. Ibid.

54. Ibid.

55. Ibid.

56. Ibid.

Notes to Chapter Nine

1. Fr. Aleksandr delivered the fourth volume to his editor, Zoia Afanas'evna Maslenikova, in 1969. Zoia Afanas'evna Maslenikova, "Moi dukhovnik," January 4, 1970, in *Zhizn' ottsa Aleksandra Menia* (Moscow: Pristsel's, 1995), 307.

2. Sergei Sergeevich Averintsev, "Predislovie," in *Istoki religii*, vol. 1 of *Istoriia religii v semi tomakh: V poiskakh puti, istiny, i zhizni*, by Aleksandr Men (Moscow: Slovo, 1991), 6.

3. Sergei Zheludkov and Kronid Arkad'evich Liubarskii, "1982: Izdatel'stvo Zhizn' s Bogom," in *Khristianstvo i ateizm* (Brussels: Zhizn' s Bogom, 1982), 248.

4. Friedrich Engels, "On the History of Early Christianity," *About.com*, http://atheism.about.com/library/marxism/bl_EngelsEarlyChrist.htm; Vladimir Il'ich Lenin, "Socialism and Religion," in *Collected Works* (Moscow: Progress, 1965), 11:83–87.

5. Mikhail Aksenov-Meerson, "Zhizn' svoiu za drugu svoi," in *Pamiati protoiereia Aleksandra Menia*, ed. T. V. Gromova (Moscow: Rudomino, 1991), 118; see also Mark Tunick, "Hegel and the Consecrated State," in *Hegel on Religion and Politics*, ed. Angelica Nuzzo (Albany: State University of New York Press, 2013), 19–38.

6. Aksenov-Meerson, "Zhizn' svoiu," 118; Richard Kroner, "Introduction: Hegel's Philosophical Development," in *On Christianity: Early Theological Writings*, by George Wilhelm Friedrich Hegel, trans. T. M. Knox, with an introduction and fragments translated by Richard Kroner (New York: Harper, 1961), 11–15, 33–34, 51–55; Walter Kaufmann, *Hegel: A Reinterpretation* (Garden City, NY: Anchor Books, 1966), 36–37, 41–45.

7. George Wilhelm Friedrich Hegel, "The Positivity of the Christian Religion," and "The Spirit of Christianity and Its Fate," in *On Christianity*, 67–181 and 182–301.

8. Hegel, "Positivity," 180–81.

9. Ibid., 181.

10. Ibid.

11. Robert C. Tucker, *Philosophy and Myth in Karl Marx*, 3rd ed. (New Brunswick, NJ: Transaction Publishers, 2001), 39–41.

12. Hegel, quoted in Tucker, *Philosophy and Myth*, 40.

13. Aksenov-Meerson, "Zhizn' svoiu," 118.

14. Ibid. See also Kevin Thompson, "Hegel, the Political, and the Theological: The Question of Islam," in Nuzzo, *Hegel on Religion*, 99–117.

15. Aksenov-Meerson, "Zhizn' svoiu," 118.

16. Fr. Aleksandr cited the Orthodox writers who followed Solov'ev in making this attempt but whose works did not succeed in completing Solov'ev's dream. They included A. Vvedenskii, *Religioznoe soznanie iazychestva: Opyt filosofskoi istorii estestvennykh religii*, vol. 1 (Moscow: Universitetskaia tipografiia, 1902); A. Klintin, *Istoriia religii* (Odessa, 1911); and N. Bogoliubov, *Filosofiia religii*, vol. 1 (Kiev: Tip. Imp. universiteta sv. Vladimira, 1918). Fr. Aleksandr also mentioned Fr. A. El'chaninov, who together with Pavel Florensky and Sergei Bulgakov, completed a short work on the most important moments in the history of religion. See Aleksandr V. El'chaninov, Sergei Nikolaevich Bulgakov, Pavel Aleksandrovich Florenskii, and Vladimir Frantsevich Ern, *Istoriia religii: S prilozheniem stat'i S. N. Bulgakova, "O protivorechivosti sovremennogo bezreligioznogo mirovozzreniia"* (Moscow: Russkii put', 1911); Nikolai Berdiaev's later article, "Nauka o religii i khristianskaia apologetika," which Fr. Aleksandr commended for its contribution to the study of pre-Christian religious beliefs; and Men, *Istoki religii*, 10.

17. Men, *Istoki religii*, 10.

18. Ibid.

19. Ibid., 483; the passage here uses, but modifies, the translation of the text quoted by Yves Hamant, *Alexander Men: A Witness for Contemporary Russia (A Man for Our Times)*, trans. Steven Bingham, intro. Maxym Lysack (Torrance, CA: Oakwood, 1995), 163.

20. Men, *Istoki religii*, 11.

21. Andrei Alekseevich Eremin, *Otets Aleksandr Men': Pastyr' na rubezhe vekov*, 2nd ed. (Moscow: Carte Blanche, 2001), 453.

22. Ibid., 454.

23. Aleksandr Men, *Magizm i Edinobozhie: Religioznyi put' chelovechestva do epokhi velikikh Uchitelei*, vol. 2 of *Istoriia religii: V poiskakh puti, istiny, i zhizni* (Moscow: Slovo, 1992), 58.

24. Ibid., 9–10, 57–58, 405.

25. Eremin, *Otets Aleksandr Men'*, 455.

26. Men, *Magizm i Edinobozhie*, 58.

27. Ibid.

28. Fr. Aleksandr had read the theologian Karl Jaspers's (1883–1969) *The Origin and Goal of History* (1949). He followed Jaspers's periodization of history, particularly his emphasis on the emergence of great religious traditions in the first millennium BCE and the breakthrough against paganism these religious traditions generated. Jaspers raised important issues, most notably how a sense of the spiritual unity of all humankind began during this "axial period." The "axial period," as Jaspers pointed out, became the "common starting point from which the paradigms of thought in East and West had arisen." Karl Jaspers, *The Origin and Goal of History*, trans. Michael Bullock (New Haven, CT: Yale University Press, 1953); Aleksandr Men, "K problematike 'osevogo vremeni' (nadkonfessional'naia i khristosentricheskaia traktovki)," *Narody Azii i Afriki*, no. 1 (1990): 68–77.

29. Aleksandr Men, *U vrat molchaniia*, vol. 3 of *Istoriia religii: V poiskakh puti, istiny, i zhizni* (Moscow: Slovo, 1991), 175. Men thought it important that the followers of Christianity have knowledge of Buddhism and Confucianism, given their cultural richness and world prominence.

30. Men, *U vrat molchaniia*, 180.

31. Ibid., 153–54, 163, 180.

32. Aleksandr Men, *Dionis, Logos, Sud'ba: Grecheskaia religiia i filosofiia ot epokhi kolonozatsii do Aleksandra*, vol. 4 of *Istoriia religii: V poiskakh puti, istiny, i zhizni* (Moscow: Slovo, 1991), 7.

33. Ibid., 67–68, 78–85, 116–18, 212–14, 218–20.

34. Ibid., 22–23, 25–27, 28–30, 231–32.

35. Ibid., 162.

36. A. Harnack, "Vzgliad na Sokrata tserkovnykh pisatelei pervykh vekov," quoted by Men, *Dionis, Logos, Sud'ba*, 162.

37. Eremin, *Otets Aleksandr Men'*, 471.

38. Aleksandr Men, *Vestniki tsarstva Bozhiia: Bibleiskie proroki ot Amosa do Restavratsii (VIII– IV vv. do n.e.)*, vol. 5 of *Istoriia religii: V poiskakh puti, istiny, i zhizni* (Moscow: Slovo, 1992), 11. As Fr. Aleksandr described them, the prophets had their own individual style: "God's voice was an internal voice, crying out in the depths of the soul, where, in the words of Meister Eckhart, the human being finds God" (12).

39. Ibid., 22, 284–93.

40. Ibid., 319.

41. Aleksandr Men', *Na poroge Novogo Zaveta: Ot epokhi Aleksandra Makedonskogo do propovedi Ioanna Krestitelia*, vol. 6 of *Istoriia religii: V poiskakh puti, istiny, i zhizni* (Moscow: Slovo, 1993).

42. Eremin, *Otets Aleksandr Men'*, 470.

43. Fr. Aleksandr completed his writing of the sixth volume in 1979, delivering it to Maslenikova in this year. It took her three years to complete the editing, possibly because of illness. See Maslenikova, "Moi dukhovnik," January 4, 1979, 423–25.

44. The volume opens with a vast panorama of ancient Roman culture in which Fr. Aleksandr examines the origins of Roman law, the influence of Greek thought and Hellenistic culture, the Stoics, and the diverse religious models present in the Roman world. He traces the appearance of Buddhist missionaries and Eastern sects and Roman efforts to deal with a multiconfessional political and religious order.

45. Men, *Na poroge Novogo Zaveta*, 272–75.

46. Ibid., 454.

47. According to Fr. Aleksandr, no one among the ancient thinkers spoke about this in such a way as Philo. Others had reverence and the thirst to penetrate into the mystery of existence, but "only the metaphysician, inspired by the word of God, saw in love the very essence of the understanding of God" (Eremin, *Otets Aleksandr Men'*, 454–55).

48. Ibid., 477–79. Fr. Aleksandr differed from Philo in some respects, particularly on the significance of matter. As Eremin points out, Philo of Alexandria held the human body as the ideal, whereas the ideal for Fr. Aleksandr centered on the transformation of matter.

49. Men, *Na poroge Novogo Zaveta*, 476–81.

50. Eremin, *Otets Aleksandr Men'*, 480.

51. Pavel Vol'fovich Men, interview by author, Moscow, June 2, 2006.

52. Sergei Sergeevich Bychkov, "Pravoslavnyi prikhod," in *Khronika neraskrytogo ubiistva* (Moscow: Russkoe reklamnoe izdatel'stvo, 1996), 88.

53. Eremin, *Otets Aleksandr Men'*, 403; A. Belavin, "Predislovie," in *Mirovaia dukhovnaia kul'tura, khristianstvo, tserkov': Lektsii i besedy*, by Aleksandr Men, ed. Anastasiia Andreeva et al., 2nd ed. (Moscow: Fond imeni Aleksandra Menia, 1997), 7.

54. Georgii P. Fedotov, "Berdyaev the Thinker," *Chebucto Community Net*, http://www.chebucto.ns.ca/Philosophy/Sui-Generis/Berdyaev/essays/fedotov.htm.

55. Nikolai A Berdiaev, *Filosofiia svobody: Smysl tvorchestva; Opyt opravdaniia cheloveka* (1911; repr., Moscow: Pravda, 1989), 37, 95–96, 194–95, 255–57, 428.

56. Berdiaev abhorred the objectification of nature, as well as of human beings, which turned them into passive objects for profit or human pleasure. He strongly objected to all forms of slavery, and any attempts to delimit the "freedom of the creative act" (Ibid., 37, 95–96). Fr. Aleksandr, too, understood such acts as sin, because they distorted the relationship between human beings and God.

57. Men, *Magizm i Edinobozhie*, quoted by Artūras Lukaševičius, "A Critical Evaluation of Fr. Aleksandr Vladimirovich Men's Approach to the Religions of the World, in the Light of the Declaration 'Dominus Iesus'" (PhD diss., Open University, Maryvale Institute, 2006), 65.

58. Aleksandr Men, *O sebe: Vospominaniia, interv'iu, besedy, pis'ma* (Moscow: Zhizn' s Bogom, 2007), 214; Men, "K problematike," 282–83; Christopher H. Dawson, *Progress and Religion: An Historical Enquiry* (Westport, CT: Greenwood Press, 1970). Fr. Aleksandr cites the English edition of *Progress and Religion*, published in London in 1960.

59. Fr. Aleksandr defined his basic approach at the beginning of *Istoki religii*, 13–14.

60. Dawson, *Progress and Religion*, 249.

61. Men, *Istoki religii*, 32.

62. Ibid., 22, 74. Men's references are specifically to Anglican bishop John A. T. Robinson, author of *Honest to God* (1963), and German theologian Rudolf Bultmann, author of *Jesus Christ and Mythology* (1958), who became major proponents of this line of thought.

63. Ibid., 13.

64. Pierre Teilhard de Chardin, *The Human Phenomenon*, trans. Sarah Appleton-Weber, with a foreword by Brian Swimme (Brighton, UK: Sussex Academic Press, 1999). This new edition and translation corrects many errors in the older English translation from the French, in 1959, including the title, earlier rendered as *Phenomenon of Man*. The Russian translation, which Men read, is P'er Teiiar de Sharden, *Fenomen cheloveka*, trans. N. A. Sadovskii (Moscow: Progress, 1965). Teilhard's *Le phénomène humain* was originally published in 1955.

65. Eremin, *Otets Aleksandr Men'*, 451–52; see also George L. Kline's comments on the publication of Teilhard's book in Russian, "Religious Ferment among Soviet Intellectuals," in *Religion and the Soviet State: A Dilemma of Power*, ed. Max Haywood and William C. Fletcher (New York: Praeger, 1969), 64n28.

66. Men, *Istoki religii*, 228–29. In addition to *The Human Phenomenon*, Fr. Aleksandr was familiar with Teilhard's *Hymne de l'Univers* (1961).

67. Men, "O Teiiare De Shardene," appendix 10, in *Istoki religii*, 225–42; Aleksandr Men, *Ot rabstva k svobode: Lektsii po Vetkhomu Zavetu* (Moscow: Zhizn' s Bogom, 2008), 42; Aleksandr Men, "Interv'iu na sluchai aresta," in *Kul'tura i dukhovnoe voskhozhdenie*, comp. R. I. Al'betkova and M. T. Rabotiaga (Moscow: Iskusstvo, 1992), 360. Fr. Aleksandr in his letter to Sister Ioanna, written in 1976, cites his interest in Teilhard de Chardin, and recommends him to her. Men, *Umnoe nebo: Perepiska protoiereia Aleksandra Menia s monakhinei Ioannoi (Iu. N. Reitlinger)* (Moscow: Fond imeni Aleksandra Menia, 2006), 120. Fr. Aleksandr disagreed with Teilhard on several issues, most especially in the Jesuit scientist's and philosopher's views on the origins of evil.

68. Men, "O Teiiare De Shardene," 226, 230–31, 242.

69. Teilhard de Chardin, *Human Phenomenon*, 14–15.

70. Fr. Aleksandr specifically mentioned such current authors as "Albert Camus, Jean-Paul Sartre and others, who spoke about the terrible absurdity of existence"; understandably so, Fr. Aleksandr said, when human beings are "surrounded by something menacing, inhuman, meaningless, absurd, something which cannot be trusted—a cold and lifeless world." Alexander Men, "Christianity for the Twenty-First Century," in *Christianity for the Twenty-First Century: The Life and Work of Alexander Men*, ed. Elizabeth Roberts and Ann Shukman (London: SCM Press, 1996), 182; Eremin, *Otets Aleksandr Men'*, 452.

71. Men, "O Teiiare De Shardene," 242.

72. Men, *Istoki religii*, 171.

73. "Science . . . steadily solves the mysteries of the universe and extends man's power over nature, leaving no room for religious inventions about supernatural forces." *Program of the Communist Party, Twenty-Second Party Congress*, 1961, quoted by April French, "Spiritual Dissident: The Writings of Father Aleksandr Men as Dissent from Soviet Ideology" (MA thesis, Regent College, Vancouver, BC, 2011), 100n97.

74. Men, *Istoki religii*, 111.

75. See Mikhail Iosifovich Shakhnovich, *Lenin i problemy ateizma: Kritika religii v trudakh V. I. Lenina* (Moscow: Izd-vo Akademiia Nauk SSSR, 1961), 184–211.

76. Men, *Istoki religii*, 171.

77. Ibid.

78. Ibid., 172.

79. Ibid., 176–77.

80. Fr. Aleksandr' observations share similarities with John Polkinghorne's views about the relationships between science and religion and the importance of dialogue between individuals in both fields (John Polkinghorne, "Science and Theology in Dialogue," lecture, international conference on "Alexander Men'—His Life and Legacy," Moffat, Scotland, September 16, 2012).

81. V. P. Zubov, S. M. Grambakh, V. V. Danilevskii, and Iu. Ia. Kogan, "Nauka i tekhnika," in *Ocherki istorii SSSR: Period feodalizma, Rossii vo vtoroi polovine XVIII v.*, ed. A. I. Baranovich, B. B. Kafengauz et al. (Moscow: Izd-vo Akademii nauk SSSR, 1956), 464, also 23, 455–56, 462–63, 469, 506–7.

82. I. S. Bak, "M. V. Lomonosov v bor'be za razvitie proizvoditel'nykh sil Rossii," in *Istoriia russkoi ekonomicheskoi mysli*, vol. 1, *Epokha feodalizma*, pt. 1, *IX–XVIII vv.*, ed. A. I. Pashkov (Moscow: Gosudarstvennoe izd-vo politicheskoi literatury, 1955), 403.

83. Men, *Istoki religii*, 181.

84. Ibid.

85. Artūras Lukaševičius, "Critical Evaluation," 50, and *Aleksandr Men's Approach to the World's Religions: A Critical Evaluation in Light of the Declaration Dominus Iesus* (Saarbrücken: VDM Verlag Dr. Müller, 2009), 154.

86. Men, *Istoki religii*, 17.

87. Hamant, *Alexander Men*, 165.

88. Men, *Dionis, Logos, Sud'ba*, 67.

89. Ibid.

90. Ibid. Fr. Aleksandr cited Albert Einstein, Niels Bohr, and Bertrand Russell. He referenced for these observations the study of Iu. Shreider, "Nauka—istochnik znanii i sueverii," *Novyi mir*, no. 10 (1969): 207–26.

91. Thomas Henry Huxley, "We Are All Scientists," *Darwiniana* (1863), excerpted in *A Treasury of Science*, 2nd ed., ed. Harlow Shapley, Samuel Rapport, and Helen Wright with an introduction by Harlow Shapley (New York: Harper, 1946), 15.

92. See, for example, Aleksandr Men, *Syn chelovecheskii*, 4th ed. (Moscow: Slovo, 1992), 63, 69, 70, 73, 96, 110, 131. I owe this observation to Professor John Polkinghorne's lecture, "Science and Theology."

93. Walter Isaacson, *Einstein: His Life and Universe* (New York: Simon and Schuster, 2007), 20. Fr. Aleksandr appreciated the contributions of Charles Darwin, whose *Origin of Species*, uncovered the "endless complexity" of natural processes, and whose theory of evolution "did not undermine religion, but enriched it" (Men, *Istoki religii*, 104).

94. Men, *Istoki religii*, 177.

95. Sergei Borisovich Filatov, "Russkaia pravoslavnaia tserkov' i politicheskaia elita," in *Religiia i politika v postkommunisticheskoi Rossii*, ed. L. N. Mitrokhin (Moscow: Institut filosofii RAN, 1994), 99–118; Wallace L. Daniel, *The Orthodox Church and Civil Society in Russia* (College Station, TX: Texas A&M University Press, 2006), 33–35.

96. See Ann Shukman's introductory comments to Alexander Men, "A Credo for Today's Christian," in Roberts and Shukman, *Christianity*, 68. Fr. Aleksandr's perspectives on the relationship between church and state will be treated in more detail later in this study.

97. Men, "Credo for Today's Christian," 68–69.

98. Men, "Interv'iu na sluchai aresta," 360.

99. Men, "Credo for Today's Christian," 69.

100. Men, *Istoki religii*, 178.

101. Aleksandr Men, "Faith and Its Enemies," in Roberts and Shukman, *Christianity*, 56–57.

102. Men, *Istoki religii*, 178.

103. Ibid.

104. Ibid., 58.

105. Sergei Bychkov, quoted by Lukaševičius, "Critical Evaluation," 50.

106. Men, *Istoki religii*, 11.

107. Ibid., 13.

108. Ibid., 177.

109. Ibid., 90. Fr. Aleksandr makes a similar point about the creative process later in this volume, quoting the Russian poet Gavriil Derzhavin (*Istoki religii*, 104).

110. Men, "Faith and Its Enemies," 64.

111. Fr. Georgii Chistiakov, interview by author, Moscow, May 30, 2006.

112. Ibid.

113. Iurii Tabak, interview by author, Moscow, October 14, 2008.

114. Ibid.; Andrei Cherniak, interview by author, Moscow, May 24, 2007.

115. Nadezhda Mandelstam is the author of two superb books on the Russian intelligentsia and the Soviet suppression of Russia's cultural heritage: *Hope against Hope: A Memoir*, trans. Max Hayward, intro. Clarence Brown (New York: Atheneum, 1976) and *Hope Abandoned*, trans. Max Hayward (New York: Atheneum, 1974). "She was very close to Fr. Aleksandr," said a friend who knew both of them well. "She was impressed with his personality, the depth of his knowledge of Russian literature, his humor, and his open-mindedness. They spent a lot of time together at his house and sometimes at her place in Moscow" (Iurii Tabak, interview by author, Moscow, October 19, 2008).

116. Ludmila Evgen'evna Ulitskaia, *Sviashchennyi musor: Rasskazy, esse* (Moscow: Astrel', 2012), 94–95.

117. Ibid., 96.

118. See Ulitskaia's full account and what Fr. Aleksandr meant to her; ibid., 94–100.

119. On Anatolii Krasnov-Levitin, see Jane Ellis, *The Russian Orthodox Church: A Contemporary History* (New York: Routledge, 1986), 290–91.

120. "Conversation with Anatolii Krasnov-Levitin," interview by Michael Bourdeaux. The transcript of the interview is located in the Keston Archive, Anatolii Krasnov-Levitin file, SU/Ort 2/file 3.

121. Michael Aksenov-Meerson, "The Dissident Movement and *Samizdat*," in *The Political, Social, and Religious Thought of Russian "Samizdat": An Anthology*, ed. Michael Aksenov-Meerson and Boris Shragin, trans. Nicholas Lupinin (Belmont, MA: Nordland, 1977), 40n43. I have made minor grammatical corrections to the quotation.

122. Ibid., 42n47.

123. Ibid., 42–43.

124. Eremin, *Otets Aleksandr Men'*, 480.

125. On these various editions, see the bibliography of Fr. Aleksandr Men's writings, in *Dvadtsat' let bez ottsa Aleksandra, i s nim*, ed. Evgenii Borisovich Rashkovskii, with a foreword by Elena Iur'evna Genieva (Moscow: Rudomino, 2010), 328, 333, 335, 337, 339. From 2000 to 2003, the Aleksandr Men Foundation in Moscow republished the entire six-volume work.

126. Editorial note to Aleksandr Men, "K problematike," 77.

127. Andrei Kuraev, "Somnitel'noe pravoslavie ottsa," *Nezavisimaia gazeta*, March 18, 1993, 5.

Notes to Chapter Ten

1. Aleksandr Men, letter to Zoia Afanas'evna Maslenikova, November 1,1976, in *Zhizn' ottsa Aleksandra Menia*, by Zoia Afanas'evna Maslenikova (Moscow: Pristsel's, 1995), 375–76.

2. Aleksandr Men, letter to Iuliia Nikolaevna Reitlinger, January–February 1979, in *O sebe: Vospominaniia, interv'iu, besedy, pis'ma* (Moscow: Zhizn' s Bogom, 2007), 219.

3. Ibid. Fr. Aleksandr's correspondence with Sister Ioanna has been published as *Umnoe nebo: Perepiska protoiereia Aleksandra Menia s monakhinei Ioannoi (Iu. N. Reitlinger)* (Moscow: Fond im. Aleksandra Menia, 2006).

4. Pavel Vol'fovich Men, interview by author, Moscow, July 3, 2013.

5. Zoia Afanas'evna Maslenikova, "Moi dukhovnik," June 16, 1978, in Maslenikova, *Zhizn' ottsa Aleksandra Menia*, 367, and July 19, 1978, 368. Also Maslenikova, *Zhizn' ottsa Aleksandra Menia*, 247.

6. These biographical facts about Fr. S. Sredi are drawn from Maslenikova, *Zhizn' ottsa Aleksandra Menia*, 247. Fr. Stefan Sredi served as senior priest at Novaia Derevnia until March 1983, when he was transferred to the city of Krasnogorsk. See also Men, *O sebe*, 239n1.

7. Maslenikova, *Zhizn' ottsa Aleksandra Menia*, 247.

8. Andrei Alekseevich Eremin, *Otets Aleksandr Men': Pastyr' na rubezhe vekov*, 2nd ed. (Moscow: Carte Blanche, 2001), 79.

9. See for example, Iurii Iakovlevich Glazov, *V kraiu ottsov: Khronika nedavnego proshlogo* (Moscow: Istina i Zhizn', 1998), 54–55, 68, 174–75.

10. In 1978, the journal *Nauka i religii* remained prominent and extremely visible; its circulation of 440,000 reached a wide reading public. The Communist youth organization, the *Znanie* (Knowledge) Society, designed to popularize scientific information, sponsored lectures attended by over 1.25 billion people in 1983. Created in 1947 to support public lectures, broadcasts, television productions, and "people's universities," the society was originally called the All-Union Society for the Dissemination of Political and Scientific Knowledge. In 1962, the association changed its name to the *Znanie* Society; it dealt with a large range of topics, but antireligious education comprised a substantial part of its mission and programming. See Paul D. Steeves, "Znanie Society," in *The Modern Encyclopedia of Russian and Soviet History*, ed. Joseph L. Wieczynski (Gulf Breeze, FL: Academic International Press, 1987), 46:114–16.

11. Fr. Aleksandr Men, "Otvet na pros'bu Z. A. Maslenikovoi o svoem puti k Bogu, o svoem dukhovnom opyte," in Men, *O sebe*, 226; Aleksandr Men, "Interv'iu na sluchai aresta," in Aleksandr Men, *Kul'tura i dukhovnoe voskhozhdenie*, comp. R. I. Al'betkova and M. T. Rabotiaga (Moscow: Iskusstvo, 1992), 359; Men, *O sebe*, 30, 32; Aleksandr Men, "Pis'mo k E. N.," in *"AEQUINOX": Sbornik pamiati o. Aleksandra Menia*, ed. I. G. Vishnevetskii and E. G. Rabinovich (Moscow: Carte Blanche, 1991), 185, and "O vremeni i o sebe," in *Khronika neraskrytogo ubiistva*, by Sergei Bychkov (Moscow: Russkoe reklamnoe izdatel'stvo, 1996), 167.

12. Aleksandr Men, "Vospominaniia o studencheskikh godakh," in Bychkov, *Khronika neraskrytogo ubiistva*, 144.

13. These mentors included Boris Aleksandrovich Vasil'ev and Tat'iana Ivanovna Kupriianova. Men, *O sebe*, 27; Tat'iana Ivanovna Kupriianova, "Avtobiograficheskie zapiski," in *Maroseika*:

Zhizneopisanie ottsa Sergiia Mecheva: Pis'ma, propovedi, vospominaniia o nem, comp. Sergei S. Bychkov (Moscow: Martis, Sam and Sam, 2001), 443; Pavel Vol'fovich Men, "Ierei Boris Vasil'ev. Ego zhizn', sluzhenie i tvorchestvo," in *Tserkovnaia zhizn' XX veka: Protoierei Aleksandr Men' i ego dukhovnye nastavniki; Sbornik materialov Pervoi nauchnoi konferentsii "Menevskie chenteniia" (9–11 Sentiabria 2006 g.)*, ed. M. V. Grigorenko (Sergiev Posad: Izdanie prikhoda Sergievskoi tserkvi v Semkhoze, 2007), 149–55.

14. Eremin, *Otets Aleksandr Men'*, 25; see also Sergei Sergeevich Bychkov's comparision of Men to the Mechevs, in Bychkov, *Khronika neraskrytogo ubiistva*, 61–62.

15. Biographical details here and in the next paragraphs are drawn from Bychkov, *Maroseika*; Pavel Aleksandrovich Florenskii, "Otets Aleksei Mechev," in *Sochineniia v chetyrekh tomakh*, comp. and ed. Igumen Andronikov (A. S. Trubachev), P. V. Florenskii, and M. S. Trubachev (Moscow: Mysl', 1996), 2:621–27; and Nikita A. Struve, ed., *Otets Aleksei Mechev: Vospominaniia S. Durylina, o. Vladimira, Episkopa Arseniia, A. Iarmolovich, i dr. Pis'ma, Propovedi, Nadgrobnoe slovo o sebe samom* (Paris: YMCA-Press, 1970).

16. Florenskii, "Otets Aleksei Mechev," 623.

17. Ibid.

18. Fr. Aleksei treated her with deep affection; she had been and remained the "love of his life," and his letters to her are filled with tenderness. See *Zhizneopisanie Moskovskogo startsa ottsa Alekseia Mecheva*, comp. Monakhiniia Iulianiia, 2nd. ed. (Moscow: Russkii Khronograf, 1999), 23–24.

19. Bychkov, *Maroseika*, 34.

20. Florenskii, "Otets Aleksei Mechev," 623–24; Bychkov, *Maroseika*, 34.

21. He also learned from his experience of serving the Divine Liturgy with Saint John of Kronstadt, whose approach he incorporated and who had shown him what it meant to "pray with the love of God burning in me." Bychkov, *Maroseika*, 34–35.

22. Florenskii, "Otets Aleksei Mechev," 624.

23. Ibid., 625.

24. Bishop Arsenii Zhadonovskii, quoted in *Zhizneopisanie Moskovskogo startsa*, 58.

25. Bychkov, *Maroseika*, 36–37.

26. Ibid., 38. "Pis'ma S. A. Mecheva iz Italii," in Bychkov, *Maroseika*, 200, 201, 202. Sergei Alekseevich had a superb education that included several fields of study. He entered Moscow University, where he enrolled in the medical faculty, although he did not remain there for long, soon transferring to the literature-philological faculty. After volunteering as a male nurse in World War I and serving on the Russian front in Poland (where he met and fell in love with a Russian Sister of Mercy, Evfrosiniia Nikolaevna Shaforostova, whom he later married), he returned to the university. He completed his studies in the literature-philological faculty in 1917, concentrating on ancient Russian literature, in which he had a great interest. But his education did not end there; his work in the university also focused on the psychology of creativity, the history of the Russian Orthodox Church, to which he devoted himself after his first degree, and then the spiritual fathers of the ancient Eastern Church. In the student theological circle he joined at the university, he applied himself to study of the sacred writings of his own country. He had not yet made the decision to become a priest, as his father had long wished, but he had come to know in depth the theological and cultural history of Russia and to place that history in a larger setting (Bychkov, *Maroseika*, 41–43; *Zhizneopisanie Moskovskogo startsa*, 75–76).

According to Bychkov's account, Sergei Alekseevich met Evfrosiniia Nikolaevna in late 1914 or early 1915. She recalled that their first meeting took place in the middle of the night, when a German aircraft dropped a bomb on the square in front of the house where she and other Russian Sisters of Mercy were sleeping. An alarm sounded, causing her and other medical personnel to flee; she first encountered Sergei Alekseevich during this event. Subsequently, they became close friends and married in 1918, in a wedding ceremony conducted by Fr. Aleksei.

27. See Florenskii, "Otets Aleksei Mechev," 626. See the definition and discussion of the elder in Russian Orthodoxy, in chapter 4 (and n31) of this study.

Fr. Nektarii, who died in 1928, is recognized as the "last Elder of Optina Pustyn." The Bolsheviks closed the monastery in 1923, and, as Florensky recounts, Fr. Nektarii was incarcerated in the Kozel'skii prison. After his release, he settled in the nearby village of Plokhino, then the village of Kholmishcha; see Florenskii, "Otets Aleksei Mechev," 800n5.

28. Sergei Durylin, quoted in *"Pastyr' dobryi": Zhizn' i trudy moskovskogo startsa protoiereia Alekseia Mecheva,* comp. Sergei Fomin, 2nd ed. (Moscow: Serda-Press, 2000), 6.

29. Bychkov, *Maroseika,* 37.

30. Ibid., 45.

31. Nikolai Berdiaev, *Dream and Reality: An Essay in Autobiography* (New York: Macmillan, 1951), 204.

32. Fr. Aleksei, Florensky points out, "taught with his life"; in the Maroseiskaia Obshchina [Community], "life was built around spiritual experience." Florenskii, "Otets Aleksei Mechev," 626–27.

33. Pavel Aleksandrovich Florenskii, "Rassuzhdenie na sluchai konchiny ottsa Alekseia Mecheva," in *Sochineniia,* 2:616.

34. Ibid., 617.

35. Ibid., 612–13. Fr. Aleksei believed that the listings of regulations, taken as a whole, spoke about love and compassion; according to Florensky, his opponents, who wanted to substitute a singular regulation, failed to understand the meaning of love.

36. *Zhizneopisanie Moskovskogo startsa,* 87.

37. Bychkov, *Maroseika,* 24–26. After his arrest in 1929, Fr. Sergei was exiled and spent the next four years in Ust-Sysolsk (Sykyvkar), in the northwestern Komi Republic. In 1934, he was again arrested and spent the next seven years in prison in Vologda. The Soviet government transferred him to a Iaroslavl' prison after the German invasion in June 1941, where he was killed.

38. Fomin, *Pastyr' dobryi,* 266.

39. Vladimir Arkhipov, interview by author, Novaia Derevnia, July 1, 2009; Vladimir Arkhipov, *Slovo ob ottse Aleksandre: Stat'i* (Moscow: Blagovest, 2008), 37, 39, 89.

40. Arkhipov, *Slovo ob ottse Aleksandre,* 37.

41. The activities of the "circles" are described in Bychkov, *Maroseika,* 49–51; Florenskii, "Otets Aleksei Mechev," 626–27. Sergei Nikolaevich Durylin, born in 1877 in Moscow, graduated from the Moscow Archeological Institute but in 1918 left his profession to become a priest. He served in the parish of Fr. Aleksei Mechev; see Struve, *Otets Aleksei Mechev,* 14.

42. Florenskii, "Otets Aleksei Mechev," 626. Fr. Sergei knew well that the religious traditions of Orthodoxy and the connections to Russian culture were being lost. The members of the brotherhood had little knowledge of such traditions and memories, and his teachings aimed to fill that gap. He also led excursions of students to the religious sites related to the country's cultural memory, experiences that forged close bonds between the people who traveled with him, as well as captured for them Russia's history. On one occasion, in 1924, for example, Fr. Sergei conducted an excursion to the Nikolo-Ugreshskii Monastery, in the Moscow region. A member of the group, a young woman who had known other participants only casually before, describes her experience of developing new friendships:

"It was especially joyous to go together on the train, and to see among us Fr. Sergii [Sergei]—animated, in conversation first with one, then with another group. When we left the train and walked across the field to the monastery, the sisters began to sing. Fr. Sergii [Sergei] joined in, and such a joy it was to be in the midst of these close friends—lightly breathing the air, singing harmoniously. . . . Our large company settled in for the night, and, early in the morning the next day, Fr. Sergii [Sergei] heard confessions and gave us the possibility of receiving communion. After these days, I significantly felt myself having closer connections with everyone. My understanding of 'family' took on much greater reality" (Anonymous student, quoted in Bychkov, *Maroseika,* 99).

43. Aleksandr Men, letters to Raisa Il'inichna Kolesinkova, summer 1985, and letter to Iuliia Nikolaevna Reitlinger, September 1981, in Vladimir Iliushenko, *Otets Aleksandr Men': Zhizn', Smert', Bessmertie,* 2nd ed. (Moscow: VGBIL im. M. I. Rudomino, 2010), 471–72, 477, 589; Alexander Men,

An Inner Step toward God: Writings and Teachings on Prayer, ed. and intro. April French, trans. Christa Belyaeva (Brewster, MA: Paraclete Press, 2014), 13–14, 54, 57, 67–68.

44. *Zhizneopisanie Moskovskogo startsa*, 87.

45. Ibid.; Fomin, *Pastyr' dobryi*, 6; *Moskovskii batiushka: Vospominaniia ob o. Aleksee Mecheve* (Moscow: Izdanie Moskovskogo Sviato-Danilova Monastyria, 1994), 16; Florenskii, "Otets Aleksei Mechev," 627. Berdiaev notes that during the Russian Civil War even soldiers in the Red Army sometimes visited Fr. Aleksei at night; Berdiaev, *Dream and Reality*, 204.

46. The Mechevs' reputation spread also among students at Moscow University, who came in large numbers, some perhaps from curiosity, others seeking community and a direction for their lives during these chaotic times. A student from the philosophy section recalls the courses she took with Viacheslav Ivanov and others on the philosophy faculty and how she became deeply engaged in them. After a year or so, perhaps through such courses, she and others "felt the insufficiency of philosophy, and all of us came to the realization that it was necessary to study the experiences of the sacred fathers and that only here would we find stability, the eternal, and the vitally essential" (Elena Vladimirovna Apushkina, "Zhizn', ozarennaia svetom," in Bychkov, *Maroseika*, 360).

47. Florenskii, "Otets Aleksei Mechev," 625.

48. Yves Hamant, interview by author, Moscow, January 19, 2010.

49. Ibid. The importance of connecting the secular and the sacred worlds is a major theme of Men's lecture, "Khristianstvo i tvorchestvo," in *Radostnaia vest': Lektsy*, ed. M. V. Sergeeva (Moscow: Vita-Tsentr, 1992), 256–63; this subject is also treated by Fr. Aleksandr in his discussion of his own spiritual experiences, "O. Aleksandr pro svoi dukhovnyi opyt," in Maslenikova, *Zhizn' ottsa Aleksandra Menia*, 447–51.

50. *Zhizneopisanie Moskovskogo startsa*, 100.

51. Ibid., 99–100.

52. Eremin, *Otets Aleksandr Men'*, 49.

53. Metropolitan Iuvenalii, "Slovo, proiznesennoe pered otpevaniem protoiereia Aleksandra Menia v sele Novaia Derevnia, 11 Sentiabria 1990 goda," in *Pamiati protoiereia Aleksandra Menia*, ed. T. V. Gromova (Moscow: Rudomino, 1991), 20–21; Fr. Aleksandr Borisov, interview by author, Moscow, May 31, 2006; Eremin, *Otets Aleksandr Men'*, 60, 158.

54. Anonymous, in Fomin, *Pastyr' dobryi*, 266; Florenskii, "Otets Aleksei Mechev," 624.

55. Florenskii, "Otets Aleksei Mechev," 625.

56. Arkhipov, *Slovo ob ottse Aleksandre*, 149–50. In her excellent study of religious policy in Russia, Geraldine Fagan challenges the view that Russia upholds a narrow interpretation of religiosity and that this narrowness is an inherent part of Russia's heritage. Despite the public statements about nationhood and Orthodoxy as identical, fostered by Russian governments from Tsar Nicholas I and subsequent political leaders, religious unity is far from the reality. See Geraldine Fagan, *Believing in Russia: Religious Policy after Communism* (New York: Routledge, 2013). Fr. Aleksandr had recognized and appreciated this heterodoxical religious context from his student years in Irkutsk, and this appreciation characterized his priesthood.

57. Aleksandr Borisov, "Dukhovnyi realizm ottsa Aleksandra Menia," in Grigorenko, *Tserkovnaia zhizn'*, 166–67.

58. Ibid., 167.

59. Aleksandr Men, *Magizm i Edinobozhie: Religioznyi put' chelovechestva do epokhi velikikh Uchitelei*, vol. 2 of *Istoriia religii: V poiskakh puti, istiny, i zhizni* (Moscow: Slovo, 1991), 56–58.

60. Fr. Aleksandr Men, *Byt' khristianinom: Interv'iu i posledniaia lektsiia* (Moscow: Anno Domini, 1994), 22; Borisov, "Dukhovnyi realizm," 166.

61. Yves Hamant, interview by author, Moscow, January 19, 2010.

62. Aleksandr Men, "Lichnost' Iisusa Khrista," in *Kniga Nadezhdy: Lektsii o Biblii* (Moscow: Zhizn' s Bogom, 2011), 262–63.

63. Florenskii, "Otets Aleksei Mechev," 627.

64. Fr. Aleksandr also rejected the materialistic approach to life that had dominated Russian thought during much of the last century: "We are given faith not as an opiate, but as a life force, the power of struggle and of hope, not as our anesthetic," he wrote. "If we don't prove to Marx that for

us religion is not an opiate, we'll be bad Christians." Alexander Men, "There Must Be Differences among You," in *About Christ and the Church*, trans. Alexis Vinogradov (Torrance, CA: Oakwood, 1996), 25–40.

65. Alexander Men, "The Authority of the Church," in *About Christ*, 84, 85–86, and "A Conversation about Redemption," ibid., 91.

66. Aleksandr Men, "Nadlezhit byt' raznomysliiu," in *O Khriste i tserkvi: Besedy i lektsii* (Moscow: Khram sviatykh bessrebrenikov Kosmy i Damiana v Shubine, 2002), 58. For an English language translation of Fr. Aleksandr's talk, see Men, "There Must Be Differences," 25–40.

67. Alexander Men, "The Church and History," in *About Christ*, 16–17; "Nadlezhit byt' raznomysliiu," in *Mirovaia dukhovnaia kul'tura, Khristianstvo, Tserkov': Lektsii i besedy*, 2nd ed., ed. Anastasiia Andreeva et al, comp. Aleksandr Belavin, 2nd ed. (Moscow: Fond imeni Aleksandra Menia, 1997), 596-607; and, in the same volume, "Zhizn' v Tserkvi," 620-24; and "Rol' tserkvi v sovremennom mire," 625-632. Fr. Aleksandr's talk on the role of the church is republished in *O Khriste i tserkvi*, 65–81.

68. Men, "Nadlezhit byt' raznomysliiu," 57–58, and "Rol' tserkvi," 11.

69. Eremin, *Otets Aleksandr Men'*, 100.

70. Ibid., 48.

71. Fr. Aleksandr Men, *Syn chelovecheskii*, vol. 7 of *Istoriia religii: V poiskakh puti, istiny i zhizn'* (Moscow: Slovo, 1992), 101, 104. Although *Syn chelovecheskii* is listed here as part of this multivolume work, I argued earlier in my study that the book should be considered as a separate, but related, volume. As mentioned earlier, for an English language translation of *Syn chelovecheskii*, see Alexander Men, *Son of Man*, trans. Samuel Brown (Torrance, CA: Oakwood, 1998).

72. Men, *Syn chelovecheskii*, 103.

73. Ibid.

74. See ibid., 104.

75. Ibid., 103.

76. Aleksandr Men, "Liubit' Boga i liubit' cheloveka," in *Liubit' Boga i liubit' cheloveka: Domashnie besedy*, ed. Roza Adamiants et al. (Moscow: Zhizn' s Bogom, 2012), 110–24.

77. Ibid., 119.

78. Miroslav Volf, *A Public Faith: How Followers of Christ Should Serve the Common Good* (Grand Rapids, MI: Brazos Press, 2011), 71. Italics are Volf's.

79. Men, "Liubit' Boga," 116.

80. In theological terms, as Fr. Aleksandr defined it, flourishing specifically meant the "sense of completion, which comes to us when we fulfill that to which we are called." Ibid., 115–16.

81. Ibid., 115.

82. Ibid., 121.

83. Ibid.

84. Ibid., 123.

85. N. N. "V etom moe sluzhenie Bogu (Vospominaniia o D. E. Melekhove)," in Bychkov, *Maroseika*, 389–90, 394–98.

86. The Russian Student Christian Movement (RSKhD) (*Russkoe studentcheskoe khristianskoe dvizhenie*) predated the First World War. The organization survived the war and the revolution and continued to meet in the 1920s. Composed largely of students who rejected the official church's connections to the Soviet government, the RSKhD met in small groups, engaged in Bible studies, and provided assistance to each other. Most of the students in the RSKhD identified themselves as Orthodox. The organization, associated with the international YMCA, continued its activities until 1934, when many of its members were arrested. For more details on the RSKhD, see Matthew Lee Miller, *The American YMCA and Russian Culture: The Preservation and Expansion of Orthodox Christianity, 1900-1940* (Lanham, MD: Lexington Books, 2013). Established in Paris, the publishing house of the Russian Student Christian Movement and its influential journal, the *Journal of the Russian Christian Movement* (*Zhurnal khristianskogo dvizheniia*), have had an extremely large impact, as Miller argues, both in Orthodox circles abroad and in the former Soviet Union, on furthering the goals of unifying Orthodox believers and developing a Christian philosophy.

87. Men, "Liubit' Boga," 121n1.

88. Aleksandr Men, "Beseda v dome prestarelykh i invalidov," in *Liubit' Boga*, 192. In this talk, which took place on August 30, 1989, Fr. Aleksandr continued many of the same themes he discussed in his previous "house group talks" and for that reason it is included here.

89. Ibid., 198.

90. Fr. Aleksandr Men, *Otets Aleksandr Men' otvechaet na voprosy*, 2nd ed., ed. Roza Adamiants, Nataliia Vtorushina, and Pavel Men (Moscow: Zhizn' s Bogom, 2008), 282.

91. See Daniel Pipes, "The Problem of Soviet Muslims," *Asian Outlook (Taipei)* (March–April 1991), http://www.danielpipes.org/206/the-problem-of-soviet-muslims.

92. Men, *Otets Aleksandr Men' otvechaet*, 282.

93. Ibid., 289.

94. Ibid., 289–90.

95. Ibid., 283.

96. Ibid., 282–83. Fr. Aleksandr referenced the work of his mentor V. S. Solov'ev, who wrote, in the nineteenth century, what Men called one of the best works on Islam. Solov'ev had called on Christians to remember that, like Christians, "Mohammed had professed faith in a single true God." Fr. Aleksandr also critically assessed historians, philosophers, and others, who, "either consciously or unconsciously," confused people by their translations of the term "Allah." The term, he noted, is not as simple as translators have made it out to be, but rather represents a term used in many ancient languages signifying God.

97. See the list of books mentioned in Vladimir Il'ich Iliushenko, "Vospominaniia," in *Otets Aleksandr Men': Zhizn', Smert', Bessmertie*, 2nd ed. (Moscow: VGBIL im. M. I. Rudomino, 2010), 350.

98. Aleksandr Men, "Trudnyi put' k dialogu: O romane Grema Grina 'Monsen'or Kikhot,'" in *Kul'tura i dukhovnoe voskhozhdenie*, 328.

99. Maslenikova, "Moi dukhovnik," June 2, 1980, 465. Maslenikova also mentioned her work with Fr. Aleksandr on this translation in her diary entries for October 27, 1980, 467, and March 12, 1983, 503. Fr. Aleksandr's translation of Greene's novel has recently been published: Grem Grin [Graham Greene], *Sila i slava: Roman*, trans. Aleksandr Men, with an introduction by Ekaterina Genieva, afterword by Kseniia Atarova (Moscow: Rudomino, 2012). I am grateful to Dr. Ann Shukman for this citation.

100. Men, "Trudnyi put' k dialogu," 343.

101. Irina Ivanovna Maslova, "Sovet po delam religii pri sovete ministrov SSSR i russkaia pravoslavnaia tserkov' (1965–1991 g.g.)," *Otechestvennaia istoriia*, no. 6 (2005): 59.

Notes to Chapter Eleven

1. Otto Luchterhandt, "The Council for Religious Affairs," in *Religious Policy in the Soviet Union*, ed. Sabrina Petra Ramet (New York: Cambridge University Press, 1993), 55–83.

2. Christopher Andrew and Vasili Mitrokhin, *The Sword and the Shield: The Mitrokhin Archive and the Secret History of the KGB* (New York: Basic Books, 1999), 490.

3. Irina Ivanovna Maslova, "Sovet po delam religii pri sovet ministrov SSSR i russkaia pravoslavnaia tserkov' (1965–1991 g.g.)," *Otechestvennaia istoriia*, no. 6 (2005): 52, 57–58. Maslova's research, which is heavily based on the archives of the Council for Religious Affairs, emphasizes how representatives of the Council, in coordination with certain bishops, attempted to "nip in the bud" the aspirations of priests who "tried to steer believers toward oppositional activities" (ibid., 57-58).

4. Andrew and Mitrokhin, *Sword and the Shield*, 5.

5. Document 161, KGB, March 25, 1974, No. 788-A, Moscow, Secret, "To the CC CPSU," from KGB chairman Iuri Andropov, in Felix Corley, ed. and trans., *Religion in the Soviet Union: An Archival Reader* (New York: New York University Press, 1996), 267–69.

6. Ibid., 268.

7. The report professes great suspicion of methods used by the Vatican, including the widespread "use of the method of tourism, scientific and technical exchanges and private visits." Andropov

also cites the names of certain Catholic professors and officials who had attempted to strengthen the relationship with the Russian Orthodox Church (ibid).

8. Ibid., 267.

9. Sergei Bychkov, "KGB protiv sviashchennika Aleksandra Menia," *Vestnik russkogo khristianskogo dvizheniia*, n.s., no. 196 (2010): 119–20.

10. Document 161, KGB, in Corley, *Religion*, 268.

11. Bychkov, "KGB," 120. See the previous discussion of the Brussels press, "La Vie avec Dieu," in chapter 7.

12. Ibid., 127.

13. Ibid.

14. Vladimir Il'ich Iliushenko, *Otets Aleksandr Men': Zhizn' i smert' vo Khriste* (Moscow: Pik, 2000), 353; Andrei Mikhailovich Tavrov, *Syn chelovecheskii: Ob ottse Aleksandre Mene* (Moscow: Eksmo, 2014), 41–42. Sergei Sergeevich Bychkov, *Khronika neraskrytogo ubiistva* (Moscow: Russkoe reklamnoe izdatel'stvo, 1996), 37–40.

15. Document 199. "Report on the work of the 4th department of the 5th directorate of the KGB," January 1977, in Corley, *Religion*, 365.

16. "The KGB tried to make him into a dissident," said Mikhail Aleksandrovich Men. "They wanted to frame him as a dissident. But he was never much interested in politics. He always thought that his main task was to preach the Gospels, but, indirectly, his activities, his books, sermons, and slides went against Soviet power" (Mikhail Aleksandrovich Men, interview by author, Ivanovo, July 1, 2013).

17. Irina Ivanovna Maslova, "Russkaia Pravoslavnaia Tserkov' i KGB (1960–1980-e gody)," *Voprosy istorii*, no. 12 (2005): 86.

18. Ibid.

19. Ibid., 87.

20. Ibid.

21. Ibid., 89–90. Maslova notes that nearly all the resolutions demanded the beginning of negotiations with the Vatican, rebuilding the administrative structure of the Greek-Catholic Church, providing "moral and material compensation" for the servitors of the Greek-Catholic Church, and giving religious believers the constitutional guarantees of freedom of speech, press, and assembly.

22. Mikhail Vital'evich Shkarovskii, *Russkaia Pravoslavnaia Tserkov' v XX veke* (Moscow: Veche, Lepta, 2010) 3–4, 6–9; Mikhail Ivanovich Odintsov, *Gosudarstvo i tserkov' v Rossii: XX vek* (Moscow: Luch, 1994), 16–18. Odintsov speaks to the years early in the Bolshevik era when these issues commanded central attention in defining the society and government.

23. Such divided loyalty marked the entire reign of Patriarch Pimen, whose long tenure (1971–1990) served the KGB, and who, in the words of a critic, lived in a "dense shroud of icy darkness." Gleb Yakunin, "Report to the Christian Committee for the Defense of Believers' Rights in the USSR on the Current Situation of the Russian Orthodox Church and the Prospects for a Religious Renaissance in Russia," August 15, 1979, in *Documents of the Christian Committee for the Defense of Believers' Rights in the USSR* (San Francisco, CA: Washington Research Center, 1980), 11:xvii. According to Yakunin, the patriarch took no independent action apart from those who controlled him. He "is invested with the eyes and ears of the KGB. . . . Informers are included among those who surround him [the patriarch] most closely—the novices, subdeacons, and his personal secretary. And even his personal chauffeur is a KGB officer, a retired major."

24. "Zapiska Nachal'nika 4 otdela 5 Upravleniia KGB pri SM SSSR podpolkovnik Fitsev, 1973"; "Zapiska Nachal'nika 4 otdela 5 Upravleniia KGB pri SM SSSR podpolkovnik E. D. Kubyshkin," May 1977; "Zapiska V. I. Timoshevskogo," January 1989, Keston Archive, Anita Deyneka Collection, Box 1. These clerical agents, reporting under the code names "Adamant," "Abbot," "Antonov," and others, at various meetings of the World Council of Churches in the 1970s and '80s, gathered information, collected what KGB officials called "operational materials of interest," and sought to influence Western clerical circles ("Zapiska Nachal'nika 4 otdela 5 Upravleniia KGB pri SM SSSR podpolkovnik Fitsev," January 1977; "Zapiska Nachal'nika 4 otdela 5 Upravleniia KGB pri SM SSSR podpolkovnik N. N.

Romanov," 1982," Keston Archive, Anita Deyneka Collection, Box 1. "Adamant" was the code name for Metropolitan Iuvenalii of Krutitsk and Kolomna, "Antonov" for Metropolitan Filaret of Kiev, and "Abbat" for Metropolitan Pitirim of Volokolamsk and Iur'ev. See Keith Armes, "Chekists in Cassocks: The Orthodox Church and the KGB," *Demokratizatsiya* 1, no. 4 (Fall 1992): 72–73.

25. Patriarch Pimen, "Speech at the Reception in Honour of the Participants in the Conference," June 10, 1977, *Journal of the Moscow Patriarchate*, no. 8 (1977): 59; Andrew and Mitrokhin, *Sword and the Shield*, 491.

26. Patriarch Pimen, "Congratulatory Telegram to Leonid Il'ich Brezhnev, General Secretary of the CC CPSU," December 17, 1976, *Journal of the Moscow Patriarchate*, no. 2 (1977): 4; Andrew and Mitrokhin, *Sword and the Shield*, 491. Earlier that year, Pimen, Metropolitan Aleksii of Tallinn and Estonia, who would eventually succeed Pimen, and other members of the Holy Synod received special state awards for their "manifold and fruitful activities" in promoting international peace and friendship ("Soviet Peace Funds Awards," *Journal of the Moscow Patriarchate*, no. 4 [1976]: 4).

27. Viktor Mikhailovich Chebrikov, deputy chairman of the KGB under Andropov and later chairman from 1982 to 1988, in a communication in January 1971, acknowledged that the majority of the Orthodox clergy was loyal to the Soviet government. Nevertheless, he wrote, "we have a small group of clergy and church activists, in the main religious fanatics, who incorrectly understand the situation of the church and believers. They undertake steps to change the governance of the Russian Orthodox Church, for the purpose of strengthening its position and escaping the control of the government" (Maslova, "Russkaia Pravoslavnaia Tserkov," 93).

28. Maslenikova, "Moi dukhovnik," February 15, 1980, in *Zhizn' ottsa Aleksandra Menia* (Moscow: Pristsel's, 1995), 460.

29. Maslenikova describes step-by-step the events of this conflict, which began with Fr. Aleksandr's creation of a choir, made up mostly of young people, many of whom were the children of newcomers to the parish. While he had kept them separate from the traditional choir, made up nearly exclusively of elderly women, Fr. Stefan mixed the two, an act that led to an explosion among the older choir members, who placed the blame on Fr. Aleksandr for organizing the new choir. Their resulting resentment led to the writing of a denunciation to the authorities, which accused Fr. Aleksandr of organizing a "Jewish choir" in the Novaia Derevnaia parish. Maslenikova, *Zhizn' ottsa Aleksandra Menia*, 247–50.

30. Maslenikova, "Moi dukhovnik," February 15, 1980, 460. Despite the pressures he had to bear, Fr. Aleksandr stayed at Novaia Derevnia. His nemesis, Fr. Stefan, remained only until 1983, when the church transferred him to another parish.

31. Yves Hamant, *Alexander Men: A Witness for Contemporary Russia (A Man for Our Times)*, trans. Steven Bigham, intro. Maxym Lysack (Torrance, CA: Oakwood, 1995), 177.

32. Jane Ellis, *The Russian Orthodox Church: A Contemporary History* (New York: Routledge, 1986), 255.

33. Ibid., 194.

34. For the above restrictions, see ibid., 255–56; Decree of the Chairman of the State Committee of the USSR Council of Ministers for Publishing, Printing Presses, and the Book Trade I, No. 346/DSP, Moscow, June 6, 1975, and Chief Directorate for the Preservation of State Secrets in Print Attached to the USSR CM, Leningrad Directorate, October 12, 1977, No. 215S, Copy No. 1, in Corley, *Religion*, 270–74.

35. Maslova, "Russkaia Pravoslavnaia Tserkov," 89.

36. Maslenikova, "Moi dukhovnik," March 11,1980, 462–64.

37. Iv. Aman (Yves Hamant), "Razmatyvaia nit' vospominanii," in *Pamiati protoiereia Aleksandra Menia*, ed. T. V. Gromova (Moscow: Rudomino, 1991), 103.

38. Ibid.

39. See Vladimir Poresh, "Secret Police Harass Poresh," *Religion in Communist Lands* 8, no. 2 (Summer 1980): 103–6. This account appeared originally in Russian, in *Obshchina*, no. 2 (1978): 149–58; Philip Walters, "The Ideas of the Christian Seminar," *Religion in Communist Lands* 9, nos.

3–4 (Autumn 1981): 111–22; Aleksandr Ioilovich Ogorodnikov, "Ot sostavitelei," *Obshchina*, no. 2 (1978): 1.

40. Aleksandr Men, "Interv'iu na sluchai aresta," in *Kul'tura i dukhovnoe voskhozhdenie*, comp. R. I. Al'betkova and M. T. Rabotiaga (Moscow: Iskusstvo, 1992), 356–63.

41. Ibid., 357.

42. Ibid., 361.

43. Ibid., 361–62.

44. Aleksandr Men, *Kak Chitat' Bibliiu* (1981; repr., Moscow: Fond Aleksandra Menia, 2005). This represented the second of three works on *Life in the Church* (*Zhizn' v Tserkvi*). There is much more on Fr. Aleksandr's *Kak Chitat' Bibliiu* in April French, "Spiritual Dissent: The Writings of Father Aleksandr Men as Dissent from Soviet Ideology" (MA thesis, Regent College, Vancouver, BC, 2011), 121–46.

45. Maslenikova, "Moi dukhovnik," March 11, 1980, 463–64.

46. Ibid., April 21, 1980, 464.

47. Ibid., March 21, 1980, 464.

48. Ibid., April 21, 1980, 464.

49. Ibid.

50. Maslenikova, "Moi dukhovnik," June 11, 1981, 483.

51. Ibid., August 21, 1981, 483.

52. Bychkov, *Khronika neraskrytogo ubiistva*, 28.

53. Maslenikova, "Moi dukhovnik," n.d., 1983, summary, 504.

54. Bychkov, *Khronika neraskrytogo ubiistva*, 29.

55. Hamant, *Alexander Men*, 181–82.

56. Ibid.

57. Bychkov, *Khronika neraskrytogo ubiistva*, 29.

58. Patriarch Pimen, "His Holiness's Address Before Panikhida in the Patriarchal Cathedral of the Epiphany in Moscow," February 12, 1984, *Journal of the Moscow Patriarchate*, no. 3 (1984): 3.

59. Shkarovskii, *Russkaia Pravoslavnaia Tserkov'*, 398.

60. Ibid.

61. Bychkov, *Khronika neraskrytogo ubiistva*, 29; Peter Jarman, "East-West Dialogue during the Cold War years: Possibilities and Limitations," paper presented to a conference on the role of the peace movements during the Cold War held at the London School of Economics, February 2, 2008, http://www.oldsite.transnational.org/Resources_Treasures/2008/Jarman_East-West_Quaker.pdf.

62. Bychkov, *Khronika neraskrytogo ubiistva*, 43. Ironically, as Sergei Bychkov points out, this initial meeting with Sychev and Mikhailov took place exactly five years to the day before Fr. Aleksandr's murder.

63. Maslenikova, "Moi dukhovnik," May 20, 1986, 511; Bychkov, *Khronika neraskrytogo ubiistva*, 44. See also, on the Fr. Dmitrii Dudko case, Oliver Bullough, *The Last Man in Russia: The Struggle to Save a Dying Nation* (New York: Basic Books, 2013), 193–201; Ellis, *Russian Orthodox Church*, 422–27.

64. Aleksandr Men, "Zaiavlenie," in *Informatsionyi Biulleten*, no. 13, November 25, 1985, 42–43, in Keston Archive, SU/Ort/8/2/Men'.

65. Ibid.

66. Materials from the available KGB sources in the late 1970s and early 1980s contain little evidence that the police recognized Fr. Aleksandr as the author of manuscripts published in Brussels. But archival materials of the KGB do reveal knowledge of an exchange of written materials with a foreign emissary in late 1985. This transfer of documents from Fr. Aleksandr "to the West" led, in the words of KGB officer Vladimir Sychev, to "prepare for conducting a criminal investigaton of him" (V. Sychev, December 1985, "Podborka vypisok iz materialov Tsentral'nogo arkhiva KGB i arkhiva TsK KPSS o deiatel'nosti sovetskoi vlasti i organov KGB vnutri Russkoi Pravoslavnoi Tserkvi za 1921–1990," Keston Archive, Anita Dayneka Collection, Box 1.

67. Bychkov, *Khronika neraskrytogo ubiistva*, 47.

68. Details of this plan in the Central Committee are included in Bychkov, *Khronika neraskrytogo ubiistva*, 43–44. The report to the Central Committee was signed by V. Sychev and V. Makarov and dated March 1986.

69. Ibid., 45.

70. N. Dombkovskii, "Krest na sovesti," *Trud*, April 10 and 11, 1986, appendix no. 14, in Bychkov, *Khronika neraskrytogo ubiistva*, 208–18.

71. Ibid., 209.

72. Ibid., 212. Dombkovskii noted Meyendorff's membership on the editorial board of the *Bulletin of the Russian Christian Movement* (*Vestnik russkogo khristianskogo dvizheniia*), a publication, he wrote, engaged in slandering the Soviet Union.

73. See the discussions of "reconstructing the self" for key elements in the emotional transformation of the self from former ways of thinking and behaving to becoming more public spirited and part of the new order, in Igal Halfin, *Terror in My Soul: Communist Autobiographies on Trial* (Cambridge, MA: Harvard University Press, 2003), especially the chapter "A Voyage toward the Light," 43–95.

74. Dombkovskii, "Krest na sovesti," 215.

75. Ibid., 217–18. The article mentions the Reverend Canon Michael Bourdeaux and his reception of the Templeton Prize for Progress in Religion, awarded by the John Templeton Foundation in 1984.

76. Mikhail Aleksandrovich Men, interview by author, Ivanovo, July 1, 2013.

77. Maslenikova, "Moi dukhovnik," May 20, 1986, 510.

78. Ibid.

79. Ibid., 511. This and other entries in late May to mid-June 1986 are undated because of Fr. Aleksandr's advice to Maslenikova not to maintain a daily account, since he expected a KGB search of her house.

80. Ibid.

81. Ibid., 512.

82. Ibid.

83. Dombkovskii, "Krest na sovesti," 219.

84. Ibid.

85. Ibid., 221; Maskenikova, "Moi dukhovnik," September 21, 1986, 519.

86. Dombkovskii, "Krest na sovesti," September 21, 1986, 221.

87. Ibid.

88. In the summer of 1986, the KGB discovered an anonymously written article in the Paris journal *Vestnik russkogo khristianskogo dvizheneniia*, which they immediately associated with Fr. Aleksandr. Titled "Seven Questions and Answers about the Russian Orthodox Church" (*"Sem' voprosov i otvetov o Russkoi Pravoslavnoi Tserkvi"*), the two-part article began by evaluating the present condition of the church, in which the anonymous author subjected the church to a withering critique, both of its external and internal circumstances and capacities. ("Sem' voprosov i otvetov o Russkoi Pravoslavnoi Tserkvi," *Vestnik russkogo khristianskogo dvizheniia* 137 (1982): 233–60, and 138 (1983): 215–28.

In the beginning of the article, the author(s) defined how the church existed in a contradictory, nearly impossible situation: an "atheistic government," which openly "proclaims its goal to be the full and final annihilation of religion." The author(s) went on to explore the devastating consequences: the lack of any kind of religious literature, the small number of prayer and church service material for religious believers, the non-existence of nearly all religious instruction, the overwhelming conservatism of the clergy and the fear of religious creativity, the narrowly prescribed framework for dialogue of any kind, the psychological and cultural dependency on the government, and many other factors—all of which, in combination, led to a crisis within the church, but also more broadly, within the society.

The discovery of this article led to a fresh round of interrogations, conducted by the KGB official Vladimir Sychev. The anonymity of the author, the publication in what Sychev labelled an "anti-Soviet journal," and the article's "slanderous content" prompted the questioning of Fr. Aleksandr to determine the author's identity. Fr. Aleksandr did not write the article, as the KGB discovered, but the whole event signified yet another step in a process of threat and intimidation. (Sychev's recollections of this event are included in Bychkov, *Khronika neraskrytogo ubiistva*, 45–46.)

89. Maslova, "Russkaia Pravoslavnaia Tserkov," 86; Corley, *Religion*, 360.

90 . Maslenikova, "Moi dukhovnik," May 20, 1986, 510-512; August 24,1986, 517-518. Men was also summoned earlier to Metropolitan Iuvenalii's residence; see Bychkov, *Khronika neraskrytogo ubiistva*, 47.

91. Maslenikova, "Moi dukhovnik," August 21, 1986, 518.

92. Maslenikova, "Moi dukhovnik," August 24, 1986, 518.

93. Bychkov, *Khronika neraskrytogo ubiistva*, 44; the passage cited is from Luke 21:12–15, and the translation is from *The Orthodox Study Bible* (Nashville, TN: Thomas Nelson, 2008).

Notes to Chapter Twelve

1. Alexander Kremlev, "Father Alexander Men," slidefilm narrated by Sergei Bessmertnyi, August 25, 2012, Youtube.com, http://youtube/Bmhrp4VNY10.

2. Mikhail Sergeevich Gorbachev, quoted in Michael Bourdeaux, *Gorbachev, Glasnost, and the Gospel* (London: Hodder and Stoughton, 1990), 44.

3. Sergei Borisovich Filatov, "Russkaia Pravoslavnaia Tserkov' i politicheskaia elita," in *Religiia i politika v postkommunisticheskoi Rossii*, ed. L. N. Mitrokhin (Moscow: Institut filosofii RAN, 1994): 99–100.

4. Nathaniel Davis, *A Long Walk to Church: A Contemporary History of Russian Orthodoxy*, 2nd ed. (Boulder, CO: Westview Press, 2003), 63.

5. Davis references a lecture by the Very Reverend Leonid Kishkovsky, presented in Claremont, California, on March 8, 1989, in which Kishkovsky underscored the significance of the dialogue between secular and church scholars. See Davis, *Long Walk to Church*, 275n11.

6. Mikhail Vital'evich Shkarovskii, *Russkaia Pravoslavnaia Tserkov' v XX veke* (Moscow: Veche, Lepta, 2010), 403–4.

7. President Gorbachev to Patriarch Pimen, quoted in Shkarovskii, *Russkaia Pravoslavnaia Tserkov'*, 404. As the president had promised the patriarch, the government had already begun the complex transfer to the church of previously nationalized religious buildings, as well as several sacred relics, and had given permission to open new churches, spiritual academies, and monasteries, and to increase the publication of church literature. According to official sources, in 1988, the Soviet government returned 528 church buildings to the Orthodox Church, and gave 44 permits for new church construction. In the same year, 809 new Orthodox societies were registered, bringing the total registered church societies, on January 1, 1989, to 7,549 in the Soviet Union (ibid., 406; Davis, *Long Walk to Church*, 69).

8. The remaining five included Metropolitan Makarii of Moscow (1482–1563); the Rev. Paisii Velichkovskii (1722–1794); the blessed Xenia of Saint Petersburg (1732 to the beginning of the nineteenth century); Saint Ignatius Brianchaninov (1807–1867); and Saint Feofan the Recluse (1815–1894).

9. Shkarovskii, *Russkaia Pravoslavnaia Tserkov'*, 406.

10. "Message from Patriarch Tikhon, dated 19 January 1918," in *Christians in Contemporary Russia*, by Nikita A. Struve, trans. Lancelot Sheppard and A. Manson, 2nd rev. ed. (New York: Scribner, 1967), 343–45; see also Matthew Spinka, *The Church and the Russian Revolution* (New York: Macmillan, 1927), 118–22. As the reader will recall, Patriarch Tikhon served under great political pressure, abdicated his position in 1922, later proclaimed his loyalty to the government, and reclaimed his patriarchal throne.

11. Zoia Afanas'evna Maslenikova, *Zhizn' ottsa Aleksandra Menia* (Moscow: Pristsel's, 1995), 179; Aleksandr Men, *Otets Aleksandr Men' otvechaet na voprosy* (Moscow: Zhizn' s Bogom, 2008), 238, 324.

12. See, for example, the physicist Boris Raushenbakh's account of Fr. Aleksandr's appearance at a meeting of professors in the Russian Academy of Sciences, in Wallace L. Daniel, "Religion, Science, Russia: An Interview with Boris Raushenbakh," *Christian Century*, 28 February 1996, 232–35.

13. Fr. Aleksandr Men, quoted by Yves Hamant, *Alexander Men: A Witness for Contemporary Russia (A Man for Our Times)*, trans. Steven Bigham, intro. Maxym Lysack (Torrance, CA: Oakwood, 1995), 203.

14. At the time, the high stakes at issue in this discussion, James H. Billington wrote, were "based on the large-scale determination of the Russian people to rediscover everything meaningful in their shared experience that Stalin attempted to destroy and that Stalin's successors continued to defile: traditional village culture, the soil and rivers of a once pristine ecology, the long-suffering compassion of grass-roots Russian Orthodoxy, the artistic majesty of a pioneering monastic culture that carried that faith across the forbidding Siberian frontier on to Alaska, and above all, a unique, modern literary tradition permeated with moral passion. There is a desire not just to recover but to learn from and make restitution to the old Russian culture." James H. Billington, "Russia: Continuity or Radical Change?" *Texas Journal of Ideas, History, and Culture* 13, no. 1 (Fall/Winter 1990): 66.

15. These are the questions Billington posed in "Russia."

16. Fr. Vladimir, "Ne khlebom edinym," *Nash sovremennik*, no. 6 (1990): 55–56.

17. Metropolitan Ioann, "The West Wants Chaos," in *Christianity after Communism: Social, Political, and Cultural Struggle in Russia*, ed. Niels C. Nielsen, Jr. (Boulder, CO: Westview Press, 1994), 107–12; Ralph Della Cava, "Reviving Orthodoxy in Russia: An Overview of the Factions in the Russian Orthodox Church in the Spring of 1996," *Cahiers du Monde russe* 38, no. 3 (1997): 387–414.

18. Fr. Vladimir, "Ne khlebom edinym," 55–56.

19. On *symphonia* and related aspects of the church-state relationship, see Gregory Freeze, "Handmaiden of the State: The Church in Imperial Russia Reconsidered," *Journal of Ecclesiastical History* 36, no. 1 (January 1985): 82–102; Igor' Kornil'evich Smolich, *Geschichte der Russischen Kirche, 1700–1917* (Leiden: E. J. Brill, 1964); Valerie Kivelson and Robert H. Greene, eds., *Orthodox Russia: Belief and Practice under the Tsars* (University Park: Pennsylvania State University Press, 2003).

20. Pilar Bonet, "Poslednee interv'iu Aleksandra Menia," in *Kul'tura i dukhovnoe voskhozhdenie*, comp. R. I. Al'betkova and M. T. Rabotiaga (Moscow: Iskusstvo, 1992), 446.

21. Ibid., 447.

22. Aleksandr Men, "Chto proiskhodit s nashei kul'turoi? (Interv'iu)," in *Trudnyi put' k dialogu: Sbornik*, by Aleksandr Men, ed. N. Matiash, foreword by Antonii, Metropolitan of Sourozh (Moscow: Raduga, 1992), 81.

23. Ibid.

24. Ibid.

25. Ibid., 82.

26. Ibid., 79.

27. Kirill (Gundiaev), "Tserkov' v otnoshenii k obshchestvu v usloviiakh perestroiki," *Zhurnal Moskovskoi Patriarkhii* 47, no. 2 (1990): 38. On October 1, 1990, the Soviet Parliament passed the long-awaited Soviet Law on Freedom of Conscience and Religious Organizations, which turned upside down the values articulated in the Soviet Constitution of 1977 and many previous enactments of the Soviet government. The law abrogated the onerous legal requirement that forced religious communities to register with the government. It also affirmed the separation of church and state. Both in law and in practice, however, the 1990 Soviet Law on Freedom of Conscience and Religious Organizations would be severely challenged in the next decade, and major parts of it would be declared nonbinding and redefined. See Wallace L. Daniel, Peter L. Berger, and Christopher Marsh, Introduction to *Perspectives on Church-State Relations in Russia* (Waco, TX: J. M. Dawson Institute of Church-State Studies, 2008), 1–6.

28. Patriarch Aleksii II, quoted by Serge Schmemann, "An Awakened Church Finds Russia Searching for Its Soul," *New York Times*, April 26, 1992, section 4.

29. G. Alimov and G. Charodeev, "Faith without Deeds Is Dead—An Interview with Patriarch Aleksii II," trans. Suzanne Oliver, *Religion in Communist Lands* 18, no. 3 (Autumn 1990): 266; Aleksii II, "Education and the Christian View of Man," *Russian Social Science Review* 35, no. 6 (November–December 1994), 45–48.

30. Fr. Aleksandr's discussions of such social needs are exemplified in his "Fenomen cheloveka: O dukhovnom i nravstvennom," in *Pravoslavnye vesti*, ed. Vladimir Erokhin (Moscow: Tip. Informatsionno-blagotvoritel'nogo tsentra Put', Istina i Zhizn', 2005), 4–8; Aleksandr Men, "Slovo pered kreshcheniem," in *Radost' sluzheniia: Domashnie besedy*, ed. Roza Adamiants et al. (Moscow: Zhizn' s Bogom, 2013), 48–49, and *Ot rabstva k svobode: Lektsii po Vetkhomu Zavetu* (Moscow: Zhizn' s Bogom, 2008), 41–43.

31. Aleksandr Men, "Khristianskaia kul'tura na Rusi," in *Radostnaia vest': Lektsii*, comp. A. A. Andreeva (Moscow: Vita Tsentr, 1991) 251.

32. Ibid., 251–52.

33. Ibid., 251.

34. Aleksandr Men, "Rol' tserkvi v sovremennom mire," in *Mirovaia dukhovnaia kul'tura, Khristianstvo, Tserkov': Lektsii i besedy*, 2nd ed., ed. Anastasiia Andreeva et al, comp. Aleksandr Belavin, 2nd ed. (Moscow: Fond imeni Aleksandra Menia, 1997), 625-32. Fr. Aleksandr also pointed out the church's limited social role and how, in the provinces, the physical condition of a large majority of the clergy was little distinguished from the poorest villagers. Given these circumstances, he did not find it surprising that the church as an institution engendered little respect in the eyes of Russia's educated class. Nor did he find it difficult to understand why the church fell easily and quickly after the Bolsheviks came to power. The church lacked the popular support, social respect, and deeply rooted creativity to withstand the Bolsheviks' ferocious attacks.

35. Aleksandr Men, "Sushchnost' khristianstva," in *Kniga Nadezhdy: Lektsii o Biblii* (Moscow: Zhizn' s Bogom, 2011), 228.

36. Ibid.

37. Men, "Khristianskaia kul'tura na Rusi," 249–50.

38. Ibid., 250.

39. Ibid., and "Rol' tserkvi," 11.

40. Men, "Khristianskaia kul'tura na Rusi," 251.

41. Men, "Rol' tserkvi," 11. Many nineteenth- and early twentieth-century religious-philosophical thinkers had emphasized the need for an independent church, and from them Fr. Aleksandr again sought guidance. Elsewhere, Fr. Aleksandr had criticized the government's relationship with the church: "The government has always intended that the church would neither develop independent thoughts, nor take an independent position whatsoever on any kind of concrete real-life problem" ("Mozhno li reformirovat' pravoslavnuiu tserkov'? Neizvestnoe interv'iu Aleksandra Menia," *Nezavisimaia gazeta*, January 2, 1992, 6; Fr. Aleksandr's interview was also published as "Problemy tserkvi iznutri," in Men, *Kul'tura i dukhovnoe voskhozhdenie*, 440–45).

42. Bonet, "Poslednee interv'iu Aleksandra Menia," 445–46; Aleksandr Men, "Chto proiskhodit," 85–86. For an English translation, see "Russia in Crisis," in *Christianity for the Twenty-First Century: The Life and Work of Alexander Men*, ed. Elizabeth Roberts and Ann Shukman (London: SCM Press, 1996), 139–50. Aleksandr Men, *Otets Aleksandr Men' otvechaet na voprosy* (Moscow: Zhizn' s Bogom, 2008), 236–37, 300–301. Men's conception of freedom was critical of the church's frequent misinterpretation of one of the Gospel's central teachings: the need for freedom of the soul. Speaking about the philosopher Vladimir Solov'ev, his predecessor, Fr. Aleksandr recalled Solov'ev's claim that "Orthodox Christianity had degraded us as a country, degraded us because of its protectionism, its support for censorship, and its connection to the government"; see Aleksandr Men, "Vladimir Solov'ev," in *Russkaia religioznaia filosofiia: Lektsii*, ed. Marina Nasonova (Moscow: Khram sviatykh bessrebrennikov Kosmy i Damiana v Shubine, 2003), 41.

43. Aleksandr Men, "Religiia, 'kul't lichnosti' i sekuliarnoe gosudarstvo," in Men, *Kul'tura i dukhovnoe voskhozhdenie*, 394–96.

44. Ibid., 396–98, 400–401.

45. Aleksandr Men, "Khristianstvo i tvorchestvo," in *Radostnaia vest'*, 257–58.

46. Vladimir Il'ich Iliushenko, interview by author, Moscow, June 6, 2006.

47. Ibid.

48. Men, *Russkaia religioznaia filosofiia*.

49. Alexander Men, "Christianity: The Universal Vision," in Roberts and Shukman, *Christianity*, 94. He offered hope, giving free play to the imagination to make the world a better and more spiritually hospitable place. See Lesley Chamberlain, *Motherland: A Philosophical History of Russia* (New York: The Rookery Press, 2007), 62.

50. Aleksandr Men, "Vladimir Sergeevich Solov'ev," in *Mirovaia dukhovnaia kul'tura, khristianstvo, tserkov': Lektsii i besedy*, 2nd ed., ed. Anastasiia Andreeva et al., comp. A. Belavin (Moscow: Fond imeni Aleksandra Menia, 1997), 425–26.

51. Mikhail Gershenzon, "Preface to First Edition," in *Vekhi: Landmarks; A Collection of Articles about the Russian Intelligentsia*, trans. and ed. Marshall S. Shatz and Judith E. Zimmerman (Armonk, NY: M. E. Sharpe, 1994), xxxvii. These metaphysical writers thus did not support the social order the Bolsheviks aspired to build and, as mentioned earlier, Lenin forced them into exile. Yet, as Fr. Aleksandr told his listeners, even in exile, such remarkable thinkers "never lost their connection to their homeland and to their native spiritual culture," despite the difficulties of their fate (Men, "Khristianskaia kul'tura na Rusi," 253). The story of their exile and subsequent life is well told by Lesley Chamberlain, *The Philosophy Steamer: Lenin and the Exile of the Intelligentsia* (London: Atlantic Books, 2006).

52. Aleksandr Men, "Nikolai Berdiaev," in *Russkaia religioznaia filosofiia*, 157.

53. Ibid., 156.

54. Aleksandr Men, "Fr. Sergei Bulgakov," in *Russkaia religioznaia filosofiia*, 177.

55. Ibid., 179. Catherine Evtuhov's study of Bulgakov has illuminating chapters on his upbringing and university education, in Catherine Evtuhov, *The Cross and the Sickle: Sergei Bulgakov and the Fate of Russian Religious Philosophy* (Ithaca, NY: Cornell University Press, 1997), 21–27, 28–37.

56. Men, "Fr. Sergei Bulgakov," 180.

57. Ibid., 181.

58. Rowan Williams, General Introduction to *Sergii Bulgakov: Towards a Political Theology*, ed. and intro. Rowan Williams (Edinburgh: T & T Clark, 1999), 4.

59. In his lecture on Bulgakov's intellectual evolution, Fr. Aleksandr singled out a book that Bulgakov wrote in 1911 titled *Karl Marx as a Religious Type* (Sergei Nikolaevich Bulgakov, *Karl Marks kak religioznyi tip* [1907; repr., Paris: YMCA-Press,1929]). Marx extolled a "scientific, objective, dialectical methodology" in his study of economic history, but, Bulgakov argued, when the careful reader examined the assumptions that underlay Marx's methodology, one saw nonscientific reasoning. The hard-minded exterior of Marx's scientific analysis and his renunciation of Christianity hid a personality that drew heavily on Christianity. Marx had put forth a holistic, apocalyptic vision that, like Christianity, contained a passionate belief in humankind's ultimate deliverance from oppression. Unlike Christianity, a central piece of that vision displayed a "desire to recognize the self as God" (Men, "Fr. Sergei Bulgakov," 185). Bulgakov's book, according to Fr. Aleksandr, was a "remarkable work" about the "spiritual personality," a quality Marx had renounced but which, nevertheless, characterized his thinking (ibid.).

60. Ibid., 194.

61. Ibid.

62. Ibid., 197.

63. Aleksandr Men, "Sergei i Evgenii Trubetskie," in *Russkaia religioznaia filosofiia*, 49.

64. Ibid., 59.

65. Unlike many of the clergy, Sergei Nikolaevich did not fear biblical criticism, and viewed it as helpful to understanding the context in which the Gospels were written; ibid., 50–51, 59. Deeply influenced by the German scholar Adolph Harnack, under whom he studied at the University of Berlin, Sergei Nikolaevich also differed from his teacher. He admired Harnack's critical approach and his extensive knowledge of biblical sources, but he did not agree with the conclusions Harnack reached in his cycle of public lectures on "The Essence of Christianity," which he presented, in 1899–1900, at the University of Berlin and which caused a sensation. Trubetskoi, Fr. Aleksandr pointed out, "understood that the path to reality for the human being is not closed," and, on this point, he very much departed from Harnack (ibid., 53).

66. Ibid., 55.

67. Evgenii Nikolaevich Trubetskoi, *Mirosozertsanie V. S. Solov'eva*, 2 vols. (Moscow: Put', 1913), and *Religiozno-obshchestvennyi ideal zapadnogo khristianstva*, 2 vols. (1892; repr., St. Petersburg: Izd-vo Russkogo khristianskogo gumanitarnogo instituta, 2004).

68. Men, "Sergei i Evgenii Trubetskie," 68.

69. Evgenii Nikolaevich Trubetskoi, *Tri ocherka o russkoi ikone* (Moscow: InfoArt, 1991).

70. Men, "Sergei i Evgenii Trubetskie," 70.

71. Ibid., 69.

72. The later years of Evgenii Trubetskoi's life were filled with world war, revolutions, and civil war, as Fr. Aleksandr reminded his audience. The extreme violence that marked this period easily promoted a sense of meaninglessness. Against this meaninglessness, Trubetskoi posited the elements that were meaningful: love and unity, both of which ancient icons exhibited. A sacred painting could not be separated into pieces, cut up into fragments, without losing its meaning, Fr. Aleksandr said in his lecture. The same process applies to life; by separating the parts, the whole organism loses its meaning (ibid., 70).

73. Ibid., 69.

74. Morozova's significant contributions to and support for the discussion of philosophy, theology, art, and the circle of intellectuals she encouraged are well described in Evgenii Aleksandrovich Gollerbakh, *K nezrimomu gradu: Religiozno-filosofskaia gruppa "Put'" (1910-1919) v poiskakh novoi russkoi identichnosti* (St. Petersburg: Aleteiia, 2000), 61–75.

75. Ibid., 66.

76. Ibid.

77. Slavophile is the name for an independent group of individuals who represented a certain intellectual approach to Russia's major problems of the times. The group flourished in the 1840s and 1850s. Its members were influenced by German philosophers Georg Wilhelm Friedrich Hegel and Friedrich Wilhelm Joseph von Schelling and by German romanticism. The group's leaders were prominent landlords of broad cultural and intellectual interests; among their outstanding spokesmen were Petr and Ivan Kireevskii, Aleksei Khomiakov, and Konstantin Aksakov. The Slavophiles developed an ideology emphasizing Russia's unique historical destiny and the superiority of Russian Orthodoxy over Western religions. According to Ivan Kireevskii, Russia's most distinctive cultural characteristic was its "sobornost," or conciliarity, which set it apart from Western egoism, commercialism, and extreme individualism.

78. Ibid., 67.

79. Men, "Sergei i Evgenii Trubetskie," 70–71.

80. Men, "Khristianstvo i tvorchestvo," 260.

81. Men, "Two Understandings of Christianity," in Roberts and Shukman, *Christianity*, 159–60.

82. Men, "Khristianstvo i tvorchestvo," 262.

Notes to Chapter Thirteen

1. Fr. Vladimir Arkhipov, interview by author, Novaia Derevnia, July 1, 2009; Pavel Men, interview by author, Moscow, July 3, 2014; Fr. Georges Chistiakov, interview by author, Moscow, May 30, 2006; Aleksei Bodrov, "The Open University," *Religion, State, and Society* 22, no. 2 (1994): 199–204. In 1989, Fr. Aleksandr founded this organization to assist children facing lengthy hospital stays, and it is called the Help and Charity Service at the Russian Children's Clinical Hospital, in Moscow.

2. Organizers of the event celebrating the seventy-fifth anniversary of Fr. Aleksandr's birth, on January 22, 2010, selected a partial recording of this lecture to open the ceremony. The celebratory event was held in the Great Hall of the Library of Foreign Literature in Moscow, the same hall in which Fr. Aleksandr gave many of his lectures. The lecture hall that evening was filled to capacity with people who came to pay their respects, and the author was present.

3. Aleksandr Men, "Two Understandings of Christianity," in *Christianity for the Twenty-First Century: The Life and Work of Alexander Men*, ed. Elizabeth Roberts and Ann Shukman (London: SCM Press, 1996), 152.

4. Other literary scholars, however, dispute such a likeness, pointing out significant differences between Dostoevsky's character and the famous Amvrosii. But, Fr. Aleksandr emphasized, definite similarities existed between the literary figure and the religious leader that distinguished both of them.

5. Men, "Two Understandings of Christianity," 152–53.

6. Ibid., 153.

7. Ibid., 154.

8. Ibid., 155.

9. Ibid.

10. Ibid.,157.

11. Ibid., 156.

12. Ibid., 155, 157, 159.

13. This is also one of the main points in Nikolai Berdiaev's essay "Salvation and Creativity (Two Understandings of Christianity)," *Berdyaev.com*, http://www.berdyaev.com/berdiaev/berd_lib/1926_308.html.

14. Men, "Two Understandings of Christianity," 162–63.

15. Vladimir Il'ich Iliushenko, *Otets Aleksandr Men': Zhizn', Smert', Bessmertie*, 2nd ed. (Moscow: VGBIL im. M. I. Rudomino, 2010), 227.

16. Ibid., 360, 361.

17. Ibid., 325.

18. Men, "Khristianstvo i tvorchestvo," in *Radostnaia vest': Lektsy*, ed. M. V. Sergeeva (Moscow: Vita-Tsentr, 1992), 256.

19. Larissa Rudova, "Bergsonism in Russia: The Case of Bakhtin," *Neophilologus* 80, no. 2 (April 1996): 175–88.

20. Men, "Interv'iu na sluchai aresta," in *Kul'tura i dukhovnoe voskhozhdenie*, comp. R. I. Al'betkova and M. T. Rabotiaga (Moscow: Iskusstvo, 1992), 360.

21. Paola Marrati, "James, Bergson, and an Open Universe," in *Bergson, Politics, and Religion*, ed. Alexandre Lefebvre and Melanie White (Durham, NC: Duke University Press, 2012), 310.

22. Henri Bergson, *The Two Sources of Morality and Religion*, trans. R. Ashley Audra and Cloudesley Brereton, with the assistance of W. Horsfall Carter (Garden City, NY: Doubleday, Anchor Books, 1935), 266.

23. Ibid., 206, 266. These attributes are explored more fully in Bergson's preceding, related book, *Creative Evolution*, trans. Arthur Mitchell (New York: Henry Holt, 1911), 137–76.

24. Bergson, *Two Sources*, 206–7.

25. Ibid., 267. The open society is not static, but constantly seeks self-renewal, which comes from the interaction with other religions. The open society is not one that has simply expanded its boundaries, but is qualitatively different. See Frédéric Worms, "The Closed and the Open in the Two Sources of Morality and Religion: A Distinction That Changes Everything," in Lefebvre and White, *Bergson, Politics, and Religion*, 37–38.

26. Men, "Razum i isstuplenie mass," in Men, *Kul'tura i dukhovnoe voskhozhdenie*, 374–78. Fr. Aleksandr's essay first appeared in the newspaper *Sovetskaia kul'tura*, on July 28, 1990.

27. Ibid., 376. Earlier, in his *History of Religion*, Fr. Aleksandr contrasted Plato's view of the city-state with Socrates's, clearly voicing his support for the more open model advanced by Socrates.

28. Men, "Razum i isstuplenie mass," 376.

29. Aleksandr Men, *Bibliia i literatura: Lektsii* (Moscow: Khram dviatykh bessrebrenikov Kosmy i Damiana v Shubine, 2002).

30. Men, *Bibliia i literatura*, 34. See also his statement, "As long as we breathe, we must create. And this creativity must be multifaceted; in its essence, creativity comes from the soul." Men, "Khristianskaia kul'tura na Rusi," in *Radostnaia vest'*, 263.

31. See, for example, Lev Vladimirovich Cherepnin, *Obrazovanie russkogo tsentralizovannogo gosudarstva v XIV–XV vekakh: Ocherki sotsial'no-ekonomicheskoi i politicheskoi istorii Rusi* (Moscow: Izd-vo sotsial'no-ekonomicheskoi literatury, 1960); M. S. Bodnarskii, *Ocherki po istorii*

russkogo zemlevedeniia, vol. 1 (Moscow: Izd-vo Akademii nauk SSSR, 1947); and Sergei Vladimirovich Bakhruskin, *Nauchnye Trudy*, 4 vols. (Moscow: Izd-vo Akademii nauk SSSR, 1952–1959).

32. Men, *Bibliia i literatura*, 35.

33. Ibid., 37.

34. Ibid., 39.

35. Ibid., 57, 62.

36. Ibid., 47–48.

37. Ibid., 51.

38. Ibid., 128–29.

39. Ibid., 130.

40. Ibid., 132.

41. Ibid., 131–32.

42. Ibid., 135.

43. Ibid., 139.

44. Ibid., 141.

45. Ibid., 145–46.

46. Ibid., 163.

47. Ibid., 145.

48. Ibid., 173. Fr. Aleksandr referred to S. N. Bulgakov's statement that "Tolstoy, in an epoch of spiritual crisis, stirred up the conscience of society."

49. Jonathan Sutton, "The Religious Roots of Change in Present-Day Russia," *Religion, State, and Society* 21, no. 2 (1993): 231; Veniamin (Novik), *Pravoslavie, Khristianstvo, Demokratiia: Sbornik statei* (St. Petersburg: Aleteiia, 1999), 278–91.

50. Men, *Bibliia i literatura*, 174–75. Fr. Aleksandr makes special reference to Solov'ev's "Istoriia i budushchnost' teokratii." See Vladimir Sergeevich Solov'ev, *Issledovanie vsemirno-istoricheskogo puti k istinnoi zhizhi* (Zagreb: Aksionernaia tipografiia, 1887).

51. Ibid., 180.

52. Ibid., 183.

53. Ibid., 243.

54. Ibid., 277–78.

55. Ibid., 247–49, 251–53, 254–56, 272–74, 280–85, 328–30, 333–35. Taken together, the images of Christ in these revolutionary years were much different than the standard view of Christ as a myth that predominated later in the Soviet Union.

56. Evgenii Nikolaevich Trubetskoi, "Dva mira v drevnerusskoi ikonopisi," in *Tri ocherka o russkoi ikone: "Inoe tsarstvo" i ego iskateli v russkoi narodnoi skazke*, 2nd ed. (Moscow: Lenta-Press, 2003), 96. The English translation is used here: Eugene N. Trubetskoi, "Two Worlds in Old-Russian Icon Painting," in *Icons: Theology in Color*, trans. Gertrude Vakar, intro. George M. A. Hanfmann (New York: St. Vladimir's Seminary Press, 1973), 55.

57. Men, *Bibliia i literatura*, 288–89; Boris Pasternak, *Doctor Zhivago*, trans. Richard Pevear and Larissa Volokhonsky, intro. Richard Pevear (New York: Pantheon Books, 2010), 464.

58. Men, *Bibliia i literatura*, 289–90.

59. Ibid., 292; Pasternak, "The Garden of Gethsemane," in *Doctor Zhivago*, 496.

60. Men, *Bibliia i literatura*, 296. On the life and writings of Iurii Dombrovskii, see Peter Doyle, *Iurii Dombrovskii: Freedom under Totalitarianism*, ed. Peter I. Barta, Studies in Russian and European Literature 4 (Amsterdam: Harwood Academic, 2000).

61. Klara Turumova-Dombrovskaia, "Ubit za roman," *Novaia gazeta*, May 22, 2008, http://www.novayagazeta.ru/society/40145.htlm.

62. Men, *Bibliia i literatura*, 297.

63. Ibid.

64. See the perceptive comments on this phenomenon by Oliver Bullough, *The Last Man in Russia: The Struggle to Save a Dying Nation* (New York: Basic Books, 2013), 186–87.

65. Trubetskoi, *Icons*, 87, 89.

66. Ibid., 84.

67. Men, *Bibliia i literatura*, 297.

68. Ibid., 299–300.

69. Ibid., 301.

70. In his lecture, Fr. Aleksandr discussed the publishing industry in the 1930s. On religious subjects, the publishing house "Atheist" dominated the industry, producing massive quantities of books deriding religious views and extolling atheism. In this atmosphere, Bulgakov worked on his masterpiece, taking a much different approach than the perspectives of this industry (ibid., 302).

71. Ibid., 304.

72. Ibid.

73. Mikhail Aleksandrovich Men, interview with author, Ivanovo, July 1, 2013.

Notes to Chapter Fourteen

1. Fr. Vladimir Arkhipov, interview by author, Novaia Derevnia, July 1, 2009.

2. Sergei Bulgakov, "Heroism and Asceticism: Reflections on the Religious Nature of the Russian Intelligentsia," in *Vekhi: Landmarks; A Collection of Articles about the Russian Intelligentsia*, trans. and ed. Marshall S. Shatz and Judith E. Zimmerman (Armonk, NY: M. E. Sharpe, 1994), 17–49.

3. Mikhail Aleksandrovich Men, interview by author, Ivanovo, July 1, 2013. The interview took place in Mikhail Aleksandrovich's office in Ivanovo, where he served as governor-general of the province of Ivanovo.

4. Ibid.

5. Ibid.

6. Ibid.

7. Jack F. Matlock, Jr., *Autopsy of an Empire: The American Ambassador's Account of the Collapse of the Soviet Union* (New York: Random House, 1995), 295–330.

8. See Geoffrey Hosking, *Russia and the Russians: A History* (Cambridge, MA: The Belknap Press of Harvard University Press, 2001), 589–90.

9. David Remnick, *Lenin's Tomb: The Last Days of the Soviet Empire* (New York: Random House, 1993), 302.

10. Andrei Borisovich Zubov, ed. *Istoriia Rossii XX vek*, vol. 2, *1939–2007* (Moscow: Astrel', 2009), 560–61; Hosking, *Russia and the Russians*, 586–87; Vladimir Viktorovich Sogrin, *Politicheskaia istoriia sovremennoi Rossii, 1985–2001: Ot Gorbacheva do Putina* (Moscow: Ves' Mir, 2001), 25–44.

11. V. Pazlova, "Dialog? Tol'ko znakomstvo," *Nauka i religiia*, no. 6 (1988): 30–31.

12. John Garrard and Carol Garrard, *Russian Orthodoxy Resurgent: Faith and Power in the New Russia* (Princeton, NJ: Princeton University Press, 2008), 51–58.

13. See especially Irina Papkova, *The Orthodox Church and Russian Politics* (New York: Oxford University Press, 2011).

14. Zubov, *Istoriia Rossii XX vek*, 539.

15. A comprehensive listing of the large number of articles in Russian newspapers and journals concerning the debate over religion during 1989 and 1990 can be found in T. Ia. Kashirina, V. I. Mordvinova, and M. D. Afanas'ev, eds., *Sovetskoe gosudarstvo i Russkaia Pravoslavnaia Tserkov': K istorii vzaimootnoshenii (Metodiko-bibliograficheskie materialy v pomoshch' rabote bibliotek-metodicheskikh tsentrov)* (Moscow: Gosudarstvennaia publichnaia istoricheskaia biblioteka RSFSR, 1990). For analysis of the long-awaited Soviet Law on Freedom of Conscience and Religious Organizations, passed on October 1, 1990, by the Congress of People's Deputies, see Giovanni Codevilla, "Commentary on the New Soviet Law on Freedom of Conscience and Religious Organizations," *Religion in Communist Lands* 19, nos. 1–2 (Summer 1991): 119–45.

16. "Individual'noe i massovoe soznanie," *Inostrannaia literatura*, no. 11 (1990): 203.

17. The first symposium, in 1989, had included the British novelist Graham Greene. All three of the symposia featured major writers, artists, literary scholars, and theologians. The materials of the

symposia were presented in detail in *Inostrannaia literatura*, as follows: "Kommunizm i khristianstvo," no. 5 (1989): 203–24; "Khudozhnik i vlast," no. 5 (1990): 177–201; and "Individual'noe i massovoe soznanie," no. 11 (1990): 203–22.

18. "Individual'noe i massovoe soznanie," 203.

19. Ibid., 205.

20. Ibid., 204.

21. Ibid., 213.

22. Ibid.

23. Ibid.

24. Aleksandr Men, "K novomu perevodu knigi Ekklesiasta (predislovie)," *Detektiv i politika*, no. 3 (1989): 324.

25. "Individual'noe i massovoe soznanie," 222.

26. Ibid.

27. N. I. Basovskaia, "Predislovie," in *Ot rabstva k svobode: Lektsii po Vetkhomu Zavetu*, by Aleksandr Men (Moscow: Zhizn' s Bogom, 2008), 6.

28. Ibid.

29. Ibid., 7.

30. See, for example, Men, *Ot rabstva k svobode*, 29, 36–37, 56, 65–67, 69, 195–97, 203; Basovskaia, "Predislovie," 7; Fr. Aleksandr also included references to early Russian philosophers/ theologians, Nikolai Berdiaev and Sergei Bulgakov.

31. Men, *Ot rabstva k svobode*, 29, 240–41.

32. Fr. Vladimir Arkhipov, interview by author, Novaia Derevnia, July 1, 2009.

33. Yves Hamant, *Alexander Men: A Witness for Contemporary Russia (A Man for Our Times)*, trans. Steven Bigham, intro. Maxym Lysack (Torrance, CA: Oakwood, 1995), 189.

34. Aleksandr Men, "Religiia, 'kul't lichnosti' i sekuliarnoe gosudarstvo," in *Kul'tura i dukhovnoe vozkhozhdenie*, comp. R. I. Al'betkova and M. T. Rabotiaga (Moscow: Iskusstvo, 1992), 402–3, English translation: "Religion, the 'Cult of Personality,' and the Secular State," in *Christianity for the Twenty-First Century: The Life and Work of Alexander Men*, ed. Elizabeth Roberts and Ann Shukman (London: SCM Press, 1996), 378–413; Men, "Khristianskaia kul'tura na Rusi," in *Kul'tura i dukhovnoe vozkhozhdenie*, 151–52; Men, "Rol' tserkvi v sovremennom mire," *Mirovaia dukhovnaia kul'tura, khristianstvo, tserkov': Lektsii i besedy*. 2nd ed., ed. Anastasiia Andreeva et al. and comp. A. Belavin (Moscow: Fond imeni Aleksandra Menia, 1997), 625–32; Men, *Otets Aleksandr Men' otvechaet na voprosy*, 2nd ed. (Moscow: Zhizn' s Bogom, 2008), 236–37, 254; Pilar Bonet, "Poslednee interv'iu Aleksandra Menia," in Men, *Kul'tura i dukhovnoe voskhozhdenie*, 445.

35. Vladimir L'vovich Fainberg, *Vse detali etogo puteshestviia: Skrizhali; Vospominaniia ob o. Aleksandre Mene* (Moscow: Zarech'e, 2011), 441.

36. Aleksandr Men, "Chto proiskhodit s nashei kul'turoi? (Interv'iu)," in *Trudnyi put' k dialogu: Sbornik*, by Aleksandr Men, ed. N. Matiash, foreword by Antonii, Metropolitan of Sourozh (Moscow: Raduga, 1992), 81.

37. Mikhail Aleksandrovich Men, interview by author, Ivanovo, July 1, 2013.

38. Metropolitan Iuvenalii was an exception. He greatly valued and encouraged Fr. Aleksandr's activities throughout this period; Pavel Vol'fevich Men, interview by author, Moscow, July 2, 2013.

39. Aleksei Il'ich Osipov, interview by author, Sergiev Posad, June 11, 1994.

40. "Bez blagosloveniia," is referenced in *Vokrug imeni ottsa Aleksandra*, comp. A. I. Zorin and V. I. Iliushenko (Moscow: Obshchestvo "kul'turnoe vozrozhdenie" imeni Aleksandra Menia, 1993), 35; Vasilenko offered a summary and response to these accusations, in "Vokrug imeni ottsa Aleksandra Menia," 9–34, and in the same volume, see Vladimir Il'ich Iliushenko, "Kompleks sal'eri," 94–95.

41. John Anthony McGuckin, *The Orthodox Church: An Introduction to Its History, Doctrine, and Spiritual Culture* (Malden, MA: Blackwell, 2008), 17.

42. Hamant, *Alexander Men*, 194; Aleksandr Markovich Verkhovskii, *Politicheskoe pravoslavie: Russkie pravoslavnye natsionalisty i fundamentalisty, 1995–2001 gg.* (Moscow: Oktiabr', 2003), 5–12.

43. Hannah Arendt, *The Origins of Totalitarianism*, 2nd ed. (Orlando, FL: Harcourt Brace Jovanovich, 1979), 268–69, 364; James H. Billington, *Russia in Search of Itself* (Washington, DC: Woodrow Wilson Press Center, 2004), 86–89, 104, 141, 164.

44. Vasil'ev earlier worked under the guidance of the nationalist artist Il'ia Glazunov, whom he served as assistant and secretary. Aleksandr Verkhovskii and Vladimir Pribylovskii, *Natsional-patrioticheskie organizatsii v Rossii: Istoriia, ideologiia, ekstremistskie tendentsii* (Moscow: Izd-vo "Institut eksperimental'noi sotsiologii," 1996), 10–15, 28–29, 154–56, 167.

45. Yeltsin agreed to meet with the leaders of Pamiat' in an effort to learn more about their identity and perspectives. He came away from the meeting extremely concerned about their extremist and aggressive views.

46. This was a charge Fr. Aleksandr's enemies often leveled against him. In addition, Fr. Aleksandr's public statements about inner freedom, the openness it required, and the allegiance to a different pursuit of truth than what the state espoused was also anathema to the KGB. His views on the individual and mass consciousness moved in the opposite direction from KGB leaders' desire for social order and a powerful, unified Russian state. The threat that Fr. Aleksandr's public statements posed increasingly became a source of irritation.

47. For the resolutions of Pamiat' and additional primary materials on other national-patriotic groups, see Verkhovskii and Pribylovskii, *Natsional-patrioticheskie organizatsii*, 15–18, 105–83; Wallace Daniel, "The Vanished Past: Russia's Search for Identity," *The Christian Century*, March 17, 1993, 293–96.

48. Bonet, "Poslednee interv'iu Aleksandra Menia," 449.

49. Fr. Aleksandr asked what would lead Russia out of the spiritual and moral abyss. As a first step, he called for repentance, an old and sacred call, deeply embedded in the Gospels. "Repentance is not some sterile 'grubbing around in one's soul,' not some masochistic self-humiliation, but a re-evaluation leading to action, the action John the Baptist called 'the fruits of repentance'" (Aleksandr Men, "Russia in Crisis," in Roberts and Shukman, *Christianity*, 142). See, for the full interview, Men, "Chto proiskhodit, 78–92; Men, "K novomu perevodu," 323–24.

50. Bonet, "Poslednee interv'iu Aleksandra Menia," 449.

51. "Pis'mo Sviashchenniku Aleksandru Meniu," in *Khronika neraskrytogo ubiistva*, by Sergei Bychkov (Moscow: Russkoe reklamnoe izd-vo, 1996), appendix 13, 194.

52. Fr. Aleksandr maintained that his manner and commitments consistently stayed the same—to serve a higher purpose than himself: "I work now as I have always worked: with my face into the wind. This is not as easy as it may sometimes seem. At the present time, the wind is obviously stronger, especially from the Black Hundreds. I have to stand solidly on my two feet, legs spread, in order not to be overturned. In short, don't be worried about me. . . . I am only an instrument that God is using for the moment. Afterwards, things will be as God wants them" (Aleksandr Men, quoted in Hamant, *Alexander Men*, 204).

53. Alekander Men, "Christianity for the Twenty-First Century," in Roberts and Shukman, *Christianity*, 179.

54. Ibid., 185.

55. Ibid., 191.

56. Ibid., 180.

57. Ibid., 191–92.

Notes to Chapter Fifteen

1. Vladimir Il'ich Iliushenko, *Otets Aleksandr Men': Zhizn', Smert', Bessmertie*, 2nd ed. (Moscow: VGBIL im. M. I. Rudomino, 2010), 399–400, 401, 402, 405; Andrei Alekseevich Eremin, *Otets Aleksandr Men': Pastyr' na rubezhe vekov*, 2nd ed. (Moscow: Carte Blanche, 2001), 435–36.

2. Pilar Bonet, "Poslednee interv'iu Aleksandra Menia," in *Kul'tura i dukhovnoe voskhozhdenie*, by Aleksandr Men, comp. R. I. Al'bertkova and M. T. Rabotiaga (Moscow: Iskusstvo, 1992), 445.

3. Eremin, *Otets Aleksandr Men'*, 429–30.

4. The Centre of Religious Literature in the Library of Foreign Literature is dedicated to Fr. Aleksandr Men. Consecrated by Patriarch Aleksii II shortly after Fr. Aleksandr's death, the Centre's collections display books and other resources featuring a wide assortment of world religions and communicating Fr. Aleksandr's lifelong efforts to engage in dialogue with them.

5. Vladimir Andreevich Skorodenko, *Margarita Rudomino All-Russian State Library for Foreign Literature* (Moscow: Rudomino, 2004), 15.

6. Ekaterina Genieva, "Posledniaia strecha," *Znamia*, no. 9 (September 1991): 201–203.

7. Ibid., 203.

8 . Editors' introductory comments to Fr. Aleksandr Men, "Christianity for the Twenty-First Century," in *Christianity for the Twenty-First Century: The Life and Work of Alexander Men*, ed. Elizabeth Roberts and Ann Shukman (London: SCM Press, 1996), 179; Andrei Mikhailovich Tavrov, *Syn chelovecheskii: Ob ottse Aleksandre Mene* (Moscow: Eksmo, 2014), 269–70.

9. Men, "Christianity," 191.

10. Anastasiia Iakovlevna Andreeva, "V nem zhilo bessmertie . . . ," in *Taina zhizni i smerti*, ed. A. I. Andreeva (Moscow: Znanie, 1992), 3–4.

11. Ibid., 5. Fr. Aleksandr had continually raised eternal questions and had put them squarely before us, Andreeva said, and they now would remain before the Russian people.

12. Aleksandr Minkin, "Ne rydaite obo mne . . . ," in *Pamiati protoiereia Aleksandra Menia*, ed. T. V. Gromova (Moscow: Rudomino, 1991), 76.

13. "Pis'mo Patriarkha Moskovskogo i Vseia Rusi Aleksiia II posle ubiistva protoiereia Aleksandra Menia," September 11, 1990, *Alexandermen.ru*, http://www.alexandermen.ru/biogr/slovopat.html.

14. See also the metropolitan's moving prayer, which he gave after the burial and addressed to Fr. Aleksandr, stating his assurance that Fr. Aleksandr will have a "place by the Throne of the Sovereign Christ, where you will pray for your spiritual children, as they will offer prayers from the heart for you. Eternal memory to you, beloved brother in Christ" (Metropolitan Iuvenalii, "Slovo, skazannoe posle otpevaniia protoiereia Aleksandra Menia v sele Novaia Derevnia," September 11, 1990, *Alexandermen.ru*, http://www.alexandermen.ru/biogr/juvenal.html.

15. Iuvenalii, "Slovo."

16. Stephen Handelman, "Soviet Priest's Murder Sends Shock Waves Through Nation," *Toronto Star*, September 23, 1990, Sunday Second Edition.

17. The *Star's* correspondent quoted Father Aleksandr Borisov, a member of the Moscow city council, who gave one of the graveside eulogies at Fr. Aleksandr's funeral on September 11, as saying: "It is as though God wants to tell us something very important with the death of Alexander. . . . The struggle for the soul of Russia and its people has only just begun, and those who are in front will always fall first" (Handelman, "Soviet Priest's Murder").

18. Michael Bourdeaux, "Obituary: Fr. Alexander Men," *Independent* (London), September 14, 1990, gazette page. See also "Father Aleksandr Men," *Times*, September 15, 1990, Sunday edition. Appearing in the *Washington Post* forty days after Fr. Aleksandr's death, David Remnick's assessment had a similar theme. "During the Brezhnev years, Fr. Aleksandr was one of the few priests who did not compromise with the regime; he showed everyone what it meant to live honestly, to hold high ideals, and to seek spiritual independence." Remnick referenced these virtues as he cited Fr. Aleksandr's frenetic activities in the last several years of his life. "Now, he told his brother Pavel, he felt like an 'arrow finally sprung from the bow,' able to preach and lecture in churches and auditoriums, on radio and television all without fear. His murder, on a narrow asphalt path on the way to the train station, silenced that active voice." David Remnick, "Lament for a Murdered Russian Priest: On the Brink of Religious Freedom, a Reminder of the Need for Fear," *Washington Post*, October 18, 1990.

19. Irina Ilovaiskaia, "Pastyr', ispovednik, muchenik: Ego zaveshchanie—propoved' liudei i neustannoe iskanie pravdy," *Russkaia mysl'*, no. 3845, September 14, 1990, 8. Andrei Sakharov died in December 1989.

20. Ibid.

21. *Izvestiia*, quoted by Handelman, "Soviet Priest's Murder."

22. Minkin, "Ne rydaite obo mne . . . ," quoted in Remnick, *Lenin's Tomb*, 364.

23. Sergei Sergeevich Bychkov, *Khronika neraskrytogo ubiistva* (Moscow: Russkoe reklamnoe izd-vo, 1996), 10.

24. Ibid.

25. Larisa Kislinskaia, "Ubiistvo sviashchennika: Sledstvie prodolozhaetsia," *Leninskoe znamia*, September 18, 1990.

26. Oxana Antic, "Series of Assaults on Russian Orthodox Priests," *Report on the USSR*, February 22, 1991, 4.

27. Mary Dejevsky, "Third Priest Murdered in Moscow Crime Wave," *Times* (London), February 6, 1991.

28. Jeanne Vronskaya, "Obituary: Father Superior Lazar," *Independent* (London), January 16, 1991.

29. Dejevsky, "Third Priest Murdered"; Antic, "Series of Assaults," 4.

30. Fr. Aleksandr's death, Aleksandr Minkin wrote, has brought Russia to a crucial juncture. What also troubled Minkin was the public's reaction: he compared Fr. Aleksandr's murder to the assassination of President Kennedy in the United States, which stirred the entire country, and the assassination of the charismatic Polish priest and supporter of Solidarity, Jerzy Popieluszko, in 1994, by three members of Poland's internal intelligence agency. The latter event triggered a national protest against abuses of power by Communist authorities. In contrast, Fr. Aleksandr's death in Russia fomented no such soul-searching or expressions of public outrage, Minkin wrote, but prompted a casual indifference: "people are standing in line talking about other things." Minkin, "Ne rydaite obo mne . . . ," 76, 78.

31. The letter was signed by Il'ia Zaslavskii, and, in addition to President Gorbachev, was addressed to the director of the Committee on State Security of the USSR, V. A. Kriuchkov, and minister of Internal Affairs, V. V. Bakatin.

32. Il'ia Zaslavskii, "Prezidentu SSSR M. S. Gorbachevu," in Gromova, *Pamiati protoiereia Aleksandra Menia*, 23.

33. Ibid.

34. Oxana Antic speculated that the murders might have represented intentional acts ("Series of Assaults," 4).

35. Minkin, "Ne rydaite obo mne . . . ," 76.

36. Kislinskaia, "Ubiistvo sviashchennika."

37. News summary, Keston Archive, Aleksandr Men file, SU 18/05/1991.

38. Ibid.

39. See Sergei Bychkov's account of the case of Mikhail Potemkin, whom the police arrested shortly after the murder of Fr. Lazar (Viacheslav Solnyshko), in the winter of 1990. Potemkin claimed that members of a Zionist organization in Russia killed Fr. Lazar, and Potemkin confessed to being part of the plot to murder Fr. Aleksandr Men. According to Bychkov, Potemkin's story fascinated the chief of the investigating committee, Ivan Leshchenko. After fleshing out the details, Leshchenko planned to make public Potemkin's story, before learning that Potemkin had served as a KGB provocateur during the Brezhnev era and afterward. In September 1986, he had been the KGB agent who passed classified Soviet information to the American journalist Nicholas Daniloff, a provocation that precipitated charges of espionage against Daniloff and provoked a diplomatic crisis (Bychkov, *Khronika neraskrytogo ubiistva*, 17).

40. James H. Billington, "Rossiia v poiskakh sebia," *Nezavisimaia gazeta*, April 6, 1991, 5.

41. Aleksandr Verkhovskii and Vladimir Pribylovskii, *Natsional-patriotichtskie organizatsii v Rossii: Istoriia, ideologiia, ekstremistskie tendentsii* (Moscow: Izd-vo "Institut eksperimental'noi sotsiologii," 1996), 28–29; Aleksandr Verkhovskii, *Politicheskoe pravoslavie: Russkie pravoslavnye natsionalisty i fundamentalisty, 1995–2001* (Moscow: Oktiabr', 2003), 5–6, 21–22, 277–78; Vladimir Viktorovich Sogrin, *Politicheskaia istoriia sovremennoi Rossii, 1985–2001: Ot Gorbacheva do Putina* (Moscow: Ves' Mir, 2001), 43–44.

42. Aleksandr Verkhovskii et al., "Tserkov' v politike i politika v tserkvi," in *Politicheskaia ksenofobiia: Radikal'nye gruppy, predstavlenniia liderov, rol' tserkvi* (Moscow: Panorama, 1999), 134, 136–37, 141–42.

43. Such themes were repeatedly conveyed in the journals *Nash sovremennik* and *Molodaia gvardiia* in 1988–1989, and also in the mass-produced novels of the popular writer V. Pikul' (Sogrin, *Politicheskaia istoriia*, 43–44).

44. The 1976 "Pis'mo sviashchenniku Aleksandru Meniu" (in Bychkov, *Khronika neraskrytogo ubiistva*, appendix 13, 194–207), which questioned the correctness of Fr. Aleksandr's teachings and his authenticity as an Orthodox believer, exemplified the tenor of these disparaging contentions.

45. Ioann, metropolitan of Saint Petersburg and Ladoga, quoted in Bychkov, *Khronika neraskrytogo ubiistva*, 85. Metropolitan Ioann falls both within the fundamentalists and the anti-Semites.

46. Bychkov, *Khronika neraskrytogo ubiistva*, 19.

47. Ibid.,18–19; "Pis'mo sviashchenniku Aleksandru Meniu," 194-207.

48. Bychkov, *Khronika neraskrytogo ubiistva*, 19.

49. Bonet, "Poslednee interv'iu Aleksandra Menia," 448–49.

50. Ibid., 449.

51. On charges of an alleged alliance between Jews and Catholics, see Iurii Tabak, "President Rossii v zerkale mifologicheskogo soznaniia radikal'nykh grupp," in *Sumerki shovinizma: Analiz rossi-iskikh ksenofobskikh izdanii*, 2nd ed. (Moscow: Academia, 2008), 209.

52. Bychkov, *Khronika neraskrytogo ubiistva*, 12.

53. Vladimir Il'ich Iliushenko, interview by author, Moscow, June 5, 2006.

54. Bonet, "Poslednee interv'iu Aleksandra Menia," 445.

55. "Individual'noe i massovoe soznanie," *Inostrannaia literatura*, no. 11 (1990): 222; and Leonid Ivanovich Vasilenko, "Khristianstvo i kul'tura v trudakh protoeireia Aleksandra Menia," in Men, *Kul'tura i dukhovnoe voskhozhdenie*, 480.

56. Bonet, "Poslednee interv'iu Aleksandra Menia," 446. Vasilenko helpfully reminds the reader of Fr. Aleksandr's earlier discussion, in *Magizm i Edinobozhie*, of the process in which individuals had sought freedom from patrimonial ways of thinking. In contemporary Russia and elsewhere, Fr. Aleksandr had seen aspects of patrimonial consciousness reasserting themselves in "aggressive forms in mass neo-pagan social movements" (Vasilenko, "Khristianstvo i kul'tura," 479; Aleksandr Men, "Razum i isstuplenie mass," in *Kul'tura i dukhovnoe voskhozhdenie*, 377.

57. Vladimir Il'ich Iliushenko, interview by author, Moscow, June 5, 2006.

58. Mikhail Aleksandrovich Men, interview by author, Ivanovo, July 1, 2013.

59. Ibid.

60. The details about Sychev's visit with Fr. Aleksandr, in June 1990, were recorded by Sergei Bychkov, "KGB protiv sviashchennika Aleksandra Menia," *Vestnik russkogo khristianskogo dvizheniia*, n.s., no. 196 (2010): 127.

61. Pavel Vol'fovich Men, interview by author, Moscow, July 3, 2013.

62. Ibid.

63. Pavel Vol'fovich Men, interview by author, Moscow, June 2, 2007.

64. Ibid.

65. Bonet, "Poslednee interv'iu Aleksandra Menia," 446. In the 1960s, Fr. Aleksandr told Bonet, the church had a group of outward-looking, energetic, reform-minded priests who were capable of leading the Orthodox Church in a positive, appealing direction. They had, however, been crushed by bishops in the hierarchy of the church. At present, Fr. Aleksandr said, this situation was reversed. Among the elite of the church were hierarchs who believed that significant reforms had to be enacted to make the church more appealing. But the reformist elements were opposed by the broad, middle level of the Orthodox clergy, who aspired, most of all, to recover the status and privileges the church had enjoyed in the pre-Bolshevik past.

66. Pavel Vol'fovich Men, interview by author, Moscow, July 3, 2013. During his investigations, Sergei Bychkov reported that an independent medical examiner, in 1995, who carefully studied

the head wound of Fr. Aleksandr, found that the instrument used in the assault was not an axe. The medical examiner announced that a sapper's spade (*sapernaia lopatka*), a weapon common to KGB professionals, served as the murder weapon. Bychkov quoted from a KGB training manual, which describes the militant quality of the instrument: "with the sharpened edge of the spade, one may easily cut the throat, break the skull into halves, separate the fingers from the hand, and, with a strong blow to the stomach, render an opponent defenseless." The original investigators of Fr. Aleksandr's murder pursued an incorrect track, as they searched for the axe used in the killing of Fr. Aleksandr, according to Bychkov. He reported seeing in the chief investigator's office a display of nearly twenty axes, supposed models of the murder weapon. But this, like so much else in the case, sent the investigators down a false trail. Bychkov was convinced that only highly skilled professionals could have carried out Fr. Aleksandr's murder (Bychkov, "KGB," 128).

67. Fr. Viktor Grigorenko, interview by author, Semkhoz, July 4, 2013.

68. Andrei Fadin, "Filosov Iurii Senokosov ob ubiistve o. Aleksandra Menia," *Vek XX i mir*, no. 1 (1991): 33.

69. Ibid., 33–34. Fr. Aleksandr's murder, Senokosov maintained, repeated similar acts in Russia's past, carried out by people who were convinced that murder could resolve a religious or a political crisis. Senokosov had in mind the religious crisis of the sixteenth century and the creation of Tsar Ivan Groznyi's *oprichniki*, the group of terrorists who sought to purify the country. The Russian philosopher referred to the analysis in Georgii Petrovich Fedotov's seminal work, *Sviatye drevnei Rusi*, recently published for the first time in Russia. He had also in mind the assassination of Tsar Aleksandr II in 1881, a political murder carried out under much different circumstances. Fr. Aleksandr's killing, Senokosov argued, had parallels to these two earlier events, in which murder was viewed as a sacrificial act.

70. Aleksandr Men, "Chto takoe liubov'? V chem smysl zhizni?" *Sreten'e*, no. 2 (1990): 9–13, reprinted as "Otvety na voprosy," in Men, *Kul'tura i dukhovnoe voskhozhdenie*, 144.

Notes to Epilogue

1. An extended description of the courtyard is included in Wallace L. Daniel, "Aleksandr Men and Russian Orthodoxy: The Conflict between Freedom and Power," *Religion in Eastern Europe* 29, no. 4 (November 2009): 1–20.

2. Leonid Ivanovich Vasilenko, "Posmertnaia travlia ottsa Aleksandra Menia," *Vestnik russkogo khristianskogo dvizheniia*, no. 180 (2000): 275.

3. *Zemshchina*, no. 1 (May 1991), quoted by Yves Hamant, *Alexander Men: A Witness for Contemporary Russia (A Man for Our Times)*, trans. Steven Bingham, intro. Maxym Lysack (Torrance, CA: Oakwood, 1995), 5.

4. Feliks Karelin, Sergei Antiminsov, and Andrei Kuraev, *O bogoslovii protoiereia Aleksandra Menia* (Zhitomir: Ni-Ka, 1999).

5. Olga Loukmanova, review of *O bogoslovii protoiereia Aleksandra Menia*, by Feliks Karelin, Sergei Antiminsov, and Andrei Kuraev, in *East-West Church and Ministry Report* 7, no. 3 (Summer 1999): 3.

6. Feliks Karelin's arrival at Novaia Derevnia, his personality, and relationship to Fr. Aleksandr are described in Aleksandr Men, *O sebe: Vospominaniia, interv'iu, besedy, pis'ma*. (Moscow: Zhizn' s Bogom, 2007), 145–53, 170–74.

7. Karelin's essay is titled "O domostroitel'nykh predelakh bogoizbrannosti evreiskogo naroda," in Feliks Karelin, Sergei Antiminsov, and Andrei Kuraev, *O bogoslovii protoiereia Aleksandra Menia* (Zhitomir: Ni-Ka, 1999), 4–21.

8. Ibid., 12.

9. Ibid., 21.

10. Sergii Antiminsov, "Protoierei Aleksandr Men' kak kommentator Sviashchennogo Pisaniia," in Karelin et al., *O bogoslovii*, 22–23.

11. Ibid., 33–34.

12. A major source of criticism concerned Fr. Aleksandr's interpretation of evil. The reader will recall Fr. Aleksandr's belief, which he based on the Gospels, that good and evil had existed in the world from the beginning, and human beings had to choose between them. Antiminsov adamantly objected to this view, claiming it had no basis in Christianity. Maintaining God to be absolute Good, everything in God's creation was also good; evil arose because of man's original sin, not because of a continuing battle between the powers of good and evil. According to Antiminsov, Fr. Aleksandr attempted "to turn sacred history into something else," an amorphous, superfluous account in which his "god of history" remained indifferent to good and evil, and which Antiminsov labeled as a "Theology of Chaos," the way of the Antichrist. Ibid., 34, 35, 60–61.

13. Andrei Kuraev, "Aleksandr Men': Poteriavshiisia missioner," in Karelin, Antiminsov, and Kuraev, *O bogoslovii*, 76–104.

14. Ibid., 79–82, 90–91.

15. Andrei Kuraev, *Okkul'tizm v Pravoslavii* (Moscow: Blagovest, 1998). Kuraev devoted the first chapter in his book to Fr. Aleksandr, again labelling Fr. Aleksandr a Uniate. *Okkul'tizm v Pravoslavii* had a press run of thirty thousand copies.

16. They included, most notably, book outlets in the Church of the Sacred Martyrs Kosma and Damian in central Moscow, where Fr. Aleksandr Borisov, Fr. Aleksandr's former associate, served as head priest, and the several different churches served by Fr. Georgii Kochetkov.

17. Leonid Vasilenko, "Za chto nenavidiat ottsa Aleksandra Menia," *NG-religii* 18, no. 65 (2000), http://www.vehi.net/men/vasilenko2.html, and Vasilenko, "Posmertnaia travlia," 259–89.

18. Vasilenko, "Za chto nenavidiat."

19. Aleksandr Ermolin, "Mesto ottsa Aleksandra v Pravoslavnom predanii," *Alexandermen. com*, http://www.alexandrmen.ru/biogr/ermolin.html.

20. Ibid.

21. Ibid. Fr. Aleksandr expressed and explained in detail these relationships of the priest with his spiritual children in *Prakticheskoe rukovodstvo k molitve* (Riga: Fond im. Aleksandra Menia, 1991).

22. Ermolin specifically cited the teachings of Saint Grigorii the Great and Saint Paul. His reference is to Fr. Aleksandr's "Pis'mo ob ekumenizme." http://www.alexandrmen.ru/letters/ecumenzm. html.

23. Ermolin, "Mesto ottsa Aleksandra."

24. Kuraev, *Okkul'tizm*, 31, 38–39.

25. Dmitrii Efimovich Furman, interview by author, Moscow, June 6, 1994.

26. Mikhail Aleksandrovich Men, interview by author, Ivanovo, July 1, 2013.

27. Fr. Aleksandr's *Mir Biblii* was issued in 300,000 copies by the publishing house Knizhnaia palata, in 1990 (Iakov Krotov, "Fr. Aleksandr: Bibliografiia," *Biblioteka Iakova Krotova*, http://krotov. info/library/13_m/myen/_bibl_menn.htm). In the same year, beginning in June and in five subsequent issues, the journal *Smena: Ezhemesiachnyi literaturno-khudozhestvennyi publitsisticheskii zhurnal* published Fr. Aleksandr's *Syn chelovecheskii*.

28. Krotov, "Fr. Aleksandr."

29. Mikhail Aleksandrovich Men, interview by author, Ivanovo, July 1, 2013; Aleksandr Men, *Syn chelovecheskii*, 7th ed. (Moscow: Zhizn' s Bogom, 2014).

30. Sergei Borisovich Filatov, interview by author, Moscow, June 15, 1994.

31. Fr. Aleksandr Borisov, interview by author, Moscow, May 31, 2006.

32. On Fr. Georgii Kochetkov's background and ministry, see Wallace L. Daniel, *The Orthodox Church and Civil Society in Russia* (College Station, TX: Texas A&M University Press, 2006), 74–108.

33. Fr. Aleksandr Men, untitled statement announcing the founding of the "Cultural Renaissance Society" (1988), Keston Archive, Aleksandr Men File, SU 18/05/1991.

34. Obshchestvo "Kul'turnoe Vozrozhdenie" imeni Aleksandr Menia, *Biulleten' No. 3*, Keston Archive, Aleksandr Men File, SU 18/05/1991.

35. Ibid.

36. Ibid.

37. Vladimir Il'ich Iliushenko, *Otets Aleksandr Men': Zhizn', Smert', Bessmertie*, 2nd ed. (Moscow: VGBIL im. M. I. Rudomino, 2010), 391–92. Iliushenko served as one of the organizers of the society.

38. This educational mission reflects Fr. Aleksandr's thinking; participants invited to the first organizational meeting of the society in 1988 included the well-known folk singer Bulat Okudzhava, writer Iulii Kim, philologist Mikhail Gasparov, poets Aleksandr Zorin and Vladimir Kornilov, director of the Library of Foreign Literature Ekaterina Genieva, director of the Museum of Fine Arts Irina Antonova, director of the Center for Education, Russian Ministry of Education and Culture Evgenii Iamburg, and many others. Ibid., 391.

39. Ibid., 141.

40. Ibid., 391.

41. "Pomogite spasti detei!," *Deti.msk.ru*, http://deti.msk.ru.

42. Ibid.

43. Aleksandr Aleksandrovich Bessmertnyi-Anzimirov, "Poslednii li novomuchenikov rossi-iskikh?" in *Pamiati protoiereia Aleksandra Menia*, ed. T. V. Gromova (Moscow: Rudomino, 1991), 97–98.

44. Fr. Georgii Petrovich Chistiakov, *Putevoi bloknot*, comp. N. F. Izmailovaia (Moscow: Tsentr knigi Rudomino, 2013), 117, and Ekaterina Iur'evna Genieva, "Zhivoi golos ottsa Georgii," preface to *Putevoi bloknot*, 7.

45. Fr. Georgii Chistiakov, interview by author, Moscow, May 30, 2006. See also the description of Fr. Georgii in Iliushenko, *Otets Aleksandr Men, 332–35.*

46. Sophia Kishkovsky, "At a Russian Hospital, Art Inspires Children," *New York Times*, January 7, 2006. In 1997, the society was registered as the Regional Public Charity Foundation for Seriously Ill and Abandoned Children (Regional'nyi blagotvoritel'nyi obshchestvennyi fond pomoshchi tiazh-elobol'nym i obezdolennym detiam), and the following year began fundraising through the Internet. The hospital has received support from local and foreign organizations, including the Russian émigré organization, the Orthodox Christian organization ACER-Russie, in Paris, and the Italian organiza-tion *Aiutateci a Salvare i Bambini* (Help Us Save the Children) (Kishkovsky, "At a Russian Hospital").

47. For example, in the summer of 2005, in cooperation with the Russian State University for the Humanities and the Latvian Ministry of Foreign Affairs, the Center helped organize a summer camp for students. The Russian State University selected Riga "so that the students might learn more about Latvia's positive experience with people of different nations and religious confessions living side by side in harmony." Ministry of Foreign Affairs of the Republic of Latvia, "Summer Camp Held in Riga for Students of the Russian State University for the Humanities," http://www.mfa.gov.lv/en/security/news/4457/?pg=6070. The almanac published by the Center contains materials written by academicians, theologians, pastors, and former parishioners of Fr. Aleksandr, on various aspects of his life and min-istry. Currently issued under the title *Khristianos*, the almanac is a valuable resource on Fr. Aleksandr's teachings, as well as the connections he made between religion and culture. See especially the large volume, dedicated to his memory, on the twentieth anniversary of his death, *Khristianos* 19 (2010).

48. Pavel Men supplied the author with these publication figures (interview by author, Moscow, July 3, 2013).

49. "Patriarkh Kirill prevetstvoval uchastnikov v Menevskikh chtenii," September 10, 2010. http://blagovest-info.ru/index.php?ss=2&s=8&id=36566; "Patriarch Kirill blagoslovil rasprostrane-nie trudov ottsa Aleksandra Menia v khramakh Russkoi tserkvi," September 10, 2010. http://www.interfax-religion.ru/?act=news&div=42164.

50. Fr. Vladimir Arkhipov, interview by author, Novaia Derevnia, July 1, 2009.

51. Fr. Vladimir has written a small book in which these points are developed, largely through his understanding of Fr. Aleksandr's teachings. Vladimir Arkhipov, *Slovo ob ottse Aleksandre* (Moscow: Blagovest, 2008).

52. Fr. Vladimir Arkhipov, interview by author, Novaia Derevnia, July 1, 2009.

53. Ibid.

Selected Bibliography

Archival Sources

Keston Archive, Baylor University
  Aleksandr Mèn file, SU 18/05/1991
  Anatolii Krasnov-Levitin file, SU/Ort 2/file 3
  KGB files, Anita Deyneka Collection, Box 1
  Gleb Yakunin file, SL/Ort8/2

Interviews by Author

Fr. Mikhail Aksenov-Meerson, Bethesda, MD, July 27, 2011.
Fr. Vladimir Arkhipov, Novaia Derevnia, July 1, 2009.
Fr. Aleksandr Borisov, Moscow, May 31, 2006.
Andrei Cheniak, Moscow, May 24, 2007.
Fr. Georgii Chistiakov, Moscow, May 30, 2006, and June 8, 2006.
Sergei Borisovich Filatov, Moscow, June 15, 1994.
Dmitrii Efimovich Furman, Moscow, June 6, 1994.
Ekaterina Iur'evna Genieva, Moscow, June 5, 2006, and July 3, 2009.
Fr. Viktor Grigorenko, Moffat, Scotland, September 16, 2012, and Semkhoz, Russia, July 4, 2013.
Yves Hamant, Moscow, January 20, 2010.
Vladimir Il'ich Iliushenko, Moscow, June 5, 2006.
Mikhail Aleksandrovich Men, Ivanovo, July 1, 2013.
Pavel Vol'fovich Men, Moscow, June 5, 2006; June 2, 2007; July 3, 2013.
Andrei Il'ich Osipov, Sergiev Posad, June 11, 1994.
Iurii Mikhailovich Tabak, Moscow, October 19, 2008.
Gleb Yakunin, Moscow, May 10, 2007.

Writings by Father Aleksandr Men

About Christ and the Church. Translated by Alexis Vinogradov. Torrance, CA: Oakwood, 1996.
"The Authority of the Church." In Men, *About Christ*, 77–86.
"Beseda ob apostole Pavle." In Men, *Tserkov' i my*, 77–100.
"Beseda ob iskuplenii." In Men, *Mirovaia dukhovnaia kul'tura*, 648–55.
"Beseda v dome prestarelykh i invalidov." In Men, *Liubit' Boga*, 181–202.
Bibliia i literatura: Lektsii. Moscow: Khram sviatykh bessrebrenikov Kosmy i Damiana v Shubine, 2002.
Byt' khristianinom: Interv'iu i posledniaia lektsiia. Moscow: Anno Domini, 1994.
"Christianity for the Twenty-First Century." In Roberts and Shukman, *Christianity*, 179–92.
Christianity for the Twenty-First Century: The Life and Work of Alexander Men. Edited by Elizabeth Roberts and Ann Shukman. London: SCM Press, 1996.
"Christianity: The Universal Vision." In Roberts and Shukman, *Christianity*, 75–103.
"Chto proiskhodit s nashei kul'turoi? (Interv'iu)." In Men, *Trudnyi put' k dialogu*, 78–93.
"Chto takoe liubov'? V chem smysl zhizni?" *Sreten'e*, no. 2 (1990): 9–13. Reprinted as "Otvety na voprosy." In Men, *Kul'tura i dukhovnoe voskhozhdenie*, 140–44.
"A Conversation about Redemption." In Men, *About Christ*, 87–96.

"A Credo for Today's Christian." In Roberts and Shukman, *Christianity*, 68–74.

Dionis, Logos, Sud'ba: Grecheskaia religiia i filosofiia ot epokhi kolonozatsii do Aleksandra. Vol. 4 of *Istoriia religii: V poiskakh puti, istiny, i zhizni*. Moscow: Slovo, 1991.

"Faith and Its Enemies." In Roberts and Shukman, *Christianity*, 54–67.

"Fenomen cheloveka." In *Pravoslavnye vesti*. Edited by Vladimir Erokhin, 4–8. Moscow: Tip. Informatsionno-blagotvoritel'nogo tsentra Put', Istina i Zhizn', 2005.

"Fr. Sergei Bulgakov." In Men, *Russkaia religioznaia filosofiia*, 177–97.

"'Gospod' moi i Bog moi,'" *Zhurnal Moskovskoi patriarkhii*, no. 4 (1964): 54–57.

An Inner Step toward God: Writings and Teachings on Prayer. Edited and introduced by April French. Translated by Christa Belyaeva. Brewster, MA: Paraclete Press, 2014.

"Interv'iu na sluchai aresta." In Men, *Kul'tura i dukhovnoe voskhozhdenie*, 356–63.

Istoki religii. Vol. 1 of *Istoriia religii v semi tomakh: V poiskakh puti, istiny, i zhizni*. Moscow: Slovo, 1991.

Kak Chitat' Bibliiu. 3 pts. 1981. Reprint, Moscow: Fond Aleksandra Menia, 2005.

"Khristianskaia kul'tura na Rusi." In *Radostnaia vest': Lektsii*. Complied by A. A. Andreeva, 248–56. Moscow: Vita-Tsentr, 1992.

"Khristianstvo i tvorchestvo." In Men, *Radostnaia vest'*, 256–63.

Kniga Nadezhdy: Lektsii o Biblii. Moscow: Zhizn' s Bogom, 2011.

"K novomu perevodu knigi Ekklesiasta (predislovie)." *Detektiv i politika*, no. 3 (1989): 322–26.

"K problematike 'osevogo vremeni' (nadkonfessional'naia i kristosentricheskaia traktovki)." *Narody Azii i Afriki*, no. 1 (1990): 68–77.

"K problematike 'Osevogo vremeni' (O dialoge kul'tury i religii)." In Men, *Trudnyi put' k dialogu*, 248–90.

"Krest." *Zhurnal Moskovskoi patriarkhii*, no. 9 (1960): 36–38. Reprinted in Grigorenko and Men, *Navstrechu khristu*, 83–90.

Kul'tura i dukhovnoe voskhozhdenie. Compiled by R. I. Al'betkova and M. T. Rabotiaga. Moscow: Iskusstvo, 1992.

"Lichnost' Iisusa Khrista." In Men, *Kniga Nadezhdy*, 241–63.

"Liubit' Boga i liubit' cheloveka." In Men, *Liubit' Boga*, 110–24.

Liubit' Boga i liubit' cheloveka: Domashnie besedy. Edited by Roza Adamiants, Nataliia Vtorushina, Nataliia Grigorenko, and Pavel Men. Moscow: Zhizn' s Bogom, 2012.

Magizm i Edinobozhie: Religioznyi put' chelovechestva do epokhi velikikh Uchitelei. Vol. 2 of *Istoriia religii v semi tomakh: V poiskakh puti, istiny, i zhizni*. Moscow: Slovo, 1992.

"Mif ili deistvitel'nost?" In *Syn chelovecheskii*. 4th ed. Appendix 1, 234–84. Moscow: Slovo, 1992.

Mirovaia dukhovnaia kul'tura, khristianstvo, tserkov': Lektsii i besedy. 2nd ed. Edited by Anastasiia Andreeva et al. and compiled by A. Belavin. Moscow: Fond imeni Aleksandra Menia, 1997.

"Mozhno li reformirovat' pravoslavnuiu tserkov'? Neizvestnoe interv'iu Aleksandra Menia." *Nezavisimaia gazeta*, January 2, 1992.

"Nadlezhit byt' raznomysliiu." In Men, *Mirovaia dukhovnaia kul'tura*, 596–607.

"Na poroge Novogo Goda." *Zhurnal Moskovskoi patriarkhii*, no. 1 (1960): 15–17. Reprinted in Grigorenko and Men, *Navstrechu Khristu*, 42–49.

Na poroge Novogo Zaveta: Ot epokhi Aleksandra Makedonskogo do propovedi Ioanna Krestitelia. Vol. 6 of *Istoriia religii: V poiskakh puti, istiny, i zhizni*. Moscow: Slovo, 1993.

"Nazaret—kolybel' khristianstva." *Zhurnal Moskovskoi patriarkhii*, no. 9 (1959): 61–64. Reprinted in Grigorenko and Men, *Navstrechu Khristu*, 31–41.

"Neskol'ko slov k kontsu spora." In Men, *Kul'tura i dukhovnoe voskhozhdenie*, 450–69.

"Nikolai Berdiaev." In Men, *Russkaia religioznaia filosofiia*, 153–76.

"O. Aleksandr pro svoi dukhovnyi opyt." In *Zhizn' ottsa Aleksandra Menia*, by Zoia Afanas'evna Maslenikova, 447–51. Moscow: Pristsel's, 1995.

O Khriste i tserkvi: Besedy i lektsii. Moscow: Khram sviatykh bessrebrenikov Kosmy i Damiana v Shubine, 2002.

Ot rabstva k svobode: Lektsii po Vetkhomu Zavetu. Moscow: Zhizn' s Bogom, 2008.

O sebe: Vospominaniia, interv'iu, besedy, pis'ma. Moscow: Zhizn' s Bogom, 2007.

"Osnovye cherty khristianskogo mirovozzreniia (Po ucheniiu Slova Bozhiia i opytu Tserkvi)." In Men, *Kul'tura i dukhovnoe voskhozhdenie*, 26–30.

"O Teiiare de Shardene." Appendix no. 10. In Men, *Istoki religii*, 225-42.

Otets Aleksandr Men otvechaet na voprosy. Compiled by Anastasiia Andreeva. 2nd ed. Moscow: Zhizn' s Bogom, 2008.

"Otets Pavel Florenskii." In Men, *Russkaia religioznaia filosofiia*, 198–223.

Otvechaet na voprosy. Moscow: Zhizn' s Bogom, 2008.

"Otvety na voprosy." In Men, *Kul'tura i dukhovnoe voskhozhdenie*, 469–70.

"O vremeni i o sebe." In Bychkov, *Khronika neraskrytogo ubiistva*, 155–71.

"Piatidesiatnitsu prazdnuem." *Zhurnal Moskovskoi patriarkhii*, no. 5 (1961): 55–58. Reprinted in Grigorenko and Men, *Navstrechu Khristu*, 135–46.

"Pis'mo k E. N." In Vishnevetskii and Rabinovich, *"AEQUINOX,"* 182–202.

"Pis'mo ob ekumenizme." http://www.alexandrmen.ru/letters/ecumenzm.html.

"Poeziia sv. Grigoriia Bogoslova." *Zhurnal Moskovskoi patriarkhii*, no. 3 (1959): 62–67. Reprinted in Grigorenko and Men, *Navstrechu Khristu*, 7–30.

Prakticheskoe rukovodstvo k molitve. Riga: Fond im. Aleksandra Menia, 1991.

"Predislovie." In Vasilevskaia, *Katakomby XX vek*, 7–16.

"Problemy tserkvi iznutri." In Men, *Kul'tura i dukhovnoe voskhozhdenie*, 440–45.

Radostnaia vest': Lektsii. Compiled by A. A. Andreeva. Moscow: Vita-Tsentr, 1992.

Radost' sluzheniia: Domashnie besedy. Edited by Roza Adamiants, Nataliia Vtorushina, Nataliia Grigorenko, and Pavel Men. Moscow: Zhizn' s Bogom, 2013.

"Rasizm pered sudom khristianstva." *Zhurnal Moskovskoi patriarkhii*, no. 3 (1962): 22–27. Reprinted in Grigorenko and Men, *Navstrechu Khristu*, 198–216.

"Razum i isstuplenie mass." In Men, *Kul'tura i dukhovnoe voskhozhdenie*, 374–78.

"Religiia, 'kul't lichnosti' i sekuliarnoe gosudarstvo." In Men, *Kul'tura i dukhovnoe voskhozhdenie*, 378–413.

"Religion, Knowledge, and the Problem of Evil." In Roberts and Shukman, *Christianity*, 39–53.

"Rol' tserkvi v sovremennom mire." In Men, *Mirovaia dukhovnaia kul'tura*, 625–32.

"Russia in Crisis." In Roberts and Shukman, *Christianity*, 139–50.

Russkaia religioznaia filosofiia: Lektsii. Edited by Marina Nasonova. Moscow: Khram sviatykh bessrebrennikov Kosmy i Damiana v Shubine, 2003.

"Sergei i Evgenii Trubetskie." In Men, *Russkaia religioznaia filosofiia*, 48–71.

"Slovo pered kreshcheniem." In *Radost' sluzheniia: Domashnie besedy*. Edited by Roza Adamiants et al, 32–51. Moscow: Zhizn' s Bogom, 2013.

Son of Man. Translated by Samuel Brown. Torrance, CA: Oakwood, 1998.

"Sv. Apostol Luka kak deepisatel' tserkvi." *Zhurnal Moskovskoi patriarkhii*, no. 12 (1963): 50–52. Reprinted in Grigorenko and Men, *Navstrechu Khristu*, 287–95.

"Svetochi pervokhristianstva." *Zhurnal Moskovskoi patriarkhii*, no. 7 (1961): 58–66. Reprinted in Grigorenko and Men, *Navstrechu Khristu*, 147–74.

"Sviatiia sviatykh." *Zhurnal Moskovskoi patriarkhii*, no. 11 (1960): 51–52. Reprinted in Grigorenko and Men, *Navstrechu Khristu*, 91–100.

"Sv. Liverii, papa Rimskii (K 1600-letiiu so dnia prestavleniia)." *Zhurnal Moskovskoi patriarkhii*, no. 8 (1966): 52–57. Reprinted in Grigorenko and Men, *Navstrechu Khristu*, 296–308.

Syn chelovecheskii. Vol. 7 of *Istoriia religii v semi tomakh: V poiskakh puti, istiny, i zhizni.* Moscow: Slovo, 1992.

"'Syn gromov' (ocherk zhizni i tvorenii apostola Ioanna Bogoslova)." *Zhurnal Moskovskoi patriarkhii*, no. 5 (1962): 49–60. Reprinted in Grigorenko and Men, *Navstrechu Khristu*, 244–79.

"Taina Volkhov." *Zhurnal Moskovskoi patriarkhii*, no. 1 (1962): 60–67. Reprinted in Grigorenko and Men, *Navstrechu Khristu*, 91–100.

"There Must Be Differences among You." In *About Christ*, 25–40.

"Trudnyi put' k dialogu: O romane Grema Grina 'Monsen'or Kikhot.'" In Men, *Kul'tura i dukhovnoe voskhozhdenie*, 328–43.

Trudnyi put' k dialogu: Sbornik. Edited by N. Matiash. Foreword by Antonii, Metropolitan of Surozh. Moscow: Raduga, 1992.

Tserkov' i my: Domashnie besedy. Moscow: Zhizn' s Bogom, 2012.

"Tserkov' v istorii." In Men, *Mirovaia dukhovnaia kul'tura*, 587–95.

"Two Understandings of Christianity." In Roberts and Shukman, *Christianity*, 151–63.

Umnoe nebo: Perepiska protoiereia Aleksandra Menia s monakhinei Ioannoi (Iu. N. Reitlinger). Moscow: Fond im. Aleksandra Menia, 2006.

U vrat molchaniia. Vol. 3 of *Istoriia religii: V poiskakh puti, istiny, i zhizni.* Moscow: Slovo, 1991.

Vestniki tsarstva Bozhiia: Bibleiskie proroki ot Amosa do Restavratsii (VIII–IV vv. do n.e.). Vol. 5 of *Istoriia religii: V poiskakh puti, istiny, i zhizni.* Moscow: Slovo, 1992.

"Vladimir Solov'ev." In Men, *Russkaia religioznaia filosofiia*, 25–47.

"Vospominaniia o studencheskikh godakh." In Bychkov, *Khronika neraskrytogo ubiistva*, appendix 8, 144–50.

"Zhizn' v Tserkvi." In Men, *Mirovaia dukhovnaia kul'tura*, 620–24.

Primary Texts and Published Works

Akademiia nauk SSSR. *Istoriia Sibiri s drevnikh vremen do nashikh dnei v piati tomakh.* Vol. 5, *Sibir' v periode zaversheniia stroitel'stva sotsializma i perekhoda k kommunizmu.* Leningrad: Nauka, 1969.

Akademiia nauk SSSR. Institut filosofii. *Filosofskaia entsiklopediia.* Vol. 5. Edited by Fedor Vasil'evich Konstantinov. Moscow: Sovetskaia entsiklopediia, 1970.

Aksenov-Meerson, Michael. "The Dissident Movement and *Samizdat.*" In *The Political, Social, and Religious Thought of Russian "Samizdat": An Anthology.* Edited by Michael Aksenov-Meerson and Boris Shragin, translated by Nicholas Lupinin, 19–43. Belmont, MA: Nordland, 1977.

———. [Mikhail Aksenov-Meerson]. "Zhizn' svoiu za drugu svoi." In Gromova, *Pamiati*, 116–20.

Alekseev, Valerii Arkad'evich. *"Shturm nebes" otmeniaetsia? Kriticheskie ocherki po istorii bor'by s religiei v SSSR.* Moscow: Rossiia molodaia, 1992.

Aleksii II. "Education and the Christian View of Man." *Russian Social Science Review* 35, no. 6 (November–December 1994): 45–48.

Alexeyeva, Ludmilla. *Soviet Dissent: Contemporary Movements for National, Religious, and Human Rights.* Translated by Carol Pearce and John Glad. Middletown, CT: Wesleyan University Press, 1985.

Alimov, G., and G. Charodeev, "Faith without Deeds Is Dead—An Interview with Patriarch Aleksii II." Translated by Suzanne Oliver. *Religion in Communist Lands* 18, no. 3 (Autumn 1990): 262–75.

Aman, Iv. [Yves Hamant]. "Razmatyvaia nit' vospominanii." In Gromova, *Pamiati*, 100–104.

Andreeva, Anastasiia Iakovlevna. "V nem zhilo bessmertie . . ." In *Taina zhizni i smerti*, edited by A. Ia. Andreeva, 3–11. Moscow: Znanie, 1992.

Andrew, Christopher, and Vasili Mitrokhin. *The Sword and the Shield: The Mitrokhin Archive and the Secret History of the KGB.* New York: Basic Books, 1999.

Antic, Oxana. "Series of Assaults on Russian Orthodox Priests." *Report on the USSR*, February 22, 1991, 4.

Antiminsov, Sergii. "Protoierei Aleksandr Men' kak kommentator Sviashchennogo Pisaniia." In *O Bogoslovii Protoiereia Aleksandra Menia*, edited by Sergii Antiminsov, Feliks Karelin, and Andrei Kuraev, 3–63. Moscow: Pravilo very, 1993. Reprint Zhitomir: Ni-Ka, 1999.

Appleby, Scott R. *The Ambivalence of the Sacred: Religion, Violence, and Reconciliation.* Lanham, MD: Rowman and Littlefield, 2000.

Apushkina, Elena Vladimirovna. "Zhizn', ozarennaia svetom." In Bychkov, *Maroseika*, 358–86.

Arendt, Hannah. *The Origins of Totalitarianism*. 2nd ed. Orlando, FL: Harcourt Brace Jovanovich, 1979.

Arkhipov, Vladimir. *Slovo ob ottse Aleksandre*. Moscow: Blagovest, 2008.

Armes, Keith. "Chekists in Cassocks: The Orthodox Church and the KGB." *Demokratizatsiya* 1, no. 4 (Fall 1992): 72–84.

Armstrong, Terence, ed. *Yermak's Campaign in Siberia: A Selection of Documents*. Translated by Tatiana Minorsky and David Wileman. Hakluyt Society Publications, 2nd ser., no. 146. London: Hakluyt Society, 1975.

Averintsev, Sergei Sergeevich. "Predislovie." In Men, *Istoki religii*, 5–6.

———. *Religiia i literatura: Sbornik statei*. Ann Arbor, MI: Hermitage, 1981.

———. "Vmesto nekrologa." In Gromova, *Pamiati*, 37–42.

Avrutin, Eugene M. *Jews and the Imperial State: Identification Politics in Tsarist Russia*. Ithaca, NY: Cornell University Press, 2010.

Bak, I. S. "M. V. Lomonosov v bor'be za razvitie proizvoditel'nykh sil Rossii." In *Istoriia russkoi ekonomicheskoi mysli*. Vol. 1, *Epokha feodalizma*. Pt. 1, *IX–XVIII vv.*, edited by A. I. Pashkov, 402–31. Moscow: Gosudarstvennoe izd-vo politicheskoi literatury, 1955.

Bakhruskin, Sergei Vladimirovich. *Nauchnye trudy*. 4 vols. Moscow: Izd-vo Akademii nauk SSSR, 1952–1959.

Bakusev, V. M. et al., eds. *Optina Pustyn': Russkaia pravoslavnaia dukhovnost'*. Compiled by A. Gorelov. Moscow: Kanon+, 1997.

Ball, Alan M. "The Roots of *Bezprizornost'* in Soviet Russia's First Decade." *Slavic Review* 51, no. 2 (Summer 1992): 247–70.

———. *Russia's Last Capitalists: The Nepmen, 1921–1929*. Berkeley: University of California Press, 1987.

Basov, V. "Vse urovni znaniia." *Nauka i zhizn'*, no. 6 (1982): 2–13.

Basovskaia, N. I. "Predislovie." In Men, *Ot rabstva k svobode*, 5-8.

Beeson, Trevor. *Discretion and Valor: Religious Conditions in Russia and the Soviet Union*. 1974. Reprint, Philadelphia: Fortress Press, 1982.

Beglov, Aleksei L'vovich. "Starchestvo v trudakh russkikh tserkovnykh uchenykh i pisatelei." In *Put' k sovershennoi zhizni: O russkom starchestve*, edited by A. L. Beglov, 5–29. Moscow: Pravoslavnyi Sviato-Tikhonovskii gumanitarnyi universitet, 2006.

Belavin, Aleksandr. "Sviashchennik Aleksandr Men'." In Gromova, *Pamiati*, 28–36.

Benjamin, Walter. *Moscow Diary*. Edited by Gary Smith. Translated by Richard Sieburth. Cambridge, MA: Harvard University Press, 1986.

Benyowsky, Maurice Auguste. *The Memoirs and Travels of Mauritius Augustus, count de Benyowsky: In Siberia, Kamchatka, Japan, the Liukiu Islands and Formosa*. Translated from the original manuscript (1741–1771) by William Nicholson. Edited by Pasfield Oliver. New York: Macmillan, 1898.

Berdiaev, Nikolai Aleksandrovich. *Dream and Reality: An Essay in Autobiography*. New York: Macmillan, 1951.

———. *Filosofiia svobody: Smysl tvorchestva; Opyt opravdaniia cheloveka*. 1911. Reprint, Moscow: Pravda, 1989.

———. "Nauka o religii i kristianskaia apologetika." *Put'*, no. 6 (1927): 50–68.

———. "Salvation and Creativity (Two Understandings of Christianity)." Berdyaev.com, http://www.berdyaev.com/berdyaev/berd_lib/1926_308.html.

Bergson, Henri. *Creative Evolution*. Authorized translation by Arthur Mitchell. New York: Henry Holt, 1911.

———. *The Two Sources of Morality and Religion*. Translated by R. Ashley Audra and Cloudesley Brereton, with the assistance of W. Horsfall Carter. Garden City, NY: Doubleday, Anchor Books, 1935.

Berry, Wendell. *Imagination in Place: Essays*. Berkeley, CA: Counterpoint, 2010.

Bershtein, Evgenii. "'The Withering of Private Life': Walter Benjamin in Moscow." In *Everyday Life in Early Soviet Russia: Taking the Revolution Inside*, edited by Christine Kiaer and Eric Naiman, 217–29. Bloomington: Indiana University Press, 2006.

Bessmertnyi-Anzimirov, Aleksandr Aleksandrovich. "Poslednii li novomuchenikov rossiiskikh?" In Gromova, *Pamiati*, 97–99.

Beyrau, Dietrich. *Intelligenz und Dissens: Die russischen Bildungsschichten in der Sowjetunion 1917–1985*. Göttingen: Vandenhoeck and Ruprecht, 1999.

"Bez blagosloveniia." In Zorin and Iliushenko, *Vokrug imeni ottsa Aleksandra*, 35.

Billington, James H. *The Icon and the Axe: An Interpretive History of Russian Culture*. New York: Vintage Books, 1970.

———. "Rossiia v poiskakh sebia." *Nezavisimaia gazeta*, April 6, 1991, p. 5.

———. "Russia: Historic Continuity or Radical Change?" *Texas Journal of Ideas, History, and Culture* 13, no. 1 (Fall/Winter 1990): 66–67.

———. *Russia in Search of Itself*. Washington, DC: Woodrow Wilson Center Press, 2004.

———. *Russia Transformed: Breakthrough to Hope; Moscow, August 1991*. New York: The Free Press, 1992.

Bodnarskii, M. S. *Ocherki po istorii russkogo zemlevedeniia*. Vol. 1. Moscow: Izd-vo Akademii nauk SSSR, 1947.

Bodrov, Aleksei. "The Open University." *Religion, State, and Society* 22, no. 2 (1994): 199–204.

Bogdanov, D. P. "Optina pustyn' i palomnichestvo v nee russkikh pisatelei." *Istoricheskii vestnik*, no. 122 (October 1910): 327–39.

Bonet, Pilar. "Poslednee interv'iu Aleksandra Menia." In Men, *Kul'tura i dukhovnoe voskhozhdenie*, 445–50.

Borisov, Aleksandr. "Dukhovnyi realizm ottsa Aleksandra Menia." In Grigorenko, *Tserkovnaia zhizn'*, 161–71.

Bourdeaux, Michael. "Father Aleksandr Men." *Times* (London), September 15, 1990.

———. *Gorbachev, Glasnost, and the Gospel*. London: Hodder and Stoughton, 1990.

———. *Patriarch and Prophets: Persecution of the Russian Orthodox Church Today*. New York: Praeger, 1970.

Braun, Leopold L. S. *In Lubianka's Shadow: The Memoirs of an American Priest in Stalin's Moscow*. Edited by G. M. Hamburg. Notre Dame, IN: University of Notre Dame Press, 2006.

Bulgakov, Sergei Nikolaevich. "Heroism and Asceticism: Reflections on the Religious Nature of the Russian Intelligentsia." In Shatz and Zimmerman, *Vekhi*, 17–49.

———. *Karl Marks kak religioznyi tip*. 1907. Reprint, Paris: YMCA-Press, 1929.

———. *The Orthodox Church*. With a foreword by Thomas Hopko. Translation revised by Lydia Kesich. 1935. Reprint, Crestwood, NY: St. Vladimir's Seminary Press, 1988.

Bullough, Oliver. *The Last Man in Russia: The Struggle to Save a Dying Nation*. New York: Basic Books, 2013.

Butinova, Mariia Sidorovna, and Nikolai Petrovich Krasnikov. *Muzei istorii religii i ateizma: Spravochnik-putevoditel'*. Moscow: Nauka, 1965.

Bychkov, Sergei Sergeevich. "KGB protiv sviashchennika Aleksandra Menia." *Vestnik russkogo khristianskogo dvizheniia*, n.s., no. 196 (2010): 105–31.

———. *Khronika neraskrytogo ubiistva*. Moscow: Russkoe reklamnoe izdatel'stvo, 1996.

———, comp. *Maroseika: Zhizneopisanie ottsa Sergeiia Mecheva, pis'ma, propovedi, vospominaniia o nem*. Moscow: Martis, Sam and Sam, 2001.

———. "Pravoslavnyi prikhod." In *Khronika neraskrytogo ubiistva*, 82–89.

Chamberlain, Lesley. *Motherland: A Philosophical History of Russia*. New York: The Rookery Press, 2007.

———. *The Philosophy Steamer: Lenin and the Exile of the Intelligentsia*. London: Atlantic Books, 2006.

Chelpanov, Georgii Ivanovich. *Mozg i dusha: Kritika materializma i ocherk sovremennykh uchenii o dushie: Publichnyia lektsii, chitannyia v Kieve v 1898–1899 godu*. St. Petersburg: Mir Bozhii, 1900.

Cherepnin, Lev Vladimirovich. *Obrazovanie russkogo tsentralizovannogo gosudarstva v XIV–XV vekakh: Ocherki sotsial'no-ekonomicheskoi i politicheskoi istorii Rusi*. Moscow: Izd-vo sotsial'no-ekonomicheskoi literatury, 1960.

Chertkov, A. "Sviatoi rozhdestvenskii obman." *Nauka i religiia*, no. 12 (1962): 24–27.

Chetverikov, Sergii. *Optina Pustyn'*. 2nd ed. Paris: YMCA-Press, 1988.

Chistiakov, Georgii Petrovich. "Mariia Iudina." In *V poiskakh vechnogo grada*, 63–66. Moscow: Put', 2002.

———. *Putevoi bloknot*. Compiled by N. F. Izmailovaia. Moscow: Tsentr knigi Rudomino, 2013.

Chumachenko, Tatiana Aleksandrovna. *Church and State in Soviet Russia: Russian Orthodoxy from World War II to the Khrushchev Years*. Edited and translated by Edward E. Roslof. Armonk, NY: M. E. Sharpe, 2002.

Clark, Katerina. *Moscow, the Fourth Rome: Stalinism, Cosmopolitanism, and the Evolution of Soviet Culture, 1931–1941*. Cambridge, MA: Harvard University Press, 2011.

Codevilla, Giovanni. "Commentary on the New Soviet Law on Freedom of Conscience and Religious Organizations." *Religion in Communist Lands* 19, nos. 1–2 (Summer 1991): 119–45.

Collins, P. McDonough. *Siberian Journey: Down the Amur to the Pacific, 1856–1857*. Madison: University of Wisconsin Press, 1962.

Colton, Timothy J. *Moscow: Governing the Socialist Metropolis*. Cambridge, MA: Harvard University Press, 1995.

Corley, Felix, ed. and trans. *Religion in the Soviet Union: An Archival Reader*. New York: New York University Press, 1996.

Daniel, Wallace L. "Aleksandr Men and Russian Orthodoxy: The Conflict between Freedom and Power." *Religion in Eastern Europe* 29, no. 4 (November 2009): 1–20.

———. "Aleksandr Men, the Russian Orthodox Church, and the Connection between Religion and Culture." *Modern Greek Studies Yearbook* 28–29 (2012–2013): 29–49.

———. "The Church and the Struggle for Renewal: The Experience of Three Moscow Parishes." In *Burden or Blessing? Russian Orthodoxy and the Construction of Civil Society and Democracy*, edited by Christopher Marsh, 61–68. Boston, MA: Boston University, Institute on Culture, Religion, and World Affairs, 2004.

———. "The New Religious Press in Russia." In *Christianity after Communism: Social, Political, and Cultural Struggle in Russia*, edited by Niels C. Nielsen, Jr., 47–62. Boulder, CO: Westview Press, 1994.

———. *The Orthodox Church and Civil Society in Russia*. College Station, TX: Texas A&M University Press, 2006.

———. "Religion and Science: The Evolution of Soviet Debate." *Christian Century*, January 29, 1992, 98–100.

———. "Religion, Science, Russia: An Interview with Boris Raushenbakh." *Christian Century*, February 28, 1996, 232–35.

———. "The Vanished Past: Russia's Search for Identity." *Christian Century*, March 17, 1993, 293–96.

Daniel, Wallace L., Peter L. Berger, and Christopher Marsh. Introduction to *Perspectives on Church-State Relations in Russia*, edited by Wallace L. Daniel, Peter L. Berger, and Christopher Marsh, 1–6. Waco, TX: J. M. Dawson Institute of Church-State Studies, 2008.

Danilenko, Vladimir. "The Beilis Case Papers: Documents on the Beilis Case from the State Archive of the Kiev Oblast," Fonds 2, 183, 864. http//www.eastview.com/docs/IntroductionEng.pdf.

Davis, Nathaniel. *A Long Walk to Church: A Contemporary History of Russian Orthodoxy*. 2nd ed. Boulder, CO: Westview Press, 2003.

Dawson, Christopher H. *Progress and Religion: An Historical Enquiry*. Westport, CT: Greenwood Press, 1970.

Dejevsky, Mary. "Third Priest Murdered in Moscow Crime Wave." *Times* (London), February 6, 1991.

Della Cava, Ralph. "Reviving Orthodoxy in Russia: An Overview of the Factions in the Russian Orthodox Church in the Spring of 1996." *Cahiers du Monde russe* 38, no. 3 (1997): 387–414.

Dobb, Maurice. *Soviet Economic Development since 1917.* Rev. ed. New York: International Publishers, 1968.

Dombkovskii, N. "Krest na sovesti." In Bychkov, *Khronika neraskrytogo ubiistva*, appendix 14, 208–18.

Dosifeia (Verzhblovskaia). "O Matyshke Marii." In Vasilevskaia, *Katakomby XX veka*, 279–306.

Dostoevsky, Anna Grigor'evna Snitkina. *Dostoevsky: Reminiscences.* Translated and edited by Beatrice Stillman, with an introduction by Helen Muchnic. New York: Liveright, 1975.

Dostoevsky, Fyodor. *The Brothers Karamazov.* Translated and annotated by Richard Pevear and Larissa Volokonsky. New York: Vintage, 1991.

Douroff, Anastasia, and Evgeniia Svin'ina. *Rossiia—ochishchenie ognem: Iz dnevnika khristianki, Moskva, 1964–1977.* Moscow: Rudomino, 1996.

Doyle, Peter. *Iurii Dombrovskii: Freedom under Totalitarianism.* Edited by Peter I. Barta. Studies in Russian and European Literature 4. Amsterdam: Harwood Academic, 2000.

Drews, Arthur. *The Christ Myth.* Translated by C. Delisle Burns. Westminster College-Oxford Classics in the Study of Religion. Amherst, NY: Prometheus Books, 1998.

———. *Die Christusmythe.* Part 2, *Die Zeugnisse für die Geschichtlichkeit Jesu, eine Antwort an die Schriftgelehrten mit besonderer Berücksichtugung die theologischen Methode.* Jena: Diederich, 1911.

Dunlop, John B. *Staretz Amvrosy: Model for Dostoevsky's Staretz Zossima.* Belmont, MA: Nordland Publishing, 1972.

Duranty, Walter. *I Write as I Please.* New York: Simon and Schuster, 1935.

El'chaninov, Aleksandr V., Sergei Nikolaevich Bulgakov, Pavel Aleksandrovich Florenskii, and Vladimir Frantsevich Ern. *Istoriia religii: S prilozheniem stat'i S. N. Bulgakova "O protivorechi-vosti sovremennogo bezreligioznogo mirovozzreniia."* Moscow: Russkii put', 1911.

Ellis, Jane. *The Russian Orthodox Church: A Contemporary History.* New York: Routledge, 1986.

Engels, Friedrich. "On the History of Early Christianity." *About.com.* http://atheism.about.com/library/marxism/bl_EngelsEarlyChrist.htm.

Eremin, Andrei Alekseevich. *Otets Aleksandr Men': Pastyr' na rubezhe vekov.* 2nd ed. Moscow: Carte Blanche, 2001.

Erickson, John. "Soviet War Losses: Calculations and Controversies." In *Barbarossa: The Axis and Allies,* edited by John Erickson and David Dilks, 255–77. Edinburgh: Edinburgh University Press, 1994.

Ermolin, Aleksandr. "Mesto ottsa Aleksandra v Pravoslavnom predanii." *Alexandermen.ru.* http://www.alexandrmen.ru/biogr/ermolin.html.

Eshliman, Nikolai Ivanovich, and Gleb Pavlovich Yakunin. "An Open Letter to His Holiness, the Most Holy Patriarch of Moscow and All Russia, Alexi." In Bordeaux, *Patriarch and Prophets,* 194–223.

———. "To the Chairman of the Presidium of the Supreme Soviet of the Union of Soviet Socialist Republics." In Bordeaux, *Patriarch and Prophets,* 189–94.

Etkind, Alexander. "Soviet Subjectivity: Torture for the Sake of Salvation?" *Kritika: Explorations in Russian and Eurasian History* 6, no. 1 (Winter 2005): 171–86.

Evdokimov, Michel. *Father Alexander Men: Martyr of Atheism.* Translated by Margaret Parry. Foreword by Neville Kyrke-Smith. Introduction by Metropolitan Kallistos of Diokleia. Leominster, Herefordshire, England: Gracewing, 2011.

Evtuhov, Catherine. *The Cross and the Sickle: Sergei Bulgakov and the Fate of Russian Religious Philosophy.* Ithaca, NY: Cornell University Press, 1997.

Fadin, Andrei. "Filosov Iurii Senokosov ob ubiistve o. Aleksandra Menia." *Vek XX i mir,* no. 1 (1991): 32–35.

Fagan, Geraldine. *Believing in Russia: Religious Policy after Communism.* New York: Routledge, 2013.

Fainberg, Vladimir L'vovich. *Vse detali etogo puteshestviia: Skrizhali; Vospominaniia ob o. Aleksandre Mene.* Moscow: Zarech'e, 2011.

Farrar, Frederic William. *The Early Days of Christianity.* London: Cassell, 1882.

———. *Skvoz mrak k svetu, ili na rassvete khristianstva (povest' iz vremen Neronovskogo goneniia na kristian): V izlozhenii, s angliiskogo podlinnikov F. Volgina.* St. Petersburg: P. P. Soikin, 1897.

Farson, Negley. *Black Bread and Red Coffins.* New York: Century, 1930.

Fedotov, Georgii P. "Berdyaev the Thinker." *Chebucto Community Net.* http://www.chebucto.ns.ca/Philosophy/Sui-Generis/Berdyaev/essays/fetodov.htm.

Figes, Orlando. *The Whisperers: Private Life in Stalin's Russia.* New York: Henry Holt, 2007.

Filatov, Sergei Borisovich. "Russkaia Pravoslavnaia Tserkov' i politicheskaia elita." In *Religiia i politika v postkommunisticheskoi Rossii,* edited by L. N. Mitrokhin, 99–118. Moscow: Institut filosofii RAN, 1994.

———. *Sovremennaia religioznaia zhizn' Rossii: Opyt sistematicheskogo opisaniia.* Vol. 1. Edited by Michael Bourdeaux and Sergei Borisovich Filatov. Moscow: Logos, 2004.

"Filosofskie i sotsialogicheskie problemy nauchno-tekhnicheskoi revoliutsii." *Voprosy filosofii,* no. 4 (1969): 3–15.

Florenskii, Pavel Aleksandrovich. "Otets Aleksei Mechev." In *Sochineniia v chetyrekh tomakh,* compiled and edited by Igumen Andronikov (A. S. Trubachev), P. V. Florenskii, and M. S. Trubachev, 2:621–27. Moscow: Mysl', 1996.

———. "Rassuzhdenie na sluchai konchiny ottsa Alekseia Mecheva." In *Sochineniia v chetyrekh tomakh,* compiled and edited by Igumen Andronikov (A. S. Trubachev), P. V. Florenskii, and M. S. Trubachev, 2:591–600. Moscow: Mysl', 1996.

Fomin, Sergei Vladimirovich, ed. and comp. *"Pastyr' dobryi": Zhizn' i trudy moskovskogo startsa protoiereia Alekseia Mecheva.* 2nd ed. Moscow: Serda-Press, 2000.

Forsyth, James. *A History of the Peoples of Siberia: Russia's North Asian Colony, 1581–1900.* Cambridge: Cambridge University Press, 1992.

Frank, Joseph. *Dostoevsky: The Mantle of the Prophet, 1871–1881.* Princeton, NJ: Princeton University Press, 2002.

Frazier, Ian. *Travels in Siberia.* New York: Farrar, Straus and Giroux, 2010.

Freeze, Gregory L. "Handmaiden of the State: The Church in Imperial Russia Reconsidered." *Journal of Ecclesiastical History* 36, no. 1 (January 1985): 82–102.

———. "The Stalinist Assault on the Parish." In *Stalinismus vor dem Zweiten Weltkrieg: Neue Wege der Forschung,* edited by Manfred Hildermeier and Elisabeth Müller-Luckner, 209–32. Munich: Oldenbourg, 1998.

French, April. "Spiritual Dissent: The Writings of Father Aleksandr Men as Dissent from Soviet Ideology." MA thesis, Regent College, Vancouver, BC, 2011.

French, R. A., and Alan Wood, eds. *The Development of Siberia: People and Resources.* Basingstoke: The Macmillan Press, 1989.

Furman, Dmitrii Efimovich. "Nasha politicheskaia sistema i ee tsikly." *Svobodnaia mysl',* no. 11 (2003): 9–30.

Furman, Dmitrii Efimovich, and Kimmo Kääriänen. "Veruiushchie, ateisty i prochie: Novoe issledovanie rossiiskoi religioznosti." *Voprosy filosofii,* no. 1 (January 1997): 79–91.

Garadzha, Viktor Ivanovich. "Na urovne trebovanii zhizni." *Nauka i religiia,* no. 1 (January 1988): 10–12.

Garadzha, Viktor Ivanovich, and Elena Dmitrievna Rutkevich, eds. *Religiia i obshchestvo: Khrestomatiia po sotsiologii religii.* Moscow: Aspekt, 1996.

Garrard, John, and Carol Garrard. *Russian Orthodoxy Resurgent: Faith and Power in the New Russia.* Princeton, NJ: Princeton University Press, 2008.

Geldern, James von. "The Center and the Periphery: Cultural and Social Geography in the Mass Culture of the 1930s." In *New Directions in Soviet History,* edited by Stephen White, 62–80. Cambridge, MA: Cambridge University Press, 1992.

Genieva, Ekaterina. "Posledniaia strecha." *Znamia,* no. 9 (September 1991): 201–3.

Gilbert, Peter. Introduction to *On God and Man: The Theological Poetry of St. Gregory of Nazianzus.* Translated by Peter Gilbert. Crestwood, NY: St. Vladimir's Seminary Press, 2001.

Gitelman, Zvi. "Soviet Political Culture: Insights from Jewish Emigres." *Soviet Studies* 24, no. 4 (October 1977): 543–64.

Glazov, Iurii Iakovlevich. *V kraiu ottsov: Khronika nedavnego proshlogo*. Moscow: Istina i Zhizn', 1998.

Gnucheva, Vera Fedorovna, comp. *Materialy dlia istorii ekspeditsii Akademii nauk v XVIII i XIX vekakh: Khronologicheskie obzory i opisanie arkhivnykh materialov*. Trudy Arkhiva Akademii nauk SSSR 4. Moscow: Izd-vo Akademii nauk SSSR, 1940.

Gollerbakh, Evgenii Aleksandrovich. *K nezrimomu gradu: Religiozno-filosofskaia gruppa "Put'" (1910–1919) v poiskakh novoi russkoi identichnosti*. St. Petersburg: Aleteiia, 2000.

Gorbachev, Mikhail. *Perestroika: New Thinking for Our Country and the World*. New York: Harper and Row, 1987.

Gorbachev, Mikhail, and Zdeněk Mlynář. *Conversations with Gorbachev on Perestroika, the Prague Spring, and the Crossroads of Socialism*. Translated by George Shriver. New York: Columbia University Press, 2002.

Graham, Loren, and Jean-Michel Kantor. *Naming Infinity: A True Story of Religious Mysticism and Mathematical Creativity*. Cambridge, MA: The Belknap Press of Harvard University Press, 2009.

Greenberg, Louis. *The Jews in Russia*. Vol. 2, *The Struggle for Emancipation, 1881–1917*. Edited by Mark Wischnitzer. 1951. Reprint, New York: Schocken Books, 1976.

Grigorenko, M. V., ed. *Tserkovnaia zhizn' XX veka: Protoierei Aleksandr Men' i ego dukhovnye nastavniki; Sbornik materialov Pervoi nauchnoi konferentsii "Menevskie chenteniia" (9–11 Sentiabria 2006 g.)*. Sergiev Posad: Izdanie prikhoda Sergievskoi tserkvi v Semkhoze, 2007.

Grigorenko, Nataliia, and Pavel Men, eds. *Navstrechu khristu: Sbornik statei*. Moscow: Zhizn' s Bogom, 2009.

Grigorenko, Viktor, Fr. "Zhiznennyi put' Arkhimandrita Serafima (Batiukova)." In Grigorenko, *Tserkovnaia zhizn'*, 109–16.

Grin, Grem [Greene, Graham]. *Sila i slava: Roman*. Translated by Aleksandr Men, with an introduction by Ekaterina Genieva, afterword by Kseniia Atarova. Moscow: Rudomino, 2012.

Gromova, T. V., ed. *Pamiati protoiereia Aleksandra Menia*. Moscow: Rudomino, 1991.

Halfin, Igal. *Terror in My Soul: Communist Autobiographies on Trial*. Cambridge, MA: Harvard University Press, 2003.

Halfin, Igal, and Jochen Hellbeck. "Rethinking the Stalinist Subject: Stephen Kotkin's 'Magnetic Mountain' and the State of Soviet Historical Studies." *Jahrbücher für Geschichte Osteuropas* 44, no. 3 (1996): 456–63.

Hamant, Yves. *Alexander Men: A Witness for Contemporary Russia (A Man for Our Times)*. Translated by Steven Bigham, introduction by Maxym Lysack. Torrance, CA: Oakwood, 1995.

———. *Alexandre Men, un témoin pour la Russie de ce Temps*. Preface by J.-M. Lustiger. Paris: Mame, 1993.

Handelman, Stephen. "Soviet Priest's Murder Sends Shock Waves Through Nation." *Toronto Star*, September 23, 1990, Sunday Second Edition.

Harrison, Mark. *Accounting for War: Soviet Production, Employment, and the Defence Burden, 1940–1945*. Cambridge: Cambridge University Press, 1996.

Havriljukova, Ludmila. "Biographical, Theological and Ecumenical Aspects of the Correspondence between Alexandr Men (1935–1990) and Ioanna (Yu. N. Reitlinger) (1898–1988). MA thesis, University of Leeds, 2009.

Haywood, A. J. *Siberia: A Cultural History*. New York: Oxford University Press, 2010.

Hegel, George Wilhelm Friedrich. "The Positivity of the Christian Religion." In *On Christianity: Early Theological Writings*, translated by T. M. Knox, with an introduction and fragments translated by Richard Kroner, 67–181. New York: Harper, 1948.

———. "The Spirit of Christianity and Its Fate." In Hegel, *On Christianity*, 182–301.

Hellbeck, Jochen. "Fashioning the Stalinist Soul: The Diary of Stepan Podlubnyi (1931–1939)." *Jahrbücher für Geschichte Osteuropas* 44, no. 3 (1996): 345–73.

———. *Revolution on My Mind: Writing a Diary under Stalin.* Cambridge, MA: Harvard University Press, 2006.

———. "Russian Autobiographical Practice." In Hellbeck and Heller, *Autobiographical Practices,* 279–98.

———. "Self-Realization in the Stalinist System: Two Soviet Diaries of the 1930s." In *Stalinismus vor dem Zweiten Weltkrieg: Neue Wege der Forschung,* edited by Manfred Hildermeier and Elisabeth Müller-Luckner, 275–90. Munich: Oldenbourg, 1998.

Hellbeck, Jochen, and Klaus Heller, eds. *Autobiographical Practices in Russia/Autobiographische Praktiken in Russland.* Göttingen: V and R Unipress, 2004.

Hosking, Geoffrey. *Ruler and Victims: The Russians in the Soviet Union.* Cambridge, MA: The Belknap Press of Harvard University Press, 2006.

———. *Russia and the Russians: A History.* Cambridge, MA: The Belknap Press of Harvard University Press, 2001.

Huxley, Thomas Henry. "We Are All Scientists." In *Darwiniana* (1863). Excerpted in *A Treasury of Science.* 2nd ed. Edited by Harlow Shapley, Samuel Rapport, and Helen Wright, with an introduction by Harlow Shapley, 14–20. New York: Harper, 1946.

Iazykova, I. K. "Dobry pastyr'—Otets Nikolai Golubtsov." In Grigorenko, *Tserkovnaia zhizn',* 139–48.

Iliushenko, Vladimir Il'ich. "Kompleks sal'eri." In Zorin and Iliushenko, *Vokrug imeni ottsa Aleksandra,* 93–118.

———. *Otets Aleksandr Men': Zhizn', Smert', Bessmertie.* 2nd ed. Moscow: VGBIL im. M. I. Rudomino, 2010.

———. *Otets Aleksandr Men': Zhizn' i smert' vo Khriste.* Moscow: "Pik," 2000.

———. "Vospominaniia." In Iliushenko, *Otets Aleksandr Men,* 339–412.

Ilovaiskaia, Irina. "Pastyr', ispovednik, muchenik: Ego zaveshchanie—propoved' liudei i neustannoe iskanie pravdy." *Russkaia mysl',* no. 3845, September 14, 1990.

"Individual'noe i massovoe soznanie." *Inostrannaia literatura,* no. 11 (1990): 203–22.

Ioann, Metropolitan. "The West Wants Chaos." In *Christianity after Communism: Social, Political, and Cultural Struggle in Russia,* edited by Niels C. Nielsen, Jr., 107–12. Boulder, CO: Westview Press, 1994.

Iossel, Mikhail. "Ray Bradbury in the U.S.S.R." *The New Yorker,* June 8, 2012. http:www.newyorker.com/books/page-turner/ray-bradbury-in-the-u-s-s-r.

Isaacson, Walter. *Einstein: His Life and Universe.* New York: Simon and Schuster, 2007.

Iskander, Fazil'. "Svetiashchiisia chelovek." *Znamia,* no. 9 (September 1991): 203–6.

Isupov, V. A. *Demograficheskie katastrofy i krizisy v Rossii v pervoi polovine XX veka: Istoriko-demograficheskie ocherki.* Novosibirsk: Sibirskii khronograf, 2000.

Iuvenalii, Metropolitan. "Slovo, proiznesennoe pered otpevaniem protoiereia Aleksandra Menia v sele Novaia Derevnia, 11 Sentiabria 1990 goda." In Gromova, *Pamiati,* 20–21.

———. "Slovo, skazannoe posle otpevaniia protoiereia Aleksandra Menia v sele Novaia Derevnia." September 11, 1990. *Alexandermen.ru.* http://www.alexandermen.ru/biogr/juvenal.html.

"Iz interv'iu ottsa Dmitriia Dudko." In Zorin and Iliushenko, *Vokrug imeni ottsa Aleksandra,* 44.

Jarman, Peter. "East-West Dialogue during the Cold War Years: Possibilities and Limitations." Paper presented to a conference on the role of the peace movements during the Cold War held at the London School of Economics, February 2, 2008. http://www.oldsite.transnational.org/Resources_Treasures/2008/Jarman_East-West_Quaker.pdf.

Jaspers, Karl. *The Origin and Goal of History.* Translated by Michael Bullock. New Haven, CT: Yale University Press, 1953.

Kallistos (Ware), Bishop of Diokleia. *The Inner Kingdom.* Crestwood, NY: St. Vladimir's Seminary Press, 2000.

Karelin, Feliks. "O domostroitel'nykh predelakh bogoizbrannosti evreiskogo naroda." In Karelin et al., *O bogoslovii,* 4–21.

Karelin, Feliks, Sergei Antiminsov, and Andrei Kuraev. *O bogoslovii protoiereia Aleksandra Menia.* Zhitomir: Ni-Ka, 1999.

Kashirina, T. Ia., V. I. Mordvinova, and M. D. Afanas'ev, eds. *Sovetskoe gosudarstvo i russkaia pravoslavnaia tserkov': K istorii vzaimootnoshenii (Metodiko-bibliograficheskie materialy v pomoshch' rabote bibliotek-metodicheskikh tsentrov).* Moscow: Gosudarstvennaia publichnaia istoricheskaia biblioteka RSFSR, 1990.

"Katalog 1982: Izdatel'stvo Zhizn' s Bogom." In Sergei Zheludkov and Kronid Arkad'evich Liubarskii. *Khristianstvo i ateizm,* 243–50. Brussels: Zhizn' s Bogom, 1982.

Kaufmann, Walter. *Hegel: A Reinterpretation.* Garden City, NY: Anchor Books, 1966.

Kenworthy, Scott M. *The Heart of Russia: Trinity-Sergius, Monasticism, and Society after 1825.* New York: Oxford University Press, 2010.

Kerblay, Basile H. *Modern Soviet Society.* Translated by Rupert Sawyer. London: Methuen, 1983.

Kheisserman, E. *Potentsial'nye vozmozhnosti psikhicheskogo razvitiia normal'nogo i nenormal'nogo rebenka.* Translated by Vera Iakovlevna Vasilevskaia. Moscow: Prosveshchenie, 1964.

Khoruzhii, Sergei Sergeevich. "Fenomen russkogo starchestva v ego dukhovnykh i antropologicheskikh osnovaniikh." *Tserkov' i vremia* 21, no. 4 (2002): 208–26.

"Khudozhnik i vlast'." *Inostrannaia literatura,* no. 5 (1990): 177–201.

Kirill (Gundiaev). "Tserkov' v otnoshenii k obshchestvu v usloviiakh perestroiki." *Zhurnal Moskovskoi patriarkhii* 47, no. 2 (February 1990): 32–38.

Kishkovsky, Sophia. "At a Russian Hospital, Art Inspires Children." *New York Times,* January 7, 2006.

Kislinskaia, Larisa. "Ubiistvo sviashchennika: Sledstvie prodolozhaetsia." *Leninskoe znamia,* September 18, 1990.

Kivelson, Valerie, and Robert H. Greene, eds. *Orthodox Russia: Belief and Practice under the Tsars.* University Park: Pennsylvania State University Press, 2003.

Klier, John Doyle. *Russia Gathers Her Jews: The Origins of the "Jewish Question" in Russia, 1772–1825.* DeKalb: Northern Illinois University Press, 2011.

———. *Russians, Jews, and the Pograms of 1881–1882.* New York: Cambridge University Press, 2011.

Kline, George L. "Religious Ferment among Soviet Intellectuals." In *Religion and the Soviet State: A Dilemma of Power,* edited by Max Hayward and William C. Fletcher, 57–69. New York: Praeger, 1969.

Koenker, Diane. "Urbanization and Deurbanization in the Russian Revolution and Civil War." *The Journal of Modern History* 57, no. 3 (September 1985): 424–50.

Komaromi, Ann. "Samizdat as Extra-Gutenberg Phenomenon." *Poetics Today* 29, no. 4 (Winter 2008): 629–67.

"Kommunizm i khristianstvo." *Inostrannaia literatura,* no. 5 (1989): 203–24.

Kornblatt, Judith Deutsch. *Doubly Chosen: Jewish Identity, the Soviet Intelligentsia, and the Russian Orthodox Church.* Madison: University of Wisconsin Press, 2004.

Korneeva, Vera Alekseevna. "Vospominaniia o khrame Svv. Bessrebrenikov Kira i Ioanna na Solianke." In Vasilevskaia, *Katakomby XX veka,* 251–59.

Krasnov-Levitin, Anatolii Emmanuilovich. "Freedom of Belief and of Atheism: Face to Face." In Bordeaux, *Patriarch and Prophets,* 264–70.

Kremlev, Alexander. "Father Alexander Men.'" Slidefilm narrated by Sergei Bessmertnyi. August 25, 2012. *Youtube.com.* http://youtube/Bmhrp4VNYI0.

Kriuchev, Vladimir. "Poniatnyi kazhdomy." *Vpered,* September 10, 2014, 3.

Kroner, Richard. "Introduction: Hegel's Philosophical Development." In *On Christianity: Early Theological Writings,* translated by T. M. Knox, with an introduction and fragments translated by Richard Kroner, 1–66. New York: Harper, 1961.

Krotov, Iakov. "Fr. Aleksandr: Bibliografiia." *Biblioteka Iakova Krotova.* http://krotov.info/library/13_m/myen/_bibl_menn.htm.

Kryvelev, Iosif Aronovich. *Christ: Myth or Reality?.* Translated by S. Galynsky. Religious Studies in the USSR, series 2. Moscow: "Social Sciences Today" Editorial Board, 1987.

———. *Chto znaet istoriia ob Iisuse Khriste?* Moscow: Sovetskaia Rossiia, 1969.

———. *Istoriia religii: Ocherki.* 2 vols. Moscow: Mysl', 1975–1976.

Kupriianova, Tat iana Ivanovna. "Avtobiograficheskie zapiski." In Bychkov, *Maroseika*, 442–49.

Kuraev, Andrei. "Aleksandr Men': Poteriavshiisia missioner." In Karelin et al., *O bogoslovii*, 76–104.

———. *Okkul'tizm v Pravoslavii.* Moscow: Blagovest, 1998.

Kyrlezhev, Aleksandr. "Tserkov' i mir v sotsial'noi kontseptsii Russkoi Pravoslavnoi Tserkvi." *Russkaia mysl'*, September 21–27, 2000.

Lenin, Vladimir Il'ich. *Materialism and Empirio-Criticism: Critical Comments on a Reactionary Philosophy.* https://www.marxists.org/archive/lenin/works/1908/mec/two4.htm.

———. "O znachenii voinstvuiushchego materializma." In *Polnoe sobranie sochenenii*, 45:23–33. 5th ed. Moscow: Izd-vo Politicheskoi Literatury, 1964.

———. "Socialism and Religion." In *Collected Works*, 11: 83–87. Moscow: Progress, 1965.

"Letter from His Grace, Sergius, Metropolitan of Nijny Novgorod, *locum tenens* of the Keeper of the Patriarchal Throne to the clergy and faithful of the Patriarchate of Moscow; Moscow, 16th/29th June 1927." In *Christians in Contemporary Russia* by Nikita Struve, translated by Lancelot Sheppard and A. Manson, 362–64. 2nd ed. New York: Scribner, 1967.

Levin, M. G., and L. P. Potapov. *The Peoples of Siberia.* Chicago, IL: University of Chicago Press, 1964.

Lezov, Sergei. "Est' li u russkogo pravoslaviia budushchee? (Ocherki sovremennogo pravoslavnogo liberalizma)." *Znamia*, no. 3 (March 1994): 171–90.

Lodyzhenskii, Mitrofan Vasil'evich. *Misticheskaia trilogiia.* Vol. 1, *Sverkhsoznanie i puti ego dostizheniiu: Indusskaia radzhaioga i khristianskoe podrizhnichestvo; Opyt issledovaniia.* Petrograd: Ekaterininskaia tip., 1915.

Loukmanova, Olga. Review of *O bogoslovii protoiereia Aleksandra Menia*, by Feliks Karelin, Sergei Antiminsov, and Andrei Kuraev. *East-West and Church Ministry Report* 7, no. 3 (Summer 1999): 3.

Louterbach, Richard E. *Through Russia's Back Door.* New York: Harper, 1950.

Löwe, Heinz-Dietrich. "Pogroms in Russia: Explanations, Comparisons, Suggestions." *Jewish Social Studies* 11, no. 1 (2004): 16–23.

Luchterhandt, Otto. "The Council for Religious Affairs." In *Religious Policy in the Soviet Union*, edited by Sabrina Petra Ramet, 55–83. New York: Cambridge University Press, 1993.

Lukasevicius, Arturas. *Aleksandr Men's Approach to the World's Religions: A Critical Evaluation in Light of the Declaration Dominus Iesus.* Saarbrücken: VDM Verlag Dr. Müller, 2009.

———[Artūras Lukaševičius]. "A Critical Evaluation of Fr. Aleksandr Vladimirovich Men's Approach to the Religions of the World, in the Light of the Declaration 'Dominus Iesus.'" PhD diss., Open University, Maryvale Institute, 2006.

Mandelstam, Nadezhda. *Hope Abandoned.* Translated by Max Hayward. New York: Atheneum, 1974.

———. *Hope against Hope: A Memoir.* Translated by Max Hayward with an introduction by Clarence Brown. New York: Atheneum, 1976.

Maron, Gottfried. "Frieden und Krieg: Ein Blick in die Theologie- und Kirchengeschichte." In *Glaubenskriege in Vergangenheit und Gegenwart*, edited by Peter Hermann, 17–35. Göttingen: Vandenhoeck und Ruprecht, 1996.

Marrati, Paola. "James, Bergson, and an Open Universe." In *Bergson, Politics, and Religion*, edited by Alexandre Lefebvre and Melanie White, 299–312. Durham, NC: Duke University Press, 2012.

Maslenikova, Zoia Afanas'evna. "K istorii knigi o. Aleksandra Menia 'Syn chelovecheskii.'" In Vishnevetskii and Rabinovich, *"AEQUINOX,"* 178–81.

———. "Moi dukhovnik." In *Zhizn' ottsa Aleksandra Menia*, 271–552.

———. "Otets Aleksandr—pisatel'." In Gromova, *Pamiati*, 133–40.

———. *Zhizn' ottsa Aleksandra Menia.* Moscow: Pristsel's, 1995.

Maslova, Irina Ivanovna. "Russkaia Pravoslavnaia Tserkov' i KGB (1960–1980-e gody)." *Voprosy istorii*, no. 12 (2005): 86–96.

———. "Sovet po delam religii pri sovete ministrov SSSR i russkaia pravoslavnaia tserkov' (1965–1991 gg.)." *Otechestvennaia istoriia*, no. 6 (2005): 52–65.

Matlock, Jack F., Jr. *Autopsy of an Empire: The American Ambassador's Account of the Collapse of the Soviet Union*. New York: Random House, 1995.

McGuckin, John Anthony. *The Orthodox Church: An Introduction to Its History, Doctrine, and Spiritual Culture*. Malden, MA: Blackwell, 2008.

Mechev, Aleksei. *Moskovskii batiushka: Vospominaniia ob o. Aleksee Mecheve*. Foreword by Mikhail Trukhanov. Moscow: Izdanie Moskovskogo Sviato-Danilova Monastyria, 1994.

Mechev, Sergei Alekseevich. "Pis'ma iz Italii." In Bychkov, *Maroseika*, 200–202.

Medvedev, Roy Aleksandrovich. *Lichnost' i epokha: Politicheskii portret L. I. Brezhneva*. Moscow: Novosti, 1991.

Meerson, Michael. "The Life and Work of Father Aleksandr Men." In *Seeking God: The Recovery of Religious Identity in Orthodox Russia, Ukraine, and Georgia*, edited by Stephen K. Batalden, 13-27. DeKalb: Northern Illinois University Press, 1993.

Men, Elena Semenovna. "Moi put'." In Vasilevskaia, *Katakomby XX veka*, 208–50.

Men, Pavel Vol'fovich. "Ierei Boris Vasil'ev. Ego zhizn', sluzhenie i tvorchestvo." In Grigorenko, *Tserkovnaia zhizn'*, 149–55.

Merridale, Catherine. *Night of Stone: Death and Memory in Twentieth-Century Russia*. New York: Viking, 2001.

Miklukho-Maklai, Nikolai Nikolaevich. *Travels to New Guinea: Diaries, Letters, Documents*. Moscow: Progress, 1982.

Miller, Matthew Lee. *The American YMCA and Russian Culture: The Preservation and Expansion of Orthodox Christianity, 1900-1940*. Lanham, MD: Lexington Books, 2013.

Ministry of Foreign Affairs of the Republic of Latvia. "Summer Camp Held in Riga for Students of the Russian State University for the Humanities." http://www.mfa.gov.lv/en/news/latest-news/6025.

Minkin, Aleksandr. "Ne rydaite obo mne. . ." In Gromova, *Pamiati*, 75–78.

Mitrofanova, E. N. "Otets Aleksandr Men' i ego dukhovnye nastavniki." In Grigorenko, *Tserkovnaia zhizn'*, 156–60.

Monkhouse, Allan. *Moscow, 1911–1933*. Boston: Little, Brown, 1934.

Morozov, Boris. *Evreiskaia emigratsiia v svete novykh dokumentov*. Tel Aviv: Ivrus, 1998.

Mysh, Mikhail Ignat'evich. *Rukovodstvo k russkim zakonam o evreiakh*. 2nd ed. St. Petersburg: Tipolitografiia M. P. Frolovoi, 1898.

Naumov, Igor V. *The History of Siberia*. Edited by David N. Collins. New York: Routledge, 2006.

N. N. "V etom moe sluzhenie Bogu (Vospominaniia o D. E. Melekhove)." In Bychkov, *Maroseika*, 387–98.

Norman, Henry. *All the Russias: Travels and Studies in Contemporary European Russia, Finland, Siberia, the Caucasus, and Central Asia*. New York: Charles Scribner's Sons, 1903.

Odintsov, Mikhail Ivanovich. *Gosudarstvo i tserkov' v Rossii: XX vek*. Moscow: Luch, 1994.

Ogorodnikov, Aleksandr Ioilovich. "Ot sostavitelei." *Obshchina*, no. 2 (1978): 1.

Okun, Semen Bentsianovich. *The Russian-American Company*. Edited with introduction by B. D. Grekov. Translated by Carl Ginsburg. Preface by Robert J. Kerner. Cambridge, MA: Harvard University Press, 1951.

Ordina, O. N. *Fenomen starchestva v russkoi dukhovnoi kul'ture XIX veka*. Kirov: Viatskii sotsial'no-ekonomicheskii institut, 2003.

Osipova, Irina Ivanovna. "Dokumenty po regionam i godam: Iz istorii gonenii Istinno-Pravoslavnnoi (Katakombnoi Tserkvi): Konets 1920-kh–nachalo 1970-kh godov." *Mezhdunarodnoe istoriko-prosvetitel'skoe pravozashchitnoe i blagotvoritel'noe obshchestvo MEMORIAL*. http://www.histor-ipt-kt.org/doc.html.

———. "Kniga Pamiati po regionam i alfavitu: Iz istorii gonenii Istinno-Pravoslavnnoi (Katakombnoi) Tserkvi: Konets 1920-kh–nachalo 1970-kh godov." *Mezhdunarodnoe istoriko-prosvetitel'skoe pravozashchitnoe i blagotvoritel'noe obshchestvo MEMORIAL*. http://www.histor-ipt-kt.org/kniga.html.

———, comp. "O, Premiloserdyi ... Budi s nami neotstupno ...": Vospominaniia veruiushchikh Istinno-Pravoslavnoi (Katakombnoi) Tserkvi: Konets 1920-kh–nachalo 1970-kh godov. St. Petersburg: Kifa, 2011.

Paert, Irina. *Spiritual Elders: Charisma and Tradition in Russian Orthodoxy.* DeKalb: Northern Illinois University Press, 2010.

Papkova, Irina. *The Russian Orthodox Church and Russian Politics.* New York: Oxford University Press, 2011.

Pasternak, Boris Leonidovich. *Doctor Zhivago.* Translated by Richard Pevear and Larissa Volokhonsky, with an introduction by Richard Pevear. New York: Pantheon Books, 2010.

"Patriarkh Kirill blagoslovil rasprostranenie trudov ottsa Aleksandra Menia v khramakh Russkoi tserkvi." September 10, 2010. http://www.interfax-religion.ru/?act=news&div=42164.

"Patriarkh Kirill privetstvoval uchastnikov v Menevskikh chtenii," September 10, 2010. http://blagovest-info.ru/index.php?ss=2&s=8&id=36566.

Pazlova, V. "Dialog? Tol'ko znakomstvo." *Nauka i religiia,* no. 6 (1988): 30–31.

Petrov, Aleksandr Iur'evich. *Rossiisko-amerikanskaia kompaniia: Deiatel'nost' na otechestvennom i zarubezhnom rynkakh (1799–1867).* Moscow: Institut vseobshchei istorii RAN, 2006.

Petrunina, L. Iu., ed. *Vasilii Alekseevich Vatagin: K 125-letiiu so dnia rozhdeniia; Materialy mezhdunarodnoi muzeinoi konferentsii, Moskva, 5–6 fevralia 2009 (s prilozheniiu: CD).* Moscow: Ekspress 24, 2010.

Pimen, Patriarch. "Congratulatory Telegram to Leonid Il'ich Brezhnev, General Secretary of the CC CPSU," December 17, 1976. *Journal of the Moscow Patriarchate,* no. 2 (1977): 4.

———. "His Holiness's Address before Panikhida in the Patriarchal Cathedral of the Epiphany in Moscow," February 12, 1984. *Journal of the Moscow Patriarchate,* no. 3 (1984): 3.

———. "Speech at the Reception in Honour of the Participants in the Conference," June 10, 1977. *Journal of the Moscow Patriarchate,* no. 8 (1977): 59.

Pipes, Daniel. "The Problem of Soviet Muslims." In *Asian Outlook (Taipei)* (March–April 1991). http://www.danielpipes.org/206/the-problem-of-soviet-muslims.

"Pis'mo Patriarkha Moskovskogo i Vseia Rusi Aleksiia II posle ubiistva protoiereia Aleksandra Menia," September 11, 1990. *Alexandermen.ru.* http://www.alexandermen.ru/biogr/slovopat.html.

"Pis'mo Sviashchenniku Aleksandru Meniu." In Bychkov, *Khronika neraskrytogo ubiistva,* appendix 13, 194–207.

Polkinghorne, John. "Science and Theology in Dialogue." Lecture, international conference on "Alexander Men'—His Life and Legacy." Moffat, Scotland, September 16, 2012.

"Pomogite spasti detei!" *Deti.msk.ru.* http://deti.msk.ru.

Poresh, Vladimir. "Secret Police Harass Poresh." *Religion in Communist Lands* 8, no. 2 (Summer 1980): 103–6.

Pospielovsky, Dimitry V. *The Orthodox Church in the History of Russia.* Crestwood, NY: St. Vladimir's Seminary Press, 1998.

———. *Russkaia pravoslavnaia tserkov' v XX veke.* Moscow: Respublika, 1995.

———. *Soviet Studies on the Church and the Believer's Response to Atheism.* Vol. 3, *A History of Soviet Atheism in Theory and Practice, and the Believer.* New York: St. Martin's Press, 1988.

Put' chelovecheskii; K 75-letiiu so dnia rozhdeniia protoiereia Aleksandra Menia. Compiled by Fr. V. A. Grigorenko. Moscow: Zhizn' s Bogom, 2010.

Pyman, Avril. *Pavel Florensky: A Quiet Genius; The Tragic and Extraordinary Life of Russia's Unknown da Vinci.* Foreword by Geoffrey Hosking. New York: Continuum, 2010.

Rashkovskii, Evgenii Borisovich, ed. *Dvadtsat' let bez ottsa Aleksandra, i s nim.* Foreword by Elena Iur'evna Genieva. Moscow: Rudomino, 2010.

"The Regulations for the Council of Russian Orthodox Church Affairs," October 7, 1943, Decree No. 1095. *Zhurnal Moskovksoi patriarkhii,* no. 4 (1945): 54.

Remnick, David. *Lenin's Tomb: The Last Days of the Soviet Empire.* New York: Random House, 1993.

Roberts, Elizabeth, and Ann Shukman, eds. *Christianity for the Twenty-First Century: The Life and Work of Alexander Men*. Introduction by Ann Shukman, foreword by Richard Harries. London: SCM Press, 1996.

Rogger, Hans. "Conclusion and Overview." In *Pogroms: Anti-Jewish Violence in Modern Russian History*, edited by John D. Klier and Shlomo Lambroza, 314–72. Cambridge: Cambridge University Press, 1992.

Sal'skii, Frantsisk [Francis de Sales]. *Vvedenie v blagochestivuiu zhizn'*. Translated by Vera Iakovlevna Vasilevskaia. Moscow: Stella Aeterna, 1999.

Semenev, Iurii Ivanovich. "Razvitie obshchestvenno-ekonomicheskikh formatsii i ob'ektivnaia logika evolutsii religii." *Voprosy nauchnogo ateizma* 20 (1976): 43–61.

"Sem' voprosov i otvetov o Russkoi Pravoslavnoi Tserkvi." *Vestnik russkogo khristianskogo dvizheniia* 137 (1982): 233–60; and 138 (1983): 215–28.

Serafim (Leonid Mikhailovich Chichagov). *Obrashchenie Preosviashchennogo Serafima, Episkopa Kininevskogo k dukhovenstvu eparkhii po voprosy o vozrozhdenii prikhodskoi zhizni*. Kishinev: Eparkhial'naia tipografiia, 1909.

Seraphim, Sigrist. *A Life Together: Wisdom of Community from the Christian East*. Brewster, MA: Paraclete Press, 2011.

Sergii (Stragorodskii). "Pastyriam i pasomym khristovoi pravoslavnoi tserkvi," June 22, 1941. In *Russkaia pravoslavnaia tserkov' i Velikaia Otechestvennaia Voina: Sbornik tserkovnykh dokumentov*, 4–5. Moscow: 1-ia Obraztsovaia tipografiia Ogiza, 1943.

Service, Robert. *Lenin: A Political Life*. Vol. 1, *The Strengths of Contradiction*. Bloomington: Indiana University Press, 1985.

Shakhnovich, Mikhail Iosifovich. *Lenin i problemy ateizma: Kritika religii v trudakh V. I. Lenina*. Moscow: Izd-vo Akademiia Nauk SSSR, 1961.

Shatz, Marshall S., and Judith E. Zimmerman, eds. and trans. *Vekhi: Landmarks; A Collection of Articles about the Russian Intelligentsia*. Armonk, NY: M. E. Sharpe, 1994.

Shkarovskii, Mikhail Vital'evich. *Russkaia Pravoslavnaia Tserkov' v XX veke*. Moscow: Veche, Lepta, 2010.

Shreider, Iu. "Nauka—istochnik znanii i sueverii." *Novyi mir*, no. 10 (1969): 207–26.

Skorodenko, Vladimir Andreevich. *Margarita Rudomino All-Russian State Library for Foreign Literature*. Moscow: Rudomino, 2004.

Smokin-Rothrock, Victoria. "The Ticket to the Soviet Soul: Science, Religion, and the Spiritual Crisis of Late Soviet Atheism." *Russian Review* 73, no. 2 (April 2014): 171–197.

Smolich, Igor' Kornil'evich. *Geschichte der russischen Kirche, 1700–1917*. Leiden: E. J. Brill, 1964.

Sogrin, Vladimir Viktorovich. *Politicheskaia istoriia sovremennoi Rossii, 1985–2001: Ot Gorbacheva do Putina*. Moscow: Ves' Mir, 2001.

Solov'ev, Vladimir Sergeevich. "Chteniia o bogochelovechestve." In *Sobranie sochineniia Vladimira Sergeevicha Solov'eva*. Brussels: Zhizn' s Bogom, 1966, 3:79–102, 103–19.

———. *Lectures on Divine Humanity*. Translated by Peter Zouboff, revised and edited by Boris Jakim. Hudson, NY: Lindisfarne Press, 1995.

———. *The Philosophical Principles of Integral Knowledge*. Translated by Valeria Z. Nollan. Grand Rapids, MI: William B. Eerdmans, 2008.

———. *Sobranie sochinenii Vladimira Sergeevicha Solov'eva*. 12 vols. Brussels: Zhizn' s Bogom, 1966–1969.

———. "Ob upadke srednevekovogo mirosozertsaniia." In *Sobranie sochinenii Vladimira Sergeevicha Soloveva*. Brussels: Zhizn' s Bogom, 1966, 6:381–93.

Solzhenitsyn, Alexander I. *The Oak and the Calf: Sketches of Literary Life in the Soviet Union*. Translated by Harry Willetts. New York: Harper and Row, 1980.

"Soviet Peace Funds Awards." *Journal of the Moscow Patriarchate*, no. 4 (1976): 4.

Spinka, Matthew. *The Church and the Russian Revolution*. New York: Macmillan, 1927.

Stalin, I. "O proekte konstitutsii Soiuza SSR (Doklad na Chrezvychainom VIII Vsesoiuznom s"ezde Sovetov, 25 November 1936)." In *Voprosy Leninizma*, 507–34. 11th ed. Moscow: Gosudarstvennoe izd-vo politicheskoi literatury, 1947.

Stanton, Leonard J. *The Optina Pustyn Monastery in the Russian Literary Imagination: Iconic Vision in Works by Dostoevsky, Gogol, Tolstoy, and Others*. Middlebury Studies in Russian Language and Literature 3, edited by Thomas R. Beyer, Jr. New York: Peter Lang, 1995.

Steeves, Paul D. "Znanie Society." In *The Modern Encyclopedia of Russian and Soviet History*, edited by Joseph L. Wieczynski, 46:114–16. Gulf Breeze, FL: Academic International Press, 1987.

Stevens, Jennie A. "Children of the Revolution: Soviet Russia's Homeless Children (*Besprizorniki*) in the 1920s." *Russian History* 9, nos. 2–3 (1982): 242–64.

Stolee, Margaret K. "Homeless Children in the USSR, 1917–1957." *Soviet Studies* 40, no. 1 (January 1988): 64–83.

Strumilin, Stanislav Gustavovich. *O piatiletnem plane razvitiia narodnogo khoziaistva SSSR: Diskussiia v kommunisticheskoi akademii*. Moscow: Izd-vo kommunisticheskoi akademii, 1928.

Struve, Nikita A. *Christians in Contemporary Russia*. Translated by Lancelot Sheppard and A. Manson. 2nd rev. ed. New York: Scribner, 1967.

———, ed. *Otets Aleksei Mechev: Propovedi, pis'ma, vospominaniia o nem*. 2nd ed. Compiled by Boris Aleksandrovich Vasil'ev. Paris: YMCA-Press, 1989.

———, ed. *Otets Aleksei Mechev: Vospominaniia S. Durylina, o. Vladimira, Episkopa Arseniia, A. Iarmolovich, i dr.; Pis'ma, Propovedi, Nadrobnoe slovo o sebe samom*. Paris: YMCA-Press, 1970.

Sukhikh, A., and L. Bondarenko. "Sovremennoe Pravoslavie i dvoistvennaia istina." *Nauka i religiia*, no. 3 (March 1964): 14.

Sutherland, Christine. *The Princess of Siberia: The Story of Maria Volkonsky and the Decembrist Exiles*. London: Metheun, 1984.

Sutton, Jonathan. *The Religious Philosophy of Vladimir Solovyov: Towards a Reassessment*. Basingstoke: Macmillan, 1988.

———. "The Religious Roots of Change in Present-Day Russia." *Religion, State, and Society* 21, no. 2 (1993): 229–35.

Tabak, Iurii Mikhailovich. *Sumerki shovinizma: Analiz rossiiskikh ksenofobskikh izdanii*. 2nd ed. Moscow: Academia, 2008.

Tavrov, Andrei Mikhailovich. *Syn chelovecheskii: Ob ottse Aleksandre Mene*. Moscow: Eksmo, 2014.

Teilhard de Chardin, Pierre. *The Human Phenomenon*. Translated by Sarah Appleton-Weber, with a foreword by Brian Swimme. Brighton, UK: Sussex Academic Press, 1999.

Telesin, Julius. "Inside 'Samizdat.'" *Encounter* 40, no. 2 (February 1973): 25–33.

Tepnina, Mariia Vital'evna. "Iz vospominanii-interv'iu." In Vasilevskaia, *Katakomby XX veka*, 260–69.

Tertz, Abram [Andrei Sinyavsky]. *The Trial Begins and On Socialist Realism*. New York: Vintage, 1965.

Thompson, Kevin. "Hegel, the Political, and the Theological: The Question of Islam." In *Hegel on Religion and Politics*, edited by Angelica Nuzzo, 99–117. Albany: State University of New York Press, 2013.

Thrower, James. *Marxist-Leninist "Scientific Atheism" and the Study of Religion and Atheism in the USSR*. Berlin: Mouton, 1983.

Tillich, Paul. *A History of Christian Thought*. Edited by Carl E. Braaten. New York: Harper and Row, 1968.

Tokarev, Sergei Aleksandrovich. *Rannie formy religii i ikh razvitiia*. Moscow: Nauka, 1964.

———. *Religiia v istorii narodov mira*. 3rd ed. Moscow: Polizdat, 1976.

Trapani, Nina Vladimirovna. "Iz vospominanii ob ottse Petre Shipkove." In Vasilevskaia, *Katakomby XX veka*, 270–78.

Trubetskoi, Evgenii Nikolaevich. *Icons: Theology in Color*. Translated by Gertrude Vakar, with an introduction by George M. A. Hanfmann. New York: St. Vladimir's Seminary Press, 1973.

———. *Mirosozertsanie V. S. Solov'eva*. 2 vols. Moscow: Put', 1913.

———. *Religiozno-obshchestvennyi ideal zapadnogo khristianstva*. 2 vols. 1892. Reprint, St. Petersburg: Izd-vo Russkogo khristianskogo gumanitarnogo instituta, 2004.

———. *Tri ocherka o russkoi ikone. "Inoe tsarstvo" i ego iskateli v russkoi narodnoi skazka*. 2nd. ed. Moscow: "Lapta-Press," 2003.

———. "Umozrenie v kraskakh." In *Tri ocherka*, 7–66.

————. "Dva mira v drevnerusskoi ikonopisi." In *Tri ocherka*, 67-128.

————. "Rossiia v ee ikone." In *Tri ocherka*, 129-184.

Tucker, Robert C. *Philosophy and Myth in Karl Marx*. 3rd ed. New Brunswick, NJ: Transaction Publishers, 2001.

Tunick, Mark. "Hegel and the Consecrated State." In *Hegel on Religion and Politics*, edited by Angelica Nuzzo, 19-38. Albany: State University of New York Press, 2013.

Turumova-Dombrovskaia, Klara. "Ubit za roman." *Novaia gazeta*, May 22, 2008. http://www.novayagazeta.ru/society/40145.html.

Ugrinovich, Dmitrii Modestovich. *Vvedenie v teoreticheskoe religiovedenie*. Moscow: Mysl', 1973.

Ulitskaia, Liudmila Evgen'evna. "Aleksandr Men'." In *Sviashchennyi musor: Rasskazy, esse*, 94-100. Moscow: Astrel', 2012.

Vasilenko, Leonid Ivanovich. "Khristianstvo i kul'tura v trudakh protoiereia Aleksandra Menia." In Men, *Kul'tura i dukhovnoe voskhozhdenie*, 471-81.

————. "Posmertnaia travlia ottsa Aleksandra Menia." *Vestnik russkogo khristianskogo dvizheniia*, no. 180 (2000): 259-89.

————. "Vokrug imeni ottsa Aleksandra Menia." In Zorin and Iliushenko, *Vokrug imeni ottsa Aleksandra*, 9-34.

————. "Za chto nenavidiat ottsa Aleksandra Menia." *NG-religii*, 18, no. 65 (2000). http://www.vehi.net/men/vasilenko2.html.

Vasil'ev, Boris Aleksandrovich. *Dukhovnyi put' Pushkina*. Moscow: Sam and Sam, 1994.

Vasil'eva, Olga Iur'evna. *Russkaia pravoslavnaia tserkov' v politike sovetskogo gosudarstva v 1943-1948 gg*. Moscow: Institut rossiiskoi istorii RAN, 1999.

Vasilevskaia, Vera Iakovlevna. *Katakomby XX veka: Vospominaniia*, edited by Roza Adamiants et al. and compiled by Nataliia Grigorenko and Pavel Men. Moscow: Fond imeni Aleksandra Menia, 2001.

————. "N. I. Pirogov i voprosy zhizni." In *Psikhiatriia i aktual'nye problemy dukhovnoi zhizni: Sbornik pamiati professora D. E. Melekhova*, edited by V. Ia. Vasilevskaia, Georgii Kochetkov, and M. G. Gal'chenko, 62-79. Moscow: SF MVPKhSh, 1997.

————. *Ponimanie uchebnogo materiala uchashchimisia vspomogatel'noi shkoly*. Moscow: Akademiia pedagogicheskikh nauk RSFSR, 1960.

Vath, Christopher. "Maria Yudina: The Pianist Who Moved Stalin." Crossroads Cultural Center and the Siena Forum for Faith and Culture. September 17, 2011. http://www.crossroadsculturalcenter.org/events/2011/9/17/maria-yudina-the-pianist-who-moved-stalin.html.

Veniamin (Novik). *Pravoslavie, Khristianstvo, Demokratiia: Sbornik statei*. St. Petersburg: Aleteiia, 1999.

Verkhovskii, Aleksandr Markovich. *Politicheskoe pravoslavie: Russkie pravoslavnye natsionalisty i fundamentalisty, 1995-2001 gg*. Moscow: Oktiabr', 2003.

Verkhovskii, Aleksandr, Ekaterina Mikhailovskaia, and Vladimir Pribylovskii. "Tserkov' v politike i politika v tserkvi." In *Politicheskaia ksenofobiia: Radikal'nye gruppy, predstavlenniia liderov, rol' tserkvi*, 60-122. Moscow: Panorama, 1999.

Verkhovskii, Aleksandr, and Vladimir Pribylovskii. *Natsional-patrioticheskie organizatsii v Rossii: Istoriia, ideologiia, ekstremistskie tendentsii*. Moscow: Izd-vo "Institut eksperimental'noi sotsiologii," 1996.

Vipper, Robert Iur'evich. *Rim i rannee khristianstvo*. Moscow: Izd-vo Akademii nauk SSSR, 1954.

————. *Vozniknovenie khristianskoi literatury*. Moscow: Nauka, 1946.

Vishnevetskii, I. G., and E. G. Rabinovich, eds. *"AEQUINOX": Sbornik pamiati o. Aleksandra Menia*. Moscow: Carte Blanche, 1991.

Vladimir, Fr. "Ne khlebom edinym." *Nash sovremennik*, no. 6 (1990): 55-56.

Volf, Miroslav. *Exclusion and Embrace: A Theological Exploration of Identity, Otherness, and Reconciliation*. Nashville, TN: Abingdon, 1996.

————. *A Public Faith: How Followers of Christ Should Serve the Common Good*. Grand Rapids, MI: Brazos Press, 2011.

Volkogonov, Dmitrii. *Lenin: A New Biography*. Translated and edited by Harold Shukman. New York: The Free Press, 1994.

Vronskaya, Jeanne. "Obituary: Father Superior Lazar." *Independent* (London), January 16, 1991.

Vysheslavtseva, O. N. *Pastyr' vo vremena bezbozhiia: Ob ottse Nikolae (Golubtsove)*. St. Petersburg: Satis', 1994.

Walters, Philip. "The Ideas of the Christian Seminar." *Religion in Communist Lands* 9, nos. 3–4 (Autumn 1981): 111–22.

Webster, Elsie May. *The Moon Man: A Biography of N. N. Miklouho-Maclay*. Berkeley: University of California Press, 1984.

Werth, Alexander. *Russia at War, 1941–1945*. New York: Carroll and Graf, 1964.

Williams, Rowan. General Introduction to *Sergii Bulgakov: Towards a Russian Political Theology*. Edited and introduced by Rowan Williams. Edinburgh: T & T Clark, 1999.

Worms, Frédéric. "The Closed and the Open in the Two Sources of Morality and Religion: A Distinction That Changes Everything." In *Bergson, Politics, and Religion*, edited by Alexandre Lefebvre and Melanie White, 25–39. Durham, NC: Duke University Press, 2012.

Yakunin, Gleb. "Report to the Christian Committee for the Defense of Believers' Rights in the USSR on the Current Situation of the Russian Orthodox Church and the Prospects for a Religious Renaissance in Russia," August 15, 1979. In *Documents of the Christian Committee for the Defense of Believers' Rights in the USSR*, 11:xvi–xxx. San Francisco, CA: Washington Research Center, 1980.

"Zapiska G. G. Karpova o prieme I. V. Stalinym ierarkhov Russkoi Pravoslavnoi Tserkvi, September 1943." In *Russkie patriarkhi XX veka: Sud'by Otechestva i Tserkvi na stranitsakh arkhivnykh dokumentov*. Pt. 1, *"Delo" patriarkha Tikhona; Krestnyi put' patriarkha Sergiia*, edited by Mikhail Ivanovich Odintsov, 283–91. Moscow: Izd-vo RAGS, 1999.

Zaslavskaya, Olga. "From Dispersed to Distributed Archives: The Past and the Present of Samizdat Material." *Poetics Today* 29, no. 4 (Winter 2008): 669–712.

Zaslavskii, Il'ia. "Prezidentu SSSR M. S. Gorbachevu." In Gromova, *Pamiati*, 23.

Zernov, Nicholas. *The Russian Religious Renaissance of the Twentieth Century*. New York: Harper and Row, 1963.

Zhelnavakova, Mariia Sergeevna. "Iz pisem." In Vasilevskaia, *Katakomby XX veka*, 307–10.

Zheludkov, Sergei. "Letter to Pavel Litvinov." In Bourdeaux, *Patriarch and Prophets*, 339–41.

Zhizneopisanie Moskovskogo startsa ottsa Alekseia Mecheva. Compiled by Monakhinia Iulianiia. 2nd ed. Moscow: Russkii Khronograf, 1999.

Zorin, A. I., and V. I. Iliushenko, comps. *Vokrug imeni ottsa Aleksandra*. Moscow: Obshchestvo "Kul'turnoe vozrozhdenie" imeni Aleksandra Menia, 1993.

Zubok, Vladislav. *Zhivago's Children: The Last Russian Intelligentsia*. Cambridge, MA: The Belknap Press of Harvard University Press, 2009.

Zubov, Andrei Borisovich, ed. *Istoriia Rossii XX vek*. Vol. 2, *1939–2007*. Moscow: Astrel', 2009.

Zubov, V. P., S. M. Grambakh, V. V. Danilevskii, and Iu. Ia. Kogan. "Nauka i tekhnika." In *Ocherki istorii SSSR, Period feodalizma Rossiia vo vtoroi polovine XVIII v*. Edited by A. I. Baranovich, B. B. Kafengauz et al., 428–69. Moscow: Izd-vo Akademii nauk SSSR, 1956.

Index

W

X

Y

Z